The Dynamics of Persuasion

Now in its seventh edition, this essential text continues to provide students with a comprehensive yet accessible overview of the study and practice of persuasive communication.

Attuned to the swift changes in the world of persuasion in the twenty-first century, this book covers how theories and research illuminate and adapt to our present digital era, with continued attention to ethical implications and today's big topics. This new edition features updated definitions of key terms in the field as they relate to present-day practice; an integration of persuasion theories and the ubiquity of online influence; new examples and cases to illustrate persuasive communication's approach to health campaigns, attitudes, communicator appeals, dissonance, and ethics; and a thorough reflection of the most current scholarship in the field.

The Dynamics of Persuasion, Seventh Edition provides a solid foundation for undergraduate students in communication studies and psychology to grasp the key concepts and practices of persuasive communication today.

The book is complemented by online resources for both instructors and students, including an instructor's manual, lecture slides, sample test questions, and links to relevant articles and videos illustrating concepts presented in the text. Please visit www.routledge.com/cw/perloff.

Richard M. Perloff, Professor of Communication, Psychology, and Political Science at Cleveland State University, is a nationally recognized scholar of persuasion and psychological perceptions of media. His *Dynamics of Persuasion*, first published in 1993, has emerged as a major scholarly textbook in the field. His articles on communication theories and psychological perceptions of news have appeared in *Communication Theory*, *Communication Research*, and *Mass Communication and Society.* A dedicated teacher, he has received teaching awards at Cleveland State University.

D0022385

Routledge Communication Series

Jennings Bryant/Dolf Zillmann, Series Editors

Selected titles include:

Family Communication, 3rd Edition
Chris Segrin and Jeanne Flora

Advertising Theory, 2nd Edition
Shelley Rodgers and Esther Thorson

An Integrated Approach to Communication Theory and Research, 3rd Edition
Edited by Don W. Stacks, Michael B. Salwen, and Kristen C. Eichhorn

Analyzing Media Messages, 4th Edition
Using Quantitative Content Analysis in Research
Daniel Riffe, Stephen Lacy, Brendan R. Watson, and Frederick Fico

The Media Handbook, 7th Edition
A Complete Guide to Advertising Media Selection, Planning, Research, and Buying
Helen Katz

Media Effects, 4th Edition
Advances in Theory and Research
Edited by Mary Beth Oliver, Arthur A. Raney, and Jennings Bryant

Communication Research Measures III
A Sourcebook
Edited by Elizabeth E. Graham & Joseph P. Mazer

Political Public Relations: Concepts, Principles and Applications, 2nd Edition
Edited by Jesper Strömbäck and Spiro Kiousis

African American Communication, 3rd Edition
Exploring Identity and Culture
Edited by Ronald L. Jackson II, Amber L. Johnson, Michael L. Hecht and Sidney A. Ribeau

Handbook of Visual Communication, 2nd Edition
Theory, Methods, and Media
Edited by Sheree Josephson, James D. Kelly and Ken Smith

The Dynamics of Persuasion, 7th Edition
Communication and Attitudes in the 21st century
Richard M. Perloff

For a full list of titles please visit: https://www.routledge.com/Routledge-Communication-Series/book-series/RCS.

The Dynamics of Persuasion

Communication and Attitudes in the **Twenty-First Century**

7th edition

Richard M. Perloff

Routledge
Taylor & Francis Group

NEW YORK AND LONDON

Seventh edition published 2021
by Routledge
52 Vanderbilt Avenue, New York, NY 10017

and by Routledge
2 Park Square, Milton Park, Abingdon, Oxon, OX14 4RN

Routledge is an imprint of the Taylor & Francis Group, an informa business

© 2021 Taylor & Francis

First edition published by Lawrence Erlbaum Associates 1993
Sixth edition published by Routledge 2017

Library of Congress Cataloging-in-Publication Data

Names: Perloff, Richard M., author.
Title: The dynamics of persuasion : communication and attitudes in the
   21st century / Richard M Perloff.
Description: 7th edition. | New York, NY : Routledge, 2020. | Includes bibliographical
   references and index. |
Identifiers: LCCN 2020004547 (print) | LCCN 2020004548 (ebook) | ISBN 9780367185787
   (hardback) | ISBN 9780367185794 (paperback) | ISBN 9780429196959 (ebook)
Subjects: LCSH: Persuasion (Psychology) | Mass media–Psychological aspects. |
   Attitude change.
Classification: LCC BF637.P4 P39 2020 (print) | LCC BF637.P4 (ebook) | DDC 153.8/52–dc23 LC
   record available at https://lccn.loc.gov/2020004547LC ebook record available at https://lccn.
   loc.gov/2020004548

ISBN: 978-0-367-18578-7 (hbk)
ISBN: 978-0-367-18579-4 (pbk)
ISBN: 978-0-429-19695-9 (ebk)

Typeset in Sabon
by Swales & Willis, Exeter, Devon, UK

Visit the companion website: www.routledge.com/cw/Perloff

Contents

Contents

Preface

Dark digital changes and abiding communicative consistencies. Sexual exploitation with roots in classic coercive techniques. Harmful products that call up memories of older risky brands. A new marketing craze that works for familiar psychological reasons.

These striking changes reflect time-honored continuities in persuasion processes and effects. They are hallmarks of the seventh edition of *The Dynamics of Persuasion: Communication and Attitudes in the Twenty-First Century*. The text adapts classic theories and research to the present era, as I discuss the many digital and social transformations that bear on persuasion. These include online disinformation that fuels prejudice, cyber propaganda, examples of wanton sexual abuse, the diffusion of Juul, and influencer marketing.

The seventh edition offers an abundance of contemporary academic studies that question and extend classic studies. This includes new sections on problems replicating key research findings, reassessments of the Milgram study, new research on confirmation biases, applications of strong attitude research to anti-vaccination activists, priming (totally new section), and illustrations of attitude measurement that go beyond traditional gender roles to incorporate same-sex, transgender, and non-binary role definitions. I have thoroughly reviewed the social scientific literature on persuasion, scouring online data bases, journals, and books, while at the same time seizing on practical applications that showcase the dynamic processes and effects of persuasion.

I have cut, added, and reorganized. I have had to cut many sections from the previous edition to make way for changes reflecting the contemporary dynamics of persuasive communication.

To more cohesively explain newer, dark changes in persuasive communications, I have confined the first chapter to an introduction of continuities and changes, pushing definitions into a second chapter. This includes a thorough discussion of propaganda, in light of online disinformation, as well as expanded definitions of propaganda and persuasion. The long-standing discussion of cults has been moved, for ease of reading, from a box to the text itself, with application to online cult-like groups. Given the expanding literature criticizing the classic Milgram study, I devote a full chapter to charisma and authority (now Chapter 9), placing credibility and social attractiveness in the next chapter. There are now 16 chapters, offering more crystallized, in-depth discussions.

In the tradition of the six previous editions, I have tried to convey the liveliness and richness of everyday persuasion, offering a flavor redolent less of a text than an engaging book on persuasive communication. And yet, theory and research remain the core of the book, the mainstays through which all else is interpreted. Specific changes include the following:

Chapter 1 discusses dark digital falsehoods, noting that these, unfortunately, characterize contemporary persuasion. Chapter 2 extends the discussion of complex definitional issues, examining #MeToo era sexual abuse reports through the lens of the coercion–persuasion continuum, with emphasis on its coercive nature. There is an expanded discussion of propaganda and an elaborated definition to incorporate digital disinformation and gray areas.

Chapter 3 introduces the much-ballyhooed replication crisis in social psychology. I discuss problems in replicating key persuasion-related research, emphasizing the importance of replication, while also looking critically at the replication approach and the difficult questions it raises. Chapter 4 covers the latest work on attitudes, buttressed by a new discussion of liberal/conservative values and a contemporary example of symbolic attitudes toward immigration. Chapter 5 expands the discussion of strong attitudes with a box on anti-vaxxers and a thorough introduction to priming theory and applications. Chapter 6, focusing on attitude functions and attitude-behavior consistency, updates research and offers reasoned action and planned behavior applications to a health problem du jour: Adolescents' attitudes and behavior toward the e-cigarette Juul. Chapter 7 expands the description of attitude measurement to include same-sex, transgender, and non-binary gender attitudes.

Chapter 8, the first chapter in the third section, offers new research and online examples of the Elaboration Likelihood Modal. Chapter 9, now focusing on charisma and the Milgram study, expands the charisma section to include the problematic nature of President Trump's charisma, as well as an extended discussion revaluating Milgram in light of new scholarship. Chapter 10 describes contemporary aspects of credibility, including questions about the decline in expertise, along with a host of new applications of social attractiveness. Chapter 11, focusing on message factors, updates the literature on evidence and narrative, with implications for climate change, along with an application of how language research illuminates the role played by credibility and gender in Christine Blasey Ford's riveting accusations against Justice Brett Kavanaugh, along with his response, during the 2018 Senate Judiciary Committee hearings. The next two chapters, Chapters 12 and 13 on emotional appeals and cognitive dissonance respectively, are filled with new research from the empirical vineyards of persuasion scholarship.

In the final part of the book, Chapter 14, which examines interpersonal persuasion, offers new applications to the opioid crisis. Chapter 15 is richly revised, with new sections on the psychology of influencer marketing, and marketing ethics in an era of privacy violation. The final chapter, Chapter 16, extends classic health marketing research with online examples, newer studies and distinctions, along with discussion of health campaigns in an online age.

The end result, I hope, is an expanded, enriched book. Throughout the text, I emphasize the power of persuasion, its ethical cornerstones, use by malevolent influence agents, but also its capacity to heal and self-liberate. I stress the abiding importance of psychological processes, how you can't appreciate the contemporary message without understanding the mind, and persuasion's fraught role in society, all the more today given the blurred distinctions among social influence categories. Finally, I highlight the many insights research offers into persuasion's perils, its subtle, unfathomable effects, and its constructive potential to liberate the mind and improve our collective health.

Acknowledgments

I am grateful to many people for their thoughtful comments and support.

Thank you, first, to Felisa Salvago-Keyes, Communication Studies Publisher at Routledge, for her insights, understanding, and all-in dedication to this project. Thanks to Elizabeth Riley for her meticulous copyediting and Grant Schatzman at Routledge for his conscientious, super-efficient work. Thank you once again to the conscientious, ever-talented Sharon Muskin for her aesthetic care and meticulous assistance with word processing, art work, and manuscript preparation. We have worked on many books together, and each time her perseverance improves the final product.

I want to thank four colleagues who offered astute, discerning comments on my discussion of social influence, #MeToo, and sexual abuses. Thanks to Kyra Rothenberg, Elizabeth Pask, Julie Andsager, and Elizabeth Thomas, for their excellent suggestions. These four faculty members really thought over the issues and came up with perceptive, insightful ideas that improved my discussion of these complex issues. I also am indebted to a variety of expert, well-recognized persuasion researchers for encouraging comments, critical pointers, or supportive reactions to chapters I sent them. Thank you so much, David Ewoldsen, Lijiang Shen, Jim Dillard, Dan O'Keefe, Icek Ajzen, Katie Stansberry, Carlina DiRusso, Jeff Niederdeppe, Xiaoli Nan, Dolores Albarracín, Richard Griggs, George White-head III, Eddie Harmon-Jones, and Eliot Aronson. I also appreciate suggestions from the Routledge reviewers who perused my prospectus and two key chapters.

My thanks also to Cleveland State students, including Nicole Merlino, whose class presentation prompted a social media update to the accessibility discussion in Chapter 15, and the ever-positive School of Communication coordinator, Rashelle Baker, for her great sense of humor.

Finally, thanks, as always to my family: my son, Michael, lawyer-persuader par excellence, daughter Catherine, effervescent, perceptive writer about social influence in the financial sector, and my wife Julie for her abiding support.

Part One

Foundations

Chapter 1

Introduction to Persuasion

When you think of persuasion, what comes to mind? Advertising, perhaps? The ad for running shoes that pops up everywhere on your phone? Retail stores that electronically track your shopping patterns, then send a push notification on your smartphone promoting a product they know you like? Those ubiquitous social media influencers who peddle products to devoted online followers? That's persuasion, right? Powerful stuff – the kind of thing that wields strong effects on society and spells success for its purveyors. But what about you? What does persuasion mean to you personally? Can you think of times when the media or attractive communicators changed your mind about something? Anything come to mind? "Not really," you say. You've got the canny ability to see through what other people are trying to sell you.

Well, that's perhaps what we like to think. "It's everyone else who's influenced, not me or my friends – well, maybe my friends, but not me." But wait: What about those Levi's jeans, UGG boots, Juicy Couture sweater, or Nike sneakers you bought? Marketing had to play a role in that decision somehow. What about the book you purchased on Amazon after reading all the favorable customer reviews? You have to admit that other people's comments may have swayed you more than a smidgeon. And, if you search your mind, you probably can think of lots of times when you yielded to another's pushy persuasion, only to regret it later – the time you let yourself get talked into allowing a car repair that turned out to be unnecessary or agreed to loan a friend some money, only to discover she had no intention of paying you back.

But that's all negative. What of the positive side? Have you ever been helped by a persuasive communication – an antismoking ad or a reminder that it's not cool or safe to drink when you drive? Have you ever had a conversation with a friend who opened your eyes to new ways of seeing the world or a teacher who said you had potential you didn't know you had?

You see, this is persuasion too. Just about anything that involves molding or shaping attitudes involves persuasion. Now there's another term that may seem foreign at first: Attitudes. Attitudes? There once was a rock group that called itself that. But we've got attitudes as surely as we have arms, legs, cell phones, or Facebook pages. We have attitudes about music, politics, money, sex, race, even God. We don't all share the same attitudes, and you may not care a whit about issues that intrigue your acquaintances. But we have attitudes and they shape our world in ways we don't always recognize. Persuasion is the study of attitudes and how to change them.

Persuasion calls to mind images of salespeople and manipulators, such as clever strategists on classic TV shows like *Survivor* – which prizes plying physical attractiveness and verbal manipulation (Murphy, 2018) – and con artists, such as the swindlers who devise false profiles on dating sites like Match.com. These online crooks pilfer photos of attractive women and men from Instagram, allure lonely victims to click onto the site, sweet talk them, and hit them up for money (Murphy, 2016). Let's also not forget the online prescription drug sites that deliver to your doorstep drugs promising to cure everything from public speaking anxiety to erectile dysfunctions, in the total absence of medical counsel from a licensed M.D. (Singer & Thomas, 2019). On a more whimsical note, persuasion brings to mind the hopelessly, worrisomely gullible people who fall prey to scams, such as those playfully perpetrated by *Candid Camera* television host Peter Funt: The Denver residents who believed they would be getting mail delivered via drone, and the folks from Scottsdale, Arizona who fell for the policeman's story that he was enforcing a "2 m.p.h. pedestrian speed limit" (Funt, 2014, p. A21)!

There is another side too: Persuasion harnessed in the service of social change. Activists have doggedly employed persuasion to help change attitudes toward race, gender roles, and climate change. Consumer advocates have tirelessly warned people about dishonest business practices. Health communicators have launched countless campaigns to change people's thinking about cigarettes, alcohol, drugs, and unsafe sex. Political leaders have relied on persuasion when attempting to influence opinions toward policy issues or when trying to rally the country behind them during national crises. Some of our greatest leaders have been expert persuaders – Abraham Lincoln, Martin Luther King, Jr., and Franklin Delano Roosevelt come immediately to mind, as do the crop of current political persuaders, working in the thicket of the social media age (see Figure 1.1). And the health specialists who helped convince Americans to change their hygiene habits in the wake of the coronavirus pandemic certainly harnessed persuasion for the public good.

Persuasion, alas, intrigues and repels us. We are fascinated by charisma, why some people have it and others don't. We are riveted by courtroom trials, both in television fiction and in real life. Many women waited in line to watch the 2011 trial of Casey Anthony, charged with killing her two-year-old daughter, Caylee with chloroform and duct tape. Some curiosity-seekers longed to see if the prosecution could make the case that Casey killed her daughter because she grew frustrated with motherhood, which kept her away from the sybaritic life of cocktails and men. Others found themselves drawn in by the courtroom drama, intrigued by the strategies her lawyers ingeniously devised to poke holes in the prosecution's arguments. At the same time as we are piqued by persuasion in cases like the Anthony trial, we recoil when reading about its horrific excesses, such as its use by charismatic cult leaders and terrorists who lure vulnerable young people into their lairs, only to later exploit their innocence in a deadly fashion. The power of persuasion – its ability to captivate and connive – fascinates people the world over.

In our own unprecedented era, where YouTube influencers recruit millions of followers through catchy, charismatic marketing of a personal brand and online provocateurs create false Facebook pages that can be difficult to distinguish from legitimate counterparts, influence intrigues and unnerves. We willingly give apps intimate information about our personal lives – body weight, pregnancy date, location of the fast food restaurant we binge at on weekends – only to discover these details have been shared with companies which hope to use this information to snooker us into buying their products. Our fascination with persuasion reflects realistic fears and hopes, as well as exaggerations about effects of the global, glitzy media. Sorting out the real from the fanciful and, more broadly, understanding the processes by which persuasion occurs is the focus of this book.

This text examines these issues, exploring them through the keen lens of social scientific theory and research. It delves into persuasive communications, their effects, and the dynamics of attitudes

Figure 1.1 Steve Jobs, the Computer and Marketing Guru, Showcased the Ways That Persuasion Could Be Harnessed for Positive Purposes, Unleashing His Communication Skills to Develop and Promote Apple Computers, the iPod, iPhone, and iPad. Like all people and professional persuaders, Jobs was imperfect: He was widely viewed as contemptuous and disparaging of others. Yet he was also a visionary whose ideas – and captivating persuasive abilities – revolutionized the world of products and technology

Image courtesy of iStock photos

communicator hope to change. It takes you through theories, classic applications, and subtle implications of the persuasion craft. And on a more personal note, I endeavor to show how you can use persuasion insights to become a more effective persuasive speaker, a more critical judge of social influence attempts, and a more sensitive, ethical communicator.

This introductory chapter sets the stage for the chapters that follow, placing persuasion in its historical context and explaining, with examples that encompass LeBron James, "Make America Great Again," and fake Facebook posts, the distinctive characteristics of persuasion today.

Persuasion: Constancies and Changes

The study and practice of persuasion are not new. Persuasion can be found in the Old Testament – for example, in Jeremiah's attempts to convince his people to repent and establish a personal relationship with God. We come across persuasion when we read about John the Baptist's exhortations for Christ. John traveled the countryside, acting as Christ's "advance man," preaching that "Christ is coming, wait till you see him, when you look in his eyes you'll know that you've met Christ the Lord" (Whalen, 1996, p. 110).

Long before professional persuaders hoped to turn a profit from books on closing a deal, traveling educators known as the Sophists paraded through ancient Greece, charging money for lectures on public speaking and the art of political eloquence. Five centuries before political consultants advised presidential candidates how to package themselves on television, the Italian diplomat Niccolo Machiavelli rocked the Renaissance world with his how-to manual for political persuaders, entitled *The Prince*. Machiavelli believed in politics and respected crafty political leaders. He offered a litany of suggestions for how politicians could maintain power through cunning and deception.

In the United States, where persuasion has played an outsized role in politics and commercial sales, it should come as no surprise that communication campaigns are as American as media-advertised apple pie! The first crusade to change health behavior did not occur in 1970 or 1870, but in 1820. Nineteenth-century reformers expressed concern about increases in binge drinking and pushed for abstinence from alcohol. A few years later, activists committed to clean living tried to persuade Americans to quit using tobacco, exercise more, and adopt a vegetarian diet that included wheat bread, grains, fruits, and vegetables (Engs, 2000).

As they say in France: *Plus ça change, plus c'est la même chose* (the more things change, the more they remain the same). Yet, for all the similarities, there are important differences between our era of persuasion and those that preceded it. Each epoch has its own character, feeling, and rhythm. Contemporary persuasion differs from the past in the following ways, encapsulated in Table 1.1.

The Number and Reach of Persuasive Communications Have Grown Exponentially

Online advertising, public service announcements, negative political commercials, and those daily interruptions from telephone marketers are among the most salient indicators of this trend. Eons ago, you could go through a day with preciously little exposure to impersonal persuasive messages. This is no longer true during an epoch in which there are countless persuasive appeals (Rhoads, 1997), and messages are conveyed through mediated channels, via colorful language, emoticons, and emoji. People frequently showcase persuasive messages on their bodies, on T-shirts, bracelets, and tattoos. Even tragedies have become fair game. Shortly after terrorists slaughtered 12 people in an attack on the French satirical magazine, *Charlie Hebdo*, in 2015, "Je Suis Charlie" ("I Am Charlie") items began selling on Amazon, Etsy, and other online retail sites. Appearing at the Golden Globe Awards, the elegant Amal Clooney sported a black-and-white "Je Suis Charlie" button, all the more eye-catching since it fit with her black Dior dress and her white gloves; she and other communicators showed their affinity for a persuasive cause "by wearing it, literally," on their sleeve (Friedman, 2015).

Persuasion's reach extends well beyond the United States, to countries and communities linked into worldwide media marketing and attuned to sports celebrities. Some years back, a U.S. college student traveling in remote areas of China reported that, while stranded by winter weather, he came across a group of Tibetans. After sharing their food with the student, the Tibetans began to discuss an issue that touched on matters American. "Just how," one of the Tibetans asked the young American, "was Michael Jordan doing?" (LaFeber, 1999, p. 14). In our own time, another basketball superstar – LeBron James, who famously played for the Cleveland Cavaliers – has become an international phenomenon, known for his basketball prowess worldwide.

While traveling in France several years back, a Cleveland newspaper columnist, Phillip Morris, spotted a man at a subway stop near Paris sporting jeans, headphones, and a LeBron James jersey, with the iconic number 23 that once graced James' Cleveland Cavaliers jersey. Morris gave the guy a thumbs up and the man returned the sign, raising his thumb too. "Common ground between strangers had been established without a single word being exchanged. That is the power of sports and the undeniable global magnetism of LeBron James," Morris (2018, p. E3) concluded, underscoring the iconic appeal of James – athletic superstar, graceful actor in a blockbuster movie, and bodacious, sometimes-controversial spokesperson for political causes, ranging from impassioned statements about police shootings of African Americans to an oddly unartful defense of the authoritarian Chinese regime in 2019.

James' tweeted criticism of freedom of speech to oppose the Chinese government, which seemed to showcase pocketbook over principle since James has benefited handsomely from sales of his merchandise in China, became an immediate global cause celebre, destined to hurt him with Hong Kong's anti-Chinese protesters, while increasing his cachet with the lucrative Chinese market. James' appeal is

Table 1.1 Key Ways Today's Persuasion Differs from Previous Eras

1. Number of messages
2. Speed and brevity
3. A hybrid industry – part institutional, part gig
4. Subtlety
5. Complexity and digital mediation
6. Entwined with online and social media (exposure to short, metaphorical messages, with simultaneous message exchange among millions of strangers, that may confirm biases, as well as expand beliefs)
7. Spread of dark digitized falsehoods, aided by automated bots

emblematic of the power of a brand, the image of triumph in sports, the magnetism of celebrity, as well as its dark glare, all the symbolic stuff that lies at the heart of so much mediated persuasion, ubiquitous as it is in contemporary life (e.g., Rhoads, 1997).

Persuasive Messages Travel Faster Than Ever Before

Advertisements "move blindingly fast," one writer observes (Moore, 1993, p. B1). Ads quickly and seamlessly combine cultural celebrities (Beyoncé), symbols (success, fame, and athletic prowess), and commodity signs (the Nike swoosh). By pressing "send," political marketing specialists can recruit volunteers.

Texts, tweets, and short posts have become the signatures of instantaneous contemporary persuasion, characterized as much by their brevity as their speed. Consider how, in the wake of police killings of unarmed African American men, tweets sprang up almost instantly. Tweets with hashtags like the now-famous "Black Lives Matter" diffused across the nation soon after the death of Michael Brown on August 9, 2014, arousing passions and activating attitudes. These simple metaphoric statements, emblematic of time-honored outrage at racial injustice, spread like wildfire across social networks, allowing social activists to mobilize the committed, as activists have done for centuries. There was a contemporary twist: They could reach millions instantly with messages packed with powerful words and vivid pictures, perhaps changing attitudes and winning converts, without once directly exchanging a persuasive message face-to-face.

Twitter is the epitome of terse persuasive messaging. The hashtag #lovewins, joyously developed to celebrate the Supreme Court's ruling in favor of same-sex marriage, moved with warp speed to convey, distill, and mobilize attitudes toward racial prejudice and gay rights. #lovewins took off like few other hashtags. The Supreme Court announced its same-sex marriage decision on Friday morning, June 26, 2015. By 3 p.m. on Friday, 2.6 million tweets with that hashtag had been posted, at the rate of about 20,000 tweets per minute (Flynn, 2015). While the metaphoric hashtag undoubtedly stimulated tweets among those who already agreed with the Court's decision, its popularity and emotional content likely affirmed attitudes toward same-sex marriage in ways not possible before the current era. In a similar fashion, in the wake of news exposés of celebrity sexual harassment and the spontaneous growth of the online discussion of sexual abuse, #MeToo hashtags proliferated, tweeted more than 19 million times.

Persuasion Is a Hybrid Industry – Part Institutional, Part Gig

In the old days, it was pretty straightforward. Persuasion is institutionalized, older editions of this book blared, an activity that occurs in large organizations that test-market and vet persuasive messages before officially releasing them. This is still true but, with millions of gig workers marketing themselves feverishly on social media, the term "hybrid" is more apt, calling attention to the ways that persuasion occurs in both macro (institutional) and micro (hustler on her smartphone) contexts.

To be sure, numerous companies are in the persuasion business. Advertising agencies, public relations firms, marketing conglomerates, lobbying groups, social activists, pollsters, speech writers, image consultants – companies big and small – are involved with various facets of persuasion. The list is long and continues to grow. Persuasion is a critical weapon in the arsenal of powerful companies. Tobacco companies and vaping giants like Juul use public relations agents to massage their images in the face of broad public criticism. Political interest groups spend millions to influence the votes of members of Congress. Energy companies hire persuasion specialists to deflate the arguments of environmentalists concerned about global warming. Wealthy, powerful organizations have more resources to use persuasion effectively than do less politically connected groups. They can depend upon networks of connections spread across society's most influential institutions.

But not all persuasion occurs this way. In the gig economy, persuasion has gone freelance. More than nine in ten new jobs created in recent years were outsourced to individual entrepreneurs, getting paid by the hour. Some 18 million Americans are doing sales or multilevel marketing work, buying everything from leggings to vitamins with their own cash, and then trying to recoup their losses by hustling them to friends on social media. Nearly half of all millennials have worked in this way, doing persuasion not in big organizations, but solo, peddling an entrepreneurial initiative or social cause (Whippman, 2018).

It is a non-stop pursuit. "Share my blog post, buy my book, click on my link, follow me on Instagram, visit my Etsy shop, donate to my Kickstarter, crowdfund my heart surgery," writer Ruth Whippman exclaimed, describing the persuasion pursuits of many millennials. The goal is to create a persuasive online brand, then tweet, retweet, tweet again, and blog, frequently besieging your friends to share your posts so you can develop a distinctive "social media presence," to call on that hackneyed, over-used phrase. The form and content of these gig, entrepreneurial messages differ dramatically from the more committee-tested communications developed in organizational settings.

In today's hybrid persuasion, the old and the new offer possibilities and pitfalls. Doing persuasion in a big organization brings excitement and the prospect of riches. However, one gives up freedom and must rationalize (another persuasion factor), reducing dissonance that can occur when one devises messages that please corporate bosses, but offend a personal moral compass. Solo persuasion in the gig economy lets you do what you want and pursue the dream of becoming the next Warby Parker. However, the non-stop pressure to promote yourself on every online site creates its own type of contemporary angst. In today's persuasion, there is no free lunch, on or offline.

Persuasive Communication Has Become More Subtle and Devious

We are long past the days in which brash salespeople knocked on your door to pitch encyclopedias or hawk Avon cosmetics directly. Nowadays, salespeople know all about flattery, empathy, non-verbal communication, and likeability appeals. Walk into a Nordstrom clothing store and you see a fashionably dressed man playing a piano. Nordstrom wants you to feel like you're in a special, elite place, one that not-so-incidentally sells brands of clothing that jibe with this image.

Advertising no longer relies only on hard-sell, "hammer it home" appeals, but also on soft-sell messages that play on emotions. Some years back, the United Colors of Benetton clothing company showed attention-grabbing pictures of a dying AIDS patient and a desperately poor Third World girl holding a White doll from a trash can. The pictures appeared with the tag line, "United Colors of Benetton." What do these images have to do with clothing? Nothing – and everything. Benetton was selling an image, not a product. It appealed to consumers' higher sensibilities, inviting them to recognize that "the world we live in is not neatly packaged and cleansed as most ads depict it ... at Benetton we are not like others, we have vision" (Goldman & Papson, 1996, p. 52; see Figure 1.2).

Figure 1.2 Today's Persuasive Communications Are Characterized by the Use of Indirect and Subtle Appeals. What message do you think this ad for United Colors of Benetton, a clothing and fashion accessories company, is trying to convey?

Image courtesy of Benetton

Benetton was promoting a brand, the image of a company that was not like all the others, but one that cared about the poor and oppressed – one with soul. "In corporate America, the branding conceit of the moment includes just the right dash of social activism," a writer observes (Egan, 2015, p. A17). It's all so soft-sell and even a little bit devious.

Other examples abound, almost amusing in their irony. Chick-fil-A restaurants place to-go orders filled with fatty waffle potato fries and high-sodium nuggets in bags inscribed with exercise tips suggesting you "play hopscotch, dodgeball or other outdoor games" to burn calories and stay healthy. Similarly, McDonald's, world famous for quick meals but also heart-clogging transfat, has playgrounds at some of its restaurants, a similar attempt to cleverly link the restaurant with an active, healthy lifestyle.

There are other, more serious, examples of the subtle, devious use of persuasion. Persuaders also manipulate Internet technology, disguising persuasion intent. Advertisers deliberately place sponsored stories and blog posts next to bona fide news articles on websites (Ember, 2015). They cleverly blend them into the page to suggest to consumers that these posts are not actually ads, but news articles written by journalists or Web producers. Thus, a drug company's sponsored article on sleep deprivation that promotes a sleeping pill may be interpreted by consumers as a credible news story written by an impartial reporter rather than what it is: An advertiser's sly attempt to hawk a product. When shared on social media, the deception may be magnified.

These techniques fall into the category of promotional content that bears stylistic similarities to the news or mimics legitimate news articles, but is intended to promote a commercial product or service (Glasser, Varma, & Zou, 2019). The term "native" reinforces the deception because it suggests the content belongs naturally in a news space when it is deceptively designed to mimic news.

There are other, more serious examples of the subtle, devious use of persuasion. Consider the organized attempts to denigrate the science of climate change, part of an institutionalized effort to weaken U.S. government efforts to mitigate ecological damage. Although the science is complicated, there is a preponderance of evidence in support of global warming and stratospheric ozone depletion, with environmental scientists in agreement that the gradual warming of the earth has occurred as a result of human activities. Yet a conservative countermovement, which rejects environmental science, disdains government regulation, and (to be fair) fears that efforts to tame global warming will cause a massive loss in American jobs, has mounted a "war on climate science," and on the canons of respectable scientific study (Dunlap & Jacques, 2013, p. 713).

More than 92 percent of the books questioning the seriousness of climate change over a 30-year period have been linked to conservative think tanks (Jacques, Dunlap, & Freeman, 2008). Some authors, while promoting themselves as honest seekers of truth, have worked for the well-heeled fossil fuels industry, raising questions about the objectivity of their conclusions (Dunlap & Jacques, 2013). Their goal is to exploit the principles of persuasion in an effort to mold public attitudes and influence policy decisions, despite the strong scientific consensus that failure to take meaningful steps to reduce global warming will, over the long haul, exert profound impacts on the health of the planet (Gillis, 2015). Sadly, their efforts may have paid off, as they convinced many people that the facts on climate change are open to dispute, when global warming is an incontrovertible, woeful fact.

Political movements like these, along with discoveries of their masked persuasive intent, have left an imprint on the public. They have made Americans more cynical about persuasion. Bombarded by communications promoted as truth but actually misleading, as well as by blogs that identify factual inaccuracies in these slickly packaged messages, consumers have grown wary of the truthfulness of persuaders' claims. They seem to recognize that this is an age of spin in which commercial and political communicators regard the truth as just another strategy in the persuasion armamentarium. While skepticism is a useful attribute in an age of ubiquitous mediated persuasion, it also breeds cynicism, the problematic refusal to trust scientifically valid messages, and knee-jerk rejection of research based on carefully gathered empirical facts that can help people take appropriate steps to ward off environmental dangers.

Persuasive Communication Is More Complex and Digitally Mediated

Once upon a time long ago, persuaders knew their clients. Everyone lived in the same small communities. When cities developed and industrialization spread, persuaders knew fewer of their customers, but could be reasonably confident that they understood their clients because they all shared the same cultural and ethnic background. As the United States has become more culturally and racially diverse, persuaders and consumers frequently come from different sociological places. A marketer cannot assume that her client thinks the same way that she does or approaches a communication encounter with the same assumptions. The intermingling of people from different cultural groups is a profoundly positive phenomenon, but it makes for more dicey and difficult interpersonal persuasion.

What's more, persuasive communication seems to bombard in multiple directions, from a plethora of media. Advertisements, political advertisements, and even computer-mediated interpersonal appeals from Facebook friends to see this movie, join this cause, or reject another friend's manipulative stance are emblematic of the contemporary age. Technology increasingly mediates – comes between – the communicator and message recipient.

Digital technology has changed the nature of persuasion in several key respects. It has increased complexity, blurring lines among information, entertainment, and influence. For example, a website intended to inform or amuse may capture the eye of a blogger, who combines it with imagery and sends the modification over the Internet. It's now a persuasive message, taking on a meaning the original communicator never intended. An older (but still classic) example involves a song originally sung by the musical group Green Day, "Wake me up when September ends," a political song about war and romance. When a blogger known as Zadi linked the song with TV news coverage of Hurricane Katrina and posted it on her website in September 2005, it became a musically conveyed persuasive message about society's indifference to Katrina's victims (Boxer, 2005). The pairing of lyrics like "summer has come and passed, the innocent can never last" with images of devastation created an eerie, haunting message. When combined with suggestions that the Bush administration had been callous in its response to hurricane victims, the mélange conveyed a potent political message, one that might be at odds with the original Green Day song, with its more ambiguous stand toward the war in Iraq.

Over the ensuing decade, millions of people have routinely performed the same digital editing strategy on less storied persuasive messages. Contemporary technologies make it possible for people to alter the content of persuasive messages, giving messages meanings they did not have and that the original communicator did not intend. From a purist's perspective, this raises questions. How dare someone remix the Bible, or Shakespeare? To a purist, it seems almost … blasphemous. On the other hand, the freedom to modify the content of persuaders' messages empowers receivers, offering them opportunities to challenge powerful persuaders in innovative ways. And it's also fun, suggesting that the "p" in persuasion can also stand for playful.

Interactivity allows endless two-way communication between senders and receivers, enabling receivers to transform the meaning of messages so they no longer comport with the original communication, producing a seemingly infinite potpourri of sender–receiver intersections. Thus, the Internet has democratized persuasive discourse, creating a mechanism by which "regular citizens, possessing nothing more than a cheap video camera (or just a cell phone or computer cam) can have a significant impact on an election, a public debate, a business controversy, or any other form of public issue" (Gurak & Antonijevic, 2009, p. 504).

Yet this heady optimism about persuasive discourse on the Internet has given way to skepticism and uneasy philosophical issues, in light of the upsurge in venomous online speech. Political activists regularly remix messages, changing the meaning of the original message in controversial ways. Several years back, a right-wing activist edited the violent ending from an action movie, "Kingsman: The Secret Service," in which the main character guns downs some 40 people in the space of three minutes, as a song, "Free Bird," plays in the background. The remixed version shows President Trump's face superimposed on the top of the main character's in a "Church of Fake News," as he shoots church members, whose superimposed faces are those of his political opponents, journalists, and depict the logos of political and news organizations, like Black Lives Matter and CNN on their bodies. The video, condemned by Trump, could be viewed as sophomoric satire, excerpt that it was shown at a conference of Trump supporters at his Miami resort and occurs in the context of deadly outbreaks of violence at houses of worship (Warzel, 2019; for a German example, see Satariano, 2019). This case highlights the fuzzy line between protecting freedom of online persuasive speech and government's concern that online messages will exert pernicious effects on like-minded Internet users.

Persuasion Has Become Entwined with Online and Social Media Technologies

Interactive technologies have done much to eviscerate the boundary between persuader and persuadee. As one writer notes, "the line between persuader and persuaded is becoming less like the one between labor and management and more like the one between driver and pedestrian – one we might cross over frequently in a single day" (Johnson, 2011, p. 18; see also Figure 1.3).

Figure 1.3 Social Media and the Internet Have Changed the Topography of Persuasive Discourse, Normalizing Short, Emotionally Fraught Posts That Can Polarize Attitudes, But Can Also Bridge Cultural Differences, Engaging More Individuals Than Possible in Earlier Eras. More ominously, the ability of cyberagents and extremist groups to circulate false, inflammatory messages – some automated by social bots – that cannot easily be traced has darkened the contours of online persuasion. It has disturbingly showcased how malevolent persuaders exploit free speech to circulate messages that can activate prejudiced attitudes

The ubiquitous social media blurs these boundaries even more. Many persuasion encounters now occur online – via tweets, posts, hashtag, and emoji – rather than face-to-face. Does this change the nature of persuasion? No and yes. On the one hand, persuasion, as we will see, involves the symbolic process by which messages influence beliefs and attitudes. This occurs through social media, just as it has for centuries in interpersonal communication or, in the twentieth century, via film and television. Regardless of the media platform, persuasive communicators must convince another person to rethink an idea, belief, or feeling about an issue. There are no guarantees that online persuasion will work, and social media posts can have wonderful influences when they induce someone to look at the world through different eyes, malevolent effects when culturally insensitive posts inflame old prejudices, and unspeakable impact when terrorists harness horrific, technologically savvy videos to recruit new members.

Social media and online communication are unique in that messages, as in tweets, are frequently terse, calling on "the economy of the form," where powerful meanings are distilled into a simple meaning-packed phrase, like "#BlackLivesMatter" or, on the other side of the political ledger, "MakeAmericaGreatAgain" (Cobb, 2016, p. 35). These simple hashtag phrases can, like haiku, exert powerful effects through literary simplicity and conveyance of strong symbolic meanings, via both words and visual images, like emoji and emoticons. When people tweet regularly, their ease at sending simple, even one-word, emotive tweets, may propel them to rely more on simple, even politically extreme, thoughts, when expressing their attitudes (Gandarillas et al., 2018).

Contemporary social media persuasive message effects are unique in that they: (a) can involve simple catchphrases; (b) diffuse more quickly and widely than previous technologies; (c) enable others to participate in meaning conferral; and (d) are capable of mobilizing individuals across national boundaries.

Online media can exert a variety of positive effects on beliefs and attitudes. They delightfully expose individuals to a multitude of communicators, some offering viewpoints that contrast with users' political attitudes (Manjoo, 2015). On the other hand, people frequently come into contact with political media messages with which they already agree (Stroud, 2011). Thus, persuasive messages that are shared on social networking sites are apt to be those that reaffirm a particular worldview or political perspective. A pro-life message is posted on Facebook walls of individuals who earnestly oppose abortion for religious reasons, and it is never seen by those on the pro-choice side of the issue. A tweet that opposes affirmative action, arguing that it is not fair to working-class White students, is cheered by conservative members of the tweeter's social network, but is never glimpsed by affirmative action supporters, who might gain another perspective from the conservative tweet. More nuanced messages that try to balance the strong and weak points of different positions may be shared less frequently. This can make social media an echo chamber, where messengers preach to the choir and individuals end up feeling all the more strongly that their position is correct. If social media favor the congenial, rather than the confrontationally challenging, positions that help shake up our assumptions, it is doing us a disservice. We need perspectives that expand, enrich, excite, and propel us to change. That's persuasion too.

Persuasion Is Frayed by Dark, Digital Falsehoods and Automated Devices

This final facet of contemporary persuasion highlights the dark side. Of course, persuasion has always involved distortions, falsehoods, and lies. Sexist men branded innocent women witches in the 1600s, racist tropes stereotyped and stigmatized African Americans, and Jews have historically been targeted with anti-Semitic slurs. Traveling salesmen have long peddled falsehoods. Deception in advertising dates back decades. Even the term "propaganda" dates back to Alexander the Great, the Roman Empire, the Catholic Church (in its efforts to excoriate the Protestant Reformation), and most infamously to Nazi Germany, with its heinous use of films and radio in the 1930s (Jowett & O'Donnell, 2019). Yet, despite these similarities with classic persuasion in the past, today's digital deceptions have several distinctive characteristics.

First, in the past, fakery lacked the capacity to permeate deeply and broadly across multiple social networks, producing and reproducing effects, as it does today, through the mixed blessings of online media. Persuaders perpetrating false messages could not hope to gain simultaneous access to so many people of different backgrounds. Beginning during the white-hot 2016 presidential election, Russian agents trying to foment discord and turn the election in Donald Trump's favor created hundreds of thousands of false messages, phony Facebook accounts, fictitious personae, and automated bots that reached millions of users. On Facebook, the Internet Research Agency, the computer-savvy Russian spy agency, posted some 80,000 incendiary messages that reached 126 million Americans on Facebook, who liked the messages or spread them to other Facebook users (Isaac & Wakabayashi, 2017).

On the domestic front, left-wing and right-wing ideologues have adapted these techniques. Liberal political operatives created a fake Facebook page that deliberately linked an Alabama Republican running for re-election with numerous Russian accounts to suggest he was in cahoots with the Russians (Shane & Blinder, 2018). Right Wing News posted a story about Dr. Christine Blasey Ford, falsely claiming that lawyers for the psychologist, who accused Justice Brett Kavanaugh of sexual assault in 2018, had been bribed by Democrats; the site then proceeded to share the story on Facebook pages so the disinformation spread online quickly. "There are now well-developed networks of Americans targeting other Americans with purposefully designed manipulations," a social media expert said (Frenkel, 2018, p. A1). Old-style deceptive, propagandistic persuasion – though more on the propaganda term in the next chapter – never had this reach and speed of influence.

A second noteworthy aspect of today's dark online deceptions involves mechanisms by which these messages can attract an audience using digital techniques unavailable in previous eras. Communications can be so cleverly constructed that it can be impossible to differentiate fake from real posts on feminism and racial issues (Collins & Frenkel, 2018). False, heinous messages have an initial psychological luster, spreading more quickly, deeply, and broadly on Twitter than accurate information, in part because they are novel, elicit strong negative emotions, and provoke people to share the messages with others (Vosoughi, Roy, & Aral, 2018).

The third distinctive aspect of deceptive digital messages is the capacity of malicious software to influence human minds. This is truly novel, the stuff of science fiction movies and Philip K. Dick novels, but now quite real. The key is the *social bot*, an automated software that is capable of automatically generating messages and advocating positions by appearing to be a follower or fake account that may solicit followers. Social bots perform a host of human activities, like tweeting, posting status updates, sharing pictures, making friend requests, and conversing online with others. Stealthily passing themselves off as humans through artificial intelligence or automatically mimicking other online participants, "they are designed to appear human" to social networking site users, offering up a sense of self, posing "as a subject with personal biography" with whom the user might develop an online social relationship (Gehl & Bakardjieva, 2017, p. 2). In fact, the messages are machine-generated, intended to fool people by diffusing artificially inflated support for popular and subversive political causes and infiltrating online discussions, inserting, via algorithms, misinformation and slander (Ferrara et al., 2016).

While there is no doubt that fake and social bot-originated messages are out there in force, there is debate about the extent of their effects. It is easy to assume these new-fangled digital posts are effective, but if you do, you may be guilty of the *third-person effect*, presuming that, of course, *you* see through these messages and recognize they're false, but *others* (the masses of third persons) fall prey to their sinister influence (Perloff, 2009). You may, in short, buy into the prevailing wisdom and exaggerate others' susceptibility to these automated posts, assuming they are effective, in the absence of evidence, because they malevolently exploit artificial intelligence and other sexy technologies.

It turns out there are good arguments on both sides of the issue. Some scholars emphasize the ways that fake social media sites exploit classic persuasion principles, such as similarity between the communicator and target audience member, and access strong attitudes. A 2016 site created by Russian political operatives hyped similarity, illustrated by the fictitious Facebook page of a supposedly friendly (but Russian-created) American, Melvin Redick, of Harrisburg, Pennsylvania, shown with the familiar backward baseball cap and smiling young daughter, as he promoted a website that promised to show the "hidden truth" about Hillary Clinton (Shane, 2017).

In other instances, social media sites primed partisans' strong attitudes, in particular their identification with ethnic, religious, or racial groups. Amplified by sounds and colors, these posts have accessed extreme attitudes, pushing them to the surface, putting people with strong attitudes in touch with their most prejudiced sentiments.

Some scholars remain dubious about the extent of these effects. While acknowledging that social media influences can occur, they point out they are relatively rare, in any case blown out of proportion by a conflict-driven, ratings-hungry news media. Harking back to the controversial 2016 election, research finds that Russian bots comprised only 1 percent of all election-related tweets, and it is likely fewer of these were even seen, let alone acted on (Nyhan, 2018). What's more, these messages may not have changed attitudes so much as reached people who already were true believers and disliked the other side. On the other hand, if they achieved this impact, that constitutes a persuasive influence, polarizing attitudes, even stoking hate in an age of white-hot strong ideological passions.

Terrorists who have attacked places of worship, like Jewish synagogues or churches, have, in extreme cases, turned to social media platforms popular with White supremacists, where they either posted hateful messages themselves or found psychological support from bigoted messages posted by many others. This can deliver "psychological proof" (Cialdini, 2009) that extremists' ideas are valid and otherwise douse antisocial impulses with the fire of sustenance, lent by support from a welcoming online community of prejudiced others. Extremism is hardly new; it dates to antiquity (Berger, 2018). However, social media platforms can pump up hate, distributing hateful manifestos within seconds to politically similar others, who share it with thousands more.

The forces at work here are the stuff of attitudes and involve the power of persuasion. Online networks offer a venomous gathering place for people who could never have located each other before, and, through the synergistic power of social contagion and selective perception, fortify partisan attitudes and prime deep-seated prejudice. This is new, a disturbing characteristic of our age.

Conclusions

Persuasion is a ubiquitous part of contemporary life. If you search the term on the Web, you may find hundreds of topics, including "brainwashing controversies," "marketing," "how to get people to like you," or "15 secrets of really persuasive people." The Internet is a persuader's paradise, with websites promoting millions of products and services. Social media is filled with opinionated message exchanges among strangers spanning the globe. However, persuasion has more personal components. We can all think of times when we yielded to a parent's heart-felt influence attempt, tried to persuade friends to go along with us, or scratched our heads to figure out ways we could have done a better job of getting a colleague to accept our plan.

Persuasion is an ancient art. It dates back to the Bible and ancient Greece. Yet there are important aspects of contemporary persuasion that are unique to this era, notably the volume, speed, subtlety, complexity, digitization, and remixing of modern messages. Social media have transformed some of the contours of persuasion, elevating terse text messages, fraught with cultural meanings, compressing distances between persuader and persuadee, highlighting the versatility of persuasion, where individuals are simultaneously message sender and message receiver on different social networking sites, and expanding choices almost endlessly, while paradoxically amplifying exposure to like-minded others that reinforce pre-existing worldviews.

Finally, deceptions, a long-standing feature of persuasion, have taken on darker hues in recent years, with the capacity of digitized falsehoods to permeate more broadly and deeply, in some cases aided by automated social bots. Scholars differ in their assessment of the degree to which these falsehoods influence attitudes, but there is little doubt they have provided extremist elements with digital weapons of influence. Our task is to unpack and understand the multitude of messages, good and bad, malevolent and benign. A theme of this book is that these message effects are best understood through the time-honored processes of persuasion, with their emphasis on the complex interplay between the message and the mind.

References

Berger, J. M. (2018). *Extremism*. Cambridge, MA: MIT Press.

Boxer, S. (2005, September 24). Art of the internet: A protest song, reloaded. *The New York Times*, A17.

Cialdini, R. B. (2009). *Influence: Science and practice* (5th ed.). Boston, MA: Pearson Education.

Cobb, J. (2016, March 14). The matter of Black lives. *The New Yorker*, 34–40.

Collins, K., & Frenkel, S. (2018, September 5). Spotting the deceptive Facebook posts. *The New York Times*, B4.

Dunlap, R. E., & Jacques, P. J. (2013). Climate change denial books and conservative think tanks: Exploring the connection. *American Behavioral Scientist*, 57, 699–731.

Egan, T. (2015, April 4). Conscience of a corporation. *The New York Times*, A17.

Ember, S. (2015, December 23). F.T.C. guidelines for native ads aim to prevent deception. *The New York Times*, B1, B2.

Engs, R. C. (2000). *Clean living movements: American cycles of health reform*. Westport, CT: Praeger.

Ferrara, E., Varol, O., Davis, C., Menczer, F., & Flammini, A. (2016, July). The rise of social bots. *Communications of the ACM*, 59, 96–104.

Flynn, K. (2015, June 26). How #LoveWins on Twitter became the most viral hashtag of the same-sex marriage ruling. *International Business Times*. Retrieved from www.ibtimes.com/how-lovewins-twitter-became-most-viral-hashtag-same-sex-marriage-ruling-1986279

Frenkel, S. (2018, October 12). Made in U.S.: Untruths infest social websites. *The New York Times*, A1, A12.

Friedman, V. (2015, August 6). Taking stock of Tom Brady. *The New York Times*, D2.

Funt, P. (2014, September 27). Curses, Fooled again! *The New York Times*, A21.

Gandarillas, B., Briñol, P., Petty, R. E., & Díaz, D. (2018). Attitude change as a function of the number of words in which thoughts are expressed. *Journal of Experimental Social Psychology, 74,* 196–211.

Gehl, R. W., & Bakardjieva, M. (2017). Socialbots and their friends. In R. W. Gehl & M. Bakardjieva (Eds.), *Socialbots and their friends: Digital media and the automation of sociality* (pp. 1–16). New York: Routledge.

Gillis, J. (2015, December 1). Short answers to hard climate questions. *The New York Times,* D6.

Glasser, T. L., Varma, A., & Zou, S. (2019). Native advertising and the cultivation of counterfeit news. *Journalism, 20,* 150–153.

Goldman, R., & Papson, S. (1996). *Sign wars: The cluttered landscape of advertising.* New York: Guilford Press.

Gurak, L. J., & Antonijevic, S. (2009). Digital rhetoric and public discourse. In A. A. Lunsford, K. H. Wilson, & R. A. Eberly (Eds.), *The Sage handbook of rhetorical studies* (pp. 497–507). Thousand Oaks, CA: Sage.

Isaac, M., & Wakabayashi, D. (2017, October 31). Broad reach of campaign by Russians is disclosed. *The New York Times,* B1, B3.

Jacques, P. J., Dunlap, R. E., & Freeman, M. (2008). The organisation of denial: Conservative think tanks and environmental scepticism. *Environmental Politics, 17,* 349–385 (Ch.1).

Johnson, C. (2011). *Microstyle: The art of writing little.* New York: W. W. Norton.

Jowett, G. S., & O'Donnell, V. (2019). *Propaganda & persuasion* (7th ed.). Thousand Oaks, CA: Sage.

LaFeber, W. (1999). *Michael Jordan and the new global capitalism.* New York: Norton.

Manjoo, F. (2015, May 8). Facebook finds opposing views trickle through. *The New York Times,* A1, B7.

Moore, M. T. (1993, June 15). Visual overload: Fleeing ad images catch viewers. *USA Today,* B1.

Morris, P. (2018, July 4). LeBron's impact goes far beyond the courts with NBA players. *The Plain Dealer,* E3.

Murphy, C. (2018). Persuasion techniques in the game of *Survivor. Student paper, Persuasion and Attitude Change,* Cleveland State University.

Murphy, K. (2016, January 17). Seeking love, getting scammed. *The New York Times* (Sunday Review), 4.

Nyhan, B. (2018, February 13). Fake news and bots may be worrisome, but their political power is overblown. *The New York Times.* Retrieved April 11, 2019, from www.nytimes.com/2018/02/13/upshot/fake-news-and-bots-may-be-worrisome

Perloff, R. M. (2009). Mass media, social perception, and the third-person effect. In J. Bryant & M. B. Oliver (Eds.), *Media effects: Advances in theory and research* (3rd ed., pp. 252–268). New York: Taylor & Francis.

Rhoads, K. (1997). Everyday influence. In *Working psychology: Introduction to influence.* Retrieved May 4, 2013, from www.workingpsychology.com/evryinfl.html

Satariano, A. (2019, May 6). As Europe polices Tech, critics demand a guard for free speech. *The New York Times,* A1, A8.

Shane, S. (2017, September 8). To sway vote, Russia used army of fake Americans. *The New York Times,* A1, A10–A11.

Shane, S., & Blinder, A. (2018, December 19). Secret experiment in Alabama Senate race imitated Russian tactics. *The New York Times.* Retrieved April 9, 2019, from /www.nytimes.com/2018/12/19/us/alabama-senate-roy-jones

Singer, N., & Thomas, K. (2019, April 3). Prescription drugs to your door, nearly as easy as ordering pizza. *The New York Times,* A1, A14.

Stroud, N. J. (2011). *Niche news: The politics of news choice.* New York: Oxford University Press.

Vosoughi, S., Roy, D., & Aral, S. (2018). The spread of true and false news online. *Science*, 359(6380), 1146–1151.

Warzel, C. (2019, October 16). Violent Trump video is dumb for a reason. *The New York Times*, A26.

Whalen, D. J. (1996). *I see what you mean: Persuasive business communication*. Thousand Oaks, CA: Sage.

Whippman, R. (2018, November 24). Everything is for sale now. Even us. *The New York Times* (Sunday Review). Retrieved November 26, 2018, from www.nytimes.com/2018/11/24/opinion/sunday/gig=econom

Chapter 2

Foundations of Persuasion

At first blush, it seems pretty obvious. Academics, you sometimes think, make too big a deal about what is right there in front of us. You know persuasion when you see it. Coercion involves force. Propaganda is everywhere, and manipulation is something that clever, canny people do to hoodwink friends or consumers. Brainwashing is a bizarre, but real, phenomenon that describes extremities of human behavior.

Those may be the short-hand, informal ways you describe social influence. However, the concepts mentioned above that bear on the ways communications mold behavior are a lot more complicated and interrelated, as well as sharply delineated, than the simple ideas sketched out above suggest. Actions that seem to fall under the persuasion rubric may not actually constitute bona fide persuasion. Coercion is more than force and overlaps with persuasion in deeply psychological ways. Propaganda differs from persuasion in ways you might not expect. Manipulation has a very clear meaning in the scholarly field of persuasive communication. Brainwashing is a much-abused term that is more boogeyman than a basic element of persuasion.

Definitions are a key part of the social scientific mission because they delineate concepts, clarify ways that a construct differs from related ideas, and set up the parameters of a field of study. This chapter lays out the foundations of persuasion by defining and differentiating coercion, persuasion, propaganda, and manipulation, discussing their fraught implications for the world of unsavory persuasion, and debunking the much-mystified notion of brainwashing, with its applications to religious and terrorist cults. I begin with a novel, but important, issue: The quintessentially human aspects of persuasion.

Foundations

Do Animals Persuade?

Persuasion is celebrated as a quintessential human activity, but here's a subversive thought: Suppose we're not the only ones who do it? What if our friends in the higher animal kingdom also use a little homespun social influence? Frans de Waal painstakingly observed chimpanzees in a Dutch zoo and chronicled his observations in a book aptly called *Chimpanzee Politics* (1982). His conclusion: Chimps use all sorts of techniques to get their way with peers. They frequently resort to violence, but not always. Chimps form coalitions, bluff each other, and even show some awareness of social reciprocity, as they seem to recognize that favors should be rewarded and disobedience punished.

Does this mean that chimpanzees are capable of persuasion? Some scientists would answer "yes" and cite as evidence chimps' subtle techniques to secure power. Indeed, there is growing evidence that apes can form images, use symbols, and employ deception (Angier, 2008; Miles, 1993). To some scientists, the difference between human and animal persuasion is one of degree, not kind.

Wait a minute. Do we really think that chimpanzees persuade their peers? Perhaps they persuade in the Godfather sense of making people an offer they can't refuse. However, this is not persuasion so much as it is coercion.

As we will see, persuasion involves the persuader's awareness that he or she is trying to influence someone else. It also requires that the "persuadee" makes a conscious or unconscious decision to change his mind about something. With this definition in mind, chimpanzees' behavior is better described as social influence or coercion than persuasion (see definitions of these terms that appear later in the chapter).

"Okay," you animal lovers say, "but let me tell you about my cat." "She sits sweetly in her favorite spot on my sofa when I return from school," one feline-loving student told me, and then "curls up in my arms, and purrs softly until I go to the kitchen and fetch her some milk. Isn't that persuasion?" Well – no. Your cat may be trying to curry your favor, but she has not performed an act of persuasion. The cat is not cognizant that she is trying to "influence" you. What's more, she does not appreciate that you have a mental state – let alone a belief – that she wants to change.

Some animals, like apes, do have cognitive abilities. For example, they are aware of themselves; they can recognize that a reflected image in a mirror is of them (Fountain, 2006). Animals also experience emotions, sometimes poignantly, as when a dying chimpanzee grinned, cried, and caressed the face of a friend, a Dutch biologist who had come to bid goodbye to the chimp as she lay stricken on her deathbed (de Waal, 2019; Montgomery, 2019). However, as one leading moral philosopher convincingly argued, it makes no sense to believe that higher animals are motivated by a self-interested, abstract conception of their long-term goals, an attribute that is necessary to develop a persuasive message (Korsgaard, 2006). There is also no evidence that animals have well-developed beliefs or attitudes toward social objects and that they can articulate these through language. Nor do their attempts to influence humans appear directed at changing human attitudes, as opposed to simpler behaviors that bear on their lives.

There is one other reason why it does not make sense to say that animals engage in persuasion. Persuasion has moral components; individuals choose to engage in morally beneficent or morally reprehensible actions. However, as philosopher Carl Cohen (Cohen & Regan, 2001) points out,

> with all the varied capacities of animals granted, it remains absolutely impossible for them to act morally, to be members of a moral community … A being subject to genuinely moral judgment must be capable of grasping the maxim of an act and capable, too, of grasping the generality of an ethical premise in a moral argument.
>
> (p. 38)

Cohen and Reagan overstate this a little, given evidence that apes have some moral perspective-taking skills (de Waal, 2006).

Figure 2.1 Higher Animals Like Apes and Gorillas Can Coerce Their Peers. They can also engage in considerable social influence. However, they do not seem to be capable of persuasion, a human activity
Image courtesy of Shutterstock

Yet even granting that animals have mental and emotional capacities, and clearly possess moral impulses, they do not have the capacity to formulate morally based arguments. Nor do they possess the ability to use language to develop morally focused messages that are intended to influence cognitions or feelings associated with attitudes (see Figure 2.1).

At the same time, we need to remember that the difference between the capacity of humans and higher animals to persuade is frequently one of degree, as Darwin himself observed (de Waal, 2016). In light of increasing evidence that monkeys have rudimentary abilities to read intentions, draw mental inferences and behave (if not think) in morally relevant ways (Hauser, 2006), as well as experience an array of emotions, we should keep an open mind. Animals are certainly capable of social influence, and we may yet discover that higher animals can engage in elemental persuasion processes. But when it comes to highly symbolic communication that takes into account beliefs, attitudes, and messages designed to shape them, animals do not possess an ability to change attitudes in a manner that could be characterized as persuasion.

In sum, persuasion matters and strikes to the core of our lives as human beings. This means that we must define what we mean by persuasion and differentiate it from related terms. Scholars have defined persuasion in different ways. I list the following major definitions to show you how different researchers approach the topic. Persuasion, according to communication scholars, is:

- a communication process in which the communicator seeks to elicit a desired response from his receiver (Andersen, 1971, p. 6);
- a conscious attempt by one individual to change the attitudes, beliefs, or behavior of another individual or group of individuals through the transmission of some message (Bettinghaus & Cody, 1987, p. 3);
- a symbolic activity whose purpose is to effect the internalization or voluntary acceptance of new cognitive states or patterns of overt behavior through the exchange of messages (Smith, 1982, p. 7);
- a successful intentional effort at influencing another's mental state through communication in a circumstance in which the persuadee has some measure of freedom (O'Keefe, 2016, p. 4).

All of these definitions have strengths. Boiling down the main components into one unified perspective (and adding a little of my own recipe), I define *persuasion* as a symbolic process in which communicators try to convince other people to change their own attitudes or behaviors regarding an issue through the transmission of a message in an atmosphere of free choice. There are five components of the definition.

Persuasion Is a Symbolic Process

Contrary to popular opinion, persuasion does not happen with the flick of a switch. You don't just change people's minds – snap, crackle, pop. On the contrary, persuasion takes time, consists of a number of steps, and actively involves the recipient of the message. As Mark Twain quipped, "Habit is habit, and not to be flung out of the window, but coaxed downstairs a step at a time" (cited in Prochaska et al., 1994, p. 471).

Many of us view persuasion in one-sided, mechanistic ways. Persuaders are seen as tough-talking salespeople, strongly stating their position, hitting people over the head with arguments, and pushing the deal to a close. But this oversimplifies matters. It assumes that persuasion is a boxing match, won by the fiercest competitor. In fact, persuasion is different. It's more like teaching than boxing. Think of a persuader as a teacher, moving people step by step to a solution, helping them appreciate why the advocated position solves the problem best. Persuasion, in short, is a process.

Persuasion also involves the use of symbols. A symbol is a form of language in which one entity represents a concept or idea, communicating rich psychological and cultural meaning. Symbols include words like freedom, justice, and equality; non-verbal signs like the flag, Star of David, or Holy Cross; and images that are instantly recognized and processed like the Nike swoosh or McDonald's golden arches. Symbols are persuaders' tools, harnessed to change attitudes and mold opinions. Thus, persuasion frequently does not operate on a literal level. Language is subject to multiple interpretations. Meanings differ, depending on the way words and pictures pique audience members' imaginations, and the interpretations individuals apply to the same message. A rose is not always a rose. It may be a blossoming beauty to one audience and a thorn to another.

A message that uses the word "fetus" or "unborn child" has strikingly different meanings to pro-life and pro-choice audiences. To Jews, Christians, and Muslims who inhabit the Middle East, Jerusalem is not a neutral place, but calls up different religious meanings. It is a place of holiness to Jews, embedded in Jewish consciousness as the spiritual ancestral homeland of the Jewish people. For Christians, Jerusalem is the city where Jesus preached and healed, and prophetically sat at his Last Supper. For Muslims, Jerusalem is a sacred place, the site of the Prophet Muhammad's ascent to heaven.

In political persuasive communications, you find that some of the most vociferous debates involve different symbols attached to material objects. To many conservatives, guns are about the Second

Amendment to the Constitution, protection against intruders, and freedom that cuts to the core of gun owners' identities. To many liberals, guns connote killing, death of innocents, and a psychological insecurity cloaked in Second Amendment verbiage.

Meanings, multiple and shifting, inhabiting the rich tableau of the human mind: these are centerpieces of persuasion.

The centerpieces are powerful and in flux. For decades, the Confederate flag was, to many outside the South, a symbol of the region's despicable embrace of slavery. However, to some residents of South Carolina, it meant something different, serving as a striking "symbol of things southern," an emblem of the region's ancestral past (Coski, 2005, p. 305). But when online pictures appeared showing Dylann Roof, the White man who, in 2015, murdered nine African Americans in a historic Black church in Charleston, holding the flag and a gun, the iconography changed. It became untenable, even to those who saw the flag as a marker of southern pride, to adhere to this interpretation. The event wiped out – eviscerated and destroyed – these meanings, at least on a national level, imbuing the flag's white stars and red and blue colors with a vastly different cultural topography.

And yet, because this issue involves the South, with its conflicted views about the Confederacy (even today), one harks back to writer William Faulkner's classic observation that "the past is never dead; it's not even past." After a Charlottesville, Virginia rally by White nationalists in August, 2017 protesting the planned removal of a statue of Robert E. Lee erupted in violence, and a White supremacist smashed his car into a crowd of counter-protesters, killing a young woman, President Donald Trump blamed both sides, lamenting the removal of the "beautiful" Confederate statutes and monuments. The notion, frequently touted by White southerners, that the monuments represent "heritage, not hate," turns out to be an inversion of symbols, showcasing the ways symbolic meanings, always controversial and debated by proponents of different perspectives, change over time and come to be reinterpreted in light of new historical knowledge.

Far from commemorating the pastoral heritage of the South, historians now believe the Confederate statues represented efforts by White political leaders, marginalized during Reconstruction but politically ascendant – as elected leaders of southern state governments between 1890 and 1920 – to legitimize racially prejudiced ideas and recapture symbolic glory. They sought to do this by building monuments to certain southerners (Confederate leaders), while ignoring others, like dissenting southern generals and nineteenth century Black legislators (Foner, 2017; Robertson, Blinder, & Fausset, 2017). The Confederate monuments were more than symbols of heritage; they enshrined racial prejudice, glorifying men who fought a war to enslave other human beings (Lipstadt, 2019).

In a democratic society, symbols are the focus of continued debate, exemplified by discussions about whether the Confederate monuments should be toppled because they represent racism, preserved because society should not censor artworks, even if they are offensive, or should be balanced with alternative monuments to courageous Black protesters of the Jim Crow era. Symbols, with their rich tapestry of meanings that represent an intersection between the iconography of the object (the flag or the statue) and the perceptions that the perceiver brings to the object in a specific culture at a particular time, are a core component of persuasion.

Persuasion Involves an Attempt to Influence

Although it can have dramatic effects, persuasion does not always or inevitably succeed. Sometimes it fails to influence attitudes or behavior. Just as some companies go out of business soon after they open, persuasive communications do not always influence target audiences. But persuasion does involve a deliberate attempt to influence another person. Persuaders must intend to change another individual's attitude or behavior and must be aware (at least at some level) that they are trying to accomplish this goal.

For this reason it does not make sense to say that chimpanzees persuade each other. As noted earlier, chimps, smart as they are, do not seem to possess high-level awareness that they are trying to change another primate, let alone modify a fellow chimp's mind. Indeed, it is unlikely that they can conceptualize that the other animal has a mind that they seek to change, let alone an attitude that they would like to modify.

In a similar fashion, we should not make the claim that very young children are capable of persuasion. True, a mother responds to an infant's cry for milk by dashing to the refrigerator (or lending her breast, if that's her feeding preference). Yes, we have all shopped in toy stores and watched as two-year-olds point to toys seen on television and scream, "I want that." And we have been witness to the sight of parents, who pride themselves on being competent professionals, helplessly yielding to prevent any further embarrassment.

Yet the baby's cry for milk and the toddler's demand for toys do not qualify as persuasion. These youngsters have not reached the point where they are aware that they are trying to change another person's mental state. Their actions are better described as coercive social influence than persuasion. In order for children to practice persuasion, they must understand that other people can have desires and beliefs; recognize that the persuadee has a mental state that is susceptible to change; demonstrate a primitive awareness that they intend to influence another person; and realize that the persuadee has a perspective different from theirs, even if they cannot put all this into words (Bartsch & London, 2000; Lapierre, 2015). As children grow, they appreciate these things, rely less on coercive social influence attempts than on persuasion, and develop the ability to persuade others more effectively (Kline & Clinton, 1998).

The main point here is that persuasion represents a conscious attempt to influence the other party, along with an accompanying awareness that the persuadee has a mental state that is susceptible to change. It is a type of social influence. *Social influence* is the broad process in which the behavior of one person alters the thoughts or actions of another. Social influence can occur when receivers act on cues or messages that were not necessarily intended for their consumption (Dudczak, 2001). Persuasion occurs within a context of intentional messages that are initiated by a communicator in the hope of influencing the recipient (Frymier & Nadler, 2017). This is pretty heady stuff, but it's important because, if you include every possible influence attempt under the persuasion heading, you count every communication as persuasion. That would make for a very long book.

The larger question is whether persuasion should be defined from the perspective of the audience member or of the communicator. If you define it from the audience member's point of view, then every message, including countless ones relayed via social media, that conveys an opinion, or ends up altering someone's attitude, gets counted as persuasion. This is democratic, but unwieldy. It means that communication and persuasion are identical. It says that every Facebook post with an idea or emotion is persuasion, an attempt to convince. Do we really view social media messages through the lens of persuasion? People do a lot of communicating – talking, gossiping, disclosing things about themselves online and offline – that are not attempts to persuade. Some may be experienced as social influence, others less so. In any case, much everyday communication is not intended to change attitudes. For this reason, it is more useful to stipulate that persuasion involves some sort of deliberate effort to change another's mind.

Mind you, it gets messy in the blurred lines world of social media, where you encounter messages all day long that aren't intended to change your attitude, but can have that effect. These kinds of influences were dramatically experienced in the blizzard of posts women read, sent, and processed concerning sexual abuse, in the wake of media exposés of famous men's sexual abuse and later the emergence of the symbolic #MeToo movement. Women who posted pained personal recollections of sexual abuse weren't necessarily trying to influence others so much as share their experiences. Their messages moved others they never met in a myriad of ways, undoubtedly increasing people's empathy for victims who had experienced sexual abuse, perhaps inducing them to view their own victimization in a different light, even empowering them to take action against those who wronged them. The #MeToo posts weren't necessarily persuasive messages intended to change specific attitudes toward sexual assault. Instead, they influenced people who perused the posts, in this way pointing up the blurred conceptual boundary areas between concepts, the power of symbolic social influence, and the role intent plays in the particular type of social influence called persuasion.

People Persuade Themselves

One of the great myths of persuasion is that persuaders convince us to do things we really don't want to do. They supposedly overwhelm us with so many arguments or such verbal ammunition that we acquiesce. They force us to give in. This overlooks an important point: People persuade themselves to change attitudes or behavior. Communicators provide the arguments. They set up the bait. We make the change, or refuse to yield. As D. Joel Whalen puts it:

> You can't force people to be persuaded – you can only activate their desire and show them the logic behind your ideas. You can't move a string by pushing it, you have to pull it. People are the same. Their devotion and total commitment to an idea come only when they fully understand and buy in with their total being.
>
> (Whalen, 1996, p. 5)

The observation of the legendary psychologist William James remains true today: "The greatest discovery of our generation is that human beings can alter their lives by altering their attitudes of mind. As you think, so shall you be" (quoted in Johnson & Boynton, 2010, p. 19).

You can understand the power of self-persuasion by considering an activity that does not at first blush seem to involve persuasive communication: Therapy. Therapists undoubtedly help people make changes in their lives. But have you ever heard someone say, "My therapist persuaded me"? On the contrary, people who seek psychological help look into themselves, consider what ails them, and decide how best to cope. The therapist offers suggestions and provides an environment in which healing can take place (Kassan, 1999). But if progress occurs, it is the client who makes the change and the client who is responsible for making sure that there is no regression to the old ways of doing things. Of course, not every self-persuasion is therapeutic. Self-persuasion can be benevolent or malevolent. An ethical communicator will plant the seeds for healthy self-influence. A dishonest, evil persuader convinces a person to change her mind in a way that is personally or socially destructive. Note also that persuasion typically involves change. It does not focus primarily on forming attitudes, but on inducing people to alter attitudes they already possess. This can involve shaping, molding, or reinforcing attitudes, as is discussed later in the chapter.

Persuasion Involves the Transmission of a Message

The message may be verbal or non-verbal. It can be relayed interpersonally, through mass media, or social networking sites. It may be reasonable or unreasonable, factual or emotional. The message can consist of arguments or simple cues, like music in an advertisement that brings pleasant memories to mind. Persuasion is a communicative activity; thus, there must be a message for persuasion, as opposed to other forms of social influence, to occur.

Life is packed with messages that change or influence attitudes. In addition to the usual contexts that come to mind when you think of persuasion – advertising, political campaigns, and interpersonal sales – there are other domains that contain attitude-altering messages. News unquestionably shapes attitudes and beliefs (McCombs, 2014). Talk to older Americans who watched TV coverage of White policemen beating Black protesters in the South or chat with people who viewed television coverage of the Vietnam War, and you will gain first-hand evidence of how television news can shake up people's worldviews. News of more recent events – terrorist killings of innocent Americans, calamitous climate change occurrences, school shootings, and heart-rending stories of children separated from parents entering the United States – have left indelible impressions on people's views of politics and the world as a whole.

Art – books, movies, plays, and songs – also has a strong influence on how we think and feel about life. Artistic portrayals can transport people into different realities, changing the way they see life (Green & Brock, 2000; Igartua & Barrios, 2012). If you think for a moment, I'm sure you can call to mind books, movies, and songs that shook you up and pushed you to rethink your assumptions. Dostoyevsky's discussions of the human condition, a Picasso painting, movies like *12 Years a Slave*, *Schindler's List*, *American Sniper*, *Green Book*, and *Bohemian Rhapsody*, *The Simpsons* television show, a folk melody or hip-hop song, like "To Pimp a Butterfly" – these can all influence and change people's worldviews. Indeed, Harper Lee's classic, *To Kill a Mockingbird*, with its portrayal of lawyer Atticus Finch's crusading battle against racial prejudice, inspired many Americans, propelling them to model Finch's single-minded dedication to social justice. Little wonder that so many readers once transported by *Mockingbird* found themselves disturbed and disoriented by Lee's subsequently published novel, *Go Set a Watchman*, with its depiction of Finch as a racist who attended a meeting of the Ku Klux Klan.

Yet although novels, even powerful ones, works of art, and investigative news stories contain messages that change attitudes, they are not pure exemplars of persuasion.

Recall that persuasion is defined as an attempt to convince others to change their attitudes or behavior. In many cases, journalists are not trying to change people's attitudes toward a topic. They are describing events so as to provide people with information, offer new perspectives, or entice viewers to watch their programs. In the same fashion, most artists do not create art to change the world. They write, paint, or compose songs to express important personal concerns, articulate vexing problems of life, or soothe, uplift, or agitate people. In a sense, it demeans art to claim that artists attempt only to change our attitudes. Thus, art and news are best viewed as borderline cases of persuasion. Their messages can powerfully influence our worldviews, but because the intent of these communicators is broader and more complex than attitude change, news and art are best viewed as lying along the border of persuasion and the large domain of social influence.

For example, you can easily think of movies that have a clearly persuasive purpose. Michael Moore definitely hoped that *Fahrenheit 9/11* would convince Americans to change their attitudes toward former President Bush and the war in Iraq, and that his 2016 documentary, *Where to Invade*

Next, with its emphasis on European-style social reforms, would goad Americans into considering these reforms as models for the United States.

However, other directors' motives are less clear-cut. Alfonso Cuarón directed the celebrated movie, *Roma*, an affecting story of male–female relationships, sexual callousness, and family dynamics, focusing on the tribulations of a domestic worker in Mexico City, who is treated cruelly by her employer and the man who impregnates her, but shows uncommon dedication to others in grueling circumstances. The movie called attention to the plight of domestic workers, perhaps triggering changes in Mexico's treatment of domestic workers, but this was not Cuarón's intent (Tillman, 2019). As an internationally acclaimed director, he sought to create a movie that honestly discussed webs of interpersonal relationships, abuses of power, and human devotion to others. His intent was not purely persuasive, yet the film influenced people, transporting them to different realms of social reality (see Chapter 11).

Persuasion Requires Free Choice

If, as noted earlier, self-persuasion is the key to successful influence, then an individual must be free to alter her own behavior or to do what he wishes in a communication setting. But what does it mean to be free? Philosophers have debated this question for centuries, and if you took a philosophy course, you may recall those famous debates about free will versus determinism.

There are more than 200 definitions of freedom, and, as we will see, it is hard to say precisely when coercion ends and persuasion begins. I suggest that individuals are free when they have ability to act otherwise – to do other than what the persuader suggests – or to reflect critically on their choices in a situation (Smythe, 1999). Even so, it is important to remember that people do not have absolute freedom, even in a democratic society like ours that enshrines human rights. Americans do not have the same access to international media, such as the Middle East television network Al Jazeera, that offer critical portraits of U.S. policies, as they do to American media that provide a more positive picture. Are Americans free to sample all media? Theoretically, yes, but practically, no. From an early age, American children are exposed to advertisements that tout the blessings of commercial products, but have virtually no exposure to communications that question the virtues of the capitalist system. Given the powers of socialization, how free are these individuals to reject the trappings of capitalism when they become adults? In America, girls and boys learn (partly through advertising) that diamond rings symbolize marital bliss and that marriage is a desirable life-pursuit. What is the likelihood that, as adults, these individuals could reject wedding rings and marriage after, say, reading articles that criticize the spiritual emptiness of material possessions and the rigidities of marital roles?

I ask these questions not to argue that wedding rings or marriage are without value, but to suggest that none of us are as free as we think – not in America or in any other culture, and that the concept of freedom that underlies persuasion is a relative, not an absolute, concept.

Culture and social environmental constraints can limit the freedom to choose, constraining individuals' experience of how much choice they have. People are always, at some (complex) level, free to accept and reject alternatives presented to them. However, when their options are restricted by the power of the communicator who delivers the message, it makes less sense to argue that persuasion has occurred. One might argue that, for persuasion to occur, the individual must be faced with choices that do not thwart his or her physical or psychological well-being in substantive ways. In persuasion, the choices can be tough and painful, but the power of the communicator cannot unduly restrict the individual or involve choices that cause physical or significant psychological harm.

Summary

This section has offered a definition of persuasion, delineating its main, intriguingly complex, features. Throughout the book, we will trace the ways in which these distinctive characteristics of persuasion play out in real life. The key attributes of persuasion are that it operates as a process, not a product; relies on symbols; involves the communicator's intent to influence; entails self-persuasion; requires the transmission of a message; and assumes free choice. Of all these attributes, the one that cuts to the core of persuasion is self-persuasion. In the end, we persuade ourselves. We decide to change our own minds about issues, people, and ideas. Persuaders transmit messages, call on their most attractive features, play word games, and even manipulate verbal cues in hopes of convincing us to change our attitudes about an issue.

Now that persuasion has been defined, it is important to differentiate it from related aspects of social influence. To truly understand the nature of persuasion, you have to appreciate how it overlaps with and diverges from coercion, propaganda, and manipulation.

Persuasion versus Coercion

How does persuasion differ from coercion? The answer may seem simple at first. Persuasion deals with reason and verbal appeals, while coercion employs force, you suggest. It's not a bad start, but there are subtle relationships between the terms – fascinating overlaps – that you might not ordinarily think of. Consider these scenarios:

- Tom works for a social service agency that receives some of its funding from United Way. At the end of each year, United Way asks employees to contribute to the charity. Tom would like to donate, but he needs every penny of his salary to support his family. One year, his boss, Anne, sends out a memo strongly urging employees to give to United Way. Anne doesn't threaten, but the implicit message is: I expect you to donate, and I'll know who did and who didn't. Tom opts to contribute money to United Way. Was he coerced or persuaded?
- Elizabeth, a high school junior, has been a football fan since grade school and throughout middle school. Waiting eagerly for the homecoming game to start, she glances at the field, catching a glimpse of the senior class president as he strides out to the 50-yard line. Much to her surprise, the class president asks the crowd to stand and join him in prayer. Elizabeth is squeamish. She is not religious and suspects that she's an atheist. She notices that everyone around her is standing, nodding their heads, and reciting the Lord's Prayer. She glances to her left and sees four popular girls shooting nasty looks at her and shaking their heads. Without thinking, Elizabeth rises and nervously begins to speak the words herself. Was she coerced or persuaded?

Before we can answer these questions, we must know what is meant by coercion. Philosophers define coercion as a technique for forcing people to act as the coercer wants them to act – presumably contrary to their preferences. It usually employs a threat of some dire consequence if the actor does not do what the coercer demands (Feinberg, 1998, p. 387) or a willingness to do harm to the message receiver (Powers, 2007).

Tom's boss and Elizabeth's classmates pushed them to act in ways that were contrary to their preferences. The communicators employed a direct or veiled threat. It appears that they employed coercion.

Things get murkier when you look at scholarly definitions that compare coercion with persuasion. Mary J. Smith (1982) takes a relativist perspective, emphasizing the role of perception. According to this view, it's all a matter of how people perceive things. Smith argues that when people believe that they are free to reject the communicator's position, as a practical matter they are free, and the influence attempt falls under the persuasion umbrella. When individuals perceive that they have no choice but to comply, the influence attempt is better viewed as coercive.

One problem with this definition is the problem with relativism and subjectivism: We have different criteria for different people. But this makes it high-nigh impossible to come up with yardsticks to apply consistently across people and situations. It would be like saying that a law applied if you perceived you understood it, but not if you didn't think you understood it, which is obviously unsatisfactory from a legal perspective.

You can now appreciate how difficult it is to differentiate persuasion and coercion. Scholars differ on where they draw the line between the two terms. Some would say that both influence agents used a little bit of both persuasion and coercion. My own view is that the first case is a relatively clear instance of coercion. The communicator employed a veiled threat. What's more, Tom's boss wielded power over him, leading to the reasonable perception that Tom had little choice but to comply. The other scenario is more ambiguous; arguably, it is more persuasion than coercion because most people would probably assume that they could resist the communicators' appeals. In addition, no direct threats of any kind were employed. What's more, Elizabeth did not seem to be faced with a choice that thwarted her physical or psychological well-being in substantive ways.

These examples highlight the importance of coming up with clear, definite ways of defining persuasion and coercion. And yet, they emphasize the point suggested earlier, that persuasion and coercion are not polar opposites but, rather, overlapping concepts. In contemporary life, we glimpse examples of this. From the all-too-common cases of spousal abuse to the manipulative rituals of Alcoholics Anonymous to prosaic fraternity (along with sorority) pressures to conform, the psychological truth is that coercion and persuasion shade into one another in subtle, complex ways (see Figures 2.2 and 2.3). And yet, from a scientific perspective, it is important to differentiate the terms clearly.

Those who say it all comes down to perception must wrestle with the ambiguity (unsatisfactory in a court of law) that an influence attempt can be persuasion for one person (if he claims to be free to reject the communicator's position), yet coercive for another (if she claims she has no choice but to comply). This means that two individuals could be influenced by the same message, but one (who

Coercion _____ Persuasion

Nature of psychological threat
Ability to do otherwise
Request runs counter to one's preferences

Coercion and persuasion are not polar opposites. They are better viewed as lying along a continuum of social influence.

Figure 2.2 Coercion and Persuasion

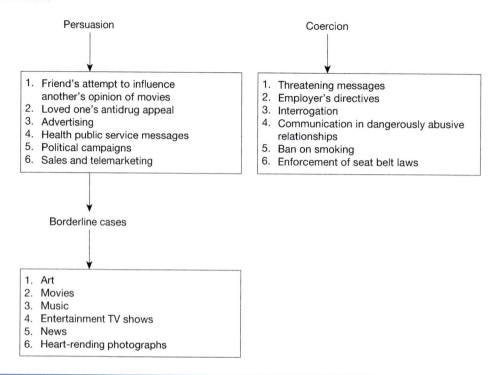

Figure 2.3 Understanding Persuasion, Coercion, and Borderline Cases of Persuasion. Note that coercion can be negative or positive (as in smoking bans and enforcement of seat belt laws). Borderline cases focus on persuasion rather than coercion. They lie just outside the boundary of persuasion because the intent of the communicator is not to explicitly change an individual's attitude toward the issue, but is, instead, broader and more complex (Gass & Seiter, 2014)

claimed it was persuasion) would be held accountable for his actions, while the other (who perceived coercion) could be exonerated on the grounds that she lacked the freedom to reject the message. An individual could claim she was coerced in a situation where reasonable observers would maintain the individual had the ability to do otherwise. This is clearly unsatisfactory. Interesting as the perceptual approach is, it does not provide a clear boundary line between persuasion and coercion. A more concrete approach is needed.

Based on contemporary approaches, we can say that coercion occurs when the influence agent: (a) delivers a believable threat of significant physical or emotional harm to those who refuse the directive, (b) deprives the individual of some measure of freedom or autonomy, and (c) attempts to induce the individual to act contrary to her preferences (Dahl, 1989; Feinberg, 1998; Rosenbaum, 1986). Persuasion, by contrast, occurs in an atmosphere of free choice: It assumes the individual is capable of resisting an influence attempt or of willingly persuading him or herself to alter an attitude about an issue. It's complex. While coercion can have salutary ethical features, as in bans on e-cigarettes, persuasion also can be morally objectionable, as when someone lies to get her way.

The most troubling cases are those in which unsavory communicators blend the two, preying on people's weaknesses. The next section discusses one such instance, an issue of highly contemporary significance where powerful communicators exploited the occupational, social, and psychological vulnerabilities of their victims.

Sexual Abuse in Hollywood, #MeToo, and the Psychology of Coercion

Some years back, investigative stories in major news media revealed the litany of repulsive acts of sexual abuse that the high-profile Hollywood producer Harvey Weinstein reportedly engaged in over many years, the news stories causing many other women to offer online support and share similar experiences of abusive woes in what became known as the #MeToo Movement (Kantor & Twohey, 2017).

As more journalistic exposés salaciously revealed how other powerful, famous men – former *Today* show host Matt Lauer, comedian Louis CK, and elite Manhattan restaurateurs – had engaged in sexual misconduct, with #MeToo stories cascading across social media, many women began rethinking their own experiences and recognizing instances when they acquiesced in ways they now regretted. How had men forced them to partake in sexual acts? Had men coerced them, and if so how? And, with the benefits of wisdom that time affords, what insights now accrued that could help them understand why they did not resist and object in the ways they most certainly would today? These questions cut to the core of issues discussed in this chapter, offering insights about the dynamics of the psychological forces that operate in sexually abusive situations (see Figure 2.4).

Let's look at Weinstein. The Hollywood mogul – the once proud co-founder of Miramax Films who produced dozens of popular and artistic film successes that ironically (or perhaps not) included *Sex, Lies, and Videotape*, as well as strong portraits of women, such as *Shakespeare in Love* – invited young women, who caught his lecherous eye, to come by his room for what the women thought were work-related reasons, only to learn he had very different motives. Four women said he had touched them in ways that could be legally regarded as an assault and three others said that he had forcibly performed sexual acts (Farrow, 2017).

Were these women persuaded rather than coerced? Certainly not. Based on investigative news articles – the exposés are impeccably reported and participants meticulously detailed in their recollections – it is clear that coercion occurred. Weinstein threatened them (and worse), deprived them of freedom, and forced them to act contrary to their preferences. These aren't just coercive acts; they constitute assault.

More psychologically provocative are cases where Weinstein didn't physically force himself on women, but used emotionally exploitive tactics. For example, he invited a 20-year aspiring actress, Tomi-Ann Roberts, to his room for an audition, explaining that her audition would go much better if she performed naked, adding that if she could not show her breasts to him in private, she would not be able to do it in the topless scene in his film. People told young actresses this was the way the business worked, and who were they, these youthful actress-wannabees? "I was nobody," Tomi-Ann Roberts said, and he was Harvey Weinstein (Kantor & Abrams, 2017). It was "coercive bargaining," as Ashely Judd described it (Kantor & Twohey, 2017), and worse for women, like Mira Sorvino, whose rejections of Weinstein damaged their careers.

Figure 2.4 The International #MeToo Movement Against Sexual Harassment Calls Attention to the Malevolent Powers of Social Influence, the Psychological, as well as Physical, Underpinnings of Coercion, and the Powerful Impact That Culture Plays in Enabling Psychological Exploitation of Some Women's Occupational, Social, and Psychological Vulnerabilities. The movement highlights the feelings of empowerment women experience when they label wanton acts as sexual abuse and recognize that they have recourse to call out sexual exploiters

Adding to the psychological pressure, there was "a culture of silence about sexual assault" inside Weinstein's production companies and the culture of Hollywood; people knew, but didn't talk for fear they would be fired or worse (Farrow, 2017). And yet, some women did refuse, walking out of his hotel room when he persisted. Years later, some of the women who acquiesced to powerful predators, like Weinstein, as well as intimidating male executives in the tech industry, regretted that they didn't do more. They lamented that they didn't have "enough spine or backbone" to do what they should have done, as one woman put it (Wakabayashi & Benner, 2018, p. A16).

There were psychological elements to these situations, highlighting the overlap between persuasion and coercion in some complex instances where accusers continued to have friendly contact with the alleged aggressor after the attack (Ransom, 2020; Twohey & Kantor, 2020). Yet given the nature of the ways sexual influence was exploited, these incidents, complex but heinous as they are, clearly fall into the coercion category. Think of it this way. Definitions should make intuitive sense. Does it sound reasonable for a woman who acquiesced to Weinstein's sadistic requests to tearfully relate to a friend that "he persuaded me"? It doesn't in the slightest, because the phrase "he persuaded me" implies the individual was, in some sense, a willing participant in the process, felt psychologically free to reject his request, and willingly consented because he appealed to her emotions, attitudes, or values. But this is a distortion of what happened. It makes more intuitive – and conceptual – sense for the woman to state, to friends, colleagues, or the police, that "he coerced me." The differential powers between the two – seniority, wealth, gender (Weinstein "a man in an industry in which men dominate, and … often used that dominance to claim sexual favors") – are hallmarks of coercion (Chiu, 2019, p. 7).

What's more, if we look at the core qualities of coercion, it becomes obvious. Coercion involves the transmission of a believable threat, a request that runs counter to one's preferences, and a deprivation of an individual's freedom. These all operated here. Aspiring actresses had a choice – say yes, go up to his room, and possibly face some kind of unwanted act – or say no and possibly get fired, shutting down dreams of a promising career. This is not a choice embracing freedom of opportunity, but a foreclosing of opportunities, the embodiment of coercion. In these situations, it all can happen so quickly, within seconds or minutes, in a context where one feels barricaded by threats, walled in by fears, precisely the kind of situation that occludes persuasion. The psychological battery is all the more wicked when it happens to a young woman, full of hope, eyes open to possibilities, until they are cruelly crushed by a man and his complicit compatriots.

But this is how predators operate. They deliberately deceive and manipulate vulnerable women (and men), exploiting a multitude of persuasive and coercive techniques. As communication scholar Kyra Rothenberg (2019) perceptively observes:

> Predators target, plot, and scheme the vulnerable. They deceive and manipulate, creating illusion of legitimacy. They count on people trusting them because of their distinguished positions. They isolate so victims cannot prove fault. They surprise. They've ruminated on a variety of scenarios in their minds. They are confident, whereas victims are caught off guard, surprised and unprepared, shocked that this important person could actually be behaving this way.

In these ways, predatory men exploit classic persuasion and social influence techniques – among them, authority, credibility, distraction, compliance-gaining, and cognitive heuristics – in the service of despicable ends.

This examination of celebrity men's sexual abuse, punctuated by the painful stories thousands of women have shared in online posts, has important implications for readers of this book. First, the examples remind us of that social influence can be exploited for harmful ends in ways that are both powerful and subtle. Second, they highlight the role that time-honored cultural norms play in the persuasion process. For decades, male bosses' sexual harassment of aspiring female employees was so normatively accepted that women felt they had no choice but to comply or, if not, to suppress their anger, go about their jobs, and never report the abuse to authorities.

Now, in the wake of long-overdue social reckoning, men's harassment is recognized as the physically and psychologically coercive act that it is. Women are also more aware that they have significant legal and psychological remedies they can bring to bear to reap social justice. And it's not only women: Men in authority positions can exploit other male underlings with sexual influence techniques, injustices that men of different gender orientations can effectively challenge interpersonally and in the courts.

Coercion, persuasion, and perceived freedom are inextricably linked with contemporary cultural practices, helping us understand the reasons why people sometimes feel unable to resist oppressive authorities and the feeling of empowerment they experience when they reject unseemly requests.

The Bad Boys of Persuasion

There are two additional terms that are bandied about when social influence and persuasion are discussed: Propaganda and manipulation. The first is more sinister, has more problematic implications for democratic communication, and has recently been rebooted from a rather exclusive association with totalitarian governments, such as Nazi Germany in the 1930s and North Korea in the present era, to concerns about how Russia harnessed propaganda to sow chaos in the 2016 U.S. presidential election. What is propaganda? What isn't? These are important, fascinating questions worthy of extended discussion below.

Propaganda

Persuasion and propaganda, like persuasion and coercion, are not polar opposites, but overlap, yet differ, as in a Venn diagram. They are hard to disentangle, partly because it can be arbitrary whether you use propaganda or persuasion to describe mass influence attempts. It is, to some degree, a matter of academic orientation. Scholars of political rhetoric, as well as radical mass communication scholars, prefer the propaganda label, partly because it highlights the nefarious ways that governments and social institutions exploit communications to further their own ends (Herman & Chomsky, 2002; Jowett & O'Donnell, 2019). Social scientists gravitate to the persuasion construct, because it has a more neutral connotation, boasts a long intellectual lineage from Aristotle through Hovland, Lumsdaine, and Sheffield (1949) World War II-era studies of how messages can boost war-time morale, and has spawned a litany of theory-driven research on message effects that helps identify the psychological underpinnings of mass social influence.

Given the historical importance of propaganda, and its recent resurgence, how do we define this fraught concept?

First, propaganda refers to instances in which a group has near or total control over the transmission of information and dissent is prohibited or forcibly discouraged. Classic examples include Hitler's Germany, the Communist Party under the repressive Mao Zedong, the current North Korean government, and extremist groups, like the Islamic State or ISIS, and the African Islamist group, Boko Haram.

North Korea provides a chilling example. Religion is banned; citizens' communications are closely monitored. Access to the Internet and social media is strictly controlled. Every morning, the all-controlling state sends forth a message, a veritable connection from Big Brother, to every home or village. Through its controlled communications over the years, the government has drummed in the idea that the United States is a hateful enemy and North Korea will destroy the United States in a nuclear conflict, enforcing through coercive messaging a single-minded unity around the strong, unassailable wisdom of the supreme leader, Kim Jong-un. The message is conveyed through ubiquitous images of missiles – in billboards that depict missiles obliterating the U.S. Capitol, on state TV, even at a dolphin show in Pyongyang – and more generally in songs, art, and movies (Kristof, 2017; Osnos, 2017; see Figure 2.5).

Figure 2.5 This Rally in Pyongyang, North Korea, With the Visible Picture of North Korea's Leadership, Features Throngs of People Shouting Slogans in Support of the North Korean Leader Kim Jong-un, a Classic Example of State-Organized Government Propaganda. Other examples of propaganda, such as Russian cyberagents' creation of fake Facebook pages and even negative political campaign ads that can't be easily traced to a source, blur the lines more

Critics might argue that the United States also propagandistically showcases its symbols of national values, via historic monuments in Washington, D.C., reverence shown the president during televised addresses, and commercial advertising, the emblem of a capitalist state. This is quite correct. However, these do not constitute propaganda per se because the government does not control the display of national symbols. Indeed, as discussed earlier, symbols, on topics like immigration, candidates, and election-year advertising, are highly contested, objects of widespread debate. Even a president as concerned with controlling appearances as Donald Trump found that, in a democratic society, he cannot control the way the media portray him, and his policies (and rambunctious tweets) are held up for praise, ridicule, scorn, and bilious discussion on media outlets that endlessly dissect and challenge his statements. This isn't to say the U.S. government doesn't try to use symbols to influence or that powerful groups don't manipulate media to achieve their goals. They do, sometimes with nefarious purposes. It's just not propaganda.

Nations – those, in the extreme, like North Korea and, to a lesser extent, China or Turkey – are not the only groups that wield the one-sided cudgel of propaganda. Propaganda can also be digital and has gone viral, with ISIS posting gruesome YouTube videos of medieval-style beheading of American journalists, clad in orange jump suits to deliberately mock the garb worn by prisoners at the U.S. Guantanamo Bay detention camp. The murderous African extremist group, Boko Haram, even created its own media outlet, with a logo, Twitter account, and slick videos (Callimachi, 2015). For Boko Haram, ISIS, and other violent political cults, propaganda is the communicative order of the day. There are no alternative, dissident messages available to members of these groups, when they gather in isolated locales. It is their view or the information highway. Propaganda aptly describes the nature and structure of their social environments, for members are exposed only to the ruling group's perspective.

Let's turn now to a second characteristic of propaganda: Its falsehood. Unlike persuasion, propaganda is always deceptive, presenting only one sliver of the facts – the one propagandists want people to hear. Propagandists deliberately hide or distort opposing positions, and their media systems make it high-nigh impossible for citizens to have access to alternative viewpoints. Persuasion, by contrast, can be honest, up-front, and transparent, offering a truthful perspective on the issue. It isn't always, of course. Persuasion usually involves some kind of sleight of hand, and its truth level lies on a continuum from totally veracious to entirely fallacious and underhanded. On a more systemic level, persuasion, as it works in democratic societies, involves a relatively free flow of information, where people have access to perspectives that challenge the government and powerful political groups.

But the Internet and social media have added another component, allowing not just nations or non-state terrorist organizations like ISIS to spread falsehoods widely, but domestic extremist groups, who can disseminate false information via algorithms and social bots. Communication scholar Sharon Meraz (2019) felicitously calls this "computational propaganda," adding another layer to the propaganda term.

There is a key third difference between propaganda and persuasion. Propaganda necessarily involves the media, both the mass and social media, like Facebook and Twitter. Persuasion, by contrast, occurs in mediated settings, but also in interpersonal and organizational contexts – one-on-one, in group meetings on the job, and at large political rallies. Propaganda, by contrast, is impossible without dissemination by media.

A fourth feature of propaganda is that the source of a message designed to appeal to masses of individuals is frequently obscured, deliberately hidden, or of unknown provenance. Citizens who receive the message have no way of determining the actual source of the communication because it has been deliberately shrouded in secrecy. The Russian viral campaign to influence the 2016 presidential election was an exercise in propaganda because the true sources of the fake Facebook accounts, false social media posts, and inflammatory online messages regarding Hillary Clinton were hidden from view.

It gets more complicated, though, when you consider that negative political advertisements in America can employ some of the same dark techniques as Russian propagandists. Hidden financial donors with patriotic-sounding names like Alliance for a Free Society have doled out millions of dollars to candidates, but the sources of the money are difficult to locate, donors are not revealed, and the groups are often nothing more than shell companies for special interests that created the ads (Confessore & Willis, 2014). Does this make political advertising propaganda? No – but the lines blur.

As a communicative institution in a political democracy, political advertisements are not controlled by a ruling junta or the party in power. People have easy access to messages from the opposing candidate that challenge a particular negative commercial and can quickly locate fact-checking corrections on websites like PolitiFact. However, particular ads that make it impossible to identify the source have propagandistic features, illustrating the gray areas that blur differences between persuasion and propaganda, paralleling the overlaps between persuasion and coercion discussed in the previous section.

The final difference between the two terms – the one you come up against every time the word "propaganda" is invoked – lies not so much in the arenas in which the two terms operate. The difference is semantics, in this case the connotation of the terms. Propaganda has come to acquire a negative connotation; it is associated with our enemies, foreign powers that a particular nation dislikes, or revolutionary groups that are linked with values "we" dislike. Persuasion can convey negative images as well, like exploiting another person's weaknesses or pulling the wool over someone's eyes, but the connotations are not as sinister as with propaganda. Persuasion also is widely viewed as exerting positive influences on health, consumer purchases, and lifestyle. Not so, propaganda.

Subjectively, we use the term propaganda to refer to a persuasive communication with which one disagrees and to which the individual attributes hostile intent. Liberals claim that the news is unadulterated propaganda for Republicans; conservatives contend that the news is propaganda for the left. When you hear people call a persuasive communication propaganda, beware. The speakers are using language to denounce a message with which they disagree. Think about it: You wouldn't hear a salesperson come home from work and tell a spouse, "I had a great day, dear – wielded some really juicy propaganda and sold a few cars!" Of course not! What we do is regarded as persuasion, what our foes convey, well that's propaganda!

The best example of this is the ubiquitous news media labeling of Russian meddling in American elections as propaganda. To be sure, the Russian interference fell under the propaganda label. However, the semantics are illuminating. The United States government readily labeled the Russian social media campaign "propaganda," but is reluctant to apply this label to similar U.S. efforts to covertly swing elections to advance American interests or secretly print millions of brochures to defeat a candidate in Serbia (Shane, 2018). Instead, we call them foreign policy interventions, covert intelligence, or perhaps even patriotic persuasion!

Thus, a clear difference between propaganda and persuasion lies in semantics: Propaganda has a negative connotation, evoking unfavorable images, partly because it frequently relies on covert techniques harnessed by groups that deny citizens access to alternative viewpoints, but also because political groups have deliberately used the term as a cudgel to condemn their adversaries. From an academic perspective, the strong popular association of propaganda with negative attributes weakens its utility as a scholarly construct to explain social influence. (This is a problem with Jowett and O'Donnell's (2019) thorough work on propaganda; the overwhelmingly negative connotation of the term "propaganda" makes it difficult to see how propaganda can exert positive effects, and this is complicated by conflating propaganda with persuasion.)

With all this in mind, we can define propaganda clearly. *Propaganda* is a system of communicating information, in which the communicator has near or total control over the transmission of information, and relies on media to reach masses of individuals with false, deceptive, frequently covert messages; the term evokes negative connotations and meanings in others.

Manipulation

Let's move now to a related term, frequently used synonymously with persuasion. It's a familiar term: Manipulation. Manipulation does not have the same deeply unfavorable meanings, but it does conjure up negative associations. People frequently use the term "manipulation" to criticize persuaders for employing underhanded techniques. "She's so manipulative," someone charges. "That's another example of media manipulation," a friend observes. Is manipulation the same as persuasion? Is all persuasion manipulative? Although the terms overlap, there are key differences. *Manipulation* is a persuasion technique that occurs when a communicator hides his or her true persuasive goals, hoping to mislead the recipient by delivering an overt message that disguises its true intent. Flattery, sweet talk, and false promises are manipulative techniques.

All persuasion is not manipulative. A persuader whose motives are honest and transparent is not employing manipulation. At the same time, message recipients can naively trust a communicator, failing to notice that the persuader is disguising more sinister intentions. A trusting receiver may fall prey to manipulative con artists, who run the gamut from sweet-talking salesmen promising infirmed elderly individuals "miracle" pain products at exorbitant prices to the celebrated case of financier Bernard Madoff, who bilked thousands of trusting clients of their life-savings in a $50 billion scam that was revealed in 2008.

Because manipulation can be sneaky and has negative connotations, it is sometimes linked with coercion. But manipulation is not the same as coercion. Manipulation assumes free choice; it is a mildly duplicitous form of persuasion. Coercion occurs when choice and freedom are compromised. Manipulative persuaders who have their, rather than our, interests at heart can pull the wool over our eyes, and it is up to us to see through their subtle ploys.

Coercion. Persuasion. Propaganda. Manipulation. You now have an appreciation of what they are how and how we delineate their major characteristics (see Table 2.1). There is something else to consider, an implication that is at once strange and devastatingly representative – an application of

Table 2.1 Definitions of Core Terms

Social influence has different features and different constructs. The four key components – persuasion, coercion, propaganda, and manipulation – can overlap and shade into one another. Each has distinctive characteristics, summarized below:

Persuasion: a symbolic process in which communicators try to convince other people to change their own attitudes or behaviors regarding an issue through the transmission of a message in an atmosphere of free choice.

Coercion: a type of social influence that occurs when the influence agent delivers a believable threat of some consequence, deprives the individual of some measure of freedom or autonomy, and attempts to induce the individual to act contrary to his or her preferences. (Coercion can be implemented on a societal level, with positive consequences, as with bans on cigarette smoking. On the individual level, it frequently has more negative effects, overlapping complexly with persuasion. If a choice offered by a communicator could reasonably result in physical or significant psychological harm to the individual's well-being, coercion rather than persuasion can be said to occur.)

Propaganda: a system of communicating information, in which the communicator has near or total control over the transmission of information, and relies on media to reach masses of individuals with false, deceptive, frequently covert messages that semantically evoke negative connotations.

Manipulation: a persuasion technique that occurs when a communicator hides his or her true persuasive goals, hoping to mislead the recipient by delivering an overt message that disguises its true intent.

persuasion and social influence more broadly you wouldn't think about ordinarily, but one that begs for consideration. From deadly examples in the twentieth century to more high-tech examples today, this sadly real-life arena offers an important perspective on persuasion. The domain is cults – religious, terrorist, and online communities – worthy of explanation, consideration, and sober analysis.

The Cult of Persuasion, Coercion, and Social Influence

Edison Jessop, a resident of the Yearning for Zion Ranch in west Texas, had no complaints. "We've got 300 pounds of cabbage out of there already, and a couple hundred more coming," he said, as he drove by a garden (Kovach, 2008). Jessop regarded the ranch, home to followers of the Fundamentalist Church of Latter Day Saints, as a wonderful place to raise children. However, the church was also a polygamist community that followed the strict teachings of leader Rulon Jeffs and his son, Warren. Television and Internet were forbidden. Laughter was against the law. All the women wore old-fashioned "Little House on the Prairie Dresses." Some of the men had as many as five wives. Warren Jeffs is believed to have fathered more than 100 children (Atlas et al., 2008). Most disturbingly, there was evidence of possible sexual abuse. When a 16-year-old girl called a domestic abuse hotline, claiming she had been abused by her 50-year-old husband, state authorities raided the compound. Although there was disagreement about the merits – and legality – of the state's action, there was little doubt that the church bore the earmarks of a religious cult.

It was hardly the first time that a religious cult attracted national attention. In March 1997, the nation learned the tragic fate of the 39 members of the Heaven's Gate cult, all of whom committed suicide. Many wondered why 39 intelligent, committed men and women willingly took their own lives, joyfully announcing their decision in a farewell videotape and statement on their web site. The suicide was timed to coincide with the arrival of the Hale–Bopp comet. Believing that a flying saucer was traveling behind the comet, members chose to leave their bodies behind to gain redemption in a Kingdom of Heaven (Robinson, 1997). To many people, this provided yet another example of the powerful, but mysterious, technique called brainwashing. The cult leader, Marshall Applewhite, known to his followers as "Do," supposedly brainwashed cult members into committing mass suicide in their home in Rancho Santa Fe, California.

Although Heaven's Gate was the first Internet cult tragedy, one that drove millions of curiosity-seekers to the group's web site, it was only the most recent in a series of bizarre cult occurrences that observers could describe only as brainwashing (see Figure 2.6).

Famous though it may be, brainwashing is not a satisfactory explanation for what happens in cults. It does not tell us why ordinary people choose to join and actively participate in cults. It does not explain how leaders wield influence or are able to induce followers to engage in self-destructive behavior. Instead, the brainwashing term condemns people and points fingers.

How can we explain the cult phenomenon? Although they are on the outer limits of social influence, cults provide a window on the power of coercion and persuasion, helping us appreciate the ways malevolent leaders secure compliance. In this way, they offer insights about the nature of persuasion and the ways extremist groups work and adapt to twenty-first century life.

How Cults Influence

First, we need to define a cult. A cult is a group of individuals who are: (a) excessively devoted to a charismatic leader, himself or herself "the object of worship"; (b) effectively isolated from the rest of

Figure 2.6 The Residues of Cults: The Dead at Jonestown, Where More Than 900 Individuals Followed the Directive of Cult Leader Jim Jones to Drink Cyanide-Laced Kool-Aid at the Cult's Home in Guyana, South America in 1978 (left). Some two decades later, members of the Heaven's Gate cult wore identical clothing and displayed a common group identity, following the messianic message of their leader, Marshall Applewhite, known as "Do" (right). Thirty-nine cult members committed suicide en masse (middle), announcing their decision in a farewell videotape on the cult's website in March 1997

Images courtesy of the Associated Press

society; (c) denied access to alternative points of view; and (d) subjected to exploitative social influence techniques (see Lifton, 2003, p. xii). To appreciate how cults influence individuals, we need to consider the dynamics of persuasion and coercion.

People join cults for many reasons. They are lonely and confused, and the cult provides a loving home. Simple religious answers beckon and offer a reason for living. Isolated from parents and friends, young people come to depend more on the cult for social rewards. The cult leader is charismatic and claims to have supernatural powers. He gains followers' trust and devotion. Purposelessness is relieved; order replaces chaos. The more people participate in the group's activities, the better they feel; the better they feel, the more committed they become; and the more committed they are, the more difficult it is to leave.

Initially, cult leaders employ persuasive appeals. Over time they rely increasingly on coercive techniques. Heaven's Gate leaders told followers that they must learn to deny their desires and defer to the group. Everyone woke at the same time to pray, ate the same food, wore short haircuts and nondescript clothing, and sported identical wedding rings on their fingers to symbolize marriage to each other. Individual identity was replaced by group identity. Autonomy gave way, slowly replaced by the peacefulness of groupthink (Goodstein, 1997). Once this happens – and it occurs slowly – cult members no longer have free choice; they are psychologically unable to say no to leaders' demands. Coercion replaces persuasion. Conformity overtakes dissent. Persuasion and coercion coexist, shading into one another. Simple demarcations are hard to make. The outcome is inevitably tragic.

Terrorist Cults

It would be a happy ending if Heaven's Gate were the last cult that exploited individuals' vulnerabilities. However, in recent years, we have witnessed the growth of cross-national terrorist cults composed of men who are convinced that America is the enemy of Islam and are willing to kill innocent people or themselves, if directed by their *maulanas* or masters (Goldberg, 2000). It is tempting to view these individuals as victims of terrorist brainwashing – automatons directed into action by receipt of a social media post. Once again, the brainwashing metaphor simplifies and distorts. These individuals have frequently joined Muslim religious schools out of their own volition. Bereft of meaning and purpose in a changing world, grasping for an outlet to express decades-long simmering hate, and seeking a way to exact revenge or seek recognition, they join terrorist cells. There they are groomed, influenced, even coerced by "teachers" and assorted leaders of an international political-religious cult emphasizing a violent, destructive interpretation of Islam (Goldberg, 2000; Zakaria, 2001).

Attuned to the psychology of persuasion, terrorist cult leaders hook sympathetic young people into embarking on a series of steps that take them from naïveté to commitment to martyrdom. They invite sympathizers to say how much they love the Islamic cause, convince them to commit to a small elite cell of suicide bombers, dress up the cell symbolically in the trappings of honor and prestige, and induce them to make a videotape in which they publicly declare they are "the living martyr" for Islam, which "binds them to the final deed, because it is sent to their families." Then they sweeten the deal by promising they will earn a place in Heaven next to Allah (Zimbardo, 2007, p. 292). For young men and women, who grow up in desolate environments, poor and bereft of hope, the promise of immortality and achievement of a grand vision that will outlive one's life on earth are potent promises. They lift the spirits and give would-be terrorists a reason to live.

Increasingly, these groups rely heavily on social media and the Internet to recruit the disaffected. Some 5,000 sites diffuse messages and graphic videos that promote extremist ideologies and political violence (Koomen & van der Pligt, 2016). The Islamic State or ISIS, which has launched horrific attacks on Western targets, is distressingly savvy in the construction of propaganda videos that depict the cult-like organization in romantic terms, combining video clips of dedicated, heroic fighters, along with children in ISIS's thrall, with vicious beheadings, and eerie montages from CNN and Fox News. These messages, cut Hollywood style with music and powerful cinematic images, appeal to some deeply disaffected, angry, and identity-searching young men and women, reared on social media and alluring video games, for whom the messages resonate, offering a surrealistic aura of romance, thrill, and even hope (Zakaria, 2015; see Figure 2.7a–b).

(a)

(b)

Figure 2.7a–b In an Age of Social Media, Terrorists Exploit Social Media to Do Their Persuasive Bidding, Posting Videos That Recruit the Angry and Disaffected to Their Cause. These videos, while hateful to the overwhelming majority of citizens across the world, offer a powerful allure to the chronically disenchanted, suggesting that ISIS soldiers are role models to children and are part of a larger collective, unified and strong

Images courtesy of the Associated Press

To be sure, not every young man or woman who is isolated or is tempted by self-sacrifice will join ISIS or become a suicide bomber. Far from it. Only an unusual handful will execute evil actions. As scholar Alan Wolfe notes, "political evil recruits those attracted to brutality, motivated by a burning sense of victimhood, anxious to right what they believe to be longstanding wrongs, and in extreme cases willing to die for their beliefs" (2011, pp. 78–79).

Groups like ISIS can appeal to these needs. Like the old in-person religious cults, they harness manipulative persuasion techniques, now relayed through Twitter, that include vibrating iPhone messages complete with emoticons and status updates, to draw in lonely and confused young adults. From an academic perspective, there is a question as to whether such viral terrorist messages fall under the rubric of a cult. After all, recruits who access these posts on mobile phones are not isolated from the rest of society or living in some far-away, sequestered place under the dominion of a charismatic leader. Increasingly, as terrorist or domestic extremist groups recruit via social media, it is harder to apply the cult label to their activities. In a social media age, older persuasion distinctions become fuzzier and more complicated. Virulent, White supremacist online communities are cult-like in their appeals, the successors to the twentieth century exploitative cults, except their charismatic appeals "are delivered digitally, and recruits' isolation from others occurs not through geographic separation but through algorithmic manipulation" (Perloff, 2019, p. A28).

Cults and cult-like communities are by definition persuasion in extremis, deviant, unusual, if powerful, examples of persuasion, coercion, propaganda, and manipulation. With this perspective in mind, let's return to the everyday world of persuasive communication, appreciating the powers of social influence, and focusing on definitions again, but with a new twist.

Understanding Persuasive Communication Effects

Up to this point, the definitional emphasis has been on differences between persuasion and related terms. However, persuasion, alas, is not of one piece; there are different kinds of persuasive communications, and they have different types of effects. Some messages dramatically influence attitudes; others exert smaller or more subtle impacts. Taking note of this, Miller (1980) proposed that communications exert three different persuasive effects: shaping, reinforcing, and changing responses.

Shaping

Today everyone has heard of the Nike "swoosh." You've seen it on hundreds of ads and on the clothing of celebrity athletes. It's a symbol that resonates and has helped make Nike a leader in the athletic shoe business. The now-classic ad campaigns featuring Michael Jordan and Bo Jackson in their era – and Colin Kaepenick, LeBron James, and Serena Williams in theirs – helped mold attitudes toward Nike by linking Nike with movement, speed, and superhuman athletic achievement.

A nastier example is e-cigarette marketing. The vaping giant Juul has exploited contemporary media and social media to target teenagers, calling on sleek, time-tested association-based ads that show cool-looking young people posing flirtatiously with their Juuls, as well as those featuring attractive young women with taglines like "Vaporized." These and interpersonal persuasive messages have led to what some experts call an epidemic of adolescent nicotine addiction, with more than 3.5 million middle and high school students enjoying "the head rush" of a Juul puff, their attitudes and behavior shaped by manipulative ads (Hoffman, 2018, p. A1; see Chapters 6, 11, and 14).

On a more positive level, socialization can be regarded as an example of attitude shaping or formation. Influential social agents model a variety of pro-social values and attitudes, such as self-discipline, altruism, and religion.

Reinforcing

Contrary to popular opinion, many persuasive communications are not designed to convert people, but rather to reinforce a position they already hold. As will be discussed in Chapter 5, people have strong attitudes toward a variety of topics, and these attitudes are hard to change. Thus, persuaders try to join 'em, not beat 'em.

In political campaigns, candidates try to bolster party supporters' commitment to their cause. Democratic standard-bearers have made late-campaign appeals to African American voters, the overwhelming majority of whom are registered Democrats. Republican candidates have won elections by appealing to religious conservatives. Increasingly, political consultants argue that elections are not solely about winning over undecided voters, but, rather, concerned with appeals to the base.

In a similar fashion, health education experts try to reinforce individuals' decisions to quit smoking or to abstain from drinking in excess. Persuaders recognize that people can easily relapse under stress, and they design messages to help individuals maintain their commitment to giving up unhealthy substances. Thus, persuasion involves bolstering, reinforcing, and strengthening attitudes. While these are not the mass transformations somewhat simplistically associated with persuasion, they count because they involve the individual's alteration of an attitude or decision to commit to a behavior based on attitude reinforcement. If you are a marketing consultant, attitude strengthening can translate to increased purchase of a product, a palpable instance of persuasion.

Changing

This is perhaps the most important persuasive impact and the one that comes most frequently to mind when we think of persuasion. Communications can markedly change attitudes. Just think how far this country has come in the past 50 years on the subject of race. In the 1950s and 1960s, Black people were lynched for being in the wrong place at the wrong time, many southerners openly opposed school desegregation, and northern Whites steered clear of socializing with Black friends or colleagues. This changed as civil rights campaigns, heart-rending media stories, and increased dialogue between Blacks and Whites led Whites to rethink their prejudiced attitudes toward African Americans (Thernstrom & Thernstrom, 1997). In 1958, interracial marriage was favored by 4 percent of Americans. More than half a century later, the proportion in support of marriage between men and women of a different race increased more than 20-fold, to 87 percent (Leonhardt & Parlapiano, 2015). And while institutionalized racial prejudice continues to afflict people of color in America, widespread attitude changes have greatly improved the social environment.

Negative attitudes toward gay marriage have also changed dramatically. In American cities where gay couples would have been flogged or killed decades ago, prejudice has given way to tolerance. Consider Jacksonville, Florida. A gay church was bombed there in the 1980s. Nowadays, eight churches accept gay parishioners and one seeks out couples who have children. The city has one of the largest populations of gay parents in the United States (Tavernise, 2011). Polls consistently show that the majority of Americans support gay marriage, a sea change in attitudes that achieved legal significance when the Supreme Court legalized same-sex marriage in 2015. On other topics too, spanning gender roles, diet, and exercise, Americans and, in many instances, people worldwide have changed their attitudes. On the critical issue of global warming, more than three-fourths of Americans regard climate change as a "crisis" or a "major problem" (Kolbert, 2019, p. 20). Persuasive communications have clearly exerted psychological effects. They have influenced attitudes and, in some cases, behavior.

Important as these effects are, they rarely occur overnight. Persuasion is a process; change can be slow and painstaking. A bigot does not become more open-minded after one persuasive encounter. It takes many years of exposure to people of color, rethinking of prejudices, and self-insight. Persuasion is a process. It happens over time, step by step, with each step counting as an instance of self-persuasion.

Conclusions

Persuasion is a quintessentially human pursuit. While social influence is practiced by higher animals, it is more difficult to argue that animals, smart as they are, emotionally tuned in as they can be, have attitudes, or are cognizant at some level that they are trying to change a critter or human's belief or attitude. Persuasion is one of the forces that make us human, with its emphasis on language, cognizance of others' attitudes, and psychological shaping of messages to fit the target's attributes, for good but also malevolent ends.

Persuasion is defined as a symbolic process in which communicators try to convince other people to change their own attitudes or behavior regarding an issue through the transmission of a message, in an atmosphere of free choice. One of the vexing aspects of this definition is the emphasis on the intentional component of persuasion, as opposed to other forms of social influence, where intent is less significant. It can be difficult to determine whether a persuader is, at some level, hoping to change attitudes, rather than trying to simply communicate ideas or emotions without a deliberate intent to change attitudes.

In the digital milieu, we receive many messages from communicators who may not be trying to change our own attitudes, but can end up influencing us, provoking emotions and priming stereotypes. During earlier eras, when communicators' intentions were more transparent (though not necessarily more benign), persuasion was a handy term to invoke to describe the powers of attitude-changing messages. Nowadays, persuasion sits alongside a multiplicity of platforms for social influence, and it inexactly describes remixed messages, where the original persuader's intent has been altered by new online persuaders. For now, it is important to appreciate that persuasion is distinctive in its recognition that a communicator is deliberately trying to change receivers' attitudes through messages. This requires an appreciation of the psychological dynamics of the communicator, message receivers, and context.

A key aspect of persuasion is self-persuasion. Communicators do not change people's minds; people decide to alter their own attitudes or to resist persuasion. There is something liberating about self-persuasion. It says that we are free to change our lives in any way that we wish. We have the power to become what we want to become – to stop smoking, lose weight, modify dysfunctional behavior patterns, change career paths, or discover how to become a dynamic public speaker. Obviously, we can't do everything: There are limits set by both our cognitive skills and society. But in saying that people ultimately persuade themselves, I suggest that we are partly responsible if we let ourselves get conned by dishonest persuaders. I argue that people are capable of throwing off the shackles of dangerous messages and finding positive ways to live their lives.

Of course, this is not always easy. The tools of self-persuasion can be harnessed by both beneficent and malevolent communicators. Persuaders can be honest and truthful, appealing to the best angels in the message recipient. Or they can be dishonest and manipulative, trying to pull the wool over people's eyes. Trying to see the best in a persuader or hoping that a persuader's ministrations will bring them wealth, love, or happiness, people can coax themselves into accepting messages advanced by unsavory communicators. When this occurs, persuaders are ethically responsible for the choices they make.

Social influence is a powerful phenomenon. It can be viewed as a continuum, with coercion lying on one end and persuasion at the other. There are not always black-and-white differences between persuasion and coercion. They can overlap, as in situations involving authority, religious cults, and sexual abuse, as experienced by famous and ordinary, but valorous, women who chronicled their experiences in online posts that spawned the informal #MeToo movement and sadly documented the ubiquity of exploitive sexual influence attempts.

Still, with clear definitions we can disentangle coercion and persuasion. Coercion occurs when the influence agent delivers a believable threat of some consequence, deprives the individual of some measure of freedom or autonomy, and attempts to induce the individual to act contrary to his or her preferences. Persuasion occurs in an atmosphere of free choice, where the individual is autonomous, capable of saying no, and able to change his or her mind about the issue. In such situations, individuals are responsible for their choices and accountable for their decisions. Of course, terms like free choice, autonomy, and threats are not absolute, but, in some sense, relative and contextual. Their meanings are constructed by individuals in social situations, with meanings and the psychology of choices shaped by the cultural norms of a particular time. Freedom, coercion, and persuasion are closely linked with contemporary cultural practices, helping us appreciate why people feel unable to resist sexually abusive authorities, as well as the ennobling power they feel when they recognize they are free to reveal and reject untoward social influence attempts. Broad social changes expand psychological choices, changing and humanizing the contours of persuasion.

Persuasion overlaps with propaganda and manipulation. Propaganda, dormant for years, has returned with a visceral, viral vengeance with Russian cyberagents and later domestic extremists, who have sown discord by creating false messages and phony Facebook accounts that reached millions of Americans. The differences between propaganda and persuasion are particularly fraught, and overlap in intriguing ways, as seen in the difficulty of determining if particular deceptive political ads constitute persuasion or propaganda.

Still, one can tease out differences between the terms. In the main, propaganda occurs when leaders have near or total control over transmission of information and rely on media to target masses of individuals with false, deceptive, frequently covert messages. In systems where propaganda is dominant, dissent is discouraged. Propaganda has a negative connotation, in the eyes of observers; we call the techniques that our adversaries use propaganda, but when we harness them, they are righteously called persuasion. Manipulation occurs when a persuader disguises his or her intent, hoping to mislead the message recipient with a charming or otherwise disingenuous message. While manipulation also has a negative connotation, unlike propaganda, it can be used for positive purposes, as when someone flatters someone who is down in the dumps to enhance their mood, or tells someone who is struggling with an addiction that they are doing really well to motivate them to quit the habit.

Persuasion, broadly defined, has a host of effects on individuals, subtly and obtrusively influencing beliefs, emotions, and actions. Persuasion helps form, reinforce, and change attitudes. It can humanize, but also belittle. Just as humans are full of complicated emotions – strong and weak, good and bad – so is persuasion a fascinating amalgam of communication effects varying in their power and goodness, a time-honored facet of contemporary life. Like the human beings who created it, persuasion is not simple, but messy, overlapping with other constructs, yet distinct in its psychological properties and potential for liberation of the human spirit.

References

Andersen, K. (1971). *Persuasion: Theory and practice*. Boston, MA: Allyn & Bacon.

Angier, N. (2008, December 23). A highly involved propensity for deceit. *The New York Times*, D1, D4.

Atlas, D., Dodd, J., Lang, A., Bane, V., & Levy, D. S. (2008, April 28). Life in the cult. *People*, 62–67.

Bartsch, K., & London, K. (2000). Children's use of mental state information in selecting persuasive arguments. *Developmental Psychology, 36*, 352–365.

Bettinghaus, E. P., & Cody, M. J. (1987). *Persuasive communication* (4th ed.). New York: Holt, Rinehart & Winston.

Callimachi, R. (2015, February 21). In newly sophisticated Boko Haram videos, hints of Islam State ties. *The New York Times*, A9.

Chiu, R. (2019, October 6). I can finally tell my Weinstein story. *The New York Times* (Sunday Review), 7.

Cohen, C., & Regan, T. (2001). *The animal rights debate*. Lanham, MD: Rowman & Littlefield.

Confessore, N., & Willis, D. (2014, November 3). Hidden donors spend heavily on attack ads. *The New York Times*, A1, A16.

Coski, J. M. (2005). *The Confederate battle flag: America's most embattled emblem*. Cambridge, MA: Belknap Press of Harvard University Press.

Dahl, R. A. (1989). *Democracy and its critics*. New Haven, CT: Yale University Press.

de Waal, F. (1982). *Chimpanzee politics: Power and sex among apes*. London: Jonathan Cape Ltd.

de Waal, F. (2006). Morally evolved: Primate social instincts, human morality, and the rise and fall of "veneer theory". In S. Macedo & J. Ober (Eds.), *Primates and philosophers: How morality evolved* (pp. 1–80). Princeton, NJ: Princeton University Press.

de Waal, F. (2016). *Are we smart enough to know how smart animals are?* New York: W.W. Norton.

de Waal, F. (2019). *Mama's last hug: Animal emotions and what they tell us about ourselves*. New York: Norton.

Dudczak, C. A. (2001, January). *Comments on the Dynamics of Persuasion*. Prepared for Lawrence Erlbaum Associates.

Farrow, R. (2017, October 10). From aggressive overtures to sexual assault: Harvey Weinstein's accusers tell their stories. *The New Yorker*. Retrieved April 15, 2019, from www.newyorker.com/news/news-desk/from-aggressive=over

Feinberg, J. (1998). Coercion. In E. Craig (Ed.), *Routledge encyclopedia of philosophy* (pp. 387–390). London: Routledge.

Foner, E. (2017, August 21). Confederate statues and "our" history. *The New York Times*, A25.

Fountain, H. (2006, October 31). Observatory: The elephant in the mirror. *The New York Times*, D3.

Frymier, A. B., & Nadler, M. K. (2017). *Persuasion: Integrating theory, research, and practice* (4th ed.). Dubuque, IA: KendallHunt.

Gass, R. H., & Seiter, J. S. (2014). *Persuasion: Social influence and compliance gaining* (5th ed.). Boston, MA: Pearson.

Goldberg, J. (2000, June 25). The education of a holy warrior. *The New York Times Magazine*, 32–37, 53, 63–64, 70–71.

Goodstein, L. (1997, April 7). No one put a gun to their heads. *The Washington Post National Weekly Edition*, 32.

Green, M. C., & Brock, T. C. (2000). The role of transportation in the persuasiveness of public narratives. *Journal of Personality and Social Psychology, 79*, 701–721.

Hauser, M. D. (2006). *Moral minds: How nature designed our universal sense of right and wrong.* New York: HarperCollins.

Herman, E. S., & Chomsky, N. (2002). *Manufacturing consent: The political economy of the mass media* (2nd ed.). New York: Pantheon.

Hoffman, J. (2018, November 17). One drag on a Juul hooked a teenager for years. *The New York Times*, A1, A14, A15.

Hovland, C. I., Lumsdaine, A. A., & Sheffield, F. D. (1949). *Experiments on mass communication.* Princeton, NJ: Princeton University Press.

Igartua, -J.-J., & Barrios, I. (2012). Changing real-world beliefs with controversial movies: Processes and mechanisms of narrative persuasion. *Journal of Communication, 62,* 514–531.

Johnson, B. T., & Boynton, M. H. (2010). Putting attitudes in their place: Behavioral prediction in the face of competing variables. In J. P. Forgas, J. Cooper, & W. D. Crano (Eds.), *The psychology of attitudes and attitude change* (pp. 19–38). New York: Psychology Press.

Jowett, G. S., & O'Donnell, V. (2019). *Propaganda & persuasion* (7th ed.). Thousand Oaks, CA: Sage.

Kantor, J., & Abrams, R. (2017, October 10). Gwyneth Paltrow, Angelina Jolie and others say Weinstein harassed them. *The New York Times.* Retrieved April 15, 2019, from www.nytimes.com/2017/10/10/us/gwyneth-paltrow-angelina

Kantor, J., & Twohey, M. (2017, October 5). Harvey Weinstein paid off sexual harassment accusers for decades. *The New York Times.* Retrieved April 15, 2019, from www.nytimes.com/2017/10/05/us/harvey-weinstein-harassment

Kassan, L. D. (1999). *Second opinions: Sixty psychotherapy patients evaluate their therapists.* Northvale, NJ: Jason Aronson Press.

Kline, S. L., & Clinton, B. L. (1998). Developments in children's persuasive message practices. *Communication Education, 47,* 120–136.

Kolbert, E. (2019, September 30). A climate change? *The New Yorker,* 19–20.

Koomen, W., & van der Pligt, J. (2016). *The psychology of radicalization and terrorism.* New York: Routledge.

Korsgaard, C. M. (2006). Morality and the distinctiveness of human action. In S. Macedo & J. Ober (Eds.), *Primates and philosophers: How morality evolved* (pp. 98–119). Princeton, NJ: Princeton University Press.

Kovach, G. C. (2008, June 6). A sect's families reunite, and start to come home. *The New York Times.* Retrieved April 24, 2019, from www.nytimes.com/2008/06/06/us/06polygamy.html

Kristof, N. (2017, October 8). War drums inside the North. *The New York Times* (Sunday Review), 1, 4.

Lapierre, M. A. (2015). Development and persuasion understanding: Predicting knowledge of persuasion/selling intent from children's theory of mind. *Journal of Communication, 65,* 423–442.

Leonhardt, D., & Parlapiano, A. (2015, June 30). A march toward acceptance when civil rights is the topic. *The New York Times,* A3.

Lifton, R. J. (2003). Foreword. In M. T. Singer (Ed.), *Cults in our midst* (Rev ed., pp. xi–xiii). San Francisco, CA: Jossey-Bass.

Lipstadt, D. E. (2019, September 8). Confronting the evils of the past. *The New York Times Book Review,* 14.

McCombs, M. E. (2014). *Setting the agenda: The mass media and public opinion* (2nd ed.). Cambridge, England: Polity.

Meraz, S. (2019, November). Networked gatekeeping in the age of Trump. *Paper presented to panel on news at the annual convention of the Midwest Association for Public Opinion Research,* Chicago, IL.

Miles, H. L. (1993). Language and the orangutan: The old "person" of the forest. In P. Cavalieri & P. Singer (Eds.), *The great ape project: Equality beyond humanity* (pp. 42–57). New York: St. Martin's Griffin.

Miller, G. R. (1980). On being persuaded: Some basic distinctions. In M. E. Roloff & G. R. Miller (Eds.), *Persuasion: New directions in theory and research* (pp. 11–28). Beverly Hills, CA: Sage.

Montgomery, S. (2019, March 3). Animal care. *The New York Times Book Review*, 1, 16.

O'Keefe, D. J. (2016). *Persuasion: Theory and research* (3rd ed.). Thousand Oaks, CA: Sage.

Osnos, E. (2017, September 18). On the brink. *The New Yorker*, 34–53.

Perloff, R. M. (2019, June 26). Online cults are different. *The New York Times* (Letter to the Editor), A28.

Powers, P. (2007). Persuasion and coercion: A critical review of philosophical and empirical approaches. *HEC Forum*, 19, 125–143.

Prochaska, J. O., Redding, C. A., Harlow, L. L., Rossi, J. S., & Velicer, W. F. (1994). The transtheoretical model of change and HIV prevention: A review. *Health Education Quarterly*, 21, 471–486.

Ransom, J. (2020, February 1). Rape and relationship: A Weinstein accuser's complicated testimony. *The New York Times*, A23.

Robertson, C., Blinder, A., & Fausset, R. (2017, August 19). Monument debate spurs calls for a reckoning in the south. *The New York Times*, A1, A10.

Robinson, W. G. (1997). Heaven's Gate: The end? *Journal of Computer Mediated Communication*. Retrieved May 4, 2013, from http://jcmc.indiana.edu/vol3/issue3/robinson/html

Rosenbaum, A. S. (1986). *Coercion and autonomy: Philosophical foundations, issues, and practices*. Westport, CT: Greenwood.

Rothenberg, K. P. (2019, October 7). *The predatory nature of events in cases of sexual abuse*. Email to Richard M. Perloff.

Shane, S. (2018, February 18) America meddles in elections, too. *The New York Times* (Sunday Review), 4.

Smith, M. J. (1982). *Persuasion and human action: A review and critique of social influence theories*. Belmont, CA: Wadsworth.

Smythe, T. W. (1999). Moral responsibility. *Journal of Value Inquiry*, 33, 493–506.

Tavernise, S. (2011, January 19). Gay parents are thriving in South, census says. *The New York Times*, A1, A15.

Thernstrom, S., & Thernstrom, A. (1997). *America in black and white: One nation, indivisible*. New York: Simon & Schuster.

Tillman, L. (2019, January 20). "Roma" star uses her moment. *The New York Times* (Arts & Leisure), 1, 12.

Twohey, M., & Kantor, J. (2020, February 8). Weinstein case presents jurors with quandary. *The New York Times*, A1, A25.

Wakabayashi, D., & Benner, K. (2018, October 26). How Google has protected its elite men. *The New York Times*, A1, A16.

Whalen, D. J. (1996). *I see what you mean: Persuasive business communication*. Thousand Oaks, CA: Sage. Retrieved November 26, 2018, from www.nytimes.com/2018/11/24/opinion/sunday/gig=econom

Wolfe, A. (2011). *Political evil: What it is and how to combat it*. New York: Knopf.

Zakaria, F. (2001, October 15). Why do they hate us? *Newsweek*, 22–30, 32–38, 40.

Zakaria, F. (Anchor). (2015, November 17). *Blindsided: How ISIS shook the world*. CNN television documentary.

Zimbardo, P. (2007). *The Lucifer effect: Understanding how good people turn evil*. New York: Random House.

Chapter 3

Historical, Scientific, and Ethical Foundations

Persuasion has many attributes. It is subtle, powerful, liberating, and manipulative. But one thing it is not is new. Persuasion dates back to ancient times, to classical rhetoric of Greece and Rome that emphasized the importance of oratory in civic life (Hogan, 2013). Over time the focus on rhetoric, with its unfortunate linkage with doubletalk and empty words, has been supplanted by a social scientific focus, showcasing another quality of persuasion scholarship: It is never static.

Calling on the past as prologue, this chapter presents historical and ethical perspectives on persuasion, introducing you to hallmarks in the scholarly study of persuasion over many centuries. After a brief introduction to the classical rhetorical tradition of ancient Athens, the chapter takes a contemporary turn, introducing the distinctive features of twenty-first-century scholarship on persuasion, including its main features and critical perspectives. In the final portion of the chapter, I call on time-honored perspectives on the philosophy of ethics, as I explore their implications for persuasion.

Historical Review of Persuasion Scholarship

Ancient Greece: "It's All *Sophos* to Me"

Rhetoric refers to the use of argumentation, language, and public address to influence audiences. "If any one group of people could be said to have invented rhetoric," James L. Golden and colleagues note, "it would be the ancient Greeks" (Golden, Berquist, & Coleman, 2000, p. 1). The Greeks loved public speech. Trophies were awarded for skill in oratory. Citizens frequently acted as prosecutors and defense attorneys in lawsuits that were daily occurrences in the Athenian city-state (Golden et al., 2000). Before long, citizens expressed interest in obtaining training in rhetoric, or the art of public persuasion.

To meet the demand, a group of teachers decided to offer courses in rhetoric, as well as in other academic areas. The teachers were called Sophists, after the Greek word, *sophos*, for knowledge. The Sophists traveled from city to city, peddling their intellectual wares for a fee; the Sophists were dedicated to their craft but needed to make a living. Two of the traveling teachers – Gorgias and Isocrates – taught classes on oratory, placing considerable emphasis on style.

The Sophists attracted a following, but not everyone who followed them liked what they saw. Plato, the great Greek philosopher, denounced their work in his dialogues. To Plato, truth was a supreme value. Yet the Sophists sacrificed truth at the altar of persuasion, in Plato's view. Thus, he lamented that "he who would be an orator has nothing to do with true justice, but only that which is likely to be approved by the many who sit in judgment" (Golden et al., 2000, p. 19). The Sophists, he charged, were not interested in discovering truth or advancing rational, "laborious, painstaking" arguments, but, rather, in "the quick, neat, and stylish argument that wins immediate approval – even if this argument has some hidden flaw" (Chappell, 1998, p. 516). To Plato, rhetoric was like cosmetics or flattery: Not philosophy and therefore not deserving of respect (see Figure 3.1).

Figure 3.1 The Great Greek Philosopher Plato Distrusted Persuasion Because It Seemed to Rely so Frequently on Style, Not Substance
Image courtesy of Shutterstock

The Sophists, for their part, saw persuasion differently. They surely believed that they were rocking the foundations of the educational establishment by giving people practical knowledge rather than "highfalutin" truth. They also were democrats, willing to teach any citizen who could afford their tuition.

Why do we care about the differences of opinion between Plato and the Sophists some 2,500 years later? We care because the same issues bedevil us today. Plato is the friend of all those who hate advertisements because they "lie" or stretch the truth. He is on the side of everyone who turns off the television during elections to stop the flow of "political speak," or candidates making any argument they can to win elections. The Sophists address those practical persuaders – advertisers, politicians, salespeople – who have to make a living, need practical knowledge to promote their products, and are suspicious of "shadowy" abstract concepts like truth (Kennedy, 1963). The Sophists and Plato offer divergent, dueling perspectives on persuasive communication. Indeed, one of the themes of this book is that there are *dual approaches* to thinking about persuasion: One that emphasizes in-depth thinking and cogent arguments and the other focusing on style, oratory, and simpler persuasive appeals that date back to some of the Sophist writers.

The First Persuasion Theorist

Plato's greatest contribution to persuasion – or rhetoric, as it was then called – may not have been the works he created but, rather, his intellectual offspring. His best student – a Renaissance person before there was a Renaissance, a theorist before "theories" gained adherents – was Aristotle. Aristotle lived in the fourth century BC and wrote 170 works, including books on rhetoric. His treatise "Rhetoric" is regarded as "the most significant work on persuasion ever written" (Golden et al., 2000, p. 2; see Figure 3.2). He rescued rhetoric from the rock-bottom low point Plato had dropped it, emphasizing its virtues and viewing it through different lenses.

Bridging Plato and the Sophists, Aristotle's great insight was that both Plato and the Sophists had a point. Plato was right that truth was important, and the Sophists were correct that persuasive communication is a practical tool. Aristotle's great contribution was to recognize that rhetoric could be viewed in a more analytical fashion – as a phenomenon that could be described with precise concepts and by invoking probabilities (Golden et al., 2000; McCroskey, 1997). Drawing on his training in biology, Aristotle developed the first scientific approach to persuasion.

Rather than dismissing persuasion, as did Plato, the more practical Aristotle embraced it. "Aristotle said the goal of rhetoric wasn't so much finding the truth of a matter as convincing an audience to make the best decision about that matter," noted Martha D. Cooper and William L. Nothstine (1998, p. 25). To Aristotle, rhetoric had argumentative, practical virtues. He articulated a host of specific concepts on the nature of argumentation and the role of style in persuasion. He proposed methods by which persuasion occurred, described contexts in which it operated, and made ethics a centerpiece of his approach. During an era in which Plato was railing against the Sophists' pseudo-oratory, teachers were running around Greece offering short courses on rhetoric, and great orators made fortunes by serving as ghostwriters for the wealthy, Aristotle toiled tirelessly on the academic front, developing the first theories of persuasion.

Aristotle proceeded to argue that persuasion had three main ingredients: *Ethos* (the nature of the communicator), *pathos* (the emotional state of the audience), and *logos* (message arguments). Aristotle was also an early student of psychology, recognizing that speakers had to adapt to their audiences by considering in their speeches those factors that were most persuasive to an audience member. He

Figure 3.2 Aristotle Developed the First Systematic Approach to Persuasion Effects and Ethics

Image courtesy of Shutterstock

valued the development of cogent arguments that could stimulate thoughtful debate in the civic sphere, an ideal that many find lacking in contemporary public life, but which is a cornerstone of success and ethical citizenship (Infante & Rancer, 1996; Rancer & Avtgis, 2014). Aristotle regarded ethics as an important component of persuasion, calling attention to the personal character of the orator and proclaiming that "we believe good men more fully and more readily than others."

Aristotle's Greece was a mecca for the study and practice of persuasion. Yet it was not always pretty or just. Women were assumed to be innately unfit for engaging in persuasive public speaking;

they were denied citizenship and excluded from the teaching professions (Waggenspack, 2000). Although slaves outnumbered free men in ancient Athens, they could not participate in the vaunted democratic government. Aristotle, though he preached admirably and credibly about ethics, had blind spots that reflected the biases of the era in which he lived.

When Greek civilization gave way to Rome, the messengers were lost, but not the message. The practical Romans preserved much of Athenian civilization, adapting classic rhetorical works to Roman culture. Their rhetoricians also proclaimed that oratory was a virtue. Over the course of the ensuing centuries, a series of spectacular events occurred: The fall of the Roman Empire, the growth of Christianity, the Black Death, the Italian Renaissance, and the European wars. Rhetorical thought paled in comparison to these events. Nonetheless, the work of the early rhetoricians survived and influenced the political philosophy of subsequent generations, including the founders of the United States, and scholars of both dictators and social movements spanning the civil rights protesters of the 1960s to feminists of the late twentieth century (Burke, 1950; Waggenspack, 2000; see also Campbell, 1989).

From an academic perspective, rhetorical scholarship continues apace, but has been supplemented and to some degree replaced by social scientific approaches. Rhetorical approaches offer intriguing insights on the basic arguments employed in contemporary persuasion. However, they do not provide evidence about the effects that persuasive communications exert in everyday situations. Social science perspectives, by drawing on theories and scientific methods, yield a wealth of knowledge of the impact of persuasion and the processes by which it achieves its effects.

Origins of the Social Scientific Approach

Social scientific studies of persuasion were born in the 1930s with early research on attitudes (Allport, 1935). Psychologists were fascinated by the power of this new mental construct – *attitude* – and intrigued by the possibility of devising questionnaire methods to study social attitudes. For the first time, something mental and amorphous could be measured with the new techniques of social science. The heady excitement that greeted the development of new attitude measurement techniques was accompanied by a foreboding concern about the powers of propaganda and persuasion, evident in World War I government propaganda campaigns and the disturbing effects of a social movement in Germany that exploited communications for destructive purposes. Hitler's mastery of the new technologies of twentieth-century media raised new questions about the ways persuasion could be harnessed for nefarious purposes. America needed to launch its own communication initiative to explore ways of using persuasive messages to mobilize soldiers and the Allied war effort.

Scholarship received a boost when the U.S. War Department commissioned a group of researchers to explore the effects of a series of documentary films. The movies were designed to educate Allied soldiers on the Nazi threat and to boost morale. The War Department asked Frank Capra, who had previously directed such classics as *Mr. Smith Goes to Washington*, to direct the films. They were called simply *Why We Fight* (see Figure 3.3).

Asked to evaluate the effects of the wartime documentaries, the social scientists received the added benefit of working, albeit indirectly, with Capra. It must have been a heady experience, assessing the effects of a Hollywood director's films on beliefs and attitudes. The studies offered some of the first hard evidence that communications influenced attitudes, albeit complexly (Hovland, Lumsdaine, & Sheffield, 1949). The experiments showed that persuasion research could be harnessed by government for its own ends – in this case, beneficial ones, but certainly not value-neutral objectives.

Figure 3.3 The *Why We Fight* Films Offered an Opportunity to Test the Psychological Effects of Morale-Boosting Wartime Communications
Image courtesy of Eye of History, Wesleyan University

Several of the researchers working on the *Why We Fight* research went on to do important research in the fields of psychology and communication. One of them, Carl Hovland, seized the moment, brilliantly combining experimental research methodology with the ideas of an old persuasion sage, the first scientist of persuasion, the A-man: Aristotle. Working in a university setting, Hovland painstakingly conducted a series of experiments on persuasive communication effects (see Figure 3.4). What the researchers discovered – for example, that credible sources influenced attitudes – was less important than how they went about their investigations. Hovland and colleagues devised hypotheses, developed elaborate procedures to test predictions, employed statistical procedures to determine whether

Figure 3.4 Carl Hovland Conducted Path-Breaking Experiments on the Psychological Effects of Persuasive Communications
Image courtesy of Seminarioteorico01.blogspot.com

predictions held true, and reported findings in scientific journals that could be scrutinized by critical observers (Hovland, Janis, & Kelley, 1953).

From a historical perspective, the distinctive element of the persuasion approach that began in the mid-twentieth century and continues today is its empirical foundation. Knowledge is gleaned from observation and evidence rather than armchair philosophizing. Researchers devise scientific theories, tease out hypotheses, and dream up ways of testing them in real-world settings. No one – not the Greeks, Romans, or twentieth-century Western rhetorical theorists – had taken this approach. Capitalizing on the development of a scientific approach to behavior, new techniques for measuring attitudes, advances in statistics, and American pragmatism, early researchers were able to forge ahead, asking new questions and finding answers.

Scholarly activity continued apace from the 1960s onward, producing a wealth of persuasion concepts far surpassing those put forth by Aristotle and classical rhetoricians. These terms include attitude, belief, cognitive processing, cognitive dissonance, social judgments, and interpersonal compliance. We also have a body of knowledge – thousands of studies, books, and review pieces on persuasion. More articles and books on persuasion have been published over the past 50 years than in the previous 2,500 years.

What once was a small field that broke off from philosophy has blossomed into a multidisciplinary field of study, comprising social psychology, communication, and marketing. If you look up "persuasion" under PsycINFO or in Communication Abstracts, you will find thousands of studies, journal articles, and books.

What's more, research plays a critical role in everyday persuasion activities. Advertising agencies spend millions on research. When Nike plans campaigns geared to young people (with ads resembling music videos), company executives plug in facts gleaned from marketing research. Brands harness Millennials' social media posts and friends' product likes, to develop micro-targeted Facebook ads. Plato, the purist, would be horrified by these developments. Aristotle, the practical theorist, would be pleased that persuasion had become a respected field of academic study. But he would lament ethical shortcomings in the practice of persuasion: Mean-spirited political debates and society's failure to insist that moral character serve as a prerequisite for a career in public office. Both would be amazed by the sheer volume of persuasion research and its numerous applications, pro and con, to everyday life. Who knows? Maybe they'll be talking about our age 500 years from now! So, sit back and enjoy. You're about to embark on an exciting intellectual journey, fraught with intriguing findings and complex applications to everyday life.

The Contemporary Study of Persuasion

Contemporary scholars approach persuasion from a social science point of view. This may seem strange. After all, you may think of persuasion as an art. When someone mentions the word "persuasion," you may think of such things as "the gift of the gab," "manipulation," or "subliminal seduction." You may feel that by approaching persuasion from the vantage point of contemporary social science, we are reducing the area to something antiseptic. However, this is far from the truth. Social scientists are curious about the same phenomena that everybody else is: For example, what makes a person persuasive, what types of persuasive messages are most effective, and why do people go along with the recommendations put forth by powerful persuaders? The difference between the scientist's approach and that of the layperson is that the scientist formulates theories about attitudes and persuasion, derives hypotheses from these theories, and puts the hypotheses to empirical test. By empirical test, I mean that hypotheses are evaluated on the basis of evidence and data collected from the real world.

Theory plays a major role in the social scientific enterprise. A *theory* is a large, umbrella conceptualization of a phenomenon that contains hypotheses, proposes linkages between variables, explains events, and offers predictions. It may seem strange to study something as dynamic as persuasion by focusing on abstract theories. But theories contain ideas that yield insights about communication effects. These ideas provide the impetus for change. They are the pen that is mightier than the sword.

In fact, we all have theories about human nature and about persuasion (Roskos-Ewoldsen, 1997; Stiff, 1994). We may believe that people are basically good, parents have a major impact on kids' personalities, or men are more competitive than women.

We also have theories about persuasion. Consider these propositions:

- Advertising exploits people.
- You shouldn't persuade people by scaring them.
- The key to being persuasive is physical appeal.

At some level these are theoretical statements – propositions that contain interesting, testable ideas about persuasive communication. But there are problems with the statements from a scientific perspective. They are not bona fide theories of persuasion.

The first statement is problematic because it uses a value-laden term, *exploit*. Exploitation evokes negative images. Perhaps advertising doesn't exploit so much as guide consumers toward outcomes they sincerely want. The first rule of good theorizing is to state propositions in value-free language.

The second statement – you shouldn't persuade people by merely scaring them – sounds reasonable until you start thinking about it from another point of view. One could argue that giving people a jolt of fear is just what is needed to get them to rethink dangerous behaviors like drug abuse or binge drinking. You could suggest that appeals to fear motivate people to take steps to protect themselves from dangerous outcomes.

The third statement – that physical appeal is the key to persuasion – can also be viewed with a critical eye. Perhaps attractive speakers turn audiences off because people resent their good looks or assume they made it because of their bodies, not their brains. I am sure you can think of communicators who are trustworthy and credible, but aren't so physically attractive.

Yet, at first blush, the three statements made sense. They could even be called intuitive "theories" of persuasion. But intuitive theories – our homegrown notions of what makes persuasion tick – are problematic. They lack objectivity. They are inextricably linked with our own biases of human nature (Stiff, 1994). What's more, they can't be easily scientifically tested or disconfirmed. By contrast, scientific theories are stated with sufficient precision that they can be empirically tested (through real-world research). They also contain formal explanations, hypotheses, and corollaries.

Researchers take formal theories, derive hypotheses, and test them in real-world experiments or surveys. If the hypotheses are supported over and over again, to a point of absolute confidence, we no longer call them theories but, rather, laws of human behavior. We have preciously few of these in social science. (Darwinian evolution counts as a theory whose hypotheses have been proven to the point that we can call it a law.)

At the same time, there are many useful social science theories that can forecast behavior, shed light on people's actions, and suggest strategies for social change.

The beauty of research is that it provides us with a yardstick for evaluating the truth value of ideas that at first blush seem intuitively correct. It lets us know whether our gut feelings about persuasion – for example, regarding fear or good looks – amount to a hill of beans in the real world. Moreover, research provides a mechanism for determining which notions of persuasion hold water, which ones leak water (are no good), and, in general, which ideas about persuasive communication are most accurate, compelling, and predictive of human action in everyday life.

Researchers study persuasion in primarily two ways. They conduct *experiments*, or controlled studies that take place in artificial settings. Experiments provide convincing evidence that one variable causes changes in another. Because experiments typically are conducted in university settings and primarily involve college students, they don't tell us about persuasion that occurs in everyday life among diverse population groups. For this reason, researchers conduct surveys. *Surveys* are questionnaire studies that examine the relationship between one factor (e.g., exposure to a social media anti-e-cigarette campaign) and another (e.g., reduced smoking). Surveys do not provide unequivocal evidence of causation.

In the preceding example, it is possible that people may reduce e-cigarette use shortly after a media campaign, but the effects may have nothing to do with the campaign. E-cig users may have decided to quit because friends bugged them or they wanted to save money on vaping.

Most studies of persuasive communication effects are experiments. Studies of attitudes and media applications of persuasion are more likely to be surveys. Both experiments and surveys are useful, although they make different contributions (Hovland, 1959).

Scientific Questions, Replication Shortcomings, and Conceptual Virtues

Questions cut to the heart of the scientific enterprise. Social scientists question the fabric of society. They dream up queries about the human condition, wondering about the dynamics of strong attitudes, curious about the ways persuasive messages can prime these attitudes in malevolent and beneficent ways. They also turn the interrogatives on themselves, raising questions about the validity of the social science enterprise.

The self-reflective aspect has increased dramatically, beginning decades ago with questions about the generalizability of social psychological experiments conducted in university laboratories, mounting in recent years with strong criticisms of once-sanctified research, like Milgram's obedience studies (see Chapter 9), and amplifying at crescendo-like proportions with questions about the replicability of social psychological experiments.

Replication is the ability to obtain the same findings when an experiment is conducted under identical or extremely similar circumstances, using the same procedures, materials, and measuring instruments. Replication lets social scientists see if the original findings can be repeated or duplicated, providing confidence in the robustness – reliability, validity, and generalizability – of the results. If the same findings do not emerge when the original study is repeated, in a virtually identical manner to the original experiment, scholars wonder if the initial results were a fluke, sloppily conducted, or, even in weirdly unusual cases, falsified (Diener & Biswas-Diener, 2019). They may question if the original investigators were too quick to declare the results were valid. Alternatively, they may decide that the newer studies did not mirror the procedures the original researchers employed, or that other factors intervened to result in different findings.

These questions have come to a head in recent years with a flurry of evidence that many studies, particularly in social psychology, which bears on persuasion, do not replicate or obtain weaker findings than the original experiments (Bohannon, 2015; Carey, 2015). In one case, only 39 percent of 100 prominent studies could be clearly replicated (Open Science Collaboration, 2015). These findings collectively drew dismay from scientists, who feared that the hypotheses they thought they had confirmed were far less solid – the knowledge base shakier – than they had long presumed.

Not so fast, said other thoughtful scholars. Gilbert and his colleagues (2016) reexamined the replication critique, paying close attention to methodological protocol. And guess what? They found a number of irregularities in the replication studies. Many replication attempts employed procedures that substantially differed from those used by the original investigators. In one dramatic instance, the original study, which focused on social psychological issues, assessed Americans' attitudes toward African Americans. However, it was replicated with Italian respondents, who did not harbor the same stereotypes. In another case, an original investigation that asked college students to imagine being called on in class by a professor was replicated with students who had never attended college. Pointing to these procedural and other methodological artifacts, as well as evidence from another group of researchers who found a much higher replication rate, Gilbert et al. concluded that "the reproducibility of psychological science is quite high" (p. 1037-b).

In a similar fashion, other researchers, while acknowledging the failure to replicate classic studies, have counterargued that researchers conducting the replications may not always accurately mirror the original study's experimental procedures. Still others have taken up a compromise position, noting that our knowledge of psychological – and persuasion principles – is not at the point that we can expect a particular variable to hold under all conditions, circumstances, and people (Cesario, 2014). In addition, when persuasion researchers repeat a persuasion study today, using a message that was in vogue in the early 2000s but was insensitive, let's say, to the gender norms of our current era, it is no wonder they don't replicate the results. This may not mean that the original concept is faulty, only that things have changed, we need a more appropriate message, or should more precisely pinpoint the contextual factors that determine when the phenomenon occurs and when it doesn't (Van Bavel et al., 2016).

And yet, critics have helpfully called attention to the importance of replication, reminding us that social scientific findings should not be flukes, particular to one research laboratory, but should gain validity by emerging through replication by different social scientists using similar procedures. There are now a variety of outlets where failed and successful replication attempts can be published, highlighting what we know and don't, which is all to the good.

The field of persuasion is plagued by far too many studies that were conducted at one point in time, but have not been reexamined, to see if they hold water today. What's more, fascinating as the results can sometimes be, they are also based on studies of young people – frequently college students, often White – from the American culture, raising questions about the generalizability of results to societies far away and characterized by different cultural norms. Yet, on another level, to the extent that findings from classic social psychological studies of attitudes do not obtain the same results when reproduced in the current era, we may conclude that the original theoretical postulates should be modified to fit the contours of today. The foundations of knowledge change with cultural transformations, as classic concepts take on new meanings or are enhanced by ideas that emerge in today's sociocultural arena.

In discussing the empirical field of persuasion throughout the book, I will call attention to the limits of what we know, but also the field's strengths – the ways imaginative concepts and bold theories offer incisive clues about the perils and promises of persuasion. These classic theories need to be appreciated for what they are – not perfect templates to predict each and every persuasion situation, but ideas, constructs, and promising propositions to generate broader understanding of persuasion than are suggested by everyday intuitions and biased beliefs. Research guided by these concepts provides us with insights – hardly predicting each and every persuasion situation, to be sure, but evidence that enriches understanding of the warp and woof of persuasive communication in everyday life.

Research is important because, guided by penetrating theories, it advances knowledge. Yet one must not lose sight of the big picture: The role that persuasion plays in society and the fundamental ethics of persuasive communication. The final section of the chapter, building on the preceding discussion, examines these broader concerns.

Seeing the Big Picture

Persuasion is so pervasive that we often don't ask the question: What sort of world would it be if there were no persuasive communications? It would be a quieter world, that's for sure – one with less buzz, especially around dinnertime when telemarketers phone! But, without persuasion, people would have to resort to different means to get their way. Many would resort to verbal abuse, threats, and coercion to accomplish personal and political goals. Argument would be devalued or non-existent. Force – either physical or psychological – would carry the day.

Persuasion, by contrast, is a profoundly civilizing influence. It prizes oratory and argument. It says that disagreements between people can be resolved through logic, empathy-based appeals, and the rough-and-tumble banter of group discussion. Persuasion provides us with a constructive mechanism for advancing our claims and trying to change institutions. It offers a way for disgruntled and disenfranchised people to influence society. Persuasion provides a mechanism for everybody – from teens sharing opinions about school policies on Yik Yak to Wall Street brokers selling stocks – to advance in life and achieve their goals.

Persuasion is not always pretty. It can be mean, vociferous, and ugly. Persuasion, as Winston Churchill might say, is the worst way to exert influence – except for all the others. Were there no persuasion, Democrats and Republicans would have settled their disagreement about how to help Americans facing the coronavirus pandemic not in Congress, but on the battlefield. Conversely, if persuasion were the accepted way to resolve problems among terrorist militia operating in the Middle East, peace, not deadly violence, would reign supreme.

Persuasion is not analogous to truth. As Aristotle recognized, persuasive communications are designed to influence, rather than uncover universal truths (Cooper & Nothstine, 1998). In fact, persuaders sometimes hide truth, mislead, or lie outright in the service of their aims or clients. The field of ethics is concerned with determining when it is morally appropriate to deviate from truth and when such deviations are ethically indefensible.

Persuasion assumes without question that people have free choice – that they can do other than what the persuader suggests. This has an important consequence. It means that people are responsible for the decisions they make in response to persuasive messages. Naturally, people can't foresee every possible consequence of choices that they make. They cannot be held accountable for outcomes that could not reasonably have been foreseen.

But one of the essential aspects of life is choice – necessarily based on incomplete, and sometimes inaccurate, information. Provided that individuals have freedom of choice, a foundation of persuasion, they are responsible for the decisions they make. As religious scholar P. J. O'Rourke observed:

> One of the annoying things about believing in free will and individual responsibility is the difficulty of finding somebody to blame your problems on. And when you do find somebody, it's remarkable how often his picture turns up on your driver's license!
>
> (quoted in Genzlinger, 2011, p. C6)

At the same time, persuaders also make choices. They must decide how best to appeal to audiences. They necessarily must choose between ethical and unethical modes of persuasion. Persuaders who advance their claims in ethical ways deserve our respect. Those who employ unethical persuasion ploys should be held accountable for their choices. This raises an important question: Just what do we mean by ethical and unethical persuasion? The final portion of the chapter addresses this issue.

Persuasion and Ethics

Is persuasion ethical? This simple question has engaged scholars and practitioners alike. Aristotle and Plato discussed it. Machiavelli touched on it. So have contemporary communication scholars and social psychologists. And you can bet that practitioners – fashion designer Michael Kors, Facebook's Mark Zuckerberg, and the late Steve Jobs – mulled it over, some more than others, to be sure.

Yet persuasion ethics demand consideration. As human beings, we want to be treated with respect, and we value communications that treat others as an end, not a means, to use Immanuel Kant's famous phrase. At the same time, we are practical creatures, who want to achieve our goals, whether they be financial, social, emotional, or spiritual. The attainment of goals – money, prestige, love, or religious fulfillment – requires that we influence others in some fashion somewhere along the way. Is the need to influence *incompatible* with the ethical treatment of human beings?

Some scholars would say it invariably is. Plato, who regarded truth as "the only reality in life," was offended by persuasive communication (Golden et al., 2000, p. 17). As noted earlier, he regarded rhetoric as a form of flattery that appealed to people's worst instincts. Although Plato did believe in an ideal rhetoric admirably composed of truth and morality, he did not think that ordinary persuasion measured up to this standard.

The German philosopher Immanuel Kant would view persuasion as immoral for a different reason: In his view, it uses people, treating them as means to the persuader's end, not as valued ends in themselves (Borchert & Stewart, 1986). This violates Kant's ethical principles. As thoughtful as these perspectives are, they set up a rather high bar for human communication to reach. What's more, these philosophers tend to lump all persuasive communication together. Some communications are indeed false, designed to manipulate people by appealing to base emotions, or are in the interest of the sender and not the receiver. But others are not. Some messages make very intelligent appeals, based on logic and evidence. In addition, not all persuaders treat people as a means. Therapists and health professionals ordinarily accord clients a great deal of respect. Many people who do volunteer work – such as those who counsel teens in trouble or HIV/AIDS victims – do not receive great financial benefit from their work. Their communications can be very much in the best interest of those receiving the message.

On the other extreme are philosophers who argue that persuasion is fundamentally moral. Noting that people are free to accept or reject a communicator's message, conservative thinkers tend to embrace persuasion. Believing that people are sufficiently rational to distinguish between truth and falsehood, libertarian scholars argue that society is best served by diverse persuasive communications that run the gamut from entirely truthful to totally fallacious (Siebert, Peterson, & Schramm, 1956). Persuasion, they say, is better than coercion, and people are in any event free to accept or reject the communicator's message.

There is some wisdom in this perspective. However, to say that persuasion is inherently moral is an extreme, absolute statement. To assume that people are capable of maturely rejecting manipulative communicators' messages naively neglects cases in which trusted but evil people exploit others' vulnerability. What of persuaders who trick or emotionally exploit poor people and then take advantage of their dependence to demand they pony up more money for a fraudulent loan? Perhaps we would argue that the people chose to go along with the request – they're persuaded, not coerced – but it would be heartless to suggest that such persuasion is moral.

Consider also those nasty car salespeople who stretch the truth or lie outright to make a sale. Don't forget history's legions of con men – the snake oil salesmen of the nineteenth century who promised that new nutritional cures would work magic on those who purchased them, and their modern counterparts, the hosts of infomercials who tell you that vitamin supplements will enhance your libido. Social media has added a new wrinkle to the historical litany of nefarious persuasion, with the emergence of Twitter feeds from White supremacists, terrorists, and child pornographers.

This brings us to a third viewpoint, and it hues closest to truth. Persuasion can be used for a host of good or bad purposes, with ethical and unethical intentions. Aristotle endorsed this view. He argued that persuasion could be used by anyone: "by a good person or a bad person, by a person seeking worthy ends or unworthy ends" (McCroskey, 1997, p. 9). Thus, charisma can be employed by a Hitler or a Martin Luther King, by a bin Laden or a Gandhi. Step-by-step persuasion techniques that begin with a small request and hook the person into larger and larger commitments have been used by North Korean captors of American soldiers during the Korean War and by religious cult leaders – but also by Alcoholics Anonymous.

What determines whether a particular persuasive act is ethical or unethical? How do we decide if a communicator has behaved in a moral or immoral fashion? In order to answer these questions, we must turn to moral philosophy. Philosophers have offered many perspectives on these issues, beginning with Plato and continuing to the present day.

Normative Theories of Ethics

A normative theory of ethics adopts a prescriptive approach. Social scientific theories describe and explain the world as it is. Normative theories prescribe, suggesting what people *ought* to do, in light of moral philosophy and a vision of the good life. Two classical normative perspectives with important implications for persuasion are utilitarianism and Kantian deontological thought.

Utilitarianism offers a series of common-sense solutions to moral dilemmas. It also contains an elaborate set of postulates that can help people to decide whether particular actions are morally justified. Developed by British philosophers Jeremy Bentham and John Stuart Mill and adapted by American thinkers over the years, utilitarianism emphasizes *utility* or *consequences*. Actions are judged based on whether they produce more positive than negative consequences. To utilitarians, the moral act is the one that promotes the greatest good for the greatest number of people.

There is a certain elegant simplicity to utilitarianism. And while it may seem intuitively obvious, it is important to appreciate that when it was originally articulated in the eighteenth and nineteenth centuries, it represented a radical repudiation of contemporary ethical doctrines that emphasized fidelity to God. Rather than focusing on divine rules that came from the heavens, morality was intended to improve the happiness of human beings living on earth. Utilitarianism bespoke a compassion for mortal men and women.

Yet, as utilitarianism came under scrutiny, it became clear that it contained serious flaws. Consider this example. A guard is falsely accused of killing a prisoner in a maximum security prison. Prisoners begin to riot. The guard is innocent, but if he signs a confession and succumbs to arrest, the rioting will stop. The utilitarian would support this option. Although the confession and arrest might cause pain to the guard, it would forestall a riot, which would cause more harm to more people. But this solution seems unjust (Rachels, 1986).

Utilitarianism thus seems wrong because it places consequences ahead of other considerations, such as fairness and truth. It assumes that what is right is that which produces the most good. But there are instances in which something can be wrong, even though it leads to positive consequences. Utilitarianism gives short shrift to other values such as fairness and justice.

Kant's deontological theory. The writings of the great eighteenth-century German philosopher Immanuel Kant offer a devastating critique of utilitarianism that still makes sense today (see Figure 3.5).

According to Kantians, "just because something gives many people pleasure doesn't make it right. The mere fact that the majority, however big, favors a certain law, however intensely, does not make the law just" (Sandel, 2009, p. 106). A *deontological or duty-based theory* emphasizes moral duties, universal obligations, and according respect to individuals as ends in and of themselves.

The deonotological approach argues that the moral value of an act derives not from the consequence it produces, but in the *intention* from which the act is performed (Sandel, 2009). The late communication scholar James C. McCroskey was a proponent of intention-based morality. He argued, "If the communicator seeks to improve the well-being of his audience through his act of communication, he is committing a moral act. If he seeks to produce harm for his audience, the communicator is guilty of an immoral act" (1972, p. 270).

But how do we know what the communicator's intentions are? Perhaps a seemingly well-meaning social activist operates from more self-aggrandizing, publicity-enhancing motives. It can be difficult to pinpoint the content of another individual's intentions. Deontological theory assumes that, to the extent that we can appreciate another's true intentions, the morally right act is one that is performed for the right reason. But motives are multifaceted, intentions are complicated, and can be evaluated differently, depending on the evaluator's moral rubric.

Immanuel Kant.

Figure 3.5 Immanuel Kant's Philosophy Emphasized That the Morality of Persuasion Should Be Based on Intentions and Moral Duty, Not Simply the Consequences of an Action

Image courtesy of Shutterstock

To appreciate the basic distinction between the utilitarian and deontologial approaches, consider this example. Juul, the hugely popular vaping company, launched an advertising campaign several years back that featured testimonial statements from ex-cigarette smokers, who exchanged their nicotine-laden cigarettes for the seemingly more benign Juul e-cigarette (Roose, 2019).

Utilitarians would evaluate the campaign entirely by its effects. If ex-smokers' stories, which emphasized that cigarette smoking created interpersonal tensions with family members, helped them kick the habit, utilitarian philosophers would give the campaign high marks on the moral metric.

However, deontological thinkers would beg to differ. They would point out that that Juul received loads of negative publicity for shamelessly marketing its product to vulnerable teenagers, as well as earning the wrath of consumers, who sued Juul for deceptively claiming its product was safe when it has had adverse health effects (see Chapters 6 and 12). Faced with this avalanche of bad press, Juul realized it had to embark on the "Make the Switch" ad campaign to improve its brand image and fend off further lawsuits.

Viewed through deontological eyes, the campaign lacked moral value. The company's intentions were selfish, not altruistic, a "convenient smoke screen" (Roose, 2019). Juul wasn't so much interested in helping people quit smoking so much as polishing its image as a public health advocate to ward off negative publicity in the press and social media, in this way elevating its brand in the eyes of the public, as well as corporations, like tobacco colossus Altria that paid more than $12 billion for a 35 percent stake in Juul. By not taking into account motives and intrinsic moral duties, deontological thinkers argue that effects-based utilitarians understate the essence of morality. Utilitarians, for their part, would respond that intentions are hard to measure, no one's motives are perfectly pure, and overall aggregate improvements in health is what matters.

Additional Complicating Factors

In his classic statement of *deontological thought*, the categorical imperative, Kant famously exhorted that we should never treat others as a means, but always as an end, not using them for our purposes, but respecting their fundamental, essential humanity. His philosophical rule is non-negotiable – it applies to all situations. It is an elegant statement, one worthy of emulation. However, it also raises difficult questions. Should a rule apply to all situations when different contexts contain complex quandaries that require moral flexibility? Kantians would say that lying is never permissible in persuasion, a worthwhile precept. Yet clearly, there are times when exceptions must be made to this rule. As Hauser (2006) notes:

> If an adult sexually abuses a child and then tells the child to keep this a secret, it seems morally permissible, perhaps obligatory, for the child to report the abuse to an authority. Once again, a rigid deontological stance is problematic, because it is sometimes permissible to lie, breaking a promise to keep a secret.
>
> (pp. 269–270)

Or consider this more familiar contemporary example that calls on deontological and other philosophical principles. Is it ethical for charities to exploit tragedy? After the slaughter of 12 people at the French newspaper, *Charlie Hebdo*, in 2015, "Je Suis Charlie" items became the rage, retailing online. Shortly after the Boston Marathon bombing, memorabilia of the tragedy (jackets, shirts, and pins) were sold on eBay. In the wake of riots over police violence against unarmed African Americans, a designer developed a T-Shirt that showcased victims' names in big black capital letters under the heading, "They Have Names." Deontological theorists would rightly cry foul, pointing out that consumers are using victims as a means to their self-promotion, and retailers are cashing in on others' misfortune. But some (not all) of the profits from the sales go to charities to help families of the victims. And if people can find meaning in a tragedy, even wearing a shirt to proclaim their affinity with the victims, why should we be so quick to condemn them? These are not simple issues.

Deontological theory, although not without flaws, complements results-oriented approaches by calling attention to human dignity. It emphasizes the importance of duty and acting on the basis of morally upright intentions. Other philosophers would add that to treat someone with respect and dignity means treating her as a responsible being, one who is accountable for her actions. People have autonomy, and freely decide what to do based on their beliefs. Thus, a persuader who delivers an uplifting, respectful message deserves praise. A communicator who chooses to mislead, lie, or distort in the service of persuasion deserves to be held accountable for his deeds (see Box 3.1 for a summary of key points in these theories).

BOX 3.1

Understanding Persuasion Ethics: Primer on Two Philosophical Theories

Utilitarianism judges ethics in terms of outcomes. The moral act is one that promotes the greatest good for the greatest number of people.

A shortcoming of utilitarianism is that it does not consider the communicator's intentions or moral obligations.

Deontological theory emphasizes moral duty, moral obligation, and according respect to individuals as ends in and of themselves. Actions are judged based on their adherence to obligations and universal moral rules.

A shortcoming of deontological thought is its rigidity. It does not allow for exceptions that ought to be made in particular situations.

Utilitarianism and deontological thought provide helpful yardsticks to judge the morality of persuasive communications.

Becoming an Ethical Persuader

What criteria do we employ to evaluate the ethics of a persuader's conduct? Utilitarianism urges that we examine the consequences of the action or underlying rule. Deontological thought steers us toward the intentions of the communicator, emphasizing that moral acts flow from our universal obligation to treat people with respect.

One choice people have is not to be ethical at all, to pursue self-interest at any cost. This is the emphasis of ethical egoism, a flawed approach to ethical decision-making. In the end, philosophers cannot persuade people to make ethical judgments; they cannot convince unsavory characters to behave in humane ways or to use morally acceptable strategies to influence others. One can give many arguments on behalf of ethical persuasion, from the Golden Rule to moral duty to the Aristotelian notion that virtue is inextricably linked with a good life.

An ethical approach to persuasion emphasizes the development of thoughtful, humane arguments, advanced forcefully, but not aggressively. Ethical persuaders affirm the dignity of each person, treat audience members as free and autonomous agents, present facts and opinions fairly, and provide different perspectives on an issue to enable people to make the most thoughtful decision possible (e.g., Wallace, 1967). It is easy to be an ethical egoist, placing your self-interest on others. It is difficult to reflect on what constitutes the morally right thing to do and even harder to implement this in practice. We all lapse, opting to get what we want rather than listening to our higher ethical angel. Some people choose – notice, it's a choice – to ignore their moral conscience, and others, due to upbringing or socialization, don't always know what the right thing to do is. Prosaic as it may sound, doing the right thing – practicing ethical persuasion – is a worthwhile goal, an important personal attribute, and a foundation of the good life. In a society wracked by polarization and sundered by hate, and imperilled by global challenges, ethical, tolerant persuasion remains a salve we need, a lifeline for amelioration of the human condition.

The Present Approach

There are thousands of books on persuasion, hundreds of thousands of articles, probably more. "How to persuade" books, apps, and websites proliferate. No surprise here: A search for the keys to persuasion is surely among the most basic of human desires. Who among us has not entertained the thought that somewhere out there lies the secret to persuasion? Who has not dreamed that he or she might, with luck or perseverance, find the simple trick or magic elixir that contains the formula for social influence?

We may yet find the secret to persuasion or, failing that, we may someday understand perfectly why people need to believe that simple solutions exist. But you won't find a simple formula here. Instead, you will discover intriguing theories, bundles of evidence, creative methodologies, and rich applications of research to everyday life. This book, focusing on academic scholarship on persuasion, attempts to increase your knowledge of attitudes and persuasion.

The book is divided into four parts. The first part, which you have just completed, described the foundations of persuasion, defining terms, providing a historical overview, and introducing major theories of ethics. The second part focuses on attitudes. The third part examines theories and research on persuasion and attitude change, using theory as a fulcrum to explain how communications change attitudes. The final part explores persuasion contexts – interpersonal, advertising and marketing, and health campaigns. Thus, I move from a general conceptual overview to a focus on the individual mind, expand the focus to the attitude-changing effects of sources and messages, and in the final section take an ever-broader perspective, exploring persuasion in interpersonal and societal contexts.

Throughout the book, I explore what it means to persuade and be persuaded, the contexts in which this occurs, and ethics of persuasive communications.

Certain themes predominate and run through the book:

- the central role persuasion performs in contemporary life (from social media to interpersonal compliance-gaining);
- the way ideas and concepts shade into each other, blurring simple distinctions that characterize our initial perspective on persuasion;
- the important part that theory and research play in illuminating persuasive communication effects;
- the centrality of self-persuasion, as we convince ourselves and change our own minds in response to persuasive messages;

- the two very different ways people frequently process persuasive information, one effortful, the other more automatic;
- the endless complexity of human behavior;
- persuasion's capacity to deceive and stoke hate, and its potential to liberate and heal psychological wounds;
- the importance of adopting an ethical approach to persuasion, particularly in an era of ever-subtle technological tricks.

Conclusions

Persuasive communications have been studied for thousands of years, beginning with the early Greeks. The Greeks grappled with some of the same issues we discuss today. The Sophists defended the art of persuasion, offering courses on oratory that usefully appealed to large numbers of citizens, but may have prized style over substance. Plato, an idealist, criticized the Sophists' philosophy, charging that it placed superficial arguments and appearance over truth. Thanks to Plato, we use the term sophistry to refer to persuasive arguments that are glib and favor style over more substantive concerns.

Aristotle, the first scholar of persuasion, argued that persuasion has virtues. He developed a series of principles to help shed light on the effects of rhetorical messages, as they were then known. Novel in his day, his principles called attention to source and message characteristics. Aristotle coupled his persuasion theorizing with a healthy respect for ethics. He emphasized that a broad education and development of moral character were essential characteristics in those who aspired to deliver compelling oratory. It was the Romans who elevated oratory to a higher plane. Cicero and Quintilian extolled the virtues of persuasion, emphasizing that the ideal citizen is the "good man speaking well." The emphasis on "man" was no accident. It would be centuries before women were brought into the realm of persuasion and public address.

Building on rhetorical perspectives and integrating them with scientific methods, the social science approach evolved, offering a framework to articulate principles about persuasion. It focuses on the development of theories, specific hypotheses, and research methods to test hypotheses in social settings. At the heart of the scientific enterprise are questions – questions about the whys and wherefores of persuasion effects, but also the social science mission itself. Contemporary scholars have called attention to the importance of replicating studies, demonstrating that the same findings hold when different researchers conduct the experiments under similar conditions, a key component of scientific validity. There is robust debate about the degree to which social psychological studies – and persuasion experiments – can be successfully replicated, as well as the generalizability of persuasion studies to diverse cultural populations. There are shortcomings, as well as strengths, in persuasion research. Yet the thoughtful scientific concepts and overarching theories that undergird the persuasion field, tested in contemporary studies in diverse ways, offer promising insights about the role persuasion plays in everyday life. The continued effort to test hypotheses and accumulate knowledge that explains persuasion in our irreverent, digital age attests to the importance of the social scientific mission.

Persuasion is also noteworthy for its focus on big questions. What would society be like if there were no persuasion? Persuasion, at its best, offers a civilized means to solve human dilemmas, one that prizes language, argumentation, and the rough banter of verbal give and take. It assumes that people have free choice and are responsible for the persuasive messages they deliver.

At the heart of persuasion are ethical dilemmas. Persuasive communication can be used with great effectiveness by both moral and immoral persuaders. This does not mean that persuasion is amoral, as is sometimes believed. There is ethical and unethical persuasion.

To help adjudicate the ethics of persuasion, different normative or prescriptive theories have been developed. Utilitarianism emphasizes that we should judge actions based on their consequences. Utilitarianism offers a common-sense, explicit, and quantifiable series of principles to resolve moral problems. However, it gives moral duty, intentions, and universal obligations short shrift.

Kantian deontological theory emphasizes that the moral value of an act derives from the respect it accords individuals as ends in and of themselves. It also places a premium on duty and the persuader's intention, according weight to good intentions in the calculus of moral behavior. However, deontological theory can lead to rigid enforcement of obligations, underplaying instances where exceptions should be made to serve an uplifting moral end.

In the end, there are many reasons to practice ethical persuasion, not least that it is one of the requirements of being a good person and part of the curriculum of the good life. Calling on the respect for moral oratory that infused the writings of classical rhetorical theorists, J. Michael Hogan (2013) offers a ringing endorsement of how persuasion can be harnessed for positive purposes and to enhance the common good. "The challenge," he says, "lies in reviving the spirit of the classical rhetorical tradition – particularly its emphasis on the *ethics* of speech and the *responsibilities* of citizenship – in a culturally diverse and technologically advanced society" (p. 16). He calls for "a healthy politics of persuasion" in which "reasoned argument prevails over appeals to fears or prejudices, and diverse perspectives and opinions are encouraged and respected" (p. 16). It is a perspective that the classical rhetoricians, in their finest and most egalitarian moments, would passionately embrace.

References

Allport, G. W. (1935). Attitudes. In C. Murchison (Ed.), *A handbook of social psychology* (Vol. 2, pp. 798–844). Worcester, MA: Clark University Press.

Bohannon, J. (2015). Many psychology papers fail replication test. *Science, 349*(6251), 910–911.

Borchert, D. M., & Stewart, D. (1986). *Exploring ethics*. New York: Macmillan.

Burke, K. (1950). *A rhetoric of motives*. New York: Prentice Hall.

Campbell, K. K. (1989). *Man cannot speak for her: A critical study of early feminist rhetoric* (Vol. 1). New York: Greenwood.

Carey, B. (2015, August 27). Many psychology findings not as strong as claimed, study says. *The New York Times*. Retrieved May 4, 2019, from www.nytimes.com/2015/08/28/science/many-social-science-findings-not-as-strong-as-claimed-study-says.html

Cesario, J. (2014). Priming, replication, and the hardest science. *Perspectives on Psychological Science, 9*, 40–48.

Chappell, T. (1998). Platonism. In R. Chadwick (Ed.), *Encyclopedia of applied ethics* (Vol. 3, pp. 511–523). San Diego, CA: Academic Press.

Cooper, M. D., & Nothstine, W. L. (1998). *Power persuasion: Moving an ancient art into the media age* (2nd ed.). Greenwood, IN: Educational Video Group.

Diener, E., & Biswas-Diener, R. (2019). The replication crisis in psychology. In R. Biswas-Diener & E. Diener (Eds.), *Noba textbook series: Psychology*. Champaign, IL: DEF Publishers. Retrieved from www.nobaproject.com

Genzlinger, N. (2011, May 16). Housewives, sure, but what makes them real? *The New York Times*, C1, C6.

Gilbert, D. T., King, G., Pettigrew, S., & Wilson, T. D. (2016). Comment on "Estimating the reproducibility of psychological science". *Science, 351*(6277), 1037–b.

Golden, J. L., Berquist, G. F., & Coleman, W. E. (2000). *The rhetoric of Western thought* (7th ed.). Dubuque, IA: Kendall/Hunt.

Hauser, M. D. (2006). *Moral minds: How nature designed our universal sense of right and wrong.* New York: HarperCollins.

Hogan, J. M. (2013). Persuasion in the rhetorical tradition. In J. P. Dillard & L. Shen (Eds.), *The Sage handbook of persuasion: Developments in theory and practice* (2nd ed., pp. 2–19). Thousand Oaks, CA: Sage.

Hovland, C. I. (1959). Reconciling conflicting results derived from experimental and survey studies of attitude change. *American Psychologist, 14*, 8–17.

Hovland, C. I., Janis, I. L., & Kelley, H. H. (1953). *Communication and persuasion: Psychological studies of opinion change.* New Haven, CT: Yale University Press.

Hovland, C. I., Lumsdaine, A. A., & Sheffield, F. D. (1949). *Experiments on mass communication.* Princeton, NJ: Princeton University Press.

Infante, D. A., & Rancer, A. S. (1996). Argumentativeness and verbal aggressiveness: A review of recent theory and research. In B. Burleson (Ed.), *Communication yearbook 19* (pp. 319–351). Thousand Oaks, CA: Sage.

Kennedy, G. (1963). *The art of persuasion in Greece.* Princeton, NJ: Princeton University Press.

McCroskey, J. C. (1972). *An introduction to rhetorical communication.* Englewood Cliffs, NJ: Prentice Hall.

McCroskey, J. C. (1997). *An introduction to rhetorical communication* (7th ed.). Boston, MA: Allyn and Bacon.

Open Science Collaboration (2015). Estimating the reproducibility of psychological science. *Science, 349* (6251). Retrieved May 4, 2019, from https://science.sciencemag.org/content/349/6251/aac4716

Rachels, J. (1986). *The elements of moral philosophy.* Philadephia, PA: Temple University Press.

Rancer, A. S., & Avtgis, T. A. (2014). *Argumentative and aggressive communication: Theory, research, and application* (2nd ed.). New York: Peter Lang Publishers.

Roose, K. (2019, January 12). Juul's convenient smoke screen. *The New York Times,* B1, B4.

Roskos-Ewoldsen, D. R. (1997). Implicit theories of persuasion. *Human Communication Research, 24*, 31–63.

Sandel, M. J. (2009). *Justice: What's the right thing to do?* New York: Farrar, Straus & Giroux.

Siebert, F. S., Peterson, T., & Schramm, W. (1956). *Four theories of the press: The authoritarian, libertarian, social responsibility, and Soviet communist concepts of what the press should be and do.* Urbana, IL: University of Illinois Press.

Stiff, J. B. (1994). *Persuasive communication.* New York: Guilford.

Van Bavel, J. J., Mende-Siedlecki, P., Brady, W. J., & Reinero, D. A. (2016). Contextual sensitivity in scientific reproducibility. *PNAS (Proceedings of the National Academy of Sciences), 113*(23), 6454–6459.

Waggenspack, B. (2000). Women's role in rhetorical traditions. In J. L. Golden, G. F. Berquist, & W. E. Coleman (Eds.), *The rhetoric of Western thought* (7th ed., pp. 340–370). Dubuque, IA: Kendall/Hunt.

Wallace, K. R. (1967). An ethical basis of communication. In R. L. Johannesen (Ed.), *Ethics and persuasion: Selected readings* (pp. 41–56). New York: Random House.

Part Two

The Nature of Attitudes

Chapter 4

Attitudes
Definition and Structure

You scan this long post on Facebook about the beauties of performance art, are impressed, but can't believe someone would care so much about this aesthetic. But when your friend tells you about her passion – constructing statues and human shapes that make a potent political statement about urban squalor, all from metal scraps in city junkyards – you send a lengthy, heart-felt message about the times in which we live and the importance of her work. Meanwhile, your mom is busy posting about the locavore movement, with its devotion to eating only locally grown food products, your sister is emailing you approvingly about pro-Life feminists who dislike #MeToo, your dad is boasting about his bracket choices for the impending March Madness (along with goofy emojis about how great basketball is) and your roommates can't stop talking about how businesses callously produce greenhouse gas emissions that are destroying the planet. I know, I know, you say, it's a problem, I agree – but can you leave me alone for just a little while? I don't care as much about this as you do, and how come you never said anything when I've talked about things that I'm passionate about. You're not the only one with attitudes, you know.

That's the word, the term, the concept that cuts to the heart of who we are, and the fundamentals of persuasion. You see, even today, when we communicate through text, cell phones, and Instagram, *attitudes* are ubiquitous. They can be weak, muddled, impassioned, and strong. In fact, it's when they are strong that we truly grasp the central role they play in our lives and the process of persuasion.

Attitudes – indispensable aspects of our psychological makeup – are the subject of this chapter and the ones that follow. Attitudes and their close cousins (beliefs and values) have been the focus of much research over the past 50 years. They are the stuff of persuasion – objects persuaders try to change, possessions we cling to tenaciously, badges that define us, categories that organize us, and constructs that marketers want to measure and manipulate. The first portion of the chapter defines attitude and discusses its main components. The second section focuses on the structure of attitudes, ambivalence, and how people cope with inconsistency. Chapter 5 follows this up with an exploration of the psychology of strong, deeply held attitudes. Chapter 6 examines why we hold the attitudes we do and their effects on behavior. Chapter 7 then takes a more down-to-earth approach, examining how researchers measure attitudes with survey instruments.

The Concept of Attitude

"She's got an attitude problem," someone says, telegraphing familiarity with the term *attitude*. But being familiar with a term does not mean one can necessarily articulate a clear, comprehensive definition. This is a task that we look to scholars to perform, and social scientists have offered a litany of definitions of attitude, dating back to the nineteenth century. Darwin regarded attitude as a motor concept (a scowling face signifies a "hostile attitude"; see Petty, Ostrom, & Brock, 1981). Freud, by contrast, "endowed [attitudes] with vitality, identifying them with longing, hatred and love, with passion and prejudice" (Allport, 1935, p. 801). Early-twentieth-century sociologists Thomas and Znaniecki placed attitude in a social context, defining it as an individual's state of mind regarding a value (Allport, 1935).

Their view resonated with a growing belief that the social environment influenced individuals, but then-contemporary terms like *custom* and *social force* were too vague and impersonal to capture the complex dynamics by which this occurred. *Attitude*, which referred to a force or quality of mind, seemed much more appropriate. By the 1930s, as researchers began to study the development of racial stereotypes, Gordon Allport (1935) declared that attitude was the most indispensable concept in contemporary social psychology.

Over the past century, attitude research has flourished. Social scientists have conducted surveys of people's attitudes, examining political, religious, consumer, and sex-role attitudes, to name but a few (Cohen & Reed, 2006). They have explored the structure and functions of attitudes and documented relationships between attitudes and behavior. "A recent search for the term *attitude* in the American Psychological Association's comprehensive index to psychological and related literature (PsycINFO) yielded 180,910 references," Dolores Albarracín and her colleagues declared with perhaps a little bit of pride (Albarracín, Johnson, & Zanna, 2005, p. vii).

More than a decade later, aided by technological improvements in informational searches, Albarracín and her associates (2019) reported that Amazon listed more than 30,000 books with the word *attitude* in the title, while the number of scholarly citations for the attitude concept grew by leaps and bounds over the past 50 years. No surprise. "Attitudes are part of the fabric of culture and society," Blair T. Johnson and his colleagues (2019) observe. "Without attitudes, humans would not be very human, nor *could* they be very human without possessing and using attitudes" (p. 637).

Attitude is a psychological construct. It is a mental and emotional entity that inheres in, or characterizes, the person. It has also been called a "hypothetical construct," a concept that cannot be observed directly but can only be inferred from people's actions. An exemplar of this approach is the University of Michigan psychology professor who ran through the halls of his department shouting (in jest), "I found it. I found it. I found the attitude." His comment illustrates that attitudes are different from the raw materials that other scientific disciplines examine – materials that can be touched or clearly seen, such as a rock, plant cell, or an organ in the human body.

Although in some sense we do infer a person's attitude from what he or she says or does, it would be a mistake to assume that for this reason attitudes are not real or are "mere mental constructs." This is a fallacy of behaviorism, the scientific theory that argues that all human activity can be reduced to behavioral units. Contemporary scholars reject this notion. They note that people have thoughts, cognitive structures, and a variety of emotions, all of which lose their essential qualities when viewed exclusively as behaviors. Moreover, they argue that an entity that is mental or emotional is no less real than a physical behavior. As Allport noted perceptively:

Attitudes are never directly observed, but, unless they are admitted, through inference, as real and substantial ingredients in human nature, it becomes impossible to account satisfactorily either for the consistency of any individual's behavior, or for the stability of any society.

(1935, p. 839)

Over the past century, numerous definitions of attitude have been proposed. The following views of attitude are representative of the population of definitions. According to scholars, an attitude is:

- an association between a given object and a given evaluation (Fazio, 1989, p. 155);
- a psychological tendency that is expressed by evaluating a particular entity with some degree of favor or disfavor (Eagly & Chaiken, 1993, p. 1);
- a learned predisposition to respond in a consistently favorable or unfavorable manner with respect to a given object (Fishbein & Ajzen, 1975, p. 6); or
- a more or less permanently enduring state of readiness of mental organization which predisposes an individual to react in a characteristic way to any object or situation with which it is related (Cantril, quoted in Allport, 1935, p. 804).

Notice that these definitions emphasize different aspects of the attitude concept. Fazio focuses simply on the mental association of an object and a feeling. Eagly and Chaiken stress that attitudes involve a person's evaluation of an issue. Fishbein and Ajzen, as well as Cantril, take a behavioral view, suggesting that attitudes predispose people to behave in a particular way. Which is right, you ask? Which definition is the correct one?

There are no objective answers to these questions. As was the case with the definition of persuasion, scholars differ in how they view a particular phenomenon. You cannot say that one definition is more correct than another because defining terms is a logical, not empirical, exercise. If you find the lack of certainty frustrating, you're not alone. But take heart! Science has to start somewhere. Someone has to come up with a workable definition of a term before the empirical explorations can begin. Science requires a leap of faith. Yet this does not mean that one must settle with definitions that are inadequate or incomplete. Definitions are evaluated on the basis of their clarity, cogency, and comprehensiveness. The above definitions of attitude are erudite and perceptive. So which definition is correct? All are, in varying degrees. In this, a textbook that offers multiple approaches, I offer an integrative approach that combines these definitions and emphasizes commonalities.

Attitude is defined as: a learned, global evaluation of an object (person, place, or issue) that influences thought and action. Psychologically, an attitude is not a behavior, though it may consist of acquired patterns of reacting to social stimuli. It is not pure affect, though it is most assuredly emotional. It is a predisposition, a tendency, a state of readiness that guides and steers behavior in certain predictable, though not always rational, ways.

Characteristics of Attitudes

Attitudes Are Learned

People are not born with attitudes. They acquire attitudes over the course of socialization in childhood and adolescence. This has important implications. A critical application is this: No one is born prejudiced. Children don't naturally discriminate against kids with different skin color or religious preferences. Over time, kids acquire prejudiced attitudes. Or to be blunt, human beings learn to hate.

Fortunately, not all attitudes are so negative. Think about the rush you get when "The Star-Spangled Banner" is played after a U.S. victory at the Olympics. Sports fans across the world experience a similar thrill when their national anthem is performed at the Olympic Games. People have positive sentiments toward all sorts of things – hometown sports teams, teachers who lift our spirits, children, pets, cool cars – you get the drift. These are all learned.

Attitudes vary widely. They depend to a considerable degree on what individuals have learned in their course of cultural and social upbringing. Do you think abortion should be legal? Do you feel that homosexuality should be accepted or discouraged by society? Your attitude depends in part on your religious background. Eighty-seven percent of atheists think abortion should be legal in most cases, but less than half of Catholics and fewer than one in three Mormons feel this way. Fifty-five percent of evangelical Protestants believe homosexuality should be discouraged by society, compared to 23 percent of Catholics and 18 percent of Jews (Pew Research Center, 2015). Attitudes vary as a function of religion, social upbringing, even the cultural landscape in which an individual was raised. People tend to cluster with those who share their attitudes (Bishop, 2008). This is why they are frequently surprised to learn that people from different groups have vastly different outlooks on social issues than they do.

A Biological Basis of Attitudes?

For generations it was an article of faith that attitudes were entirely a product of the environment. Nurture, not nature, was assumed to be the foundation of attitudes. Over the past decades, with the explosion of research on biological determinants of behavior, psychologists have begun to rethink this thesis, wondering if genes might play some role in the development of our attitudes.

Some years back, Tesser (1993) explored this question. He acknowledged that there is not "a gene for attitudes toward jazz in the same way as there is a gene for eye color" (p. 139). But he argued that inherited physical differences in taste and hearing might influence attitudes toward food and loud rock music. Perhaps those who are born with higher activity levels gravitate to vigorous exercise or sports.

Others make a similar argument. There is a genetic basis for certain personality traits, like impulsivity (Albarracín & Vargas, 2010). If we find that impulsive people have more positive attitudes toward trying new experiences, we would have evidence that genes might play an indirect role in the formation of attitudes. At the same time, there is evidence that some political attitudes have a genetic basis (Alford, Funk, & Hibbing, 2005; Banaji & Heiphetz, 2010). Thus it is fair to say that nature – in the form of genes and heredity – shapes some attitudes, although considerably more research needs to be conducted before we can understand exactly the processes by which this occurs.

Even those who argue that genes play a role in attitude formation are quick to acknowledge that genes do not operate in isolation. Whatever influence they exert is in combination with the social environment. And culture exerts a mighty impact. There is no gene that causes attitudes toward race, gun safety, or religion. Whatever influence genes exert is critically filtered through environmentally experienced lenses. For example, a person might be genetically predisposed to like tomatoes, but if tomatoes are not available (or affordable), she cannot develop a positive attitude toward the popular vegetable. In addition, if the first time she tastes a tomato she develops a rash or gets bitten by a dog, she is apt to evaluate tomatoes more negatively.

Consider similar implications from contemporary research on the role genes play in another social arena – gay sexual preferences. Research finds that genetics has an impact on proclivity for same-sex partners, but the likelihood that someone will act on their desire depends on social factors, like the degree to which society tolerates gay or lesbian intimacy, their family's tolerance of same-sex behavior, and even personality characteristics, like propensity to take risks (Belluck, 2019).

Thus, even if attitudes have genetic antecedents, these inherited preferences are not equivalent to attitudes. Attitudes develop through encounters with social objects. "Individuals do not have an attitude until they first encounter the attitude object (or information about it) and respond evaluatively to it," Alice H. Eagly and Shelly Chaiken declare (1998, p. 270).

Attitudes Are Global, Typically Emotional, Evaluations

Attitudes are, first and foremost, evaluations (Cooper, Blackman, & Keller, 2016). Having an attitude means that you have categorized something and made a judgment of its net value or worth. It means that you are no longer neutral about the topic. That doesn't mean you can't have mixed feelings, but your view on the issue is no longer bland or without color.

Attitudes invariably involve affect and emotions. "Attitudes express passions and hates, attractions and repulsions, likes and dislikes," note Eagly and Chaiken (1998, p. 269).

Affect usually plays an important part in how attitudes are formed or experienced. I say "usually" because some attitudes may develop more intellectually, by absorbing information, while others are acquired through reward and punishment of previous behavior (Dillard, 1993; Zanna & Rempel, 1988).

Attitudes are complex. They have different components and are formed in different ways. A classic tripartite model emphasizes that attitudes can be expressed through thoughts, feelings, and behavior (Breckler, 1984). What's more, some attitudes are more based on affect and emotion (like our knee-jerk positive attitude toward our college's sports teams), while others may be more cognitive (for example, an attitude toward climate change; Edwards, 1990).

Our attitudes are not always internally consistent, and you may have contradictory attitudes toward the same issue. What's more, as Justin Hepler and Dolores Albarracín (2013) have shown, individuals can differ in the degree to which they have positive or negative attitudes toward life's constellation of issues. Some people are positive types, harboring favorable attitudes toward a variety of topics, spanning architecture, camping, and public speaking; others are more negative – not grouchy, just more apt to dislike public speeches, outdoor camping, or certain buildings, for example. Attitudes are a function of the object under consideration and the person doing the evaluating.

Attitudes are fascinating, complex, large summary evaluations of issues and people. (They are global, or macro, not micro.) Your attitude toward gender roles is a large, complex entity composed of a number of beliefs and feelings. For this reason, researchers speak of "attitude systems" that consist of several subcomponents. Attitudes involve beliefs, feelings, intentions to behave, and behavior itself, although these are best viewed as separate entities.

Attitudes Influence Thought and Action

Attitudes (and values) organize our social world. They allow us to categorize people, places, and events quickly and to figure out what's going on. They are like notebook dividers, labels to categorize a collection of favorite books, or ways to organize smartphone apps. Attitudes shape perceptions and influence judgments. If you're a Republican, you probably evaluate Republican political leaders favorably and have a negative, gut-level reaction to some Democratic politicians. And vice versa if you are a Democrat. On the other hand, if you hate politics and distrust politicians, you filter the political world through a skeptical set of lenses.

Attitudes also influence behavior. They guide our actions and steer us in the direction of doing what we believe. In our society, consistency between attitude and behavior is valued, so people try hard to "practice what they preach." As will be discussed, people usually translate attitudes into behavior, but not always.

Attitudes come in different shapes and sizes. Some attitudes are strong; others are weaker and susceptible to influence. Still others contain inconsistent elements. Some attitudes exert a stronger impact on thought and behavior than others. In sum: Attitudes are complex, dynamic entities – like people. The pioneering persuasion scholar Muzafer Sherif (1967) noted that when we talk about attitudes, "we are talking about the fact that (a person) is no longer neutral in sizing up the world around him; he is *attracted* or *repelled, for* or *against, favorable* or *unfavorable*" (1967, p. 2).

Evaluation – a constellation of positive or negative feelings about an issue, wrapped around thoughts – is at the heart of an attitude across different societies and cultures. Yet intriguing cultural differences persist. Western models of attitudes emphasize the individual and personal preferences. Non-Western models, such as in Asian cultures, focus more on collectivistic aspects that stress meeting important others' expectations, stretching beyond the individual to take into account group norms and social roles, as Shavitt (2019) notes. Complicating matters, some people living in Western cultures, like the United States, are also concerned with fitting in with the expectations of a group, such as a religious organization, and ambitious young people in technologically sophisticated societies like South Korea can adopt a more individualistic, career-oriented focus than their less competitive peers. And yet, even if intra-cultural differences exist, group norms may exert a stronger effect on public expressions of behavior than attitudes in certain non-Western countries (Eom et al., 2016). The intersection between culture and attitude remains important, particularly when one considers the most effective ways to adapt cultural sensitivities to the development of messages designed to change attitudes, as well as values and beliefs, the focus of the next sections.

Values and Beliefs

What do you value? What do you believe about life and society? To answer these questions, it helps to define value and belief clearly. Both concepts play an important role in persuasion. Like attitudes, values and beliefs are learned and shape the ways we interpret information.

Values are enduring ideals, guiding principles in one's life, or overarching goals that people strive to obtain (Maio & Olson, 1998). They are "conceptions of the preferable"; our views of the advantageous means and end-points of action (Rokeach, 1973, p 9; Kluckhohn, 1951). More comprehensively, values are "desirable end states or behaviors that transcend specific situations, guide selection or evaluation of behavior and events, and are ordered by relative importance" (see Schwartz & Bilsky, 1987, p. 551). Values can either transcend or celebrate selfish concerns. Freedom, equality, and a world of beauty are universal values that extend beyond individual interests (Rokeach, 1973; Schwartz, 1996). Self-fulfillment, excitement, and recognition express strong desires to enrich our own lives. Power and achievement are self-enhancement values. Warm relationships with others and a sense of belonging emphasize love and security (Kahle, 1996).

Values are large macro constructs that underlie attitudes. Consider the different attitudes people hold toward research on animals. Those who support scientific research on animals place a greater value on human life, arguing that we owe to humans obligations that we do not owe to animals. Those who strenuously oppose animal research retort that this reeks of "speciesism." They accord equal value to all living sentient beings, whether animals or humans. Your attitude toward animal research derives from your more general, spiritual values. Thus, values can have strong moral components.

Social psychologist Jonathan Haidt (2013) has examined the moral foundations of values, focusing on the political domain. He has argued that political liberals and conservatives look at the world through very different lenses of moral virtue. Liberals believe the best way to maintain social stability is by teaching people to respect the rights of others. They adopt an individualizing orientation, professing concern about protecting individuals from harm, while also embracing fairness and social justice for individual citizens. To liberals, showing compassion for victims of societal oppression is the most sacred moral value.

By contrast, conservatives, hoping to preserve societal norms by strengthening people's ties to groups, view the larger group as the focus of moral virtues. Although they do value individualizing attributes, conservatives are more concerned with loyalty to one's in-group or nation; preserving respect for authority; and embracing sanctity and moral purity, even regarding some actions as wrong because they are fundamentally unnatural (Graham, Haidt, & Nosek, 2009). To spiritual conservatives, the most sacred moral value is safeguarding the traditions and institutions that maintain a moral community.

By appreciating these value differences, we gain exquisite insight into how liberals and conservatives harbor such dramatically different attitudes toward social issues like immigration, abortion, and capital punishment.

Liberals tend to be more accepting of illegal immigration because they emphasize social justice and compassion for individuals who experience life-threatening harm, such as asylum seekers escaping from gangs in Central America. Conservatives favor a wall to block illegal immigration because they value respect for authority (not breaking the law), legal citizenship as the cornerstone of allegiance to country, and the purity of the American in-group. Similarly, conservatives can oppose abortion in all circumstances because they view abortion as unnatural and a violation of religious sanctity. By contrast liberals, stressing harm to the pregnant woman, are willing to make trade-offs, supporting abortion under many conditions.

There are nuanced aspects to these value differences. Conservatives can also oppose programs to allow illegal (or undocumented) immigrants into the country because they too are concerned with perceived harm, such as that illegal immigrants will take jobs from Americans. In a similar fashion, conservatives passionately oppose abortion because of harm to a fetus. (This becomes complicated as liberals don't believe the fetus is a person or a human entity that can experience pain.) There are clearly ambiguities and gray areas in Haidt's moral foundations approach (Frimer et al., 2013). And, of course, it is more complicated in today's political world, where staunch liberals and conservatives frequently view politics through the cloistered lens of their in-group rather than more abstract philosophical perspectives.

Nonetheless, there is wisdom in the insight that liberals and conservatives differ not because they are simply biased (as each side views the other), but as a result of some legitimate differences in the moral (and ideological) underpinnings of their social worlds. In many cases, neither side is wrong or evil, but instead, views morality through different cultural lenses than the other. The recognition of "not bad, just different" can help breed tolerance, while also suggesting ways to develop persuasive messages that will appeal to the different values that underlie each group's attitudes toward social problems, a topic broached in Chapter 10.

In contrast to values, *beliefs* are more specific and cognitive. Freedom encompasses attitudes toward censorship, entrepreneurship, political correctness, and smoking in public. People have hundreds of attitudes, but dozens of values (e.g., Rokeach, 1973). Even more than attitudes, values strike to the core of our self-concepts. Values are more global and abstract than attitudes. In contrast, beliefs are more specific and cognitive. You can think of values as the broad macro term that encompasses attitudes (see Figure 4.1).

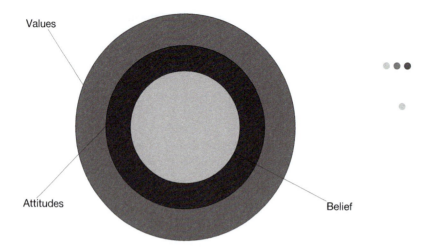

Values

Attitudes

Belief

> **Figure 4.1** Schematic Diagram of Values, Attitudes, and Beliefs. The diagram shows that values encompass attitudes, and attitudes incorporate beliefs, offering one perspective on how these concepts are structured in our minds

While attitudes involve the organization of beliefs around a particular topic, values refer to a singular, holistic idea, a broad conception of the desirable, important, or socially significant end-state (Rokeach, 1973). A broad value like equality encompasses different attitudes, such as toward affirmative action, diversity in education, and income redistribution. A value like liberty includes attitudes toward government, welfare, and guns. These different attitudes include a variety of beliefs too.

Beliefs number in the hundreds, perhaps thousands! These are typical:

- Stricter gun control laws reduce violent crime.
- Maintaining a vegetarian diet improves your state of mind.
- Video games are addictive.
- College students drink too much.
- Girls talk more about relationships than do guys.
- A daily dose of religion uplifts the spirits.

Beliefs are more cognitive than values or attitudes. Beliefs are cognitions about the world – subjective probabilities that an object has a particular attribute or that an action will lead to a particular outcome (Fishbein & Ajzen, 1975; though see Rokeach, 1960, for another, enriching view of beliefs).

People frequently confuse beliefs with facts. Just because we fervently believe something to be true does not make it so. Almost half of the American public does not accept the theory of evolution, believing instead that God created human beings in their present form (Collins, 2006). Yet more than a century's worth of scientific studies offers incontrovertible support for evolution and principles such as natural selection and adaptation (Dennett, 2005; Scott, 2004).

Beliefs can be patently and unequivocally false. A Taliban leader from Afghanistan claimed that in America, parents do not show love to their children and the only good thing to come out of the United

States is candy (Goldberg, 2000). In the United States, opinion polls show that more than a fourth of American adults believe there is no solid evidence in support of global warming when, in fact, there is considerable empirical evidence that global warming exists. About a third of U.S. adults think that vaccines cause autism, despite the preponderance of scientific research to the contrary (Dixon et al., 2015). Unfortunately, beliefs like these are tenaciously held and highly resistant to change.

Other beliefs can be strongly held, but impossible to verify. You probably did not know that 68 percent of Americans believe in life after death, 62 percent believe in hell, and 59 percent believe in the devil (Schott, 2008). Try verifying these beliefs and then convincing believers they are wrong! Increasingly, fallacious, deeply prejudiced beliefs circulate on extremist sites like 4chan, including the notion that satanic pedophiles control the government or White Americans will be replaced by non-White migrants, aided by global leaders (McIntire, Yourish, & Buchanan, 2019). True believers not only buy into these notions, but retweet them, lending falsehoods a scary verisimilitude.

Beliefs of all sorts can be categorized into different subtypes. *Descriptive beliefs*, such as those previously discussed, are perceptions or hypotheses about the world that people carry around in their heads. *Prescriptive beliefs* are "ought" or "should" statements that express conceptions of preferred end-states. Prescriptive beliefs, such as "prostitution should be legal" or "capital punishment should be banned," cannot be tested by empirical research. They are part of people's worldviews.

In sum, values are broad, deeply held principles, the large macromolecules of our social brains. Attitudes spring from values and contain beliefs, the smaller cognitive atoms that are part of the attitude molecule. For example, a strong conservative value of individual rights can lead to the development of a favorable attitude toward gun ownership. This in turn consists of beliefs, such as that if school teachers were armed, they would be more likely to prevent school shootings. The descriptive belief is just that, a belief, one that would be shared by those with a favorable attitude toward gun rights and opposed by those with a negative attitude toward this position. In contrast, a strong liberal value of government control over social policy leads to the development of pro-gun control attitudes. This in turn consists of beliefs, such as that the passage of gun control legislation, such as background checks, will reduce gun violence. Conservatives and liberals clash over these beliefs, with each side questioning the evidence in favor of beliefs advanced by the other. Given the polarization between people on both sides of issues like gun rights, it is helpful to understand the dynamics of beliefs and values in hopes of increasing understanding and tolerance.

From an academic perspective, beliefs and values are fascinating and important. Yet they have been the focus of somewhat less empirical research study than attitudes. This is because, historically, the attitude concept helped bridge behaviorist and cognitive approaches to psychology. It explained how people could be influenced by society, yet could also internalize what they learned. It articulated a process by which social forces could affect behavior and not merely stamp their response on the organism.

I should also note that the present focus – values shape attitudes, attitudes contain beliefs, and attitudes are the core construct – is not the only way to approach this issue. You could also argue that beliefs are of key importance because they are the underlying building blocks; profoundly influence political attitudes (as when people hold conspiracy theories about 9/11, the spread of AIDS, or enemies plotting America's destruction); and are the focus of a time-honored human institution, religion, with adherents' faith-based belief in God. The luminary social psychologist of the 1960s, Milton Rokeach, emphasized the power of beliefs in his prodigious work (e.g., Rokeach, 1968). An approach that privileges beliefs is not necessarily wrong or unhelpful; Rokeach's books have rich implications for attitudes today, when so many individuals in extremist groups harbor false, deluded beliefs.

Ultimately, the orientation authors choose reflect their own scholarly synthesis of an area and sense of which structural approach best fits the current times. Attitudes represent our focus because: (1) they have been the thrust of so much research across disciplines; (2) they provide a centerpiece that encompasses other critical cognitive constructs; (3) they integrate cognition and effect in a parsimonious fashion; (4) they capture the dogged resistance of human beings to change; and (5) with their strong emotional aspects, underscore the passions and polarization of current and earlier historical epochs.

Structure of Attitudes

Suppose we could glimpse an attitude up close. Let's say we could handle it, feel its shape and texture, and then inspect it carefully. What would we see?

We cannot observe attitudes with the same exactitude that scientists employ when examining molecules under electron microscopes. We lack the attitudinal equivalent to the human genome, the long strand of DNA that contains our 23 critical chromosome pairs. Instead, we infer attitudes from what people do or say, and what they report on carefully constructed survey instruments. This does not make attitudes any less real than chemical elements on the periodic table, the 30,000 human genes, rocks, plants, or any other material that scientists scrutinize. It simply makes our job of uncovering their basic content more challenging and perhaps more subject to human fallibility. Just as the human genome and physical substances have structure, attitudes also possess a certain organization. How are attitudes organized? What are their major components? Scholars have studied these issues, highlighting the underlying bases of attitudes, their complexity, ambivalence, and a host of fascinating factors (Fabrigar, MacDonald, & Wegener, 2019). Over the years, social scientists have proposed several models to help us understand the dynamics of attitude structure.

Expectancy–Value Approach

The *expectancy–value approach* asserts that attitudes have two components: Cognition and affect (or head and heart). Your attitude is a combination of what you believe or expect of a certain object and how you feel about (evaluate) these expectations.

The theory was developed by Martin Fishbein and Icek Ajzen in 1975 and is still going strong today! According to Fishbein and Ajzen, attitude is a multiplicative combination of (a) strength of beliefs that an object has certain attributes, and (b) evaluations of these attributes (see Figure 4.2).

The prediction is represented by the following mathematical formula:

$$A = \text{sum } b(i) \times e(i)$$

where $b(i)$ = each belief and $e(i)$ = each evaluation.

Formulas like these are helpful because they allow for more precise tests of hypotheses. There is abundant evidence that attitudes can be accurately estimated by combining beliefs and evaluations. Fishbein and Ajzen showed that beliefs (particularly personally important ones) and evaluations accurately estimate attitudes toward a host of topics, ranging from politics to sex roles (Ajzen & Fishbein, 2008, 1975). Beliefs are the centerpiece of attitude and have provided researchers with rich insights into the dynamics of attitudes and behaviors.

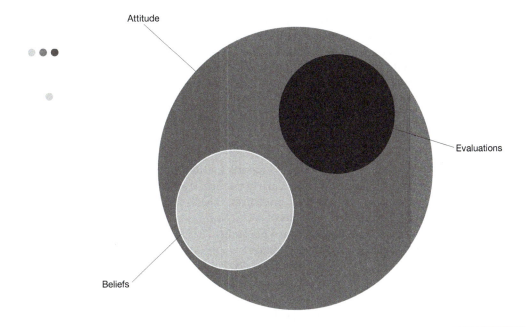

Figure 4.2 Expectancy–Value Approach to Attitudes

Diane M. Morrison and her colleagues (1996) systematically examined beliefs about smoking in an elaborate study of elementary school children's decisions to smoke cigarettes. They measured *beliefs* about smoking by asking kids whether they thought that smoking cigarettes would:

- hurt your lungs;
- give you bad breath;
- make your friends like you better;
- make you feel more grown up; or
- taste good.

The researchers assessed *evaluations* by asking children if they felt that these attributes (e.g., hurting your lungs, making your friends like you better) were good or bad. An evaluation was measured in this general fashion:

Do you think that making your friends like you better is: *very good, good, not good or bad, bad, or very bad*?

Morrison and colleagues gained rich insights into the dynamics of children's attitudes toward smoking. Had they just measured attitude, they would have discovered only how kids evaluated cigarette smoking. By focusing on beliefs, they identified specific reasons why some children felt positively toward smoking. By assessing evaluations, the researchers tapped into the affect associated with these attributes. Their analysis indicated that two children could hold different attitudes about smoking because they had different beliefs about smoking's consequences or because they held the same beliefs but evaluated the consequences differently.

Some children evaluate smoking favorably because they believe that their friends will like them better if they smoke or that smoking makes them feel grown up. Kids who value these outcomes may be particularly inclined to start smoking before they hit adolescence. This information is clearly useful to health educators who design antismoking information campaigns. It is important too, given that about a third of high school students use tobacco products, such as e-cigarettes or cigarettes (Hoffman & Kaplan, 2019).

Affect and Symbols

A second perspective on attitude structure places emotion and symbols at center stage. According to the *symbolic attitude approach*, attitudes – particularly political ones – are characterized by emotional reactions, sweeping sentiments, and powerful prejudices. These, rather than molecular beliefs, are believed to lie at the core of people's evaluations of social issues.

Consider racism, sexism, or attitudes toward abortion. These evaluations are rife with symbols and charged with affect. According to David O. Sears, people acquire affective responses to symbols early in life from parents, peers, and mass media (Sears & Funk, 1991). Symbols include the flag, religious ornaments, and code words associated with minority groups (see also Sears, Henry, & Kosterman, 2000).

As a result of early learning experiences, people develop strong attitudes toward their country, as well as religious values, ethnic loyalties, and racial prejudices. These "symbolic predispositions," as they are called, lie at the core of people's attitudes toward social issues.

As an example, consider attitudes toward immigration, an issue that surfaced during President Trump's term. The issue became controversial in the wake of record numbers of Central American migrants trying to cross the southern border (at one point via a caravan of immigrants, desperately fleeing political violence in their home countries, who were maligned by Trump). Trump, arguing the migrants represented a symbolic and tangible threat to America, pledged to protect Americans from "criminals" bent on an invasion of the United States. He took many measures to keep illegal immigrants out, including separating children from parents and pressing for a wall at the southern border (Shear, Jordan, & Fernandez, 2019).

As Figure 4.3 shows, a symbolic view of attitudes toward immigration would begin with a semantic node, the term "illegal immigrant," which can provoke more negative attitudes than "undocumented workers" (Pearson, 2019). As a symbol, "illegal immigration" encapsulates a variety of attributes that are accessed when the topic of illegal immigrants is broached. From a symbolic perspective, a negative attitude toward immigration – a complex topic with cultural and economic components – would spring from the social groups that the concept calls up, their psychological meaning, and feelings they elicit. To the extent that attitudes toward immigration are composed of constructs like illegal aliens, immigrants of color, crimes allegedly committed by migrants, a disease-bearing and terrorist-infested caravan, and job threat to Americans, all of which elicit strong negative affect, the attitude will be rich in negative symbolic valence or value.

Underscoring the role that subjective beliefs play, even in the symbolic approach, there is strong evidence challenging the perceptions that undocumented or illegal immigrants are invasion-bent criminals who threaten Americans' safety, that the Central American caravan contained disease-bearing or violent individuals, and immigrants are taking jobs from working-class Americans (see Flagg, 2019; Timm, 2017). Research suggests these beliefs rest on stereotypes and false assumptions.

STRUCTURE OF ATTITUDES

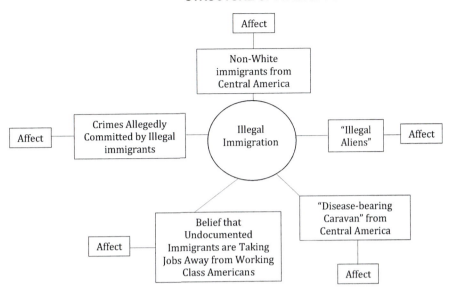

Figure 4.3 A Symbolic View of Attitudes Toward Illegal Immigration. Affect, or emotion, is attached to, or experienced with, each of the various aspects of the illegal immigration concept. Each of the attributes, like "non-White immigrants from Central America," evoke feelings, frequently negative for strong opponents of illegal immigration. Illegal immigration thus comes to represent the collective semantic meanings the attributes call to mind. See Pryor and Reeder (1993) for an example involving HIV/AIDS, from which this more current illustration was adapted

Yet facts can be outgunned by affect when attitudes are based on symbolic meanings. The symbolic approach reveals how some Americans can harbor a strongly negative attitude toward illegal immigration, based on the melange of incorrect beliefs, stereotypes, and unfavorable emotional associations the concept calls to mind. This is obviously a negative take on attitudes toward illegal immigration, not one that describes all Americans or attitudes toward legal immigration, for that matter. However, it helps unpack the viscerally unfavorable views some individuals have developed on the freighted immigration issue. Persuasive messages can access or prime these feelings, an intriguing – sometimes ethically problematic – outgrowth of the symbolic approach, a topic broached in Chapter 5.

The symbolic attitude perspective goes a long way toward helping us to deconstruct people's views on contemporary issues. It calls attention to the role that associations play in attitude structure (as well as the effect of more elaborated beliefs). We will shortly touch on implications of the symbolic approach for understanding contemporary prejudiced attitudes toward Muslims.

The Role of Ideology

A third view of attitude organization emphasizes ideology, or worldview. Unlike the symbolic approach, which emphasizes the power of emotions evoked by symbols and stereotypes, the ideological perspective focuses on the influence of strong, well-developed political beliefs. Indeed, for some people, attitudes are an outgrowth of broad ideological principles or a coherent political philosophy (see Figure 4.4).

Individuals with ideologically based attitudes typically forge stronger connections among diverse political issues than do those who don't think much about abstract political ideas. For example, conservatives, whose worldviews emphasize self-reliance, responsibility, and reward for hard work, typically oppose welfare because it gives money to those who don't hold down jobs. Conservatives support across-the-board tax cuts because they reward with tax refunds those who have earned the most money (Lakoff, 1996). Attitudes toward welfare and taxes, flowing from a conservative ideology, are therefore interrelated.

By contrast, liberals – who value nurturance, fairness, and compassion for the disadvantaged – favor welfare because it helps indigent individuals who have been left behind by society. Liberal thinkers also oppose across-the-board tax cuts because (in their view) these tax reductions favor the rich; liberals prefer targeted tax cuts that redistribute money to low- and middle-income people. Attitudes toward welfare and tax cuts go together – are correlated – in liberals' minds.

As a general rule, individuals with strong ideological positions view social and political issues differently from the way ordinary citizens do. Unlike many people, who respond to political issues primarily on the basis of simple symbolic predispositions, those who hold a strong ideological viewpoint begin with an ideology, and their attitudes flow from this (see Lavine, Thomsen, & Gonzales, 1997).

The *ideological approach to attitudes* asserts that attitudes are organized "top-down." That is, attitudes flow from the hierarchy of principles (or predispositions) that individuals have acquired and developed.

A shortcoming with this approach is that it assumes that people operate on the basis of one set of ideological beliefs. In fact, individuals frequently call on a variety of prescriptive beliefs when thinking about social issues (Conover & Feldman, 1984). For instance, a student might be a social liberal,

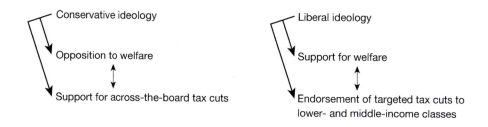

Figure 4.4 Large Arrow Depicts Influence of Ideology on Attitudes and Smaller Arrow Denotes Association Between Two Attitudes

believing affirmative action is needed to redress societal wrongs. She could also be an economic conservative, believing that government should not excessively regulate private companies. The student might also have strong religious convictions and a deep belief in a Supreme Being. Her social attitudes are thus structured by a variety of belief systems (sometimes called schema), rather than by one singular ideological set of principles.

Attitude Structure and Persuasion

These perspectives on attitude structure contain insights about the underlying dynamics of people's attitudes. They also are of interest to communicators who hope to change attitudes. For example, suppose you were asked to develop a campaign to influence Americans' attitudes toward Muslim Americans, hoping to enhance empathy, in the wake of the rise in anti-Muslim sentiments that occurred following the growth of ISIS and ISIS-led or inspired attacks in Paris and San Bernardino, California. "If a Muslim hasn't been called a terrorist in middle school, lower school or high school, then they're probably in a really great school – and I'm happy for them!" said Hebh Jamal, a 15-year-old from the Bronx. She plaintively noted that "I feel like the past two months have probably been the hardest of my life" (Semple, 2015, pp. A1, A28). Here she is, a normal teenager from New York, and she, like many other Muslim Americans, has experienced prejudice from her fellow Americans. How can you, calling on persuasion theories, develop messages to change attitudes? The three attitude structure approaches offer insights, emphasizing that an understanding of the structure of attitudes can suggest ways to develop messages to change these attitudes.

First, the expectancy–value approach suggests you should first explore beliefs some Americans might hold about Muslim Americans, such as erroneous beliefs that they support ISIS or do not obey American laws. You would then then find information to counteract these beliefs, pointing out that overwhelming numbers of Muslims despise ISIS, adhere to U.S. laws, and support U.S. institutions.

The symbolic approach would focus on the affective basis of attitudes – chiefly the negative feelings some Americans call up when thinking about Muslims, like biased perceptions that they are weird or different because, for example, some Muslim women wear a hijab, a traditional head covering worn in public. Communications might show pictures of young Muslim teens frolicking with cell phones, madly sharing pictures on Instagram, or, in the case of New Yorker Hebh Jamal, cheering for the New York Yankees in Yankee Stadium.

The ideological approach would locate the bedrock principle underlying a particular ideological perspective. For instance, when targeting conservatives, who put a premium on authority, self-reliance, and responsibility, the campaign might emphasize that Muslim parents are just as apt as non-Muslim moms and dads to demand discipline and personal responsibility from their kids. When appealing to liberals, who value equality and compassion, communicators could emphasize that the liberal American ethos demands that we treat different ethnic groups equally, respecting their traditions. There is no guarantee that these approaches would change attitudes, for as we will see, changing attitudes is hard, but they might make some headway, tethered, as they are, in an appreciation of the psychology of attitude structure.

Are Attitudes Internally Consistent?

As we have seen, expectations, symbols, and ideology influence attitudes and persuasion. This raises a new question, one filled with intriguing dimensions. Given that attitudes are complex macromolecules with so many different components, are they in harmony or in disarray? Are attitudes at peace or ready to ignite, due to the combustible combination of cognitions, affect, and behavior? In other words, when we have an attitude toward an issue, are we all of one mind, consistent in our thoughts and feelings, or are we divided and ambivalent? These are questions that many of us have probably asked in one way or another. We have heard people say, "Intellectually, I agree, but emotionally I don't," or "You're a hypocrite; you say one thing and do another."

Intra-Attitudinal Consistency

It is pleasant when we are all of one mind on an issue – when our general attitude is in sync with specific beliefs about the topic or has the same "electrical charge" as our feelings. However, life does not always grant us this pleasure. We are ambivalent about many issues. Ambivalence occurs when we feel both positively and negatively about a person or issue (Fabrigar et al., 2019; Thompson, Zanna, & Griffin, 1995). Ambivalence, characterized by uncertainty or conflict among attitude elements, is a particularly interesting aspect of attitude structure, and it has complex relations with different aspects of attitudes.

Ambivalence can frequently be found among young women who love the power and responsibility that come with high-powered jobs, yet also worry that their commitment to a career will compromise their chances of raising a family when they reach their 30s (Orenstein, 2000).

Ambivalence is also a reasonable response to the complex issues women face in another arena: Abortion. In contrast to the "us-versus-them" and pro-life versus pro-choice polarities that characterize the media debate, in reality, most women find themselves on shakier ground, balancing moral values against practical realities, "weighing religious, ethical, practical, sentimental and financial imperatives that [are] often in conflict" (Leland, 2005, p. 29). Women who learn that their child will be born with a severe birth defect must balance their fear of raising a child with this condition against a religious belief in the sanctity of life. Poor women who received abortions at an Arkansas medical clinic readily admitted their ambivalence and pain. "I know it's against God," said Tammy, who works in a coffee shop in Tennessee:

> But you have three kids, you want to raise them good. My friends and sister-in-law say, "You care about money problems but don't care about what God will do," I believe it's wrong. I pray to God to forgive me. This will be the last one. Never, never again.
>
> (Leland, 2005, p. 29)

Echoing these sentiments and discussing the moral ambiguities, one activist observed, "We either want to ban abortion outright or see abortion as good, as empowering. But most people think it's a tough decision. It's a hard issue" (Peters, 2019, p. 19).

Balancing Things Out

Ambivalence drives some people berserk. They will do anything to resolve it. More generally, psychologists argue that individuals dislike inconsistency among cognitive elements and are motivated to reconfigure things mentally so as to achieve a harmonious state of mind. Fritz Heider (1958) proposed an algebraic model of attitudes, called *balance theory*. Heider's model involves a triad of relationships: A person or perceiver (P), another person (O), and an issue (X). Heider argued that people prefer a balanced relationship among P, O, and X.

Borrowing from chemistry, Heider suggested that cognitive elements have a positive or negative valence (or charge). A positive relationship, in which P likes O or X, is symbolized with a plus sign. A negative relationship, in which P dislikes O or X, is assigned a minus sign. A visual thinker, Heider diagrammed his model with a series of triangles. Each of the three relationships (P, O; P, X; and O, X) is assigned a plus or minus. Attitudes are in harmony when the signs multiplied together yield a plus. If you remember your elementary arithmetic, you recall that a plus – a plus is a plus, a minus – a minus is a plus, and a plus – a minus yields a minus. Let's see how this works in real life to understand how people cope with inconsistency among attitudinal elements.

Consider for a moment the contemporary quandary of an individual – let's call him Sam – who believes in evolution. A religious friend, Samantha, a devotee of intelligent design, believes God created human beings in their present form. She questions the validity of Darwinian evolution. Sam's belief in evolution is symbolized by a + in the model. Sam's liking of Samantha is conveyed by a +. Samantha's disagreement with evolution is symbolized by a –. Multiplying the three terms, one gets a minus, suggesting that Sam's attitude is imbalanced, or not entirely consistent (Figure 4.5a). Presumably, Sam would find the inconsistency uncomfortable and would feel impelled to restore mental harmony. Balance theory says that he has several options. He could change his attitude toward evolution and question the notion that human beings evolved from earlier species of animals (Figure 4.5b). Or he could alter his attitude toward Samantha, deciding that he can't be friendly with someone who harbors such opinions, perhaps going so far as to unfriend her on Facebook (Figure 4.5c).

Balance theory helps us understand many situations in which people face cognitive inconsistency. For example, one anti-abortion activist told a researcher that she could not be friends with somebody who disagreed with her on abortion (Granberg, 1993). Unfortunately, balance theory does not describe many subtleties in people's judgments. It also fails to describe those situations in which people manage to like people with whom they disagree (Milburn, 1991). Thus, we need another approach to explain how people grapple with inconsistency. A time-honored model proposed by Robert P. Abelson (1959) is more helpful. Abelson suggested that people resolve cognitive conflict in four ways: (a) denial, (b) bolstering, (c) differentiation, and (d) transcendence, or what could also be called integration.

Consider how this could work in the earlier example:

Denial. Sam could try to forget about the fact that he and Samantha disagree about evolution.

Bolstering. Sam could add mental elements to his attitude, noting that there is strong empirical support for the idea of natural selection and no scientific challenge to the notion that human beings evolved from earlier species of animals. In this way, he might feel more strongly about the belief, thereby reducing cognitive imbalance.

Differentiation. He might differentiate his liking of Samantha from her disbelief in evolution. In effect, Sam could agree to disagree with Samantha, noting they have been long-time friends and agree about other issues.

Integration. Sam could try to integrate his views with those of Samantha in a way that suggests both can peacefully coexist. He could acknowledge that there is no contradiction between his belief in evolution and her belief in God. Integrating his beliefs with hers, he could conclude that science explains *how* human beings evolve, while religion explains *why* humans developed in the first place. By combining the views in a way that allows him to see good in both perspectives, he might reconcile his belief in evolution with Samantha's theist principles.

As this example suggests, people regularly struggle with inconsistencies among different elements of their attitudes. Mental inconsistencies are part of life. Balance theory and the modification discussed

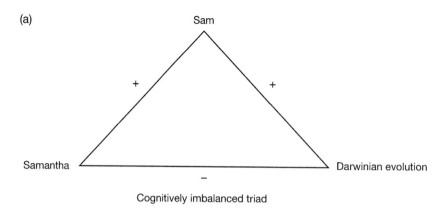

(a)

Sam

+   +

Samantha   Darwinian evolution

−

Cognitively imbalanced triad

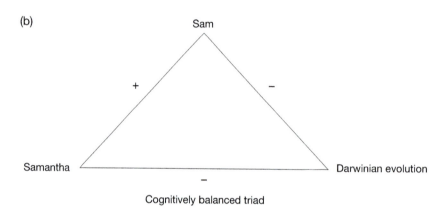

(b)

Sam

+   −

Samantha   Darwinian evolution

−

Cognitively balanced triad

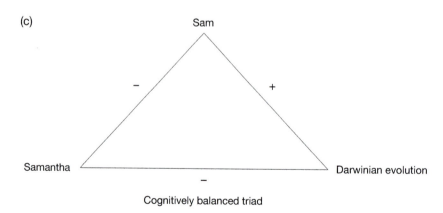

(c)

Sam

−   +

Samantha   Darwinian evolution

−

Cognitively balanced triad

Figure 4.5a–c Balance Theory Analysis of Sam's Attitudes toward Darwinian Evolution and Those of a Friend Who Does Not Believe in Evolution ("+" indicates positive sentiments; "−" shows negative ones)

above suggest that people try to find ways to reduce cognitive imbalance. They do not always succeed. Finding ambiguity uncomfortable, many people prefer to deny or derogate a position that conflicts with an aspect of an attitude. On the other hand, there are times when the strain to achieve cognitive balance can produce changes in attitude. This is evident in the ways many conventional parents reconciled discomfort with same-sex marriage with love for a gay child, deciding, as one mom put it, to "err on the side of love" (Cooper & Peters, 2012, p. A16).

Conclusions

Attitudes – emotional, evaluative, frequently formed at a young age – are a core dimension of persuasion. Attitudes, after all, are the entities that communicators seek to shape, reinforce, mold, and change. An attitude is defined as a learned, global evaluation of an object (person, place, or issue) that influences thought and action.

Values underlie or shape attitudes. Values are guiding principles in an individual's life. They include universal values, like freedom, and self-enhancing values, such as achievement. Differences in moral values help explain some of the fractious arguments between liberals and conservatives; it's not that they hate each other personally (though this can happen), but begin with different evaluative assumptions about the world, which in turn structure their attitudes and beliefs in ways that place them on different sides of complex social issues.

Beliefs, defined as cognitions about the world, in turn are viewed as components of attitudes. People cling tenaciously to beliefs, sometimes assuming their beliefs are facts. (They're not.) There are two types of beliefs: Descriptive beliefs, the perceptions of the world that people carry in their heads, and prescriptive beliefs, or mental prescriptions of what should or ought to happen in life.

One of the interesting questions about attitudes concerns their structure or organization. Expectancy–value theory says that attitudes are composed of expectations (beliefs) and evaluations of these beliefs. It emphasizes the role that salient, or psychologically relevant, beliefs play in shaping attitudes. Expectancy–value theory helps break down the macro-concept of attitude into component parts, yielding rich information about the human mind. The symbolic attitude approach argues that symbolic predispositions, like prejudice and deep-seated values, lie at the heart of attitudes. It calls attention to the many affective attributes that are associated with the attitude object. An ideological perspective contends that attitudes are organized around ideological principles, like liberalism–conservatism.

Because people are complex, attitudes are not always internally consistent. Individuals frequently experience ambivalence, feeling both positively and negatively about a person or issue. Preferring harmony to discord, people strive to reduce inconsistency among cognitive elements. Balance theory and other cognitive consistency models describe ways that individuals can restore mental harmony. We don't always succeed in this endeavor, and inconsistency is inevitably a fact of life.

Persuaders can change attitudes by gaining insights into their complex structure. They can focus on changing beliefs, altering the symbolic affect associated with beliefs, or target messages at bedrock moral principles. They can also encourage individuals to alter elements of their attitudes so as to gain cognitive harmony. In some cases, these persuasion attempts can fail, but in other instances, guided by a deft persuader who combines the science and art of persuasion, the appeals can prove stunningly successful.

References

Abelson, R. P. (1959). Modes of resolution of belief dilemmas. *Journal of Conflict Resolution*, 3(4), 343–352.

Ajzen, I., & Fishbein, M. (2008). Scaling and testing multiplicative combinations in the expectancy–value model of attitude. *Journal of Applied Social Psychology*, 38, 2222–2247.

Albarracín, D., Johnson, B. T., & Zanna, M. P. (2005). Preface. In D. Albarracín, B. T. Johnson, & M. P. Zanna (Eds.), *The handbook of attitudes* (pp. vii–ix). Mahwah, NJ: Lawrence Erlbaum Associates.

Albarracín, D., Sunderrajan, A., Lohmann, S., Chan, M.-P. S., & Jiang, D. (2019). The psychology of attitudes, motivation, and persuasion. In D. Albarracín & B. T. Johnson (Eds.), *The handbook of attitudes* (Vol. 1: Basic principles, pp. 3–44). New York: Routledge.

Albarracín, D., & Vargas, P. (2010). Attitudes and persuasion: From biology to social responses to persuasive intent. In S. T. Fiske, D. T. Gilbert, & G. Lindzey (Eds.), *Handbook of social psychology* (Vol. 1, 5th ed., pp. 394–427). Hoboken, NJ: Wiley.

Alford, J., Funk, C., & Hibbing, J. (2005). Are political orientations genetically transmitted? *American Political Science Review*, 99, 153–167.

Allport, G. W. (1935). Attitudes. In C. Murchison (Ed.), *A handbook of social psychology* (Vol. 2, pp. 798–844). Worcester, MA: Clark University Press.

Banaji, M. R., & Heiphetz, L. (2010). Attitudes. In S. T. Fiske, D. T. Gilbert, & G. Lindzey (Eds.), *Handbook of social psychology* (Vol. 1, 5th ed., pp. 353–393). New York: Wiley.

Belluck, P. (2019, August 30). Research finds not one "gay gene," but a multitude of influences. *The New York Times*, A1, A23.

Bishop, B. (with R. G. Cushing) (2008). *The big sort: Why the clustering of like-minded America is tearing us apart*. Boston, MA: Houghton-Mifflin.

Breckler, S. J. (1984). Empirical validation of affect, behavior, and cognition as distinct components of attitude. *Journal of Personality and Social Psychology*, 47, 1191–1205.

Cohen, J. B., & Reed, A., II. (2006). A multiple pathway anchoring and adjustment (MPAA) model of attitude generation and recruitment. *Journal of Consumer Research*, 33, 1–15.

Collins, F. S. (2006). *The language of God: A scientist presents evidence for belief*. New York: Free Press.

Conover, P. J., & Feldman, S. (1984). How people organize the political world: A schematic model. *American Journal of Political Science*, 28, 95–126.

Cooper, H., & Peters, J. W. (2012, May 15). For some, same-sex marriage is not politics, it's personal. *The New York Times*, A16.

Cooper, J., Blackman, S. F., & Keller, K. T. (2016). *The science of attitudes*. New York: Routledge.

Dennett, D. C. (2005, August 28). Show me the science. *The New York Times* [Week in Review], 11.

Dillard, J. P. (1993). Persuasion past and present: Attitudes aren't what they used to be. *Communication Monographs*, 60, 90–97.

Dixon, G. N., Weberling McKeever, B., Holton, A. E., Clarke, C., & Eosco, G. (2015). The power of a picture: Overcoming scientific misinformation by communicating weight-of-evidence information with visual exemplars. *Journal of Communication*, 65, 639–659.

Eagly, A. H., & Chaiken, S. (1993). *The psychology of attitudes*. Fort Worth, TX: Harcourt, Brace, Jovanovich.

Eagly, A. H., & Chaiken, S. (1998). Attitude structure and function. In D. T. Gilbert, S. T. Fiske, & G. Lindzey (Eds.), *Handbook of social psychology* (Vol. 1, 4th ed., pp. 269–322). Boston, MA: McGraw-Hill.

Edwards, K. (1990). The interplay of affect and cognition in attitude formation and change. *Journal of Personality and Social Psychology, 59*, 202–216.

Eom, K., Kim, H. S., Sherman, D. K., & Ishii, K. (2016). Cultural variability in the link between environmental concern and support for environmental action. *Psychological Science, 27*, 1331–1339.

Fabrigar, L. R., MacDonald, T. K., & Wegener, D. T. (2019). The origins and structure of attitudes. In D. Albarracín & B. T. Johnson (Eds.), *The handbook of attitudes* (Vol. 1: Basic principles, pp. 109–157). New York: Routledge.

Fazio, R. H. (1989). On the power and functionality of attitudes: The role of attitude accessibility. In A. R. Pratkanis, S. J. Breckler, & A. G. Greenwald (Eds.), *Attitude structure and function* (pp. 153–179). Hillsdale, NJ: Lawrence Erlbaum Associates.

Fishbein, M., & Ajzen, I. (1975). *Belief, attitude, intention and behavior: An introduction to theory and research.* Reading, MA: Addison–Wesley.

Flagg, A. (2019, May 15) Undocumented population and crime rate. *The New York Times*, A13.

Frimer, J. A., Biesanz, J. C., Walker, L. J., & MacKinlay, C. W. (2013). Liberals and conservatives rely on common moral foundations when making moral judgments about influential people. *Journal of Personality and Social Psychology, 104*, 1040–1059.

Goldberg, J. (2000, June 25). The education of a holy warrior. *The New York Times Magazine*, 32–37, 53, 63–64, 70–71.

Graham, J., Haidt, J., & Nosek, B. A. (2009). Liberals and conservatives rely on different sets of moral foundations. *Journal of Personality and Social Psychology, 96*, 1029–1046.

Granberg, D. (1993). Political perception. In S. Iyengar & W. J. McGuire (Eds.), *Explorations in political psychology* (pp. 70–112). Durham, NC: Duke University Press.

Haidt, J. (2013). *The righteous mind: Why good people are divided by politics and religion.* New York: Vintage Books.

Heider, F. (1958). *The psychology of interpersonal relations.* New York: Wiley.

Hepler, J., & Albarracín, D. (2013). Attitudes without objects: Evidence for a dispositional attitude, its measurement, and its consequences. *Journal of Personality and Social Psychology, 104*, 1060–1076.

Hoffman, J., & Kaplan, S. (2019, December 6). Data shows one in three teenagers use tobacco. *The New York Times*, A14.

Johnson, B. T., Landrum, A. R., & McCloskey, K. (2019). Attitudes in the 21st century: Accomplishments, challenges, and gaps. In D. Albarracín & B. T. Johnson (Eds.), *The handbook of attitudes* (Vol. 1: Basic principles, pp. 627–652). New York: Routledge.

Kahle, L. R. (1996). Social values and consumer behavior: Research from the list of values. In C. Seligman, J. M. Olson, & M. P. Zanna (Eds.), *The psychology of values: The Ontario symposium* (Vol. 8, pp. 135–151). Mahwah, NJ: Lawrence Erlbaum Associates.

Kluckhohn, C. (1951). Values and value-orientations in the theory of action: An exploration in definition and classification. In T. Parsons & E. A. Shils (Eds.), *Toward a general theory of action* (pp. 388–433). Cambridge, MA: Harvard University Press.

Lakoff, G. (1996). *Moral politics: What conservatives know that liberals don't.* Chicago, IL: University of Chicago Press.

Lavine, H., Thomsen, C. J., & Gonzales, M. T. (1997). The development of inter-attitudinal consistency: The shared-consequences model. *Journal of Personality and Social Psychology, 72*, 735–749.

Leland, J. (2005, September 18). Under din of abortion debate, an experience shared quietly. *The New York Times*, 1, 29.

Maio, G. R., & Olson, J. M. (1998). Values as truisms: Evidence and implications. *Journal of Personality and Social Psychology, 74*, 294–311.

McIntire, M., Yourish, K., & Buchanan, L. (2019, November 3). Noxious undertow in president's feed: Conspiracy-mongers, racists and spies. *The New York Times* (Special section: The Twitter presidency), 6–8.

Milburn, M. A. (1991). *Persuasion and politics: The social psychology of public opinion*. Pacific Grove, CA: Brooks/Cole.

Morrison, D. M., Gillmore, M. R., Simpson, E. E., Wells, E. A., & Hoppe, M. J. (1996). Children's decisions about substance use: An application and extension of the theory of reasoned action. *Journal of Applied Social Psychology, 26*, 1658–1679.

Orenstein, P. (2000). *Flux: Women on sex, work, kids, love, and life in a half-changed world*. New York: Doubleday.

Pearson, M. R. (2019). How "undocumented workers" and "illegal aliens" affect prejudice toward Mexican immigrants. *Social Influence, 5*, 118–132.

Peters, J. W. (2019, June 16). On abortion, many say it's complicated. *The New York Times*, 1, 19.

Petty, R. E., Ostrom, T. M., & Brock, T. C. (1981). Historical foundations of the cognitive response approach to attitudes and persuasion. In R. E. Petty, T. M. Ostrom, & T. C. Brock (Eds.), *Cognitive responses in persuasion* (pp. 5–29). Hillsdale, NJ: Lawrence Erlbaum Associates.

Pew Research Center (Religion & Public Life). (2015, November 3). U.S. public becoming less religious. Retrieved February 23, 2016, from www.pewforum.org/2015/11/03/u-s-public-becoming-less-religious/.

Pryor, J. B., & Reeder, G. D. (1993). Collective and individual representations of HIV/AIDS stigma. In J. B. Pryor & G. D. Reeder (Eds.), *The social psychology of HIV infection* (pp. 263–286). Hillsdale, NJ: Lawrence Erlbaum Associates.

Rokeach, M. (1960). *The open and closed mind; Investigations into the nature of belief systems and personality systems*. New York: Basic Books.

Rokeach, M. (1968). *Beliefs, attitudes, and values: A theory of organization and change*. San Francisco, CA: Jossey-Bass.

Rokeach, M. (1973). *The nature of human values*. New York: Free Press.

Schott, B. (2008, December 20). The way we were, 1968. *The New York Times*, A21.

Schwartz, S. (1996). Value priorities and behavior: Applying a theory of integrated value systems. In C. Seligman, J. M. Olson, & M. P. Zanna (Eds.), *The psychology of values: The Ontario symposium* (Vol. 8, pp. 1–24). Mahwah, NJ: Lawrence Erlbaum Associates.

Schwartz, S. H., & Bilsky, W. (1987). Toward a universal psychological structure of human values. *Journal of Personality and Social Psychology, 53*, 550–562.

Scott, E. C. (2004). *Evolution vs. creationism: An introduction*. Berkeley, CA: University of California Press.

Sears, D. O., & Funk, C. L. (1991). The role of self-interest in social and political attitudes. In M. P. Zanna (Ed.), *Advances in experimental social psychology* (Vol. 24, pp. 1–91). San Diego, CA: Academic Press.

Sears, D. O., Henry, P. J., & Kosterman, R. (2000). Egalitarian values and contemporary racial politics. In D. O. Sears, J. Sidanius, & L. Bobo (Eds.), *Racialized politics: The debate about racism in America* (pp. 75–117). Chicago, IL: University of Chicago Press.

Semple, K. (2015, December 15). Muslim youths in U.S. feel strain of suspicion. *The New York Times*, A1, A28.

Shavitt, S. (2019). Culture and attitude theorizing: Attitudes in Western and non-Western contexts. in D. Albarracín & B. T. Johnson (Eds.), *The handbook of attitudes* (Vol. 1: Basic principles, pp. 602–624). New York: Routledge.

Shear, M. D., Jordan, M., & Fernandez, M. (2019, April 10). The U.S. immigration system may have reached a breaking point. *The New York Times*. Retrieved May 13, 2019, from www.nytimes.com/2019/04/10/us/immigration-border-r

Sherif, M. (1967). Introduction. In C. W. Sherif & M. Sherif (Eds.), *Attitude, ego-involvement, and change* (pp. 1–5). New York: Wiley.

Tesser, A. (1993). The importance of heritability in psychological research: The case of attitudes. *Psychological Review*, *100*, 129–142.

Thompson, M. M., Zanna, M. P., & Griffin, D. W. (1995). Let's not be indifferent about (attitudinal) ambivalence. In R. E. Petty & J. A. Krosnick (Eds.), *Attitude strength: Antecedents and consequences* (pp. 361–386). Hillsdale, NJ: Lawrence Erlbaum Associates.

Timm, J. G. (2017, June 28). Fact check: No evidence undocumented immigrants commit more crimes. *NBC News*. Retrieved May 12, 2019, from www.nbcnews.com/politics/white-house/fact-check-no-evid

Zanna, M. P., & Rempel, J. K. (1988). Attitudes: A new look at an old concept. In D. Bar-Tal & A. Kruglanski (Eds.), *The social psychology of knowledge* (pp. 315–334). New York: Cambridge University Press.

Chapter 5

The Power of Our Passions

Theory and Research on Strong Attitudes

What is it about a player, wearing the uniform of his nation, dribbling, kicking, and pummelling a funny-looking spherical ball that drives Europeans berserk? Why does the emotional temperature of so many ordinarily tame and sober Europeans skyrocket as World Cup fever draws closer? What causes a handful of European men to access their inner hooligan when the start of a fierce cross-national soccer rivalry commences? Why did a qualifying match between Italy and Serbia have to be cancelled after just seven minutes of play in Genoa? You want to know why? It's football, baby! Football! It's athletic greats Paul Pogba, Oliver Giroud, Luke Modrić, Cristiano Ronaldo, Lionel Messi, and – yes, them too from years ago – Pelé and David Beckham.

It's the 2019 U.S. women's soccer team, following in the footsteps of the 1999 U.S. World Cup Champions they admired as girls; successors to the 2015 U.S. victors, who drubbed Japan with three hat-trick goals; a fearsome group of spirited, "in your face," competitors, who pummelled outstanding women's teams from France, England, and the Netherlands, enthralling screaming fans sporting red, white, and blue face paint as they hoisted the American flag after a 2–0 victory in the finals, capped by stunning kicks from Megan Rapinoe and Rose Lavelle.

It's vintage soccer: 11 players, a field of grass, a fake, quick pass, a game-winning boot that vanquishes the hopes of the rivals and swells the pride of a nation.

Football, as it is known in Europe, and soccer in American parlance, is one of many topics that elicits *strong attitudes*. A host of social issues – including gender roles, prayer in school, and contentious topics like gun control and abortion – also arouse powerful passions. Why do people hold attitudes with such tenacity? What is the nature of these attitudes? Why are some partisans frequently so dogmatic and impervious to argument? These are some of the topics discussed in this chapter, as I continue the exploration of attitude dynamics and implications for persuasion (see Figure 5.1).

Guided by academic research and theory, the first section of the chapter examines the nature of strong attitudes, while the second portion focuses on social judgment theory, with an examination of the concepts of selective perception, selective exposure, and confirmation biases. The third section delves into the more subtle, less conscious processes of accessibility, while the fourth and fifth portions describe related constructs of implicit attitudes and priming. The final section offers an overview of the neuroscience approach to attitudes. The chapter is enlivened by examples from everyday life – in some

Figure 5.1 American Women Soccer Stars Megan Rapinoe and Rose Lavelle (With feet in the Air) Celebrate Their Goals as the United States Defeated the Netherlands to Win the 2019 Women's World Cup. Soccer – or football as it is popularly called in Europe – arouses strong nationalistic attitudes, swelling patriotic pride, as well as gender-role attitudes sparked by charges that women soccer players are paid less and accorded less respect than their male counterparts

Image courtesy of Getty Images

cases depicting the vehemence with which strong attitudes are held, in others offering prescriptions for change. There's a lot here, but it should help you appreciate the power of our passions with new insights.

What Are Strong Attitudes?

From the French Revolution to violence perpetrated against doctors who perform abortion, "the incidents that attract our attention are often those associated with strong sentiments," Jon A. Krosnick and Richard E. Petty observed (1995, p. 1; see Figure 5.2). Intrigued by the dynamics of such attitudes, social psychologists have embarked on a series of studies exploring strong attitude characteristics and effects.

This might all seem obvious at first blush. People with strong attitudes have lots of passion and care a lot; isn't that what one would expect? Yes – but remember that persuasion scholars take a scientific approach. They want to understand what a strong attitude looks like, what it means psychologically to feel deeply about an issue, and how strong attitudes differ from weaker or more ambivalent ones. Remember also that people have acted brutally in the name of strong attitudes. They have killed innocent people and destroyed themselves. The more we can understand such attitudes, the more likely it is that we can devise ways to convince troubled or violent people to rethink their approaches to life.

Attitudes, by definition, influence thought and action. But strong attitudes are particularly likely to: (a) persist over time, (b) affect judgments, (c) guide behavior, and (d) prove resistant to change (Krosnick & Petty, 1995). Why is this so? Why are strong attitudes stable? As psychological experts explain, strong attitudes are buttressed by foundational beliefs and values, steeped in social knowledge, reinforced by similar others, cognitively elaborated, and readily accessible at the moment of a spontaneous argument on the topic (Wang Erber, Hodges, & Wilson, 1995).

The symbolic approach discussed in Chapter 4 suggests that people acquire strong attitudes at an early age. They are learned, rehearsed, and associated with positive aspects of a child's upbringing. Attitudes are also formed through observation of role models and reinforced when models, such as parents or peers, reward children for displaying the attitude (Bandura, 1971). Consider the example of a sportsman who has a staunchly favorable (yet complicated) attitude toward hunting. Hunter Steve Tuttle explained how he acquired his attitude:

> I remember the first time I ever killed something. It was a rabbit, and I was about 12 years old. I put my gun to my shoulder and aimed – taking care to lead the target – and pulled the trigger. The animal seemed to tumble end over end in slow motion … My father … looked up at me and said, "Good shot, boy!" and handed me the rabbit. I was proud and devastated all at once … The other men in the hunting party came over and slapped me on the back. Little did they know that I would have given anything to bring that rabbit back to life. I would feel sad about it for weeks … I went on to shoot a lot more game over the years, but none ever had the same emotional impact, nor did I ever get teary-eyed at the moment of the kill. In my culture, in the rural America of western Virginia, that was the day I began to change from boy to man.
>
> (2006, pp. 50–51)

Notice that during this pivotal experience the boy was rewarded for shooting the rabbit by a role model, his father ("Good shot, boy"), as well as by the other men in the hunting party, who slapped him on the back. In this way the positive aspects of an attitude toward guns were formed.

(a)

(b)

Figure 5.2a–b Abortion Is One of Many Issues That Evokes Strong Passions. Could part of its power stem from its linkage with strong values, such as freedom and religion?

Images courtesy of Getty Images

The ideological approach takes another tack, emphasizing that strong attitudes are likely to be organized around principles and values. For example, pro-gun partisans anchor their support of gun owners' rights in fidelity to values like freedom and self-reliance. Anti-gun activists support gun control, based on an equally heartfelt concern with the terrible effects of gun violence.

Social psychologists who study strong attitudes offer additional insights. They emphasize that strong attitudes, such as support for and opposition to gun control, possess different attributes from weak attitudes (Holbrook et al., 2005). Strong attitudes are characterized by:

- importance (we care deeply about the issue);
- ego-involvement (the attitude is linked to core values or the self);
- extremity (the attitude deviates significantly from neutrality);
- certainty (we are convinced that our attitude is correct);
- accessibility (the attitude comes quickly to mind);
- knowledge (we are highly informed about the topic);
- hierarchical organization (the attitude is internally consistent and embedded in an elaborate attitudinal structure).

Attitudes and Information-Processing

Strong attitudes influence message evaluations and judgments of communications. Two theories – social judgment theory and the attitude accessibility approach – shed light on how this occurs. Both are theories about attitudes in general, but they offer insights into the dynamics of strong attitudes.

Social Judgment Theory

On the eve of a Subway Series between the New York Yankees and New York Mets a few years back, a reporter filed this tongue-in-cheek report on how Yankee and Mets fans saw each other, based on interviews with New York baseball fans. It is a case study in how partisans on opposite sides of an issue perceive their antagonists:

> "Yankee fans are much more highly educated," [Allen Sherman, a Yankee fan] said. "… We have to be. It's harder to spell Yankees than Mets. And we can curse in so many different languages. We earn more, so when we throw a beer can it's those high-priced beer cans …" Fred Sayed, 26, a technical support manager from Queens and an ardent Mets fan, was able to be pretty explicit himself in defining Yankee fans: "All Yankee fans are just flat-out stupid."
>
> (Kleinfield, 2000, p. A1)

Lest we ignore partisanship in other sports, I invite you to consider LeBron James, just about the most hated person in Cleveland, Ohio because he dissed the city's beloved Cleveland Cavaliers professional basketball team by joining the Miami Heat in 2010. Frustrated by his inability to win a championship ring as a Cavalier, James announced, in a nationally televised announcement that followed a much-publicized series of interviews with other NBA team executives who courted the talented athlete, that he was taking "his talents to South Beach." While Miami fans applauded the decision and others credited James with having the entrepreneurial guts to break the umbilical cord that had locked him into a contract with the Cavaliers since he joined the team at the age of 19, Cleveland fans were furious, to the point of violence. Longing for a national championship that had eluded the city for more than four decades, Clevelanders felt betrayed, first by James's decision and then by the way he announced it, teasing them for weeks by raising hopes that (in the eyes of fans) he knew would be dashed. Fans called him "narcissistic" and said they felt their "hearts been ripped out." One long-time fan called him the "the whore of Akron" (Sandomir, 2011). Others burned replicas of his jersey or threw rocks at a downtown billboard that featured James. Police had to be called out to stem the riots. Cleveland fans were overjoyed when James joined the team in 2014 as euphoria overtook anger and hope supplanted despair.

In 2018, after the Cavaliers had won the NBA championship two years earlier, Clevelanders displayed a change of heart. Still jubilant about the victory and ever-grateful to James, they turned the other cheek and accepted with equanimity his decision to join the Los Angeles Lakers after delivering the city its desperately sought national championship.

These anecdotes show that people have very strong – actually extremely strong – attitudes toward sports, affect that intriguingly has neurological roots (Cikara, Botvinick, & Fiske, 2011). Yet the examples tell us more than this. They speak to the biases individuals have when they harbor strong feelings about a topic, and, in this way, illustrate the social judgment approach to attitudes. Pioneered by Muzafer Sherif and Carolyn Sherif (1967), social judgment theory emphasizes that people evaluate issues based on where they stand on the topic. As Sherif and Sherif noted:

> The basic information for predicting a person's reaction to a communication is *where* he places its position and the communicator relative to himself. The way that a person appraises a communication and perceives its position relative to his own stand affects his reaction to it and what he will do as a result.

> (p. 129)

Social judgment theory emphasizes that receivers do not evaluate a message purely on the merits of the arguments. Instead, the theory stipulates that people compare the advocated position with their attitude and then determine whether they should accept the position advocated in the message. Like Narcissus preoccupied with his reflection in the water, receivers are consumed with their own attitudes toward the topic. They can never escape their own points of view (see Figure 5.3).

Social judgment theory, so named because it emphasizes people's subjective judgments about social issues, articulates several core concepts. These are: (a) latitudes of acceptance, rejection, and non-commitment; (b) assimilation and contrast; and (c) ego-involvement.

Latitudes

Attitudes consist of a continuum of evaluations – a range of acceptable and unacceptable positions, as well as positions toward which the individual has no strong commitment. The *latitude of acceptance* consists of all those positions on an issue that an individual finds acceptable, including the most acceptable position. The *latitude of rejection* includes those positions that the individual finds objectionable, including the most objectionable position. Lying between these two regions is the *latitude of non-commitment*, which consists of those positions on which the individual has preferred to remain non-committal. This is the arena of the "don't know," "not sure," and "haven't made up my mind" responses (see Figure 5.4).

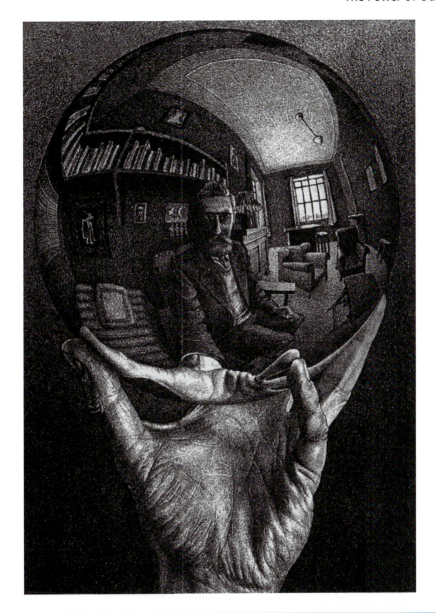

Figure 5.3 This Painting, *Hand with Reflecting Sphere*, by the Artist M. C. Escher, Illustrates a Central Principle of Social Judgment Theory. It highlights the notion that people are consumed by their own attitudes toward a topic. They cannot escape their own perspectives on the issue

From M. C. Escher's *Hand with Reflecting Sphere* © 2007 The M. C. Escher Company – Holland. www.mescher.com. With permission

(a)

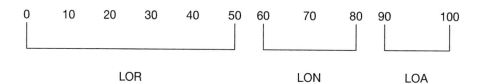

(b)

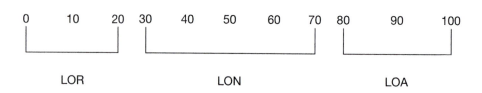

Figure 5.4 Latitude of Rejection (LOR), Latitude of Non-commitment (LON), and Latitude of Acceptance (LOA) of Individuals with Strong and Moderate Attitudes on an Issue. Panel (a) illustrates latitudes of an individual with a strong attitude. Note the large size of the latitude of rejection and the small size of the latitude of acceptance. Panel (b) shows latitudes of an individual with a moderate attitude. This individual's latitudes of acceptance and non-commitment are larger and the latitude of rejection is smaller, signifying greater openness to alternative points of view. The hypothetical scale goes from 0 to 100, where 100 indicates a message in total agreement with an individual's position and 0 a position in total disagreement

Think of the latitude of acceptance as the area in your mind that contains all the favorable ideas you have about an issue, the latitude of rejection as the arena containing all the things you don't like about the issue, and the latitude of non-commitment the middle ground where you stash the thoughts that are ambivalent or middle-of-the-road.

Early research focused on the relationship between extreme attitudes and size of the latitudes. Studies indicated that extremity of position influenced the size of the latitudes of rejection and acceptance (Sherif, Sherif, & Nebergall, 1965). Individuals with strong – in particular, extreme – views on a topic have large latitudes of rejection. They reject nearly all opposing arguments and accept only statements that are adjacent to their own stands on the issue. This is one reason why it is hard to change these folks' minds.

Assimilation and Contrast

One way to appreciate these terms is to focus on an entirely different issue for a moment: The weather. For example, if the weather is unseasonably warm in Chicago one January afternoon (say, 45°), Chicagoans will excitedly talk about the temperature, remarking on how warm it is outside. Expecting the temperature to register 25° or below, they are pleasantly surprised, so much so that some giddy Chicago residents will slip on shorts, take a long jog around Lake Michigan – and a day later get really sick because, for most people, 45° is still too cold for a long run in shorts! This is a *contrast effect*, in which we focus on how different reality is from expectation.

On the other hand, if the Chicago thermometer reads 32° during the frigid days of January, people think nothing of it. Expecting the temperature to be in the 20s, they are hardly surprised. They *assimilate* the temperature to what they expected, neglecting the fact that 32° is somewhat warmer than average for the Windy City in January.

Assimilation and contrast are perceptual mistakes, distortions that result from the tendency to perceive phenomena from the standpoint of a personal reference point or anchor. People judge message positions not objectively but, rather, subjectively. Their initial attitude serves as the reference point. In *assimilation*, people pull a somewhat congenial message toward their own attitude, assuming that the message is more similar to their attitude than it really is. They overestimate the similarity between a speaker's attitude and their own. In the case of *contrast*, individuals push a somewhat disagreeable message away from their attitude, assuming that it is more different than it really is. They overestimate the difference between the communicator's attitude and their own (Granberg, 1993).

Thus, we assimilate our friends' attitudes toward our own, assuming that their views are more similar to ours than they really are. This is one reason why people who fall in love are so shocked at their first disagreement. At the same time, we contrast our foes, exaggerating the degree to which their attitudes are different from ours. "You mean, we actually agree," we jokingly say to an opponent at the office.

Assimilation and contrast are natural human biases that occur because we perceive events through our own frames of reference, not objectively. Both processes can help people cope with everyday persuasion events. However, they have psychological costs as well. When we assimilate, we assume everyone shares our attitudes and thereby close our eyes to instances where others have intriguingly different perspectives. When we contrast, we may automatically assume that others with whom we disagree on an issue are "bad people" or disagree with us about everything.

An unfortunate example of this occurred some years back when a long-time pro-gun journalist was banished by pro-gun zealots for offering the mildest defense of gun control legislation. Dick Metcalf, a widely known columnist for *Guns & Ammo* magazine and star of a television show touting guns, was a persona non grata, "vanished, disappeared" as he put it, when in October, 2013 he penned a column called "Let's Talk Limits" that suggested that "all constitutional rights are regulated, always have been, and need to be" (Somaiya, 2014, p.1). The retribution was fierce and came immediately. *Guns & Ammo* readers threatened that they would cancel their subscriptions, angry pro-gun advocates emailed death threats, and the magazine cancelled his column and fired him. Although Metcalf is a proud gun owner who showcases the heads of 23 large bucks on the walls of his shooting club, his smidgeon of a mention that there was another side to the debate led to an outpouring of contrast effects. Pro-gun activists swiftly distanced themselves from him, exaggerating the difference between his position and theirs, viewing him as an enemy. Metcalf committed the "unforgivable sin of trying to be reasonable regarding arms regulation" (Lehman, 2014, p. A20).

In fairness, it is likely if a politician long associated with gun control praised concealed-carry gun laws, noting that states that permit their citizens to carry concealed weapons have lower violent crime rates, he or she would be condemned by liberal gun control advocates. On both sides of the gun issue (as in other arenas of extreme attitudes), there is little room for debate and scant interest in listening to moderate voices that could bridge strident differences between opposing perspectives. Such is the power of virulently strong attitudes.

Messages

Social judgment theory has interesting implications for persuasion. In the main, it suggests that persuaders have a tough road to hoe. People's existing attitudes serve as anchors, serving as filters through which individuals evaluate incoming messages. Messages that land within the latitude of acceptance are assimilated or assumed to be closer to the individual's own position than they actually are (Eagly & Chaiken, 1993). A communication that resonates with the individual's initial attitude, but advocates a stronger position moderately discrepant with the person's viewpoint, can actually persuade the individual – so long as it falls in the latitude of acceptance. The person will assimilate the message, figure that it's something he or she pretty much agrees with, and accept the advocated position. The same holds true for a message that lands in the latitude of non-commitment, provided the message is ambiguous. (This is a reason why sometimes it's good to be vague and hedge your bets.)

But if the message raises too many hackles – is too discrepant with the individual's initial attitude – it is a very different story. When a communicator delivers a message with which the person strongly disagrees, forces of resistance set in. Once the message ends up in the latitude of rejection, it's "Goodbye Charlie." The message recipient will contrast the message, perceiving it to be more disagreeable than it actually is (see Box 5.1 for a summary of the main aspects of social judgment theory).

Ego-involvement

If you had to say which concept from social judgment theory exerted the greatest influence on research, it would be involvement. Social scientists have found involvement fascinating because it seems to have such a strong impact on latitudes and assimilation/contrast. Practitioners have been intrigued because of its many implications for intractable conflict on social and political issues.

Ego-involvement is "the arousal, singly or in combination, of the individual's commitments or stands in the context of appropriate situations" (Sherif et al., 1965, p. 65). People are ego-involved when they perceive that the issue touches on their self-concepts or core values. Highly involved individuals differ from less involved persons in two ways. First, when people are involved in or care deeply about a social issue, they have larger latitudes of rejection relative to their latitudes of acceptance and non-commitment. This means that they reject just about any position that is not in sync with their own. Second, when deeply concerned about an issue, people are apt to assimilate ambiguous messages only when the arguments are generally consistent with their preconceived attitudes (Sherif et al., 1965). Individuals with ego-involved stances are hard to persuade: They are stubborn or resilient, depending on your point of view (see Figure 5.4).

There has been much research exploring the psychology of ego-involved attitudes. Studies have shown that when individuals are ego-involved in an issue (as people frequently are with the environment, religion, or animal rights), they engage in what is known as *selective perception*. They perceive events so that they fit their preconceived beliefs and attitudes (e.g., Edwards & Smith, 1996; Hastorf

& Cantril, 1954; Hovland, Harvey, & Sherif, 1957). An intriguing study by Charles G. Lord, Lee Ross, and Mark R. Lepper (1979) provides a snapshot of current thinking on this issue. The study was conducted more than 30 years ago, but is regarded as a classic in the field.

Partisanship and Capital Punishment

Lord and his colleagues sought out individuals with strong views on the contentious topic of the death penalty. One group favored the death penalty, believing it to be an effective deterrent against crime. The second group opposed it, maintaining that capital punishment was inhumane or an ineffective deterrent. Individuals from each group read brief descriptions of two purported investigations of the death penalty's deterrent effects. One study always reported evidence that the death penalty was effective (e.g., "in 11 of the 14 states, murder rates were *lower* after adoption of the death penalty"). The other study used similar statistics to make the opposite point – that the death penalty was an ineffective deterrent against crime (e.g., in 8 of the 10 states, "murder rates were *higher* in the state *with* capital punishment").

BOX 5.1

Understanding Theory: Primer on Social Judgment Theory

1 Social judgment theory emphasizes that individuals do not assess a message based on its objective qualities, but compare the message to their own attitudes.

2 People assimilate congruent messages to their own attitude, presuming the message is more consonant with their attitude than it actually is. They contrast discrepant messages from their attitude, presuming the message differs more sharply from their attitude than it actually does.

3 There are three layers of an attitude: Latitude of acceptance, or the positions an individual finds acceptable, latitude of rejection, those that are seen as intolerable or absolutely unacceptable, and the latitude of non-commitment, the area where the person has preferred to remain noncommittal, an area of potential attitude change.

4 When people are high in ego-involvement or have strong views on the issue, they are especially resistant to persuasion.

5 Persuasion requires a match between the message and the individual's existing attitude. Communicators can persuade an individual to adopt a message that is somewhat discrepant from his or her initial position, provided the message lands in the latitude of acceptance. But persuaders cannot veer too far from the individual's preexisting position if they hope to nudge the individual to change his or her attitude on the issue. Once a message lands in the latitude of rejection, it is likely to be discarded.

6 The theory is vague on where you shoot the message arrow so it persuades individuals. It does not tell you how to frame your arguments to maximize success.

7 Social judgment theory suggests that persuaders should try to figure out at the outset which positions will fall within audience members' latitudes of acceptance and latitudes

of rejection. In this way, they can tailor the message to fit an individual's preexisting sentiments. This can be helpful in an election when candidates hope to push voters from "leaning strongly in favor" to "definitely likely to cast a vote in favor" of the candidate.

8   In other cases, the theory suggests that persuaders can succeed by convincing message recipients that the advocated position falls within their latitude of non-commitment. A public policy advocate may not need to convince voters that a policy is the best, only that it is *not* unacceptable or not without some moral basis (O'Keefe, 2016). "The job of those trying to bring about change is not to hector it into the agenda of the necessary but to move it into the realm of the plausible," Gopnik (2015, p. 31) observed. Attitude change toward gay marriage – from opposition to broad-based support – illustrates this. Many Americans became more favorable toward same-sex marriage, not because they liked all aspects, but because it became more difficult to view gay marriage as unreasonable or untenable.

Thus, students read one study that supported and one study that opposed their position on the death penalty. The evidence in support of the death penalty's deterrent effect was virtually the same as the evidence that questioned its impact.

If people were objective and fair, they would acknowledge that the evidence for both sides was equally strong. But that is not how these ego-involved partisans responded. Proponents of capital punishment found the pro-death penalty study more convincing, and opponents found the anti-death penalty study more persuasive. For example, *a supporter of capital punishment* said this about a study supporting the individual's position on the death penalty:

> The experiment was well thought out, the data collected was valid, and they were able to come up with responses to all criticisms.

The same person reacted to the anti-capital-punishment study by remarking that:

> There were too many flaws in the picking of the states and too many variables involved in the experiment as a whole to change my opinion.

An *opponent of capital punishment* said this of a sympathetic study that opposed the death penalty:

> The states were chosen at random, so the results show the average effect capital punishment has across the nation. The fact that 8 out of 10 states show a rise in murders stands as good evidence.

The opponent reacted in this way to the pro-capital-punishment study:

> The study was taken only 1 year before and 1 year after capital punishment was reinstated. To be a more effective study they should have taken data from at least 10 years before and as many years as possible after.
>
> (Lord et al., 1979, p. 2103)

You can appreciate what happened. Individuals liked studies that supported their position on capital punishment and managed to find fault with studies that opposed their position. They processed information very selectively, exhibiting what the authors called *biased assimilation*. They assimilated ambiguous information to their point of view, believing that it was consistent with their position on capital punishment. What's more, proponents and opponents managed to feel even more strongly about the issue by the study's conclusion. Proponents reported that they were more in favor of the death penalty than they had been at the study's start. Opponents indicated that they were more opposed than they had been at the beginning of the experiment. Reading the arguments did not reduce biased perceptions; it caused partisans to become even *more* polarized, *more* convinced that they were right! (See Figure 5.5.)

These classic findings were published in 1979, but they have continued to hold up over the years, as seen in supportive, though complicating, results by Miller et al. (1993), and findings from an intriguing study published more than 35 years later by Dan Kahan and his colleagues (2017).

Figure 5.5 Supporters and Opponents of Capital Punishment Have Such Strong Attitudes That They Hold Steadfastly to Their Positions, Even When the Evidence Appears to Support the Other Side. Opponents rally against the death penalty

Image courtesy of Shutterstock

Kahan and his associates wondered whether the ability to understand complex scientific findings would overpower the tendency to perceive evidence through the lens of one's own biases. Perhaps, they argued, people high in numeracy or skill in quantitative reasoning appreciate the gist of empirical findings, and this cognitive understanding tempers their inclination to see evidence through biased lenses. The researchers found that people high in "numeracy," or skill in quantitative reasoning, had a more accurate understanding of complicated empirical findings on a neutral issue, the effects of skin cream on treating skin rashes, than those lower in this ability. Aided by their quantitative reasoning skills, they could ferret through numerical data and get to the heart of the issue, correctly determining when the treatment reduced or increased skin rashes. But when the evidence touched on their strong attitudes toward gun control – specifically banning concealed guns in public – their attitudes overwhelmed their capacity to be rational. Liberals read the evidence as indicating that banning concealed handguns in public reduces crime. By contrast, conservatives interpreted the same evidence as suggesting that banning guns in public increases crime because it prevents citizens from protecting themselves from gun-toting criminals.

The researchers had cleverly constructed contingency (row by column) tables, in which the numbers were exactly the same for the effects of skin treatment on rashes as they were for banning concealed handguns in public. For example, liberals with strong numerical skills nailed a complex series of findings on skin rashes, correctly noting that patients who used a skin cream were nearly two times more likely to see their rash get better than worse, compared to patients who did not use the skin cream. Ditto for conservatives with strong numerical skills.

By contrast, when the same numerical data showed cities that banned handguns in public were nearly twice as likely to experience an increase rather than a decrease in crime, compared to cities that did not ban carrying concealed handguns (a conclusion liberals wouldn't like), liberal quantitative experts rejected the conclusion. Similarly, when the data, with exactly the same numbers, showed that cities that banned concealed guns in public were nearly twice as likely to experience a decrease rather than an increase in crime, compared to cities that did not ban handguns, a conclusion conservatives wouldn't like, the conservative quantitative experts couldn't abide by the conclusion. When people had to decide between accepting facts they didn't like because they were correct, or rejecting these facts because they didn't support their beliefs, they called on their quantitative skills oh-so-selectively, flat out rejecting information that didn't conform with their beliefs, as the capital punishment students had done nearly 40 years earlier. You could headline the results: Biases Win! Logic Loses! Biases Continue to Overwhelm Analytical Thinking!

Of course, the headlines over simplify a little. When attitudes aren't quite so strong or polarizing, the ability to cognitively reflect can help people get beyond their biases (Pennycook & Rand, 2018). But, in the main, the research offers a cautionary tale, documenting the persistence of confirmatory biases in the face of contradictory evidence.

From Then to Now: Why Biased Beliefs Persevere and Why It Matters

Psychological Explanations

Over the past several decades, social psychologists, fascinated by the cognitive underpinnings of attitude polarization, have tried to piece together what happens inside an individual's mind when he or she is faced with conflicting evidence on an issue. In particular, they have sought to probe the mental and emotional dynamics of strong attitudes, exploring why people tenaciously hold onto ego-involved beliefs in the face of daunting evidence that they are questionable, problematic, or simply not true (Albarracín, Chan, & Jiang, 2019).

One explanation for the persistence of biased beliefs is that people are very familiar with their strong attitudes and beliefs. Having systematically, deeply processed them, they are easily accessible, well-integrated into latitudes of acceptance, linked with values, and frequently rehearsed, making them highly resistant to change. A second view takes a more motivational approach, emphasizing that strong attitudes are part of people's self-system, helping them cope and performing psychological functions (see Chapter 6). People may be defensively motivated to protect their attitudes from change, holding onto these beliefs, like cherished possessions, determined to process information so they preserve beliefs in the face of hostile attack (Kunda, 1990).

A third view, process-oriented, emphasizes that people, approaching new information with no intention of mentally searching for facts that might prove their position wrong, engage in a "biased memory search" at the get-go. Convinced that their position is correct, they search memory for facts that support their view of the world, conveniently overlooking or rejecting evidence on the other side that might call their ideas into question (Edwards & Smith, 1996). This biased search is facilitated by the tendency to focus on the "gist" of the issue – the thrust or overarching narrative – rather than specific details in the message (Reyna & Brainerd, 1995). Thus, beliefs persevere in the face of challenging facts because people remember the big picture and forget specific information that questions their view. It is also more difficult to efficiently process inconsistent information; it is less familiar and may contradict well-learned congruent beliefs (Albarracín et al., 2019).

More generally, people invoke, frequently unreasonably and defensively, a higher threshold to refute preexisting sentiments, erecting a criteria for refutation that no argument could satisfy, one they conveniently do not apply to less important or congenial beliefs. For example, global warming opponents can pounce on one small finding that purports to show the earth is not warming, even though it may not be statistically significant and is overwhelmed by opposing findings from thousands of other studies. Or they might point to a bitterly cold day to argue that global warming is a hoax, when climate change is a global planetary phenomenon that describes a broad pattern of effects that occur in many places, not a particular finding in one small place on one particular day.

Thus, for a variety of reasons – cognitive, motivational, emotional – people hold onto strongly held beliefs, selectively perceiving information in light of their enduring attitudes.

Think of it all as a blind spot, "a bias blind spot," (Pronin, Lin, & Ross, 2002) exemplifying a *confirmation bias*, the psychological tendency to process social information by seeking out and selectively interpreting evidence so it confirms one's preexisting view, a subset of humans' need for cognitive consistency (Tsang, 2019; see Chapter 13). Confirmation bias has several related conceptual cousins, such as selective exposure (the tendency to seek out attitude-confirming information), biased recall, and rejection of perspectives that are incompatible with existing strong attitudes and beliefs.

Applications

Research on confirmation biases has real-life implications. Let's see how this works.

Selective Perception

We're accustomed to cases where Republicans and Democrats credit national economic success to the policies of a president from their party, while denying that it could have anything to do with the actions of a president from the opposing political party (Casselman & Tankersley, 2018). And, of course, partisans see political scandals and political cataclysms, like impeachment, through the lens of their own partisan viewpoints (Peters, 2019; Shear & Fandos, 2019).

Intriguingly, selective perception extends beyond politics. It has rich applications to partisan support for sports teams. If you have ever had the experience of "knowing" that the referee's game-changing call was definitely biased against your team and in favor of your opponents in football, basketball, or any sport, you can appreciate how this works. There is empirical evidence to support this notion. In January, 2015 the New England Patriots defeated the Indianapolis Colts in an American Football League championship game, amid swirling controversy that New England quarterback Tom Brady had knowingly and illegally deflated the air pressure in the football to make it easier to grip the football before he passed. Some months later, researchers polled fans of the New England Patriots, Indianapolis Colts, and other teams. Just 16 percent of Patriots fans said Brady broke the rules, compared to 67 percent of fans of other teams. A jaw-dropping 90 percent of fans of the defeated Colts were sure Brady broke the rules (Nyhan, 2015). Even knowledge didn't make a difference. Patriots fans who were knowledgeable about the ins and outs of different aspects of the controversy were still overwhelmingly likely to say that Brady broke no rules, even as other knowledgeable partisans from other teams undoubtedly perceived Brady's behavior in exactly the opposite fashion.

Sadly, selective perceptions are a ubiquitous subtext in the seemingly endless, tragic cases of police violence against minorities. Individuals more sympathetic with the plight of police will view a forensic video through different eyes than those more critical of police decisions. For example, on November 22, 2014 in Cleveland, a police officer killed 12-year-old Tamir Rice because he thought he was reaching for a gun (it turned out to be a toy pellet gun, but, amazingly, the dispatcher who received an earlier 911 call failed to inform the officer that the gun was probably fake). A forensic video of the incident elicited strikingly different reactions. Those sympathetic with the police pointed to video evidence that the 12-year-old walked toward a police cruiser that arrived at the scene and lifted his right shoulder and arm in the instant before the officer shot him, suggesting the officer could have feared for his life, rendering his decision reasonable, though tragic. Lawyers for the family argued that the police officers created the problem by failing to follow police procedure: They drove their car within feet of Tamir and then shot him instantly, without issuing a verbal command or knowing for certain if the youngster was the individual described in the 911 call (Danylko, 2015). Selective perceptions in these cases, understandable as they are, impede collective efforts to devise sensible reforms to improve police–community relations.

Selective Exposure in Action

Another selective bias also intercedes in many real-life situations: *Selective exposure.* Selective exposure is the tendency to seek out communications that embrace one's worldview, and to prefer information consistent, rather than inconsistent, with one's overall attitudes. As a general rule, an exhaustive study of the issue reveals people are much more likely to select information that reflects their social attitude (Hart et al., 2009). However, this is not always the case. There are situations in which people seek out information that challenges their position, such as when they are trying to make an important financial or medical decision and realize that they need both sides to make an informed choice (Frey, 1986). Indeed, when strong values are not in play or people are relatively open-minded on a topic, they seek out messages that challenge their beliefs (Hart et al., 2009; see also Jang, 2014; Manjoo, 2015).

However, this is not the norm in partisan politics; staunch liberals and conservatives are frequently motivated to avoid listening to their adversaries' opinions, even passing up the chance to win $3 to avoid hearing the other side of the same-sex marriage issue! In one study, partisans willingly declined a $3 reward because listening to their opponents made them feel angry or required too much effort on their part (Frimer, Skitka, & Motyl, 2017).

In subtle ways, selective exposure is a norm. People select social worlds – neighborhoods, friends, even websites and blogs – that reinforce their preexisting viewpoints (Iyengar & Hahn, 2009). Many of us grew up in neighborhoods peopled by individuals who shared our social attitudes and lifestyles. People tend to cluster or segregate by attitudes, so that voters are most likely to live and talk with those who share their political points of view (Bishop, 2008; Mutz, 2006; though see Abrams and Fiorina, 2012), for a different view).

Preferences for like-minded others runs so deep that a number of Americans say they would be disgruntled if a close family relative married someone who harbors a different political viewpoint. Thirty percent of strong conservatives say they would be unhappy if a close relative chose a Democrat for their mate. Twenty-three percent of strong liberals profess they would be displeased if an immediate family member married a political conservative (Cohn, 2014). Nearly a third of individuals in one survey said they had quit talking to a family member or friend because of political disagreements over the contentious 2016 election (Peters, 2018).

The problem is exacerbated by the tendency for selective exposure to strengthen partisan beliefs (Krosnick & MacInnis, 2015; Westerwick et al., 2017). New apps that offer one-sided partisan feeds, like a National Rifle Association campaign app that bars messages that challenge the NRA position, allow people to live in universes that spit back and reinforce what they already believe (Singer & Confessore, 2018).

The rub is this: When people live in ideological bubbles that reinforce their convictions, they feel comforted and cocooned, but, as philosopher John Stuart Mill observed more than 150 years ago, they are "deprived of the opportunity of exchanging error for truth" (Mill, 1859/2009, p. 20). They don't see how their viewpoints are at odds with the facts. They miss out on the wisdom that comes from an appreciation of the complexity of truth.

One final point: As you considered these examples, you may have concluded that this discussion applied only to the strong-minded political partisans you have seen on television and whose posts you encountered on social media – those driven to protest and agitate. But this misses the reality of everyday life.

Everybody – me, you, our friends – has strong attitudes on certain topics. It may not be global warming or animal research or electoral politics. It could be fashion, Facebook, football, or video games. There are certain issues on which we all are biased and psychologically intransigent. Social judgment research leaves no doubt that when we encounter messages on these topics, we will selectively perceive information, reject viewpoints that actually might be congenial to our own, even assume the communicator harbors hostile intentions. Such is the power of strong social attitudes. Once one recognizes this, one can take steps to counteract selective biases – for example, by considering that the other individual has a legitimate point of view and that one's own perspective may blind one to the cogent arguments in the other's position. It is sage advice, hardly new, for it dates back to the Sermon on the Mount when Jesus profoundly advised, "First take the plank out of your own eye, and then you will see clearly to remove the speck from your brother's eye."

The Contemporary Problem with Selectivity

Unfortunately, our age of algorithmic social media sites makes removing these specks more difficult. When the information people receive on social media tends to comport with their preexisting beliefs, they see only their side of the issue, not another side. What's more, ideologically slanted news articles and biased posts can be grossly inaccurate, offering a version of reality that is grotesquely incongruent with scientific or consensually accepted facts on an issue. Posts claiming that vaccines cause autism (see Box 5.2), climate change is a hoax, evolution is just a theory, or any number of White supremacist conspiracy theories arguing that minorities will soon replace Whites circulate among like-minded followers, reinforcing biased beliefs, allowing dogmatically held falsehoods to overwhelm facts. The danger is that truth is forsaken because people are too committed to extremist dogma to consider other, more reasonable perspectives. Persuasion research offers insights into the psychological roots of these biases, as well as ways to change strong attitudes and beliefs (see Box 5.3 and Chapter 10).

BOX 5.2

Anti-Vaxxers: A Case Study in the Power and Distortions of Strong Attitudes

They're hardly bashful. Quite the contrary, they defiantly proclaim, with public Facebook groups named Wrong Vaccines and Instagram hashtags #AntiVax and #CDCWhistleBlower, their contempt for medical science, loathing of vaccines, and unshakeable religious beliefs that vaccines interfere with humans' "God-given immunity" to illness and the body's natural ability to ward off disease (Stansberry & DiRusso, 2016).

Vaccines have names too. They call them "poison, the evil beast," and "demonic concoctions." With their language and social media pronouncements, a small, but vocal, group of Americans showcase their belligerent opposition to vaccines, attitudes that persevere and only seem to have become more virulent over time, in spite of the proven medical facts that vaccines (a signature achievement of medical science) are safe, do not cause autism (another bugaboo), and that failure to vaccinate children causes epidemic outbreak of deadly diseases like measles (Kinch, 2018; Pager, 2019; Wiznitzer, 2009).

In a fascinating study of anti-vaccination opponents' online communication networks, Kathleen Stansberry and Carlina DiRusso (2016) documented the defiant, hostile attitudes toward vaccines and medical science displayed by anti-vaxxers, characterized by selective exposure to their own communication networks; selective interpretation of findings that challenge their beliefs; and adroit ability to reframe doctors' commitment to disease prevention as exemplifying doctors' efforts to "forcibly injecting children with toxic chemicals" (Stansberry & DiRusso, 2016, p. 18), a perspective that flies in the face of physicians' Hippocratic oath.

Anti-vaccination activists' attitudes are textbook examples of the generalizability of Lord and his colleagues' capital punishment study, Kahan's research on attitudes toward gun rights, and strong attitude theory, amplified by a populist distrust of empirical facts and the communicative powers of online media.

While the number of anti-vaccination groups is small, they are virally loud, and, as one writer noted, "more widely available thanks to the concentration of social activity on a few platforms and the substantial reach of a small number of anti-vax media organs" (Madrigal, 2019).

From their own vantage point, anti-vaccination opponents, operating from their own social judgment anchors, viewing everything from the reflecting pool of their own attitudes (as in Escher's famous portrait), are well-intentioned, understandably concerned about children's susceptibility to disease, and doing their best to educate an American public they view as "sheep" that need to "wake up" to the greed of the medical community (Stansberry & DiRusso, 2016, p. 19). Unfortunately, their beliefs are filled with ad hominem attacks, such as comparisons of pediatricians administering vaccines to Nazis, and false claims on Facebook pages and elsewhere

Figure 5.6 Opponents of Vaccination Protest Against Vaccination, Charging That Vaccines Are Unsafe and Cause Autism. Their claims are incorrect, flying in the face of voluminous medical evidence. Although they represent a small minority of the public, anti-vaxxers, as they are known, are vocal, illustrating anew the ways that biased perceptions and confirmation biases are at the root of strong attitudes. The refusal of a handful of vaccination opponents to get vaccinations contributed to an unprecedented outbreak of measles in the United States in 2019

Image courtesy of Shutterstock

that eating papaya can ward off measles, or, in some bizarre cases, that children's souls are on a journey that vaccines would impede (Sommer, 2018; de Freytas-tamura, 2019, p. A18; see Figure 5.6). Some extremists have targeted a leading vaccine expert, sending so many death threats that the FBI provided him with a bodyguard (Interlandi, 2019).

Confirmation biases at the root of these actions are magnified by the cascading effects of social contagion, where socially congenial "contagious collectives" composed of anti-vaccination advocates spread misinformation across geographical boundaries, with great speed and perceived influence (González-Bailón, 2017, p. 85).

Let's be clear. Vaccines – notably the MMR (measles, mumps, and rubella) vaccine – do not cause autism or other diseases. Medical experts, armed with scientific facts, have debunked this myth for years. Yet, emboldened by biased beliefs trumpeted interpersonally or online, a handful of closed-minded religious and secular communities have shunned the measles vaccine, clinging to a variety of misconceptions, including the notion that the final vaccine product is impure, in violation of religious laws (Kinch, 2018; Pager, 2019). In 2019, this led to an outbreak of more than 1,000 cases of measles across the United States. Measles can cause pneumonia, deafness, and even death in children and was declared eliminated in the United States in 2000, but recurred due to vaccination opponents' determination not to immunize their children.

BOX 5.3

Changing Strong Attitudes

They are the most difficult facets of attitudes to change, but changing them may be the most important task that persuaders face. When you consider the power of strong attitudes – race, abortion, immigration – the ways they can polarize and hamper attempts to bring people together, you can appreciate why we should figure out ways to influence rigidly held attitudes and beliefs. A variety of persuasion theories offer clues. Here are several ideas of what persuaders might do:

- *Call on balance theory by pointing out that the person whose prejudiced attitude you want to modify has friends who embrace a more tolerant view.* Balance theory emphasizes that inconsistencies among elements of an attitude can create internal pressures to change. This is what happened in the case of attitudes toward gay marriage, as noted in Chapter 4. Some Americans who opposed same-sex marriage had gay friends or relatives who passionately felt the other way. To maintain balance in the P-O-X triad, and valuing their interpersonal relationships, gay marriage opponents altered their attitudes so they were in sync with their friends' views. This restored cognitive balance, setting the stage for the development of more favorable attitudes toward same-sex marriage.
- *Find a persuasive role model to showcase the attitude you want to change.* Exposure to the role model on mass or social media can influence attitudes via a host of psychological processes, and the changes can be enduring. Consider racial prejudice. Viewing Barack Obama's 2008 presidential campaign reduced racial prejudice, with the largest reductions occurring among conservatives and Republicans (Goldman & Mutz, 2014). Although

Americans were divided on Obama's policies, they perceived him as charismatic, intelligent, and successful. These perceptions sharply reduced racial prejudice, perhaps by encouraging deeper reflection or showing how the prejudice was untenable in view of Obama's bias-disproving, positive traits.

- *Induce the individual to contemplate the other side of the issue.* Although this requires that the target audience member engage in sympathetic role-taking, a difficult task for people with strong views, the strategy can help people see the issue from the other side, reducing biased perceptions (Lord, Lepper, & Preston, 1984). By considering the opposite position (guided by a trusted communicator), individuals may formulate positive thoughts, articulated in their own words. They may also gain empathy for those who have been hurt by a policy they support. This can set the stage for change, helping people think through strong beliefs and develop new feelings that can cause them to question long-held attitudes.
- *Remind the person whose attitude you want to change that he or she values fairness and consideration of different points of view.* Then suggest that it would be inconsistent with your receiver's value system not to consider sound arguments in favor of the other point of view (see Chapter 13).
- *Frame the position in terms that are consistent with the individual's own perspectives on the issue.* By emphasizing ways that the advocated position derives from a receiver's long-held attitudes or social values, a communicator can nudge the individual into considering an alternative viewpoint. We frequently look at issues from our point of view, forgetting that if we want to persuade others we have to frame or articulate the issue in their terms (see Chapter 10).
- *Tread carefully.* Don't say things that will fall into the individual's latitude of rejection. Point to instances where both sides agree. Expect that persuasion will occur slowly, in stages. Try to build sympathy and compassion for those from the opposing position, while not arousing anger from those with strong positions on the issue. For example, on the fractious issue of guns, gun control advocates frequently raise the ire of strong pro-gun activists by inviting activists to believe that government will take their guns away. If gun control supporters recognized the political reality – that military-style rifles will be here for many years to come – it would reduce gun owners' fears at the outset, reducing contrast effects, and building common ground (Kingsbury, 2019). In the end, on attitudes toward guns and other ego-involved issues, we need to find ways to tolerate the attitudes of those with whom we emphatically disagree. In civil society, we must live, coexist, and respect each other.

Attitude Accessibility

The event happened years ago, but those old enough to remember it will never forget. On September 11, 2001, Americans received a massive, tragic jolt from their quiescence. The terrorist attacks on the World Trade Center and Pentagon exerted enormous impacts, altering Americans' view of the world and changing the calculus of U.S. foreign policy. A particularly dramatic – and ironically positive – effect was the outpouring of patriotism that the events unleashed. Flags flew everywhere. They could be seen on houses, cars, clothing, book bags, even tattoos. People sang the national anthem and "America the Beautiful" proudly and with feeling, not mumbling the words in private embarrassment. Subsequent anniversaries of 9/11 brought out some of the same emotions.

Tragically, for many people the events of September 11 accessed emotion-packed attitudes – toward loved ones, the United States, and the preciousness of human life. They thus provide a poignant introduction to the concept of attitude accessibility, a helpful approach to attitude dynamics developed by Russell H. Fazio. Fazio (1995) views attitude as an association between an object (person, place, or issue) and an evaluation. It's a linkage between a country (United States) and a great feeling; an ethnic identity (Black, Hispanic, Asian) and feelings of pride; or a product (Nike tennis shoes) and exhilaration. Prejudiced attitudes, by contrast, are associations between the object and feelings of disgust or hatred.

Attitudes vary along a continuum of strength. Weak attitudes are characterized by a familiarity with the object, but a lukewarm evaluation of its net worth. Your attitudes toward Denmark, Eskimos, or an infrequently advertised brand of sneakers probably fall under the weak label. You have heard of the entities, but don't have particularly positive or negative feelings toward them. You can retrieve your attitude toward these objects, but not automatically or without effort. Strong attitudes – toward country, an ethnic group, a celebrity, or favorite product – are characterized by well-learned associations between the object and your evaluation. These attitudes are so strong and enduring that we can activate them automatically from memory. Simply reading the name of the object in print will trigger the association and call the attitude to mind. (Thought experiment: Look at the word "Denmark" and observe what comes to mind. Now try "U.S.A." or a religious group with which you identify. What thoughts leap to mind? What emotions do you feel? According to accessibility theory, a global feeling about America, or your religion, should come to mind when you see the word on the page; see Figure 5.7.)

The key constructs of the theory are accessibility and association. *Accessibility* refers to the degree to which attitude is automatically activated from memory. If you want a simple colloquial phrase, think of accessibility as "getting in touch with your feelings." Associations are links among different components of the attitude. The stronger the linkages are, the stronger is the attitude. Accessibility theory calls on a cognitive model of associative networks to explain attitude strength (see Roskos-Ewoldsen, Roskos-Ewoldsen, & Carpentier, 2009). It is a complex model, so an example may help you to appreciate the associative notion.

Consider attitude toward America, mentioned previously. Imagine the attitude is located somewhere in your mind, with "pathways" or "roads" connecting different components of the attitude. Each component is linked with a positive or negative evaluation. Fourth of July is associated with positive affect, which radiates out (in red, white, and blue) to fireworks and hot dogs, also evaluated positively. Other components of the America concept could be freedom of speech, Thomas Jefferson, the "Star-Spangled Banner," baseball, land of opportunity, and rock 'n' roll. Many people have good feelings about these concepts. The stronger the association between the overall concept, America, and a positive evaluation is, the more likely it is that a strong, favorable attitude will come quickly to mind when people see the word "America."

Needless to say, not everyone loves America. Some Americans have a negative attitude toward their country. Racial prejudice, school violence, and poverty might be images of the United States that these individuals have conjured up many times. Having learned to strongly associate America with negative feelings, they have a strongly unfavorable attitude that would come automatically to mind when they encounter the name of their country (see Figure 5.8).

Stimulated by the accessibility notion, researchers have conducted numerous experiments over the past couple of decades. They have examined factors that make it more likely that we are "in touch with" our attitudes. They also have explored the influence of accessibility on processing information

Figure 5.7 The American Flag Evokes Strong Sentiments, Typically Pride and Reverence for Country. What comes to mind when you see these flags?
Photograph by William C. Rieter

(Fazio, 1990, 2000; Roskos-Ewoldsen, 1997; Roskos-Ewoldsen, Arpan-Ralstin, & St. Pierre, 2002). In order to measure this deep-seated construct, researchers have used reaction time procedures. Participants in the study view the name or picture of an attitude object on a computer screen and indicate whether they like or dislike the object. The speed with which they push a button on the computer indexes accessibility. The quicker their *response time*, the more accessible the attitude. Guided by this and related procedures, psychologists have learned a great deal about attitude accessibility. Key findings include:

- *The more frequently that people mentally rehearse the association between an object and evaluation, the stronger the connection will be.* For example, hatred of terrorist groups, on the negative side, and love of country, on the positive side, are strong attitudes. People have come over time to frequently associate terrorists with horrific outcomes and commonly link one's country with

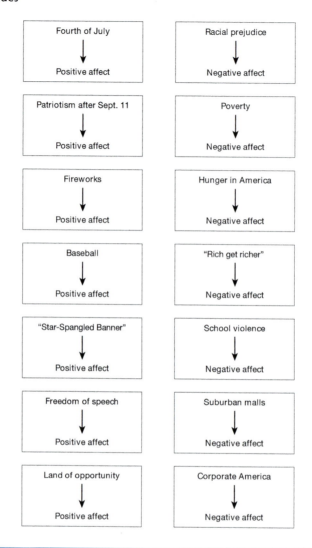

Figure 5.8 Associations and Accessibility. Associative networks for an individual with a positive attitude toward America (left) and for an individual with a negative attitude toward America (right). When attitudes are strong, they can be accessed immediately – in this case, as soon as individuals see the word "America." Of course, associative networks about one's country are not limited to Americans. We could chart positive and negative associative networks for individuals from a host of other countries – for example, the United Kingdom, the Netherlands, Germany, Russia, and China. The stronger the associations between country and evaluations, the more likely the attitude should come quickly to mind

good feelings. These attitudes have increased in strength over time and can influence our behavior, sometimes without our being aware of it. Intriguingly, the more attitudes are based on emotions, the more accessible from memory they are (Rocklage & Fazio, 2018).

- *Objects toward which we have accessible attitudes are more likely to capture attention* (Roskos-Ewoldsen & Fazio, 1992). Objects that are strongly associated in memory with good or bad feelings are more likely to get noticed. Intriguingly, this has a variety of implications for advertising, as is discussed in Chapter 15.
- *Accessible attitudes serve as filters for processing information.* Attitudes that people can call up quickly from their minds influence how they interpret incoming information. An attitude cannot influence thinking if people cannot call it to mind, and attitudes based on strong linkages between the issue and feelings are more apt to be activated when people encounter the issue in real life. These attitudes should serve as filters that influence how people interpret messages.

Attitude accessibility, pioneered over 20 years ago, has become such a popular staple in social psychology that it has generated criticism as well as praise. Although intrigued by the concept, some researchers question whether accessibility has the strong effects Fazio attributes to it (Doll & Ajzen, 1992). Others have suggested that accessibility is less important than other aspects of attitude strength, such as the ways in which attitudes are mentally structured (Eagly & Chaiken, 1995). These are complex issues. Some researchers, like Fazio, believe that accessibility is the key aspect of attitude strength. Other researchers maintain that personal importance of the attitude is what differentiates strong from weak attitudes; still other scholars believe that ego-involvement is critical. (And you thought strong attitudes were simple!) Despite their differences, social psychologists agree that accessibility is an intriguing construct, with fascinating implications for information processing and persuasion.

Implicit Attitudes

Some strong attitudes are characterized by a feature not discussed thus far in the book: They are outside conscious awareness. In other words, we are not consciously aware that we harbor certain feelings about the person or issue. Consider prejudiced attitudes – instances in which people blindly hate other people from different racial, ethnic, or religious groups. Prejudiced persons do not give the despised group member much chance; the mere thought or sight of the other elicits a volcanically negative response. Consider the case of Amadou Diallo (see Figure 5.9).

Diallo, born in Guinea, worked in 1999 as a peddler selling videotapes on a sidewalk in lower Manhattan. While he was standing on the steps of his apartment building one February night, his behavior aroused the suspicion of four White plainclothes police officers wearing sweatshirts and baseball caps.

Convinced that Diallo fit the description of a serial rapist who had stalked the neighborhood a year ago, one of the policemen confronted Diallo and asked to have a word with him. Frightened, Diallo ran into a nearby building. The police followed, demanding that he take his hands out of his pockets. His hand on the doorknob, Diallo began slowly pulling an object from his pocket, an object that looked unmistakably to the officers like the slide of a black gun. Fearing for their lives, the officers opened fire. It was only when they examined Diallo's dead body and looked at his open palm that they could see the object up close. It was a wallet. Diallo, the dark-skinned immigrant, perhaps thinking the police wanted to see his ID, had reached for a wallet.

Figure 5.9 Amadou Diallo, a Dark-Skinned Immigrant, May Have Automatically Evoked Implicit Stereotyped Attitudes on a February Night in Manhattan, Leading to Tragic Consequences

Image courtesy of the Associated Press

Had the policemen, in that split second when impressions are formed and attitudes jell, misperceived Diallo based on stereotypes of his race? Had they categorized him as Black and therefore, at lightning-quick speed, accessed a negative attitude that led them to infer he was a criminal ready to gun them down? Perhaps. Did the same unconscious bias operate more recently, in March 2018, when an unarmed Black man, Stephen Clark, was fatally shot holding a cell phone in his grandmother's home in Sacramento by officers who read racial prejudice into the cell phone Clark carried (Baker, 2018)? What about similar tragic instances when White police officers fatally shot unarmed Blacks in Ferguson, Missouri, Staten Island New York, and North Charleston, South Carolina?

We can't say for sure; there were a variety of complex factors operating. Police officers are in the line of fire and they have been gunned down for just doing their jobs. We need to be careful about assuming that violence is caused by unconscious biases. But certainly these cases, when considered in light of what we know about the power of implicit attitudes, raise troubling questions (Eberhardt, 2019). They highlight the power of implicit attitudes. *Implicit attitudes* are defined as:

> evaluations that (a) have an unknown origin (i.e., people are unaware of the basis of their evaluation); (b) are activated automatically; and (c) influence implicit responses, namely uncontrollable responses and ones that people do not view as an expression of their attitude and thus do not attempt to control.
>
> (Wilson, Lindsey, & Schooler, 2000, p. 104)

Implicit attitudes are habitual; they emerge automatically, in the absence of conscious thought and can be measured through subtle psychological measures (see Chapter 7). Implicit attitudes are likely formed at an early age. As early as six years of age, White children display a pro-White, anti-Black evaluation (Baron & Banaji, 2006). In fairness, as children grow up, they learn about the prejudice African Americans faced in this country and are exposed to egalitarian role models. This encourages the development of favorable attitudes toward people of different racial groups. What happens to the implicit, negative evaluation acquired at an early age? Some psychologists argue that it persists, even coexists, with a positive attitude toward the ethnic group.

Timothy D. Wilson and colleagues (2000) argue that people have *dual attitudes*: An explicit attitude that operates on a conscious level and guides much everyday behavior, and an implicit attitude that influences non-verbal behaviors and other responses over which we lack total control.

The implicit attitude can be activated automatically, perhaps in highly charged emotional situations in which the individual is not able to keep feelings at bay. This may have happened to the police officers who confronted Amadou Diallo that cold February night, as well other unarmed African American men more recently.

There is much discussion about these issues among scholars and in the academic journals. One problem is that the implicit attitude notion is somewhat vague. Critics point out that all attitudes may not have dual components; a moderately held pro-environmental attitude may operate only on the conscious level. It may lack the preconscious primitive dimension. It is also possible that people don't have dual attitudes at all, but instead have one rather complex attitude that contains aspects they are aware of and others that elude conscious awareness. Pulling different ideas together, Albarracín and her colleagues (2019) note that implicit attitudes refer to initial, spontaneous, less-than-conscious affective processes, while explicit attitudes are more deliberate, guided by goals, a desire to present oneself positively and broader values. Attitudes being complex, changing implicit attitudes does not always produce changes in everyday, explicit behavior on issues like race (Forscher et al., 2019).

There is much that we need to know about implicit attitudes and how dual attitudes operate. For now, these new approaches provide new insights on strong attitudes. They suggest that when people harbor highly prejudiced attitudes, the negative, gut-level feelings acquired at a young age can overwhelm or override social norms or positive attitudes acquired later. Hateful attitudes may be impervious to influence because they are so much a part of the individual or because the person is not aware of the depths of prejudice. This raises troubling questions for those of us who believe in persuasion. To what degree can prejudice be unlearned? Can positive attitudes, formed by newly acquired associations between race and favorable attributes, override the negative feelings learned at a young age (Forscher et al., 2019)? Can people be taught to recognize stereotypes within themselves (like the assumption that tall African Americans are on a football team or rural Whites are staunch Republicans) and replace them with non-biased beliefs (Devine et al., 2012)? Or, when stereotypes turn to hardened prejudice and prejudice morphs into hate, is argumentation powerless? Can people who hate ever change their minds?

Priming

The latter questions suggest interesting, important intersections between persuasion and implicit attitudes, particularly those rooted in prejudice. The key concept here is priming. *Priming*, in its most general form, involves the impact of a prior stimulus or message on reactions to a subsequent stimulus or message (e.g., Roskos-Ewoldsen, Klinger, & Roskos-Ewoldsen, 2007; Roskos-Ewoldsen et al., 2009).

As David Roskos-Ewoldsen and his colleagues helpfully note, the process is analogous to priming a well: The act of priming allows the well to generate water when it is later pumped. In the psychological arena, a prime contained in a first message serves as the wellspring, so to speak, of responses to the second message. Priming thus occurs when exposure to an initial stimulus increases the salience and accessibility of thoughts and feelings psychologically related to that stimulus. Priming is an automatic process, about which individuals may be relatively oblivious, one that involves little thinking and frequently operates on a level below conscious awareness (Bargh & Williams, 2006). In this sense, it differs from ideas like reasoned action theory (Chapter 6) and central processing (Chapter 8) that focus on more conscious consideration of persuasive messages. Priming is relevant to many aspects of social influence, but is most germane to persuasion in cases when messages access strong attitudes involving racial and political prejudice. It is intriguingly relevant to contemporary life, where captivating, inflammatory messages circulate around the Internet, stoking biases among individuals who gravitate to polarizing social media sites.

Priming evolved from cognitive psychological research that examined how information was represented in memory. It emphasizes that information is encoded in memory by nodes that represent concepts, which are in turn related to other concepts by associative pathways in the mind. When concepts are activated or primed, they spread their meaning, like wildfire through a forest, to related nodes, conferring powerful meanings and emotionally packed associations.

From a persuasion perspective, primes qualify as intentional attempts to influence in political ads that contain deliberately inserted racially or otherwise coded associational messages. In instances where the presence of an unarmed minority male primes prejudiced feelings on the part of police officers that lead, in extreme cases, to police violence, one can't say that this is a case of persuasion per se; the racial cue did not represent a deliberate attempt to persuade. It is instead an example of social influence, broadly defined. In addition, priming cues, visuals, and verbal messages can have negative repercussions, as in prejudice, and positive effects, as when they elicit prideful patriotism. There is scholarly discussion about the level of consciousness required for priming effects to occur; the extent to which priming occurs for all attitudes, or primarily strong attitudes; and tendency to conflate myths of subliminal advertising impact with priming, the latter a bona fide phenomenon.

Research Evidence

A host of studies have applied priming to activation of social stereotypes. Political messages have deliberately, but subtly, employed racially coded themes, linking Central American migrants with crime and disease via words or pictures, or employed fake images of immigrants entering the United Kingdom illegally. By priming racial stereotypes, calling them to mind at a preconscious level, persuasive messages can help access deep-seated attitudes, in some cases propelling people to vote for candidates who implicitly or explicitly embrace prejudiced ideas (Mendelberg, 2001, 2008; Valentino, Hutchings, & White, 2002). (Note that it's not just stereotypes about minorities; candidates could also prime class, gender, and stereotypes of rural White Americans to influence voting in subtle ways.) Obviously, to the extent this happens, it is not a good or moral way to use persuasion, but, as we know, persuasion is frequently used for unsavoury purposes. Alas, as David Ewoldsen, who has done extensive research on priming, has noted, such media primes can exert strong persuasive effects in the political domain. Priming, he has argued in his substantial work in this area, can exert important effects on political and social attitudes, working through complex psychological mediators.

There are complications. First, priming can influence attitudes, but the effects are greater when primes are more intense and there is a smaller lag time between presentation of the prime and target (Carpentier, Roskos-Ewoldsen, & Roskos-Ewoldsen, 2008; Roskos-Ewoldsen et al., 2007). This makes priming ideal for the tail end of election campaigns, although negative ads that prime strong attitudes can backfire, as well as succeed. Second, primes exert stronger attitudinal effects when they resonate with meanings already in people's heads. Coded racial stereotypes work best on those who buy into racial themes – those high in prejudice who implicitly reject values of racial equality (e.g., Skinner & Cheadle, 2016, though see Goldman & Mutz, 2014). Third, subtle racial appeals typically operate on implicit attitudes that people aren't always aware of.

Applications

Priming is rich in implications for acts of prejudice, though we have to be careful in assuming that the primes exerted a causal impact in the absence of hard evidence. Still, the applications are intriguing. Priming helps explain how anti-Semitic extremist posts can activate prejudices among individuals harboring virulently negative attitudes toward Jews, contributing to an increase in anti-Semitic attacks in Germany, Europe, and in synagogues across the United States (Schuetze, 2019). Equally ominously, priming offers an explanation of how racist, virulent White nationalist messages on online message boards like 8chan can stoke hate, perhaps propelling followers, like the suspect in the 2019 El Paso massacre, who announced that the attack "is a response to the Hispanic invasion of Texas," to commit violent atrocities (Baker & Shear, 2019, p. 1). The word "invasion" was also widely used in right-wing media outlets to disparage Central American migrants illegally entering the United States (Peters, Grynbaum, Collins, & Harris, 2019). Importantly, we don't know – and probably will never know with convincing facts – that these media platforms *caused* gunmen to commit such acts of violence. Priming plausibly suggests these messages could have exerted these effects.

In one final example of social influence, priming has been richly – if sadly and controversially – studied in police contexts. There is convincing evidence that police officers primed by exposure to crime-related words like "apprehend and capture" looked more at a Black than a White face, presumably because of the time-honored stereotyped association between Blacks and criminal behavior. "Thinking about apprehending, arresting, and shooting pulled (people's) attention in the direction of the Black face," Eberhardt (2019, p. 60) noted. These and other findings suggest that there may be a prejudiced underpinning to the voluminous evidence that police are more likely to stop African American than White drivers for seemingly suspicious behaviors, although White drivers more frequently possess a firearm.

To be sure, policing is complex, can't be reduced to one trope, and police are engaged in honorable, courageous pursuits. *Importantly, criminals can also be primed by cues, as when vicious anti-police posts access criminals' deep-seated anti-police sentiments that may propel them to shoot police officers.*

On a more constructive note, priming, Fazio's approach, and Eberhardt's research broadly suggest ways of reducing prejudice by, for example, helping police appreciate unintentional implicit biases, calling attention to time-honored racial associations between race and crime, and linking minorities with positive attributes that can help extinguish implicit attitudes. Attitude change is not an easy task and can't always be achieved, but concepts rooted in an understanding of the psychology of priming implicit attitudes can help us make inroads in these problems.

A Neuroscience Approach

Building on the foregoing research, which emphasizes the powerful (sometimes non-conscious) impact of attitudes, is the *neuroscience perspective* on social behavior. Neuroscientists emphasize that attitudes have biological, as well as psychological, foundations. Articulating its core assumption, Myers (2008) explains that:

> [E]verything psychological – every idea, every mood, every urge – is simultaneously biological. We find it convenient to talk separately of biological and psychological influences, but we need to remember: To think, feel, or act without a body would be like running without legs.

(p. 35)

Neuroscience research has become a pervasive part of the cognitive and behavioral sciences over the past couple of decades. It has intriguing implications for attitudes and persuasion, and particularly interesting applications to the underpinnings of strong attitudes. It is important to first define several key terms. A *neuron* is a nerve cell, the foundation of the nervous system. Extensions of the nerve cell receive information and conduct it toward the body of the cell. The information is subsequently passed on to other neurons, glands, or muscles in an elaborate neural communication system. Chemical stimulation is fired across a synaptic junction or small gap between a sending and receiving neuron. Neurons in essence talk with each other at these synaptic gaps, facilitating information processing.

At the foundation of all mental activity is the brain, the bundle of neurons that makes possible the human mind. The brain has numerous components, including a network of nerves called the reticular formation that helps control arousal; the cerebellum, which coordinates processing of sensory information and movement; and the amygdala, associated with emotions.

Neuroscientists look into the brain by magnetic resonance imaging (MRI). Using contemporary neuroscientific methodologies (see Chapter 7), scientists have gleaned new information about neural bases of different attitudes, including politics, where research finds that, in the case of strong partisans, the reasoning areas of the brain "shut down" when they are considering information inconsistent with their political positions, and emotional areas light up brightly when they process consonant information (Westen et al., 2006; see also Tavris & Aronson, 2007). In a similar fashion, attitudes toward sports, which, as we know, can be intense, animated, even violent, have neutral underpinnings. Avid fans on both sides of the century-old rivalry between the Boston Red Sox and New York Yankees displayed different brain mechanisms, depending on whether their team played well or poorly, with particularly aggressive fans showing greater neutral activity (Cikara et al., 2011).

Neuroscience research has been particularly helpful in illuminating biological bases of implicit prejudice (in which the amygdala plays a complex role that varies with context), as well as stereotyping, which is maintained by a network of neural domains, rather than one component (Amodio, Harmon-Jones, & Berkman, 2019).

Other research has tied brain activity more directly to persuasive messages. Research participants who viewed a celebrity tennis player promoting a product within his expertise – tennis shoes – exhibited stronger brain activity in the prefrontal cortex region of the brain, linked with semantic processing, than did those who saw the player promote a product outside his expertise, an alcoholic beverage (Klucharev, Smidts, & Fernández, 2008). The findings are interesting because they show that celebrities are so powerful an influence in today's society that they actually stimulate areas of the brain. Moreover, the findings show the subtlety of neural effects, as celebrities exerted stronger influences in the prefrontal cortex region when they promoted a product within their area of expertise than when they didn't.

Neuroscience research also has implications for health persuasion. In one study, 20 young adults read persuasive messages about the importance of wearing sunscreen to protect against skin cancer. They viewed the text and images on the slides while in a functional MRI scanner, which gives a snapshot of the brain's functioning and structure. Researchers assessed neural activities in regions of the brain that have been linked with psychological processes. They also obtained self-report measures of sunscreen use before and after the scanning session.

The persuasive message increased subsequent sunscreen use. Importantly, use of sunscreen was significantly associated with brain activity. Neural activity in key regions of the brain was correlated with persuasion-produced behavior change (Falk et al., 2010).

The findings do not indicate that the brain caused people to change their sunscreen use in response to the persuasive message. It could be that attitudes led to the behavioral change and brain activity reflected this. The causal relationship between the mind and brain activity is very complex. As Satel and Lilienfeld (2013) note, "specific brain structures rarely perform single tasks, so one-to-one mapping between a given region and a particular mental state is nearly impossible. In short, we can't glibly reason backward from brain activations to mental functions" (p. 13).

It is easy to become enamored of the neuroscience approach and conclude that everything boils down to the brain, and we are wired to obey our neurons. This does not reflect an accurate understanding of the neuroscience perspective. Its insight is that persuasive message effects and attitudes have biological, brain-based underpinnings. These can offer fascinating new clues about the dynamics of complex, multifaceted attitudes, particularly strong attitudes rooted in prejudice. Armed with these insights, we can gain a more comprehensive understanding of linkages between the gray matter of the brain and the emotionally laden messages that animate everyday life (e.g., Harmon-Jones & Winkielman, 2007; Weber et al., 2015).

There is also practical relevance to this research. Social media companies like Google and YouTube are increasingly using neuroscience-type studies and artificial intelligence to mimic brain activities in an effort to recommend videos that engage viewers (Roose, 2019). In extreme cases when algorithms recommend socially problematic videos, it could be helpful to understand the mind's neural networks to help figure out ways to prevent susceptible viewers from being lured into these sites. Alas, we are a long, long way from conducing this type of research, as neuroscientific studies of persuasion are in their infancy, with many questions remaining about the breadth of effects, linkage of particular neural networks with specific persuasion processes, and a host of ethical questions about how to harness knowledge of the neuroscience of attitude change in responsible ways (Cacioppo, Cacioppo, & Petty, 2017).

Conclusions

Strong attitudes are part of what make us human. They enrich, empower, and enlighten. They showcase the willingness of people to put themselves on the line for issues that cut to the core of their convictions. Strong attitudes also exemplify the darker side of human beings: Their biases, closed-mindedness, and refusal to consider alternative points of view.

Strong attitudes have a number of characteristics, including personal importance, extremity, and certainty. Social judgment theory provides many insights into the nature of strong attitudes. The social judgment approach emphasizes the ways in which people use preexisting attitudes to filter incoming messages, interpreting persuasive arguments in light of what they already believe. It calls attention to ways that ego-involved partisans assimilate and contrast messages so as to maintain their original perspective on the issue. Social judgment theory suggests that strong attitudes are exceedingly hard to change. Messages can influence attitudes if they fall within the latitude of acceptance or within areas of susceptibility in the latitude of non-commitment. Communications that land in these areas and are perceived as congenial with the individual's initial attitude can produce attitude change. Messages that fall within the latitude of rejection are contrasted, assumed to be more discrepant from the individual's own attitude than they actually are, and are typically rejected. When people are ego-involved or care a lot about the issue, they tend to accept only those positions that are highly congenial with initial beliefs, and they reject messages that appear to lie outside their psychological comfort zones.

Strong attitudes are not without merit. They help us defend against unpleasant ideas and impel people to passionately speak out for causes, movements, and path-breaking political ideologies. But they also blind us to alternative positions, leading to selective perception, selective exposure, confirmatory biases, and resistance to change. They blind us to factual data that offer alternative views, prevent us from considering information that disconfirms our attitude, and, in cases like opposition to vaccines, can cause people to take actions that are antithetical to public health. Preexisting biases are the dark side of strong attitudes, and persuasion scholars have suggested several ways to overcome these biases, difficult as it psychologically can be.

Fazio's accessibility approach also sheds light on the nature of strong attitudes. Strong attitudes – toward religion, ethnicity, and even a favorite sports team – are characterized by well-learned associations between the object and an evaluation. These attitudes are usually so strong and enduring – or chronically accessible – that people can call them up automatically from memory. The more frequently people rehearse linkages between an object and a positive association – for example, between chocolate and memories of delicacy – the stronger their love of chocolate. Conversely, the more frequently one repeats negative associations – between chicken gizzards and disgust – the stronger the negative attitude. In this way, positive attitudes – from adoration of food to love of country – as well as negative attitudes – to both food and my country's "enemies" – inexorably develop.

Biased thinking is also likely when people harbor strong implicit attitudes, or those excluded from total awareness. Priming is one of the psychological processes that operates outside, or partly in the shady borders below, conscious awareness, making it one of the persuasion-related approaches that tap into political or racial attitudes virtually automatically. Priming effects are greater under particular conditions, notably when primes are more intense and attitudes are stronger, as well as easier to access. With its emphasis on accessing of attitudes simply and provocatively, priming has intriguing implications for political communication and prejudice, shedding light on how communications can exert subtle, sometimes disturbing, effects in areas ranging from presidential politics to police shootings. It is particularly relevant to our fragmented social media age, when toxic messages diffuse widely, tapping instantly and algorithmically into the views of prejudiced individuals.

Illuminating the biological basis of these attitudes, neuroscience studies suggest that strong attitudes have a different neurological foundation from weaker attitudes. A neuroscience approach has shed light on attitudes, identifying the biological underpinnings of strong affective evaluations, including activation in the portion of the brain involved in processing threatening information. However, direction of causation remains elusive. We can't say whether brain activity is a cause or effect of strong attitudes, only that strong implicit and political attitudes are accompanied by neural activity, sometimes centering on the amygdala. This is important, but we need to steer clear of a reductionist approach that says the brain causes people to display strong attitudes and the best way to change behavior is to manipulate the brain, in the style of the old movie, *A Clockwork Orange*. Brain, mind, and message intersect in many complex, as yet unknown ways.

As the chapter has emphasized, theory and research on strong attitudes have many practical applications. They can shed light on why partisans disagree so vehemently about contemporary social issues. Partisans size up the problem differently, perceive matters in a biased manner, and tend to be resistant to persuasive communication. Ethicists suggest that if we could just supply people with the facts, they would put aside opinions and act rationally (Frankena, 1963). Unfortunately, there are no such things as pure facts. Partisans come to the table with different interpretations of the facts. Just bringing people from different sides together cannot guarantee that they will reach agreement. This is why negotiations on issues ranging from labor–management disputes to the Middle East frequently fail.

This fact – that objective facts frequently elude us and biased perceptions are the order of the day – has become a ubiquitous part of contemporary culture. Of course, this raises the specter that one can never change strong attitudes. And, to be sure, people with strong attitudes are loath to change them, as a result of selective perception and the host of social judgment biases discussed in this chapter. But pessimists do not always have the last word.

Communications have changed strongly held attitudes on a host of topics, from high-cholesterol junk food to ethnic prejudice. Persuasion research holds out a key. Persuaders may be able to nudge people into changing their attitudes if they understand the structure, functions, and underlying dynamics of these attitudes. If communicators can help partisans from opposing groups just appreciate, rather than deny, the other side's emotion-packed attitudes, look for commonalities rather than differences, and try to build a common identity, baby steps toward reconciliation can be taken (Ellis, 2006). There is no guarantee that change will occur, but it is certainly more likely if communicators appreciate the psychology of the individuals they hope to influence.

References

Abrams, S. J., & Fiorina, M. P. (2012). "The Big Sort" that wasn't: A skeptical reexamination. *PS: Political Science & Politics, 45*, 203–210.

Albarracín, D., Chan, M.-P. S., & Jiang, D. (2019). Attitudes and attitude change: Social and personality considerations about specific and general patterns of behavior. In K. Deaux & M. Snyder (Eds.), *The Oxford handbook of personality and social psychology* (2nd ed., pp. 439–463). New York: Oxford University Press.

Amodio, D. M., Harmon-Jones, E., & Berkman, E. T. (2019). Neuroscience approaches in social and personality psychology. In K. Deaux & M. Snyder (Eds.), *The Oxford handbook of personality and social psychology* (pp. 97–131). New York: Oxford University Press.

Baker, A. (2018, July 16). Confronting bias for everyone's safety. *The New York Times*, A17.

Baker, P., & Shear, M. D. (2019, August 5). In Texas gunman's manifesto, an echo of Trump's language. *The New York Times*, A1, A15.

Bandura, A. (1971). Analysis of modeling processes. In A. Bandura (Ed.), *Psychological modeling: Conflicting theories* (pp. 1–62). Chicago, IL: Aldine-Atherton.

Bargh, J. A., & Williams, E. L. (2006). The automaticity of social life. *Current Directions in Psychological Science, 15*, 1–4.

Baron, A. S., & Banaji, M. R. (2006). The development of implicit attitudes: Evidence of race evaluations from ages 6 and 10 and adulthood. *Psychological Science, 17*, 53–58.

Bishop, B. (with R. G. Cushing) (2008). *The big sort: Why the clustering of like-minded America is tearing us apart*. Boston, MA: Houghton-Mifflin.

Cacioppo, J. T., Cacioppo, S., & Petty, R. E. (2017). The neuroscience of persuasion: A review with an emphasis on issues and opportunities. *Social Neuroscience, 13*, 129–172.

Carpentier, F. R., Roskos-Ewoldsen, D. R., & Roskos-Ewoldsen, B. B. (2008). A test of the network models of political priming. *Media Psychology, 11*, 186–206.

Casselman, B., & Tankersley, J. (2018, June 16). Is the state of the economy rosy or bleak? That depends on your politics. *The New York Times*, B1, B5.

Cikara, M., Botvinick, M. M., & Fiske, S. T. (2011). Us versus them: Social identity shapes neutral responses to intergroup competition and harm. *Psychological Science, 22*, 306–313.

Cohn, N. (2014, June 12). Polarization: It's everywhere. *The New York Times*, A3.

Danylko, R. (2015, November 29). Experts differ on the evidence: Analysts hired by family say shooting was "unreasonable". *The Plain Dealer*, A1, A4.

de Freytas-tamura, K. (2019, June 15). Vaccine scepticism takes root at progressive schools. *The New York Times*, A18.

Devine, P. G., Forscher, P. S., Austin, A. J., & Cox, W. T. L. (2012). Long-term reduction in implicit race bias: A prejudice habit-breaking intervention. *Journal of Experimental Social Psychology, 48*, 1267–1278.

Doll, J., & Ajzen, I. (1992). Accessibility and stability of predictors in the theory of planned behavior. *Journal of Personality and Social Psychology, 63*, 754–765.

Eagly, A. H., & Chaiken, S. (1993). *The psychology of attitudes*. Fort Worth, TX: Harcourt, Brace, Jovanovich.

Eagly, A. H., & Chaiken, S. (1995). Attitude strength, attitude structure, and resistance to change. In R. E. Petty & J. A. Krosnick (Eds.), *Attitude strength: Antecedents and consequences* (pp. 413–432). Hillsdale, NJ: Lawrence Erlbaum Associates.

Eberhardt, J. L. (2019). *Biased: Uncovering the hidden prejudice that shapes what we see, think, and do*. New York: Viking.

Edwards, K., & Smith, E. E. (1996). A disconfirmation bias in the evaluation of arguments. *Journal of Personality and Social Psychology, 71*, 5–24.

Ellis, D. G. (2006). *Transforming conflict: Communication and ethnopolitical conflict*. Lanham, MD: Rowman & Littlefield.

Falk, E. B., Berkman, E. T., Mann, T., Harrison, B., & Lieberman, M. D. (2010). Predicting persuasion-induced behavior change from the brain. *Journal of Neuroscience, 30*, 8421–8424.

Fazio, R. H. (1990). Multiple processes by which attitudes guide behavior: The MODE model as an integrative framework. In M. P. Zanna (Ed.), *Advances in experimental social psychology* (Vol. 23, pp. 75–109). San Diego, CA: Academic Press.

Fazio, R. H. (1995). Attitudes as object-evaluation associations: Determinants, consequences, and correlates of attitude accessibility. In R. E. Petty & J. A. Krosnick (Eds.), *Attitude strength: Antecedents and consequences* (pp. 247–282). Hillsdale, NJ: Lawrence Erlbaum Associates.

Fazio, R. H. (2000). Accessible attitudes as tools for object appraisal: Their costs and benefits. In G. R. Maio & J. M. Olson (Eds.), *Why we evaluate: Functions of attitudes* (pp. 1–36). Mahwah, NJ: Lawrence Erlbaum Associates.

Forscher, P. S., Lai, C. K., Axt, J. R., Ebersole, C. R., Herman, M., Devine, P. G., & Nosek, B. A. (2019). A meta-analysis of procedures to change implicit measures. *Journal of Personality and Social Psychology*. Retrieved June 24, 2019, from http://dx.doi.org/10.1037/pspa0000160

Frankena, W. (1963). *Ethics*. Englewood Cliffs, NJ: Prentice Hall.

Frey, D. (1986). Recent research on selective exposure to information. In L. Berkowitz (Ed.), *Advances in experimental social psychology* (Vol. 19, pp. 41–80). Orlando, FL: Academic Press.

Frimer, J. A., Skitka, L. J., & Motyl, M. (2017). Liberals and conservatives are similarly motivated to avoid exposure to one another's opinions. *Journal of Experimental Social Psychology, 72*, 1–12.

Goldman, S. K., & Mutz, D. C. (2014). *The Obama effect: How the 2008 campaign changed white racial attitudes*. New York: Russell Sage Foundation.

González-Bailón, S. (2017). *Decoding the social world: Data science and the unintended consequences of communication*. Cambridge, MA: MIT Press.

Gopnik, A. (2015, May 4). Trollope trending. *The New Yorker*, 28–32.

Granberg, D. (1993). Political perception. In S. Iyengar & W. J. McGuire (Eds.), *Explorations in political psychology* (pp. 70–112). Durham, NC: Duke University Press.

Harmon-Jones, E., & Winkielman, P. (2007). A brief overview of social neuroscience. In E. Harmon-Jones & P. Winkielman (Eds.), *Social neuroscience: Integrating biological and psychological explanations of social behavior* (pp. 3–11). New York: Guilford.

Hart, W., Albarracín, D., Eagly, A. H., Brechan, I., Lindberg, M. J., & Merrill, L. (2009). Feeling validated versus being correct: A meta-analysis of selective exposure to information. *Psychological Bulletin, 135*, 555–588.

Hastorf, A., & Cantril, H. (1954). They saw a game: A case study. *Journal of Abnormal and Social Psychology, 49*, 129–134.

Holbrook, A. L., Berent, M. K., Krosnick, J. A., Visser, P. S., & Boninger, D. S. (2005). Attitude importance and the accumulation of attitude-relevant knowledge in memory. *Journal of Personality and Social Psychology, 88*, 749–769.

Hovland, C. I., Harvey, O. J., & Sherif, M. (1957). Assimilation and contrast effects in reactions to communication and attitude change. *Journal of Abnormal and Social Psychology, 55*, 244–252.

Interlandi, J., (2019, June 3). When defending vaccines gets ugly. *The New York Times*, A20.

Iyengar, S., & Hahn, K. S. (2009). Red media, blue media: Evidence of ideological selectivity in media use. *Journal of Communication, 59*, 19–39.

Jang, S. M. (2014). Challenges to selective exposure: Selective seeking and avoidance in a multitasking media environment. *Mass Communication & Society, 17*, 665–688.

Kahan, D. M., Peters, E., Dawson, E. C., & Slovic, P. (2017). Motivated numeracy and enlightened self-government. *Behavioural Public Policy, 1*, 54–86.

Kinch, M. (2018). *Between hope and fear: A history of vaccines and human immunity*. New York: Pegasus Books.

Kingsbury, A. (2019, August 17). It's too late to ban assault weapons. *The New York Times*, A22.

Kleinfield, N. R. (2000, October 19). It's root, root, root, but for which team? *The New York Times*, A1, C27.

Klucharev, V., Smidts, A., & Fernández, G. (2008). Brain mechanisms of persuasion: How "expert power" modulates memory and attitudes. *Social Cognitive and Affective Neuroscience, 3*, 353–366.

Krosnick, J. A., & MacInnis, B. (2015). Fox and not-Fox television news impact on opinions on global warming: Selective exposure, not motivated reasoning. In J. P. Forgas, K. Fiedler, & W. D. Crano (Eds.), *Social psychology and politics* (pp. 75–90). New York: Routledge.

Krosnick, J. A., & Petty, R. E. (1995). Attitude strength: An overview. In R. E. Petty & J. A. Krosnick (Eds.), *Attitude strength: Antecedents and consequences* (pp. 1–24). Hillsdale, NJ: Lawrence Erlbaum Associates.

Kunda, Z. (1990). The case for motivated reasoning. *Psychological Bulletin, 108*, 480–498.

Lehman, S. (2014, January 8). The bitter debate over gun laws. [Letter to the Editor]. *The New York Times*, A20.

Lord, C. G., Lepper, M. R., & Preston, E. (1984). Considering the opposite: A corrective strategy for social judgment. *Journal of Personality and Social Psychology, 47,* 1231–1243.

Lord, C. G., Ross, L., & Lepper, M. R. (1979). Biased assimilation and attitude polarization: The effects of prior theories on subsequently considered evidence. *Journal of Personality and Social Psychology, 37,* 2098–2109.

Madrigal, A. C. (2019, February 27). The small, small world of Facebook's anti-vaxxers. *The Atlantic.* Retrieved May 26, 2019, from www.theatlantic.com/health/archive/2019/02/anti-vaxx–fac

Manjoo, F. (2015, May 8). Facebook finds opposing views trickle through. *The New York Times*, A1, B7.

Mendelberg, T. (2001). *The race card: Campaign strategy, implicit messages, and the norm of equality.* Princeton, NJ: Princeton University Press.

Mendelberg, T. (2008). Racial priming revived. *Perspectives on Politics, 6,* 109–123.

Mill, J. S. (1859/2009). *On liberty and other essays.* New York: Kaplan publishing.

Miller, A. G., McHoskey, J. W., Bane, C. M., & Dowd, T. G. (1993). The attitude polarization phenomenon: Role of response measure, attitude extremity, and behavioral consequences of reported attitude change. *Journal of Personality and Social Psychology, 64,* 561–574.

Mutz, D. C. (2006). *Hearing the other side: Deliberative versus participatory democracy.* Cambridge, UK: Cambridge University Press.

Myers, D. G. (2008). *Exploring psychology* (7th ed.). New York: Worth Publishers.

Nyhan, B. (2015, October 16). Team affiliation affects opinions on deflation. *The New York Times*, B13.

O'Keefe, D. J. (2016). *Persuasion: Theory and research* (3rd ed.). Thousand Oaks, CA: Sage.

Pager, T. (2019, April 10). "Monkey, rat and pig DNA": Vaccine fear drive a measles surge. *The New York Times*, A1, A19.

Pennycook, G., & Rand, D. G. (2018). Lazy, not biased: Susceptibility to partisan fake news is better explained by lack of reasoning than by motivated reasoning. *Cognition.* Retrieved May 24, 2019, from https://doi.org/10.1016/j.cognition.2018.06.011

Peters, J. W. (2018, August 20). In a divided era, political anger is all each side has in common. *The New York Times*, A12.

Peters, J. W. (2019, October 22). Trump's base is steadfast even as troubles mount. *The New York Times*, A17.

Peters, J. W., Grynbaum, M. M., Collins, K., & Harris, R. (2019, August 12). How the El Paso gunman echoed the words of right-wing pundits. *The New York Times*, A1, A14.

Pronin, E., Lin, D. Y., & Ross, L. (2002). The bias blind spot: Perceptions of bias in self versus others. *Personality and Social Psychology Bulletin, 28,* 369–381.

Reyna, V. F., & Brainerd, C. J. (1995). Fuzzy-trace theory: An interim synthesis. *Learning & Individual Differences, 7,* 1–75.

Rocklage, M. D., & Fazio, R. H. (2018). Attitude accessibility as a function of emotionality. *Personality and Social Psychology Bulletin, 44,* 508–520.

Roose, K. (2019, June 9). The making of a YouTube radical. *The New York Times*, 1, 20–21.

Roskos-Ewoldsen, D. R. (1997). Attitude accessibility and persuasion: Review and a transactive model. In B. R. Burleson (Ed.), *Communication Yearbook* (Vol. 20, pp. 185–225). Beverly Hills, CA: Sage.

Roskos-Ewoldsen, D. R., Arpan-Ralstin, L., & St. Pierre, J. (2002). Attitude accessibility and persuasion: The quick and the strong. In J. P. Dillard & M. Pfau (Eds.), *The persuasion handbook: Developments in theory and practice* (pp. 39–61). Thousand Oaks, CA: Sage.

Roskos-Ewoldsen, D. R., & Fazio, R. H. (1992). On the orienting value of attitudes: Attitude accessibility as a determinant of an object's attraction of visual attention. *Journal of Personality and Social Psychology, 63*, 198–211.

Roskos-Ewoldsen, D. R., Klinger, M. R., & Roskos-Ewoldsen, B. (2007). Media priming: A meta-analysis. In R. W. Preiss, B. M. Gayle, N. Burrell, M. Allen, & J. Bryant (Eds.), *Mass media effects research* (pp. 53–80). Mahwah, NJ: Erlbaum Associates.

Roskos-Ewoldsen, D. R., Roskos-Ewoldsen, B., & Carpentier, F. D. (2009). Media priming: An updated synthesis. In J. Bryant & M. B. Oliver (Eds.), *Media effects: Advances in theory and research* (3rd ed., pp. 74–93). New York: Routledge.

Sandomir, R. (2011, June 15). Critic of James has a happy ending for his book. *The New York Times*, B14.

Satel, S., & Lilienfeld, S. O. (2013). *Brainwashed: The seductive appeal of mindless neuroscience*. New York: Basic Books.

Schuetze, C. (2019, May 14). Anti-Semitic crime rises in Germany, and Far Right is blamed. *The New York Times*. Retrieved May 31, 2019, from www.nytimes.com/2019/05/14/world/europe-anti-semitic

Shear, M. D., & Fandos, N. (2019, October 23). Trump tied to inquiries, envoy says. *The New York Times*, A1, A14.

Sherif, C. W., Sherif, M., & Nebergall, R. E. (1965). *Attitude and attitude change: The social judgment-involvement approach*. Philadelphia, PA: W. B. Saunders.

Sherif, M., & Sherif, C. W. (1967). Attitude as the individual's own categories: The social judgment-involvement approach to attitude and attitude change. In C. W. Sherif & M. Sherif (Eds.), *Attitude, ego-involvement, and change* (pp. 105–139). New York: Wiley.

Singer, N., & Confessore, N. (2018, October 22). Let's talk politics. No liberals allowed. *The New York Times*, B1, B3.

Skinner, A. L., & Cheadle, J. E. (2016). The "Obama Effect"? Priming contemporary racial milestones increases implicit racial bias among Whites. *Social Cognition, 34*, 544–558.

Somaiya, R. (2014, January 5). Banished for questioning the gospel of guns. *The New York Times*, 1, 17.

Sommer, W. (2018, July 25). Facebook won't stop dangerous anti-vaccine hoaxes from spreading. *The Daily Beast*. Retrieved May 27, 2019, from www.thedailybeast.com/facebook-wont-stop-dangerous-anti

Stansberry, K., & DiRusso, C. (2016). UnVaxxed: A cultural study of the online anti-vaccination movement. *Paper presented to the annual convention of the Association for Education in Journalism & Mass Communication*, Minneapolis, MI.

Tavris, C., & Aronson, E. (2007). *Mistakes were made (but not by me): Why we justify foolish beliefs, bad decisions, and hurtful acts*. Orlando, FL: Harcourt.

Tsang, S. J. (2019). Cognitive discrepancy, dissonance, and selective exposure. *Media Psychology, 22*, 394–417.

Tuttle, S. (2006, December 4). The elusive hunter. *Newsweek*, 50–53.

Valentino, N. A., Hutchings, V. L., & White, I. K. (2002). Cues that matter: How political ads prime racial attitudes during campaigns. *American Political Science Review, 96*, 75–90.

Wang Erber, M., Hodges, S. D., & Wilson, T. D. (1995). Attitude strength, attitude stability, and the effects of analyzing reasons. In R. E. Petty & J. A. Krosnick (Eds.), *Attitude strength: Antecedents and consequences* (pp. 433–454). Hillsdale, NJ: Lawrence Erlbaum Associates.

Weber, R., Huskey, R., Mangus, J. M., Westcott-Baker, A., & Turner, B. O. (2015). Neural predictors of message effectiveness during counterarguing in antidrug campaigns. *Communication Monographs, 82*, 4–30.

Westen, D., Blagov, P. S., Harenski, K., Kilts, C., & Hamann, S. (2006). Neural bases of motivated reasoning: An MRI study of emotional constraints on partisan political judgment in the 2004 U. S. presidential election. *Journal of Cognitive Neuroscience*, *18*, 1947–1958.

Westerwick, A., Johnson, B. K., & Knobloch-Westerwick, S. (2017). Confirmation biases in selective exposure to political online information: Source bias vs. content bias. *Communication Monographs*, *84*, 343–364.

Wilson, T. D., Lindsey, S., & Schooler, T. Y. (2000). A model of dual attitudes. *Psychological Review*, *107*, 101–126.

Wiznitzer, M. (2009, April 3). Comments on Larry King Live. CNN *Larry King Live: Jenny McCarthy and Jim Carrey discuss autism; Medical experts weigh in*. Retrieved June 4, 2019, from www.transcripts.cnn.com/TRANSCRIPTS/0904/03/lkl.01.html

Chapter 6

Attitudes

Functions and Consequences

Leslie Maltz regards herself as a California housewife, "virtually a byword for conventionality," as a magazine reporter put it (Adler, 1999, p. 76). But a while back she ventured outside her comfort zone. She had her navel pierced and put "a diamond-studded horseshoe through it." As a result, she no longer regards herself as a housewife. "I feel like a sex symbol," she says (Adler, 1999, p. 76).

Leslie's bodacious decision illustrates a theme of this chapter: Attitudes serve functions for people, and people must decide how to translate their attitudes into action. As we will see, the issues of attitude functions and attitude–behavior consistency are intricate, complicated, and filled with implications for persuasion. This chapter calls on classic theories and research, some dating back a half-century, others more recent, but all with implications for understanding the dynamics of persuasion in our own time. I follow up on the exploration of attitudes launched in Chapters 4 and 5, focusing first on attitude function theory and research. The second section examines the venerable issue of attitude–behavior consistency, more colloquially expressed as: Do people practice what they preach?

Functions of Attitudes

Functional theories of attitude examine why people hold the attitudes they do. These approaches explore the needs that attitudes fulfill and the motives they serve. Functional approaches turn attitudes on their head. Instead of taking attitudes as a given and looking at their structure, they ask: "Just what benefits do attitudes provide? What if people did not have attitudes? What then?" Bombarded by numerous stimuli and faced with countless choices about issues and products, individuals would be forced to painstakingly assess the costs and benefits of each particular choice in each of hundreds of daily decisions (Fazio, 2000). Deprived of general attitudes to help structure the environment and position individuals in certain directions, human beings would find daily life arduous. Noting that this is not the case, theorists conclude that attitudes help people manage and cope with life. In a word, attitudes are functional.

The beauty of functional theory is that it helps us understand why people hold attitudes. This not only is interesting to theorists, but also appeals to the people watcher in us all. Ever wonder why certain people are driven to dedicate their lives to helping others, why other individuals buy fancy sports cars at the zenith of their midlives, or why younger folks, in a carefree moment, decide to get themselves tattooed? Attitude function theories shed light on these decisions, and scholars like James P. Dillard (1993), and Maria Knight Lapinksi and Franklin J. Boster (2001), have long called attention to the utility of the functional approach.

Researchers have catalogued the main functions of attitudes or the primary *benefits* that attitudes provide (Katz, 1960; Maio & Olson, 2000a; Smith, Bruner, & White, 1956; see also Carpenter, Boster, & Andrews, 2013). These are not the only functions attitudes serve, but they are the ones emphasized in persuasion research. Main attitude functions include:

Knowledge

Attitudes help people make sense of the world and explain baffling events. They provide an overarching framework, one that assists individuals in cognitively coming to terms with the array of ambiguous and sometimes scary stimuli they face in everyday life. Religious attitudes fulfill this function for many people, particularly those who have experienced personal tragedies. For example, relatives of people who were killed in the September 11 attacks found comfort in "religious certainty of a hereafter. 'A plan of exultation, a plan of salvation: they both are in a better place,'" said Margaret Wahlstrom, whose mother-in-law died at the World Trade Center (Clines, 2001, p. B8).

Utilitarian

On a more material level, attitudes help people obtain rewards and avoid punishments. Smart but mathematically challenged students say that it is functional to develop a positive attitude toward statistics courses. They figure that if they show enthusiasm, the professor will like them more. They also recognize that if they look on the bright side of the course, they can more easily muster the motivation to study. On the other hand, if they decide at the outset to blow off the course because it's too hard, they will deprive themselves of the chance to prove themselves up to the task. In a similar vein, athletes find it functional to develop a positive – rather than hostile – attitude toward a tough coach. A positive attitude can help them get along with the "drill sergeant type," thereby minimizing the chances they will earn the coach's wrath.

Social Adjustive

We all like to be accepted by others. Attitudes help us "adjust to" reference groups. People sometimes adopt attitudes not because they truly agree with the advocated position, but rather because they believe they will be more accepted by others if they take this side. For example, a student who wants to get along with a musically hip group of friends may find it functional to adopt a more favorable attitude toward alternative bands. Or teenagers, who don't have strong attitudes on the issue of global warming, may join the climate change cause to reap social approval from friends with strong passions on this issue.

Social Identity

People hold attitudes to communicate who they are and what that they aspire to be (Shavitt & Nelson, 2000). This is one reason people buy certain products; they hope that by displaying the product in their homes (or on their bodies), they will communicate something special about themselves. Women wear perfumes like Obsession and men don Polo cologne to communicate that they have money and brains (Twitchell, 1999). Others buy T-shirts with the names of brand-name stores (Hard Rock Café) or dates of rock band tours to tell passersby something of their identity ("I'm not just an ordinary student; I'm with the band. See my shirt?").

For other individuals, tattoos are personal, deeply meaningful ways of expressing who they are, both to themselves and others. There are so many creative ways that tattoos can fulfill a social identity function. They help people enhance a sense of uniqueness or express a group identity. As one woman said:

> I see tattooing as crafting your body into a piece of moving art. Look at my arms ... what is naturally attractive about a blank arm? Place a beautiful piece of art on your arm and it becomes something unique ... Tattooing might be our generation's call to be aware of artistic bodies.
>
> (Atkinson, 2004, p. 133)

Products other than tattoos, T-shirts, and perfume can fulfill social identity functions. Electronic products can do this too. In one study, young Australians maintained that their cell phones "were part of them" (Paul, 2011).

These days, iPhones and smartphones have come to play such a key social identity function for young adults that they "can feel less like devices than like extensions of their hands" (Lovett, 2014, p. 23). With their treasure trove of prized photos, texts, and friends' phone numbers, cell phones have become such personally important aspects of self that people will risk life and limb to retrieve them when they are lost (Lovett, 2014).

Value-Expressive

Another important reason people hold attitudes is to express core values and cherished beliefs. People oppose gun control laws because they fear these regulations will thwart the value they place on freedom. Others endorse affirmative action to promote egalitarian policies (Maio and Olson, 2000b). The value-expressive function is pervasive. Some young people pierce their noses, tongues, belly buttons, or ... well, other body parts to express a variety of values, including autonomy and independence from parents (see Figure 6.1).

Ego-defensive

Attitudes can serve as a "defense" against unpleasant emotions people do not want to consciously acknowledge. People adopt attitudes to shield them from psychologically uncomfortable truths. Let's say a young woman decides to break up with her boyfriend, realizing that the relationship is not going anywhere and fearing he will dump her when they go their separate ways after college. She still has feelings for her soon-to-be-ex, but to defend against these feelings and to make her position known to him clearly and with conviction, she declares in no uncertain terms that their relationship is over, kaput. Adopting a hostile attitude toward her boyfriend is functional because it helps her muster the strength she needs to call off the romance.

The ego-defensive function is so basic that it comes up in many other situations, some freighted, political, and ironic. The writer Nikole Hannah-Jones related that her father, an African American man born into a Mississippi family of sharecroppers, in a county that had lynched more Blacks than any other Mississippi county, regularly flew an American flag in their front yard, even replacing it "as soon as it showed the slightest tatter" (Hannah-Jones, 2019, p. 16). He signed up for the Army, hoping that "if he served his country, his country might finally treat him as an American" (Hannah-Jones, 2019, p. 16). His daughter could never understand why her father, having endured violent apartheid-like treatment as a child, could embrace the symbol of the country that had abused him.

Figure 6.1 Body Piercing Is Popular Among Young People. It does different things for different people, or fulfills diverse psychological functions
Photograph by William C. Rieter

Perhaps her dad, feeling understandably defensive about his own identity in the deeply prejudiced United States of his youth, flew the flag to showcase that he really was an American, despite the refusal of so many of his compatriots to convey this rudimentary respect. Hannah-Jones suggests she ultimately came to respect her father's ironic embrace of his country, showcasing the way he, like so many other Black Americans, defied the racist norms of the larger culture, developing a distinctive cultural identity, self-expression, and patriotic attitude that led them to "become the most American of all" (p. 26). Thus, the functional approach offers a special insight into the nature of attitudes, while also pointing up broader implications.

Attitudes and Persuasion

A central principle of functional theory is that the same attitudes can serve different functions for different people. In other words, different people can hold the same attitude toward a person, product, or issue; however, they may harbor this view for very different reasons.

Consider attitudes toward shopping. Some people shop for utilitarian reasons. They trek to the mall to happily purchase presents for loved ones and go home once the presents are paid for. Others shop for ego-defensive reasons, to help them forget about their problems or relieve stress. Recent immigrants to America sometimes shop to satisfy value-expressive needs. To these folks, America symbolizes the freedom to do as they wish. For those who grew up in economically and socially impoverished dictatorships, the notion that you can "buy what you want when and where you want it" is one of the great appeals of the United States (Twitchell, 1999, p. 23).

It's not just attitudes toward products that serve diverse psychological functions. People can be deeply religious for different reasons, become active in politics to satisfy different needs, even pursue identical career paths for vastly different motivations. It's fascinating to discover just how different individuals can be once you peel away the superficial attribute of attitude similarity. Such an insight emerges with particular clarity in research on the psychology of volunteerism.

Attitude Functions and Persuasion

Millions of Americans – as many as 89 million – annually volunteer their time and services to help sick, needy, homeless, and psychologically troubled individuals (Snyder, Clary, & Stukas, 2000). A functional theorist, moved by people's willingness to help others in need, would probe the reasons for these behavioral acts. What needs do these attitudes toward volunteering serve? Do different people have different motives? Mark Snyder and his colleagues found that people volunteer for very different reasons, including expressing values related to humanitarian concern for others; satisfying intellectual curiosity about the world, learning about people different from themselves; and gaining career-related benefits, such as new skills and professional contacts (Snyder et al., 2000, pp. 370–371).

These functions are intriguing. They also suggest ideas for how to promote pro-volunteering attitudes and behavior. *Functional theory* suggests that *a persuasive message is most likely to change an individual's attitude when the message is directed at the underlying function the attitude serves. Messages that match the function served by an attitude should be more compelling than those that are not relevant to the function addressed by the attitude*. The more that a persuasive appeal can explain how the advocated position satisfies needs important to the individual, the greater its impact is.

Thus, if you want to recruit volunteers or persuade people to continue engaging in volunteer activities, you must appreciate why individuals chose to volunteer in the first place. One message will not fit all. The message must match the motivational function served by volunteering. E. Gil Clary, Mark Snyder, and their colleagues dreamed up a study to test this hypothesis. They asked students to rate the importance of a series of reasons for volunteering. Reasons or functions included knowledge ("I can learn useful skills"), utilitarian ("I can gain prestige at school or work"), and value-expressive ("I believe someone would help me if I were ever in a similar situation") (Clary et al., 1994, p. 1133). The researchers then computed each student's responses to identify the volunteering function that was most and least important to him or her. Armed with this information, Clary and colleagues assigned individuals to watch a videotaped message that recommended involvement in volunteer activities. The message targeted a student's most important volunteer function (*matched* condition) or his or her least important function (*mismatched* condition). Each student watched either a matched or mismatched videotape.

For example, if a student said that volunteering mostly served a utilitarian function, he would watch a matched videotape that contained a utilitarian appeal: "You know, what I really like about all this is that I can make myself more marketable to employers and be a volunteer at the same time." If another student indicated that volunteering primarily fulfilled a value-expressive need, she would view a matched value-expressive video that noted: "By volunteering I get to turn my concerns into actions and make a difference in someone else's life" (Clary et al., 1994, pp. 1147–1148). Other students received *mismatched* videos (e.g., a student who volunteered for value-expressive reasons watched the utilitarian video).

Students then rated the effectiveness of the videotape. The results showed that matched messages were more persuasive than mismatched ones. Videotapes that targeted students' most important volunteering functions were more appealing than those that were directed at less important functions (see Figure 6.2). The implications are intriguing: They suggest that if we know the motives that volunteering fulfills, we can promote positive attitudes toward helping others. For a person who volunteers for value-expressive reasons, the message should emphasize how volunteering can relieve suffering or contribute to the social good. But a message like this will not cut it with an individual who pursues utilitarian goals. For this person, the message should emphasize how volunteering can enhance career

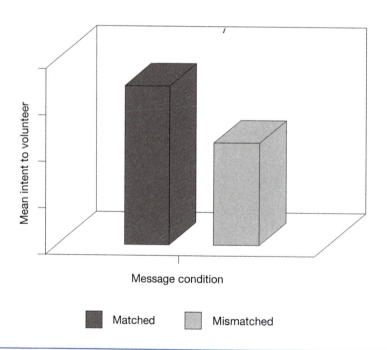

Figure 6.2 Mean Intent to Volunteer as a Function of Match of Message with Personal Motivations

From Clary et al. (1994)

skills. Idealists would find it heartless that a utilitarian message is more persuasive than an altruistic appeal. They may have a point, but such is the nature of human attitudes. To change an attitude, one must understand the function it serves and direct the message to the underlying function. This works for volunteering and other attitudes as well (Hullett, 2004, 2006; Julka & Marsh, 2005; see Box 6.1).

Of course, some scholars would note that, as persuasive as matching is, there are times when it won't work, and they are probably right. There are instances where mismatching the appeal to the function may be effective because the mismatched appeal is less psychologically threatening, or is novel (Millar & Millar, 1990). For example, if someone holds a favorable attitude toward a beer for utilitarian reasons – she likes the mellow taste – it may not be effective to suggest that another beer would deliver the same sensual feeling, because the individual is committed to her beer based on the pleasant feeling she associates with the brew. But if one offered a value-expressive reason, pointing out that her favorite beer is distributed by a company whose values the individual dislikes, she might be willing to give a competing beer a try. In general, matching message to function is the better bet, but we need to be attuned to exceptions and complexities, including the ways matching influences attitudes by working through different cognitive processes in different circumstances (Briñol & Petty, 2019; see Chapter 8).

Attitude Dysfunctions

As psychologically helpful as holding an attitude can be, there is, unfortunately, a dark side to attitude functions. An attitude that helps an individual satisfy certain needs can be detrimental in another respect. An attitude can assist the person in coping with one problem, while exerting a more harmful or dysfunctional effect in another area of the person's life. An additional complication of the functional approach is that attitudes can be functional for one person, but dysfunctional for others, as when

---

BOX 6.1

Understanding Theory: Primer on Functional Theory

1   People hold attitudes to help them cope with life.
2   Attitudes serve diverse purposes, including knowledge, utilitarian, social adjustive, social identity, value-expressive, and ego-defensive functions.
3   Two people can hold the same attitude for very different reasons.
4   An attitude can have negative or dysfunctional effects on the individual who holds the attitude, as well as on others.
5   A persuasive message is most likely to alter an attitude when the message targets the underlying function the attitude serves.
6   Functional theory offers many insights. However, it sometimes can be difficult to clearly identify the particular function an attitude serves for an individual, complicating efforts to tailor a persuasive message to a particular attitude.

yakking on a cell phone in public serves a social identity function for the yakker, but disturbs others' peace and quiet while waiting in line at the drugstore.

The foregoing discussion alerts us to several problems with the functional approach. It is hard to know whether an attitude is primarily functional or dysfunctional. If it helps the individual satisfy a need, do we call it functional, even if it has adverse consequences in other areas of the individual's life? How do we precisely weigh the benefits that the attitude provides to the individual with the negative consequences on others? It can also be difficult to identify clearly the function that an attitude serves. People may not know why they hold an attitude, lack insight into the functional bases for their attitudes, or may not want to admit that they hold an attitude for defensive reasons (Maio & Haddock, 2009). However, no theory is perfect, and on balance the functional approach is more functional than dysfunctional for persuasion scholarship! It contains hypotheses for study and generates useful insights for everyday life. These include the following nuggets:

- *People are deep and complicated creatures.* We often do things that appear inexplicable or strange, until we probe deeper and understand the needs they satisfy.
- *We should extend tolerance to others.* People have many reasons for holding an attitude. These may not be our motivations, but they can be subjectively important to that particular person.
- *Persuaders must be acutely sensitive to the functions attitudes serve.* "What warms one ego, chills another," Gordon Allport observed (1945, p. 127). A message can change attitudes only if it connects with people's needs. One may totally disagree with a person's attitude, believing it to be immoral. However, condemning the other may be less useful than probing why the individual feels the way he or she does and gently nudging the individual toward change.

Attitudes and Behavior

- Kelly has strong values, but you wouldn't guess this by observing her in everyday situations. She is charming, likeable, and adept at getting along with different kinds of people. Her friends sometimes call her a chameleon. Yet Kelly has strong views on certain issues, notably the environment and protecting endangered species. At a party, conversation turns to politics and several people advocate drilling for oil in the Arctic National Wildlife Refuge. Will Kelly take issue with their position?
- Susan is an agnostic, a skeptic who has doubts about the existence of God, and believes religion is of little use in today's society. She is a strong believer in Darwinian evolution, a forceful critic of creationist philosophy. At the same time, Susan has a soft spot for religion because it means a lot to her dad. An old friend of her dad's calls one day. He's been teaching Sunday school, but will be out of town next week when the class is scheduled to discuss the beauty of God's creation of the universe. He asks whether Susan would mind filling in for him just this once. Will Susan agree?

What is your best guess? Do these anecdotes remind you of people you know or conflicts you've experienced? These two examples are fictitious, but are based on factors studied in actual psychological experiments. They also focus on a central issue in attitude research – the connection between attitudes and behavior. The question is of theoretical and practical importance.

Theoretically, attitudes are assumed to predispose people to behave in certain ways. For example, suppose we found that attitudes had no impact on behavior. There would be less reason to study attitudes in depth. We would be better advised to spend our time exploring behavior. From a practitioner's perspective, attitudes are important only if they predict behavior. Who cares what consumers think about fast food or fast cars if their attitudes don't forecast what they buy? On the other hand, if attitudes do forecast behavior, it becomes useful for marketers to understand people's attitudes toward commercial products. Then there's us. The people watcher – intuitive psychologist – in us all is intrigued by the attitude–behavior relationship. We can all think of times when we did not practice what we preached. You probably know people who frequently say one thing and do another. The research discussed in this section sheds light on these issues.

The discussion that follows examines conditions under which people are likely to display attitude–behavior consistency. A subsequent section introduces theories of the attitude–behavior relationship. The final part of the chapter views consistency in a larger perspective.

Historical Background

For a time researchers were in a quandary. The vaunted attitude concept did not seem to predict behavior (LaPiere, 1934), suggesting to some researchers that we discard the attitude term entirely (Wicker, 1969). These conclusions characterized the field of attitude research for a time and still typify viewpoints you might hear or read about today. When someone informally laments that people never act on their plans or that acquaintances believe one thing, but always do something very different, she is echoing sentiments that date back to the early decades of the twentieth century.

It turns out these conclusions did not bear up under scientific scrutiny. Careful analyses showed that most research reported significant correlations between attitudes and behavior (Fishbein & Ajzen, 1975, 2010; Kim & Hunter, 1993). Indeed, a thorough review reports that the correlation between attitudes and behavior is a robust .52 (Albarracín, Chan, & Jiang, 2019; Glasman & Albarracín, 2006). Given the complexity and variability of human behavior, as well as imperfections in our measuring instruments, that correlation is pretty darn good.

Let's give the early scholars their due. They correctly observed that attitudes do not *always* predict behavior. They called attention to the fact that attitudes do not forecast action nearly as well as one might assume on the basis of common sense. But they threw out the attitudinal baby with the dirty behavioral bath water! Sure, attitudes do not always predict what we will do. But that does not mean they aren't useful guides or reasonable predictors, given the incredible complexity of everyday life. The consensus of opinion today is that attitudes do influence action; they predispose people toward certain behavioral choices, but not all the time. Under some conditions, attitudes forecast behavior; in other circumstances they do not. The relationship between attitude and behavior is exquisitely complex.

Now here's the good news: We can identify the factors that moderate the attitude–behavior relationship. Key variables are: (a) aspects of the situation, (b) characteristics of the person, and (c) qualities of the attitude (Fazio & Roskos-Ewoldsen, 1994; Zanna & Fazio, 1982).

Situational Factors

The context – the situation we're in – exerts a powerful impact on behavior. We are not always aware of how our behavior is subtly constrained by norms, roles, and a desire to do the socially correct thing. A *norm* is an individual's belief about the appropriate behavior in a situation. Roles are parts we perform in everyday life, socially prescribed functions like professor, student, parent, child, and friend.

Norms

Individuals may hold an attitude, but choose not to express the attitude because it would violate a social norm. You may not like an acquaintance at work, but realize that it violates conventional norms to criticize the person to his face. Someone may harbor prejudice toward co-workers, but be savvy enough to know that she had better hold her tongue lest she get in trouble on the job (Kiesler, Collins, & Miller, 1969).

Scripts

To illustrate the concept of script, I ask that you imagine you face a term paper deadline and are hard at work at your word processor. A phone rings; it's a telemarketer, the tenth to call this week. She's asking for money for injured war veterans, a cause you normally support because a relative got hurt while serving in the Afghanistan war. Not thinking and mindlessly putting on your "I'm busy, leave me alone" hat, you cut the volunteer off, telling her in no uncertain terms that you have work to do.

Your attitude obviously didn't come into play here. If it had, you would have promised a donation. Instead, you invoked a script: an "organized bundle of expectations about an event sequence" or an activity (Abelson, 1982, p. 134). Like an actor who has memorized his lines and says them on cue, you call on well-learned rules about how to handle pushy telemarketers interrupting your day. Your expectations of how the transaction with the telemarketer is going to proceed – the overly pleasant intro, follow-up for money, plea to keep you on the phone – set the tone for the conversation, and you mindlessly follow the script rather than taking the time to consult your attitude toward veterans.

Characteristics of the Person

Individuals differ in the extent to which they display consistency between attitudes and behavior. Some people are remarkably consistent; others are more variable. Social psychological research has helped pinpoint the ways in which personal factors moderate the attitude–behavior relationship. Two moderating factors are self-monitoring and direct experience.

Self-monitoring

Social psychologist Mark Snyder, whose work we glimpsed earlier, argues that he believes people can be divided into two categories. A first group consists of individuals who are concerned with managing impressions, cultivating images, and displaying appropriate behavior in social situations. Adept at reading situational cues and figuring out the expected behavior at a given place and time, these individuals adjust their behavior to fit the situation. When filling out Snyder's classic (1974) scale, they agree that "in different situations and with different people, I often act like very different persons." These individuals are called high self-monitors because they "*monitor* the public appearances of self they display in social situations" (Snyder, 1987, pp. 4–5).

A second group is less concerned with fitting into a situation or displaying socially correct behavior. Rather than looking to the situation to figure out how to behave, they consult their inner feelings and attitudes. "My behavior is usually an expression of my true inner feelings, attitudes, and beliefs," they proudly declare, strongly agreeing with this item in the self-monitoring scale. These individuals are called low self-monitors. Although there has been debate about whether there may be different dimensions of self-monitoring, researchers Gangestad and Snyder (2000) showed that, in fact, self-monitoring is a unitary personality factor, with one basic factor, the degree to which one is concerned with engaging in situationally appropriate behavior and strategically manage public impressions.

Although some of us may be a little bit of both, and our self-monitoring might fluctuate in different situations, those who are exuberantly concerned with impression management are high self-monitors, and those who are defiantly unimpressed by cultivating public appearances are low self-monitors.

There is some evidence that high self-monitors exhibit less attitude–behavior consistency than do low self-monitors (Snyder & Kendzierski, 1982; Snyder & Tanke, 1976). High self-monitors look to the situation to decide how to act. As shape-shifting "actor types" who enjoy doing the socially correct thing, they don't view each and every situation in life as a test of character. If a situation requires that they put their attitudes aside for a moment, they happily do so. Low self-monitors strongly disagree. Living by the credo, "To thine own self be true," low self-monitors place value on practicing what they preach and maintaining congruence between attitude and behavior. Not to do so would violate a personal canon for low self-monitors.

In the example given earlier, Kelly – the outgoing, chameleon-like young woman who has strong attitudes toward wildlife preservation – would be in a pickle if acquaintances at a party began taking an anti-environmental stand. Her personality description suggests she is a high self-monitor. If so, she would be unlikely to challenge her acquaintances. Instead, she might smile sweetly, nod her head, and resolve to talk up the environmental issue in situations where she could make a difference. Needless to say, a low self-monitor who shared Kelly's values would be foaming at the mouth when her friends began saying that we should drill for oil in the National Wildlife Refuge. She probably would not hesitate to tell them how she felt.

There are also interesting social media implications here. Some people are highly attuned to how they come off on social media, while others lament the phoniness they see in others' profiles. Some teens and young adults in their 20s, tired of striving to match "annoyingly perfect online avatars," or seeking a little privacy, have set up finstagrams or phony Instagram accounts geared only to friends that offer a more genuine view of themselves (Safronova, 2015, p. D1). Theory suggests that high self-monitors will be highly cognizant of how they come across on Facebook, Instagram, Snapchat, and other sites, attentive to their image, even strategizing to brand themselves in more image-conscious ways. Low self-monitors, while not unconcerned with their social media presentations, should be less interested than highs with self-branding or what they view as imagey issues. Instead, lows should be more concerned with maintaining consistency between value-expressive-based attitudes and social media posts, tweets, and profiles.

The relationship among self-monitoring, persuasion, and mediated messages are complex and can hinge on situational factors (Ajzen et al., 2019). (Interested readers should also consider refinement, modifications, and analyses of Snyder's scale that bear on persuasion in social media and other contexts; see Briggs, Cheek, & Buss, 1980; Gangestad & Snyder, 2000; Lennox & Wolfe, 1984.)

Direct Experience

Experience can also moderate the attitude–behavior relationship. Some of our attitudes are based on direct experience with an issue; we have encountered the problem in real life, it has evoked strong feelings, or led us to think through the implications of behaving in a certain way. Other attitudes are formed indirectly – from listening to parents or peers, reading books, watching television, or skimming Facebook posts. Attitudes formed through direct experience "are more clearly defined, held with greater certainty, more stable over time, and more resistant to counter influence" than attitudes formed through indirect experience (Fazio & Zanna, 1981, p. 185; see also Millar & Millar, 1996). Attitudes produced by direct experience also come more quickly to mind than attitudes acquired through indirect experiences. For these reasons, people are more apt to translate attitude into behavior when the attitude has been formed through direct experiences, at least when both attitude and behavior have a similar psychological foundation (Albarracín et al., 2019; Fazio & Zanna, 1978).

Consider a contemporary example: Adolescent drug abuse. Two teenagers may both have negative attitudes toward drug use. One formed her attitude through direct experience: She smoked a lot of marijuana, tried Ecstasy as a high school sophomore, got sick, and found the experience psychologically scary. A teenage guy formed his attitude indirectly, from reading lots of articles warning of harmful effects of drugs and getting the drug rap from parents. During the last week of high school each is tempted to try some drugs at a pulsating pre-graduation party. As she contemplates her decision, the young woman accesses and recalls the negative experiences she had a couple of years back, leading her to reject the offer. Although the guy initially says no, he finds the offer to smoke some weed tempting, his negative attitude less strongly felt, less accessible, and not sufficiently powerful to overcome the allure of a marijuana high (see Figure 6.3).

Attitudes based on direct experience are more likely to predict behavior than those formed indirectly – at least when the basis for the attitude and behavior are the same, as when both attitude and behavior are focused around emotions, or our feelings about an issue (Albarracín et al., 2019). Thus, persuaders can take advantage of people – persuading them to cast their better judgments to the wind – when individuals are uncertain about what they believe or have not thought through their attitudes

Figure 6.3 A Young Man With a Negative Attitude Toward Drugs May Not Translate Attitude into Behavior If Tempted by Peers and If He Has Little Direct Experience With Drugs to Guide Him
Image courtesy of Shutterstock

and beliefs. Adolescents may be particularly susceptible to this, suggesting that parents, teachers, and older peers should help teens recognize their gullibility when they lack experience with the particular issue.

Characteristics of the Attitude

As noted in Chapters 4 and 5, attitudes differ in their structure and strength. The nature of an attitude moderates the relationship between attitudes and behavior.

General Versus Specific Attitudes

Ajzen and Fishbein (1977) distinguished between *general* and *highly specific* attitudes. A general attitude, the focus of discussion up to this point, is the global evaluation that cuts across different situations. A specific attitude, called *attitude toward a behavior*, is evaluation of a single act, or specific behavior that takes place in a particular context at a particular time. For example, consider the issue of predicting religious behavior from religious attitudes. The general attitude is the individual's attitude toward religion. This is the sum total of the person's evaluations of many religious behaviors, such as praying, attending religious services, partaking in holiday rituals, talking about religion in everyday life, and donating money to religious causes. The specific attitude is the attitude toward one of these behaviors at a particular place and time.

A general attitude, sometimes called *attitude toward the object*, will not predict each and every religious behavior. A couple of graduate students who are deeply religious may attend only a handful of religious services over the course of six months – not because they have abandoned religion, but because they are immersed in doctoral comprehensive exams and realize they must forsake this part of their religious identity for a time. (To compensate, the students may regularly devote time to reading inspirational portions of the Bible.) The students harbor a favorable attitude toward religion, but rarely, it seems, translate attitude into behavior.

But here's the rub: If you take the dozens of other religious behaviors in which the student could (and does) partake (from praying to Bible reading), and include them in your equation, you will discover that attitude predicts behavior rather handsomely.

This is the conclusion that Fishbein and Ajzen reached in an exhaustive review of this topic. In a 1974 study – old but still good – the investigators asked people to indicate their general religious attitude, as well as how frequently they participated in each of 100 specific religious behaviors. The correlation, or association, between general attitude toward religion and any specific action was 0.15. This is a very small correlation; it means that attitude toward religion is not closely related to a particular behavior in a given situation. But when Fishbein and Ajzen (1974) looked at the overall behavior pattern, focusing not on one situation but rather on the sum total, they discovered that the relationship between attitude toward religion and religious behavior was substantial. The correlation was 0.71, approaching 1 (the latter a perfect correlation; see also Weigel & Newman, 1976).

Thus, if you want to predict people's behavior across a variety of situations, their general attitude toward the object will be a good, though imperfect predictor, because so many situational factors can understandably come up to influence intentions to behave. Attitudes predict behavior in the aggregate well, just not perfectly. On the other hand, if you want to predict behavior in a particular context, individuals' specific attitude toward the behavior should forecast intentions – and actual behavior – very well.

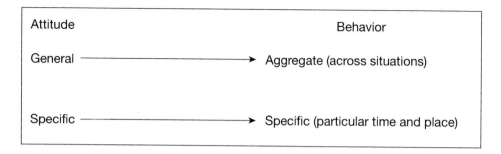

Figure 6.4 Compatibility Principle. Arrows denote strong relationships between attitude and behavior. General attitude will not predict specific behavior, and a specific attitude will not forecast behavior in the aggregate

These ideas are an outgrowth of what Ajzen and Fishbein (1977) call the *compatibility principle*. *A strong relationship between attitude and behavior is possible only if the attitudinal predictor corresponds with the behavioral criteria.* "Corresponds with," means that the attitudinal and behavioral entities are measured at the same level of specificity. Thus, specific attitudes toward a behavior predict highly specific acts. General attitudes predict broad classes of behavior that cut across different situations (see Figure 6.4).

Attitude Strength

Another moderator of the attitude–behavior relationship is the strength of the individual's attitude. Strong attitudes are particularly likely to forecast behavior (Lord, Lepper, & Mackie, 1984). This makes sense psychologically and resonates with ordinary experience. Those with strong convictions on issues ranging from abortion to immigration are the ones who are out there on the picket lines or are lobbying Congress to pass legislation favorable to their groups.

It gets more complicated when you consider those instances when we're ambivalent about issues. When people have strong feelings on both sides of an issue or are torn between head and heart, they are less apt to translate attitude into behavior (Armitage & Conner, 2000; Lavine et al., 1998). Different feelings push people in different behavioral directions. The affective aspect of an attitude (feelings) can propel people toward one choice, while the cognitive dimension (beliefs) can push them in a different direction. Faced with these cross-pressures, individuals may behave in accord with their attitude in one situation, but not so much in another.

Consider the case of Susan, the agnostic mentioned earlier who believes strongly in evolution, but has a soft spot for religion because it means a lot to her dad. Asked to teach a Sunday school class in which she has to take a creationist position on evolution, Susan is likely to have mixed feelings. Her negative views toward religion should propel her to reject the request. (Fishbein and Ajzen's model suggests that her specific negative evaluation of teaching creationism should also push her in that direction.) However, cognition clashes with affect: Susan's relationship with her dad means a lot, and the call from an old friend of her father evokes fond memories. If heart governs head and feelings overpower thoughts, she is likely to agree to teach the class. If she opts to base her decision on logic, she will politely decline. Much depends on what information comes to mind at the moment of decision, and how she goes about deciding which course to take (Wang Erber, Hodges, & Wilson, 1995).

Models of Attitude–Behavior Consistency Relations

As we have seen, people are complex. They can be consistent, practising what they preach, or they can surprise you, doing things that you would not expect based on their attitudes. Research sheds light on these phenomena. We know that attitudes frequently guide behavior, though the effects are stronger under certain circumstances, for some individuals, and with some attitudes more than others. The studies offer a patchwork – a pastiche – of conditions under which attitudes are more or less likely to influence action. Social scientists prefer more organized frameworks, such as models that explain and predict behavior. Two major theories of attitude–behavior relations have been proposed: The reasoned action and accessibility models.

The Reasoned Action Approach

Fishbein and Ajzen, who brought you the precision of the compatibility principle, also formulated a major theoretical perspective on attitude–behavior relations. Originally proposed by Fishbein and Ajzen in 1975, the conceptual framework was extended by Ajzen (e.g., 1991) in his *theory of planned behavior*. By noting that people can harbor an attitude, and believe that important others think they should engage in the behavior, but just feel they lack the personal or environmental control to accomplish the task, Ajzen contributed a keen insight. We can have all the appropriate cognitions and norms in mind, but if we don't think we have the psychological ability to do what we want, we won't perform the behaviour; our attitude won't translate into action. Perceived behavioral control has helped explain the gyrating mental dynamics of attitude–behavior relations and improved the predictive power of the model. In 2010, Fishbein and Ajzen integrated their early work, planned behavior theory, and newer ideas about norms into the reasoned action approach, clarifying, enhancing, and extending the model to take into account new processes.

The theory of planned behavior, in particular, offers the most systematic explanation in the field of the processes by which beliefs influence behavior. It offers a roadmap for the journey that thoughts in a person's head must travel before they can affect the actions he or she performs. In so doing, it generates a series of specific strategies that persuaders should employ to craft communications on any topic you can imagine.

First, a word about the name. The terms *planned behavior* and *reasoned action* imply that people engage in some measure of deliberation and planning in how they go about deciding whether to perform a particular behavior. Fishbein and Ajzen (2010) are quick to acknowledge that people do not always think their decisions through mindfully. Instead, they argue that once people form a set of beliefs, they proceed to act on these beliefs in a predictable and consistent fashion. Their beliefs provide the cognitive basis from which attitudes, intentions, and behavior subsequently follow. Beliefs, scholar Marco Yzer (2013) emphasizes, are not always rational. However, they are powerful. For example, he explains:

> Someone suffering from paranoid personality disorder may lock the door of his office because he believes that his colleagues are conspiring against him. This person acts in a reasoned manner

on a belief, even though others would deem his belief irrational. Regardless whether beliefs are irrational, incorrect (because based on false information), or motivationally biased, once beliefs are formed they are the cognitive basis from which behavior reasonably follows.

(p. 121)

There are five components of the theory: *Attitude toward the behavior*, the individual's judgment that performing the action is good or bad; *perceived norm*, perceived social pressure to perform the action; *perceived behavioral control*, the degree to which individuals believe they are capable of performing a particular behavior; *behavioral intention*, the intent or plan to perform a particular behavior; and *behavior* itself, the action in a particular situation (see Figure 6.5).

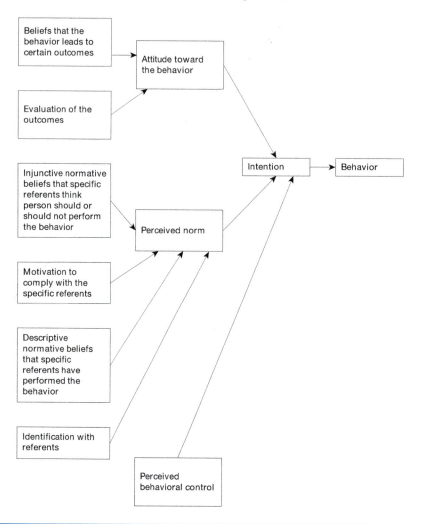

Figure 6.5 The Reasoned Action Approach
From Fishbein & Ajzen (2010)

As an example, let's suppose you stop by your high school over the summer, showing off just a little now that you are in college, but curious how the teachers are doing. A health teacher approaches you, compliments you on your communication skills (yes, flattery frequently goads us into accepting communicators' requests), then gets serious by discussing the recent upsurge in vaping; it's increased since you were a senior, the teacher adds. Unlike your friends, who think vaping is cool and not nearly as gross as cigarette smoking, you are concerned about the problem. Checking national data on your phone, you discover that 3.5 million American kids use e-cigarettes, about one in five high school students have used them, they have addictive properties, contain lots of nicotine, and can be harmful to the lungs, in some cases causing life-threatening illnesses. Indeed, more than 2,000 individuals have developed serious lung illnesses linked to vaping, and more than 35 people have died (Gupta, 2019; Kaplan & Richtel, 2019; LaVito, 2019; Richtel & Grady, 2019).

You know teenagers who are blasé about it; they're heavy users of the uber-popular Juul (which controls 70 percent of the U.S. e-cigarette market), with its sleek flash drive appearance, easy capacity to elude teacher spies with a furtive slip into a pants pocket, its intoxicating feeling of "now." Teens vape casually, in groups, with a touch of braggadocio at times, relating how they "Juul" in between classes, in their spare time, with groups of friends and talk nonchalantly about Juuling as if its effects were entirely benign (see Figure 6.6). Feeling a bit of a turncoat because you have friends who vape, but also regarding yourself as a health activist with a mission, you agree to devise some messages the school can post to persuade students to quit the Juuling habit. You opt to employ the reasoned action approach, developing a survey to get a lay of the land before creating your messages. Reflecting the specificity of reasoned action theory, you're careful to focus your questions around a highly specific vaping behavior.

Attitude

Attitude toward the behavior is a highly specific attitude. It consists of two subcomponents: *Behavioral beliefs* (beliefs about consequences of the behavior) and outcome evaluations (evaluations of the consequences). These two elements are combined as they were in the simple expectancy–value model described in Chapter 4. Each behavioral belief is multiplied by the corresponding evaluation, and results are summed across items. Beliefs and evaluations about using Juul over the course of a weekday could be measured as depicted below. (Items are phrased, using Juul, in the popular parlance, as a verb.)

Behavioral Beliefs

Juuling in My Spare Time Over the Course of a Weekday:

1 Gives me a quick lift when I'm anxious
 (Likely)   1   2   3   4   5   6   7   (Unlikely)

2 Makes me feel trendy
 (Likely)   1   2   3   4   5   6   7   (Unlikely)

3 Lets me do something adults disapprove of
 (Likely)   1   2   3   4   5   6   7   (Unlikely)

4 Gives me a good buzz when I taste the flavored pods
 (Likely)   1   2   3   4   5   6   7   (Unlikely)

5 Helps me fit in with others
 (Likely)   1   2   3   4   5   6   7   (Unlikely)

6 Can lead to serious lung illness
 (Likely)   1   2   3   4   5   6   7   (Unlikely)

Figure 6.6 That Tell-tale Puff of Smoke, Euphoric Feeling and Temporary Relief Are All Too Common Today, as Millions of Teenagers Have Turned to E-cigarettes, Particularly Juul. But e-cigarette use, or Juuling as it is popularly known, can have serious medical side effects, including addiction. The reasoned action approach, crystallized by the planned behavior model, offers insights into the role attitudes, norms, and perceived behavioral control play in the use of e-cigs like Juul, suggesting intriguing ways to persuade adolescents to dump the habit

CC image courtesy of Sarah Johnson via Flickr

Outcome Evaluations

1 Getting a quick lift when I'm anxious
   (Good)   1   2   3   4   5   6   7   (Bad)

2 Feeling trendy
   (Good)   1   2   3   4   5   6   7   (Bad)

3 Doing something adults disapprove of
   (Good)   1   2   3   4   5   6   7   (Bad)

4 Getting a good buzz from tasting flavored pods
   (Good)   1   2   3   4   5   6   7   (Bad)

5 Fitting in with others
(Good)   1   2   3   4   5   6   7   (Bad)

6 Getting a serious lung illness
(Good)   1   2   3   4   5   6   7   (Bad)

Perceived Norm

Norms refer to acceptable, recommended behavior in a society. A perceived norm is perceived social pressure to perform a particular action. The perceived norm has two components: *Injunctive norms*, or perceptions of what other people think we *should* do, and *descriptive norms*, perceptions of what others have done, are doing, or are likely to do in the future (Fishbein & Ajzen, 2010, p. 151).

Each consists of two subcomponents, which are multiplied together.

Injunctive norms consist of: (a) injunctive normative beliefs, or beliefs that individuals who are important to the person endorse the behavior; and (b) motivation to comply, the person's motivation to go along with these significant others.

Descriptive norms are composed of: (a) descriptive normative beliefs, or beliefs about how frequently important others engage in the behavior; and (b) identification, the degree to which an individual identifies with these significant others.

Injunctive Normative Beliefs

1 My mom thinks that:
(I should)   1   2   3   4   5   6   7   (I should not) Juul in my spare time over the course of a weekday

2 My dad thinks that:
(I should)   1   2   3   4   5   6   7   (I should not) Juul in my spare time over the course of a weekday

3 My best friend thinks that:
(I should)   1   2   3   4   5   6   7   (I should not) Juul in my spare time over the course of a weekday

Motivation to Comply

1 When it comes to matters of health, I want to do what my mom thinks I should do.
(Strongly agree)   1   2   3   4   5   6   7   (Strongly disagree)

2 When it comes to matters of health, I want to do what my dad thinks I should do.
(Strongly agree)   1   2   3   4   5   6   7   (Strongly disagree)

3 When it comes to matters of health, I want to do what my best friend thinks I should do.
(Strongly agree)   1   2   3   4   5   6   7   (Strongly disagree)

Descriptive Normative Beliefs

1 My mom Juuls in her spare time over the course of a weekday.
   (All of the time)   1   2   3   4   5   6   7   (Never)

2 My dad Juuls in his spare time over the course of a weekday.
   (All of the time)   1   2   3   4   5   6   7   (Never)

3 My best friend Juuls in his/her spare time over the course of a weekday.
   (All of the time)   1   2   3   4   5   6   7   (Never)

4 Most people my age Juul in their spare time over the course of a weekday.
   (All of the time)   1   2   3   4   5   6   7   (Never)

Identification

1 When it comes to matters of health, how much do you want to be like your mom?
   (A lot)   1   2   3   4   5   6   7   (Not at all)

2 When it comes to matters of health, how much do you want to be like your dad?
   (A lot)   1   2   3   4   5   6   7   (Not at all)

3 When it comes to matters of health, how much do you want to be like your best friend?
   (A lot)   1   2   3   4   5   6   7   (Not at all)

4 When it comes to matters of health, how much do you want to be like most people your age?
   (A lot)   1   2   3   4   5   6   7   (Not at all)

Descriptive and injunctive norms are then combined to produce an item measuring perceived norms.

Perceived Behavioral Control

This concept was proposed by Ajzen (1991) in his theory of planned behavior, which extended the theory of reasoned action (TRA) by emphasizing behavioral control perceptions. Perceived behavioral control is the degree to which individuals perceive they are capable of performing a particular behavior, or can control their performance of the action. The perceived behavioral control notion is fascinating, but complicated. It requires some explanation.

Let's say that a young woman has a favorable attitude toward a particular behavior, *and* believes that important others endorse the behavior and perform it themselves. You would think that she would then perform the action. However, she might be *unable* to perform the behavior because she lacks either the necessary skills or confidence that she can enact the behavior in a particular situation.

For example: A woman may feel positively toward losing weight and perceive social pressure to drop 10 pounds. But she just can't muster the self-control to stay on a diet. A young man may harbor a positive attitude toward quitting smoking and recognize that his friends all want him to quit. But every time he feels nervous, he takes a smoke. He lacks the cognitive skills and self-discipline to quit the habit. So, attitudes and norms will not predict intention or behavior in these cases. But if we add perceived behavioral control to the mix, we take into account an individual's ability to comply – or not comply – with a dietary or anti-smoking regimen, in this way improving the predictive power of attitudes and norms. Among individuals who don't think they can resist the lure of food and cigarettes, attitude and norm will not predict intention. No matter how positively they feel toward changing the behavior, and regardless of how much they value their friends' opinions, they lack the capacity to implement the intention or to carry out their plans. In these cases, we can predict at the get-go that attitudes and norms won't forecast intentions particularly well.

Thus, by adding perceived control to the model, we can come up with more accurate predictions about *when* attitudes predict intentions and behavior. And there is substantial evidence that perceived behavioral control increases our ability to accurately forecast behavior (Ajzen et al., 2019).

Okay, let's get back to the problem at hand: Measuring the degree to which teens plan to use Juul on a weekday. Simplifying Fishbein and Ajzen's measurement strategy just a bit, you might come up with these two questionnaire items to measure perceived behavioral control.

Perceived Behavioral Control

How much control do you feel you have over whether you Juul in your spare time over the course of a weekday?

(No Control) 1   2   3   4   5   6   7   (Complete Control)

How much do you feel that Juuling in your spare time over the course of a weekday is under your control?

(A lot)   1   2   3   4   5   6   7   (Not at all)

Behavioral Intention

As the name suggests, behavioral intention is the intention to perform a particular action, a plan to put behavior into effect. Intention can be predicted quite accurately from attitude toward the behavior, perceived norm, and perceived behavioral control. Intention is most likely to predict behavior when it corresponds with – is identical to – the behavior in key ways. If you want to predict whether people will use Juul over the course of a weekday, you should ask them if they intend to do just that. Asking them if they intend to use Juul in general, on weekends, or when are out of town on vacation would not predict using Juul over the course of a weekday.

The model uses a mathematical formula to determine the impact that each of the three factors exerts on intentions.

Intention to use Juul, measured as specifically as possible, could be assessed in this way:

I intend to Juul in my spare time over the course of a weekday.
(Definitely)   1   2   3   4   5   6   7   (Definitely Do Not)

Behavior

In general, intention to perform a particular behavior should predict the actual performance of the act. Thus, to provide an accurate measurement of behavior, you could ask respondents this question: Over the past month, how often have you Juuled in your spare time over the course of a weekday?

(Never)   1   2   3   4   5   6   7   (Almost Always)

The model says that intention to use Juul – determined by attitude, norm, and perceived behavioral control – should do a pretty good job of predicting behavior.

Predicting Behavior from Attitude

Recall the question guiding this section: Do attitudes predict behavior? The reasoned action approach allows us to specify the precise impact that attitudes exert on behavior. In the present case, young people who strongly *believe* that using Juul over the course of a weekday leads to positive outcomes should be especially likely to intend to Juul during the day.

In some cases, though, attitudes will not forecast action. Instead, norms dictate what people do. An adolescent might positively evaluate using Juul, but refrain because his mom does not think it is a good idea or because it is frowned on in his peer group.

Thus, the theory offers a framework for predicting behavior from attitude. Fishbein and Ajzen caution that behavior can be predicted, but you need to consider likes and dislikes (attitudes), people's natural propensity to please others (norms), and individuals' confidence that they can carry out their plans (perceived behavioral control). When strong social pressures are present, attitudes do not accurately forecast behavior (Wallace et al., 2005). When people do not have the skills or lack the confidence to execute their plans, attitudes may not predict intentions and intentions will not predict behavior. Reasoned action theory emphasizes that attitudes are a reasonably accurate indicator of what people will do, provided certain conditions are met. There will always be circumstances in which people, being complex, will behave on the basis of factors other than attitude. But the theory emphasizes that the more specific the correspondence among attitudes, norms, perceived behavioral control, intentions, and behavior, the better one can predict actual behavior. The more one can specify, in the different measures, the behavior that is performed, the context in which it takes place, and the time the behavior is enacted, the better one can forecast behavior.

The Facts on the Ground

The reasoned action approach has an outstanding track record in predicting behavior. More than 1,000 published studies have tested the model (Fishbein & Ajzen, 2010). Think about this for a moment: 1,000 studies! Each study occurred in a different setting, surveyed different individuals, and yet was carefully executed. The fact that so many empirical studies have confirmed the model should give us pause – and confidence (see model summary in Box 6.2). More than 40 years after the theory was introduced, we know that attitudes, perceived norms, and perceived behavioral control forecast intentions, and that intentions help predict behavior (Ajzen & Fishbein, 2005; Albarracín et al., 2001; Sheeran, Abraham, & Orbell, 1999; Sutton, 1998; see Icek Ajzen and his colleagues, 2019 for an excellent review). A half-century of research has provided us with a long, diverse list of intended behaviors that the model has illuminated and usefully predicted. These include:

- breast-feeding and bottle-feeding infants (Johnson-Young, 2019; Manstead, Proffitt, & Smart, 1983);
- grabbing meals in fast-food restaurants (Brinberg & Durand, 1983);
- eating a healthy diet (Booth-Butterfield & Reger, 2004);
- condom use among high-risk heterosexual and homosexual adults in the United States and abroad (Ajzen, Albarracín, & Hornik, 2007; Morrison, Gillmore, & Baker, 1995);
- texting while driving (Tian & Robinson, 2017; Wang, 2016);
- green, environmentally friendly consumption (Liu, Segev, and Villar (2017);
- intention to intervene to stop a sexual assault (Lukacena, Reynolds-Tylus, & Quick, 2019).

Shortcomings

If models could walk, this one looks like it walks on water! Well walk, for sure, but maybe only on land! As good as the model is, like all approaches, it has limitations. Some scholars protest that the attitude toward the behavior and behavioral intention measures are so highly specific and similar that the results are rather uninteresting. Others note that, contrary to the assumption that the impact of attitudes on behavior is mediated by intentions, attitudes do exert a direct impact on behavior (Bentler & Speckhart, 1979; Fazio, Powell, & Williams, 1989).

A number of critics lament that the model assumes that human beings are logical, when much behavior is spontaneous and even impulsive. As Ajzen, Fishbein, and their colleagues acknowledge, when people are in an emotional state, they can fail to execute intentions that may be in their own best interest, like not drinking or abstaining from texting when they drive (Ajzen et al., 2019). It gets even dicier when we consider implicit attitudes.

When people hold a strong implicit prejudice, their *conscious* expression of an explicit attitude on the survey may not predict negative body language toward a member of the disliked group, a behavior that the prejudiced person may not control (Ajzen & Fishbein, 2005). On the other hand, implicit prejudiced attitudes, measured on a sensitive psychological measure, might predict behaviors that prejudiced people find hard to control or are not motivated to monitor, like a White person's looking away from a person of color. However, Ajzen and colleagues (2019) caution that implicit attitudes won't predict specific prejudiced behaviors all that well since general attitudes, even of the implicit type, don't forecast specific behavior with much accuracy.

There has been a lively debate about these issues over the past decades, with Fishbein and Ajzen emphasizing that, broadly speaking, their model *can* predict a wide variety of everyday behaviors, including spontaneous and seemingly irrational behavior, like exceeding the legal speed limit and performing sex without a condom. Critics, for their part, argue that the model provides an unwieldy explanation of irrational behaviors and, in any event, not all behavior is preceded by an intention. In order to appreciate an alternative perspective based on these criticisms, the next section describes another approach to attitude–behavior relations.

BOX 6.2

Understanding Theory: Primer on the Reasoned Action Approach

1   The reasoned action approach offers a wide-ranging guide to attitudes and behavior.
2   There are five components of the theory: Attitude toward the behavior, perceived norm, perceived behavioral control, behavioral intention, and behavior.
3   Attitude toward the behavior consists of *behavioral beliefs* and outcome evaluations.
4   Perceived norm has two components: An injunctive norm, or motivation to comply with what significant others think one should do in a particular situation; and a descriptive norm, beliefs about how frequently significant others have performed the targeted behavior and identification with these others.
5   These constructs, with their subcomponents, can forecast intention to behave in a particular situation. The degree to which attitude, norm, and perceived behavioral control predict intention depends on the particular context.

6   Perceived behavioral control, or perception of whether one is psychologically capable of performing the behavior, helps determine whether attitude or norm predicts behavioral intention.

7   Behavioral intention predicts behavior, with prediction more accurate the closer and more specifically that intention corresponds to behavior.

8   There is strong support for the predictions of the model. A weakness is that the model can be laborious to study, involving so many different steps and a rather arcane phrasing of questions. Another limit is the challenge of forecasting intentions and behavior when attitudes are irrationally or implicitly held, as in the case of prejudice. This is, after all, a model of reasoned action, and not all behavior involves reasoned analysis. There is debate among researchers as to whether and when the model can account for actions that involve less mental forethought.

9   Persuasion primarily involves changing the core, salient beliefs that underlie the attitude, normative, and perceived behavioral control aspects of a particular behavior.

Accessibility Theory

It's a humid summer day, and you feel like a cold one. Glancing over the usual suspects – Miller Lite, Coors, Michelob, Bud Lite – your mouth watering, you want to make a quick choice of which six-pack to buy at the convenience store. Suddenly, the image of Clydesdale horses, a classic Budweiser branding image leaps into your mind. You smile, and reach for the Budweiser.

According to Fazio's accessibility-focused model (see Chapter 5), your attitude toward Budweiser is accessible, or capable of being quickly activated from memory. Your favorable attitude toward Bud Lite predicts your purchase behavior. Now, if we wanted, we could measure your *behavioral beliefs*, normative beliefs, perceptions of behavioral control, and other variables from the reasoned action approach. However, all this would be beside the point and far too laborious a process, according to accessibility theory. *The core notion of accessibility theory is that attitudes will predict behavior if they can be activated from memory at the time of a decision.* If a person is in touch with her attitudes, she will act on them. If not, she will be swayed by salient aspects of the situation.

This captures the gist of the model, but the core notions are more complicated. In reality, two things must transpire for an attitude to influence behavior. First, the attitude must come spontaneously to mind in a situation. That is, it must be activated from memory. Second, the attitude must influence perceptions of an issue or person, serving as a filter through which the issue or person is viewed (Fazio & Roskos-Ewoldsen, 1994, p. 85). These perceptions should then color the way people define the situation, pushing them to behave in sync with their attitude. (If people do not call up their attitude from memory, they will be susceptible to influence from other factors in the situation, such as norms or eye-catching stimuli; see Figure 6.7).

In short: You can harbor an attitude toward a person or issue, but unless the attitude comes to mind when you encounter the other person or issue, you cannot act on the attitude in a particular situation. This is one reason why it's good to be in touch with your attitudes: You can act on them when important issues come up in life.

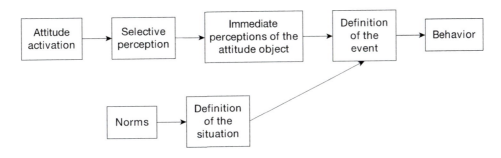

Figure 6.7 Fazio's Attitude-to-Behavior Process Model
From Fazio and Roskos-Ewoldsen (1994)

Fazio's approach derives from his MODE (Motivation and Opportunity as Determinants of Behavior) model. It extends knowledge of attitude–behavior relations by calling attention to the role accessibility plays in the process. The model suggests that attitudes guide behavior if people automatically call up attitudes from memory at the time of decision. But here is where it gets a little complicated.

Fazio argues that under some conditions people behave like Fishbein and Ajzen suggest: They consider the consequences of behaving in a particular fashion and may deliberate about pros and cons of doing x or y. But when people lack the motivation or opportunity to deliberate in this fashion, they act more spontaneously. In such situations, attitude can guide behavior if people automatically call up attitudes from memory.

Research offers some support for these propositions. For example, in one study, students who could immediately call to mind a favorable attitude toward food products were more inclined to select these products as a free gift than those with less accessible attitudes (Fazio et al., 1989). Interestingly, two students might have equally favorable attitudes toward Snickers candy bars. The student who was more "in touch" with her feelings about Snickers – who could say immediately that she liked Snickers – was more likely to select Snickers than a fellow student who had to think a little before recognizing how much she enjoyed Snickers (see Box 6.3 for a summary of accessibility theory).

At the same time, like all models, the accessibility approach is not without shortcomings, including its inability to precisely explain how general attitudes predict specific behaviors when people are low in motivation. This opens up the possibility that Fishbein-Ajzen type attitudes toward the behavior could intervene, helping to explain how attitudes influence behavior in these situations (Ajzen et al., 2019). Thus, both models could complement each other and work together in this way.

Implications for Persuasion

Both reasoned action and accessibility offer intriguing insights about attitude–behavior correspondence. As of now, reasoned action has more facts on its side, making it the most comprehensive model of beliefs, attitudes, and behavior.

What do the models suggest about persuasion? They both offer concrete ideas, demonstrating that communicators need to understand the dynamics of the mind before crafting a message. But what part of the mind do they need to change? Let's examine this question by returning to the hypothetical

> ### BOX 6.3
>
> # Understanding Theory: Primer on Accessibility Theory
>
> 1 Accessibility is a general term used to describe the degree to which an attitude is automatically activated from memory.
> 2 Objects toward which we have accessible attitudes are more likely to capture attention.
> 3 For an attitude to influence behavior, it must: (a) come spontaneously to mind in a situation; and (b) influence perceptions of the attitude object, serving as a filter through which the object is viewed.
> 4 We can harbor an attitude toward a person or issue, but unless the attitude comes to mind in the situation, we are not likely to translate it to behavior.
> 5 In contrast to the reasoned action approach, the accessibility model can help account for attitude–behavior relations in cases where a behavior is enacted spontaneously, rather than deliberately, and with minimal cognitive awareness (Rhodes & Ewoldsen, 2013; for other approaches that emphasize associative processes and implicit attitudes, see Gawronski & Brannon, 2019).
> 6 The accessibility notion, and the scientific work in this area, is fascinating. Critics, however, have suggested that accessibility may not be as essential to attitude–behavior consistency as other factors, like attitude stability (Doll & Ajzen, 1992). And while there is support for accessibility's role in moderating attitude–behavior relations, there is not as much support for the model's general propositions as there is for the reasoned action approach.

challenge that initiated this section: You are trying to devise a persuasive message to convince teenagers to quit using the e-cigarette Juul.

Here are some persuasive strategies derived from the attitude–behavior approaches. The first four are based on the reasoned action approach; the next two also call on Fazio's accessibility approach.

1 *Target relevant beliefs.* The first way to change attitudes and behaviors about vaping – or Juuling in particular – is to target beliefs, the centerpiece of the TRA. Messages could raise questions about whether teens really do get a pleasant buzz from Juul, or if, more frequently, they get a bad taste in their mouth, a burnt throat, or vaper's tongue – a loss of the ability to taste the flavors contained in the vapor. Importantly, messages could rebut the popular misconception that e-cigarettes like Juul have no serious medical side effects and can't lead to addiction.
2 *Target outcome evaluations.* Changing outcome evaluations can be difficult because you are trying to counter feelings that are gratifying. Yet persuasion can make inroads. Communicators could ask teens questions like these: Does Juul really give you a quick lift when you're anxious, or does the buzz *feel* raunchier, the anxiety reduction just short-lived? If you're doing Juul because adults don't approve, aren't you trying to get the approval of your friends, and isn't that a type of conformity too?

3 *Appeal to social norms.* This is a major influence appeal, effective in interpersonal influence and health campaigns (Goldstein & Cialdini, 2007; Park & Smith, 2007; Rimal & Lapinski, 2015). By emphasizing that individuals who are subjectively important to target audience members don't think the behavior is such a good idea, communicators can appeal to audience members' desire to stay in good psychological graces with these important others. When you can't change a belief through evidence and can't influence outcome evaluations by nudging the individual to change her affect, you switch strategies, emphasizing social norm-based appeals. You could highlight injunctive norms by emphasizing that parents or close friends would worry if the teen Juuled a lot, noting that, bottom-line, teens do care what parents and friends think about them.

You might also target descriptive norms by pointing out that everyone assumes that everyone else Juuls, but that assumption isn't backed up by evidence. A lot fewer people Juul regularly than many teens believe. By encouraging students to question their glib assumption that most people their age vape, you can flip the conformity switch, helping them recognize that their exaggerated belief about peer vaping pushes them to do something they really don't want to do (see discussion of social norms marketing in Chapter 16).

4 *Target perceived behavioral control.* A message could acknowledge that quitting Juul is difficult – a teen may feel anxious and even get the shakes a lot. However, the message would argue, it's really possible to buck the habit, people have done it, and target audience members can as well. What's more, with examples using teenagers' voices, visuals, and testimonials students can relate to, communicators can model ways that similar others have called on inner resources to dump the e-cigarette habit.

5 *Help people make good on their intentions.* As the TRA and other psychological research emphasizes, a key reason people don't always execute desired behaviors is that they don't connect intentions with behavior, or, "they simply forget to do what they intended" (Bargh, 2017, p. 270). One strategy is to put young people in touch with their feelings, helping them translate intention to quit to behavior. Research suggests that when an attitude has been recently activated or reflected on, it is relatively accessible, at least for a short amount of time (Arpan, Rhodes, & Roskos-Ewoldsen, 2007). Thus one might encourage teens to put a salient reminder of their desire to quit on their phone so that when they are faced with a choice of vaping, they quickly call their intent to quit to mind.

6 *Change attitudes through association techniques.* Research (Olson & Fazio, 2006) suggests that if campaign specialists repeatedly paired Juuling with a bad taste in the mouth, burnt throat, and ugly effects of addiction, they could help students develop more negative attitudes toward the e-cigarette. Instead of calling to mind good feelings, Juul could activate unpleasant images, deterring teens from vaping between classes.

Will these techniques work? As discussed in Chapter 5, they won't change the attitudes of adolescents with strong attitudes toward vaping and those for whom it serves deep psychological needs. But these six strategies are derived from research and, if packaged effectively, should appeal to receptive members of the audience. They won't work instantaneously; persuasion rarely does. But little by little, by planting the idea, nudging students to think about Juuling differently, they may influence attitudes and behavior.

Judging Consistency: Gray Areas and Ethical Issues

The term "hypocrisy" frequently gets bandied about when people observe inconsistencies between attitudes and behavior. It reflects an ethical concern, the belief that an individual is not living up to prescribed standards. Now that you have an appreciation for the complex underpinnings of attitude–behavior consistency, we can proceed to this more controversial aspect of the consistency issue.

Every day, it seems, we hear of famous men or women behaving badly and subsequently earning the wrath of observers, who call them hypocrites. Thomas Jefferson is the classic example. The egalitarian author of the Declaration of Independence, who penned that "all men are created equal," owned more than 100 slaves and believed that Blacks were inferior in mind and body to Whites. Was Jefferson a hypocrite, or a complicated man who harbored both revolutionary and prejudiced attitudes?

A now-classic example of alleged hypocrisy in a president involves Bill Clinton's relationship with Monica Lewinsky. During his first term and while running for re-election in 1996, Clinton championed family values, telegraphing what appeared to be a positive attitude toward marriage and monogamy. Yet he behaved quite differently, cheating on his wife and engaging in a long, sordid affair with Lewinsky. Critics pointed to the blatant contradictions between Clinton's words and actions (Bennett, 1998).

Others viewed the situation differently. We should be wary of "judging a complex being by a simple standard," one psychoanalyst said of the Clinton quandary. "To equate consistency with moral (and political) virtue, and then to demand consistency of people," wrote Adam Phillips, "can only cultivate people's sense of personal failure" (1998, p. A27). In other words, we should not ask people to be consistent. To do so is to set people up for failure, as none of us is perfect in this regard.

Consider the case of Reverend Jesse Jackson, who preached religious values, commitment to Biblical commandments like "Thou shalt not commit adultery," and counseled President Clinton regarding his sexual sins. In early 2001, the public learned that Jackson fathered a child out of wedlock. Was Jackson a hypocrite? He would seem to be, if one consults the Webster's dictionary definition. A hypocrite, the dictionary tells us, is one who pretends to be what he or she is not, or harbors principles or beliefs that he or she does not have. However, critic Michael Eric Dyson, taking a different view of hypocrisy, viewed Jackson differently. Dyson argued:

> It is not hypocritical to fail to achieve the moral standards that one believes are correct. Hypocrisy comes when leaders conjure moral standards that they refuse to apply to themselves and when they do not accept the same consequences they imagine for others who offend moral standards.
>
> (2001, p. A23)

Noting that Jackson accepted responsibility for his behavior, Dyson said he was not a hypocrite.

In 2008, critics accused Governor Sarah Palin, the Republican vice-presidential candidate, of hypocrisy. As a family-values conservative, she publicly supported abstinence-until-marriage education in schools. However, her unmarried 17-year-old daughter, Bristol, became pregnant, suggesting to some that Palin had not practiced what she preached when it came to her own family. Others were more tolerant. "The media is already trying to spin this as evidence that Governor Palin is a hypocrite," noted James Dobson, the founder of Focus on the Family. "But all it really means is that she and her family are human" (Nagourney, 2008, p. A18).

There is no end to controversy over hypocrisy among public figures. Prince, the late musical star, seems to have had an acute problem with pain pills, and his addiction may have caused his untimely death. Yet Prince brooked no tolerance for those who abused drugs on the job (Eligon, Kovaleski, & Coscarelli, 2016). Was Prince sadly hypocritical, someone who tried to deny his own dependence on drugs by castigating others, or, from a reasoned action perspective, a man whose lack of control over his own actions prevented him from displaying attitude–behavior consistency? Prince's was a tragic case, one with complex, all-too-human implications for attitude–behavior relations.

Perhaps the most seemingly incongruent example of attitude–behavior inconsistency bordering on hypocrisy is one you may have read about if you follow politics. White evangelical voters have strongly supported President Trump, sticking by him despite his committing moral breaches that clearly violate their ethical precepts, including making gross, lewd comments about grabbing women's genitals, extramarital affairs, and paying a former pornographic star hush money so she wouldn't reveal that they had sex (Goldberg, 2017; see Figure 6.8). Even White evangelical women, who are probably offended by such behavior, have stuck by him. Tempting as it is to call their behavior hypocritical, other explanations are less pejorative, helping us understand rather than condemn.

Many evangelical voters tolerate Trump's behavior because of his fidelity to issues more important to them than a husband's moral rectitude. He has offered unwavering support for the pro-life position,

Figure 6.8 Many Religious American Voters, Particularly Evangelical Christians, Have Supported President Donald Trump, Despite His Apparent Flouting of Their Values With His Marital Infidelity and Crude Comments About Women. Are they hypocritical? Not necessarily, as evangelical Christians applaud Trump's fidelity to their opposition to abortion, perhaps as well as his support for White Christian heritage. Or perhaps they are hypocritical in some way, showcasing the moral overtones in the attitude–behavior relationship

appointing two strong pro-life justices to the Supreme Court, opening up the possibility that a decision evangelicals hate far more than his sexual improprieties – Roe vs. Wade – could be overturned. To evangelicals, abortion is sin, and a president who sees things this way has shown a respect for their moral values and their religious convictions. On the other hand, you could argue evangelicals are hypocritical, their attitudes not living up to their ethical standards. They just choose to endure the hypocrisy to get what they want on abortion.

Thus, the term "hypocrite" is complicated, subject to different readings and different points of view. In trying to decide if someone behaved in a hypocritical fashion, a variety of issues emerge. What criteria do we use to say that someone is a hypocrite? Is it hypocritical if the individual displays a single inconsistency between attitude and behavior? Or is that too strict a criterion? How many inconsistencies must the person commit before the hypocrite label fits? Do certain inconsistencies get more weight than others? Does a blatant violation of an individual's deeply held values cut more to the heart of hypocrisy than other inconsistencies? Are certain kinds of attitude–behavior inconsistencies (e.g., violations of marital oaths) more ethically problematic and therefore more deserving of the hypocrite label than others? Interestingly, is hypocrisy culturally relative? Are certain kinds of inconsistencies more apt to be regarded as hypocritical in one culture than in another? Finally does application of the label "hypocrite" tell us more about the observer than the person being judged?

These strike me as valid questions, reflective of the enduring complexity of human behavior. And yet one can take this non-judgmental, relativist view too far. There are times when individuals do not practice what they have long preached. From an ethical perspective, people should be held accountable for instances in which their behavior flouts attitudes that they profess to harbor. Dictionaries tell us that hypocrisy involves pretense – pretending to have moral principles to which one's own behaviors do not conform. Such pretense violates deontological principles. Not every attitude–behavior inconsistency counts as hypocrisy. However, when an individual professes to harbor strongly held beliefs and then behaves in ways that are palpably incongruent, we can count these as instances of hypocrisy. Behaving hypocritically is not the end of the world; we all do it from time to time. When we do it, we should be held accountable.

Conclusions

Attitude research sheds light on the reasons why people hold the attitudes they do and the degree to which attitudes predict behavior.

Functional theory stipulates that people would not hold attitudes unless they satisfied core human needs. Attitudes help people cope, serving knowledge, utilitarian, social adjustive, social identity, value-expressive, and ego-defense functions. Two people can hold the same attitude for different reasons, and an attitude that is functional for one person may be dysfunctional for someone else. An attitude can help a person function nicely in one part of his or her life, while leading to negative consequences in another domain. Attitude function research also suggests strategies for attitude change. It emphasizes that persuaders should probe the function a particular attitude serves for an individual and design the message so that it matches this need.

The bottom-line question for attitude researchers is whether attitudes forecast behavior. Decades of research have made it abundantly clear that attitudes do not always predict behavior and that people are not entirely consistent. People are especially unlikely to translate attitude into behavior when norms and scripts operate, they are ambivalent about the issue, or they regard themselves as high self-monitors. Under a variety of other conditions, attitudes predict behavior handsomely. When attitudes and behavior are measured at the same level of specificity, attitudes forecast behavior. Attitudes guide and influence behavior, but not in every life situation.

The reasoned action approach, updated in 2010, offers rich insights into attitude–behavior relations. It emphasizes that once individuals develop a set of beliefs, they proceed to act on these beliefs in a predictable and consistent fashion. Beliefs are not always rational, but they can powerfully influence behavior. The model has three core components: Attitude, norm, and perceived behavioral control, with each helping determine when intention predicts behavior. With its postulates tested in more than 1,000 studies, the reasoned action approach has shown that attitudes, if carefully measured, can predict behavior in a vast array of contexts. Critics have argued that the model's weakness is that it can only usefully predict behaviors preceded by rational deliberation, when much behavior is impulsive and spontaneous.

Accessibility theory sheds light on the latter behaviors. It argues that for an attitude to affect action, it must come spontaneously to mind in a particular context and influence key perceptions of the issue or person. Fazio notes that in some circumstances people behave like Fishbein and Ajzen suggest: They consider the utilitarian consequences of acting in a particular fashion and may deliberate about the pros and cons of doing x or y. However, when people lack the motivation or opportunity to deliberate in this fashion, they behave more spontaneously. In such situations, attitude can guide behavior if people automatically call up an attitude from memory. There is less empirical evidence supporting the accessibility approach's predictions on attitude–behavior consistency than there is for reasoned action theory. However, it offers a useful counterpoint.

Both theories have implications for persuasion, though they focus on different factors. Stylistically and metaphorically, reasoned action is heavy and sturdy, like an engine, while accessibility is lithe and free form, resembling a youthful, somewhat impulsive dancer. This illustrates the dual nature of persuasion that sometimes manifests itself in everyday life: One system of our mind is geared to cognitive, effortful thinking; the other emphasizes simpler, automatic processes (Kahneman, 2011).

Attitude–behavior theories offer an excellent guide to predicting behavior. However, they cannot forecast behavior in every situation in life. There is a tension between the predictions derived from social science theory and the ultimate unpredictability of humans in everyday life. An individual may recognize the benefits of staying calm in the heat of an argument with an acquaintance, yet lash out physically against the other person. You may positively evaluate safe sex but, in the passion of the moment, conveniently forget about the condom sitting on the dresser. A co-worker may feel that it is important to complete assignments on time. However, feeling lonely and frustrated, she gets drunk the night before and fails to turn in the assignment until after the deadline has passed. People are not always consistent. Theories strive to capture the complexity of human behavior, but do not always succeed because of the many factors that come into play. Still, attitude–behavior models have done much to help shed light on the circumstances under which attitudes forecast behavior. They remind us that, even if you can't predict all the people all the time, you can do a much better job of accounting for human behavior if you take attitudes, norms, and intentions into account.

Consistency between attitude and behavior – or practicing what you preach – remains a core aspect of human character, the essence of integrity. But because we are human beings, the promise of rewards or desire to fit in can thwart attempts of the best of us to act on what we know to be our attitude or moral values. As the noted military leader Norman Schwarzkopf said, "The truth of the matter is that you always know the right thing to do. The hard part is doing it" (Dowd, 2006).

References

Abelson, R. P. (1982). Three modes of attitude–behavior consistency. In M. P. Zanna, E. T. Higgins, & C. P. Herman (Eds.), *Consistency in social behavior: The Ontario symposium* (Vol. 2, pp. 131–146). Hillsdale, NJ: Lawrence Erlbaum Associates.

Adler, J. (1999, November 29). Living canvas. *Newsweek*, 75–76.

Ajzen, I. (1991). The theory of planned behavior. *Organizational Behavior and Human Decision Processes, 50,* 179–211.

Ajzen, I., Albarracín, D., & Hornik, R. (Eds.). (2007). *Prediction and change of health behavior: Applying the reasoned action approach.* Mahwah, NJ: Lawrence Erlbaum Associates.

Ajzen, I., & Fishbein, M. (1977). Attitude–behavior relations: A theoretical analysis and review of empirical research. *Psychological Bulletin, 84,* 888–918.

Ajzen, I., & Fishbein, M. (2005). The influence of attitudes on behavior. In D. Albarracín, B. T. Johnson, & M. P. Zanna (Eds.), *The handbook of attitudes* (pp. 173–221). Mahwah, NJ: Lawrence Erlbaum Associates.

Ajzen, I., Fishbein, M., Lohmann, S., & Albarracín, D. (2019). The influence of attitudes on behavior. In D. Albarracín & B. T. Johnson (Eds.), *The handbook of attitudes* (Vol. 1: Basic principles, 2nd ed., pp. 197–255). New York: Routledge.

Albarracín, D., Chan, M.-P. S., & Jiang, D. (2019). Attitudes and attitude change: Social and personality considerations about specific and general patterns of behavior. In K. Deaux & M. Snyder (Eds.), *The Oxford handbook of personality and social psychology* (2nd ed., pp. 439–463). New York: Oxford University Press.

Albarracín, D., Johnson, B. T., Fishbein, M., & Muellerleile, P. A. (2001). Theories of reasoned action and planned behavior as models of condom use: A meta-analysis. *Psychological Bulletin, 127,* 142–161.

Albarracín, D., Sunderrajan, A., Lohmann, S., Chan, M.-P. S., & Jiang, D. (2019). The psychology of attitudes, motivation, and persuasion. In D. Albarracín & B. T. Johnson (Eds.), *The handbook of attitudes* (Vol. 1: Basic principles, 2nd ed., pp. 3–44). New York: Routledge.

Allport, G. W. (1945). The psychology of participation. *Psychological Review, 53,* 117–132.

Armitage, C. J., & Conner, M. (2000). Attitudinal ambivalence: A test of three key hypotheses. *Personality and Social Psychology Bulletin, 26,* 1421–1432.

Arpan, L., Rhodes, N., & Roskos-Ewoldsen, D. R. (2007). Attitude accessibility: Theory, methods, and future directions. In D. R. Roskos-Ewoldsen & J. L. Monahan (Eds.), *Communication and social cognition: Theories and methods* (pp. 351–376). Mahwah, NJ: Erlbaum Associates.

Atkinson, M. (2004). Tattooing and civilizing processes: Body modification as self-control. *Canadian Review of Sociology & Anthropology, 41,* 125–146.

Bargh, J. (2017). *Before you know it: The unconscious reasons we do what we do.* New York: Touchstone.

Bennett, W. J. (1998). *The death of outrage: Bill Clinton and the assault on American ideals.* New York: Free Press.

Bentler, P. M., & Speckhart, G. (1979). Models of attitude–behavior relations. *Psychological Review, 86,* 452–464.

Booth-Butterfield, S., & Reger, B. (2004). The message changes belief and the rest is theory: The "1% or less" milk campaign and reasoned action. *Preventive Medicine, 39,* 581–588.

Briggs, S. R., Cheek, J. M., & Buss, A. H. (1980). An analysis of the self-monitoring scale. *Journal of Personality and Social Psychology, 38,* 679–686.

Brinberg, D., & Durand, J. (1983). Eating at fast-food restaurants: An analysis using two behavioral intention models. *Journal of Applied Social Psychology, 13*, 459–472.

Briñol, P., & Petty, R. E. (2019). The impact of individual differences on attitudes and attitude change. In D. Albarracín & B. T. Johnson (Eds.), *The handbook of attitudes* (Vol. 1: Basic principles, 2nd ed., pp. 520–556). New York: Routledge.

Carpenter, C., Boster, F. J., & Andrews, K. R. (2013). Functional attitude theory. In J. P. Dillard & L. Shen (Eds.), *The Sage handbook of persuasion: Developments in theory and practice* (2nd ed., pp. 104–119). Thousand Oaks, CA: Sage.

Clary, E. G., Snyder, M., Ridge, R. D., Miene, P. K., & Haugen, J. A. (1994). Matching messages to motives in persuasion: A functional approach to promoting volunteerism. *Journal of Applied Social Psychology, 24*, 1129–1149.

Clines, F. X. (2001, October 21). In uneasy time, seeking comfort in the familiar frights of Halloween. *The New York Times*, B8.

Dillard, J. P. (1993). Persuasion past and present: Attitudes aren't what they used to be. *Communication Monographs, 60*, 90–97.

Doll, J., & Ajzen, I. (1992). Accessibility and stability of predictors in the theory of planned behavior. *Journal of Personality and Social Psychology, 63*, 754–765.

Dowd, M. (2006, June 3). Teaching remedial decency. *The New York Times*, A23.

Dyson, M. E. (2001, January 22). Moral leaders need not be flawless. *The New York Times*, A23.

Eligon, J., Kovaleski, S. F., & Coscarelli, J. (2016, May 5). Pain, pills, and help too late to save Prince. *The New York Times*, A1, A18.

Fazio, R. H. (2000). Accessible attitudes as tools for object appraisal: Their costs and benefits. In G. R. Maio & J. M. Olson (Eds.), *Why we evaluate: Functions of attitudes* (pp. 1–36). Mahwah, NJ: Lawrence Erlbaum Associates.

Fazio, R. H., Powell, M. C., & Williams, C. J. (1989). The role of attitude accessibility in the attitude-to-behavior process. *Journal of Consumer Research, 16*, 280–288.

Fazio, R. H., & Roskos-Ewoldsen, D. R. (1994). Acting as we feel: When and how attitudes guide behavior. In S. Shavitt & T. C. Brock (Eds.), *Persuasion: Psychological insights and perspectives* (pp. 71–93). Boston, MA: Allyn and Bacon.

Fazio, R. H., & Zanna, M. P. (1978). Attitudinal qualities relating to the strength of the attitude–behavior relationship. *Journal of Experimental Social Psychology, 14*, 398–408.

Fazio, R. H., & Zanna, M. P. (1981). Direct experience and attitude–behavior consistency. In L. Berkowitz (Ed.), *Advances in experimental social psychology* (Vol. 14, pp. 162–202). New York: Academic Press.

Fishbein, M., & Ajzen, I. (1974). Attitudes toward objects as predictors of single and multiple behavioral criteria. *Psychological Review, 81*, 59–74.

Fishbein, M., & Ajzen, I. (1975). *Belief, attitude, intention and behavior: An introduction to theory and research.* Reading, MA: Addison–Wesley.

Fishbein, M., & Ajzen, I. (2010). *Predicting and changing behavior: The reasoned action approach.* New York: Psychology Press.

Gangestad, S. W., & Snyder, M. (2000). Self-monitoring: Appraisal and reappraisal. *Psychological Bulletin, 126*, 530–555.

Gawronski, B., & Brannon, S. M. (2019). Attitudes and the implicit-explicit dualism. In D. Albarracín & B. T. Johnson (Eds.), *The handbook of attitudes* (Vol. 1: Basic principles, 2nd ed., pp. 158–196). New York: Routledge.

Glasman, L. R., & Albarracín, D. (2006). Forming attitudes that predict future behavior: A meta-analysis of the attitude-behavior relation. *Psychological Bulletin, 132*, 778–822.

Goldberg, M. (2017, January 29). The Religious Right's Trojan horse. *The York Times* (Sunday Review), 1, 3.

Goldstein, N. J., & Cialdini, R. B. (2007). Using social norms as a lever of social influence. In A. R. Pratkanis (Ed.), *The science of social influence: Advances and future progress* (pp. 167–191). New York: Psychology Press.

Gupta, V. (2019, November 21). The cowardice behind Trump's vaping-ban retreat. *The New York Times*, A25.

Hannah-Jones, N. (2019, August 18). The idea of America. *The New York Times Magazine*, 14–22, 24, 26.

Hullett, C. R. (2004). Using functional theory to promote sexually transmitted disease (STD) testing: The impact of value-expressive messages and guilt. *Communication Research*, 31, 363–396.

Hullett, C. R. (2006). Using functional theory to promote HIV testing: The impact of value-expressive messages, uncertainty, and fear. *Health Communication*, 20, 57–67.

Johnson-Young, E. A. (2019). Predicting intentions to breastfeed for three months, six months, and one year using the theory of planned behaviour and body satisfaction. *Health Communication*, 34, 789–800.

Julka, D. L., & Marsh, K. L. (2005). An attitude functions approach to increasing organ-donation participation. *Journal of Applied Social Psychology*, 35, 821–849.

Kahneman, D. (2011). *Thinking, fast and slow*. New York: Farrar, Straus and Giroux.

Kaplan, S., & Richtel, M. (2019, September 1). Vaping one day, then on a ventilator the next. *The New York Times*, 1, 16.

Katz, D. (1960). The functional approach to the study of attitudes. *Public Opinion Quarterly*, 24, 163–204.

Kiesler, C. A., Collins, B. E., & Miller, N. (1969). *Attitude change: A critical analysis of theoretical approaches*. New York: Wiley.

Kim, M. S., & Hunter, J. E. (1993). Attitude–behavior relations: A meta-analysis of attitudinal relevance and topic. *Journal of Communication*, 43(1), 101–142.

LaPiere, R. T. (1934). Attitudes vs. action. *Social Forces*, 13, 230–237.

Lapinksi, M. K., & Boster, F. J. (2001). Modeling the ego-defensive function of attitudes. *Communication Monographs*, 68, 314–324.

Lavine, H., Thomsen, C. J., Zanna, M. P., & Borgida, E. (1998). On the primacy of affect in the determination of attitudes and behavior: The moderating role of affective–cognitive ambivalence. *Journal of Experimental Social Psychology*, 34, 398–421.

LaVito, A. (2019, February 11). CDC blames spike in teen tobacco use on vaping, popularity of Juul. *CBNC*. Retrieved June 11, 2019, from www.cnbc.com/2019/02/11/e-cigarettes-single-handedly

Lennox, R. D., & Wolfe, R. N. (1984). Revision of the self-monitoring scale. *Journal of Personality and Social Psychology*, 46, 1349–1364.

Liu, Y., Segev, S., & Villar, M. E. (2017). Comparing two mechanisms for green consumption: Cognitive-affect behavior vs. theory of reasoned action. *Journal of Consumer Marketing*, 34, 442–454.

Lord, C. G., Lepper, M. R., & Mackie, D. (1984). Attitude prototypes as determinants of attitude–behavior consistency. *Journal of Personality and Social Psychology*, 46, 1254–1266.

Lovett, I. (2014, May 4). When hitting "Find My iPhone" takes you to a thief's doorstep. *The New York Times*, 1, 23.

Lukacena, K. M., Reynolds-Tylus, T., & Quick, B. L. (2019). An application of the reasoned action approach to bystander intervention for sexual assault. *Health Communication*, 34, 46–53.

Maio, G. R., & Haddock, G. (2009). *The psychology of attitudes and attitude change*. London: Sage Publications.

Maio, G. R., & Olson, J. M. (Eds.). (2000a). *Why we evaluate: Functions of attitudes*. Mahwah, NJ: Lawrence Erlbaum Associates.

Maio, G. R., & Olson, J. M. (2000b). What is a "value-expressive" attitude? In G. R. Maio & J. M. Olson (Eds.), *Why we evaluate: Functions of attitudes* (pp. 249–269). Mahwah, NJ: Lawrence Erlbaum Associates.

Manstead, A. S. R., Proffitt, C., & Smart, J. L. (1983). Predicting and understanding mothers' infant-feeding intentions and behavior: Testing the theory of reasoned action. *Journal of Personality and Social Psychology*, 44, 657–671.

Millar, M. G., & Millar, K. U. (1990). Attitude change as a function of attitude type and argument type. *Journal of Personality and Social Psychology*, 59, 217–228.

Millar, M. G., & Millar, K. U. (1996). The effects of direct and indirect experience on affective and cognitive responses and the attitude–behavior relation. *Journal of Experimental Social Psychology*, 32, 561–579.

Morrison, D. M., Gillmore, M. R., & Baker, S. A. (1995). Determinants of condom use among high-risk heterosexual adults: A test of the theory of reasoned action. *Journal of Applied Social Psychology*, 25, 651–676.

Nagourney, A. (2008, September 2). In political realm, "family problem" emerges as test and distraction. *The New York Times*, A18.

Olson, M. A., & Fazio, R. H. (2006). Reducing automatically activated racial prejudice through implicit evaluative conditioning. *Personality and Social Psychology Bulletin*, 32, 421–433.

Park, H. S., & Smith, S. W. (2007). Distinctiveness and influence of subjective norms, personal descriptive and injunctive norms, and societal descriptive and injunctive norms on behavioral intent: A case of two behaviors critical to organ donation. *Human Communication Research*, 33, 194–218.

Paul, P. (2011, December 8). Divisive devices. *The New York Times*, E14.

Phillips, A. (1998, October 2). How much does monogamy tell us? *The New York Times*, A27.

Rhodes, N., & Ewoldsen, D. R. (2013). Outcomes of persuasion: Behavioral, cognitive, and social. In J. P. Dillard & L. Shen (Eds.), *The Sage handbook of persuasion: Developments in theory and practice* (2nd ed., pp. 53–69). Thousand Oaks, CA: Sage.

Richtel, M., & Grady, D. (2019, September 7). Illness prompts warning to stop e-cigarette use. *The New York Times*, A1, A15.

Rimal, R. N., & Lapinski, M. K. (2015). A re-explication of social norms, ten years later. *Communication Theory*, 25, 393–409.

Safronova, V. (2015, November 19). The Finstagram rebellion. *The New York Times*, D1, D12.

Shavitt, S., & Nelson, M. R. (2000). The social-identity function in person perception: Communicated meanings of product preferences. In G. R. Maio & J. M. Olson (Eds.), *Why we evaluate: Functions of attitudes* (pp. 37–57). Mahwah, NJ: Lawrence Erlbaum Associates.

Sheeran, P., Abraham, C., & Orbell, S. (1999). Psychosocial correlates of heterosexual condom use: A meta-analysis. *Psychological Bulletin*, 125, 90–132.

Smith, M. B., Bruner, J. B., & White, R. S. (1956). *Opinions and personality*. New York: Wiley.

Snyder, M. (1974). Self-monitoring of expressive behavior. *Journal of Personality and Social Psychology*, 30, 526–537.

Snyder, M. (1987). *Public appearances/private realities: The psychology of self-monitoring*. New York: W. H. Freeman.

Snyder, M., Clary, E. G., & Stukas, A. A. (2000). The functional approach to volunteerism. In G. R. Maio & J. M. Olson (Eds.), *Why we evaluate: Functions of attitudes* (pp. 365–393). Mahwah, NJ: Lawrence Erlbaum Associates.

Snyder, M., & Kendzierski, D. (1982). Acting on one's attitudes: Procedures for linking attitude and behavior. *Journal of Experimental Social Psychology, 18,* 165–183.

Snyder, M., & Tanke, E. D. (1976). Behavior and attitude: Some people are more consistent than others. *Journal of Personality, 44,* 510–517.

Sutton, S. (1998). Predicting and explaining intentions and behavior: How well are we doing? *Journal of Applied Social Psychology, 28,* 1317–1338.

Tian, Y., & Robinson, J. D. (2017). Predictors of cell phone use in distracted driving: Extending the theory of planned behavior. *Health Communication, 32,* 1066–1075.

Twitchell, J. B. (1999). *Lead us into temptation: The triumph of American materialism.* New York: Columbia University Press.

Wallace, D. S., Paulson, R. M., Lord, C. G., & Bond, C. F., Jr. (2005). Which behaviors do attitudes predict? Meta-analyzing the effects of social pressure and perceived difficulty. *Review of General Psychology, 9,* 214–227.

Wang Erber, M., Hodges, S. D., & Wilson, T. D. (1995). Attitude strength, attitude stability, and the effects of analyzing reasons. In R. E. Petty & J. A. Krosnick (Eds.), *Attitude strength: Antecedents and consequences* (pp. 433–454). Hillsdale, NJ: Lawrence Erlbaum Associates.

Wang, X. (2016). Excelling in multitasking and enjoying the distraction: Predicting intentions to send or read text messages while driving. *Computers in Human Behavior, 64,* 584–590.

Weigel, R. H., & Newman, L. S. (1976). Increasing attitude–behavior correspondence by broadening the scope of the behavioral measure. *Journal of Personality and Social Psychology, 33,* 793–802.

Wicker, A. W. (1969). Attitudes vs. actions: The relationship of verbal and overt behavioral responses to attitude objects. *Journal of Social Issues, 25,* 41–78.

Yzer, M. (2013). Reasoned action theory: Persuasion as belief-based behavior change. In J. P. Dillard & L. Shen (Eds.), *The Sage handbook of persuasion: Developments in theory and practice* (2nd ed., pp. 120–136). Thousand Oaks, CA: Sage.

Zanna, M. P., & Fazio, R. H. (1982). The attitude–behavior relation: Moving toward a third generation of research. In M. P. Zanna, E. T. Higgins, & C. P. Herman (Eds.), *Consistency in social behavior: The Ontario symposium* (Vol. 2, pp. 283–301). Hillsdale, NJ: Lawrence Erlbaum Associates.

Chapter 7

Attitude Measurement

Pollsters do it with precision. Theorists do it with conceptual flair. Survey researchers do it for a living. "It," of course, is designing questionnaires to measure attitudes!

Puns and double entendres aside, attitude measurement plays a critical role in the study and practice of persuasion. It is the practical side of the field, the down-to-earth domain that provides the instrumentation to test hypotheses and to track changes in attitudes and beliefs. If there were no reliable scientific techniques to measure attitudes, we would not know how people evaluated social and political issues. We would not know the impact that persuasive communications had on people's feelings and thoughts. Documenting the effects of large-scale media campaigns would permanently elude us.

Measurement is the process of assigning individuals to different categories for the purpose of identifying their position on a factor, or variable. In quantitative social science, numbers play a key factor in these determinations. Measurement allows us to describe complex attitude and persuasion phenomena in ways that can be validated and cross-checked by other scientists, enabling the building of a coherent body of knowledge.

This chapter explores the main themes in attitude measurement. It describes scales used to tap attitudes, as well as the pitfalls and challenges researchers face when trying to assess attitudes empirically. After reading this chapter, you should know more about how to write good attitude questions and how to locate valid scales that measure specific attitudes.

Overview

Attitude questionnaires date back to 1928. It was in this year that psychologist Louis Thurstone published an article titled "Attitudes Can Be Measured." Thurstone (1928) proposed an elaborate procedure to assess people's views on social issues. An innovative student of psychologist measurement, Thurstone was the first to develop a detailed technique to empirically assess attitudes. Thanks to Thurstone and his followers, we now have established methodologies for assessing attitudes. What's more, thousands of questionnaires have been developed to tap beliefs and attitudes on countless issues.

Are you interested in attitudes toward race or affirmative action? You can find dozens of surveys, such as those developed by McConahay (1986) and Schmermund and colleagues (2001). Do you want to explore attitudes toward the homeless? Aberson and McVean (2008) developed a scale to measure biases toward homeless individuals. Did a recent trip to Las Vegas whet your intellectual appetite toward gambling? If so, you can find a valid scale tapping gambling passion in an article by Rousseau and associates (2002). Are you curious to know if people find it easier to reveal personal information online than face-to-face? Well, then you can click onto an intriguing scale that measures online communication attitudes by Ledbetter (2009). In a related fashion, if you have ever wondered if everyone feels anxious when they don't have their cell phones or believe new technology makes people waste too much time, you can tap into these perceptions with Rosen et al's (2013) validated media and technology usage and attitudes scale. More generally, there are questionnaires tapping attitudes on hundreds of issues, including climate change, prejudice against fat people, adulation of thin models, sex, sex roles, basking in the glory of sports teams, political activism, even cloning human beings.

It is not easy to write good attitude questions. You can appreciate this if you have ever tried to dream up questions assessing views on one or another issue. Administering your survey to others, you may have found respondents scratching their heads and asking, "What do you mean by this question?" Devising reliable attitude items is not as easy as it looks.

There are people who do this for a living – folks who are so proficient at devising questions that they work for professional research centers or advertising firms. There is a science to writing attitude questions, one that calls on principles of measurement, statistics, and cognitive psychology (Hippler, Schwarz, & Sudman, 1987; Tourangeau & Rasinski, 1988). It all flows from an underlying belief – core assumption – that one can measure phenomena by assigning numbers to objects on the basis of rules or guidelines (Stevens, 1950; see Figure 7.1).

Perhaps the simplest way to assess attitudes is to ask people if they like or dislike the attitude object. National opinion polls tap Americans' attitudes toward the president by asking if they approve or disapprove of the way the chief executive is handling the economy. However, there are two problems with this procedure. First, the agree–disagree scale offers people only two choices. It does not allow for shades of gray. Second, it measures attitudes with only one item. This puts all the researcher's eggs in one empirical basket. If the item is ambiguous or the respondent misunderstands the question, then all hope of accurately measuring the attitude disappears. In addition, by relying on only one item, the researcher misses the opportunity to tap complex, even contradictory, components of the attitude.

For these reasons, researchers prefer to include many survey items and to assess attitudes along a numerical continuum. Questionnaires that employ these procedures are called scales. There are three standard attitude scales: (a) Likert, (b) Guttman, and (c) the semantic differential.

To illustrate these, and make it interesting and relevant, I offer as examples scales measuring gender or sex-role attitudes. Naturally, these issues have become dicey and fraught today. Nowadays, we frequently distinguish between an individual's biological, anatomical sex, and the person's gender identity, a culturally acquired identification, which typically involves norms associated with men and women (some scholars, calling attention to complexities, have maintained that biological and cultural factors are entwined, so that sex and gender distinction cannot always be easily separated; see Shibley Hyde et al., 2019). For this chapter, gender roles (using the conventionally popular cultural perspective) provide a contemporary, easy-to-appreciate way to illustrate the variety of attitude measures. If you want to tap gender role attitudes today, you need to assess

Panel A: Stair-step scale

Question: What is your attitude toward the Republican Party?
Instructions: Place a check mark on the stairstep that best describes your attitude.

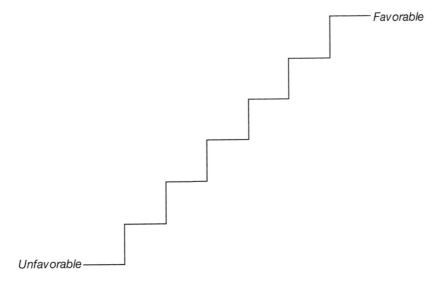

Panel B: Opinion thermometer

Question: How do you feel about Barack Obama?
Instructions: Circle the number on the thermometer scale that best describes your feelings.

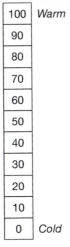

Figure 7.1 Two Different Types of Numerical Attitude Scales

Adapted from Ostrom et al. (1994)

attitudes from multiple vantage points: A traditional male–female perspective, feminist, LGBTQ, and rejection of the gender binary by individuals who don't identify as female or male (Bergner, 2019).

Thus, with a broad appreciation for fluid sexual identifications and gender roles, this chapter presents different ways of measuring attitudes in an effort to offer insights into how to empirically tap these complex, controversial, ever-changing constructs reliably and validly. If attitudes are measured skillfully and sensitively in surveys, they can predict behavior (Albarracín, Chan, & Jiang, 2019), while at the same time suggesting strategies to change behavior. Thus, it behooves us to appreciate how to measure attitudes, on the basis of explicit questionnaire surveys, unobtrusive measures, and implicit strategies.

Questionnaire Measures of Attitude

Likert Scale

The nice thing about being the first to do something is that they name it after you.

A psychologist named Rensis Likert (pronounced Lickert) refined Thurstone's procedures in 1932 (Likert, 1932). Thurstone had asked as many as several hundred individuals to serve as judges. These individuals then sort attitude items into different evaluative categories. Although the procedure is elegant, it is cumbersome and assumes judges are objective. Likert recommended that researchers devise items, thereby simplifying the Thurstone procedure and offering the template for the modern attitude scale. Before continuing, let's pause for a moment of humility: These researchers were measuring attitudes in the early years of the twentieth century. As far back as the late 1920s and early 1930s, before the dawning of World War II propaganda and regular election polling of political attitudes, psychologists had recognized that mental and emotional phenomena could be empirically assessed, and they were devising ways to do this precisely. That's impressive.

The scale named for Rensis Likert, a *Likert scale*, contains a series of opinion statements. Respondents read each item and indicate their agreement or disagreement with each statement along a numerical scale. A Likert scale assumes that each item taps the same underlying attitude and there are significant interrelationships among items. It also presumes that there are equal intervals among categories. For example, on a 5-point (*strongly agree, somewhat agree, neutral, somewhat disagree, strongly disagree*) scale, researchers assume that the psychological difference between strongly agree and somewhat agree is the same as that between strongly disagree and somewhat disagree.

Likert scales are commonplace today. No doubt you've completed dozens of these strongly agree–strongly disagree surveys. An example is the course evaluation questionnaire students complete on the last day of class. (You know, the day your professor acts oh-so-nice to you and bakes those fudge brownies!) Students indicate how much they agree or disagree with statements regarding the prof.'s teaching abilities and the course content.

Likert scales can proceed from 1 to 5, as noted previously. They can also include other numerical options, such as 1 to 7, 1 to 9, or 1 to 100. Many researchers prefer 5- or 7-point scales because they allow respondents to indicate shades of gray in their opinions, but do not provide so many categories that people feel overwhelmed by choices.

To help you appreciate how researchers measure attitudes with Likert and other scales, an example is provided, using the ever-popular issue of attitudes toward gender roles (see Figures 7.1 and 7.2).

Two sample Likert scales are provided to make this concrete and interesting. The first focuses on traditional male–female gender role attitudes (Table 7.1), while the second takes a more contemporary approach, measuring beliefs and attitudes toward less traditional, nuanced gender role issues (see Table 7.2).

A sample Likert scale, focused on traditional gender role attitudes, appears in Table 7.1.

Table 7.1 Likert Scale for Male–Female Gender Roles

Please indicate whether you Strongly Agree (SA), Agree (A), are Neutral (N), Disagree (D), or Strongly Disagree (SD) with each of these statements.

		SA	A	N	D	SD
1.	Women are more emotional than men.	1	2	3	4	5
2.	Swearing and obscenity are more repulsive in the speech of a woman than of a man.	1	2	3	4	5
3.	When two people go out on a date, the man should be the one to pay the check.	1	2	3	4	5
4.	When a couple is going somewhere by car, it's better for the man to do most of the driving.	1	2	3	4	5
5.	If both husband and wife work full-time, her career should be just as important as his in determining where the family lives.	1	2	3	4	5
6.	Most women interpret innocent remarks or acts as being sexist.	1	2	3	4	5
7.	Society has reached the point where women and men have equal opportunities for achievement.	1	2	3	4	5
8.	Even though women and men should have the same opportunities at work, women should take on more of the childrearing tasks than men.	1	2	3	4	5
9.	When women lose fairly, they claim discrimination.	1	2	3	4	5
10.	Many women have a quality of purity that few men possess.	1	2	3	4	5
11.	Women should be cherished and protected by men.	1	2	3	4	5

Sources: Statement 2 is from Spence, Helmreich, and Stapp (1973). Statements 4 and 5 are from Peplau, Hill, and Rubin (1993). Items 6, 9, 10, and 11 are from Glick and Fiske (1996). Statement 7 is from Swim et al. (1995). Items 1, 2, 6, 7, 9, and 10 can be regarded as descriptive beliefs; statements 3, 4, 5, 8, and 11 are prescriptive beliefs. Note that item 9 is an example of what Glick and Fiske call hostile sexism, while 9 and 10 exemplify benevolent sexism because they are paternalistic and objectify women through romantic chivalry. However, the latter is controversial, as some women experience so-called benevolent sexism as psychologically warm and like to be cherished and protected by men. Critics would argue that these women have internalized a stereotyped ideology, an accusation women with traditional gender role attitudes might resent.

(a)

(b)

(c)

Figure 7.2a–c Attitudes Toward Male–Female Gender Roles Have Different Aspects, Including Dating, Work, and Childrearing. Scales to measure attitudes should ideally take these different aspects into account

Images courtesy of Shutterstock

(a)

(b)

(c)

(d)

Figure 7.3a–d Attitudes Toward Contemporary Gender Roles Have Opened Up as Society Has Embraced Multiple Gender Roles and Sexual Orientations. Likert scales measuring contemporary gender roles, after many years of implicitly tapping only traditional male–female role issues, have expanded to assess beliefs and affects associated with gay, transgender, and a host of other gender/sexual concerns. Reliable, validated scales tapping these attitudes offer a scientifically precise way of understanding diverse gender role attitudes in contemporary society

Image courtesy of Shutterstock

> **Table 7.2** Likert Scale for Contemporary, Less Traditional Gender Roles. Please indicate whether you Strongly Agree (SA), Agree (A), are Neutral (N), Disagree (D), or Strongly Disagree (SD) with each of these statements

		SA	A	N	D	SD
1.	Female homosexuality is a natural expression of sexuality in women.	1	2	3	4	5
2.	Sex between two men is just wrong.	1	2	3	4	5
3.	Gay individuals should be able to adopt children.	1	2	3	4	5
4.	Transgender men are unable to accept who they really are.	1	2	3	4	5
5.	Gender is binary; you are either a woman or a man.	1	2	3	4	5
6.	Transgender individuals should be able to use public restrooms that correspond to their gender identity, not their biological sex at birth.	1	2	3	4	5
7.	Letting transgender women compete in women's sports like track and tennis would be cheating.	1	2	3	4	5
8.	Transgender individuals should be able to serve in the military.	1	2	3	4	5
9.	When describing non-binary individuals, it is best to use the pronoun "they."	1	2	3	4	5
10.	People should be allowed to report their gender identity in non-binary ways, if they want to.	1	2	3	4	5
11.	Sex change operations are morally wrong.	1	2	3	4	5
12.	God made two sexes and two sexes only.	1	2	3	4	5

Sources: Statement 1 is from Norton and Herek (2013). Statement 4 is from Billard (2018). Statement 10 is from Shibley Hyde et al. (2019). Statements 11 and 12 are from Hill and Willoughby (2005). Note that some items are phrased so that agreement signifies endorsement of contemporary non-traditional gender role options, while in other cases agreement reflects a more traditional attitude. Varying the phrasing in this way can prevent respondents from getting into a response set where they just agree with whatever the item says.

Guttman Scale

Sometimes it seems that the person with the strongest attitude toward a topic is the one willing to take the most difficult stands, those that require the greatest gumption. One may not agree with these positions, but one is hard pressed to deny that these are difficult positions to endorse. A *Guttman scale* (named after Louis Guttman) takes this approach to measuring attitudes (Guttman, 1944).

The scale progresses from items easiest to accept to those most difficult to endorse. Those who get the highest score on a Guttman scale agree with all items. Those with moderate attitudes agree with questions that are easy and moderately difficult to endorse, and those with mildly positive

Table 7.3 Guttman Scale for Male–Female Gender Roles

Least difficult to accept	1	Fathers should spend some of their leisure time helping to care for the children.
	2	Fathers should share in infant care responsibilities, such as getting up when the baby cries at night and changing diapers.
	3	If both parents work, the father and mother should divide up equally the task of staying at home when children get sick.
Most difficult to accept	4	If both parents work, the father and mother should divide up equally the task of raising the children.

attitudes agree only with items that are easy to accept. A Guttman scale for male–female gender roles appears in Table 7.3.

You could devise similar Guttman gender role scales to tap attitudes toward less traditional relationships. Least difficult to accept items could involve asking if people agreed that workplace environments should be free of bias for transgender or non-binary individuals. They could then proceed to more difficult items that ask whether straight individuals would be comfortable sharing an apartment with a trans or non-binary individual, and ending with still tougher-to-agree-with items (at least for those with a traditional socialization) that asked how comfortable individuals would feel if a son or daughter chose to marry a trans or non-binary individual.

Guttman scales are hard to construct. They are not as easy to administer as Likert scales. However, they can be useful in tapping attitudes on sensitive topics like abortion. Opposition to abortion could be scaled by examining whether respondents believe it would be acceptable for a woman to have an abortion under increasingly difficult circumstances. Many people would agree that an abortion is wrong if performed primarily because the woman has low income and cannot afford to have any more children. However, fewer would agree that abortion is wrong if the pregnancy was caused by rape or incest. Respondents with an extremely strong pro-life attitude would endorse the strongest, absolutist option: Abortion is wrong in all circumstances, even when the woman's physical health or life is endangered.

Semantic Differential

Charles Osgood and colleagues do not have a scale that bears their name. But they succeeded in developing one of the most frequently used scales in the attitude business: *the semantic differential*. Osgood, Suci, and Tannenbaum (1957) chose not to assess beliefs or agreement with opinion statements. Instead, they explored the meanings that people attach to social objects, focusing on the emotional aspect of attitude. The term *semantic* is used because their instrument asks people to indicate feelings about an object on a pair of bipolar, adjective scales. The term *differential* comes from the fact that the scale assesses the different meanings people ascribe to a person or issue.

Participants rate a concept using bipolar adjectives: One adjective lies at one end of the scale; its opposite is at the other end. Osgood and colleagues discovered that people typically employ three dimensions to rate concepts: Evaluation (Is it good or bad for me?), potency (Is it strong or weak?), and activity (Is it active or passive?) (Osgood, 1974). A semantic differential scale for gender roles appears in Table 7.4, asking people to evaluate the #MeToo Movement Against Sexual Assault, the leaderless online movement that emerged after news exposés about widespread sexual abuse in Hollywood, the media, and other major industries. You could also use this scale to tap attitudes toward female politicians, corporate leaders, rock music, vegan diets, and traditional religion.

Importantly, the semantic differential runs along a continuum, so individuals can choose any of the numbers from 1 to 7. Their particular choice would reflect their degree of affect on the issue. For example, an individual who feels feminism is good might choose a 1 or 2 on the first item, but, for one psychological reason or another, could feel more ambivalently about other aspects, opting to rate feminism as unhealthy on the sixth item, giving it a 6. Although the semantic differential has been used for more than a half-century, it continues to tap subtle aspects of our feelings about people, issues, and products.

Pitfalls in Attitude Measurement

There is no perfect attitude scale. Even the best scales can fail to measure attitudes accurately. Inaccuracies result from such factors as: (a) respondent carelessness in answering the questions, (b) people's desire to say the socially appropriate thing rather than what they truly believe, and (c) a tendency to agree with items regardless of their content, or *acquiescence* (Dawes & Smith, 1985). Acquiescence, a pervasive survey response bias, is most likely to occur among individuals with less education, lower social status, and those who do not enjoy thinking (Krosnick, Judd, & Wittenbrink, 2005, 2019). Simple dichotomous questions like true/false or yes/no can aggravate the tendency to acquiesce or automatically agree. Although these problems can be reduced through careful survey measurement techniques (see next section), some inaccuracy in responses to attitude scales is inevitable.

A particularly gnawing problem in survey research involves the format and wording of questions. The way the researcher words the question and designs the questionnaire can elicit from the respondent answers that may not reflect the individual's true attitude (Schuman & Presser, 1981; Schwarz, 1999). The manner in which the question is asked can influence the response that the researcher receives. It reminds one of what writer Gertrude Stein reportedly said on her death bed. With death

Table 7.4 Semantic Differential for Gender Roles

#MeToo Movement Against Sexual Assault								
Good	1	2	3	4	5	6	7	Bad
Strong	1	2	3	4	5	6	7	Weak
Heavy	1	2	3	4	5	6	7	Light
Active	1	2	3	4	5	6	7	Passive
Fair	1	2	3	4	5	6	7	Unfair
Valuable	1	2	3	4	5	6	7	Worthless
Important	1	2	3	4	5	6	7	Unimportant

near, she asked her long-time romantic partner, "What is the answer?" When her partner did not reply, Stein said, "In that case, what is the question?"

Two key survey design factors that can influence – or bias – attitude responses are survey context and wording.

Context

Survey questions appear one after another on a piece of paper, computer screen, or in an interview administered over the telephone. Questions occurring early in the survey can influence responses to later questions. This is because thoughts triggered by earlier questions can shape subsequent responses. The answers that individuals supply may thus be artifacts of the "context" of the survey instrument rather than reflections of their actual attitudes.

For instance, respondents asked to evaluate the morality of American business leaders might respond differently if they heard Jeffrey Epstein's name at the beginning rather than at the end of a list (e.g., Schwarz & Bless, 1992). Some years back, Epstein, a billionaire financier, sexually abused about 80 teenage girls, coercing them into performing sexual acts at his palatial Palm Beach and Manhattan homes, adding insult to injury by striking a legal deal that allowed the light sentence to be kept secret from his psychologically wounded victims. With Epstein as an anchor or standard of comparison, respondents might give other business leaders favorable ratings, noting that whatever their ethical shortcomings, they had not sexually abused teenage girls. But if Epstein's name did not appear until the end of the list, respondents would have no reason to base evaluations of other business leaders on comparisons with Epstein's morally depraved behavior. As a result, business leaders might receive comparatively less positive ratings.

Howard Schuman and Stanley Presser (1981) documented question order effects in a classic study of Americans' attitudes toward abortion. Naturally, abortion attitudes were complex, but a majority supported legalized abortion. When asked, "Do you think it should be possible for a pregnant woman to obtain a legal abortion if she is married and does not want any more children?" over 60 percent said "Yes." However, support dropped when the following question was asked first: "Do you think it should be possible for a pregnant woman to obtain a legal abortion if there is a strong chance of serious defect in the baby?" In this case, only 48 percent agreed that a married woman should be able to obtain a legal abortion if she did not want any more children. To be sure, these attitudes are controversial and would outrage those who oppose abortion in all instances. But the point here is methodological, not ideological. The order of questions influenced evaluations of abortion. Something of a contrast effect appears to have emerged.

In the first case, respondents had no other anchor than abortion in the case of a married woman who does not want any more children. A substantial majority came out in favor of abortion in this case. But after considering the gut-wrenching issue of aborting a fetus with a medical defect and deciding in favor of this option, a second group of respondents now mulled over the question of abortion for married women who did not want any more children. In comparison to the birth-defect choice, this seemed relatively unsubstantial, perhaps trivial. Using the birth-defect case as the standard for comparison, the idea that a woman should get a legal abortion if she did not want any more children seemed not to measure up to these individuals' moral criterion for abortion. Not surprisingly, fewer individuals supported abortion in this case.

It is also possible that, in light of the ambivalence many neutral or pro-choice supporters feel toward abortion, those who supported abortion in the case of a serious defect in the baby felt guilty.

To reduce guilt, some may have shifted their position on abortion for married women, saying they opposed abortion in this less taxing situation. Whatever the explanation, it seems clear that the order in which the questions appeared influenced respondents' reports of their attitudes.

Note that this study was conducted some 40 years ago. Attitudes toward abortion have changed, in light of conservatives' principled and political campaigning against the issue. Even 40 percent of Democrats, who ordinarily take a pro-choice position, indicate they oppose abortion if a woman wants one, for any reason at all (Cohn, 2019). If Schuman and Presser's study were replicated today, fewer women would probably say they thought it should be possible for a pregnant woman to get an abortion if she does not want any more children, no matter what order the questions were asked. But, altering the content of items to reflect the current political environment, one should still find question order effects, a testament to the importance of replication and the durability of subtle changes in questionnaire design.

Another, more amusing, example of order effects involves measurement of happiness and dating. When students are asked first to say how happy they are and then to indicate how often they are dating, there is no relationship between happiness and dating. However, when the questions are reversed something interesting happens. When the first question is "How often are you dating?" and the second is, "How happy are you?" responses to the questions are highly correlated. Students who date a lot say they are happy and those who do not date very much claim they are unhappy. Presumably, the daters think to themselves, "I have been dating a lot. I have been going out with lots of different guys (girls). That must make me pretty happy about my life this semester." Non-daters ruminate that, "Gosh, I haven't gone on a date for months now. No one has asked me out and I have not tried to hook up with anyone. No wonder I'm depressed!" Both daters and non-daters infer their happiness from how often they have been dating (Thaler & Sunstein, 2008; see also self-perception theory, Chapter 13). The results have everything to do with the order in which questions were asked.

Wording

As writers have long known, language is full of meaning, capable of conveying powerful sentiments. It should, therefore, come as no surprise that the way a question is worded can influence respondents' evaluations of the issue. Consider attitudes toward health care as an example.

While just about everybody agreed that the nation's health care system needed overhaul back in 2009, there were sharp disagreements among political leaders about just what type of health plan was best for America. In such a situation, public opinion exerted a pivotal influence on the debate, and the way opinion poll questions were phrased produced vastly different results. When a national poll asked respondents whether they would favor or oppose "creating a public health care plan administered by the federal government that would compete directly with private health insurance companies," only 48 percent indicated they would support such a plan.

However, when individuals were asked how important they felt it was "to give people a choice of both a public plan administered by the federal government and a private plan for their health insurance," 72 percent said they believed this was very important (Connelly, 2009, p. A17). The wording in the first question emphasizes competition with private health insurance companies, while the second focuses on choice, a positive value to Americans. Even after passage of a landmark health care law in 2010, wording effects relating to health care questions persisted. The use of the more colloquial, but disparaging, description, "Obamacare" or "Barack Obama's health care plan" elicited more negative reactions than the formal name, the Affordable Care Act or the health care law (CNN, 2013; see Holl, Niederdeppe, & Schuldt, 2018).

Health care questionnaire wording issues continued apace into Trump's presidency, particularly as Democratic challengers to Trump proposed more sweeping reforms than Obama had instituted. Democratic presidential candidate Senator Bernie Sanders, denouncing the state of American health care, promoted universal care, branded as single-payer or Medicare-for-all. Words made all the difference in how Americans evaluated plans for health care reform. When described in terms that have positive connotations, like "universal health coverage" or "Medicare-for-all," more than six in ten Americans evaluated the plan positively. However, when dubbed a "single-payer health insurance system," or branded with the unpopular socialist label, as "socialized medicine," fewer than five in ten Americans rated the plan favorably. What's more, when told that a health care plan would increase taxes or eliminate private health insurance companies, support dropped (KFF, 2019; Talbot, 2019).

This wording effect might be neutralized if interviewers explained that increased taxes would fall primarily on the rich, with taxes levied primarily on the top 1 percent of Americans. On the other hand, if the poll warned that the health care plan could increase middle-class taxes, support would drop. But if it noted that the taxes would be less than the cost of earners' current deductibles, public endorsement would undoubtedly rise. Thus, it is difficult to know what surveys measuring positive attitudes toward Medicare-for-all mean, since the actual policy would have many costs and benefits not reflected by a single question. Pollsters can easily manipulate the answers they get by wording it in strategic ways. Surveys tapping complex, controversial policy issues are inevitably tainted by wording, suggesting that public opinion on these topics should not be taken at face value.

Perhaps the most disturbing example of wording effects came from polls probing an even more emotional issue: Americans' belief that the Holocaust actually occurred (see Figure 7.4).

With some anti-Semitic groups arguing that the Holocaust had never happened and was a figment of Jews' imagination, the Roper polling organization launched a national survey to see how many Americans actually bought into this false belief. In 1992, Roper probed Americans' attitudes toward the Holocaust, tapping beliefs with this key question:

> The term Holocaust usually refers to the killing of millions of Jews in Nazi death camps during World War II. Does it seem possible or does it seem impossible to you that the Nazi extermination of the Jews never happened?

Amazingly, 22 percent of respondents said it was "possible" that the mass executions never happened, about 12 percent claimed they "didn't know," and 65 percent said it was "impossible" that the event had not happened. "The fact that nearly one fourth of U.S. adults denied that the Holocaust had happened ... raised serious questions about the quality of knowledge about recent history," observed Carroll J. Glynn and colleagues (1999, p. 76). It also raised the possibility that large numbers of Americans consciously or unconsciously subscribed to an anti-Semitic ideology.

Public opinion researchers suspected that the problem, once again, was not ideological, but methodological. They suggested that the Roper question was misleading and the double negative had confused people. Several polling organizations, including Roper, conducted new surveys, this time with clearer questions like: "Does it seem possible to you that the Nazi extermination of the Jews never happened, or do you feel certain that it happened?" This time, 91 percent said they were certain it happened. Just 1 percent of the public said it was possible the Holocaust never happened, and 8 percent did not know (Smith, 1995).

The results restored faith in the public's knowledge and good sense. They also revealed the strong influence that question wording has on reports of attitudes.

Figure 7.4 During World War II, the Nazis Exterminated Six Million European Jews. In this heart-rending image, people await possible deportation or death. Some 50 years later, pollsters measured attitudes toward the Holocaust, discovering that the wording of the question influenced responses on this profoundly disturbing issue

Image courtesy of Getty Images

Psychological Issues

As you can see, wording and context effects have stimulated much discussion among researchers. In addition to raising questions about strategic use of poll findings, researchers have elucidated more scholarly concerns. Some theorists have suggested that the reason why question wording exerts such strong effects is not just that people are sensitive to subtle variations in language, but because in many cases they don't have full-blown attitudes at all. Instead, these researchers suggest, individuals construct their attitudes on the spot, based on what happens to be on their minds at the time or on thoughts triggered by survey questions (Wilson, LaFleur, & Anderson, 1996; Zaller, 1992). In support of this position, research has found that large numbers of people volunteer opinions on fictitious issues, those that the pollster has invented for the purposes of the survey. For example, over 50 percent of respondents gave their opinion of the Monetary Control Bill, legislation dreamed up by survey researchers (Bishop, Tuchfarber, & Oldendick, 1986)!

People *do* construct attitudes on the spot in response to pollsters' questions. We should not assume that this is the norm, however. It pushes the envelope to argue that people lack attitudes; clearly, people harbor attitudes when the issue touches on strong values, is the product of socialization, or has been mentally worked through. At the same time, there are plenty of policy issues in which people lack firm beliefs or opinions. In such cases, their attitudes can be swayed by pollsters' questions, a fact that has not been lost on savvy marketers hoping to manipulate public opinion (see Box 7.1).

BOX 7.1

Skewing The Survey Results

You have probably heard television advertisements that claim that "a majority of people interviewed in a major survey" said such-and-such about the product. The results make it sound like a scientific study proved that people prefer Crest to Colgate, Coke to Pepsi, Burger King to McDonald's, or iPhone to its competitors. As you listened, you no doubt thought to yourself, "Is this research real, or what?"

"Or what" is the appropriate answer. Some of the research that companies cite on their behalf is based on questionable methods. It is a powerful example of how marketing researchers can cook the data to fit the client, or design surveys that assure that companies will receive the answers they desire. Reporter Cynthia Crossen (1991) discussed this trend in the *Wall Street Journal*. She reported that:

- When Levi Strauss & Co. asked students which clothes would be most popular this year, 90 percent said Levi's 501 jeans. They were the only jeans on the list.
- A survey for Black Flag said:

  A roach disk … poisons a roach slowly. The dying roach returns to the nest and after it dies is eaten by other roaches. In turn these roaches become poisoned and die. How effective do you think this type of product would be in killing roaches?

Not surprisingly, 79 percent said effective.

- An obviously dated, but still interesting Chrysler automobile study showing its cars were preferred to Toyota's included just 100 people in each of two tests. But more important, none of the people surveyed owned a foreign car, so they may well have been predisposed to like U.S.-made vehicles.

(pp. A1, A7)

Summarizing her report on the use of marketing research, Crossen acknowledged that some studies use valid measurement techniques. But many surveys are filled with loaded questions and are designed to prove a point rather than investigate one. "There's been a slow sliding in ethics," said Eric Miller, who reviewed thousands of marketing studies as editor of a research newsletter. "The scary part is, people make decisions based on this stuff. It may be an invisible crime, but it's not a victimless one" (Crossen, 1991, p. A1). These studies are old, but, as you will read in Chapter 15, marketing experts are exploiting the newest digital decision-making gimmicks.

Asking Good Questions

As long as surveys are constructed by human beings and administered to human beings, we will never totally eliminate order or wording effects. You have to put your questions in a certain order and use particular words to communicate meaning. These are bound to influence respondents. Nonetheless, we can minimize the impact of context factors by taking precautions when designing the survey. More generally, there are many things researchers can do to improve the quality of attitude questions (Sudman & Bradburn, 1982). The next time you are asked to develop a self-report survey, you might consider these suggestions:

1. Use words that all respondents can comprehend.
2. Write specific and unambiguous items.
3. Avoid double negatives.
4. Pretest items to make sure people understand your questions.
5. If you think order of questions will influence respondents, ask questions in different sequences to check out order effects.
6. Avoid politically correct phrases that encourage socially desirable responses.
7. Write items so that they take both the positive and negative sides of an issue (to reduce respondents' tendency to always agree).
8. Consider whether your questions deal with sensitive, threatening issues (sex, drugs, antisocial behavior). If so, ask these questions at the end of the survey, once trust has been established.
9. Allow people to say "I don't know." This will eliminate responses based on guesses or a desire to please the interviewer.
10. Include many questions to tap different aspects of the attitude.

You can also save yourself some time – and improve the quality of your questionnaire – by turning to established attitude scales. You don't have to reinvent the wheel if someone else has developed a scale on the topic you're researching. To paraphrase the lyrics of an old folk song, "You can get anything you want at Alice's Restaurant" – you can get pretty much any scale you want, if you do a thorough search.

There are many standardized scales out there that tap attitudes very effectively. The advantage of using someone else's scale (other than that it frees you up to relax!) is that the scale has passed scientific muster – it is reliable, valid, and comprehensible to respondents. You can find scales from computerized databases, such as PsycINFO, Health and Psychosocial Instruments, and Communication Abstracts, or in specialized books (for example, Robinson, Shaver, & Wrightsman, 1999; Rubin, Palmgreen, & Sypher, 1994). Of course, if you're researching a new issue or want to cook up your own questions, you will have to devise your own questionnaire.

As you construct your survey, just remember that people are complex and that you will need good questions to tap their attitudes.

Other Ways to Tap Attitudes

Attitude scales can run into difficulty when tapping prejudice or feelings respondents would rather not acknowledge. In these cases, and when trying to assess implicit attitudes, researchers prefer other less obtrusive measures (Webb et al., 1966).

Unobtrusive measures can be useful in cases where it is not possible to administer self-report scales, such as in authoritarian countries. Tweets, Facebook posts, and emoticons could tap into attitudes about products, candidates, or social issues. Of course, these might not reflect attitudes so much as public responses or simple affect. But, taken as general indicators, they offer a rich contemporary database to mine beliefs and attitudes, offering access to individuals who can't always be easily reached through older more conventional methods, as well as to broad swaths of a society that is increasingly living in digital space (Chan et al., 2019; Chung & Pennebaker, 2019).

Another strategy is to employ physiological techniques. These include *galvanic skin response*, a change in the electrical resistance of the skin (e.g., measurements of sweating); (b) *pupil dilation* (precise assessments of expansion of the pupils); and (c) *facial electromyographic (EMG) techniques* that tap movements of facial muscles, particularly in the brow, cheek, and eye regions (Cacioppo, Petty, & Marshall-Goodell, 1984).

Useful as these devices are, they can, unfortunately, tap responses other than attitudes. Sweating, pupil dilation, and facial muscle activity can occur because people are interested in or perplexed about the attitude object. Physiological reactions do not always provide a sensitive indication of the directionality (pro vs. con) of people's feelings. It is also frequently impractical or expensive to use physiological techniques. However, major advances in psychobiological measures have occurred in recent years, offering potentially more reliable measurement of perspiration, while expanding assessments of cardiovascular responses, suggesting that these measures, in concert with more direct measures of attitude, can yield new insights (Zoccola, 2019).

Neuroscientific Measures

Increasingly, researchers, impressed by measures that can assess the social brain, have sought to supplement or even replace physiological techniques with neuroscientific measurements. Neuroscience measures offer information about neutral underpinnings of attitudes that are not possible to obtain through conventional measurement strategies. Neuroscientists look into the brain by magnetic resonance imaging (MRI). An MRI scan offers detailed information about soft tissues in the brain (and body), revealing structures inside the brain. *Functional magnetic resonance imaging* or fMRI reveals blood flow, and thus brain activity, offering a snapshot of the brain's functioning and structure. Comparisons of successive MRI scans allow researchers to see the brain essentially light up as an individual engages in different mental tasks (Myers, 2008). In addition, researchers have employed a device called an electroencephalograph (EEG), which, broadly speaking, taps into brain-related electrical activity that occurs in response to a social stimulus (Cooper, Blackman, & Keller, 2016). These offer insights into the biological basis of what we commonly call the mind, as well as our attitudes.

Neuroscience research employing measures like these have documented the role played by the amygdala, the brain structure linked with emotional processing, offered insights on the speed of evaluation of social stimuli, and shed light on the neural underpinnings of exposure to dissonant or inconsistent information. These measures can complement findings about strong, prejudiced attitudes obtained through standard explicit attitude scales, which can be susceptible to denial or distortion when prejudice is assessed. Neuroscientific methods take persuasion research into new arenas, offering insights never thought possible about the neural underpinnings of social attitudes.

And yet, cautions must be sounded. Exciting as they are, neuroscience measures do not identify the fundamental essence of social attitudes. Electrical activity in the brain is not synonymous with the mental and emotional entity we call an attitude any more than the brain is equivalent to the mind, or if you want to get religious, the soul. It remains to be seen if brain activity causes attitude change, reflects change that occurs through mental processes, or involves a combination of the two that requires an exquisite appreciation of the fundamental components of attitudes. There is rarely a one-to-one relationship between brain activity and the complex, socially constructed mind.

Implicit Association Test

Just as researchers have developed methods to gain insights into neutral processes, they have developed a host of measures to tap into the automatic dynamics of attitudes. A variety of measures assess the latency or length of time it takes people to indicate if they agree or disagree with a statement. For example, individuals may sit before a computer screen and read a question (e.g., "Do you favor capital punishment?"). They are instructed to hit a button to indicate whether they do or do not favor capital punishment. Researchers do not focus on whether individuals say they are pro or con, or favorable or unfavorable, to the attitude object on a questionnaire. Their primary interest is in how long it takes an individual to make her selection (Fazio, 1995). Response time or response latency then offers insight into the favorability and strength of an individual's attitude toward a social stimulus, as will be discussed below.

The most popular response-time-based measure is the *Implicit Association Test* (IAT), developed and articulated by Anthony G. Greenwald, Mahzarin R. Banaji, Brian A. Nosek, and their colleagues (Banaji & Greenwald, 2013; Greenwald, McGhee, & Schwartz, 1998; Nosek, Greenwald, & Banaji, 2007). (You can take IATs online for a variety of attitudes, such as ethnicity, gender roles, and religion. See Project Implicit at https://implicit.harvard.edu/implicit/research/.)

The IAT has been a godsend to researchers seeking to measure deep-seated attitudes, particularly implicit attitudes that operate unconsciously. Such attitudes, especially when they involve prejudices, are notoriously hard to uncover on paper-and-pencil questionnaires. People do not like to admit they harbor prejudices or may not be conscious of their biases. The IAT can tap such prejudices because it involves a less obtrusive methodology.

For example, in a study conducted back in the election campaign of 2008, researchers deliberately darkened Barack Obama's image to highlight racial cues. Some students saw the darkened version of Obama's photograph, and others viewed a lighter version. Conservative and liberal students looked at both pictures, responding with the subtle IAT measure of prejudice. Conservatives and liberals did not differ in their reactions to Obama when viewing the lightened photograph. However, conservatives displayed more negative responses to the darker images (Nevid & McClelland, 2010). The findings suggested that the IAT picked up on conservatives' hidden prejudices in a way standard questionnaires might not.

The IAT employs an interesting, but counterintuitive, procedure to tap implicit attitudes. Here is how the IAT works: Researchers present individuals with a series of items. If the item belongs to a category in the left-hand column, they might push the letter *e*. If it belongs to a category in the right-hand column, they push the letter *i*. A couple of practice rounds ensue.

In the race IAT, the words "European American" might appear in big letters on the top left of their screen and the words "African American" could appear in big letters on the top right. Respondents are told that words or images representing these categories will appear on the middle of their screen. They are instructed to press the *e* key when the word or image belongs to the category on the left, and the *i* key when the word or image belongs to the category on the right. The practice rounds are easy. When you see a photograph of a European American, a White, you might push *e*. When you see a photo of an African American, you push *i*. Similarly, in a second practice round, the word "good" might be on the top left of the screen, and "bad" at the top right. When you see a positive word like "peace," "love," or "happy," you push *e*. When you see a negative word like "war," "evil," or "terrible," you push *i*.

The test begins when the racial category appears, along with a label, either "good" or "bad." Here is where it gets a little tricky. The categories and labels could be: (a) European American or Good; (b) European American or Bad; (c) African American or Good; and (d) African American or Bad. You could see pictures of Whites and Blacks, and positive words like *peace* and negative words like *war* or *evil* again. Basically, the IAT assesses how long it takes you to classify the photograph of the European American or White person when the category is "European American or Good," and how long to classify the Black person when the category is "African American or Bad." It also taps how long it takes to classify a word like "peace" when the category is "European American or Good" or "African American or Bad." Now, the counterattitudinal case: How long does it take to classify the photograph of the White person when the category is "European American or Bad" and the Black when the category is "African American or Good"? How long does it take to classify a word like "peace" when the category is "European American or Bad" versus when the category is "African American or Good"? (See Figure 7.5.)

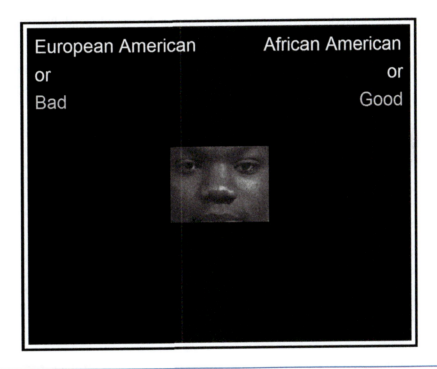

Figure 7.5 An Item in the Racial IAT. The IAT assesses the speed of individuals' response to this typically counterattitudinal pairing (from Cooper et al., 2016). If individuals respond more slowly to the pairing of the face with "European American or Bad" and "African American or Good" (shown above) than to a subsequent pairing of the face with "European American or Good" and "African American or Bad," they would be classified as having a pro-White or anti-Black IAT implicit bias. Scores are calculated after exposure to a number of such pairings, using different words

The guiding principle is people should respond quickly when evaluating two concepts that are strongly associated in memory, while reacting more slowly when evaluating two terms that are weakly or not at all associated in memory. The comparative speed, in essence the focus of the IAT, forms a way of tapping favorability of attitude. Thus, if individuals harbor a prejudice, they should take more time to punch a key when the photograph or word appears alongside counterstereotypic labels. When the item is inconsistent with the category, the attitude, in a sense, is not as easily accessible, confusion results, and it takes longer for a prejudiced individual to decide which key to push.

On the other hand, an individual reacts more quickly when the pairing taps into a stronger association reflecting a psychologically compatible association between the racial group and evaluative attribute. As noted earlier, in one round a participant would see faces of Whites paired with positive words and faces of Blacks paired with negative words. In another round, the participant would see faces of Blacks paired with positive words and Whites linked with negative words. An individual with a pro-White or anti-Black bias would react more quickly to the pairings in the first round – Whites with positive words and Blacks with negative words – than in the second round: Blacks with positive words and Whites with negative words. The faster the reaction time, the stronger the implicit psychological association.

Writer Malcolm Gladwell offers an illustrative example, describing what happened when he had to classify the photograph of a White person when the category was "White American or Bad" and a photograph of a Black person when the category was "African American or Good":

> Immediately, something strange happened to me. The task of putting the … faces in the right categories suddenly became more difficult. I found myself slowing down. I had to think. Sometimes I assigned something to one category when I really meant to assign it to the other category.
>
> (2005, pp. 82–83)

Anthony G. Greenwald, an architect of the IAT, had a similar experience, taking a variant of the race IAT for the very first time:

> I immediately saw that I was very much faster in sorting names of famous White people together with pleasant words than in sorting names of famous Black people together with pleasant words … After taking that first Race IAT and repeating it several times to see if the first result would be repeated (it was), I did not see how I could avoid concluding that I had a strong automatic racial preference for White relative to Black.
>
> (Banaji & Greenwald, 2013, p. 45)

The IAT provides a measure of the strength of an association between an attribute, such as race, and positive or negative evaluations. "When there's a strong prior association, people answer in between four hundred and six hundred milliseconds," Greenwald says. "When there isn't, they might take two hundred to three hundred milliseconds longer than that – which in the realm of these kinds of effects is huge" (Gladwell, 2005, p. 81).

Criticisms and Evaluation

The IAT is an innovative, internationally known scientific measuring instrument, the most widely used of the different measures of implicit attitudes, employed to assess a diverse range of attitudes, including race, gender, and ethnicity. It has yielded insightful findings on the subtle, sometimes prejudiced facets of attitudes that would be difficult to appreciate with traditional measures susceptible to social desirability biases. Research shows that Whites respond more quickly to the association of Black with unpleasant than to the pairing of Black and pleasant; there is also evidence that the IAT predicts prejudice, sometimes better than standard, explicit attitude measures (see Cooper et al., 2016). At the same time, there is also fierce debate about the meaning and strength of IAT findings (Arkes & Tetlock, 2004; Greenwald, Banaji, & Nosek, 2015; see also Blanton & Jaccard, 2015).

Critics argue that the test does not measure individuals' attitudes so much as the cultural associations they have learned. I may have learned that White or European American is linked with "good" in our culture, but this does not mean I personally harbor a pro-White/anti-Black attitude. For example, two psychologists note,

> in early Western movies, Hopalong Cassidy, Gene Autry, and Roy Rogers always wore white hats whereas villains always wore black. Thus, when people taking the IAT respond faster to "white/good" and "black/bad" combinations than to "white/bad" and "black/good" combinations, it is not at all clear that this is truly an indication of a prejudicial attitude toward African Americans.
>
> (Fishbein & Ajzen, 2010, p. 272)

IAT scores that are positive to Whites may not, therefore, reflect an implicit pro-White attitude so much as reflect a cultural stereotype; in support of this view, there is paradoxical evidence that many African Americans more favorably evaluate Whites than Blacks when taking the racial IAT (Cooper et al., 2016).

Similarly, it is not clear that responding to certain words on a computer test means that an individual harbors latent prejudices or deep-seated hostility toward members of minority groups. Critics worry that unfairly labeling individuals as prejudiced, based on a computerized test, can itself have dysfunctional, harmful effects on race relations (Tetlock & Arkes, 2004). Greenwald and his colleagues (2015) counter by pointing to the IAT's utility, noting that it offers empirically based insights into the psychology of racial profiling and discrimination against Blacks and women in job settings.

How robust are the findings of implicit bias obtained in IAT research? A group of social psychologists conducted a thorough meta-analysis of studies using the IAT, where researchers used high-level statistics to assess the size of empirical effects. Initially, researchers found that the IAT poorly predicted a number of relevant social attitudes and behaviors (Oswald et al., 2013). Greenwald et al. (2015) reexamined the meta-analytic research, raised methodological questions with the findings Oswald and his colleagues obtained, and argued that even small statistical effects can have significant implications for inter-group discrimination. That may be true, when one thinks about how White police officers have seemingly operated on unconscious racial biases in many killings of unarmed Blacks.

On the other hand, we don't know for sure that unconscious biases, as opposed to legitimate fears for personal safety, operated in all these cases. The IAT strongly suggests implicit biases were accessed, but we need empirical data to substantiate these conclusions. What we can say is that there is evidence that the IAT is a more sensitive measure of implicit attitudes than other measures, and can reliably predict a variety of behaviors (Jost, 2019; Kurdi et al., 2019). It also has been employed in numerous contexts, both academic and real-world, to offer insights into the dynamics of racial biases and how to tame prejudice toward a variety of groups.

The IAT, alas, has its share of methodological limitations, and debate continues regarding its generalizability to everyday situations. Nonetheless, given the subtlety of deep, prejudiced attitudes, the IAT offers a creative, useful tool to measure these attitudes. It is not without problems, highlighting the challenges of unlocking the secrets of the social mind with the innovative, but inexact, tools of social science. As even its proponents acknowledge, it is no "magic bullet," no panacea that allows researchers to gain pinpoint-accurate knowledge of unconscious racism (Jost, 2019, p. 15). However, as long as people harbor deep-seated prejudice, the IAT remains an imperfect, but intriguingly helpful instrument that offers a broad roadmap of the dynamics of implicit attitudes.

Conclusions

Attitude measurement plays a critical role in persuasion research. Persuasion is a science, as well as an art, and we need valid instruments to assess attitudes. Three venerable scales are typically employed: Likert, Guttman, and the semantic differential. A Likert scale taps agreement or disagreement with a series of belief statements. The Guttman scale focuses on items that vary in their degree of psychological difficulty. The semantic differential uses bipolar adjectives to measure the meaning associated with attitude objects. It took real ingenuity to devise these scales and they remain useful decades after they were originally developed. The Likert scale is used most frequently because it offers a viable method to tap attitudes, can be constructed easily, and its validity and reliability can be effectively documented.

There are a variety of problems in measuring attitudes through traditional self-reports, including social desirability biases, context, and wording effects. To minimize these problems, researchers have devised strategies to improve questionnaire quality that focus on asking questions clearly and thoughtfully. Supplementing self-report surveys are several indirect techniques to assess attitudes, such as unobtrusive, standard physiological, and neuroscientific measures. Indirect, subtle techniques such as the Implicit Association Test can shed light on attitudes that people are reluctant to reveal on self-report questionnaires, lest they look bad in the eyes of the researcher. The IAT can illuminate attitudes, such as prejudice, that elude conscious awareness and are difficult to accurately detect through conventional scales. The IAT focuses on response time, assuming that individuals respond relatively more quickly when evaluating two concepts that are strongly associated in memory, while reacting more slowly when evaluating two stimuli that are weakly or not at all associated in memory. The faster the reaction time, the stronger the implicit psychological association.

The IAT, for its part, is not without problems. Critics note that responses may reflect well-learned cultural associations rather than attitudes. Although the evidence for its validity is mixed, there is considerable evidence that the IAT offers a creative way to tap into prejudice and other socially sensitive attitudes that people would rather not or cannot acknowledge on a questionnaire.

In the end, as Jon Krosnick and his colleagues thoughtfully point out, "Both traditional self-report and more indirect attitude measures will continue to be used. The goal is not to come up with a single 'best' attitude measure, but rather to measure attitudes in all their complexity and all their manifestations" (Krosnick et al., 2005, p. 63). Given the complexity of attitudes, and the pervasive part they play in our lives, we need every valid measurement technique we can develop and perfect.

References

Aberson, C. L., & McVean, A. D. W. (2008). Contact and anxiety as predictors of bias toward the homeless. *Journal of Applied Social Psychology*, 38, 3009–3035.

Albarracín, D., Chan, M. P. S., & Jiang, D. (2019). Attitudes and attitude change: Social and personality considerations about specific and general patterns of behavior. In K. Deaux & M. Snyder (Eds.), *The Oxford handbook of personality and social psychology* (2nd ed., pp. 439–463). New York: Oxford.

Arkes, H. R., & Tetlock, P. E. (2004). Attributions of implicit prejudice, or "Would Jesse Jackson 'fail' the Implicit Association Test?" *Psychological Inquiry*, 15, 257–278.

Banaji, M. R., & Greenwald, A. G. (2013). *Blindspot: Hidden biases of good people*. New York: Delacorte Press.

Bergner, D. (2019, June 9). Neither/nor. *The New York Times Magazine*, 36–45.

Billard, T. J. (2018). Attitudes toward transgender men and women: Development and validation of a new measure. *Frontiers in Psychology*. Retrieved June 15, 2019, from www.ncbi.nlm.nih.gov/pmc/articles/PMC5891633/

Bishop, G. F., Tuchfarber, A. J., & Oldendick, R. W. (1986). Opinions on fictitious issues: The pressure to answer survey questions. *Public Opinion Quarterly*, 50, 240–250.

Blanton, H., & Jaccard, J. (2015). Not so fast: Ten challenges to importing implicit attitude measures to Media Psychology. *Media Psychology*, 18, 338–369.

Cacioppo, J. T., Petty, R. E., & Marshall-Goodell, B. (1984). Electromyographic specificity during simple physical and attitudinal tasks: Location and topographical features of integrated EMG responses. *Biological Psychology*, 18, 85–121.

Chan, M.-P. S., Morales, A., Farhadloo, M., Palmer, M. J., & Albarracín, D. (2019). Social media harvesting. In H. Blanton, J. M. LaCroix, & G. D. Webster (Eds.), *Measurement in social psychology* (pp. 228–264). New York: Routledge.

Chung, C. K., & Pennebaker, J. W. (2019). Textual analysis. In H. Blanton, J. M. LaCroix, & G. D. Webster (Eds.), *Measurement in social psychology* (pp. 153–173). New York: Routledge.

CNN Political Unit. (2013, September 27). Poll: "Obamacare" vs. "Affordable Care Act". Retrieved October 24, 2016, from politicalticker.blogs.cnn.com/2013/09/27/poll-obamacare-vs-affordable-care-act/

Cohn, N. (2019, June 9). Crisp battle lines on abortion blur when surveys ask voters. *The New York Times*, A1, A24.

Connelly, M. (2009, October 29). Framing the debate. *The New York Times*, A17.

Cooper, J., Blackman, S. F., & Keller, K. T. (2016). *The science of attitudes*. New York: Routledge.

Crossen, C. (1991, November 14). Studies galore support products and positions, but are they reliable? *The Wall Street Journal*, A1, A7.

Dawes, R. M., & Smith, T. L. (1985). Attitude and opinion measurement. In G. L. Lindzey & E. A. Aronson (Eds.), *Handbook of social psychology* (Vol. 1, 3rd ed., pp. 509–566). New York: Random House.

Fazio, R. H. (1995). Attitudes as object-evaluation associations: Determinants, consequences, and correlates of attitude accessibility. In R. E. Petty & J. A. Krosnick (Eds.), *Attitude strength: Antecedents and consequences* (pp. 247–282). Hillsdale, NJ: Lawrence Erlbaum Associates.

Fishbein, M., & Ajzen, I. (2010). *Predicting and changing behavior: The reasoned action approach*. New York: Psychology Press.

Gladwell, M. (2005). *Blink: The power of thinking without thinking*. New York: Little, Brown.

Glick, P., & Fiske, S. T. (1996). The ambivalent sexism inventory: Differentiating hostile and benevolent sexism. *Journal of Personality and Social Psychology, 70,* 491–512.

Glynn, C. J., Herbst, S., O'Keefe, G. J., & Shapiro, R. Y. (1999). *Public opinion.* Boulder, CO: Westview Press.

Greenwald, A. G., Banaji, M. R., & Nosek, B. A. (2015). Statistically small effects of the Implicit Association Test can have societally large effects. *Journal of Personality and Social Psychology, 108,* 553–561.

Greenwald, A. G., McGhee, D. E., & Schwartz, J. L. K. (1998). Measuring individual differences in implicit cognition: The Implicit Association Test. *Journal of Personality and Social Psychology, 74,* 1464–1480.

Guttman, L. (1944). A basis for scaling qualitative data. *American Sociological Review, 9,* 139–150.

Hill, D. B., & Willoughby, B. L. B. (2005). The development and validation of the genderism and transphobia scale. *Sex Roles, 53,* 531–544.

Hippler, H. J., Schwarz, N., & Sudman, S. (Eds.). (1987). *Social information processing and survey methodology.* New York: Springer-Verlag.

Holl, K., Niederdeppe, J., & Schuldt, J. P. (2018). Does question wording predict support for the Affordable Care Act? An analysis of polling during the implementation period, 2010-2016. *Health Communication, 33,* 816–823.

Jost, J. T. (2019). The IAT is dead, Long live the IAT: Context-sensitive measures of implicit attitudes are indispensable to social and political psychology. *Current Directions in Psychological Science, 28,* 10–19.

KFF. (Henry J. Kaiser Family Foundation). (2019, June 19). Public opinion on single—payer, national health plans, and expanding access to Medicare coverage. Retrieved June 29, 2016, from www.kff.org/slideshow/public-opinion-on-single-payer

Krosnick, J. A., Judd, C. M., & Wittenbrink, B. (2005). The measurement of attitudes. In D. Albarracín, B. T. Johnson, & M. P. Zanna (Eds.), *The handbook of attitudes* (pp. 21–76). Mahwah, NJ: Lawrence Erlbaum Associates.

Krosnick, J. A., Judd, C. M., & Wittenbrink, B. (2019). The measurement of attitudes. In D. Albarracín & B. T. Johnson (Eds.), *The handbook of attitudes* (Vol. 1: Basic principles, 2nd ed., pp. 45–105). New York: Routledge.

Kurdi, B., Seitchik, A. E., Axt, J. R., Carroll, T. J., Karapetyan, A., Kaushik, N., … Banaji, M. R. (2019). Relationship between the Implicit Association Test and intergroup behavior: A meta-analysis. *American Psychologist, 74,* 569–586.

Ledbetter, A. M. (2009). Measuring online communication attitude: Instrument development and validation. *Communication Monographs, 76,* 463–486.

Likert, R. (1932). A technique for the measurement of attitudes. *Archives of Psychology, 140,* 1–55.

McConahay, J. B. (1986). Modern racism, ambivalence, and the Modern Racism Scale. In J. F. Dovidio & S. L. Gaertner (Eds.), *Prejudice, discrimination, and racism* (pp. 91–125). Orlando, FL: Academic Press.

Myers, D. G. (2008). *Exploring psychology* (7th ed.). New York: Worth Publishers.

Nevid, J. S., & McClelland, N. (2010). Measurement of implicit and explicit attitudes toward Barack Obama. *Psychology & Marketing, 27,* 989–1000.

Norton, A. T., & Herek, G. M. (2013). Heterosexuals' attitudes toward transgender people: Findings from a national probability sample of U.S. adults. *Sex Roles, 68,* 738–753.

Nosek, B. A., Greenwald, A. G., & Banaji, M. R. (2007). The Implicit Association Test at age 7: A methodological and conceptual review. In J. A. Bargh (Ed.), *Social psychology and the unconscious: The automaticity of higher mental processes* (pp. 265–292). New York: Psychology Press.

Osgood, C. E. (1974). Probing subjective culture/Part I: Cross linguistic tool making. *Journal of Communication, 24*(1), 21–35.

Osgood, C. E., Suci, G. J., & Tannenbaum, P. H. (1957). *The measurement of meaning*. Urbana, IL: University of Illinois Press.

Ostrom, T. M., Bond, C. F., Jr., Krosnick, J. A., & Sedikides, C. (1994). Attitude scales: How we measure the unmeasurable. In S. Shavitt & T. C. Brock (Eds.), *Persuasion: Psychological insights and perspectives* (pp. 15–42). Boston, MA: Allyn and Bacon.

Oswald, F. L., Mitchell, G., Blanton, H., Jaccard, J., & Tetlock, P. E. (2013). Predicting ethnic and racial discrimination: A meta-analysis of IAT criterion studies. *Journal of Personality and Social Psychology, 105*, 171–192.

Peplau, L. A., Hill, C. T., & Rubin, Z. (1993). Sex role attitudes in dating and marriage: A 15-year follow-up of the Boston couples study. *Journal of Social Issues, 49*(3), 31–52.

Robinson, J. P., Shaver, P. R., & Wrightsman, L. S. (Eds.). (1999). *Measures of political attitudes*. San Diego, CA: Academic Press.

Rosen, L. D., Whaling, K., Carrier, L. M., Cheever, N. A., & Rokkum, J. (2013). The Media and Technology Usage and Attitudes Scale: An empirical investigation. *Computers in Human Behavior, 29*, 2501–2511.

Rousseau, F. L., Vallerand, R. J., Ratelle, C. F., Mageau, G. A., & Provencher, P. J. (2002). Passion and gambling: On the validation of the gambling passion scale (GPS). *Journal of Gambling Studies, 18*, 45–66.

Rubin, R. B., Palmgreen, P., & Sypher, H. E. (Eds.). (1994). *Communication research measures: A sourcebook*. New York: Guilford.

Schmermund, A., Sellers, R., Mueller, B., & Crosby, F. (2001). Attitudes toward affirmative action as a function of racial identity among African American college students. *Political Psychology, 22*, 759–774.

Schuman, H., & Presser, S. (1981). *Questions and answers in attitude surveys: Experiments on question form, wording, and context*. Orlando, FL: Academic Press.

Schwarz, N. (1999). Self-reports: How the questions shape the answers. *American Psychologist, 54*, 93–105.

Schwarz, N., & Bless, H. (1992). Scandals and the public's trust in politicians: Assimilation and contrast effects. *Personality and Social Psychology Bulletin, 18*, 574–579.

Shibley Hyde, J., Bigler, R. S., Joel, D., Chucky Tate, C., & van Anders, S. M. (2019). The future of sex and gender in psychology: Five challenges to the gender binary. *American Psychologist, 74*, 171–193.

Smith, T. W. (1995). Review: The Holocaust denial controversy. *Public Opinion Quarterly, 59*, 269–295.

Spence, J. T., Helmreich, R., & Stapp, J. (1973). A short version of the Attitudes Toward Women Scale (AWS). *Bulletin of the Psychonomic Society, 2*, 219–220.

Stevens, S. S. (1950). Mathematics, measurement, and psychophysics. In S. S. Stevens (Ed.), *Handbook of experimental psychology* (pp. 1–49). New York: Wiley.

Sudman, S., & Bradburn, N. M. (1982). *Asking questions*. San Francisco, CA: Jossey-Bass.

Swim, J. K., Aikin, K. J., Hall, W. S., & Hunter, B. A. (1995). Sexism and racism: Old-fashioned and modern prejudices. *Journal of Personality and Social Psychology, 68*, 199–214.

Talbot, M. (2019, January 14). Democrats in the House. *The New Yorker* (13–14).

Tetlock, P. E., & Arkes, H. R. (2004). The implicit prejudice exchange: Islands of consensus in a sea of controversy. *Psychological Inquiry, 15*, 311–321.

Thaler, R. H., & Sunstein, C. R. (2008). *Nudge: Improving decisions about health, wealth, and happiness*. New Haven, CT: Yale University Press.

Thurstone, L. L. (1928). Attitudes can be measured. *American Journal of Sociology, 33*, 529–544.

Tourangeau, R., & Rasinski, K. A. (1988). Cognitive processes underlying context effects in attitude measurement. *Psychological Bulletin, 103*, 299–314.

Webb, E. J., Campbell, D. T., Schwartz, R. D., & Sechrest, L. (1966). *Unobtrusive measures: Nonreactive research in the social sciences*. Chicago, IL: Rand McNally.

Wilson, T. D., LaFleur, S. J., & Anderson, D. E. (1996). The validity and consequences of verbal reports about attitudes. In N. Schwarz & S. Sudman (Eds.), *Answering questions: Methodology for determining cognitive and communicative processes in survey research* (pp. 91–114). San Francisco, CA: Jossey-Bass.

Zaller, J. R. (1992). *The nature and origins of mass opinion*. New York: Cambridge University Press.

Zoccola, P. M. (2019). Psychobiological measurement. In H. Blanton, J. M. LaCroix, & G. D. Webster, *Measurement in social psychology* (pp. 75–101). New York: Routledge.

Part Three

Changing Attitudes and Behavior

Chapter 8

Processing Persuasive Communications

Kate and Ben, recently married, delightfully employed, and happy to be on their own after four long years of college, are embarking on a major decision – a happy one, but an important one. They're buying a car. They have some money saved up from the wedding and have decided that, the way the stock market has been going, they'd be better off spending it than losing cash on some risky online investment.

Sitting in their living room one Thursday night watching TV, they find that they are tuning in more closely to the car commercials than the sitcoms. "That's a sign we're an old married couple," Kate jokes. Ben nods in agreement.

The next day after work, at Kate's request they click onto the *Consumer Reports* website and print out information about compact cars. On Saturday they brave the car dealerships, get the lowdown from car salesmen, and take spins in the cars. Kate, armed with her incredible memory for detail and ten Post-it notes she is reading off her iPhone, hurls questions at the car salesmen, while Ben, shirt hanging out, eyes glazed, looks dreamily at the sports cars he knows he can't afford.

By early the next week, they have narrowed down the choices to a Honda Accord and a Hyundai Sonata. Her desk covered with papers, printouts, and stacks of warranties and brochures from the dealerships, Kate is thinking at a feverish pace; she pauses, then shares her conclusions with her husband:

Okay, this is it. The Honda gets more miles per gallon and handles great on the highway. But *Consumer Reports* gives the new Sonata better ratings on safety on account of their anti-lock brakes and traction control, which is important. The Sonata also has a better repair record than the Accord. But the big thing is we get a stronger warranty with the Hyundai dealer and, Ben, the Sonata is a thousand bucks cheaper. Soooo ... what do you think?

Ben looks up.

Well, you know, I'm not into all this technical stuff like you are. I say if the Sonata gets better ratings from *Consumer Reports*, go for it. I also think the Sonata salesman made a lot of good points – real nice guy. The Honda guy basically blew us off when we told him we needed the weekend to think it over.

"There's also the other thing," says Kate, sporting a grin. "What?"

"The name."

"It's true," says Ben a bit sheepishly. "The name 'Sonata' is cool. I like it."

"What am I going to do with you?" Kate asks, with a smile and a deliberately exaggerated sigh.

"How about, take me to the Hyundai dealer, so we can buy our new car?" Ben says, smiling broadly as he strolls out the front door.

The story is fiction – but perhaps not too far from everyday experience. It is based on interviews with consumers and observations of people buying cars. The example illustrates two very different styles of processing information: Careful consideration of message arguments (Kate) and superficial examination of information and a focus on simple cues (Ben). These two ways of processing information are the main elements of contemporary theories of persuasion and form the centerpiece of the present chapter.

This chapter launches the third part of the book, which examines theory and research on the effects of persuasive communication. The chapter describes guiding models of attitude and behavior change – approaches that underlie much of the research and applications that follow. The cornerstone of these theoretical approaches is a focus on *process*. Scholars believe that if they can understand *how* people cognitively process messages, they can better explicate the impact that communications have on attitudes. They believe that the better they comprehend individuals' modes of processing information, the more accurately they can explain the diverse effects messages have on attitudes. This is what scholars mean when they say you cannot understand the effects of communications on people without knowing how people process the message.

Contemporary models evolved from earlier perspectives on persuasion – notably Hovland's path-breaking work and research conducted in the 1960s. It is important to describe these programs of research because they contributed helpful insights and also laid the groundwork for current theorizing. The first section of the chapter provides an overview of these approaches. The second portion of the chapter describes dual-process models of persuasion, focusing on a major cognitive processing model, the Elaboration Likelihood Model. Subsequent sections focus on real-life applications, fine points of the model, intellectual criticisms, and the model's contributions to persuasion.

Historical Foundations

Yale Attitude Change Approach

As noted in Chapter 2, Carl Hovland and colleagues at Yale University conducted the first detailed, empirical research on the effects of persuasive communications. The *Yale attitude change approach* was distinctive because it provided facts about the effects on attitudes of the communicator's credibility, message appeals, and audience members' personality traits. Convinced by theory and their generation's experience with World War II persuasion campaigns that communications had strong effects on attitudes, the researchers set out to examine who says what to whom with what effect (Hovland, Janis, & Kelley, 1953; Smith, Lasswell, & Casey, 1946).

Although Hovland and colleagues' findings were interesting, it was their theory-driven approach and commitment to testing hypotheses that proved enduring. The Yale researchers were also interested in understanding why messages changed attitudes. Working in an era dominated by reward-based learning theories and research on rats' mastery of mazes, Hovland naturally gravitated to explanations that focused on learning and motivation. He emphasized that persuasion entailed learning message

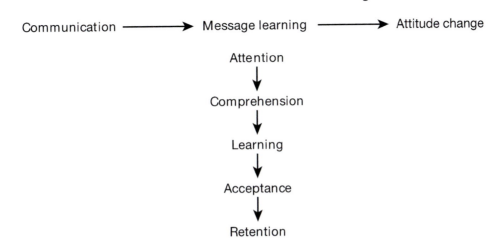

Figure 8.1 The Hovland/Yale Model of Persuasion

arguments and noted that attitude change occurred in a series of steps. To be persuaded, individuals had to attend to, comprehend, learn, accept, and retain the message (see Figure 8.1).

It sounds logical enough. Indeed there is considerable evidence that learning is a component of persuasion – the more people learn and comprehend message arguments, the more likely they are to accept the advocated positions (Chaiken, Wood, & Eagly, 1996). However, the thesis misses the mark in an important respect. It assumes that people are sponge-like creatures who passively take in information they receive. In fact, as Leon Festinger and Nathan Maccoby (1964) noted, people are actively thinking about the message, counterarguing, or even, as is common on social media, derogating the person who conveys a disagreeable message.

Think of how you react to a persuasive message. Do you sit there, taking in everything the speaker says? Are you so mesmerized by the communicator that you stifle any thoughts or mental arguments? Hardly. You actively think about the speaker, message, or persuasion context. You may remember message arguments, yet probably recall with greater accuracy your own criticisms of the speaker's point of view. This view of persuasion developed in the years that followed the publication of Hovland's research and is known as the *cognitive response approach to persuasion.*

CRA

Cognitive Response Approach

The cognitive response perspective asserts that people's own mental reactions to a message play a critical role in the persuasion process, typically a more important role than the message itself (Brock, 1967; Greenwald, 1968; Osterhouse & Brock, 1970; Petty, Ostrom, & Brock, 1981). Cognitive responses include thoughts that are favorable to the position advocated in the message (*proarguments*) and those that criticize the message (*counterarguments*). Persuasion occurs if the communicator induces the audience member to generate favorable cognitive responses regarding the communicator or message.

The cognitive response view says that people play an active role in the persuasion process. It emphasizes that people's *own* thoughts about a message are more important factors in persuasion than memory of message arguments (Perloff & Brock, 1980; see Figure 8.2). There is a good deal of evidence to substantiate this view. In fact, it may seem obvious that thoughts matter in persuasion. But remember that what is obvious at one point in time is not always apparent in an earlier era. During the 1950s and early 1960s, animal learning models of human behavior dominated psychology, and, on a broader level, Americans were assumed to follow lock, stock, and barrel the dictates of government and free-enterprise capitalism. It seemed only natural to theorize that persuasion was primarily a passive process of learning and reinforcement.

With the advent of the 1960s, all this changed. Cognitive models emphasizing active thought processes gained adherents. It became clear that older views, while useful, needed to be supplemented by approaches that afforded more respect to the individual and assigned more emphasis to dynamics of the grey matter inside the brain.

"Feed your head," the rock group Jefferson Airplane belted out during this decade. The cognitive response approach echoed the refrain. It stimulated research, bottled old scholarly wine in new explanations, and helped pave the way for new theories of attitude change. By calling attention to the role that thoughts play in persuasion, the cognitive response approach illuminated scholarly understanding of persuasion. Consider the following examples.

The first involves *forewarning*, which occurs when a persuader warns people that they will soon be exposed to a persuasive communication. This is a common occurrence in life, and research has explored what happens when people are warned that they are going to receive a message with which they will staunchly disagree. Cognitive response studies have clarified just what happens inside people's minds when this occurs. Individuals generate a large number of counterarguments, strengthening their opposition to the advocated position (Petty & Cacioppo, 1977). An old expression, "Forewarned is forearmed," describes this phenomenon, but sheds no light on why it occurs. Cognitive response analysis helps us understand it better.

When a close friend marches out of the house in the middle of an argument, vowing, "We'll talk about this when I get home," you are likely to intensify your resolve not to give in. Generating arguments on your behalf and persuading yourself that you are right, you arm yourself with a battering ram of justifications that you invoke when your friend returns. In fact, as cognitive response research predicts, forewarning someone in this general fashion significantly reduces the likelihood that a subsequent persuasive communication will succeed. "Forewarning an audience to expect a persuasive

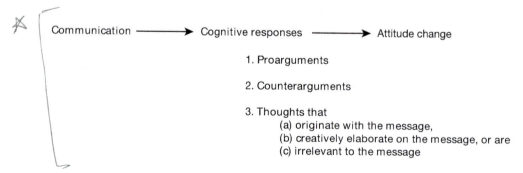

Figure 8.2 The Cognitive Response Model of Persuasion

message tends to make that message less persuasive," William L. Benoit concludes after studying this issue (1998, p. 146).

Another way of saying this is that forewarnings stiffen resistance to persuasion. Forewarnings frequently instil resistance by getting people to generate negative cognitive responses – or thoughts – about the message (though they can also work more automatically via priming; see Fransen & Fennis, 2014). On a practical level, arming individuals to resist harmful communications is important, given that people are frequently tempted to yield to peers' requests that they smoke, drink when they drive, or take drugs (Quinn & Wood, 2004).

In general, the cognitive response research has called attention to the subtle and powerful role thinking plays in the persuasion process. Thinking – and especially mentally counterarguing with persuasive messages – can stiffen resistance to persuasion, as a classic persuasion effect known as inoculation highlights (see Box 8.1).

BOX 8.1

Inoculation Theory

Persuasion not only involves changing attitudes. It also centers on convincing people not to fall prey to unethical or undesirable influence attempts. Communicators frequently attempt to persuade individuals to resist social and political messages that are regarded as unhealthy or unwise. For example, health campaigns urge young people to "say no" to drugs, smoking, drinking when driving, and unsafe sex. In the political domain, candidates attempt to persuade wavering voters to resist the temptation to bolt their party and vote for the opposing party candidate or a third-party contender.

A variety of techniques have been developed to strengthen resistance to persuasion. The techniques work by triggering counterarguments that, along with other factors, help individuals resist persuasive appeals. One of the most famous strategies evolved from a biological analogy and is known as inoculation theory. The theory is an ingenious effort to draw a comparison between the body's mechanisms to ward off disease and the mind's ways of defending itself against verbal onslaughts. In his statement of the theory, William J. McGuire noted that doctors increase resistance to disease by injecting the person with a small dose of the attacking virus, as in a flu shot (McGuire & Papageorgis, 1961; see Figure 8.3). Pre-exposure to the virus in a weakened form stimulates the body's defenses: It leads to production of antibodies, which help the body fight off disease. In the same fashion, exposure to a weak dose of opposition arguments, "strong enough to stimulate his defenses, but not strong enough to overwhelm him," should produce the mental equivalent of antibodies – counterarguments (McGuire, 1970, p. 37). Counterarguing the oppositional message in one's own mind should lead to strengthening of initial attitude and increased resistance to persuasion.

Try this analogy to help you appreciate the inoculation notion. Suppose a parent wants to prepare a college-bound son or daughter for the drinking culture on campus. The parent is concerned that their child, tempted by the thrill of boozing and the promises of wine or shots of liquor, will get uproariously drunk, or, worse, do something that he or she will regret later on. To help forestall these possibilities, and strengthen their daughter or son's resistance to

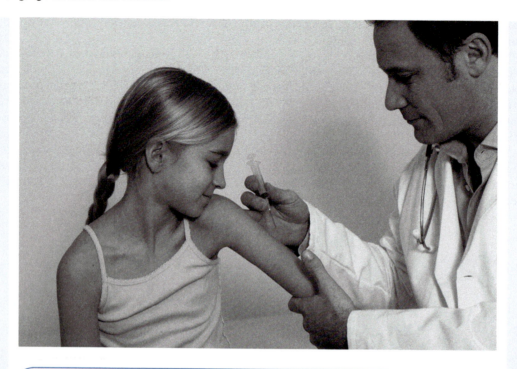

Figure 8.3 The Inoculation Perspective Draws an Analogy Between the Ability of a Flu Shot to Increase Resistance to Disease and the Ways in Which Weak Doses of Opposition Arguments Can Stiffen Resistance to Persuasion

Image courtesy of Shutterstock

pleas to hit the bars every Friday night, the parent gives the youngster a bit of the forbidden fruit. Mom or dad buys a couple of beers or a California wine, and, with some supervision (but so much that their child feels like a six-year-old), allows the youngster to imbibe. The thrill has been satiated and the teen now has some experience with the too-salty taste of beer or the sweet, vibrant taste of wine. Having received the inoculation treatment, the teen is less tempted by liquor on campus; he or she can now come up with some drawbacks of drinking and has in mind the downsides of guzzling a beer or sipping too much wine or liquor. (Of course, this may not always work, but it shows how a persuader, in this case a parent, could call on inoculation to induce resistance to persuasion.)

Importantly, as a scientific concept, inoculation has to be tested empirically to determine if it works in the real world. One of the hallmarks of inoculation research is the creativity with which it has been tested. In his original research, McGuire and his colleagues devised an innovative technique to examine inoculation. They chose to expose individuals to attacks against attitudes that had been rarely if ever criticized: Cultural truisms, or beliefs individuals learn through socialization. Cultural truisms include: "People should brush their teeth after every meal if possible," "The effects of penicillin have been of enormous benefit to mankind," and "Everyone ideally should get a yearly checkup." In essence, some participants in the experiments received a supportive defense – arguments defending the truism, such as that regularly brushing removes plaque and prevents gum disease. Others received an inoculation defense – for example, arguments *against* brushing teeth after every meal (plaque sticks between your teeth, no matter how hard you brush), and refutation of these arguments (studies show that regular brushing removes the plaque, reducing risk for bacterial infections). Individuals who received the inoculation defense were more likely to resist subsequent attacks on a brush-your-teeth-after-every-meal or yearly-checkup-type truism than those who just received supportive arguments (McGuire & Papageorgis, 1961). Presumably, the attack and refutation stimulated individuals to formulate arguments why the truism was indeed correct. They were apparently more motivated than those who heard the usual "rah-rah, it's true" supportive arguments.

These findings provided the first support for *inoculation* theory. The theory fundamentally stipulates that resistance to persuasion can be induced by exposing individuals to a small dose of arguments against a particular idea, coupled with appropriate criticism of these arguments. In essence, inoculation works by introducing a threat to a person's belief system and then providing a way for individuals to cope with the threat (that is, by refuting the counterattitudinal message; see Pfau, 1997).

Other explanations of inoculation have also been advanced, including accessibility and reframing (Pfau et al., 2003; Williams & Dolnik, 2001). Although there is healthy debate about just which processes account best for inoculation effects, there is little doubt that inoculation provides a useful way to encourage resistance to a persuasive message, in some cases providing protection against attacks on related attitudes (Banas & Rains, 2010; Benoit, 1991; Lim & Ki, 2007; Parker, Rains, & Ivanov, 2016; Pfau, 1997; Richards & Banas, 2015; Szabo & Pfau, 2002).

Indeed, inoculation theory has stimulated considerable research over the years, usefully transcending its initial focus on cultural truisms, explored exclusively in laboratory settings. Communication scholars have taken the concept to the real world, examining its applications to commercial advertising, political campaigns, and health (Compton, 2013). A number of practical conclusions have emerged from this research. They include the following:

1. **Inoculation can be useful weapons in politics and the law.** Politicians can anticipate the opposition's attacks and preempt them by using inoculation techniques (Pfau & Burgoon, 1988; Pfau & Kenski, 1990). They can acknowledge a weakness and then turn it into a persuasive strength, as President Ronald Reagan famously did in a 1984 presidential debate with Democratic challenger, Walter Mondale. The 73-year-old president implicitly acknowledged that he was considerably older than his Democratic opponent, but then punched back, quipping "I will not make an age an issue of this campaign. I am not going to exploit for political purposes, my opponent's youth and inexperience." Even Mondale had to laugh. In a similar fashion, lawyers exploit inoculation to their advantage, frequently in more serious contexts. A now-classic example of inoculation in the courtroom came in the 2011 trial of Casey Anthony, charged with the murder of her two-year-old daughter. In his closing arguments, defense attorney Jose Baez acknowledged that Casey was "a liar and a slut" and made some stupid decisions. But, he quickly added, she was not a murderer and should not pay with her life. By acknowledging the obvious – Casey had blatantly lied in the aftermath of her daughter's death – Baez helped the jury get beyond her prevarications to focus on problems with the prosecution's case.

2   **In a world filled with unethical persuaders, inoculation offers a technique to help people resist unwanted influence attempts.** The theory says that the best way to induce resistance to unethical persuasion is to provide people with a small dose of the dangerous information and then help them refute it. This offers a useful counterpoint to those who say that parents should shield children from the world's evils or shelter them from unpleasant realities. As Pratkanis and Aronson note, "We cannot resist propaganda by burying our heads in the sand. The person who is easiest to persuade is the person whose beliefs are based on slogans that have never been seriously challenged" (1992, p. 215).

Thus, teachers who want to encourage high school students to resist peer weekend appeals to binge drink or vape should mention a small positive aspect of these pursuits, following them up with relevant refutations of these arguments. And when trying to inoculate teens, who are famously reactive to what teachers advise, it's best not to use verbal overkill; instead, teachers should use refutational arguments that remind teens they have the right to make their own choice (Richards, Banas, & Magid, 2017).

Elaboration Likelihood Model   ELM

Without a doubt, the cognitive response approach advanced knowledge of persuasion. It placed thinking at the center of the persuasion process. It also provided a method to measure cognitive aspects of attitudes creatively. After a time, though, researchers realized that the approach had two limitations. First, it assumed that people think carefully about messages. Yet there are many times when people turn their minds off to persuasive communications, making decisions based on mental shortcuts. Second, the cognitive response approach failed to shed much light on the ways that messages influence people. It did not explain how we can utilize cognitive responses so as to devise messages to change attitudes or behavior. In order to rectify these problems, scholars proceeded to develop process-based models of persuasion.

 Two models currently dominate the field. The first, devised by Shelly Chaiken and Alice H. Eagly, is called the Heuristic-Systematic Model (HSM) (Chaiken, Liberman, & Eagly, 1989; Todorov, Chaiken, & Henderson, 2002). The second, articulated by Richard E. Petty, the late John T. Cacioppo, and their many colleagues, is the Elaboration Likelihood Model (ELM) (Petty & Briñol, 2012, 2015; Petty & Cacioppo, 1986; Petty & Wegener, 1999). Both approaches emphasize that you cannot understand communication effects without appreciating the underlying processes by which messages influence attitudes. Both are *dual-process models* in that they claim that there are two different mechanisms by which communications affect attitudes.

Each model has strengths. The *Heuristic-Systematic Model* offers a compelling explanation of message processing when people opt to expend relatively little effort and devote few resources to the task. Its emphasis on heuristics – a term that will be subsequently discussed – represented a substantive contribution to the academic literature on persuasion.

The *Elaboration Likelihood Model* provides a comprehensive framework for understanding the effects of a host of source, message, and receiver factors on persuasion. It also has provided a useful integration of a wealth of empirical data. This chapter focuses on the ELM because it has generated more interdisciplinary research on persuasive communication and has been applied to more communication contexts.

ELM Principles

The first question students may have when reading about an Elaboration Likelihood Model of persuasion is: "Just what does the term 'Elaboration Likelihood' mean?" This is a reasonable question. *Elaboration* refers to the extent to which the individual thinks about or mentally modifies arguments contained in the communication. *Likelihood*, referring to the probability that an event will occur, is used to point out the fact that elaboration can be either likely or unlikely. Elaboration is assumed to fall along a continuum, with one end characterized by considerable rumination on the central merits of an issue and the other by relatively little mental activity. The model tells us when people should be particularly likely to elaborate, or not elaborate, on persuasive messages.

The ELM stipulates that there are two distinct ways people process communications. These are called routes, suggesting that two different highways crisscross the mind, transporting thoughts and reactions to messages. The term *route* is a metaphor: We do not know for sure that these routes exist (any more than we know with absolute certainty that any mental construct exists in precisely the way theorists use it). Social scientists employ terms like "processing route" (or attitude) to describe complex cognitive and behavioral phenomena. As with attitude, the term "processing route" makes eminent sense and is supported by a great deal of empirical evidence. The ELM refers to the two routes to persuasion as the *central and peripheral routes*, or central and peripheral processes.

The *central route* is characterized by considerable cognitive elaboration. When people process information centrally, they carefully evaluate message arguments, ponder implications of the communicator's ideas, and relate information to their own knowledge, biases, and values. This is the thinking person's route to persuasion.

The *peripheral route* is entirely different. Rather than examining issue-relevant arguments, people examine the message quickly or focus on simple cues to help them decide whether to accept the position advocated in the message. Factors that are peripheral to message arguments carry the day. These can include a communicator's physical appeal, glib speaking style, or pleasant association between the message and music playing in the background.

When processing peripherally, people invariably rely on simple decision-making rules or *heuristics*. For example, an individual may invoke the heuristic that "experts are to be believed" and, for this reason (and this reason only), accept the speaker's recommendation. In a similar fashion, people employ a "bandwagon heuristic," illustrated by the belief that "if many other people think that something is good, then it must be good."

There are interesting social media implications in all this, calling attention to the heuristic utility of likes and tweets (Fu, 2012; Xu et al., 2012; see Chapter 15).

Thus, the ELM emphasizes that people can be simple information processors – "cognitive misers" as they are sometimes called (Taylor, 1981) under some conditions. But in other circumstances, people can take the opposite posture and function as deep, detailed thinkers. Under some conditions (when processing super-peripherally), they are susceptible to slick persuaders – and can be thus characterized by the saying attributed to P. T. Barnum: "There's a sucker born every minute!" In other circumstances (when processing centrally), individuals are akin to Plato's ideal students – seeking truth and dutifully considering logical arguments – or to Aristotelian thinkers, persuaded only by cogent arguments (logos). The model says people are neither suckers nor deep thinkers. Complex creatures that we are, we are both peripheral and central, heuristic and systematic, processors. The critical questions are when people process centrally, when they prefer the peripheral pathway, and the implications for persuasion. The nifty thing about the ELM is that it answers these questions, laying out conditions under which central or peripheral processing is most likely, and the effects of such processing on attitude change.

It comes back to the key terms of the model, *elaboration likelihood*. The model formally emphasizes that when the likelihood of elaboration of a message is low, persuasion occurs through the peripheral route, with a persuasion factor acting as a cue or heuristic. When the elaboration likelihood is high, persuasion occurs through the central route, with a persuasion occurring through more thoughtful processes, or in deep-seated ways that touch on closely held attitudes. Under these conditions, strong arguments can carry the day. Indeed, a quantitative, meta-analytic review showed that people are more persuaded by strong than weak arguments when they are centrally processing the persuasive message (Carpenter, 2015).

According to the ELM, the two basic factors that determine processing strategy are *motivation* and *ability*. When people are motivated to consider the message seriously, they process centrally. They also pursue the central route when they are cognitively able to ponder message arguments. Situations can limit or enhance people's ability to process centrally, and so too can personal characteristics. On the other hand, when people lack the motivation or ability to process a message carefully, they opt for a simpler strategy. They process superficially.

It is frequently neither possible nor functional to process every message carefully. "Just imagine if you thought carefully about every television or radio commercial you heard," note Richard Petty and colleagues. "If you ever made it out of the house in the morning, you probably would be too mentally exhausted to do anything else!" (Petty et al., 1994, p. 118). Contemporary society, with its multiple stimuli, unfathomably complex issues, and relentless social change, makes it inevitable that people will rely on mental shortcuts much of the time. Consider an issue like global warming, or climate change. More than 80 percent of Americans believe that climate change is at least partly caused by human activities, and that if no action is taken to cut emissions, global warming will become a serious problem in the future (Davenport & Connelly, 2015). Do you think most people understand the scientific basis to these conclusions? Do they think they understand the complex scientific studies that have documented global warming effects? Most certainly not. They understandably (and reasonably) rely on the opinions of scientific experts, employing a classic heuristic to help them make up their minds.

The ELM thus spells out factors that make peripheral processing most likely. The ELM also contains a variety of hypotheses about the impact that such processing exerts on persuasion. Different persuasive appeals are effective, depending on the processing route. These appeals also differ in their long-term effects on attitudes (see Figure 8.4).

Motivation to Process

1. *Involvement*

Can you think of an issue that has important implications for your own life? Perhaps it is a university proposal to raise tuition, a plan to change requirements in your major, or even a proposal to ban cell phoning while driving. Now think of an issue that has little impact on your day-to-day routines. This could be a proposal to strengthen the graduation requirements at local high schools or a plan to use a different weed spray in farming communities. You will certainly process the first issues differently from the second. Different persuasive appeals are likely to be effective in these two circumstances as well.

The topics just cited differ in their level of personal involvement, or the degree to which they are perceived to be personally relevant to individuals. *Individuals are high in involvement when they perceive that an issue is personally relevant or bears directly on their own lives. They are low in involvement when they believe that an issue has little or no impact on their own lives.*

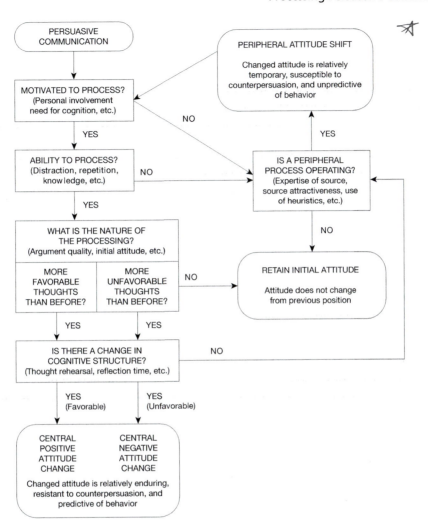

Figure 8.4 The Elaboration Likelihood Model of Persuasion. The flow chart here is interesting; the key points to keep in mind are that people process messages very differently when they are highly motivated or able to process the message than when they are low in motivation or ability. As you see on the left side of the figure, when motivated or able to process, individuals process centrally, leading to long-term attitude change. When they are not motivated or able to process messages, individuals may process peripherally (right side of the figure), relying on peripheral cues. Attitude change can result from peripheral processing, but effects are relatively temporary. But that may be all that is needed to close the deal

Adapted from Petty and Wegener (1999).

ELM Predictions and a Classic Experiment

The ELM stipulates that when individuals are high in involvement, they will be motivated to engage in issue-relevant thinking. They will recognize that it is in their best interest to consider the arguments in the message carefully. Even if they oppose the position advocated in the message, they may change their attitudes if the arguments are sufficiently compelling to persuade them that they will benefit by adopting the advocated position. Under high involvement, people should process messages through the central route, systematically scrutinizing message arguments.

By contrast, under low involvement, people have little motivation to focus on message arguments. The issue is of little personal consequence; therefore, it doesn't pay to spend much time thinking about the message. As a result, people look for mental shortcuts to help them decide whether to accept the communicator's position. They process the message peripherally, unconcerned with the substance of the communication.

These predictions are intriguing, but how do we know if they hold water in the real world? In order to discover if hypotheses are correct, researchers test them empirically.

Petty, Cacioppo, and Goldman (1981) examined these hypotheses in a now-classic study. To help you appreciate the procedures, I ask that you imagine that the experiment was being conducted again today using equivalent methods and materials. Here is how it would work:

You first enter a small room in a university building, take a seat, and wait for the experimenter. When the experimenter arrives, she tells you that the university is currently reevaluating its academic programs and is soliciting feedback about possible changes in policy. One proposal concerns a requirement that seniors take a comprehensive exam in their major area of study.

If randomly assigned to the high-involvement condition, you would be told that the comprehensive exam requirement could begin next year. That's clearly involving as it bears directly on your educational plans. How would you feel if you learned that you might have to take a big exam in your major – communication, psychology, marketing, or whatever it happened to be? You would probably feel nervous, angry, worried, or curious. Whichever emotion you felt, you clearly would be concerned about the issue.

If, on the other hand, you had been assigned to the low-involvement condition, you would be told that the exam requirement would not take effect for ten years. That clearly is low involvement. Even if you're on the laid-back, two-classes-a-semester plan, you do not envision being in college ten years from now! Realizing the message is of little personal consequence, you would gently switch gears from high energy to autopilot.

Regardless of involvement level, you would be asked now to listen to one of two messages delivered by one of two communicators. The particular message and source would be determined by lot, or random assignment.

You would listen to either strong or weak arguments on behalf of the exam. Strong arguments employ statistics and evidence ("Institution of the exams had led to a reversal in the declining scores on standardized achievement tests at other universities"). They offer cogent arguments on behalf of the exam requirement. Weak arguments are shoddy and unpersuasive (for example, "A friend of the author's had to take a comprehensive exam and now has a prestigious academic position").

Lastly, you would be led to believe that the comprehensive exam proposal had been prepared by a communicator either high or low in expertise. If assigned to the high-expertise group, you would be told that the report had been developed by the Carnegie Commission on Higher Education, which had been chaired by an education professor at Princeton University. If randomly assigned to the low-expertise communicator, you would be informed that the proposal had been prepared by a class at a local high school. You would then indicate your overall evaluation of the exam.

This constituted the basic design of the study. In formal terms, there were three conditions: Involvement (high or low), argument quality (strong or weak), and expertise (high or low). Petty and colleagues found that the impact of arguments and expertise depended to a considerable degree on level of involvement.

Under high involvement, argument quality exerted a significant impact on attitudes toward the comprehensive exam. Regardless of whether a high school class or Princeton professor was the source of the message, strong arguments led to more attitude change than did weak arguments. Under low involvement, the opposite pattern of results emerged. A highly expert source induced more attitude change than did a low-expert source, regardless of whether the arguments were strong or weak (see Figure 8.5).

The ELM provides a parsimonious explanation of the findings. Under high involvement, students believed that the senior exam would affect them directly. This heightened motivation to pay careful attention to the quality of the arguments. Processing the arguments carefully through the central route, students naturally were more swayed by strong than by weak arguments.

Imagine how you would react if you had been in this condition. Although you would hardly be overjoyed at the prospect of an exam in your major area of study, the idea would grab your attention, and you would think carefully about the arguments. After reading them, you would not be 100 percent in favor of the comprehensive exam – but having thought through the ideas and noted the benefits the exam provided, you might be more sympathetic to the idea than you would have been at the outset, and certainly more favorable than if you had listened to weak arguments on behalf of the exam.

Now imagine you had been assigned to the low-involvement and high-expertise group. You'd be on autopilot because the exam would not take place until long after you had graduated. Blasé about the whole thing, feeling little motivation to think carefully about the issue, you would understandably have little incentive to pay close attention to the quality of arguments.

You would focus on one salient cue – a factor that might help you decide what to do about this issue so that you could complete the assignment and get on with your day. The fact that the communicator was from Princeton might capture your attention and offer a compelling reason to go along with the message. "If this Princeton prof. thinks it's a good idea, it's fine with me," you might think. Click-whirr – just like that, you would go along with the message (Cialdini, 2009).

As we will see, these findings have intriguing implications for everyday persuasion. Looking back on the study findings, it may seem as if the main principle is that under high involvement, "what is said" is most important, and under low involvement, "who says it" is the key. There is some truth to this, but it greatly oversimplifies matters.

The key point is not that message appeals are more effective under high involvement and communicator appeals are more compelling under low involvement. Instead, the core issue is that people engage in issue-relevant thinking under high involvement, but under low involvement, they focus on simple cues that are peripheral to the main issues. In fact, there are times when a peripheral aspect of the message can carry the day under low involvement.

Case in point: Number of message arguments. This attribute is absolutely irrelevant, or peripheral, to the quality of the message. A speaker can have nine shoddy arguments or one extremely cogent appeal. However, the number of arguments can signify quality of argumentation in the minds of

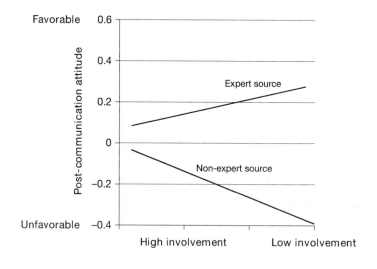

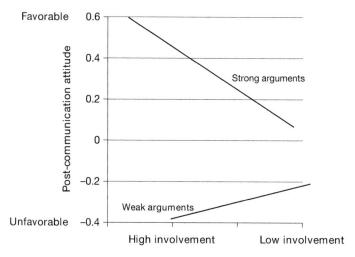

Figure 8.5 Effects of Involvement, Source Expertise, and Argument Quality on Attitudes

From Petty, Cacioppo, and Goldman (1981).

perceivers. If people would rather not think too deeply about an issue, they may fall into the trap of assuming that the more arguments a message has, the more convincing it is. This is exactly what Petty and Cacioppo (1984) discovered. When students were evaluating a proposal to institute senior comprehensive exams at their own school ten years in the future, they were more influenced by a message that had nine arguments. It didn't matter if all of them were weak. However, when contemplating a senior exam policy that would take place next year, they were naturally more motivated to devote energy to thinking about the issue. They processed arguments centrally, seeing through the shoddy ones and accepting the message only if arguments were strong.

Need for Cognition

Do you enjoy thinking? Or do you think only as hard as you have to? Do you prefer complex to simple problems? Or do you gravitate to tasks that are important, but don't require much thought?

These questions focus on another motivational factor that influences processing: A personality trait called the need for cognition. *Need for cognition* (NFC) is "a stable individual difference in people's tendency to engage in and enjoy effortful cognitive activity" (Cacioppo et al., 1996, p. 198). NFC is a need to understand the world and to employ thinking to accomplish this goal.

People high in NFC enjoy thinking abstractly. They will tell you that they "end up deliberating about issues even when they do not affect (them) personally." Ask them if they "would prefer a task that is intellectual, difficult and important to one that is somewhat important but does not require much thought," and they will readily agree.

Those on the other end of the continuum – those low in need for cognition – will tell you that, frankly, "thinking is not (their) idea of fun" and they think only as hard as they have to. They do not enjoy deliberating about issues that do not affect them personally, do not gravitate to intellectually demanding tasks, and "feel relief rather than satisfaction after completing a task that required a lot of mental effort" (see Cacioppo, Petty, & Kao, 1984). John T. Cacioppo and his colleagues developed a scale to assess NFC and they demonstrated that the scale reliably and validly taps the concept.

Need for cognition is not the same as intelligence. The two are related: you have to be somewhat intelligent to enjoy contemplating issues; thus, there is a modest relationship between verbal intelligence and need for cognition. However, two people could score high on verbal intelligence tests, yet one individual could find abstract thinking appealing, while the other could find it monotonous. People high and low in need for cognition "do not differ much in their ability to think, but primarily in their motivation to do so." (Briñol & Petty, 2019, p. 530).

What does need for cognition have to do with persuasion? Plenty. Individuals high in NFC recall more message arguments, generate a greater number of issue-relevant thoughts, seek more information about complex issues than those low in NFC, and reflect more on their thought processes (Briñol & Petty, 2005, 2019; Cacioppo et al., 1996). Given that people high in NFC like to think, they should be more influenced by quality-of-message arguments than those low in NFC. And in fact cogent issue arguments do carry more weight with high-NFC individuals. By contrast, those low in NFC are more influenced by cues that save them from effortful thought. They are frequently swayed more by a variety of simple cues, such as source credibility, communicator attractiveness, and celebrity endorsements (Cacioppo et al., 1996; Green et al., 2008; Haugtvedt, Petty, & Cacioppo, 1992; Kaufman, Stasson, & Hart, 1999; Priester & Petty, 1995). In addition, a clearly biased source who communicates the easy-to-process information that she agrees with message recipients is favored by low NFC individuals, who will do just about anything to simplify their decision-making (Westerwick, Johnson, & Knobloch-Westerwick, 2017). Indeed, even the enthusiastic endorsement of a message by others, as in outbursts of laughter, can sway low-NFC individuals (Axsom, Yates, & Chaiken, 1987).

Collectively, these findings have interesting practical implications. When persuaders direct messages to individuals who they know are high in NFC, they should make certain that they employ strong arguments or make cogent appeals to respondents' values. If, on the other hand, the message is directed at low-NFC respondents, persuaders should develop appeals that don't tax these folks' mental capacities. Simple, clear appeals – the simpler, the better – are probably advisable. For example, Bakker (1999), in a study of AIDS prevention messages, found that simple, visual safer-sex messages were highly effective for low-NFC individuals. Similar findings in different health contexts have also been reported (Braverman, 2008; Vidrine, Simmons, & Brandon, 2007; Williams-Piehota et al., 2003; see also Lee, 2013).

What's more, even a subtle cue can unleash differences in NFC. *The mere perception* that a message is complex can produce intriguing differences (e.g., See, Petty, & Evans, 2009). High-NFC individuals applied mental effort when they expected a communication to be complex, but not when they thought it would be simple. Expecting the message would pleasantly engage their thought processes, they threw themselves into the task. By contrast, individuals low in need for cognition exerted cognitive energy when they thought the message would be simple, but not when they anticipated that it would be complex. Noting that the message suited their preference for simple intellectual tasks, they expended mental effort. But when they expected it would be complex, they shied away, reluctant to devote energy to a message with undue complexity.

Two cautionary notes should be sounded. First, NFC does not always exert the hypothesized effects on attitudes (O'Keefe, 2016a). There have been cases where need for cognition does not interact with messages exactly as predicted, attesting to the complexity and intricacy of persuasion and social science research. Second, in view of the considerable support obtained for NFC on message processing, it might be reasonable to assume generally (and on a personal level) that it is better to be high than low in need for cognition. That is not necessarily so.

You can be high in NFC, enjoy thinking abstractly, but puzzle so long about a simple issue that you lose the forest for the trees. One could be low in NFC and get straight to the heart of the issue, without getting bogged down in excessive detail. The key for persuaders is to accept individuals for what and who they are. Communicators are more likely to be successful if they match messages to individuals' personality styles. Individuals who enjoy thinking are more likely to change their minds when they receive cogent messages that stimulate central processing. By contrast, people who make decisions based on intuition and gut feelings may be more swayed by messages that sketch a vision or tug at the heartstrings (Aune & Reynolds, 1994; Smith, 1993).

This underscores an important contribution that the ELM makes to knowledge of personality and persuasion. For many years, scholars hypothesized that certain individuals – for example, those with low self-esteem or low intelligence – were more gullible and susceptible to persuasion than others. Research indicated that this was not the case. There is not a gullible personality type, or if there is, researchers have had difficulty empirically identifying its contours. A more reasonable way to unravel the relationship between personality and persuasibility is to follow the directives of the ELM: Take into account the different ways that individuals who are high or low in a particular personality characteristic process persuasive messages and tailor communications to fit their processing style. A variety of personality traits, like the need to evaluate, need for closure, and self-esteem influence attitude change, working through different elaborative mechanisms (Briñol & Petty, 2019). If persuaders can tap into the different ways people high or low on these variables think, elaborate, and rely on peripheral cues, they have a better chance of guiding them toward healthy ways of adapting to life's challenges.

$2 \cdot$ Ability

A second determinant of processing strategy (besides motivation) is the person's ability to process the message. Situations can enhance or hamper individuals' ability to process a message. For example, people are less able to process a message when they are distracted, resulting in persuasive effects discussed earlier. More interestingly, we centrally or peripherally process messages depending on our cognitive ability, or knowledge. When individuals possess the ability to elaborate on a message, everything being equal, they gravitate to the central route. When they lack the ability to understand message arguments, they rely on heuristics and look to those slippery peripheral cues.

Consider knowledge as an example of ability. When people know a lot about an issue, they process information carefully and skillfully. They are better able to separate the rhetorical wheat from the chaff than are those with little knowledge of the issue. They are more capable of evaluating the cogency of information and are adept at identifying shortcomings in message arguments. It doesn't matter what the issue is: It could be nuclear physics, baseball, or roof repair. Knowledgeable people process information centrally and are ordinarily tough nuts for persuaders to crack (Wood, Rhodes, & Biek, 1995). By contrast, people with minimal knowledge on a topic lack the background to differentiate strong from weak arguments. They also may lack confidence in their opinions. They are the peripheral processors, frequently susceptible to peripheral cues on messages about these topics.

As an example, think of an issue you know a lot about – let's say, contemporary movies. Now conjure up a topic about which you know little – let's say, computer scanners. The ELM says that you will process persuasive messages on these topics very differently and that persuaders should use different techniques to change your mind on these topics. Given your expertise on modern films (you know all about different film techniques and the strengths and weaknesses of famous directors), there is every reason to believe you would centrally process a message that claims 1960s movies are superior to those of today. The message would grab your attention and could change your attitudes – provided it contained strong, compelling arguments.

A "rational" approach like this would be stunningly ineffective on the subject of scanners that digitize photos and convert words on a printed page into word-processing files. Given your ignorance of scanners, you would have difficulty processing technical arguments about optical character recognition, driver software, or high-resolution scans. On the other hand, the salesperson who used a peripheral approach might be highly effective. A salesperson who said she had been in the business ten years or who furnished ten arguments why Canon was superior to Epson might easily connect with you, perhaps changing your attitude or inducing you to buy a Canon scanner. Consistent with this logic, Wood, Kallgren, and Preisler (1985) found that argument quality had a stronger impact on attitudes among individuals with a great deal of knowledge on an issue. However, a peripheral cue, message length, exerted a stronger influence on those with little knowledge of the issue.

Peripheral Processing in Real Life

There is nothing as practical as a good theory, Kurt Lewin famously said. This is abundantly apparent in the case of the ELM. Once you appreciate the model, you begin to find all sorts of examples of how it is employed in everyday life. Four examples of peripheral processing follow, with an application to online persuasion offered in Box 8.2.

BOX 8.2

Online Bamboozling

Your older brother's 21st birthday is a week away and you haven't bought him a gift. It is not the first time you have procrastinated. He is a computer geek, a nerd's nerd, and a devotee of the old television program, *The Big Bang Theory*, because he would fit right in. You never know what to get him. You could not be more different: You are an extrovert, a people person who loves the art of conversation.

So here you are cruising the Web and a variety of apps on your smartphone – well, careening would be a more apt description, given the speed at which your fingers are moving. How do you decide what gift to purchase? What factors convince you to choose one laptop or tablet over another? An engaging study by Miriam J. Metzger, Andrew J. Flanagin, and Ryan B. Medders (2010) offers some clues. The study is important because it demonstrates that the ELM has intriguing implications for self-persuasion via the Internet, thereby enlarging its explanatory scope (see Figure 8.6).

Figure 8.6 People Frequently Shop Online, Purchasing Products as They Sit in Front of Their Personal Computers or Smartphones. The ELM reminds us that when people lack motivation or ability, they will make purchase decisions based on a host of heuristics and peripheral cues. In some cases, this makes them easy prey for unscrupulous online persuaders

Image Courtesy of Shutterstock

In ELM terms, you are a computer-searching shopper who is low in computer ability (at least compared with Einstein, your older sib). The ELM predicts that under conditions of low ability, consumers will base their product decisions on peripheral cues, relying on trusted heuristics to help them decide which products to purchase. In their study of 109 focus group participants from across the United States, Metzger, Flanagin, and Medders (2010) found that individuals relied on several key heuristics when seeking product information online. Notice that each of these represents reasonable, quite rational strategies for making a choice. At the same time, as we will see, they are short-circuited rules of thumb that leave people vulnerable to commercial manipulation. The key heuristics included the reputation of a website and endorsements. Participants trust Internet sources that were recommended by others and garnered a great deal of favorable feedback. The catch is this: As you know, just because a site has a strong reputation, ringing endorsements, or is consistent with other sites does not mean the information it contains is true or valid. People can be fooled by the patina of credibility and illusion of social proof (Cialdini, 2009).

Conniving entrepreneurs regularly sell five-star reviews to companies. "For $5, I will submit two great reviews for your business," one poster wrote on a help-for-hire site (Streitfeld, 2011, p. A1). "Do not make (the false reviews) sound like an advertisement," another faker advised. Still another, one of many who faked ratings on social media sites, spoke of outfoxing Facebook (Streitfeld, 2013, p. A17).

With companies from Penney's to Airbnb increasingly attuned to their online ratings, these digital manipulation devices can produce hefty dividends. One company, Sunday Riley Skincare, gamed the system for years, until the Federal Trade Commission discovered it had long been posting fake reviews of its water creams and night oils on Sephora's website. But the FTC declined to impose a financial penalty, doing little to discourage the practice (Maheshwari, 2019).

There may be a silver lining. As with all advertising techniques, consumers and regulators finally get wise. For instance, people now place less faith in online, user-generated restaurant reviews the more they believe that the restaurant can keep tabs on the dissemination of these reviews and the more they suspect actual consumers didn't write the reviews (DeAndrea et al., 2018). So, if you're wise to these online reviews, which you probably are, you won't be fooled. But if you are in low-involvement, make-a-quick-decision mode, relying on heuristics, you might be duped by the misleading peripheral cues of online persuasion.

The Oprah Book Club Effect

For 25 years, millions of Americans watched "Oprah's Book Club," a monthly segment of *The Oprah Winfrey Show* that featured engaging discussions of recently published novels. Book club shows involved a discussion among Winfrey, the author, and several viewers, who discussed the book and its relationship to their own lives. "The show receives as many as 10,000 letters each month from people eager to participate," a reporter related.

> By the time the segment appears, 500,000 viewers have read at least part of the novel. Nearly as many buy the book in the weeks that follow ... Oprah's Book Club has been responsible for 28 consecutive best sellers. It has sold more than 20 million books and made many of its authors millionaires.
>
> (Max, 1999, pp. 36–37)

"Oprah's Book Club" has been a great thing for books and publishing. Updated for the digital age as "Oprah's Book Club 2.0," a collaboration between Winfrey's network and her magazine, and later as a partnership with Apple's television streaming service, Apple TV Plus, it is also an example of peripheral processing in action. What convinces hundreds of thousands of people to buy these novels? What persuades them to purchase Wally Lamb's *She's Come Undone*, the story of an intelligent, overweight woman who overcomes problems stemming from sexual abuse, rather than an equally compelling novel about abuse and redemption? The answer, in a word, is Oprah. Her credibility, warmth, and celebrity status suggest to viewers that the book is worth a try. It is not that audience members are meticulously comparing one book with another, opting to integrate Oprah's advice with their literary assessments of the plot and character development. They lack motivation and perhaps ability. So, they rely on Oprah's advice and purchase the book, much to the delight of the publishing house and struggling novelist (see Figure 8.7).

Figure 8.7 Oprah Winfrey is a Charismatic, Credible Communicator. Her endorsement of a book on "Oprah's Book Club" can serve as a powerful peripheral cue, persuading some consumers to buy the book just on the basis of her say-so. Oprah has continued to wield the power of her potent peripheral appeal to low elaboration likelihood viewers on Apple's TV streaming service, Apple TV Plus
Image courtesy of Shutterstock

With the digital update of her book club, "Oprah's Book Club 2.0," Winfrey hoped that her panache, propelled by the power of peripheral cues, would continue to move promising books to the best-seller list. Even if Winfrey's current book club declines in popularity, Oprah herself remains popular, a pervasive peripheral cue in action. A day after Winfrey announced that she would purchase a 10 percent stake in Weight Watchers and accept a seat on the board, the company's sagging stock doubled, increasing its market value by some $400 million (Picker, 2015). For low-involved investors, Winfrey served as a peripheral cue; for higher-involved investors, she may have served as an argument for the future value of the company. In either case, her endorsement offered another example of what has been called the "Oprah Effect" – celebrity as powerful heuristic.

Jargon

Has this ever happened to you? Your car engine is on the blink; you take the auto to the mechanic, who looks at you with an expression that says, "You're clueless about cars, aren't you?", after which the engine pro condescendingly places hands on hips and begins to talk in tongues – invoking the most complicated car jargon you have ever heard. Impressed by the verbiage and afraid to admit you don't know much about cars, you acquiesce to the spiel (see Figure 8.8).

Figure 8.8 A Car Mechanic Can Try to Persuade a Customer to Make a Much-Needed Car Repair, Using Many Different Arguments. The ELM suggests that when the customer lacks involvement in the decision or does not know much about cars, the mechanic could pull the wool over the customer's eyes by using fancy-sounding car jargon or words like "negative torque"
Image courtesy of Shutterstock

Tom and Ray Magliozzi, who for years hosted a National Public Radio show *Car Talk*, echoed this point in a humorous but telling article. Asked by an interviewer how someone could fake being a car mechanic, they recommend a heavy use of jargon (Nitze, 2001). Use words like "the torque wrench and torquing," Tom says. Ray replies, "Torquing always sounds good." Tom adds, "I'll bet you, you could walk into some party and mention the expression 'negative torque,' there would be nobody who would have the guts to ask you what that meant. A pro included" (p. 38).

This fits right in with the ELM. Individuals with little knowledge about car mechanics have trouble following explanations involving torque or car computer systems. When a mechanic begins using the jargon, they invoke the heuristic, "Mechanics who talk this way know their stuff; if they say this, it must be so." And, just like that, the mechanic persuades these customers to make the purchase. (A similar example comes from the movie *My Cousin Vinny*, when the character played by Marisa Tomei wows a judge and jury, using jargon comprehensible only to car experts to prove that a getaway car could not possibly have been driven by the two men accused of the crime.)

Cashing in on the Power of Tweets

You see a higher follower count, or a higher retweet count, and you assume this person is important, or this tweet was well received. As a result, you might be more likely to amplify it, to share it or to follow that person, a search engine optimization developer notes, calling exquisite attention to the way the newest peripheral cues – tweets – can be exploited for profit in the billion dollar world of online marketing (Confessore et al., 2018, p 18; see Figure 8.9).

Number of tweets and retweet counts serve as peripheral cues, suggesting the popularity or worth of a product or influencer's brand to low-involved, low-ability users hopscotching through social media. Invoking the social proof heuristic that if others embrace the object, I should too – and the more who endorse it, the higher its branded import – people can make quick judgments that are tailor-made to the user low in elaboration likelihood. The trouble is that shadowy marketing companies have manipulated reliance on heuristic shortcuts, selling retweets and followers to anyone – a celeb, teenage YouTube influencer, or marketer of a fraudulent product – who hopes to game social influence on the wildly popular social networking service.

One company, Devumi, drew on some 3.5 million automated accounts, delivering customers more than 200 million faux Twitter followers, in some cases heisting the names and profile pictures of actual Twitter users – a treasure trove of manufactured followers, identity thefts, fake accounts, and bots designed to inflate the popularity of a person or product (Confessore et al., 2018). As *New York Times* reporter Nicholas Confessore and his journalistic colleagues documented, Devumi's clients include pastors, models, and reality TV stars who purchase the tweeted peripheral cues to aggrandize their reputations, exploiting consumer naiveté and low involvement processing. For YouTube influencers (see Chapter 15), it is a numbers game: The more people online influencers reach, the more money branded companies pay them. "It's fraud," said one British man who purchased 50,000 followers from Devuni (Confessore et al., 2018, p. 18).

There is a happy ending to this story, at least for now. Prompted by the journalists' investigative report, Twitter removed millions of fake accounts, dampening the manipulation of peripheral cues to deceptively enhance a brand's panache (Confessore & Dance, 2018). Alas, if past experience is a guide, this will temper the use of this social media gimmick, but marketers will find a new way to exploit ELM heuristics to their competitive advantage. The fight for truthful persuasion, if the phrase is not an oxymoron, is a constant battle.

Figure 8.9 Tweets, or More Precisely Their Quantity, Are the Latest Addition to the Long List of Peripheral Cues. A higher follower or retweet count can convey popularity and credibility to low-involved online users. Unfortunately, as is always the case with persuasion, shady companies, working on behalf of unscrupulous clients, have gamed the system by relying on automated accounts, as well as stealing names and profile pictures of actual users to artificially inflate the popularity of products or people

Central Processing

Peripheral processing is a persuader's paradise. It allows communicators to devise simplistic – sometimes deceptive – appeals to influence individuals. Tempting as it is to conclude that this is the basis for all contemporary persuasion, the fact is that much persuasion also involves careful, thoughtful consideration of message arguments. As discussed earlier, when people are motivated or able to process messages, they do not rely exclusively on peripheral cues or necessarily fall for a persuader's ploys. Instead, they attend closely to the communicator's arguments. In these situations, persuasion flows through the central route, and appeals are necessarily crafted at a higher intellectual level.

Attitudes changed through deep, central-route thinking are more likely to persist over time than those formed through short-circuited thinking or peripheral cues (Petty, Haugtvedt, & Smith, 1995). Integrated into the individual's overall cognitive structure, linked with a person's self-concept, and relatively accessible from memory, centrally processed attitudes tend to be resistant to change. This is an important point. It suggests that, once formed through central processing, attitudes endure. This is bad when the attitude is prejudice, and good when the attitude is tolerance toward different groups.

On an everyday level, central processing is ordinarily in operation when people buy big-ticket, high-involvement products like wedding rings, cars, and, of course, houses: They respond to cogent arguments in support of the particular product in question. In politics, when voters are out of work or concerned about the economy, they listen closely to candidates' plans to revitalize the nation's finances, for example by placing tariffs on Chinese products to make U.S. products more competitive, a policy implemented by President Donald Trump.

Biased Processing

Alas, policy arguments, however, do not always carry the day in persuasion. Cogent arguments can fall on deaf ears when they run counter to an individual's deep-seated attitudes or long-held values. Recall the discussion in Chapter 5 of how passionate supporters and opponents of the death penalty reacted to evidence that questioned their position. They did not alter their attitudes. On the contrary, they criticized data that disputed their point of view, praised evidence that supported their position, and emerged with renewed confidence that their view on capital punishment was correct. How could this be, one wonders, if people are supposed to consider arguments rationally when they are interested in the issue in question?

The answer points to a complexity in the ELM. All central-route processing is not rational and free of bias. Human beings are not objective thinkers. The key is the degree to which the issue touches on an individual's strong attitudes, values, or ego-entrenched positions. It is useful to distinguish between issues that are of interest because they bear on important outcomes in the individual's life – comprehensive exams, tuition increases, the economy – and those that bear on values or deep-seated attitudes. When the message focuses on a personally relevant outcome, people process arguments rationally, putting aside their biases as best they can, focusing on the merits of issue arguments. However, when the issue touches on core values or *ego-involved* schema, individuals can be extremely biased and selective in how they approach the issue.

Make no mistake: In both cases, they process centrally, engaging in considerable thinking and evaluating the basic ideas contained in the message. However, when thinking about outcomes (a comprehensive exam), they are open to cogent arguments. When considering a message that touches on core values (capital punishment, abortion), they attend to the opponent's arguments, but usually reject them (Johnson & Eagly, 1989; Wood et al., 1985, though see Park et al., 2007). Highly knowledgeable people with strong attitudes will muster all sorts of sophisticated reasons why the opponent's plan is a bad one. They will impress you with their ability to remember the other side's arguments, but in the end they will prove to be just as biased as anyone else. In these situations, people behave like ostriches, stubbornly rejecting ideas that are inconsistent with their attitude and sticking only with communications with which they already agree. This exemplifies *centrally focused, but highly biased, processing of persuasive messages.*

Central Processing and Persuasion: Arguments and Bias

What does this suggest for persuasion? It tells us persuasion practitioners should strive to increase the personal relevance of the message or issue. The more persuaders can convince individuals that an issue is relevant to their own concerns or priorities, the more likely they will centrally process the message and the more lasting persuasive effects are likely to be. In the health arena, practitioners should try to induce people to recognize that medical problems can affect them personally. If health practitioners can do this, they can encourage central processing, consideration of the personal impact of health problems, and ultimately attitude change. However, this is not always easy.

Despite the plaintive pleas of the Obama administration back in 2014 that health insurance could save them money or help avoid bankruptcy-inducing expenses, many young people did not sign up for ObamaCare, perhaps because they felt they were invulnerable to medical ailments (see Chapter 12). Once patients are convinced the issue is personally relevant, they are apt to process issues centrally, and the ELM's postulates suggest general ways to convince them to adopt medical regimen. The trick is getting them to believe they are personally susceptible to danger.

When people deny they have a problem, like drinking or anorexia, for example, they are loath to centrally process messages that can help them quit drinking or stop taking obsessive, unhealthy steps to control their body weight. The ELM is not a theory about how to motivate individuals to take these steps. It argues that once people begin to perceive that that their health problem is personally relevant, and feel they are capable of dealing with the problem, messages that get people to elaborate thoughtfully can ultimately lead to long-term attitude change. Messages must no longer rely on peripheral cues, but on issue-relevant arguments, or perhaps the affective power of engaging stories (e.g., Lane et al., 2013).

The ELM's central route also has implications for persuasion on issues where people harbour strong attitudes, like politics. It suggests that when individuals perceive a political issue to be personally relevant, they will think systematically about the issue and remain open to cogent, well-delivered arguments, sometimes in politically consequential ways. But, of course, in politics, where issues are laden with emotion and touch on long-term values, arguments that fall into the latitude of rejection are toxic. Noting that the ELM acknowledges people engage in biased processing in these cases, one harks back to social judgment theory. Voters process information in terms of their anchor, selectively and obstinately.

Social judgment theorists traditionally counselled that when individuals harbor strong political attitudes, persuaders should be political, mindful that a strident message could land them in the latitude of rejection. They need to avoid hot-button issues, encouraging recipients to assimilate their arguments and view them as a friend, not a foe. However, in a polarized era, and with so many voters turned into partisan social media sites, political persuaders are bending these rules, increasingly appealing to supporters, ignoring moderates' latitudes of non-commitment, and focusing on the biases of the base.

President Donald Trump has exemplified this style, redefining the meaning of presidential with explosive tweets and outpouring of regular insults – like calling the Speaker of the House "crazy" and Republicans who refuse to support him "human scum" (Baker, 2019). His rhetoric was applauded by his base, many of whom felt that minorities had broken society's rules by metaphorically cutting in line while they were following the rules (Hochschild, 2016). But critics lamented the ways that his rhetoric debased the nation's norms of civic discourse, a foundation of ethical persuasion.

Complexities, Complexities: The Multiple Functions Postulate

The previous section examined the nature and practical implications of central processing. In this section, I take a more theoretical direction, examining a tricky, but important, aspect of the Elaboration Likelihood Model. Petty and Cacioppo introduced the ELM more than 30 years ago. In academic circles, the theory has been extensively studied and lavishly praised; yet it has also stimulated considerable discussion, debate, criticism, and, yes, elaborations.

When we think about persuasion, we commonly think that a particular factor has a simple, dramatic effect. Focusing on the source of the message (see Chapter 10 for details), we figure that a source's credibility or physical attractiveness makes them persuasive, primarily by dint of the power of their title or how they look. The ELM blows some of this apart by emphasizing that sources, as well as other factors, don't inevitably have the same impact, or achieve their influence through the same psychological processes in every situation. Instead, a persuasion factor does different things, plays different roles, serves different functions, and does all this for different reasons in different contexts. A credible or attractive communicator can change attitudes or even have the opposite effect, inhibiting attitude change, and the speaker can achieve these effects through peripheral, central, and other processes. In short, a source, message, or personality variable can operate in different ways, exert a variety of effects, and serve diverse psychological functions, the heart of the *multiple functions postulate* (Guyer et al., 2019).

The key issue is the ability of a particular variable to do different things or serve diverse functions. Consider physical attractiveness. If you had to describe the role physical attractiveness plays in persuasion, based on the earlier discussions, you might suggest that it serves as a peripheral cue. You might speculate that when people do not care much about an issue or lack ability to process the message, they fall back on the physical appeal of the speaker. Opting not to process the message carefully, they let themselves get carried away a bit by the speaker's good looks. This analysis of attractiveness is indeed in sync with the ELM as it has been discussed thus far. Attractiveness frequently has just this effect, serving as a cue for peripheral processing.

Unfortunately, matters become more complicated when we examine other persuasion settings. For example, suppose a young woman is systematically searching for a beauty product, flips through the pages of *Glamour* magazine, and sees models promoting L'Oréal and Cover Girl lipcolors. The model's good looks represent key selling points for the products. Isn't a model's attractiveness central to the decision regarding the product, not peripheral? Couldn't the physical appeal of the model – the fact that she is beautiful and uses this product – serve as a compelling reason to purchase the particular facial cream, lipcolor, or makeup? Didn't endorsements by Jessica Simpson and Katy Perry constitute central arguments that buttressed the case for purchasing the acne medicine, Proactiv? The answer to these questions is "Yes."

The ELM argues that, theoretically, a particular variable can serve in one of a variety of capacities. For someone conscientiously comparing two beauty products, the communicator's attractiveness can serve as an *argument* for one of the products (Kahle & Homer, 1985). For example, an attractive sports celebrity promoting a sports-related product like running shoes can serve as an issue-relevant argument for purchasing the product for self-presentational reasons (Lee & Koo, 2016).

In another context – electoral politics – attractiveness can function as a *peripheral cue*, as when a low-involved voter decides to vote for a candidate because she likes her facial features, commanding non-verbal expressions, or the way he towers over the other candidates on the debate stage.

Consider a third situation involving a different aspect of politics. Let's say individuals have mixed feelings on environmental and energy issues. They believe that the United States needs to locate alternative sources of fuel, but also feel it is important to preserve breathtakingly beautiful wildlife refuges. When attractive celebrities like Robert Redford (2001), Leonardo DiCaprio, or the rock group Maroon 5 speak out about environmental preservation or climate change, they may find themselves *devoting more cognitive energy* to the communicator's arguments. They may picture Redford in their minds, link up his attractive appearance with the beauty of the wilderness, and therefore give his arguments more thought than if a less attractive communicator had advanced these positions.

Similarly, when attractive actresses like Cate Blanchett and Olivia Wilde or mega-model Gisele Bundchen lend their names to environmental causes, individuals who are ambivalent about the issue may wonder why these women signed on to environmental issues. They may picture them, think about their movies or photo-shoots, and impelled by curiosity or enchantment, consider arguments on behalf of the environment just a little more thoughtfully. Thus, attractiveness can serve as a cue, a persuasive argument, and a catalyst to thinking.

There is a fourth role that a source factor like attractiveness (or any factor, really) can play, and this merits a little discussion. Attractiveness can enhance or reduce message receivers' *confidence in the quality of their thoughts about a persuasive message*. Petty and his colleagues showed that when a message produces primarily positive thoughts, increasing confidence in these thoughts enhances persuasion (Petty, Briñol, & Tormala, 2002). This suggests that when people have mostly positive thoughts about a message *and* they are confident in the validity of those thoughts, they are especially likely to change their attitudes. On the other hand, when a message leads to mostly negative thoughts, increasing confidence in the thoughts induces people to feel more unfavorably toward the message; in this case, they are more confident that their negative reactions are correct and they reject the message. This is known as *the self-validation hypothesis* and is particularly likely to occur when people are high in elaboration likelihood – that is, motivated or able to attend to their thoughts and confidence levels.

For example, a confident, charismatic, attractive persuader may be particularly effective in convincing receivers to change their minds because she elicits positive thoughts about the message and subtly induces audience members to feel good about what they are thinking. A less confident and less attractive speaker, who struggles with his words, may produce negative cognitive responses, leading individuals to have confidence in their unfavorable reactions to the message, thus reducing persuasion.

Intriguingly, based on self-validation, if people have positive thoughts about a well-crafted message, they will be more persuaded if they nod their heads, sit up straight, or feel happy than if they shake their heads, slouch, or feel sad. Nodding your head, sitting up straight, and feeling happy suggests that your positive thoughts are valid – they're correct – and this enhances persuasion (Briñol & Petty, 2003, 2015). This can be important because increasing confidence in the quality of our thoughts can lead to more confidently held attitudes. These more confidently held attitudes can persist over time and influence behavior (Guyer et al., 2019). (Of course, this can be good or bad – it's good when our confidently-held attitudes spur us to challenge the status quo, but bad when we are so confident our attitudes are correct we close our minds to the other side.)

With this in mind, let's return to the multiple functions notion, with another example focusing on a different environmental issue: Climate change, a topic touched on earlier. Most Americans – including me – can't understand all the complex modeling and research that shows strong evidence for global warming, including data documenting that the world is hotter than it has been at any point in the last 2,000 years. Consider the authoritative report from leading environmental scientists documenting in excruciating detail the economic and health risks posed by climate change and the litany of financial and social losses that will occur if society does not make substantial changes soon. The site has the imprimatur of scientific experts and the patina of empirical sophistication (Fourth National Climate Assessment, 2018). The opinions of scientists on this issue can be influential. What does the ELM say about the role played by credibility here?

The model says credibility will perform multiple functions, depending on elaboration likelihood.

The scientists' expertise can serve as a peripheral cue for people low in ability or concern about environmental issues. These folks may say to themselves:

> Who can figure all this stuff out? But a lot of major scientists and people who know what they're talking about keep talking about global warming. And they seem to have lots of facts to back it up. I'll go with what the experts say. If they say it, it's probably right.

For those with considerable knowledge and concern about the environment, the scientists' views may actually function as an *argument*. These highly involved individuals may think:

> I know the scientific community had been reluctant to declare that temperatures are artificially rising or that carbon dioxide emissions are responsible for global warming. If scientists have changed their tune now, it must be that there is strong evidence that global warming effects are real.

To other individuals, with moderate knowledge or involvement, the scientists' proclamations about global warming may *stimulate issue-relevant thinking*. They may consider the issue more carefully now that scientific researchers across the world have concluded that significant global warming is occurring across the planet.

They may not change their minds, especially if they are conservative skeptics about scientific pronouncements. But the endorsement from a highly credible source might catalyze their thinking, leading them to develop more detailed arguments on global warming.

In addition, expert scientists speaking on the global warming issue could affect higher-involved audience members' attitudes by *bolstering their confidence in their own thoughts about the message*. After hearing the expert scientists speak in favor of global warming, people might come to evaluate their own cognitive responses more favorably. They might think: "Gee, the speaker made really good arguments. The more I think about this, the more confident I feel that global warming is a serious problem." (Note to political partisans: These examples may trend toward the moderate or liberal side of politics by illustrating the concepts with issue positions that liberals typically support. One can easily pick examples from the conservative side, showing how multiple functions work to persuade people to support, for example, tax cuts to stimulate the economy or stronger pro-gun policies. The principle should work in the same conceptual fashion, no matter which side of the political distribution the message favors.)

In short, this section showed that a particular variable can serve multiple functions. Source, message, and receiver factors are not one-dimensional, but multifaceted. Just as an attitude can serve different functions for different people, so too a persuasion factor can play different roles in different situations.

Because of the different functions variables play, working for different psychological reasons, it oversimplifies matters to say that an attractive or credible source invariably leads to more persuasion. They frequently do (see Chapter 10), but the multiple functions postulate suggests that a physically attractive speaker *could* reduce persuasion if the attractive communicator takes message receivers' attention away from the message and the message has really good arguments. Glossing over the arguments, focusing on the speaker's looks, message recipients could end up not very persuaded at all. Or, a highly credible expert might get message recipients to think rationally and focus a lot on the message. But if this message contains weak, shoddy arguments, message receivers, attending to the message because the expert called their attention to it, could end up feeling less persuaded. These aren't the typical situations; indeed, the norm is that experts and attractive sources are persuasive, under particular conditions, but these outcomes can happen, and the ELM helps us understand why.

The ELM, alas, is complicated, but very interesting once you get the gist of it. Summing up, the multiple functions postulate states that a particular factor can play different roles, such as serving as: (1) a peripheral cue under low-elaboration likelihood (low motivation and ability) circumstances; (2) a persuasive argument when elaboration likelihood is high; (3) a catalyst to thinking when ability or motivation is moderate; and (4) a determinant of confidence in one's thoughts about the message, when there is greater likelihood of elaboration.

One size does not fit all, one factor doesn't do the same thing; it's an interaction, an intersection, a lot different from the usual persuasion platitudes. The ELM is complicated because people are complex. (For a summary of its main theoretical emphases, see Box 8.3.)

BOX 8.3

Understanding Theory: Primer on the Elaboration Likelihood Model

1   The ELM argues that you cannot appreciate persuasion without understanding the underlying processes by which messages affect attitudes.

2   The model stipulates that the likelihood of elaborating on, or thinking carefully about, a message depends on individuals' motivation and ability.

3   As a dual-process model, the ELM asserts that there are two routes to persuasion: Central, characterized by careful thinking about the message, and peripheral, exemplified by a focus on simple cues and simple decision-making rules or heuristics that are irrelevant to the main arguments in the message.

4   Attitude changes that result from central processing persist longer and are more likely to predict behavior than peripherally induced attitude changes.

5   There is evidence that under low motivation – such as when people lack involvement in the issue – peripheral cues are persuasive. Under high-motivational conditions – for example, when individuals are high in involvement – central processing occurs, with strong arguments significantly influencing attitudes. Similar findings have occurred under low- and high-ability conditions. Under high elaboration, central processing can take on more open-minded and biased directions, depending on strength of initial attitude.

6   A particular persuasion factor can serve in different capacities. It can function as a peripheral cue, argument, catalyst to thinking, or a factor that enhances or reduces confidence in one's cognitive responses to a message. This is the multiple functions postulate that showcases the complexity and flexibility of the model. The postulate adds breadth to the model. But it would be useful to know the conditions under which a factor would be most likely to serve in one of these particular capacities.

7   On a practical level, the ELM emphasizes that messages should be designed to get people to think about the message, elaborate on arguments, and cogitate, because the more attitudes derive from thinking, the longer they persist over time (Briñol & Petty, 2015).

Communicators should match message content with individuals' characteristics, motivation, and ability, with message effects working by way of cues, arguments, and a variety of cognitive processes.

8   A shortcoming of the ELM is its inability to specify the type of message that will be maximally effective under high involvement, or high-elaboration likelihood. How do you design a message that gets people to think deeply about an issue and, as a consequence, to consider the merits of an alternative point of view? What types of arguments, based on the ELM, should you employ to encourage open-minded thinking and discourage biased processing and prejudice? Which messages are best at generating favorable cognitive responses? The ELM does not provide clear answers to these questions. It is better in telling us why and when certain factors work than in articulating prescriptions of how best to construct a message.

9   The model's strengths are its rich process-oriented approach and comprehensive organizing framework, which shed light on persuasion. The ELM and the Heuristic-Systematic Model offer a unified, integrative framework to the psychology of attitude change.

Criticisms and Reconciliations

Any academic model that has been around for a while will stimulate ideas – and controversy. This is as it should be: Theories are meant to be criticized and subjected to empirical scrutiny. Knowledge advances from the dueling of conflicting scholarly guns. New ideas emerge from the critical exchange of points of view.

The ELM has elicited its share of criticism, with bullets targeted at the multiple functions notion previously discussed. Critics have lamented the lack of clarity of this notion. They have argued that the ELM position permits it "to explain all possible outcomes," making it impossible in principle to prove the model wrong (Stiff & Boster, 1987, p. 251). "A persuader can conduct a post mortem to find out what happened but cannot forecast the impact of a particular message," Allen and Preiss contend (1997, pp. 117–118).

Proponents of the ELM have thundered back, arguing that critics fail to appreciate the model's strengths (Petty et al., 1987, 1993). As a general rule, proponents note, individuals will be more likely to elaborate on messages when they are high in motivation or ability, and more inclined to focus on peripheral cues when they are lower in ability or motivation. What's more, they say, if you understand the particular variable under investigation and the situation in which it operates, you can make clear predictions about the influences of persuasion factors on attitudes (Haugtvedt & Wegener, 1994; Petty & Wegener, 1998). Persuasion and human behavior are so complex, ELM proponents assert, that it is not possible to make precise predictions for every variable in each and every situation. On balance, they maintain, the ELM offers a highly useful framework for understanding how persuasion works in the panoply of situations in which it occurs in everyday life.

Both sides have a point. The multiple functions notion discussed earlier is intriguing, but it points to a problematic ambiguity in the model: The ELM is so all-inclusive that it is difficult to prove the model incorrect. We want hypotheses to be capable of being proven right – and wrong.

Yet there are ways to tease out predictions. For instance, if a model's physical attractiveness in an advertisement operates as a peripheral cue, the content of the product he or she is promoting should not influence consumers so much as the pleasing appearance of the product promoter. However, if attractiveness functions as an argument (for highly involved customers), the attractiveness cue should be a less significant predictor of persuasion than the arguments in the message (O'Keefe, 2016a). In the latter case, the consumer should generate more cognitive responses and process more deeply – perhaps verified by neuroscience data – the arguments than the cue. These nuanced hypotheses have not received adequate test.

The ELM has a variety of limitations. It does not clearly specify the type of message or theoretically derived attributes of a persuasive argument quality (Russell & Reimer, 2018) that persuaders should employ under high involvement. The only advice the model offers is to get people to cognitively elaborate, to induce them to generate positive thoughts about the message. But what type of message should you employ? How should you frame your message to get people thinking positively? Just what constitutes a high-quality, strong argument in the ELM? The model is silent on these matters, as Frymier and Nadler (2017) helpfully point out. Reinforcing this concern, Daniel J. O'Keefe (2016b), with his usual rhetorical flair, notes that the model can offer "little help to those interested in message design. If one wants to know how to construct an effective counterattitudinal persuasive message under conditions of high elaboration, the ELM provides no guidance" (p. 7; see also O'Keefe, 2016a, p. 165). In addition, the model lumps a variety of peripheral processes under the same umbrella, when one might plausibly argue that certain cues are more effective than others. And it does not do as much as it could to distinguish between a persuasive cue and an argument. Increasingly, the ELM seems to function better as a model describing the panoply of persuasion than as a deductive theory that generates hypotheses, which can be clearly tested or falsified.

Nevertheless, no conceptual framework is perfect, and the ELM has, over the long haul, helped transform the field of persuasion research. It has illuminated the psychological reasons why communications can powerfully influence attitudes. It has linked cognitive processes to communication effects in a coherent way. These are important contributions, ones that should not be minimized. Before the ELM (and the equally valuable Heuristic-Systematic Model, see Box 8.4) was formulated, there were few in-depth approaches to understanding cognitive processing and persuasive communication. There was a hodgepodge of results – findings about this type of communicator, that type of message, and this kind of message recipient. It was like a jigsaw puzzle that didn't quite fit together.

The ELM has helped provide us with a coherent perspective to understand the blooming, buzzing confusion of persuasion, offering a framework for understanding the psychology of persuasive communication. It has helped explain why different messages are effective in different circumstances, while also debunking the simple notion that a particular factor can affect attitudes through one path (O'Keefe, 2013). And some 35 years after it was introduced, it continues to offer insights to researchers and practitioners (Petty, Barden, & Wheeler, 2009), at the very least lending an umbrella conceptual framework from which to appreciate the rich complexity of persuasion effects. Although it is not without problems, the model's plasticity has generated a veritable cornucopia of persuasion findings, sometimes confirming conventional wisdom, in other cases contradicting common-sense predictions, and in a variety of other instances taking knowledge in fruitful new directions.

And yet, the model appears to have reached a point of finality. It has made its contributions to process, contributed new insights to multiple functions, and served as a source of numerous persuasion applications. Like other theoretical approaches in the psychology of persuasion, it has done its thing and made its mark, but is unlikely to generate new conceptual fruit. At the same time, it will be interesting to see how the model can be applied to take into account persuasion in a social media era, where making distinctions among persuaders, message recipients, and perhaps cues and arguments can be all the more complicated. It will be edifying to appreciate how and when tweets and emoji influence attitudes through ELM processes, and the multiple functions they play. Persuasion via social media, where peripheral cues and heuristics abound, represents an important area for future research, especially given the ways online media messages can hoodwink vulnerable individuals.

BOX 8.4

The Heuristic-Systematic Model and the Unimodel

The Heuristic-Systematic Model (HSM) complements the Elaboration Likelihood Model. It too has generated a great deal of research. No discussion on persuasion would be complete without discussing its main features.

Like the ELM, the HSM says that motivation and ability determine processing strategy. But while the ELM says the main purpose of message processing is to develop an accurate attitude in tune with reality, the HSM takes a broader approach (Dillard, 2010). It emphasizes that people can be motivated by a need to hold accurate attitudes, but also by defensive needs to maintain attitudes that bear on the self-concept, or desire to make a positive impression on others (Chen & Chaiken, 1999).

Like the ELM, the HSM emphasizes that there are two processes by which persuasion occurs. Instead of calling the routes central and peripheral, it speaks of systematic and heuristic processing. Systematic processing entails comprehensive consideration of issue-relevant arguments. Heuristic processing, discussed earlier in this chapter, involves the use of cognitive shortcuts.

A major contribution of the HSM is its suggestion that simple decision rules or heuristics play an important role in attitude change. People are viewed as "minimalist information processors" who are unwilling to devote much effort to processing persuasive arguments (Stiff, 1994). They like their shortcuts and they use them frequently in everyday life. Even so, there are some conditions under which people will gravitate to a systematic processing mode, and individuals seek a balance between relying on shortcuts and carefully processing a message.

The HSM, interestingly, emphasizes that heuristic and systematic processes are not mutually exclusive. Instead, it says that, under certain circumstances, people can rely on heuristics and systematically process a message (Eagly & Chaiken, 1993; Todorov et al., 2002). For example, a committed Democrat could glance over a social media post and make a heuristic judgment that she disapproves of the message, based on the fact that the author is a Republican. As she continues reading, she may begin processing systematically (though in a biased way), and come up with strong arguments against the author's message, confirming the initial heuristic judgment.

The HSM stipulates that two principles govern cognitive processing of persuasive messages. The first is the *least effort principle*, which stipulates that "people prefer less effortful to more effortful modes of information processing" (Eagly & Chaiken, 1993, p. 330). They frequently reject systematic processing in favor of heuristic decision-making.

The second principle is an outgrowth of the recognition that people seek to balance their desire to minimize thinking with a need to satisfy various situational objectives, such as holding accurate attitudes, defending important opinions, and conveying socially acceptable beliefs. The *sufficiency principle* stipulates that "people will exert whatever effort is required to attain a 'sufficient' degree of confidence that they have satisfactorily accomplished their processing goals" (Eagly & Chaiken, 1993, p. 330). However, once they are confident that they have developed an attitude that advances their goals, they typically quit processing the message and move on to another task.

Although most researchers like the idea of two different routes to persuasion, there are dissenters. Arie W. Kruglanski and Erik P. Thompson (1999) have argued that it is easier to think of just one pathway to persuasion; the key is how extensively people process information.

In their single-route approach or unimodel, they argue that "the function fulfilled by cues and heuristics and message arguments is essentially the same. Both serve as forms of evidence, hence they are functionally equivalent" (Kruglanski & Thompson, 1999, p. 93). It is not that cues are necessarily processed peripherally under low involvement and arguments processed centrally under high involvement. Instead, the unimodel suggests that whatever is brief and comes early in the message will naturally capture the attention of low-involved receivers, eager to complete the task. Whatever comes later and requires more thinking (cue *or* arguments) will be given relatively more scrutiny by the frequently more conscientious, high-involved participants (O'Keefe, 2016a).

In support of this notion, Kruglanski and Thompson (1999) found that when a peripheral cue is lengthy and complex, presumably requiring central processing, it can actually have a *greater* impact on high-involved participants than on low-involved individuals who are less motivated to appreciate its implications. When source expertise – theoretically a peripheral cue – contained a lot of information, expertise influenced those for whom the information was relevant rather than those for whom the issue was not particularly relevant. In another study, brief message arguments were followed by longer or lengthy arguments. Brief arguments influenced judgments under low involvement, while lengthy arguments affected judgments under high involvement (see Kruglanski et al., 2006). According to the unimodel, the cue–argument distinction is overblown and is not what distinguishes low- and high-elaboration likelihood receivers. Instead, people do not process information through two distinct routes; they simply focus on the nature of the evidence, whether a cue or an argument. In this way, their processing falls along the continuum of one factor: The nature of the data.

This is an interesting, provocative critique. But this does not entirely invalidate the idea that two different *cognitive processes* are invoked when people are high versus low in involvement and ability. The key distinction for the ELM is not cue versus argument, but degree of processing along the continuum of cognitive elaboration (O'Keefe, 2016a). Thus, in the example above, the information-filled source expertise stimuli would be processed centrally under high involvement and for individuals for whom information is relevant, because highly involved receivers are motivated to carefully scrutinize the source's background, mentally elaborating on the source's credentials. Indeed, there is evidence from some ELM experiments that the same information *is* processed through different routes (Petty & Briñol, 2012).

Yet while the unimodel has interesting implications for persuasion, it is not clear that the practical applications differ appreciably from those of the ELM. For example, both models suggest that to persuade low-involved or low-ability receivers, persuaders should capture their attention early in the message with brief, simple, easy-to-process information. To its credit, the unimodel has pointed out ambiguities in the ELM, suggesting that the cue–argument distinction is murkier than frequently assumed. However, it is not clear the unimodel can handle theoretical issues, such as the complex multiple functions notion, with any greater clarity. Certainly, there is an elegance to the peripheral versus central, dual-path approach and the emphasis on qualitative differences in processing message information. In the final analysis, the two share a basic agreement, in line with the leitmotif of this text: You cannot understand message effects without appreciating the underlying psychological process.

Conclusions

Early persuasion research tested some of the ideas about sources and messages that Aristotle developed centuries before. The Yale attitude change approach offered some of the first hard-nosed experimental tests of persuasion hypotheses. The cognitive response approach refined the Yale studies by calling attention to the role that cognitive responses play in persuasion, particularly in forewarning, distraction, and, later, inoculation. These studies paved the way for dual-process models of persuasion.

We can trace dual-process models to ancient Greece. Plato's ideal thinkers epitomized systematic, deep processing of persuasive messages; some of the Sophist writers (at least as depicted by Plato) embodied the colorful, stylistic appeals we associate with the peripheral route. Contemporary models, attempting to explain a very different world of persuasion than that which bedeviled the Greeks, hark back to the duality that preoccupied Plato in the fourth century BC.

Contemporary models stipulate that there are two routes to persuasion – one thoughtful, focusing on the main arguments in the message, the other superficial and short circuited, characterized by an attempt to make a quick choice, an easy fix. The ELM and HSM, building on the Yale attitude change and cognitive response approaches, offer insights about how people process messages in many situations. Motivation and ability determine processing strategy. Processing route, in turn, determines the type of message appeal that is maximally effective in a particular context, as well as the long-term effects of the message on attitudes. In other words, if you understand the factors impinging on someone and how he or she thinks about a persuasive message, you have a good chance of devising a message that will target the individual's attitudes.

Complications arise when we consider that persuasion factors perform multiple functions. A particular factor can serve as a cue, an argument, a catalyst to thought, or a stimulus that bolsters confidence in one's mental reactions to a persuasive message. The multiple functions notion helps explain a variety of persuasion effects; however, its ambiguity can frustrate attempts to derive clear applications of the ELM to real-life situations. Like other psychological approaches, the model does not always clearly explain how an understanding of people's thought processes can help persuaders to generate specific messages.

Yet there is much to praise in the ELM's approach. Viewed broadly, it provides an integrative framework for understanding persuasion and provides practitioners with ideas for designing effective appeals (see Box 8.5). In essence, the model tells persuaders – in areas ranging from politics to health – to understand how their audiences approach and process messages. The ELM cautions against confrontation. Instead, it instructs communicators to tailor their arguments to audience members' motives and abilities.

From an ethical perspective, the model is value-neutral. Use of heuristics can help people make efficient decisions when they lack time or resources. But peripheral cues can also mislead individuals, tricking them into buying products they do not need. Centrally processing arguments can lead to more thoughtful, reasoned decisions. However, when individuals have strong biases, such processing can reinforce prejudices, reducing openness to different points of view.

As a psychological theory, rather than a normative approach, the model does not tell us whether the motivation to carefully consider message arguments under high personal involvement balances out the drawbacks of biased, dogmatic processing or susceptibility to manipulation under low involvement. It would seem as if the most pragmatic way to resolve these conundrums is to hold persuaders responsible for their violations of ethical principles, but also remember that we are responsible for persuasive decisions we make.

BOX 8.5

Persuasion Tips

One of the nifty things about the ELM is that it contains practical, as well as theoretical, suggestions. Here are several suggestions for everyday persuasion, gleaned from the model:

1   As you prepare a presentation, ask yourself if the topic is one that engages the audience or is one of little consequence. Does the audience care a lot about the issue? Or is it of little personal relevance? If it is a high-involvement issue, you should make sure you prepare strong arguments and get the audience thinking. If it is a low-involvement matter, you should emphasize peripheral cues, simple strategies, and ways to bolster the audience's confidence that you know your stuff. But in either case, make sure you deliver your message ethically and with respect for moral values.

2   Next time you are trying to convince someone of something, you should ask yourself: What is central, or most critical, to my attempt to change the other's mind? What type of appeal will serve my goal best? For example, people are frequently scared of giving a public speech and assume that the most important thing is to look nice – buy fancy clothes, put on lots of makeup, and so forth. This can be an important aspect of persuasion, but it may be peripheral to the task. If you are trying to make a sale, you need compelling arguments that the purchase is in the client's interest. If you are trying to convince people to get more exercise, you must show them that exercise can help them achieve their goals.

   By the same token, remember that something that appears peripheral to you may be of considerable importance to the person you are trying to convince (Soldat, Sinclair, & Mark, 1997). You may spend a lot of time coming up with great arguments to convince neighbors to sign a petition against McDonald's building a new franchise near a beautiful park located down the block. But if your memo has a couple of typos or your website containing the message is overloaded with information, people may think a little less of you. They may jump to the conclusion that your arguments are flawed. To you, the typos or abundance of information are of much less consequence than the cogency of your arguments. And you may be right. But what is peripheral to you can be central to someone else. Put yourself in the minds of those receiving your message, and consider how they will react to what you say and how you package your message.

3   Pay attention to non-verbals, but for a different reason than we ordinarily assume. As noted earlier, based on self-validation, when individuals generate favorable thoughts about a message, they are more persuaded when they sit up straight, nod their heads, and feel happy than when they slouch, shake their heads, or feel sad (Briñol & Petty, 2003, 2015). When we sit up, nod our heads, feel happy and smile, we have more confidence in our positive thoughts about the message, presuming they are valid. So, when you are trying to persuade a group of people (or are going for a job interview), nod your head appropriately, stand or sit up straight, and smile. This will increase your confidence in your message, enhancing your belief in what you are communicating. As a result of your increased belief in your power of persuasion, your audience should also be more convinced.

It is our responsibility to recognize that we take mental shortcuts when we care or know little about an issue and persuaders may exploit this tendency. In the end, it is our responsibility to protect ourselves from the peripheral persuaders of the world.

References

Allen, M., & Preiss, R. (1997). Persuasion, public address, and progression in the sciences: Where we are at what we do. In G. A. Barnett & F. J. Boster (Eds.), *Progress in communication sciences* (Vol. 13, pp. 107–131). Greenwich, CT: Ablex.

Aune, R. K., & Reynolds, R. A. (1994). The empirical development of the normative message processing scale. *Communication Monographs, 61*, 135–160.

Axsom, D., Yates, S., & Chaiken, S. (1987). Audience response as a heuristic cue in persuasion. *Journal of Personality and Social Psychology, 53*, 30–40.

Baker, P. (2019, October 19). A presidency remade in Trump's image. *The New York Times*, A1, A12.

Bakker, A. B. (1999). Persuasive communication about AIDS prevention: Need for cognition determines the impact of message format. *AIDS Education and Prevention, 11*, 150–162.

Banas, J. A., & Rains, S. A. (2010). A meta-analysis of research on inoculation theory. *Communication Monographs, 77*, 281–311.

Benoit, W. L. (1991). Two tests of the mechanism of inoculation theory. *Southern Communication Journal, 56*, 219–229.

Benoit, W. L. (1998). Forewarning and persuasion. In M. Allen & R. W. Preiss (Eds.), *Persuasion: Advances through meta-analysis* (pp. 139–154). Cresskill, NJ: Hampton Press.

Braverman, J. (2008). Testimonials versus informational persuasive messages: The moderating effect of delivery mode and personal involvement. *Communication Research, 35*, 666–694.

Briñol, P., & Petty, R. E. (2003). Overt head movements and persuasion: A self-validation analysis. *Journal of Personality and Social Psychology, 84*, 1123–1139.

Briñol, P., & Petty, R. E. (2005). Individual differences in attitude change. In D. Albarracín, B. T. Johnson, & M. P. Zanna (Eds.), *The handbook of attitudes* (pp. 575–615). Mahwah, NJ: Lawrence Erlbaum Associates.

Briñol, P., & Petty, R. E. (2015). Elaboration and validation processes: Implications for media attitude change. *Media Psychology, 18*, 267–291.

Briñol, P., & Petty, R. E. (2019). The impact of individual differences on attitudes and attitude change. In D. Albarracín & B. T. Johnson (Eds.), *The handbook of attitudes (Vol. 1: Basic principles* (2nd ed., pp. 520–556). New York: Routledge.

Brock, T. C. (1967). Communication discrepancy and intent to persuade as determinants of counterargument production. *Journal of Experimental Social Psychology, 3*, 296–309.

Cacioppo, J. T., Petty, R. E., Feinstein, J. A., & Jarvis, W. B. G. (1996). Dispositional differences in cognitive motivation: The life and times of individuals varying in need for cognition. *Psychological Bulletin, 119*, 197–253.

Cacioppo, J. T., Petty, R. E., & Kao, C. F. (1984). The efficient assessment of need for cognition. *Journal of Personality Assessment, 48*, 306–307.

Carpenter, C. J. (2015). A meta-analysis of the ELM's argument quality x processing type predictions. *Human Communication Research, 41*, 501–534.

Chaiken, S., Liberman, A., & Eagly, A. H. (1989). Heuristic and systematic information processing within and beyond the persuasion context. In J. S. Uleman & J. A. Bargh (Eds.), *Unintended thought: Limits of awareness, intention, and control* (pp. 212–252). New York: Guilford.

Chaiken, S., Wood, W., & Eagly, A. H. (1996). Principles of persuasion. In E. T. Higgins & A. W. Kruglanski (Eds.), *Social psychology: Handbook of basic principles* (pp. 702–742). New York: Guilford.

Chen, S., & Chaiken, S. (1999). The Heuristic–Systematic Model in its broader context. In S. Chaiken & Y. Trope (Eds.), *Dual-process theories in social psychology* (pp. 73–96). New York: Guilford.

Cialdini, R. B. (2009). *Influence: Science and practice* (5th ed.). Boston, MA: Pearson Education.

Compton, J. (2013). Inoculation theory. In J. P. Dillard & L. Shen (Eds.), *The Sage handbook of persuasion: Developments in theory and practice* (2nd ed., pp. 220–236). Thousand Oaks, CA: Sage.

Confessore, N., & Dance, G. J. X. (2018, July 12). Twitter purges its fake followers to restore the power of influence. *The New York Times*, A1, A19.

Confessore, N., Dance, G. J. X., Harris, R., & Hansen, M. (2018, January 28). Buying online influence from a shadowy market. *The New York Times*, 1, 18–20.

Davenport, C., & Connelly, M. (2015, January 31). Most in G.O.P. say they back climate action. *The New York Times*, A1, A11.

DeAndrea, D. C., Van Der Heide, B., Vendemia, M. A., & Vang, M. H. (2018). How people evaluate online reviews. *Communication Research*, 45, 719–736.

Dillard, J. P. (2010). Persuasion. In C. R. Berger, M. E. Roloff, & D. R. Roskos-Ewoldsen (Eds.), *The handbook of communication science* (2nd ed., pp. 203–218). Thousand Oaks, CA: Sage.

Eagly, A. H., & Chaiken, S. (1993). *The psychology of attitudes*. Fort Worth, TX: Harcourt, Brace, Jovanovich.

Festinger, L., & Maccoby, N. (1964). On resistance to persuasive communications. *Journal of Abnormal and Social Psychology*, 68, 359–366.

Fourth National Climate Assessment (2018). *Vol II: Impacts, risks, and adaptation in the United States*. Retrieved June 26, 2019, from nca2018.globalchange.gov

Fransen, M. L., & Fennis, B. M. (2014). Comparing the impact of explicit and implicit resistance induction strategies on message persuasiveness. *Journal of Communication*, 64, 915–934.

Frymier, A. B., & Nadler, M. K. (2017). *Persuasion: Integrating theory, research, and practice* (4th ed.). Dubuque, IA: KendallHunt.

Fu, W. W. (2012). Selecting online videos from graphics, text, and view counts: The moderation of popularity bandwagons. *Journal of Computer-Mediated Communication*, 18, 46–61.

Green, M. C., Kass, S., Carrey, J., Herzig, B., Feeney, R., & Sabini, J. (2008). Transportation across media: Repeated exposure to print and film. *Media Psychology*, 11, 512–539.

Greenwald, A. G. (1968). Cognitive learning, cognitive response to persuasion, and attitude change. In A. G. Greenwald, T. C. Brock, & T. M. Ostrom (Eds.), *Psychological foundations of attitudes* (pp. 147–170). New York: Academic Press.

Guyer, J. J., Briñol, P., Petty, R. E., & Horcajo, J. (2019). Nonverbal behavior of persuasive sources: A multiple process analysis. *Journal of Nonverbal Behavior*, 43, 203–231.

Haugtvedt, C. P., Petty, R. E., & Cacioppo, J. T. (1992). Need for cognition and advertising: Understanding the role of personality variables in consumer behavior. *Journal of Consumer Psychology*, 1, 239–260.

Haugtvedt, C. P., & Wegener, D. T. (1994). Message order effects in persuasion: An attitude strength perspective. *Journal of Consumer Research*, 21, 205–218.

Hochschild, A. R. (2016). *Strangers in their own land: Anger and mourning on the American right*. New York: The New Press.

Hovland, C. I., Janis, I. L., & Kelley, H. H. (1953). *Communication and persuasion: Psychological studies of opinion change*. New Haven, CT: Yale University Press.

Johnson, B. T., & Eagly, A. H. (1989). Effects of involvement on persuasion: A meta-analysis. *Psychological Bulletin, 106*, 290–314.

Kahle, L. R., & Homer, P. M. (1985). Physical attractiveness of the celebrity endorser: A social adaptation perspective. *Journal of Consumer Research, 11*, 954–961.

Kaufman, D. Q., Stasson, M. F., & Hart, J. W. (1999). Are the tabloids always wrong or is that just what we think? Need for cognition and perceptions of articles in print media. *Journal of Applied Social Psychology, 29*, 1984–1997.

Kruglanski, A. W., Chen, X., Pierro, A., Mannetti, L., Erb, H. P., & Spiegel, S. (2006). Persuasion according to the unimodel: Implications for cancer communication. *Journal of Communication, 56*, S105–S122.

Kruglanski, A. W., & Thompson, E. P. (1999). Persuasion by a single route: A view from the unimodel. *Psychological Inquiry, 10*, 83–109.

Lane, R., Miller, A. N., Brown, C., & Vilar, N. (2013). An examination of the narrative persuasion with epilogue through the lens of the elaboration likelihood model. *Communication Quarterly, 61*, 431–445.

Lee, E.-J. (2013). Effectiveness of politicians' soft campaign on Twitter versus TV: Cognitive and experiential routes. *Journal of Communication, 63*, 953–974.

Lee, Y., & Koo, J. (2016). Can a celebrity serve as an issue-relevant argument in the elaboration likelihood model? *Psychology & Marketing, 33*, 195–208.

Lim, J. S., & Ki, E. J. (2007). Resistance to ethically suspicious parody video on YouTube: A test of inoculation theory. *Journalism and Mass Communication Quarterly, 84*, 713–728.

Maheshwari, S. (2019, November 29). The online star rating system is flawed … and you never know if you can trust what you read. *The New York Times*, B1, B4.

Max, D. T. (1999, December 26). The Oprah effect. *The New York Times Magazine*, 36–41.

McGuire, W. J. (1970). A vaccine for brainwash. *Psychology Today*, 36–39, 63–64. February.

McGuire, W. J., & Papageorgis, D. (1961). The relative efficacy of various types of prior belief-defense in producing immunity against persuasion. *Journal of Abnormal and Social Psychology, 62*, 327–337.

Metzger, M. J., Flanagin, A. J., & Medders, R. B. (2010). Social and heuristic approaches to credibility evaluation online. *Journal of Communication, 60*, 413–439.

Nitze, S. P. (2001, April 8). How to be an impostor. *The New York Times Magazine*, 38–40.

O'Keefe, D. J. (2013). The elaboration likelihood model. In J. P. Dillard & L. Shen (Eds.), *The Sage handbook of persuasion: Developments in theory and practice* (2nd ed., pp. 137–149). Thousand Oaks, CA: Sage.

O'Keefe, D. J. (2016a). *Persuasion: Theory and research* (3rd ed.). Thousand Oaks, CA: Sage.

O'Keefe, D. J. (2016b, November). *Two cheers for the ELM: Strengths and shortcomings after three decades*. Invited paper on panel on The ELM, Media, and Public Opinion: What Do (and Should) We Know After Thirty Years? Presented to the annual convention of the Midwest Association for Public Opinion Research, Chicago.

Osterhouse, R. A., & Brock, T. C. (1970). Distraction increases yielding to propaganda by inhibiting counterarguing. *Journal of Personality and Social Psychology, 15*, 344–358.

Park, H. S., Levine, T. R., Kingsley Westerman, C. Y., Orfgen, T., & Foregger, S. (2007). The effects of argument quality and involvement type on attitude formation and attitude change: A test of dual-process and social judgment predictions. *Human Communication Research, 33*, 81–102.

Parker, K. A., Rains, S. A., & Ivanov, B. (2016). Examining the "blanket of protection" conferred by inoculation: The effects of inoculation messages on the cross-protection of related attitudes. *Communication Monographs, 83*, 49–68.

Perloff, R. M., & Brock, T. C. (1980). "And thinking makes it so": Cognitive responses to persuasion. In M. E. Roloff & G. R. Miller (Eds.), *Persuasion: New directions in theory and research* (pp. 67–99). Beverly Hills, CA: Sage.

Petty, R. E., Barden, J., & Wheeler, S. C. (2009). The elaboration likelihood model of persuasion: Developing health promotions for sustained behavioral change. In R. J. DiClemente, R. A. Crosby, & M. C. Kegler (Eds.), *Emerging theories in health promotion practice and research* (pp. 185–214). San Francisco, CA: Wiley.

Petty, R. E., & Briñol, P. (2012). The elaboration likelihood model. In P. A. M. Van Lange, A. Kruglanski, & E. T. Higgins (Eds.), *Handbook of theories of social psychology* (Vol. 1, pp. 224–245). London, UK: Sage.

Petty, R. E., & Briñol, P. (2015). Processes of social influence through attitude change. In E. Borgida & J. Bargh (Eds.), *APA Handbook of Personality and Social Psychology (Vol. 1): Attitudes and social cognition* (pp. 509–545). Washington, DC: APA Books.

Petty, R. E., Briñol, P., & Tormala, Z. L. (2002). Thought confidence as a determinant of persuasion: The self-validation hypothesis. *Journal of Personality and Social Psychology, 82,* 722–741.

Petty, R. E., & Cacioppo, J. T. (1977). Forewarning, cognitive responding, and resistance to persuasion. *Journal of Personality and Social Psychology, 35,* 645–655.

Petty, R. E., & Cacioppo, J. T. (1984). The effects of involvement on responses to argument quantity and quality: Central and peripheral routes to persuasion. *Journal of Personality and Social Psychology, 46,* 69–81.

Petty, R. E., & Cacioppo, J. T. (1986). The Elaboration Likelihood Model of persuasion. In L. Berkowitz (Ed.), *Advances in experimental social psychology* (Vol. 19, pp. 123–205). New York: Academic Press.

Petty, R. E., Cacioppo, J. T., & Goldman, R. (1981). Personal involvement as a determinant of argument-based persuasion. *Journal of Personality and Social Psychology, 41,* 847–855.

Petty, R. E., Cacioppo, J. T., Kasmer, J. A., & Haugtvedt, C. P. (1987). A reply to Stiff and Boster. *Communication Monographs, 54,* 257–263.

Petty, R. E., Cacioppo, J. T., Strathman, A. J., & Priester, J. R. (1994). To think or not to think: Exploring two routes to persuasion. In S. Shavitt & T. C. Brock (Eds.), *Persuasion: Psychological insights and perspectives* (pp. 113–147). Boston, MA: Allyn and Bacon.

Petty, R. E., Haugtvedt, C. P., & Smith, S. M. (1995). Elaboration as a determinant of attitude strength: Creating attitudes that are persistent, resistant, and predictive of behavior. In R. E. Petty & J. A. Krosnick (Eds.), *Attitude strength: Antecedents and consequences* (pp. 93–130). Hillsdale, NJ: Lawrence Erlbaum Associates.

Petty, R. E., Ostrom, T. M., & Brock, T. C. (1981). Historical foundations of the cognitive response approach to attitudes and persuasion. In R. E. Petty, T. M. Ostrom, & T. C. Brock (Eds.), *Cognitive responses in persuasion* (pp. 5–29). Hillsdale, NJ: Lawrence Erlbaum Associates.

Petty, R. E., & Wegener, D. T. (1998). Matching versus mismatching attitude functions: Implications for scrutiny of persuasive messages. *Personality and Social Psychology Bulletin, 24,* 227–240.

Petty, R. E., & Wegener, D. T. (1999). The Elaboration Likelihood Model: Current status and controversies. In S. Chaiken & Y. Trope (Eds.), *Dual-process theories in social psychology* (pp. 41–72). New York: Guilford.

Petty, R. E., Wegener, D. T., Fabrigar, L. R., Priester, J. R., & Cacioppo, J. T. (1993). Conceptual and methodological issues in the Elaboration Likelihood Model of persuasion: A reply to the Michigan State critics. *Communication Theory, 3,* 336–363.

Pfau, M. (1997). The inoculation model of resistance to influence. In G. A. Barnett & F. J. Boster (Eds.), *Progress in communication sciences* (Vol. 13, pp. 133–171). Greenwich, CT: Ablex.

Pfau, M., & Burgoon, M. (1988). Inoculation in political campaign communication. *Human Communication Research*, 15, 91–111.

Pfau, M., & Kenski, H. C. (1990). *Attack politics: Strategy and defense*. New York: Praeger.

Pfau, M., Roskos-Ewoldsen, D., Wood, M., Yin, S., Cho, J., Lu, K. H., & Shen, L. (2003). Attitude accessibility as an alternative explanation for how inoculation confers resistance. *Communication Monographs*, 70, 39–51.

Picker, L. (2015, October 20). With Winfrey behind it, Weight Watchers stock soars. *The New York Times*, B1, B6.

Pratkanis, A. R., & Aronson, E. (1992). *Age of propaganda: The everyday use and abuse of persuasion*. New York: W. H. Freeman.

Priester, J., & Petty, R. E. (1995). Source attributions and persuasion: Perceived honesty as a determinant of message scrutiny. *Personality and Social Psychology Bulletin*, 21, 637–654.

Quinn, J. M., & Wood, W. (2004). Forewarnings of influence appeals: Inducing resistance and acceptance. In E. S. Knowles & J. A. Linn (Eds.), *Resistance and persuasion* (pp. 193–213). Mahwah, NJ: Lawrence Erlbaum Associates.

Redford, R. (2001, May 23). Bush vs. the American landscape. *The New York Times*, A29.

Richards, A. S., & Banas, J. A. (2015). Inoculating against reactance to persuasive health messages. *Health Communication*, 30, 451–460.

Richards, A. S., Banas, J. A., & Magid, Y. (2017). More on inoculating against reactance to persuasive health messages: The paradox of threat. *Health Communication*, 32, 890–902.

Russell, T., & Reimer, T. (2018). Using semantic networks to define the quality of arguments. *Communication Research*, 28, 46–68.

See, Y. H. M., Petty, R. E., & Evans, L. M. (2009). The impact of perceived message complexity and need for cognition on information processing and attitudes. *Journal of Research in Personality*, 43, 880–889.

Smith, B. L., Lasswell, H. D., & Casey, R. D. (1946). *Propaganda, communication, and public opinion*. Princeton, NJ: Princeton University Press.

Smith, R. D. (1993). Psychological type and public relations: Theory, research, and applications. *Journal of Public Relations Research*, 5, 177–199.

Soldat, A. S., Sinclair, R. C., & Mark, M. M. (1997). Color as an environmental processing cue: External affective cues can directly affect processing strategy without affecting mood. *Social Cognition*, 15, 55–71.

Stiff, J. B. (1994). *Persuasive communication*. New York: Guilford.

Stiff, J. B., & Boster, F. J. (1987). Cognitive processing: Additional thoughts and a reply to Petty, Kasmer, Haugtvedt, and Cacioppo. *Communication Monographs*, 54, 250–256.

Streitfeld, D. (2011, August 20). In a race to out-rave rivals, 5-star web reviews go for $5. *The New York Times*, A1, A3.

Streitfeld, D. (2013, September 23). Give yourself 4 stars? Online, it might cost you. *The New York Times*, A1, A17.

Szabo, E. A., & Pfau, M. (2002). Nuances in inoculation: Theory and applications. In J. P. Dillard & M. Pfau (Eds.), *The persuasion handbook: Developments in theory and practice* (pp. 233–258). Thousand Oaks, CA: Sage.

Taylor, S. E. (1981). The interface of cognitive and social psychology. In J. H. Harvey (Ed.), *Cognition, social behavior, and the environment* (pp. 189–211). Hillsdale, NJ: Lawrence Erlbaum Associates.

Todorov, A., Chaiken, S., & Henderson, M. D. (2002). The Heuristic-Systematic Model of social information processing. In J. P. Dillard & M. Pfau (Eds.), *The persuasion handbook: Developments in theory and practice* (pp. 195–211). Thousand Oaks, CA: Sage.

Vidrine, J. I., Simmons, V. N., & Brandon, T. H. (2007). Construction of smoking relevant risk perceptions among college students. The influence of need for cognition and message content. *Journal of Applied Social Psychology, 37*, 91–114.

Westerwick, A., Johnson, B. K., & Knobloch-Westerwick, S. (2017). Confirmation biases in selective exposure to political online information: Source bias vs. content bias. *Communication Monographs, 84*, 343–364.

Williams, K. D., & Dolnik, L. (2001). Revealing the worst first: Stealing thunder as a social influence strategy. In J. P. Forgas & K. D. Williams (Eds.), *Social influence: Direct and indirect processes* (pp. 213–231). Philadelphia, PA: Taylor & Francis.

Williams-Piehota, P., Schneider, T. R., Pizarro, J., Mowad, L., & Salovey, P. (2003). Matching health messages to information-processing styles: Need for cognition and mammography utilization. *Health Communication, 15*, 375–392.

Wood, W., Kallgren, C. A., & Preisler, R. M. (1985). Access to attitude-relevant information in memory as a determinant of persuasion: The role of message attributes. *Journal of Experimental Social Psychology, 21*, 73–85.

Wood, W., Rhodes, N., & Biek, M. (1995). Working knowledge and attitude strength: An information-processing analysis. In R. E. Petty & J. A. Krosnick (Eds.), *Attitude strength: Antecedents and consequences* (pp. 283–313). Hillsdale, NJ: Lawrence Erlbaum Associates.

Xu, Q., Schmierbach, M., Bellur, S., Ash, E., Oeldorf-Hirsch, A., & Kegerise, A. (2012). The effects of "friend" characteristics on evaluations of an activist group in a social networking context. *Mass Communication and Society, 15*, 432–453.

Chapter 9

"Who Says It"

Charisma, Authority, and the Controversial Milgram Study

Charisma. It is a word that comes to mind frequently when people speak of persuasion. You probably think of great speakers, a certain magnetic quality, or perhaps people you know who seem to embody this trait. Charisma is also one of those "god-terms" in persuasion (Weaver, 1953) – concepts that have positive connotations, but have been used for good and evil purposes. We can glimpse this in the tumultuous events of the twentieth century, events that were shaped in no small measure by the power of charismatic leaders. We can also observe this in speeches delivered by orators in the twenty-first century, speeches that inspired citizens.

For example: On January 12, 2016, President Barack Obama delivered his final State of the Union address, close to a dozen years after he rocked the Democratic National Convention in July 2004, giving a keynote speech that propelled him to his party's nomination and sent ripples of change through the system. On that cold January evening, he spoke forcefully and with poise. His syntax, sentence structure, and metaphoric references were distinctive. As in 2004, "his height, his prominent sober head, (and) his long arms 'lent him' a commanding aura." His voice, "with its oratorical cadences," boomed (Messud, 2008, p. 49). In a State of the Union speech marked less by specific proposals than by philosophical themes and exhortations to the citizenry, he concluded by calling on Americans to work for change:

> We need every American to stay active in our public life and not just during election time ... It is not easy. Our brand of democracy is hard. But I can promise that, a little over a year from now, when I no longer hold this office, I will be right there with you as a citizen, inspired by those voices of fairness and vision, of grit and good humor and kindness, that have helped America travel so far. Voices that help us see ourselves not first and foremost as black or white or Asian or Latino; not as gay or straight, immigrant or native born; not Democrat or Republican; but as Americans first, bound by a common creed ... And they're out there, those voices ... I see them everywhere I travel in this incredible country of ours. I see you, the American people. And, in your daily acts of citizenship, I see our future unfolding.
>
> (www.nytimes.com/2016/01/13/us/politics/obama-2016-sotu-transcript.html?_r=0)

To be sure, Obama's speech did not please everyone, and there were many Americans who did not agree with his policies. But even his critics acknowledged that the majesty of his words and soaring oratory could move audiences. Obama followed in the footsteps of another charismatic orator, Reverend Martin Luther King, Jr., whose words had inspired a movement. On August 28, 1963, King delivered his most famous address.

On that day, hundreds of thousands of people converged on Washington, DC, protesting racial prejudice and hoping to place pressure on Congress to pass a civil rights bill. The protesters marched from the Washington Monument to the Lincoln Memorial, listening to a litany of distinguished speakers, but waiting patiently for King to address the crowd. King had worked all night on his speech, a sermonic address that would prove to be among the most moving of all delivered on American soil. He alluded to Abraham Lincoln, called on Old Testament prophets, and presented "an entire inventory of patriotic themes and images typical of Fourth of July oratory," captivating the audience with his exclamation, repeated time and again, that "I have a dream" (Miller, 1992, p. 143). King's wife, Coretta Scott King, recalls the pantheon:

> Two hundred and fifty thousand people applauded thunderously, and voiced in a sort of chant, Martin Luther King … He started out with the written speech, delivering it with great eloquence … When he got to the rhythmic part of demanding freedom now, and wanting jobs now, the crowd caught the timing and shouted now in a cadence. Their response lifted Martin in a surge of emotion to new heights of inspiration. Abandoning his written speech, forgetting time, he spoke from his heart, his voice soaring magnificently out over that great crowd and over to all the world. It seemed to all of us there that day that his words flowed from some higher place, through Martin, to the weary people before him. Yea – Heaven itself opened up and we all seemed transformed.
>
> (1969, pp. 238–239)

Charisma also was in force some 30 years earlier, at a different place, during a different time. In cities like Nuremberg and Berlin, to audiences of Germans – young, old, educated, uneducated, cultured, and uncultured – Adolf Hitler spoke, using words and exploiting symbols, bringing audiences to their feet "with his overwhelming, hysterical passion, shouting the same message they had heard over and over again, that they had been done in by traitors, by conspirators …, by Communists, plutocrats, and Jews" (Davidson, 1977, p. 183). Like King's, Hitler's oratory moved people and appealed to their hopes and dreams. But his speeches malevolently twisted hope into some gnarled ghastly entity and appealed to Germans' latent, darkest prejudices. Here is how a journalist who carefully observed Hitler described the Führer's charismatic skill:

> With unerring sureness, Hitler expressed the speechless panic of the masses faced by an invisible enemy and gave the nameless specter a name. He was a pure fragment of the modern mass soul, unclouded by any personal qualities. One scarcely need ask with what arts he conquered the masses; he did not conquer them, he portrayed and represented them. His speeches are daydreams of this mass soul; they are chaotic, full of contradictions, if their words are taken literally, often senseless as dreams are, and yet charged with deeper meaning … The speeches always begin with deep pessimism, and end in overjoyed redemption, a triumphant, happy ending, often they can be refuted by reason, but they follow the far mightier logic of the subconscious, which no refutation can touch. Hitler has given speech to the speechless terror of the modern mass, and to the nameless fear he has given a name. That makes him the greatest mass orator of the mass age.
>
> (Quoted in Burleigh, 2000, pp. 100–101)

Charisma – exploited for evil purposes by Hitler, used to lift human spirits by Martin Luther King – describes the power of so many forceful speakers, including (in the political realm), American presidents John F. Kennedy, Ronald Reagan, and Bill Clinton, ex-British prime minister Tony Blair, and Silvio Berlusconi, the colorful former prime minister of Italy. Charisma aptly describes the magnetism of Malcolm X and Jesse Jackson in the domain of civil rights, Nelson Mandela and Mahatma Gandhi in the international domain of human rights, and Bono, the rock musician and tireless champion for Africans afflicted with AIDS (see Figure 9.1).

(a)

(b)

(c)

(d)

Figure 9.1a–d Charisma Has Been Harnessed in Profoundly Positive Ways by Political Leaders, Such as John F. Kennedy, the Legendary Civil Rights Leader Martin Luther King, and Michelle Obama, Who Has Inspired Women and Raised Consciousness About Health Issues. Charismatic leaders like Adolf Hitler wielded their persuasive powers in destructive ways, using words and language to deceive and devastate

Images courtesy of Getty Images

Regrettably, it also describes a legion of cult leaders, who enchanted then deceived dozens, even hundreds, of starry-eyed followers. The list of charismatic cult leaders includes Charles Manson; Jim Jones, who induced 900 people to commit suicide in Guyana; David Koresh, leader of the ill-fated Branch Davidians in Waco, Texas; Marshall Applewhite, who led 38 members of the Heaven's Gate cult to commit suicide in 1997; and, most recently, Osama bin Laden, who masterminded the September 11 attacks and, to many, was the personification of evil.

Charismatic sociopaths such as these fascinate people. "Everything that deceives," Plato declared, "may be said to enchant."

This chapter, introducing the communicator in persuasion ("Who says it?"), focuses on the ineffable, fascinating quality of charisma, explicating and unpacking the construct. This chapter and Chapter 10 proceed to discuss the major communicator concepts in persuasion: Authority, credibility, and social attractiveness. In Chapter 9, I examine authority in depth with a deep discussion of the Milgram study in obedience – its strengths, shortcomings, and applications, informed by classic and contemporary revisionist work on the study. Chapter 10 continues the focus on the communicator by harnessing theory, research, and applications to describe two other core communicator characteristics – credibility and social attractiveness.

Charisma

What is charisma? A term coined over a century ago by German sociologist Max Weber (1968), *charisma* is "a certain quality of the individual personality by virtue of which he is set apart from ordinary men and treated as endowed with supernatural, superhuman, or at least exceptional powers and qualities" (p. 241). Scholars who have studied charisma acknowledge the powerful influence it can have over ordinary people. Yet they also are quick to identify more subtle features. There are two factors that complicate charisma effects.

Characteristics

First, charisma interacts with audience factors. Followers influence the self-perception of leaders. As Ronald E. Riggio notes, "The charismatic leader inspires the crowd, but he also becomes charged by the emotions of the followers. Thus, there is an interplay between leader and followers that helps to build a strong union between them" (1987, p. 76). This happened with King and his followers – and, decades later, with a much more controversial communicator: President Donald J. Trump.

Trump exemplifies the best and the worst of the adrenalin-laced intersection between followers and leaders. His crowds line up to see him and adulate him because, despite his billionaire wealth, he comes off as one of them, speaking the emotional language of empathy, channeling their frustrations at the system, elites, and the pummelling tides of cultural change. For many of these primarily White Americans, who feel that people are metaphorically cutting in line in front of them or taking unfair advantage of their minority status to benefit from affirmative action, Trump's jeremiads and exhortations to return America to previous greatness feel like handshakes, slaps on the back by the highly charged leader of the national tribe (Hochschild, 2016). His crowds "respond to him. But he also responds to them. And they build up each other's feelings of excitement and anger" (Koerth-Baker, 2016).

You appreciate – or lament – this when you recall the ways Trump interacted with a crowd of supporters at a July 2019 North Carolina rally that offered resounding approval of his incendiary tweet that four minority Congresswomen should "go back" to the countries they came from (Baker, 2019,

p. A13), going further than even he did, chanting "Send her back." His supporters loved his tweet, and they could "egg him on with cheers and chants" that in turn encouraged him to incite the crowd with more boundary-testing, xenophobic, love-it-or-leave-it epithets (Hirschfeld Davis, Haberman, & Crowley, 2019, p. A15).

The intersection of Trump's presidential panache, credibility, and crowd adulation creates a cauldron of political energy, demonstrating that a leader can't influence followers unless followers give back and return the values and fervor the leader communicates. In Trump's case, his power is built upon his "superhuman" celebrity status with particular groups of Americans, illustrating the connection between celebrity and charisma in a society where media confer celebrity status on charismatic leaders, and celebrities become charismatic leaders in their followers' eyes by dint of media attention (Hendriks, 2017). Trump's statements offended many Americans, but not his most enthusiastic supporters, for whom his charismatic speechifying only strengthened his appeal, illustrating that, in a fragmented, multicultural society, charisma is contextual, a niche interactive attribute that resonates primarily with the charismatic leader's loyal followers (see Figure 9.2).

Figure 9.2 President Donald Trump Has Exuded a Charismatic Connection With His Crowds of Supporters, Illustrating the Emotional Interplay Between Followers and a Leader. Trump's charisma was enhanced by two other aspects of modern charismatic leaders – their celebrity status and technological prowess, in Trump's case, his emotive tweets. The interplay between his followers' adoration and Trump's impulse to play to the crowd had troubling consequences, as when he fired up the crowd with boundary-crossing, anti-democratic comments that appealed to their prejudices

A second characteristic of charisma is that it is constrained by historical factors. A person who has charisma in one era might not wield the same influences on audiences in another historical period. The chemistry between speaker and audience is a product of a particular set of circumstances, psychological needs, and social conditions. For example, Martin Luther King might not be charismatic in today's more complex multicultural era, which involves increased tolerance for racial diversity but also wariness of the costs of worthy social experiments like affirmative action. Franklin Delano Roosevelt, a grand and majestic speaker on radio, might not move millions of television viewers, who would watch a crippled president clutch his wheelchair for support. John F. Kennedy, who was captivating on television in the early 1960s, might be charismatically challenged in the fast-paced, reality TV, online media-focused era of today. Even Obama, with his non-partisan tropes, might find himself charismatically hamstrung in a politically polarizing era.

What more can be said of charisma? What role does it play in everyday persuasion? These questions are more difficult to answer. Charisma is an intriguing factor in persuasion, but an elusive one, to be sure. Granted, charisma involves a persuader's ability to command and compel an audience, but what specific traits are involved? The communicator's sociability? Attractiveness? Power? Or does it involve a host of characteristics, including charm, empathy, an ability to guide others, and skill in making people feel comfortable (Levine, Muenchen, & Brooks, 2010; Tskhay, Zhu, Zou, & Rule, 2018)? Alternatively, does charisma have more to do with the audience – individuals' own vulnerability and need to believe that a communicator has certain qualities they yearn for in life? How can one capture the seemingly ineffable power truly charismatic communicators have on their flock in more prosaic persuasive situations, in which charismatic communicators emerge but not nearly with the magic and majesty as in the grandiose, mass mediated situations described above?

These questions point to the difficulty of defining charisma with sufficient precision that it can be studied in social scientific settings, particularly those where it is wielded with outsized impact. There is no question that charisma exists and has been a powerful force in persuasion. On a practical level, it is difficult to study the concept and to determine just how it works and why. Because it is such a rare, ineffable trait that few possess, it is not a useful guide to understanding the power and processes underlying communicator characteristics.

Thus, those who wish to understand why the Martin Luther Kings and Hitlers of the world have profoundly affected audiences must take a different tack. They must either study political history or take a more finely tuned, social scientific approach to examining communicator effects.

More generally, those of us who want to comprehend how persuaders persuade are advised to chip away at the question by examining the different pieces of the puzzle. A key piece of the puzzle – a core aspect of charisma – is the communicator. His or her qualities, and the ways in which these characteristics interact with the audience, can strongly influence attitudes. This chapter continues with an overview of communicator (or source) factors. It then discusses key factors in depth, applying them to contemporary life, and harnessing concepts to shed light on the power – and limits – of communicator attributes.

Understanding the Communicator

Just as there is not one type of charismatic leader (Barack Obama differed vastly from Martin Luther King), there is not one defining characteristic of effective communicators. Communicators have different attributes and influence audiences through different processes. There are three fundamental communicator characteristics: Authority, credibility, and social attractiveness. Authorities, credible communicators, and attractive ones produce attitude change through different mechanisms (Kelman, 1958).

Authorities frequently influence others through compliance. Individuals adopt a particular behavior not because they agree with its content but, rather, because they expect "to gain specific rewards or approval and avoid specific punishments or disapproval by conforming" (Kelman, 1958, p. 53). In other words, people go along with authority figures because they hope to obtain rewards or avoid punishment.

Credible communicators, by contrast, influence attitudes through internalization. We accept recommendations advanced by credible communicators because they are congruent with our values or attitudes.

Attractive communicators – likeable and physically appealing ones – seem to achieve influence through more affective processes, such as identification. People go along with socially attractive speakers because they identify with them, or want to establish a positive relationship with the communicators (Kelman, 1958). Figure 9.3 illustrates the different processes by which sources influence attitudes. Other models, like the ELM, emphasize other mechanisms, but the point is that authority, credibility, and social attractiveness influence attitudes through different psychological processes. This chapter discusses authority in the sections that follow; credibility and social attractiveness are examined in Chapter 10.

Authority: The Classic Milgram Study

It was an amazing study – unique in its time, bold, yet controversial, an attempt to create a laboratory analogue for the worst conformity in twentieth-century history and one of the most graphic cases of criminal obedience in the history of humankind. Legendary psychologist Gordon W. Allport called the program of research "the Eichmann experiment" because it attempted to explain the subhuman behavior of Nazis like Adolf Eichmann: After ordering the slaughter of six million Jews, Eichmann said, "It was unthinkable that I would not follow orders" (Cohen, 1999, p. A1). More generally, the research was designed to shed light on the power that authorities hold over ordinary people, and how they are able to induce individuals to obey their directives, sometimes in ways that violate human decency.

You may have heard of the research program called the Milgram experiments after psychologist Stanley Milgram, who conceptualized and directed them. They are described in social psychology and social influence texts, with psychologist Muzafer Sherif calling them "the single greatest contribution

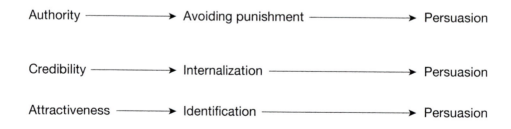

Figure 9.3 Communicators and the Influence Process

to human knowledge ever made by the field of social psychology" (cited in Reicher, Haslam, & Miller, 2014, p. 394).

A documentary film depicting the studies has been shown in thousands of college classrooms (you may have seen it). Milgram's 1974 book, *Obedience to Authority*, has been translated into 11 languages. A rock musician of the 1980s, Peter Gabriel, called on the research in his song, "We Do What We're Told – Milgram's 37." That was a long time ago, of course. If you Google "The Milgram Experiment," you will get pages of entries. If you type these words into YouTube, you see numerous videos: Footage from the actual studies, news documentaries, and psychological lectures. An episode of *The Simpsons* drew on the research when a therapist connects the family to a shock machine and they shock each other, as the town's electricity grid quivers and the streetlights vibrate. In 2015, a fictional film, *Experimenter*, profiled Milgram in seemingly ghoulish ways. There is a lot of exaggeration and hype, as well as grandiose simplifications that surround the studies. Let's look at the research, its classical implications, shortcomings, and the balance sheet for persuasion.

Experimental Procedures and Results

Milgram conducted his research – it was actually not one study, but a series of experiments – from 1960 to 1963 at Yale University and nearby Bridgeport, Connecticut. The basic procedure is described below.

On reporting to the experiment, each individual receives $4.50 for participating in the experiment, billed as a study of memory and learning. At the laboratory, participants are joined by a man introduced as a fellow subject in the study, who is actually working for the researcher.

At this point the participants are told that they will draw slips of paper to determine who will serve as the "teacher" and who will take the "learner" role. The drawing is rigged so that the naive subject is always selected to be the teacher.

The experimenter tells teacher and learner that the study concerns the effects of punishment on learning. The teacher watches as an experimenter escorts the learner to a room, seats him in a chair, straps his arms to prevent too much movement, and attaches an electrode to his wrist. The learner is told that he must learn a list of word pairs. When he makes a mistake, he will receive electric shocks, the intensity increasing with each error committed.

The teacher then is seated before a shock generator that contains a horizontal line of 30 switches varying from 15 to 450 volts and descriptions ranging from SLIGHT SHOCK to DANGER – SEVERE SHOCK. The experimenter instructs the teacher to read the word pairs to the learner, located in the next room. When the learner responds incorrectly, the teacher is to administer an electric shock, starting at the mildest level (15 volts) and increasing in 15-volt increments. After a series of shocks have been administered, the learner begins to express pain, grunting, complaining, screaming at 285 volts, and then remaining silent. Each time the teacher expresses misgivings about administering a shock, the experimenter orders him or her to continue, saying, "It is absolutely essential that you continue."

In reality, of course, the learner is not getting shocked. The experiment does not concern the effect of punishment on learning, but instead is designed to determine how far people will go in obeying an authority's directives to inflict harm on a protesting victim (Milgram, 1974). Although the shocks are not real, they seem quite authentic to individuals participating in the study. Participants frequently experience considerable tension, torn between sympathy for a suffering compatriot and perceived duty to comply with authority. As Milgram notes:

I observed a mature and initially poised businessman enter the laboratory smiling and confident. Within 20 minutes he was reduced to a twitching, stuttering wreck, who was rapidly approaching a point of nervous collapse ... At one point he pushed his fist into his forehead and muttered: "Oh God, let's stop it." And yet he continued to respond to every word of the experimenter, and obeyed to the end.

(1963, p. 377)

The businessman was the norm, not the exception. Although a group of psychiatrists predicted that about only 1 in 1,000 individuals would administer the highest shock on the shock generator, more than 65 percent went this far. And while a number of the subjects experienced distress while supposedly delivering electric shocks (Ent & Baumeister, 2014), in the end a large number of individuals complied, administering what they believed to be dangerous electric shocks (see Figure 9.4).

Figure 9.4 In the Classic Milgram Experiments, Many Participants, Such as the Man Pictured Here, Followed the Experimenter's Orders to Administer Electric Shocks, With Some Going to Dangerous Extremes. The Milgram study has been reassessed over the years, in the wake of questions about the validity of the experiments' conclusions and the ethical liberties Milgram seems to have taken with his subjects. Research conducted in one era frequently looks less impressive when viewed through the rear view window afforded by the passage of time. And yet, Milgram's obedience experiments, with all their limits, continue to offer important insights

Image courtesy of http://wikis.lib.ncsu.edu/index.php/Ethical_Concerns_in_Experimental_Research

The Milgram studies are one of many investigations of the effects of authority on behavior. There is an entire research literature on this topic (Kelman & Hamilton, 1989). The Milgram research provides a useful framework for understanding these effects – it is a window on the role authority plays in persuading individuals to comply with diverse requests.

Milgram's interest was in obedience, but not typical obedience in everyday life, like obeying traffic signs or laws prohibiting shoplifting. This obedience is not objectionable. Milgram's focus was obedience to malevolent authority, obedience that violates moral judgments, what Kelman and Hamilton call "crimes of obedience." Authority – the concept that preoccupied Milgram – is assumed to emanate not from personal qualities, *"but from (the person's) perceived position in a social structure"* (Milgram, 1974, p. 139). A legitimate authority is someone who is presumed to have "the right to prescribe behavior" for others (Milgram, 1974, pp. 142–143). In the experimental drama of the Milgram studies, the experimenter exploited his authority and led many people to administer shocks to a helpless victim.

Explanations

Why? Why would normal, upstanding human beings ignore their conscience and administer what they thought were electric shocks to a middle-aged learner? It is not so simple as to say the authority made them do it. The experimenter did not force subjects to administer dangerous electric shocks. Instead, the explanations must lie in part with the power that situations can exert on human behavior, particularly the effects of the aura – or trappings – of authority. Interpretations of the Milgram findings include:

- *Early socialization.* People are socialized to obey authority, and they get rewarded for doing so. Success in school, on sports teams, in corporate organizations, and even in Hollywood movies requires complying with the requests of authorities. "We learn to value obedience, even if what ensues in its name is unpleasant," Arthur G. Miller and colleagues note. "We also trust the legitimacy of the many authorities in our lives," they remark (Miller, Collins, & Brief, 1995, p. 9).
- *Trappings of authority.* Various aspects of the experimental situation contributed to its majesty, or "aura of legitimacy" (Kelman & Hamilton, 1989, p. 151). These included: (a) status of the institution, Yale University; (b) complex, expensive scientific equipment in the room; (c) the experimenter's clothing (his lab coat served as a symbol of scientific expertise); and (d) the experimenter's gender – men are accorded more prestige "simply by virtue of being male" (Rudman & Kilianski, 2000, p. 1315). These trappings of authority could have served as peripheral cues, calling up the rule of thumb that "you do what authorities ask" (though see Reicher et al., 2014).
- *Binding forces.* The experiment set in motion powerful psychological forces that "locked" participants into compliance. Participants did not want to harm the learner and probably harbored doubts about the necessity of administering severe electric shocks to advance scientific knowledge of memory. Still, they were reluctant to mention these concerns. Believing they lacked the knowledge or expertise to challenge the experimenter's requests, afraid of what would happen if they confronted the experimenter, concerned that he might implicitly indict them for failing to serve the noble goals of science and Yale University, they knuckled under. "To refuse to go on meant to challenge the experimenter's authority," Kelman and Hamilton note (1989, p. 153). While some people were willing to undertake this challenge, most did not. They did not perceive that they had the right or ability to question the experimenter, and thus opted to accept his view of the experimental context.

- *Power of the situation*. Pulling together these explanations, we can appreciate a core reason individuals complied: The psychological power of situational forces. By starting small, asking the teacher to start small with 15-volt shocks and then moving to ever-stronger shocks, the experimenter exploited the power of commitment and the foot-in-the-door effect, whereby individuals are more likely to comply with a large request if they have first agreed to smaller requests (see Chapter 14). In addition, the situation was novel, offering few cues for how to behave; this encouraged the uncertain, conflicted teacher to rely on the expert authority figure, who was all too happy (given the experimental requirements) to urge the administration of stronger shocks. In a similar fashion, the experiment, with its fast pace, offered few opportunities for teachers to reflect on, or centrally process, their decisions. This in turn invited learners to rely on the "click-whirr" heuristic of following the experimenter's commands.

(Burger, 2014)

Taken together, these factors help explain the Milgram results, findings that frequently astonish observers, but which become more understandable in light of the power of situational forces and psychological constructions.

The Milgram experiments illustrate the powerful impact that social influence can exert on behavior. To some degree, the experiments straddle the line between coercion and persuasion. There is a coercive aspect to the studies in that the experimenter was pushing individuals to act contrary to their preferences, and participants may have experienced the authority's directives as a threat. But the bottom line is that no one was holding a gun to participants' heads; they were free to stop the shocks whenever they wanted, and some individuals did. The experimenter set up the bait, but individuals persuaded themselves to go along with his commands.

Critiquing Milgram

Over the course of his study, Milgram made a number of refinements in the experimental situation. He found that obedience was more likely to occur under certain conditions than others and certain contexts in which disobedience prevailed. Intriguingly, substantially more individuals obeyed when the experimenter sat a few feet from the teacher than when he left the room and relayed orders by telephone. In one experiment, three individuals served as teachers. Unbeknownst to the subject, two worked for the experimenter. When the two individuals refused to shock the learner, obedience dropped sharply. This is the most hopeful aspect of the research. It suggests that authorities lose their grip if enough people resist.

Over the years, Milgram's studies have generated considerable discussion in the academic community. It would be ironic if academics accepted Milgram's findings lock, stock, and barrel – if they marched to Milgram's music in unison, just as his subjects followed the experimenter's order. I am happy to report that this is not what has occurred. Milgram's studies have been endlessly debated, criticized, and praised (Miller, 1986; Orne & Holland, 1968).

Critics have pointed out that the study involved the use of archaic, physical violence; yet much violence involves verbal or psychological abuse (Meeus & Raaijmakers, 1986). Scholars have also suggested that individuals' obedience was not as nasty as Milgram suggested. "Subjects take it for granted that the experimenter is familiar with the shock generator and that he knows that the shocks are not fatal," two researchers contended (Meeus & Raaijmakers, 1986, p. 312). In response, Milgram has noted that research participants – the teachers – perceived that the experimental situation was very real – not a game. They believed that the shocks had inflicted pain. This may be so, but it is a jump to assume that individuals who administered electric shock in the laboratory would inflict equivalent pain in real-world situations. They might, or they might not, and the outcome depends on a multitude of social and psychological factors.

Writing around the time of the 50th anniversary of Milgram's experiment, scholars continued to ruminate about the study. Some proffered the revisionist interpretation that the subject actually hesitated and questioned administering electric shocks more frequently than Milgram suggested, and the possibility that participants did not *passively* conform to authority, but actively complied because the experimenter offered a persuasive justification that shocking the learner was the appropriate way to behave (Einwohner, 2014; Griggs, 2017; Haslam, Reicher, & Birney, 2014; Reicher et al., 2014). Subjects complied with the experimenter, but it was part of a broader "submission to the requirements of an authority" (Gibson, 2019, p. 255).

Other criticisms have also been advanced. Some critics note that that the experimenter repeatedly assured teachers, who were emotionally upset about the impact of shock, that he, the experimenter, was responsible. Another line of criticism focuses on dissent, noting that, for all the talk of conformity, more than 30 percent of subjects refused to go along, some objecting strenuously to the experiment. Interesting as these arguments are, they don't detract from the fact that a substantial majority of subjects acceded to the experimenter, choosing to administer shock for which they were in some sense responsible.

An Unethical Study?

Perhaps the most significant line of criticism over the years has involved ethics, arguing that Milgram had no right to play God. Psychologist Diana Baumrind famously denounced Milgram's research, arguing that he treated his subjects disrespectfully, causing them distress; she castigated Milgram, poignantly suggesting that it was immoral to leave participants with knowledge that they could be cruel, slavishly obedient creatures (Baumrind, 1964).

The ethical critique has stimulated much discussion, with Milgram (1974) pointing out that participants in his studies had been debriefed, had not suffered harm, and actually viewed the experiment as enlightening. Yet even if one shares Milgram's positive assessment of the research, there is still something unsettling – and, at some level, wrong – about deceiving people in the name of science. Forceful ethical criticisms such as these spurred the establishment of university and federal rules to protect human subjects from harm in social science research, and policies to ensure the proper, ethical treatment of participants in their studies.

Reflecting on her courageous critique some 40 years later, the late Diana Baumrind (2013), who ventured her criticisms in 1964, held to the moral ferocity of her original critique. (Her courage is all the more impressive, given that we now know she did not have the protections of university tenure and was a young woman in the sexist 1960s, raising three young daughters at the time.) Milgram, Baumrind argued, breached the trust that experimental participants place in the researcher, violating their sense of justice, and "legitimizing lying" (p. 16). Lamenting his flagrant use of deception, she cut to the chase by asking "what code of ethics enabled Milgram" to deceive people who trusted the experimenter and experienced emotional anguish (p. 7)?

There is another side though. The noted social psychologist Carol Tavris (2013) argued that "deception itself is value neutral; it simply allows researchers to discover things about human behavior that humans aren't aware of or don't want you to know." She noted that researchers have built deception into their experimental designs to learn about important issues like prejudice reduction and conflict. Tavris is less sure that Milgram crossed an ethical boundary line than are Baumrind and other critics.

What's more, recent work published long after Milgram's studies and the endless psychological debate that ensued at the time casts doubt on (or raises questions about) the fundamental ethics of Milgram's study. As Richard A. Griggs and George I. Whitehead III (2015) persuasively explain in an important article, Milgram seems to have committed a number of ethical breaches that are rarely reported in social psychology textbooks' laudatory summaries of the study (and are getting a full airing in this edition of *The Dynamics of Persuasion*).

In a scathing attack on Milgram's ethical procedures, based on extensive research, Gina Perry (2013) reported that the experimenter took ethical liberties on recalcitrant subjects. He pushed some reluctant subjects to continue shocking the learner eight or nine times, in the case of one woman, 26 times (Tavris, 2013). Revisionist analyses indicate that Milgram's efforts to debrief his subjects, explaining that no shocks were actually administered and the learner was not harmed, "were nowhere near as thorough and effective as Milgram claimed" (Nicholson, 2011, p. 741). Contrary to his claims, Milgram did not debrief a number of participants after the study. Some reported that they felt "pretty well shook up for a few days after the experiment" and "felt so bad afterward I wanted to call and actually apologize," presumably to the learner (Nicholson, 2011, pp. 743–744). Some subjects actually "left the lab still believing they had shocked a man," having never been told that that the learner had not been harmed in the slightest by their commands (Perry, 2013, p. 77). Several subjects expressed considerable anger and distress because they were not adequately debriefed. One was shaking and shivering so much he feared he could not drive home (Perry, 2013).

Troubling as these results are, they appear to describe just a minority of subjects. A majority reported that they learned about themselves from their participation in the classic study (Nicholson, 2011). Tavris, in a careful review of Perry's book, notes that Milgram's biographer reported that only 1.5 percent of Milgram's subjects regretted having participated. Tavris acknowledges that the new revelations are important, but says Perry overlooks the good in Milgram the scientist and the many contributions his work provided.

It's a difficult issue, a quandary that is important for us to consider. One must balance legitimate criticisms of Milgram's deceptive debriefing procedures with the usual uneasy, but reasonable, caveats one must make in evaluating ethical lapses of one era in light of more nuanced, morally considered assessments observers reach at a later time, based on insights not available to scholars of the earlier epoch.

Based on normative ethical theories discussed in this book, and knowing what we know about the moral fiduciary responsibilities experimenters owe their subjects, one has to conclude that much of Milgram's study failed us on ethical grounds. He deceived his subjects into doing something that was problematic (and left even a handful of individuals with psychological distress), misled his subjects, and on deontological grounds, failed to respect the duties and obligations researchers owe those who participate in their research. On deontological grounds, the study fails morality tests.

And yet one must balance these shortcomings against the immense gains the study has produced, the many rich insights illuminating dark sides of persuasion that continue to intrigue students and scholars today. Indeed, knowledge of authority effects provided by Milgram's research can help – and probably have helped – people take steps to protect themselves against engaging in unethical obedience. The rub is that, from the standpoint of the study's participants, the experiment had moral shortcomings; a key question is whether or not the great benefits the study has produced justify this ethical lapse, and ethicists differ on this question. The research remains, as Tavris put it, a "contentious classic" (Griggs, 2017).

Revisiting Milgram: The 2009 Replication Article

This brings us to a more contemporary wrinkle in Milgram's pioneering, if troubling, research. For decades, persuasion students have wondered if Milgram's findings would be obtained today. Some scholars argued that obedience is a universal feature of the human condition. Others countered that the obedience experiments were period pieces, studies conducted a half-century ago in a profoundly different time when authorities were revered and citizens compliant. The debate has raged over the years, with some researchers contending the findings would not hold up in our more irreverent era and others pointing to recent studies that report disturbing evidence of contemporary obedience, albeit to orders that were milder than those administered by Milgram's experimenter (see Blass, 1992; Meeus & Raaijmakers, 1986). Researchers have been unable to replicate Milgram's study, in light of strong ethical proscriptions – guidelines to protect human subjects from harm – that were implemented as a result of concerns about Milgram's research.

In January 2009, the flagship journal of the American Psychological Association published a major article by Jerry M. Burger that caught the attention of persuasion scholars and others across the world who were familiar with Milgram's classic study. Burger had done what thousands of researchers had dreamed of doing. He had conducted a study that employed many of the same procedures Milgram had used, but took necessary ethical precautions. He had convinced the institutional review board at his university that the experiment satisfied guidelines designed to protect human subjects from stress and psychological harm. Burger had designed an experiment that allowed researchers to answer the time-honored question: "Would people still obey today?" (Burger, 2009).

In order to protect individuals' welfare, Burger informed participants that they could leave the experiment at any juncture and still keep the money they had been paid for participating in the experiment. They were told the confederate (the learner) had been given the same assurance. Burger also screened participants prior to the study, eliminating those who reported that they suffered from anxiety or depression. Moreover, Burger stopped the experiment when subjects administered a shock of 150 volts, rather than allowing them to continue to the stressful 450-volt level. The moment that a subject refused to continue administering electric shocks, Burger stopped the experiment and immediately debriefed the subject.

Did participants behave as their counterparts had some 40 years earlier? Or did they choose to disobey?

Burger found that the rate of obedience paralleled that obtained in Milgram's experiments. Seventy percent of participants in Burger's replication continued past 150-volt shocks, before being stopped by the experimenter; this compared to 82.5 percent in a comparable condition in Milgram's study, a non-significant difference. Although there was more obedience a half-century ago, the difference between the proportions that obeyed was not statistically significant. Obedience seems not to have meaningfully decreased over the span of four decades.

Questions remain, of course: Would the same findings emerge with different ethnic groups? (A majority of Burger's participants were White, and, in line with Milgram's study, the learner was also Caucasian.) Non-White racial groups might have different norms governing conformity. Suppose the teacher was White and the learner of a different race? Would this attenuate or increase obedience? These questions remain interesting issues to pursue and are worthwhile topics for scholarly investigation. They do not reduce the significance of Burger's findings. His replication (supported as it is by conceptually similar work over the years) showed that Milgram's experiment stands the test of time. Participants in a laboratory study of obedience readily comply with the unethical directives of an authority figure (Blass, 2009). Interestingly, from an ethical perspective, Burger did not find that subjects experienced much distress, and most felt positively about the experience (Perry, 2013).

Applications

The Milgram experiments remain "one of the most singular, most penetrating, and most disturbing inquiries into human conduct that modern psychology has produced" (quoted in Blass, 1999, p. 957). They have a number of implications for everyday life, but one must be cautious in applying these to historical and contemporary issues, for we are generalizing from a series of laboratory experiments to different, highly fraught situations in real life. There is disagreement among scholars on the extent to which one can and should extract real-life implications from Milgram's work. I think caution is warranted and care should be taken. Nonetheless, the Milgram experiments, shorn of their once-bright scientific sheen, justifiably critiqued on ethical grounds, nonetheless have value as studies of persuasion, and they continues to offer insights and explanations of troubling real-life phenomena. They help explain wartime atrocities and torture, conformity to high-profile sports authorities, and reluctance to blow the whistle on morally indefensible acts perpetrated by authorities in contexts ranging from the workplace to sexual abuse.

Milgram's research offers an interpretation – not the only one, but a powerful one – for the Holocaust of the Jews. Many German soldiers and civilians slavishly conformed to the orders of Nazi authorities. (To be sure, decades of virulent anti-Semitism laid the groundwork for German conformity and underpinned Eichmann's horrific behavior, suggesting that much more than blind obedience was involved; see, for example, Lipstadt, 2011).

More broadly, and with implications for wars the United States has fought, the Milgram findings help illuminate more recent wartime atrocities, such as in Korea, Vietnam, and Iraq, as when U.S. soldiers – responding to orders by higher-ups and peer pressure – tortured prisoners at the Abu Ghraib, Iraq prison.

Consider the case of Private Lynndie England, who was photographed holding a naked prisoner with a strap around his neck, like it was a leash (see Figure 9.5).

Lynndie grew up in a trailer park in a small town in West Virginia. As a girl, she wore her hair short, played softball, and participated in Future Farmers of America. She quit her job at a chicken-processing plant because she objected to the management's decision to send unhealthy chicken parts down the factory line (McKelvey, 2007). It was therefore ironic that she ended up doing the bidding of her commanders at Abu Ghraib, particularly Sergeant Charles A. Graner, Jr., the crude and violent man with whom she was infatuated. Brigadier General Janis L. Karpinski, who supervised detainee operations at Abu Ghraib, ventured an explanation:

> You have to understand that it builds into a crescendo … You're being mortared every night. You are breathing dust and broken concrete. It's hot. You feel dehumanized. You're drained of every bit of compassion you have. She did it because she wanted to come back from this godforsaken war and say, "We did this for the government" … She was made to believe this was of such importance to national security. It was, you know, "You stick with me, kid, and you might even win a medal."
>
> (McKelvey, 2007, pp. 238–239)

Figure 9.5 A Photo Obtained by the *Washington Post* and Released May 6, 2004, Shows U.S. Army Private Lynndie England, of the 372nd Military Police Company, with a Naked Detainee at the Abu Ghraib Prison in Baghdad

Image courtesy of the Associated Press

Thus do ordinary people, who are not cruel by nature, find themselves engaged in extraordinarily violent acts. England and others were justly punished for their actions, as they chose to perform them. Yet the higher-ups who created the conditions under which these behaviors were normative emerged scot-free. No high-ranking Army officer or general served prison time. No Defense Department or administration official was charged with torture or war crimes. England and others succumbed to the pressure of authorities and were punished for their compliance.

The Milgram findings shed light not only on compliance to authorities during wartime, but on conformity in a variety of political and organizational contexts, exemplifying how people more broadly submit to the requirements of authority figures (Gibson, 2019).

Milgram's research helps us understand why White House aides have followed presidents' commands to cover up illegal acts, lie about them, or stonewall the press. Events such as these occurred during Watergate (Kelman & Hamilton, 1989) and, to some degree, during the Clinton–Lewinsky scandal.

The results can be applied to the Penn State child abuse scandal. Former Penn State University assistant football coach Jerry Sandusky sexually abused boys for years, and university employees were afraid to take action, for fear of crossing revered head coach Joe Paterno, a Sandusky ally. In 2000, a university janitor watched as Sandusky performed oral sex on a boy in the showers. He told his co-workers, but none went to the police. "I know Paterno has so much power, if he wanted to get rid of someone, I would have been gone," one janitor said, poignantly adding that reporting the assault "would have been like going against the president of the United States in my eyes" (Mulvihill,

Armas, & Scolforo, 2012, p. A12). Like a subject in the original shock-machine studies who feared challenging the august image of Yale University, the janitor felt he had no choice but to comply.

So too did the Michigan State University coaches, trainers, and employees, who knew of the sexual abuse perpetrated by Dr. Lawrence Nasser, a former U.S.A. national gymnastics team doctor, accused by more than 150 women of sexually molesting them while serving as a doctor for Michigan State, some when they were as young as six years old. As the media reported in 2018, they were intimidated by his status and reputation and let themselves be cowed into remaining silent in the face of horrific abuse (Davey & Smith, 2018). The examples are seemingly endless, but important to review.

A famous strip-search incident at a Mount Washington, Kentucky McDonald's offers up another example of obedience to a dominating authority figure. On April 9, 2004, the Mount Washington McDonald's assistant manager, Donna Jean Summers, received a strange phone call from a man who falsely claimed to be a police detective. Claiming he had spoken with McDonald's corporate headquarters and the store manager, naming the manager correctly, he told her that a store employee, an 18-year-old girl, had stolen money from the restaurant. The so-called detective told Summers that she must search the employee immediately to recoup the money or the girl would be arrested and hauled off to jail. Amazingly – or perhaps not, given the power male authority figures can exert over the phone (Cialdini, 2009) – Summers complied, going so far as to lock the young employee into a small room, following the supposed detective's directives, as he continued to deliver them over the phone. Although the teen had a perfect record as an employee, Summers strip-searched her, just as she was ordered. The young woman was naked, crying, and humiliated.

Although the caller was later located and arrested and Summers was sentenced to probation, the psychic damage left its toll. Summers had allowed herself to follow the orders of a man who falsely claimed to be a detective, and she had to live with the consequences of her decision. The sexually harassed teenage girl, who now suffers from anxiety and depression, went along with the orders because she had been taught, her therapist said, "to do what she is told, because good girls do what they are told" (Aronson, Wilson, & Akert, 2013, p. 198).

Prescriptions

These examples are disturbing, graphic, and unusual. In one final application, the Milgram study helps explain a much more prosaic, but frequently stressful, quandary that many of us might experience when bosses ask us to commit unethical acts. Eighty-eight percent of administrative professionals admitted they had told a "little white lie" for a supervisor (Romano, 1998). Some have done worse, like the secretary for a school district who routinely complied with her boss's requests to inflate grades of college-bound students. "What am I supposed to do?" the 48-year-old woman, a single mother of two children, said to reporter Lois Romano. "I have to put food on the table. I need the benefits and so I am forced to do things I know are not correct. I have nowhere to go" (Romano, 1998, p. 29).

The woman's comments illustrate the tension people feel when faced with having to carry out orders they know are wrong. The secretary is frank about her problem, but mistaken in one respect, I maintain.

She says she has nowhere to go. Yet people always have places to go. There are always choices in life, and people can usually find a way to reconcile conscience with survival needs. The secretary may not have been able to quit her job, but she could have blown the whistle on the boss by asking a newspaper reporter to investigate the issue. Failing that, she could have kept a diary, and at a later time in life – when she could afford to leave the job or had retired – could reveal all. Or, realizing she had to put bread on the table, she might have thought through her predicament, redefined the situation as one in which her compliance was required but did not reflect her true personality, and resolved to do morally upstanding things in other aspects of her life.

The point is: There is always a way to respect conscience and resist exploitive authorities, in some way, shape, or form. If ever you are faced with a situation in which you must choose between your morals and the tempting desire to follow the crowd or a boss, remember the Milgram results. Keep them in mind also when you are tempted to join your social media friends, the thousands, tens of thousands, or even millions of people who are following, tweeting, or retweeting a Twitter post that seems weird or offensive to you. Take heart that there are courageous people out there who defy the dictates of authorities, role models who hear the voice of their own conscience, the whistle-blowers, like the CIA officer who meticulously revealed how President Trump abused his authority in pressuring the Ukrainian government to investigate Trump's political opponent, instigating the impeachment of the 45th president.

With all this in mind, I suggest when tempted to comply with an authority in a novel situation, you might ask yourself several questions: Is this something I really want to do? Is this an action I definitely embrace? How will I feel tomorrow when I realize I could have respected my own beliefs? If you ask these questions, you will be less likely to acquiesce to authority and more inclined to do something that will sit well with your inner convictions.

Conclusions

This chapter introduced the communicator – a key feature of persuasion. The concept of charisma comes to mind when we think about the communicator, and for good reason: Charismatic speakers captivate audiences, influencing attitudes in benevolent and malevolent ways. Increasingly today, charisma is a relational concept that involves the intersection of the audience with a celebrity communicator, harnessing the medium du jour – Twitter at present – to motivate, rally, and inflame the biases of followers.

Charisma involves a host of characteristics, not well understood, and for this reason scholars have tried to break down the term into constituent parts. Preferring a scientific approach to this topic, researchers have focused painstakingly on three core communicator qualities: Authority, credibility, and social attractiveness.

Authority, epitomized by the Milgram study of obedience, can influence behaviors through a process of compliance. Participants in the Milgram study obeyed a legitimate authority significantly more than experts predicted – a testament to the role of early socialization, authority's trappings, and binding psychological forces. Milgram's experiments raised serious questions about the ethics of research, as new evidence has emerged suggesting that, for all his good intentions, Milgram did not adequately debrief his subjects or relieve them of distress. The utilitarian consequences and deontological dimensions of the experiments continue to roil the scholarly community more than half a century after the studies were conducted, highlighting the significant role ethics play in social science research. Clearly, the hoopla that has traditionally been associated with the studies needs to be revised to appreciate alternative explanations of the findings, limits in its generalizability, and ethical lapses.

Difficult as it is to resolve these issues, there is probably general – though not universal – scholarly consensus that the Milgram studies generated considerable insights into the role authorities play in inducing obedience, as seen in applications spanning war-time torture, complicity with unethical employer directives, and silence in the face of sexual abuse. Milgram's procedures in his many studies of authority unwittingly, but constructively, called attention to the importance of treating research participants with dignity and respect. His study is a legacy in the social psychology of the communicator, controversial, as it should be, but enduringly important in calling attention to the ways human beings can be exploited by malevolent communicators, who are more attuned to individuals' acquiescence to authorities than the victims are themselves.

References

Aronson, E., Wilson, T. D., & Akert, R. M. (2013). *Social psychology* (8th ed.). Boston, MA: Pearson.

Baker, P. (2019, July 28). Trump accuses Black Congresman and allies of being racist, deepening feud. *The New York Times.* Online: https://www.nytimes.com/2019/07/28/us/politics/trump-elijah-cummings-baltimore.html. (Accessed: March 23, 2020).

Baumrind, D. (1964). Some thoughts on ethics of research: After reading Milgram's "Behavioral study of obedience." *American Psychologist, 19,* 421–423.

Baumrind, D. (2013). Is Milgram's deceptive research ethically acceptable? *Theoretical and Applied Ethics, 2,* 1–18.

Blass, T. (1992). The social psychology of Stanley Milgram. In M. P. Zanna (Ed.), *Advances in experimental social psychology* (Vol. 25, pp. 277–329). San Diego, CA: Academic Press.

Blass, T. (1999). The Milgram paradigm after 35 years: Some things we now know about obedience to authority. *Journal of Applied Social Psychology, 29,* 955–978.

Blass, T. (2009). From New Haven to Santa Clara: A historical perspective on the Milgram obedience experiments. *American Psychologist, 64,* 37–45.

Burger, J. M. (2009). Replicating Milgram: Would people still obey today? *American Psychologist, 64,* 1–11.

Burger, J. M. (2014). Situational features in Milgram's experiment that kept his participants shocking. *Journal of Social Issues, 70,* 489–500.

Burleigh, M. (2000). *The Third Reich: A new history.* New York: Hill and Wang.

Cialdini, R. B. (2009). *Influence: Science and practice* (5th ed.). Boston, MA: Pearson Education.

Cohen, R. (1999, August 13). Why? New Eichmann notes try to explain. *The New York Times,* A1, A3.

Davey, M., & Smith, M. (2018, January 28). Michigan State's defender led review of abuse. *The New York Times,* 1, 21.

Davidson, E. (1977). *The making of Adolf Hitler.* New York: Macmillan.

Einwohner, R. L. (2014). Authorities and uncertainties: Applying lessons from the study of Jewish resistance during the Holocaust to the Milgram legacy. *Journal of Social Issues, 70,* 531–543.

Ent, M. R., & Baumeister, R. F. (2014). Obedience, self-control, and the voice of culture. *Journal of Social Issues, 70,* 574–586.

Gibson, S. (2019). Obedience without orders: Expanding social psychology's conception of "obedience". *British Journal of Social Psychology, 58,* 241–259.

Griggs, R. A. (2017). Milgram's obedience study: A contentious classic reinterpreted. *Teaching in Psychology, 44,* 32–37.

Griggs, R. A., & Whitehead III, G. I. (2015). Coverage of Milgram's obedience experiments in social psychology textbooks: Where have all the criticisms gone? *Teaching of Psychology, 42,* 315–322.

Haslam, S. A., Reicher, S. D., & Birney, M. E. (2014). Nothing by mere authority: Evidence that in an experimental analogue of the Milgram paradigm participants are motivated not by orders but by appeals to science. *Journal of Social Issues, 70,* 473–488.

Hendriks, E. C. (2017). Breaking away from charisma? The celebrity industry's contradictory connection to charismatic authority. *Communication Theory, 27,* 347–366.

Hirschfeld Davis, J., Haberman, M., & Crowley, M. (2019, July 19). Pressed by G.O.P., Trump disavows "Send Her Back". *The New York Times,* A1, A15.

Hochschild, A. R. (2016). *Strangers in their own land: Anger and mourning on the American right.* New York: New Press.

Kelman, H. C. (1958). Compliance, identification, and internalization: Three processes of attitude change. *Journal of Conflict Resolution, 2,* 51–60.

Kelman, H. C., & Hamilton, V. L. (1989). *Crimes of obedience: Toward a social psychology of authority and responsibility.* New Haven, CT: Yale University Press.

King, C. S. (1969). *My life with Martin Luther King, Jr.* New York: Holt: Rinehart & Winston.

Koerth-Baker, M. (2016, March 15). Donald Trump incites his crowds—and his crowds incite him. *FiveThirtyEight.* Retrieved March 21, 2016, from http://fivethirtyeight.com/features/donald-trump-incites-his-crowds-a

Levine, K. J., Muenchen, R. A., & Brooks, A. M. (2010). Measuring transformational and charismatic leadership: Why isn't charisma measured? *Communication Monographs, 77,* 576–591.

Lipstadt, D. E. (2011). *The Eichmann trial.* New York: Schocken Books.

McKelvey, T. (2007). *Monstering: Inside America's policy of secret interrogations and torture in the terror war.* New York: Carroll & Graf.

Meeus, W. H. J., & Raaijmakers, Q. A. W. (1986). Administrative obedience: Carrying out orders to use psychological-administrative violence. *European Journal of Social Psychology, 16,* 311–324.

Messud, C. (2008, September 1). Some like it cool. *Newsweek,* 46–50.

Milgram, S. (1963). Behavioral study of obedience. *Journal of Abnormal and Social Psychology, 67,* 371–378.

Milgram, S. (1974). *Obedience to authority: An experimental view.* New York: Harper & Row.

Miller, A. G. (1986). *The obedience experiments: A case study of controversy in social science.* New York: Praeger.

Miller, A. G., Collins, B. E., & Brief, D. E. (1995). Perspectives on obedience to authority: The legacy of the Milgram experiments. *Journal of Social Issues, 51,* 1–19.

Miller, K. D. (1992). *Voice of deliverance: The language of Martin Luther King, Jr. and its sources.* New York: Free Press.

Mulvihill, G., Armas, G. C., & Scolforo, M. (2012, July 3). Penn State staged cover-up. *The (Syracuse) Post-Standard,* A1, A12.

Nicholson, I. (2011). "Torture at Yale": Experimental subjects, laboratory torment and the "rehabilitation" of Milgram's "Obedience to Authority". *Theory & Psychology, 21,* 737–761.

Orne, M. T., & Holland, C. H. (1968). On the ecological validity of laboratory deceptions. *International Journal of Psychiatry, 6,* 282–293.

Perry, G. (2013). *Behind the shock machine: The untold story of the notorious Milgram psychology experiments.* New York: New Press.

Reicher, S. D., Haslam, S. A., & Miller, A. G. (2014). What makes a person a perpetrator? The intellectual, moral, and methodological arguments for revisiting Milgram's research on the influence of authority. *Journal of Social Issues, 70,* 393–408.

Riggio, R. E. (1987). *The charisma quotient: What it is, how to get it, how to use it.* New York: Dodd, Mead.

Romano, L. (1998, October 19). Boss, you want me to do WHAT? *The Washington Post National Weekly Edition,* 29.

Rudman, L. A., & Kilianski, S. E. (2000). Implicit and explicit attitudes toward female authority. *Personality and Social Psychology Bulletin, 26,* 1315–1328.

Tavris, C. (2013, September 6). Book review: "Behind the shock machine" by Gina Perry. *The Wall Street Journal.* Retrieved July 20, 2019, from www.wsj.com/articles/book-review-behind-the-shock-machine-by-gina-perry-1378497014 (Accessed: March 23, 2020).

Tskhay, K. O., Zhu, R., Zou, C., & Rule, N. O. (2018). Charisma in everyday life: Conceptualizations and validation of the General Charisma Inventory. *Journal of Personality and Social Psychology, 114,* 131–152.

Weaver, R. M. (1953). *The ethics of rhetoric.* Chicago, IL: Henry Regnery.

Weber, M. (1968). *On charisma and institution building.* Chicago, IL: University of Chicago Press.

Chapter 10

"Who Says It"

Credibility and Social Attractiveness

Take a deep breath. We're about to shift gears now, moving from the transcendental moral issues of authority to everyday questions of credibility and social attractiveness.

This chapter continues the examination of the communicator, the "who says it" aspect of persuasion. The first part of the chapter discusses credibility – its components, conceptualizations, and applications. The second portion examines the more affective dimensions of social attractiveness, delineating key facets, looking at when and why they work, and implications for contemporary persuasion situations.

Credibility

Credibility is one of the "big 3" communicator factors – along with authority and social attractiveness. It dates back to Aristotle, who coined the term *ethos* to describe qualities of the source that facilitated persuasion. Hovland explored it in his early research, communication researchers deconstructed credibility in the 1960s and 1970s, and the concept continues to fascinate scholars today. Of course, corporate managers, salespeople, and politicians are very interested in what makes someone credible. Nowadays, consultants offer pointers to clients who want to improve the credibility of their commercial websites. D. Joel Whalen, in a book on persuasive business communication, says that credibility is "the single biggest variable under the speaker's control during the presentation" (1996, p. 97). Jay A. Conger, writing about the role persuasion plays in business, observes that "credibility is the cornerstone of effective persuading; without it, a persuader won't be given the time of day" (1998, p. 90).

So, what is credibility? First, let's say what it is *not*. It is not the same as authority, although the two are frequently confused. *Authority* emanates from a person's position in a social structure. It involves the ability to dispense rewards and punishments. Credibility is a psychological or interpersonal communication construct. You can be an authority, but lack credibility. Parents can be authority figures to their kids, but have zero credibility in their children's eyes due to their hypocrisy or indifference. In politics, a president is the nation's commander-in-chief – the top political authority. However, a president can lack credibility in the nation's eyes if he (or she) ignores the nation's economic problems or gets embroiled in a scandal. Dictators can do as they please; they have total, supreme authority.

But ask their citizens in private what they think of these people and you will quickly discover that authority does not translate into credibility.

Credibility is defined as "the attitude toward a source of communication held at a given time by a receiver" (McCroskey, 1997, p. 87). It is an audience member's perceptions of the communicator's qualities. Although we commonly think of credibility as something a communicator has, it is more complex. As Roderick Hart and colleagues note: "Credibility is *not a thing*. It is not some sort of overcoat that we put on and take off at will. Rather, it is a perception of us that lies inside of the people to whom we talk" (Hart, Friedrich, & Brummett, 1983, p. 204).

Credibility is more than a psychological characteristic. It is also a communication variable. It is part of the two-way interaction between communicator and message recipients – a dynamic entity that emerges from the transaction between source and audience member. This means that communicators are not guaranteed credibility by virtue of who they are, their title, or academic pedigree. As Hart reminds us, credibility "is not something we can be assured of keeping once gotten. Credibility can only be earned by paying the price of effective communication" (Hart et al., 1983, pp. 204–205). There is something democratic about credibility. It says that communicators have to enter the rough-and-tumble realm of persuasion. They must meet and greet – either interpersonally or electronically – those they seek to influence. They must earn an audience's respect and win its credibility. We observe this in many spheres of life, of which one of the most salient is public relations. Companies have engaged in splendid public relations, enhancing their credibility. Yet they also have bombed, their spokespersons making statements that have eroded corporate credibility (see Box 10.1). In addition, it is important to remember that, like all persuasion attributes, credibility can be used for both good and nefarious purposes. Confidence is a key attribute of credibility, for good and for ill, and confidence can be inferred from what persuaders say, as well as the language they use to say it (see Box 10.2 and Chapter 11).

BOX 10.1

Public Relations 101

Credibility is of central importance in public relations. "Receivers must have confidence in the sender and high regard for the source's competence on the subject," noted Cutlip, Center, and Broom (2006, p. 358) in their public relations text. Companies have garnered considerable goodwill by visibly demonstrating that they place the highest priority on consumer health and well-being. The classic case is Johnson & Johnson, the makers of Tylenol. When seven people died in Chicago from ingesting cyanide-laced Tylenol in 1982, the company acted immediately. Placing people ahead of profits and implementing deontological ethical principles (Cutlip et al., 2006), the company halted production of Tylenol capsules, pulled Tylenol packages from store shelves, and designed tamper-resistant packages. Polls showed that nine out of ten Americans did not blame the company for the poisonings. In fact, Johnson & Johnson garnered positive press for its handling of the crisis.

On the other end of the credibility spectrum sits the energy behemoth BP, which caused the worst oil spill in U.S. history in 2010. In addition to killing 11 people, the spill in the Gulf of Mexico, near the Mississippi River Delta, released nearly five million barrels of crude oil over a three-month period, extensively damaging wildlife. In contrast to Johnson & Johnson, BP eschewed personal responsibility, focusing instead on damage control and spinning excuses. Initially the company estimated that only 1,000 barrels a day spilled into the water. In fact, close to 60,000 barrels a day reached the water.

Then came the *incredible* public appearances and statements from BP CEO Tony Hayward. Hayward's pinstriped suits contrasted sharply with the coveralls worn by fishermen in the Gulf, and his British accent called up images of British royalty. Although Hayward was not born to the purple or educated at elite schools, his accent, coupled with an air of indifference, telegraphed corporate contempt.

His comments were worse. "The Gulf of Mexico is a very big ocean," he said, noting that the volume of oil "we are putting into it is tiny in relation to the total water volume." Several days later, he opined: "The environmental impact of this disaster is likely to have been very, very modest." And then, in the verbal *coup de grâce*, after apologizing to those whose lives had been torn asunder, he added, "There's no one who wants this thing over more than I do. I'd like my life back." Television happily conveyed images of his life: Wealth and attendance at a yacht race with his family. His "tin-eared utterances" suggested to many that he lacked goodwill and was disingenuous in his apologetic remarks (Goodman, 2010, p. 1; see Figure 10.1).

Figure 10.1 BP Faced Serious Moral and Public Relations Problems in the Wake of the 2010 Oil Spill in the Gulf of Mexico. CEO Tony Hayward, shown here (at right) touring the damage, made a number of public relations mistakes, further eroding BP's credibility

Image courtesy of Getty Images

In the realm of public relations, Hayward was wayward.

"It was one of the worst P.R. approaches that I've seen in my 56 years of business," said public relations expert Howard Rubinstein. "They basically thought they could spin their way out of catastrophe. It doesn't work that way." "Once you lose credibility, that's the kiss of death," added another PR specialist (Goodman, 2010, p. 6).

On the other hand, when companies gain credibility in the wake of a crisis, they can survive, stave off self-inflicted harm, and emerge with a better public image. Several years back, after a Starbucks employee in Philadelphia called the police when two Black men waiting for a business get-together, but who had not ordered anything, asked to use the restroom, a national furor erupted, besmirching Starbucks's credibility. The White employee's stereotyped assumption that the men were dangerous, decision to act on it, and the subsequent backlash against Starbucks placed Starbucks management in crisis mode, illustrating the gargantuan impact one episode massively publicized on mass and social media can exert on a company's image. Unlike BP, Starbucks did not deny the problem. On the contrary, shortly after the incident occurred, it closed 8,000 stores to hold racial bias training among its 175,000 employees, sending a widely publicized statement that it would not tolerate prejudice and was committed to racial equality, underscoring the company's determination to make good on its commitments. This in turn showcased trustworthiness and good will, two cardinal dimensions of credibility. Critics questioned the effectiveness of the training program, but one could not help but admire Starbucks' campaign to shore up its besmirched credibility (Abrams, Hsu, & Eligon, 2018).

BOX 10.2

The Con in Con Man Stands for …

How do con men connive? (And, while we're on the topic, why don't we ever talk about con women?)

The answer to the first question is confidence. Con men pull the persuasive wool over vulnerable individuals' eyes by projecting confidence and credibility. Cunning persuaders exploit peripheral credibility cues, speaking quickly to enhance expertise, exploiting smiles to convey goodwill, and projecting confidence to gain the trust of potential prey. "Confidence convinces," writer Dan Gardner (2011, p. 153) concluded, attributing its effects to a confidence heuristic. "If someone's confidence is high, we believe they are probably right; if they are less certain, we feel they are less reliable" (pp. 153–154). In a way, this is unfair, because an intelligent person who appreciates the complexity of events and fallibility of prediction should be uncertain, even humble. But we're talking persuasion – and in the world of persuasion, confidence convinces. (This is one reason President Trump has achieved stunning success in presidential politics. He is unfailingly confident, never evincing a shred of a doubt in the veracity of what he claims.)

Research documents the role played by confidence in persuasion (see Naftulin, Ware, & Donnelly, 1973 for a classic study). For example, Zarnoth and Sniezek (1997) asked students to grapple with several cognitive tasks: Math problems, a temperature forecast, and verbal analogies. Students indicated the degree to which they were confident that their answers were correct. Subsequently, students were assigned to a group and offered a collective judgment regarding the correct answer to the problems. Individuals who had displayed greater confidence exerted more impact on group judgments, even when their answers were objectively wrong!

So, the "con" in con man stands, at least in part, for confidence. But it's not just con *men* who can dupe gullible receivers. A New York City psychic, Sylvia Mitchell, was convicted of grand larceny and imprisoned for swindling unsuspecting clients of some $160,000. Over the years, women entered her plush shop, appropriately called Zena Clairvoyant, and plaintively listened as Mitchell promised to cleanse their spirits, and to refund their money. Instead, she kept the

Figure 10.2 The "Con" in Con Man Stands for Confidence. Con artists call on their all-knowing mien to exploit others' vulnerability and belief that if someone displays confidence in what they say, he (though not necessarily a "he") should be trusted. The age-old confidence scam shows no signs of disappearing, as revealed by the brazen skill that college admissions consultant William Singer displayed, as he pitched parents a message that he could get their children admitted to elite universities. Status-hungry parents doled out thousands of dollars to Singer, who fabricated their kids' credentials, gaming the corrupt elite university system, until he was arrested and pleaded guilty to racketeering charges

Image courtesy of Reuters

cash. Who would succumb to such silly scams? Explained a seasoned New York City lieutenant, the secret lies in the psychic's ability to locate a psychologically vulnerable client with money to spare. "They gain your confidence," he said. "And then you're scammed" (Wilson, 2011, p. A15).

Consider the case of con artist William Singer. "Part coach, part therapist, part motivation speaker and part name dropper," Singer, "confident and concise," the "Pied Piper" of college admissions pitched his message to attentive, believing parents: He could get their children into a prestigious university (Bosman, Kovaleski, & Del Real, 2019, p. A1).

Lured by Singer's promises, a number of parents bought into a scam that rocked the university admissions world several years back. Singer conned wealthy parents, including television stars Lori Loughlin and Felicity Huffman. Parents paid as much as $75,000 to Singer, who would pay someone else to take their child's college entrance exam ensuring the student got a high score. Parents would also pay huge sums to Singer, who, under the guise of a non-profit foundation, padded and fabricated their children's college credentials. Athletic coaches were bribed to gain admission for aspiring students who did not even play the particular sport. Singer delivered on his promises, getting many students into elite colleges, and his plan looked fool-proof, until he was caught, pleading guilty to racketeering.

His plan revealed the greedy underbelly of a corrupt university admissions system, as well as how far parents will go to gain the elixir of prestigious university admissions. "He was well dressed, he was well spoken, he had a Power Point," an Illinois father of two said, explaining why he fell for Singer's scheme (Bosman et al., 2019, A1; see Figure 10.2).

Core Characteristics

What are the main attributes of credibility? What does it mean to be a credible speaker?

Communication researchers have explored these time-honored questions, using statistical methods and survey research. Scholars asked people to evaluate the believability of famous people, giving speeches on various topics, and to rate friends or supervisors on semantic differential scales. They found that credibility is not a simple, unitary concept: It has more than one dimension, more than a single layer. Credible communicators are perceived as having expertise, trustworthiness, goodwill, dynamism, extroversion, sociability, and composure (e.g., Berlo, Lemert, & Mertz, 1969; McCroskey & Young, 1981). Keep in mind that this research was conducted decades ago, long before the onset of so many cultural, gender role, and online technology transformations that can influence the dynamics of credibility. Replication studies should be conducted to determine whether the same factors hold today.

Alas, we have to go with the knowledge base we have. And given this, and synthesizing studies, one concludes that credibility that at least three underlying characteristics: (a) *expertise*, (b) *trustworthiness*, and (c) *goodwill*. Expertise and trustworthiness have emerged with the greatest regularity, and goodwill has been uncovered in systematic research by James C. McCroskey (McCroskey & Teven, 1999). Based on the studies as a whole, one can say that a credible communicator is one who is seen as an expert, is regarded as trustworthy, and displays goodwill toward audience members. Each quality is important and deserves brief discussion.

Expertise is the knowledge or ability ascribed to the communicator. It is the belief that the communicator has special skills or know-how. You see experts used all the time in commercials. Lawyers pay for experts to testify for their side in courtroom trials. There is abundant evidence that experts are perceived as credible and can influence attitudes (Petty & Wegener, 1998).

Trustworthiness, the next core credibility component, refers to the communicator's perceived honesty, character, and safety. A speaker may lack expertise, but can be seen as an individual of integrity and character. This can work wonders in persuasion.

Goodwill, or perceived caring, is the final core communication factor. While it has emerged less frequently in factor analytic studies than the venerable expertise and trustworthiness dimensions, it is an important aspect of credibility. Communicators who display goodwill are caring, convey that they have listeners' interests at heart, and are empathic toward their audiences' needs (McCroskey & Teven, 1999). You can probably think of a doctor who knows her stuff and is honest, but seems preoccupied or uninterested in you when you complain about medical problems. The physician undoubtedly gets low marks on your credibility scale, and her advice probably has little impact on you. On the other hand, a doctor who conveys empathy with patients' needs is perceived as caring and credible, increasing patients' satisfaction and compliance with medical recommendations (Kim, Kaplowitz, & Johnston, 2004).

Role of Context

Expertise, trustworthiness, and goodwill are the primary attributes of credibility. Communicators who are credible have all or at least one of these qualities. There is a complicating factor, however: Context. As anyone who has worked in telemarketing, politics, or community organizing can tell you, the situation you are in can potently influence persuasion. This means that different facets of credibility will be influential in different social situations. This conclusion emerged from early academic studies of credibility, which found that results varied, depending on the ways in which researchers probed credibility and the circumstances in which the speeches were delivered (Cronkhite & Liska, 1976).

Importantly, the cultural context influences credibility judgments. American students evaluate political leaders on the basis of competence and character, while Japanese students sometimes employ two additional attributes: Consideration and appearance (King, Minami, & Samovar, 1985). In Western cultures, credibility may be a fixed construct, something that communicators are seen as having across contexts. In non-Western, Asian societies, where attitudes can be context-specific and there is a focus on what is appropriate in particular situations, a communicator's credibility may be seen as more variable, malleable, and tailored to what is suitable in the particular situation (Shavitt, 2019).

The Assault on Expertise

There are other, disturbing factors that afflict credibility in today's fragmented, fractious world. During a time when centrifugal cultural forces seem to be pulling us away from a consensual center of society, credibility is in the crosswinds. Cultural subgroups can question known scientifically established facts (Harmon, 2017; see Chapter 5). Many individuals are hooked into their own social media worlds, even algorithmically propelled to receive and attend to data that confirms their world-views, as you know from the discussions of selective exposure and confirmation bias. A Trump presidential adviser famously coined the oxymoronic term "alternative facts" to cast aspersions on valid factual information that ran afoul of White House statements.

In today's media environment, where their ditzy cousin's skeptical post about climate change adjoins a detail-rich global warming documentation from the National Science Foundation, some people heuristically assume that if most people in their online network question established facts, they must be correct. In a similar fashion, the easily accessible Wikipedia can carry the same clout as the more scientifically informed conclusions of the American Association for the Advancement of Sciences. The Internet is filled with so much misinformation that it is hard to know what is true and what is false. The traditional, expert gatekeepers of information are increasingly distrusted (Baker, 2019). As a result, expertise, a cardinal component of credibility, is under siege.

Some people – understandably, perhaps, but erroneously – believe that they know as much as well-trained experts. Some individuals are openly hostile to experts, smugly (or defensively) believing that their knowledge is as good as that of an expert, even when it does not constitute knowledge at all (Nichols, 2017). More and more people, presuming that everyone has an angle and can't possibly be objective, assume that experts also view evidence through the lenses of their biases (Davies, 2018), and probably even more so than in the days of Lord, Ross, and Lepper.

Nowadays, you can't simply assume that a scientific expert, who would have been viewed as credible and compelling when Hovland, Janis, and Kelley (1953) or even Petty and Cacioppo (1986) conducted their studies, carries the same cachet with audience members today. In view of widespread questioning of experts, it is important to appreciate that the degree to which a communicator's expertise carries weight with message receivers depends in important ways on how the message receiver evaluates the purveyor of expertise, the receiver's biases, and her broader values (for example, does she believe in science or subscribe to conspiracy theories?). While expertise remains one of the three pillars of credibility, it is instructive to bear in mind the Elaboration Likelihood Model's principle about sources: A particular factor, like expertise, will exert a different impact, depending on the audience members' motivation and ability to process the message, and the extent to which strong attitudes induce them to discount a persuader's expertise on an ego-involved topic.

Credibility, with its three core components, continues to be important in persuasion. Conventional experts still carry weight with most people. However, expertise is more culturally constructed and broadly questioned than in the recent past, particularly among those with impassioned positions on social issues. This is unfortunate. For all their shortcomings – experts have been wrong, after all – expertise offers a mechanism for society to determine what is factually true, providing a rational foundation for public policy decisions.

The importance of expertise, in an age of misinformation and dizzying distortion of facts on social media, took on existential importance during the early days of the coronavirus pandemic. With social media sites spreading conspiracy theories and Fox News, abetted by President Trump, telling people it was "the safest time to fly," it was the nation's sober scientists and infectious disease experts who provided the needed measure of rationality and truth. In the final analysis, expertise is psychologically complex, its impact contingent on a variety of factors; but it's also an essential resource for democracy and, in extreme cases, humanity.

A Theoretical Account of Credibility

Let's return now to more ordinary, academic issues, particularly theory. As noted earlier in the book, social scientists attempt to develop theories to explain and predict events. The ELM offered one theoretical approach to credibility, emphasizing that credibility can serve in different capacities, such as a cue, argument, or catalyst to thinking. The ELM reminds us that credibility doesn't just automatically lead to persuasion or that its effects on persuasion are simple. Instead, it highlights the fact that credibility, like other factors, is processed differently in different situations, suggesting that persuaders should be sensitive to how involved or knowledgeable about the issue their audience members are.

Another approach, characterized by its counterintuitive, surprising predictions, was developed by Alice H. Eagly and her colleagues. Eagly and her associates devised a model that assumes people are canny, skeptical observers of persuaders. Eagly, Wood, and Chaiken (1978) argue that people figure persuaders have their own motives for saying what they do. What's more, they note, audience members attribute persuaders' statements to various factors. The attribution that individuals make can exert an important influence on credibility judgments and persuasion.

Eagly et al. emphasize that individuals make predictions – or develop expectations – about what a particular communicator will say, based on what they know about him or her, and the situation. For instance, if you were told that a member of the college track team was going to talk about exercise, you probably would assume he was going to explain why running is healthy. Or, to take a political example, if informed that a candidate was speaking to a pro-environmental group, you might assume he or she was going to sing the praises of conservation.

Expectations can be confirmed – it turns out you are correct – or disconfirmed – you end up being wrong. When a speaker disconfirms your expectation, you scratch your head and want to figure out why this occurred. In such cases, you may (as we will see) conclude that the communicator is a credible source. The underpinnings for this lie in two psychological concepts: *Knowledge bias* and *reporting bias*.

Knowledge Bias

Suppose you were told that a young female professor was scheduled to give a lecture on affirmative action. If you ventured a prediction about what she was going to say, you might guess that, being young and a professor (and, therefore you assume, liberal), she would advocate affirmative action programs for women. If the speaker confirmed your prediction, you might conclude that she possessed what is called a knowledge bias. A *knowledge bias* is the presumption that a communicator has a biased view of an issue. It is an audience member's belief that the speaker's background – gender, ethnicity, religion, or age – has prevented him or her from looking objectively at the various sides of the issue. The audience member concludes that the communicator has a limited base of knowledge, produced by a need to view an issue in accord with the dominant views of her social group. "Oh, she's a modern woman; of course she'd see things that way," you might say, meaning no disrespect. Communicators who are perceived to harbor knowledge biases lack credibility and do not change attitudes (Eagly et al., 1978).

Now suppose that the speaker took the unexpected position and spoke out against affirmative action programs for women. The theory says that individuals might be taken aback by this and would feel a need to explain why the communicator defied expectation. Unable to attribute her position to gender or background, they would have to conclude that something else was operating. They might reasonably infer that the arguments against affirmative action were so compelling that they persuaded the young professor to go against the grain and take an unpopular stand. Or they might conclude that the communicator was a bit of an iconoclast, someone who defied the norm. Both these interpretations could enhance the speaker's credibility and increase the odds that she would change audience attitudes. As a general rule, when communicators are perceived to violate the knowledge bias, they gain in credibility (see Figure 10.3a).

(a)

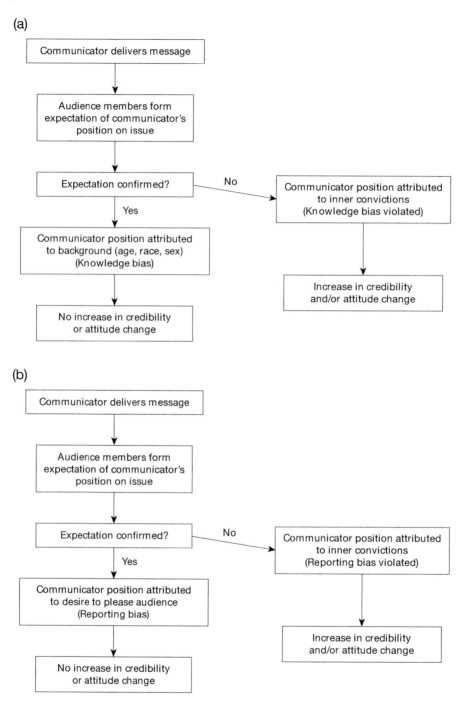

Figure 10.3 (a) Knowledge Bias; (b) Reporting Bias

Knowledge bias is admittedly a different way of looking at communicators and so it takes some getting used to. But once you appreciate the idea, it becomes an appealing way to explain seemingly paradoxical situations in everyday life. Consider the following examples:

- African American lawyer David P. Baugh defended Barry E. Black, a White member of the Ku Klux Klan accused of burning a cross. The case was intriguing because of "the paradox of an African-American defending a white supremacist, who, if he had his way, would oppress his lawyer because of his race" (Holmes, 1998, p. A14). Arguing that the principle of free speech overwhelmed any discomfort he had about the defendant's actions, the lawyer violated the knowledge bias and may have enhanced his credibility in the case.

- Celine Bonilla, at the tender age of 11, watched as police officers restrained a man on her front yard. The man and an accomplice had just murdered two of her friends and their mother, pouring gasoline on them and burning them alive in one of the most repulsive murders in Connecticut history. Yet eight years later, Celine, a nursing student, disclosed that she opposed the death penalty for the two men, viewing execution as a cruel and unusual punishment (Casey, 2015). The knowledge bias suggests that she should be a more credible spokesperson for the elimination of capital punishment than liberal ideologues. Precisely because her background experiences suggest she should support the death penalty, her opposition seems heartfelt and derived from a thoughtful reflection that enhances its believability.

- Tom Galinat is a 35-year-old Vermont farmer and hunter who owns nine guns. Jonathan Leach, a 56-year-old policy analyst from Maine, owns ten guns. Judith Pearson, a retired school principal from rural Minnesota, has a file cabinet lined with guns she uses for hunting and recreational purposes. All these gun owners have one thing in common: They vehemently disagree with the National Rifle Association's anti-gun positions and have spoken out passionately and purposefully. Their goal: To change the law to ban high-capacity rifles, or force people deemed dangerous to society to relinquish their firearms (Bidgood & Tavernise, 2018; Hsu, 2018). Once again, the knowledge bias suggests that these ardent gun owners would be more persuasive spokespersons for gun control than the usual liberal, anti-gun speakers. If you own guns and view the Second Amendment as giving you the right to unbridled gun ownership, you're unlikely to pay much attention to liberal gun opponents. The fact that these gun owners feel this way, despite their pro-gun bias, might coax you into reexamining your view.

- Perhaps the most compelling example of the knowledge bias is Jane Roe, the woman behind the Supreme Court case, Roe vs. Wade, that legalized abortion. Roe is the legal pseudonym for Norma McCorvey, the plaintiff in the case. Years after the decision, McCorvey befriended a seven-year-old girl named Emily. When she learned Emily's mother almost had an abortion, she became a pro-life advocate. From a knowledge bias perspective, the fact that McCorvey of all people came to oppose abortion suggests that the pro-life position is compelling (see Figure 10.4). (In a twist, shortly before she died, McCorvey said she switched sides only because she was paid money to do so, her motive raising questions about her credibility.)

As persuasive as these knowledge bias violations are, we need to appreciate that they have limits. A super-gun zealot or uncompromising pro-choice activist will not change her mind after hearing that gun owners or Jane Roe saw fit to change their attitudes. Viewing these issues through the lens of

Figure 10.4 Norma McCorvey (aka Jane Roe of Roe vs. Wade) Testifies Before a Senate Judiciary Committee Hearing on the 25th Anniversary of the Roe vs. Wade Supreme Court Decision That Legalized Abortion. Years after the Roe vs. Wade decision, McCorvey rethought her position and became a strong opponent of abortion rights. However, McCorvey's more recent revelation that she was paid to switch sides shows the impact people's motives exert on credibility perceptions

confirmation biases, they will be even more convinced they are right and the other side is wrong. The knowledge bias can't end entrenched polarization. However, communicators like these, who take an unexpected position, may convince people with more moderate positions and, more importantly, lend a touch of complexity and open-mindedness to policy debates.

Reporting Bias

When judging communicators, audience members also examine the extent to which speakers are taking the position merely to make points with the audience. If they believe the communicator is brown-nosing the group, they assume that the speech reflects a situational pressure to say the socially correct thing. They conclude that the communicator has withheld – or chosen not to report – facts that would upset the group. This is the *reporting bias*, the perception that the communicator has opted not to report or disclose certain facts or points of view.

When individuals believe that speakers are guilty of a reporting bias, they downgrade their credibility. Upon hearing that a candidate tailors her statements to fit the ideology of the group she is addressing, voters frequently doubt the sincerity of the candidate. "A typical politician," voters think to themselves.

On the other hand, when audience members' expectations are violated – the communicator says something that is inconsistent with group values – the speaker is seen as credible and convincing. Individuals figure that anyone who has the courage to go against the grain must truly believe what he or she is saying. They figure that the position must be so compelling and cogent that it led the speaker to ignore social conventions and adopt the position as her own (see Eagly et al., 1978; see Figure 10.3b). The reporting bias helps us understand why maverick political candidates, who are seen as having the guts to reject the politically popular group position, are perceived as credible.

There is an important exception to the reporting bias. When a speaker violates the bias, but takes a position that a group finds *highly* objectionable or offensive, the communicator will be seen as incredible, the advocated position landing in the latitude of rejection. The speaker gets points for honesty, but loses more for taking a position that is strongly inconsistent with audience members' values. People are happy to respect an unconventional communicator who seems to defy pressures to tell groups what they want to hear – until the communicator stumbles on their own group and tramples on their own attitude, particularly a strong one, such as gun rights or abortion. When it comes to strong attitudes, people seem to prefer a mildly insincere communicator who shares their values to a sincere speaker who opposes a position they believe, in their heart of hearts, to be correct.

Social Attractiveness

Credibility is an important factor in persuasion. But it is not the only communicator characteristic that influences attitudes. Socially attractive communicators – those who are likable, similar to message recipients, and physically appealing – can also induce attitude change. Let's see how.

Likability

Emma Chamberlain (eight million YouTube followers) talks a lot about herself. Like, a lot. She also uses "guys" a lot, as in "you guys," is disarmingly disclosing, self-effacing, uttering lots of familiar, sweetly said obscenities, and totally – seemingly – authentic. She appeals to followers' everyday concerns, like trying to find a Thanksgiving recipe for the *fam* and the *squad*, struggling to sew an outfit, or choosing a cool coffee shop in L.A. in the middle of the afternoon, sipping the coffee, grading it, and totally coming off like someone you guys would know.

All the while, the 21-year-old Chamberlain has been promoting products, a super well-known influencer whose trademark likability disarms, giving her a vibe of interpersonal authenticity that is almost contagious, even if her performance is far from spontaneous. By her own admission, she spends more than 20 hours editing each video before streaming it on YouTube (Bromwich, 2019).

Chamberlain epitomizes likability, an old-fashioned, but highly contemporary communicator characteristic that is as folksy as it is effective. There is evidence that likable communicators can change attitudes (Rhoads & Cialdini, 2002; Sharma, 1999). There are several reasons for this. First, a likable person makes you feel good, and the positive feelings become transferred to the message. Second, a likable persuader puts you in a good mood, which helps you access positive thoughts about the product the persuader is peddling. Third, a likable speaker may convey that she has your interest at heart, which communicates goodwill.

Likability effects appear in a variety of public arenas, from politics to corporate consulting. One context in which likability matters is one that probably would not occur to you initially: Tipping waiters and waitresses. Restaurant servers who are likable get bigger tips (e.g. Rind & Bordia, 1995). What's more, there are several techniques that waiters and waitresses can use to make themselves more likable; these, in turn, have been found to increase the amount of money customers leave on the table. If anyone reading this book is currently waiting tables, he or she may find these strategies lucrative, or at least useful! Research indicates that the following techniques increase tip size (suggestions culled from Crusco & Wetzel, 1984; Leodoro & Lynn, 2007; Lynn & Mynier, 1993; Rind & Bordia, 1995, 1996):

- writing "thank you" on the back of the check;
- drawing a happy, smiling face on the back of checks before giving them to customers;
- squatting down next to tables;
- touching the diner's palm or shoulder (waitresses only; sorry, guys).

As this discussion suggests, a communicator's *non-verbal behaviors* can enhance likability. For example, a persuader who touches a message recipient lightly on the upper arm or shoulder while making a request is more likely to gain compliance than a communicator who does not touch the target, at least in some contexts (Segrin, 1993). Making eye contact and standing closer to a target can also enhance persuasion. As you might expect, a host of contextual factors come into play, such as the nature of the touch or gaze, the relationship between communicator and recipient, and gender.

Gender, it turns out – not surprisingly – brings to the fore a disturbing aspect of touching in the workplace, with #MeToo sexual harassment implications. Waitresses who lightly touch their male customers or dress in ways that men find attractive run the risk of arousing some men's libidos and the license they feel to make crude comments about women's bodies. Waitresses with blonde hair, large breasts, or slender physiques receive larger tips than their counterparts who lack these attributes (Lynn, 2009), showcasing the role sexist norms continue to play in everyday life.

What's more, female servers say they are routinely propositioned or groped by some male customers. Klaycey Oakes, an Oklahoma waitress, told her boss that a man grabbed her thigh. Jaime Brittain, a waitress in a Louisiana steakhouse, was at a loss for words when a group of men promised her a $30 tip if only she would answer a question about her pubic hair. The women felt embarrassed and offended, but said they had to balance their anger at men's sexual abuse with pressing financial needs, like buying groceries for their families or paying the mortgage (Einhorn & Abrams, 2018). In these cases, the desire to project likability can come at the cost of waitresses' self-respect, reminding us that, in a still-sexist society, the display of even an innocuous attribute like likability can cause psychological, even physical harm to women.

Similarity

Does similarity enhance persuasion? Is a communicator who shares your values more apt to change attitudes than a dissimilar communicator? The answer is yes, especially under some conditions.

Similarity between source and receiver can facilitate persuasion in business (Brock, 1965), on academic issues (Berscheid, 1966), and even when the similarity is silly or incidental to the persuasion attempt. For example, individuals were more likely to return questionnaires in the mail if the name that appeared on the cover letter bore a similarity to their own name (Garner, 2005). Police officers dispense less costly speeding tickets when the driver shares the ticketing officer's first name (Jena, Sunstein, & Hicks, 2018). People also complied more frequently with a request to review an essay when the person making the request indicated that she shared a birthday with the research participant (Burger et al., 2004).

Similarity also can have important effects on health care. Research finds that Black patients take better care of their health and can experience more positive therapeutic outcomes when they are treated by Black physicians (Anderson & McMillion, 1995; Kalichman & Coley, 1995). Black patients frequently feel more comfortable with Black physicians and are more likely to seek them out for treatment of medical ailments (Tweedy, 2015). A legacy of insensitive, racist treatment of African Americans has left a collective toll on older African Americans, while others may feel that same-race doctors have greater appreciation of the environmental conditions that have produced crippling racial disparities in health care (Harrington, 2013; Kreps, 2006; Smedley, Stith, & Nelson, 2003).

Indeed, there is intriguing evidence that Black male patients who saw Black doctors were more likely to get diabetes screening and cholesterol tests than Black men who met with White or Asian physicians (Kolata, 2018). Given racial disparities, it's an argument for training and hiring more African American doctors, or at least trying to pair Black patients with same-race doctors who can build on a reservoir of trust and good will (see Figure 10.5).

Similarity works in commercial domains as well. Advertisers for women's fashion and clothing brands have called on similarity in their marketing spots. Christian Louboutin, which gained fame for its stylish red-soled shoes, hired a plus-size model as the star of a social media campaign for a new line of lipstick. David's Bridal, a national wedding gown retailer, selected a size 14 model, the typical size of its customers, to star in a spring bridal advertising campaign. These advertisements built on Dove's Real Beauty campaign that featured women of different body types, rather than ultra-skinny models (Olson, 2016). It became a marketing classic.

Why and When

Similarity works for several reasons. It reinforces or compliments people, telling them that their body type or personal preferences are desirable. In a cold, lonely world, the mere mention that another shares an individual's name, birthday, or appearance, to say nothing of one's political affiliation, operates as a reinforcer. It offers vicarious reward, associating the self with the implicit approval conferred by another's deliberate or incidental possession of a similar attribute. Similarity also benefits from the fruits of social comparison: I may infer that if someone who is similar to me likes a product or endorses a position, it is a good bet that the proposal will work for me as well.

When might similarity be most effective? We really don't know exactly when, but there is some reason to believe that similarity's relevance to the message plays a part (Berscheid, 1966).

In business settings, salespeople selling running shoes to high school cross-country team members may be more likely to make a sale if they explain that they ran 5K races in high school than if they

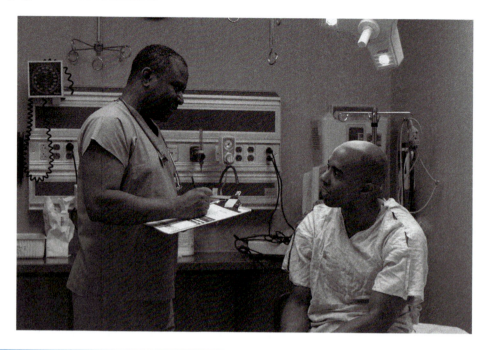

Figure 10.5 Research Finds That Black Male Patients Are More Likely to Take Diabetes and Cholesterol Preventive Steps When Seeing Black Doctors Than When Seeing Physicians From Races Different Than Their Own. The rapport, trust, and comfort level racial similarity facilitates is important, particularly because African American men have the lowest life expectancy of any ethnic or racial group in the United States

play up the fact that they grew up in the same community as the teenager. However, similarity may fail if the persuader suggests to a message receiver that he is just like the recipient – and lacks expertise.

Similarity Versus Expertise: "Just Like Me" Versus "Too Much Like Me"

The foregoing discussion raises the knotty question of when communicators should stress similarity and when they should emphasize expertise. There are no quick and easy answers. Research suggests that similarity is more effective when people must make personal and emotional decisions (Goethals & Nelson, 1973). In these cases we feel a kinship with the similar other and assume that the similar communicator is more apt to empathize with our concerns than a dissimilar speaker. By contrast, when the issue concerns factual matters, experts' intellectual knowledge may carry the day.

The question of whether a communicator should emphasize expertise or similarity comes up in many real-life persuasion situations. Politicians, advertisers, and salespeople are often faced with deciding whether to emphasize their experience or the fact that they are "just plain folks." Increasingly, it seems, companies are putting a premium on similarity, particularly similarity in appearance. Many businesses, finding that formal attire can turn off clients dressed in jeans or simple pants suits, have told employees to dress like their clients (Puente, 1999). Indeed, it would seem as if the buttoned-down business announcement has gone out of style. Few who watched the two casually dressed, youthful founders of YouTube announce in a video clip that they had sold their company to Google for $1.65 billion thought twice about the young geeks' informal attire.

Steve Constanides, an owner of a computer graphics firm, exemplifies this trend. "When you went on a sales call, you definitely got a cooler reaction if you showed up in a nice suit, because the clients would see you as just a salesman," Constanides related. "If I came in more casual attire, all of a sudden I'm like them. And it's easier to get a project," he said (Puente, 1999, p. 2D).

On the other hand, if his computer graphics sales staff abandoned expertise entirely and talked just like the clients – saying, "Hey, what's up dude?" or "Man, that's awesome!" – they would probably not sell much high-tech equipment!

Back in 2008, Republican vice-presidential candidate Sarah Palin played on similarity, as she emphasized that she was just "your average hockey mom," married to her high school sweetheart, and raising four children, including an infant son with Down syndrome. This appealed to many voters until Palin stumbled in her campaign appearances, leading one New York woman, Donna Davis, to observe that she could understand how women felt that Palin could understand their experiences. "The question for them," Davis asked, is: "'Am I ready to be vice-president of the United States?'" (Davis, 2008, p. A28). In Palin's case, her lack of expertise trumped perceived similarity.

Thus, similarity can enhance persuasion until it reduces perceptions of expertise and competence (see Box 10.3 for practical tips).

Physical Attractiveness

It is something we covet, even if we don't like to admit it. At some level, everyone wants to be physically attractive – beautiful, handsome, an object of allure. Even people who are widely acknowledged to be sexually appealing are never quite satisfied with this or that aspect of their physique. Besides the obvious advantages it bestows in capturing mates, attractiveness attracts for other reasons. We assume that physical appeal can catapult us to success, helping us land the job or deal that we privately covet. A casual glance at celebrities reveals their stunning physical features. Advertisers obviously believe that attractiveness sells. Why else would they employ the sensationally attractive to champion products?

BOX 10.3

Communicator Tips

Can research and theory offer practical suggestions on how to be a more effective communicator? You bet! Here are five ideas, gleaned from persuasion concepts and experiments:

1   If you are delivering a speech and have technical knowledge about the topic, you should let your audience know this at the outset. Don't blow your horn too much or you will come off as obnoxious. Instead, discreetly note your credentials (Allen, 2002; O'Keefe, 1987). If, on the other hand, you are new on the job and have not accumulated much technical

knowledge, don't mention this before you give the talk. There is some evidence that this could reduce your credibility in the audience's eyes (Greenberg & Miller, 1966), particularly when you are delivering a message with which audience members disagree (O'Keefe, 2016). Instead, be sure to demonstrate your qualifications as you discuss your ideas, communicating the message persuasively (Whalen, 1996).

2   Show your audience you care about both the topic and your role as a persuader. Goodwill counts for a great deal in persuasion, as discussed earlier. People forgive a lot if they believe you have their interests at heart. You should be true to yourself here: Don't fake deep caring if you don't feel it. Instead, identify one or two issues that you are legitimately interested in imparting, and focus on these.

3   Try to get the audience to like you. Likability can enhance persuasion (Sharma, 1999), so you should find a feature of your personality that you are comfortable with and let this shine through during your talk. It may be your serenity, sensitivity, gregariousness, or sense of humor. Use this as a way to connect with the audience. Promote your similarities with audience members to the extent you feel comfortable.

4   Do whatever you can to bolster your confidence. If this means engaging in positive thinking or wearing an attractive outfit, do it. Your physical appeal matters in persuasion if it can help you feel better about yourself, channel your thinking in a positive direction, and engender self-confidence. But remember: Don't let your confidence turn into arrogance. Respect your audience, stay true to your message, and deliver your message honestly and with conviction.

Hold on. Celebrities are not representative of the population as a whole. The fact that advertisers assume attractiveness works does not mean it actually does. This brings up the question: Does attractiveness enhance persuasion? You could argue that it works because physical appeal is a supremely valued commodity in America. Or you could say it doesn't because people resent extremely attractive people, or assume they're airheads, narcissists, or both. What effect does physical appeal have on attitudes? What subtle influences does it have on stereotypes? Researchers have explored these questions. Some of the answers are straightforward, confirming with intriguing evidence what we suspected. Other answers may surprise you.

In order to figure out the role physical attractiveness plays in persuasion, researchers conduct experiments pitting communicators who vary in attractiveness against one another, examining who exerts the greatest impact on attitudes. It's a little superficial, but the results do give us insights on the psychology of physical appeal. And the studies are elegant and intriguing.

In a nifty study, Chaiken (1979) recruited individuals who were high and low in physical appeal and instructed them to approach students on a university campus. Attractive and not-so-attractive communicators gave a spiel, advocating that the university stop serving meat at breakfast and lunch at the campus dining hall. Students who heard the message from the attractive speakers were more inclined to agree that meat should not be served than were students exposed to the less attractive communicators. The arguments that both sets of speakers gave were exactly the same; the only difference was that one group of communicators was nicer looking than the other. Yet this peripheral factor carried the day, inducing students to change their minds on the topic.

Why does attractiveness influence attitudes? First, people are more likely to pay attention to an attractive speaker, and this can increase the odds that they will remember message arguments. Second, attractiveness becomes associated with the message. The pleasant affect one feels when gazing at a pretty woman or handsome guy gets merged with the message, resulting in an overall favorable evaluation of the topic. Third, people like and identify with attractive communicators. At some level, perhaps unconscious, we feel we can improve our own standing in life if we do what attractive people suggest. Fourth, attractive individuals may simply be better public speakers. As psychologist Susan Fiske explains, "if you're beautiful or handsome, people laugh at your jokes and interact with you in such a way that it's easy to be socially skilled" (Belluck, 2009, p. 8).

Contextual factors

A communicator's physical appeal can add sweetness and value to a product or person. Most of us, scholar Daniel S. Hamermesh (2011) notes, "prefer as customers to buy from better-looking salespeople, as jurors to listen to better-looking attorneys, as voters to be led by better-looking politicians, as students to learn from better-looking professors" (p. 12; see also Figure 10.6).

Figure 10.6 Physical Attractiveness Can Enhance Persuasion in a Variety of Situations. The interesting questions are why attractiveness influences attitudes, when it is most likely to be effective, and how we sometimes can be goaded by attractive persuaders to perform actions we later regret

Image courtesy of Shutterstock

Attractive communicators seem to be more effective than their less attractive counterparts, everything else being equal. But everything else is never totally equal. Attractiveness influences attitudes more under certain conditions than under others.

First, attractiveness can help form attitudes. One reason people begin buying certain perfumes or toothpastes is that they link the product with attractive models, and develop a favorable attitude toward the product. Unfortunately, the same process can work with unhealthy products like cigarettes, which is one reason why cigarette advertisements feature physically attractive smokers.

Second, attractiveness can be effective when the communicator's goal is to capture attention. This is one reason why advertisers use drop-dead gorgeous models. They want to break through the clutter and get people to notice the product. Once that is accomplished, they rely on other strategies to convince people to purchase the good or service.

Third, attractiveness can be effective under low involvement, as when people are trying to decide which of two advertised convenience store products to buy or for whom to vote in a low-level election. In these cases, physical appeal acts as a peripheral cue.

Fourth, on the other extreme, attractiveness can be a deciding factor when the communicator's physical appeal is relevant to the product. In cases of beauty products or expensive clothing lines, a model's or salesperson's good looks can swing the sale. Physical appeal serves as an argument for the product, as the ELM suggests. Interestingly, attractiveness is particularly helpful in selling an appearance-related product when people are high in involvement (Trampe et al., 2010). If you are hunting for the right outfit for a job interview and are attending closely to online apparel advertisements, the ad with the nice-looking model can provide a strong argument that this is the outfit you should buy. Notice how powerful attractiveness is: It works under low and high involvement, but for different reasons.

Fifth, physical attractiveness exerts stronger effects on some people than others. Based on research on self-monitoring (see Chapter 5), Evans and Clark (2012) reasoned that attractive communicators should be more persuasive for high self-monitors, with their focus on image and socially affiliating with others; expert sources should be more impactful with low self-monitors, with their emphasis on attitudes reflecting core issues and authentic values. Evans and Clark found support for this hypothesis, suggesting that physical appeal will be more influential when it matches the needs of the message receiver, in line with functional theory.

Finally, attractiveness can influence opinions when it violates expectations. Consider the true story of Rebekka Armstrong, former *Playboy* playmate who contracted HIV from intercourse with a male model. After years of suffering, denial, and drug abuse, Armstrong went public with her story, trying to teach young people the dangers of unprotected sex. She has spoken to capacity university crowds and has her own website (Perloff, 2001). Why might she be influential?

Your image – or schema – of a *Playboy* model does not include contracting HIV. This disconfirms your expectation, and you have to think about it to put things back together mentally. As one listens to an attractive model like Armstrong talk, one discovers that she is arguing for these positions not because of a knowledge or reporting bias – but because she truly believes people must take precautions against AIDS. Thus, when attractive communicators say or do unexpected things that seem out of sync with their good looks and these events can be attributed to inner convictions, these speakers can influence attitudes.

When doesn't attractiveness make a difference?

Physical appeal cannot change deeply felt attitudes. Listening to an attractive speaker explain why abortion is necessary is not going to change the mind of a staunch pro-life advocate. Attractiveness is rarely enough to close a deal when the issue is personally consequential or stimulates considerable thinking.

Just as attractiveness can work when it positively violates expectations, it can fail when it negatively violates expectations of what is appropriate for a particular job or role (Burgoon, 1989). You would not expect your family doctor to be sensationally attractive. If the doctor accentuates his or her physical attributes, this could interfere with processing the message or lead you to derogate the doctor. "Patients and colleagues may dismiss a young doctor's skills and knowledge or feel their concerns aren't being taken seriously when the doctor is dressed in a manner more suitable for the gym or a night on the town," one medical expert noted (Marcus, 2006, p. D5). (On the other hand, some might argue that patients display a subtle prejudice when they reject an expert *because* she is good looking.)

Finally, attractiveness effects tend to be rather short-lived. As a primarily peripheral cue, attractiveness tends not to be integrated with the person's overall attitude. The person may feel positively toward the communicator, but fail to do the cognitive work necessary to develop a strong, lasting attitude toward the issue.

Beauty, in sum, has always fascinated us. It always will. Attractiveness is commonly assumed to weave a magical spell on people. Its effects are more psychological than astrological, and are inevitably due to individuals letting themselves be bowled over by an attractive person or allowing themselves to fantasize about what will happen if they go along with the communicator's recommendations.

Real-world persuaders have long recognized that attractiveness sells, even if they are less familiar with the psychological trappings of attractiveness effects. Advertisers use physical appeal as a peripheral cue to sell many products and as a central argument for beauty products. Drug companies hire former college cheerleaders to sell pharmaceutical products to doctors. In an article headlined, "Gimme an Rx! Cheerleaders Pep Up Drug Sales," a *New York Times* reporter describes how ex-cheerleaders, including a former Miss Florida USA, traipse into physicians' offices promoting pharmaceutical products. They combine physical appeal, charm, and likability to influence the nation's doctors, who are mostly men. "There's a saying that you'll never meet an ugly drug rep," one physician said (Saul, 2005, p. A1).

Discriminating *in favor* of physically attractive women is not against the law in the United States. And handsome, athletic men are also apt to be hired as pharmaceutical reps and lobbyists. Attractiveness raises ethical issues when individuals are hired solely on the basis of their physical appeal or someone less attractive is fired, as has happened with older female newscasters. The pursuit of beauty also raises ethical issues when advertisements and social media pictures of unrealistically thin models can cause some adolescent girls to devalue their bodies and themselves (see Box 10.4).

Ethics and Attractiveness

What worries most people most is that physically attractive communicators, particularly celebrities, will take advantage of others, inducing them to put aside their critical facilities, and exploiting their need to vicariously identify with the beautiful and handsome. We do not know how often this happens, but it undoubtedly does, and the theoretical ideas discussed in the chapter shed light on the process. Consider the case of Jenny McCarthy.

When McCarthy was in her early 20s, she posed nude for *Playboy* and was named Playmate of the Month. Building on her fame, she co-hosted an MTV dating show; her striking blonde hair, "buxom physique," and "girl-next-door good looks" attracted attention, along with her tendency to make upfront comments about everyday issues (Mnookin, 2011, pp. 249–250). In 2002, she gave birth to a baby boy, and subsequently, discovered he had autism. Declaring that "the University of Google is where I got my degree," she said she punched autism in Google, found information, and later decided that vaccines had caused her son's autism (Mnookin, 2011, p. 254). She went public with her allegation, making the link between autism and vaccines in interviews with Larry King and Oprah Winfrey.

Here is the problem: As you know from Chapter 5, medical experts emphatically state that vaccines do not cause autism. The incidence of autism has risen in recent years, not because of vaccines, but due to greater awareness of the condition and increased determination to diagnose and treat it. Pediatricians emphasize that vaccines play a critical role in protecting the public health. McCarthy, who has many fans, is, of course, a magnet for media attention. "Because she posed nude for Playboy, dated Jim Carrey and is blond and bellicose, she has received platforms for this message that her fellow nonsense peddlers might not have," *New York Times* columnist Frank Bruni (2014) declared. By peddling her message, McCarthy, abetted by sycophantic media coverage, may have encouraged people to buy into a false belief, one that could have real consequences if parents decide not to vaccinate their kids.

What does theory and research on physical attractiveness suggest? You probably know. By serving as a peripheral cue on a complex topic, McCarthy invites people to accept her word as truth. By virtue of the association of the anti-vaccine message with her looks, and people's identification with her as an attractive role model, her message gains credibility among some (we don't know how many) individuals. Bruni (2014) put it well:

> When did it become O.K. to present gut feelings like hers as something in legitimate competition with real science? … Are the eyeballs drawn by someone like McCarthy more compelling than public health and truth? Her exposure proves how readily television bookers and much of the news media will let famous people or pretty people or (best of all!) people who are both famous *and* pretty hold forth on subjects to which they bring no actual expertise.

BOX 10.4

Physical Attractiveness and Culture

Is attractiveness relative?

Is physical beauty culturally relative, or are standards of beauty universal phenomena? It's an interesting question, with relevance for attractiveness effects in persuasion.

Some scholars argue that signs of youth, such as cleanliness, clear skin, and absence of disease, are universally perceived as attractive. They note that there is consensus across cultures that symmetrical faces are attractive (Buss & Kenrick, 1998). Evolutionary psychologists consistently find that across different societies men like full lips, long glistening hair, symmetrical features, a small distance between the mouth and chin, and a waist-to-hip ratio of approximately .7 (Brooks, 2011). Fair enough – but culture leaves its imprint in a host of other ways.

In the United States, thin is in, even as there is increased discussion of the unhealthy consequences of an ultra-thin physique. Lean, ever-skinnier female models define the culture's standard for beauty in women (Harrison & Cantor, 1997; Kuczynski, 2006). On social media, thinness sites are pervasive, featuring ultra-skinny women, along with positive comments about looking thin or losing weight (Boepple & Thompson, 2016). Yet thinness in women – propelled by the fashion industry, advertising, and young girls' desire to emulate sometimes dangerously thin models – is a relatively new cultural invention. In earlier eras, voluptuous body shapes were regarded as sexy. "The concept of beauty has never been static," Fallon notes (1990, p. 84). Going a long, long way back in time, one finds that, between 1400 and 1700, "fat was considered both erotic and fashionable ... Women were desired for their procreative value and were often either pregnant or nursing. The beautiful woman was portrayed as a plump matron with full, nurturant breasts" (Fallon, 1990, p. 85). The art of Botticelli and Rubens reflects this ideal.

There are also subcultural variations in what is regarded as beautiful in the United States. Research shows that African American women are less likely than White women to be preoccupied with body weight (Angier, 2000). The attractiveness of other body features also varies with culture. In America, breast size is linked with beauty, as indicated by the popularity of bras that pad and surgical breast implants. Yet in Brazil, large breasts are viewed as déclassé, "a libido killer," and in Japan bosoms are less enchanting than the nape of the neck, which is seen as an erotic zone (Kaufman, 2000, p. 3). In Peru, big ears are considered beautiful, and Mexican women regard low foreheads as an indication of beauty (de Botton, 2000).

Standards for male attractiveness also vary across cultures and historical periods. Macho guys like Humphrey Bogart and Marlon Brando have been replaced by softer-looking icons of attractiveness, like Leonardo DiCaprio and Robert Pattinson a generation ago and, in current times, by the likes of Jamie Dornan, Ansel Elgort, Zac Efron, Liam Hemsworth, and Michael B. Jordan.

To be sure, there are some universals in physical appeal. Yet culture leaves a strong imprint on conceptions of physical attractiveness, and we apply these consciously and unconsciously – in evaluating everyday persuaders.

There is an interesting postscript to this. Physical attractiveness may be closely associated with the objectification of women in contemporary culture. Objectification occurs "whenever a woman's body, body parts, or sexual functions are separated out from her person, reduced to the status of mere instruments, or regarded as if they were capable of representing her" (Fredrickson & Roberts, 1997, p. 175). We see this when women are stared at more than men in interpersonal situations, depicted more sexually in the media, and even portrayed in media with a focus on the body, as opposed to men, who are more commonly represented by their heads or faces (Sparks, 2016). It also occurs when use of Facebook, with its focus on visual manipulation of physical appearance, is associated with greater objectification and body shame (Manago et al., 2015). It is likely that objectified depictions of attractive women can reinforce stereotyped attitudes. Research suggests that the cultural norm emphasizing women's appearance can lead to devaluation of their competence, warmth, and morality (Heflick et al., 2011). Message receivers, culturally socialized to focus on attractive female persuaders' appearance, may be inclined to neglect other aspects of their personality, downgrading their work and judging them by different criteria than they would apply to attractive male communicators.

Let's not end on such a traditional note. The intersection between beauty and culture has taken a new turn with the upsurge in young people who have staked out an innovative turf, one that questions hetero-normative definitions of gender and sexual identity. With people defining themselves as non-binary, refusing to limit their "sexual expression to a single definition when (they) can glissade along the Kinsey scale," marketers have now begun courting attractive models whose gender identities are fluid and unfixed (Trebay, 2018). "There is not one idea of beauty or gender anymore," said one leading hairdresser, affirming the notion of gender-nullifying beauty as in one runway look he created for non-binary and other models that alternated "lacquered bouffant updos reminiscent of the 1960s with dyed Marine crew cuts" (Trebay, 2018).

> From a social psychological and persuasion perspective, the new expansion of gender and sexuality onto a continuous, rather than dichotomous, domain raises questions. Will universally attractive features like facial symmetry continue to be perceived as appealing when expressed by a non-binary individual? Do the persuasion-enhancing effects of attractiveness persist when displayed by less societally conventional communicators? How can non-binary communicators persuade more traditional audiences to accept their gender fluidity?

Conclusions

This chapter continued our trek along the path of the persuasive communicator, focusing on credibility and social attractiveness.

Credibility, a distant cousin of authority (discussed in Chapter 9), is a critical communicator factor, the cornerstone of effective persuasion. Research suggests that expertise, trustworthiness, and goodwill are the three core dimensions of credibility. (Expertise and trustworthiness have emerged with greater regularity, and goodwill has been uncovered in more recent research.)

Each of these factors is important in its own right, and can interact with contextual factors, such as audience size, communicator role, and culture. Alas, in an Internet, social media-dominated age when even empirically documented facts are open to question and experts can be doubted by ego-involved partisans, expertise may have lost its universal sheen, raising normative questions for democratic debates.

The ELM offers insights into the factors that influence when and why credibility influences attitudes. We also gain insights from an expectancy-violation model. The latter assumes that communicators gain in credibility to the degree that they take unexpected positions on issues – stands that audiences cannot attribute to their background or situation. Communicators whose positions cannot be attributed to a knowledge or reporting bias can be perceived as highly credible, although their impact depends, as usual, on the involvement and pre-existing attitudes of audience members.

Social attractiveness consists of three elements: Likeability, similarity, and physical appeal. All three factors can influence attitudes under particular conditions and have intriguing implications for interpersonal persuasion, commercial advertising, and ubiquitous influencer-based social media messages. Attractiveness is particularly interesting, given its mythic associations with success and sex appeal. It actually works through more pedestrian, but impactful, processes like identification, and can be exploited by persuaders to con receivers into believing a variety of false claims.

Interestingly, credibility and social attractiveness continue to be important factors in the online persuasive environment (Dutta-Bergman, 2004; Fogg, 2003; Metzger, Flanagin, & Medders, 2010). In social media presentations, modality matters, with the video mode apt to increase the tendency to process communicator features peripherally and text mode likely to encourage more central processing of communicator qualities (Kim & Sundar, 2016). Once again, we see that "who says it" and the type of communicator are fundamental facets of persuasion, as critical to effective persuasion today as they were in Aristotle's age of oral communication. Messages and channels have changed, but, as the song from *Casablanca* puts it, the fundamental things apply.

References

Abrams, R., Hsu, T., & Eligon, J. (2018, May 30). Closing up shop for an afternoon to address bias. *The New York Times*, B1, B5.

Allen, M. & Associates. (2002). Effect of timing of communicator identification and level of source credibility on attitude. *Communication Research Reports, 19*, 46–55.

Anderson, R. B., & McMillion, P. Y. (1995). Effects of similar and diversified modeling on African American women's efficacy expectations and intentions to perform breast self-examination. *Health Communication, 7*, 324–343.

Angier, N. (2000, November 7). Who is fat? It depends on culture. *The New York Times*, D1–D2.

Baker, P. (2019, December 10). In a swelling age of tribalism, the trust of a country teeters. *The New York Times*, A1, A16.

Belluck, P. (2009, April 26). Yes, looks do matter. *The New York Times* (Sunday Styles), 1, 8.

Berlo, D. K., Lemert, J. B., & Mertz, R. J. (1969). Dimensions for evaluating the acceptability of message sources. *Public Opinion Quarterly, 33*, 563–576.

Berscheid, E. (1966). Opinion change and communicator–communicatee similarity and dissimilarity. *Journal of Personality and Social Psychology, 4*, 670–680.

Bidgood, J., & Tavernise, S. (2018, April 25). Calls for gun control from the well-armed. *The New York Times*, A14.

Boepple, L., & Thompson, J. K. (2016). A content analytic comparison of Fitspiration and Thinspiration. *International Journal of Eating Disorders, 49*, 98–101.

Bosman, J., Kovaleski, S. F., & Del Real, J. A. (2019, March 18). A college scam built with swagger, and secrets. *The New York Times*, A1, A13.

Brock, T. C. (1965). Communicator–recipient similarity and decision change. *Journal of Personality and Social Psychology, 1*, 650–654.

Bromwich, J. E. (2019, July 11). What if being a YouTube celebrity is actually backbreaking work? *The New York Times*, D1, D4.

Brooks, D. (2011). *The social animal: The hidden sources of love, character, and achievement.* New York: Random House.

Bruni, F. (2014, April 21). Autism and the agitator. *The New York Times*. Retrieved March 20, 2016, from www.nytimes.com/2014/04/22/opinion/bruni-autism-and-the-agitator.html

Burger, J. M., Messian, N., Patel, S., Del Prado, A., & Anderson, C. (2004). What a coincidence! The effects of incidental similarity on compliance. *Personality and Social Psychology Bulletin, 30*, 35–43.

Burgoon, M. (1989). Messages and persuasive effects. In J. J. Bradac (Ed.), *Message effects in communication science* (pp. 129–164). Newbury Park, CA: Sage.

Buss, D. M., & Kenrick, D. T. (1998). Evolutionary social psychology. In D. T. Gilbert, S. T. Fiske, & G. Lindzey (Eds.), *The handbook of social psychology* (Vol. 2, 4th ed., pp. 982–1026). Boston, MA: McGraw-Hill.

Casey, N. (2015, August 15). Death penalty ruling stirs painful memories of 3 grisly killings. *The New York Times*, A17.

Chaiken, S. (1979). Communicator's physical attractiveness and persuasion. *Journal of Personality and Social Psychology, 37*, 1387–1397.

Conger, J. A. (1998, May–June). The necessary art of persuasion. *Harvard Business Review, 76*, 84–95.

Cronkhite, G., & Liska, J. (1976). A critique of factor analytic approaches to the study of credibility. *Communication Monographs, 43*, 91–107.

Crusco, A. H., & Wetzel, C. G. (1984). The Midas touch: The effects of interpersonal touch on restaurant tipping. *Personality and Social Psychology Bulletin, 10,* 512–517.

Cutlip, S. M., Center, A. H., & Broom, G. M. (2006). *Effective public relations* (9th ed.). Upper Saddle River, NJ: Pearson Prentice Hall.

Davies, W. (2018). *Nervous states: Democracy and the decline of reason.* New York: W.W. Norton.

Davis, D. (2008, September 13). Do voters want passion, policy or both? *The New York Times [Letter to the Editor],* A28.

de Botton, A. (2000). *The consolations of philosophy.* New York: Pantheon.

Dutta-Bergman, M. J. (2004). The impact of completeness and Web use motivation on the credibility of e-health information. *Journal of Communication, 54,* 337–354.

Eagly, A. H., Wood, W., & Chaiken, S. (1978). Causal inferences about communicators and their effect on opinion change. *Journal of Personality and Social Psychology, 36,* 424–435.

Einhorn, C., & Abrams, R. (2018, March 12). Groping and harassment for a couple of dollars. *The New York Times,* A1, A14.

Evans, A. T., & Clark, J. K. (2012). Source characteristics and persuasion: The role of self-monitoring in self-validation. *Journal of Experimental Social Psychology, 48,* 383–386.

Fallon, A. (1990). Culture in the mirror: Sociocultural determinants of body image. In T.F. Cash and T. Pruzinsky (Eds.), *Body images: Development, deviance, and change* (pp. 80–109). New York: Guilford.

Fogg, B. J. (2003). Motivating, influencing, and persuading users. In J. A. Jacko & A. Sears (Eds.), *The human–computer interaction handbook: Fundamentals, evolving technologies and emerging applications* (pp. 358–370). Mahwah, NJ: Lawrence Erlbaum Associates.

Fredrickson, B. L., & Roberts, T. (1997). Objectification theory: Toward understanding women's lived experiences and mental health risks. *Psychology of Women Quarterly, 21,* 173–206.

Gardner, D. (2011). *Future babble: Why expert predictions are next to worthless, and you can do better.* New York: Dutton.

Garner, R. (2005). What's in a name? Persuasion perhaps. *Journal of Consumer Psychology, 15,* 108–116.

Goethals, G. R., & Nelson, R. E. (1973). Similarity in the influence process: The belief–value distinction. *Journal of Personality and Social Psychology, 25,* 117–122.

Goodman, P. S. (2010). In case of emergency: What not to do. P. R. missteps fueled the fiascos at BP, Toyota and Goldman. *The New York Times* (Sunday Business), 1, 6, 7.

Greenberg, B. S., & Miller, G. R. (1966). The effects of low-credible sources on message acceptance. *Speech Monographs, 33,* 127–136.

Hamermesh, D. S. (2011, August 28). Ugly? You may have a case. *The New York Times* (Sunday Review), 12.

Harmon, A. (2017, June 5). Obstacle for climate science: Skeptical, stubborn students. *The New York Times,* A1, A14.

Harrington, N. G. (2013). Introduction to the special issue: Communication strategies to reduce health disparities. *Journal of Communication, 10,* 111–123.

Harrison, K., & Cantor, J. (1997). The relationship between media consumption and eating disorders. *Journal of Communication, 47*(1), 40–67.

Hart, R. P., Friedrich, G. W., & Brummett, B. (1983). *Public communication* (2nd ed.). New York: Harper & Row.

Heflick, N. A., Goldenberg, J. L., Cooper, D. P., & Puvia, E. (2011). From women to objects: Appearance focus, target gender, and perceptions of warmth, morality, and competence. *Journal of Experimental Social Psychology, 47,* 572–581.

Holmes, S. A. (1998, November 20). Klan case transcends racial divide. *The New York Times*, A14.

Hovland, C. I., Janis, I. L., & Kelley, H. H. (1953). *Communication and persuasion: Psychological studies of opinion change*. New Haven, CT: Yale University Press.

Hsu, T. (2018, February 28). Protests are common. The boycott of the N.R.A. is different. *The New York Times*, A12.

Jena, A. B., Sunstein, C. R., & Hicks, T. R. (2018, August 5). How to avoid a ticket. *The New York Times* (Sunday Review), 9.

Kalichman, S. C., & Coley, B. (1995). Context framing to enhance HIV-antibody testing messages targeted to African American women. *Health Psychology*, 14, 247–254.

Kaufman, L. (2000, September 17). And now, a few more words about breasts. *The New York Times* [Week in Review], 3.

Kim, K. J., & Sundar, S. S. (2016). Mobile persuasion: Can screen size and presentation mode make a difference to trust? *Human Communication Research*, 42, 45–70.

Kim, S. S., Kaplowitz, S., & Johnston, M. V. (2004). The effects of physician empathy on patient satisfaction and compliance. *Evaluation & the Health Professions*, 27, 237–251.

King, S. W., Minami, Y., & Samovar, L. A. (1985). A comparison of Japanese and American perceptions of source credibility. *Communication Research Reports*, 2, 76–79.

Kolata, G. (2018, August 21). When a doctor's race matters. *The New York Times*, D3.

Kreps, G. L. (2006). Communication and racial inequities in health care. *American Behavioral Scientist*, 49, 760–774.

Kuczynski, A. (2006). *Beauty junkies: Inside our $15 billion obsession with cosmetic surgery*. New York: Doubleday.

Leodoro, G., & Lynn, M. (2007). The effect of server posture on the tips of Whites and Blacks. *Journal of Applied Social Psychology*, 37, 201–209.

Lynn, M. (2009). Determinants and consequences of female attractiveness and sexiness: Realistic tests with restaurant waitresses. *Archives of Sexual Behavior*, 38, 737–745.

Lynn, M., & Mynier, K. (1993). Effect of server posture on restaurant tipping. *Journal of Applied Social Psychology*, 23, 678–685.

Manago, A. M., Ward, L. M., Lemm, K. M., Reed, L., & Seabrook, R. (2015). Facebook involvement, objectified body consciousness, body shame, and sexual assertiveness in college women and men. *Sex Roles*, 72, 1–14.

Marcus, E. N. (2006, November 21). When young doctors strut too much of their stuff. *The New York Times*, D5.

McCroskey, J. C. (1997). *An introduction to rhetorical communication* (7th ed.). Boston, MA: Allyn and Bacon.

McCroskey, J. C., & Teven, J. J. (1999). Goodwill: A reexamination of the construct and its measurement. *Communication Monographs*, 66, 90–103.

McCroskey, J. C., & Young, T. J. (1981). Ethos and credibility: The construct and its measurement after three decades. *Central States Speech Journal*, 32, 24–34.

Metzger, M. J., Flanagin, A. J., & Medders, R. B. (2010). Social and heuristic approaches to credibility evaluation online. *Journal of Communication*, 60, 413–439.

Mnookin, S. (2011). *The panic virus: A true story of medicine, science, and fear*. New York: Simon & Schuster.

Naftulin, D. H., Ware, J. E., & Donnelly, F. A. (1973). The Doctor Fox lecture: A paradigm of educational seduction. *Journal of Medical Education*, 48, 630–635.

Nichols, T. (2017). *The death of expertise: The campaign against established knowledge and why it matters*. New York: Oxford University Press.

O'Keefe, D. J. (1987). The persuasive effects of delaying identification of high- and low-credibility communicators: A meta-analytic review. *Central States Speech Journal, 38*, 63–72.

O'Keefe, D. J. (2016). *Persuasion: Theory and research* (3rd ed.). Thousand Oaks, CA: Sage.

Olson, E. (2016, February 22). A lingerie brand offers real women as (role) models. *The New York Times*, B3.

Perloff, R. M. (2001). *Persuading people to have safer sex: Applications of social science to the AIDS crisis*. Mahwah, NJ: Lawrence Erlbaum Associates.

Petty, R. E., & Cacioppo, J. T. (1986). The Elaboration Likelihood Model of persuasion. In L. Berkowitz (Ed.), *Advances in experimental social psychology* (Vol. 19, pp. 123–205). New York: Academic Press.

Petty, R. E., & Wegener, D. T. (1998). Matching versus mismatching attitude functions: Implications for scrutiny of persuasive messages. *Personality and Social Psychology Bulletin, 24*, 227–240.

Puente, M. (1999, September 7). Casual clothes hit sour note with some. *USA Today*, 1D–2D.

Rhoads, K. V. L., & Cialdini, R. B. (2002). The business of influence: Principles that lead to success in commercial settings. In J. P. Dillard & M. Pfau (Eds.), *The persuasion handbook: Developments in theory and practice* (pp. 513–542). Thousand Oaks, CA: Sage.

Rind, B., & Bordia, P. (1995) Effect of server's "thank you" and personalization on restaurant tipping. *Journal of Applied Social Psychology, 25*, 745–751.

Rind, B., & Bordia, P. (1996). Effect on restaurant tipping of male and female servers drawing a happy, smiling face on the backs of customers' checks. *Journal of Applied Social Psychology, 26*, 218–225.

Saul, S. (2005, November 28). Gimme an Rx! Cheerleaders pep up drug sales. *The New York Times*, A1, A16.

Segrin, C. (1993). The effects of nonverbal behavior on outcomes of compliance gaining attempts. *Communication Studies, 44*, 169–189.

Sharma, A. (1999). Does the salesperson like customers? A conceptual and empirical examination of the persuasive effect of perceptions of the salesperson's affect toward customers. *Psychology and Marketing, 16*, 141–162.

Shavitt, S. (2019). Culture and attitude theorizing: Attitudes in Western and non-Western contexts. In D. Albarracín & B. T. Johnson (Eds.), *The handbook of attitudes* (Vol. 1: Basic principles, pp. 602–624). New York: Routledge.

Smedley, B. D., Stith, A. Y., & Nelson, A. R. (Eds.). (2003). *Unequal treatment: Confronting racial and ethnic disparities in health care*. Washington, DC: National Academies Press.

Sparks, G. G. (2016). *Media effects research: A basic overview* (5th ed.). Boston, MA: Wadsworth Cengage Learning.

Trampe, D., Stapel, D. A., Siero, F. W., & Mulder, H. (2010). Beauty as a tool: The effect of model attractiveness, product relevance, and elaboration likelihood on advertising effectiveness. *Psychology & Marketing, 27*, 1101–1121.

Trebay, G. (2018, September 18). For capitalism, every social leap forward is a marketing opportunity. *The New York Times*. Retrieved July 21, 2019, from www.nytimes.com/2018/09/18/style/gender-nonbinary-bra

Tweedy, D. (2015, May 17). The case for Black doctors. *The New York Times* (Sunday Review), 1, 7.

Whalen, D. J. (1996). *I see what you mean: Persuasive business communication*. Thousand Oaks, CA: Sage.

Wilson, M. (2011, May 14). Your palm's telling me you must let go. Of $27,000. *The New York Times*, A15.

Zarnoth, P., & Sniezek, J. A. (1997). The social influence of confidence in group decision making. *Journal of Experimental Social Psychology, 33*, 345–366.

Chapter 11

Fundamentals of the Message

How should you say it? Just how should you mold your message? Should you tweet the emotional phrase or stick with the dull, but venerable, statement? Should you hit the audience over the head with the argument or hedge your bets? Is it better to wow them with fancy stats or tug at their heartstrings by telling a tale of woe? If you want to convince e-cigarette users to quit, should you scare the bejeebers out of them or just frighten them a little? These questions center on the message, a time-honored factor in persuasion research, as relevant in an era of Twitter and trolls as it was during the age of persuasive speeches screamed out in the public squares of antiquity. The message, with its many features, is the focus of the next two chapters.

The message has endlessly fascinated persuasion scholars. Aristotle delineated different message factors, emphasizing that deductive syllogisms are the centerpiece of strong rhetorical arguments. Twentieth-century rhetoricians, building on Aristotle's foundations, identified key components of valid, cogent arguments (Toulmin, 1958). Contemporary scholars assume as a first principle that messages cannot be understood without appreciating the psychology of the audience. They have explored the influences of different message factors on receivers, trying to understand which components have the most impact and why. This chapter focuses on the structure, content, and style of the persuasive message. Chapter 12 explores the psychology of emotional messages, primarily fear appeals.

Understanding the Message

It seems pretty obvious.

The message – what you say and how you say it – influences people. Uh-huh, an intelligent person impatient with intellectual theories might think; now can we move on? Persuasion scholars would like to move on too – they have books to write, students to teach, and families to feed. But they – and you too, no doubt – recognize that the message construct is so big and unwieldy that it needs to be broken down, decomposed, and analyzed in terms of content and process.

This chapter explores four categories of message factor (see Table 11.1). The first concerns the structure of the message – how it is prepared and organized. The second is the specific content of the communication. The third factor is framing; and the fourth focuses on a related factor, language – how

Table 11.1 Key Message Factors

Message structure

1. Conclusion drawing
2. Message sidedness
3. Order of presentation (primacy vs. recency*)

Message content

1. Evidence
2. Narrative

Framing

1. Frames that define the problem and recommend a solution

Language

1. Speed of speech and other paralinguistic features
2. Powerless versus powerful language; forceful speech
3. Intense language

Emotional appeals

1. Fear-arousing messages
2. Guilt appeals

* Primacy occurs when an argument presented early in a message, or the first of two opposing messages, is most persuasive. Recency occurs when an argument presented later in a message, or the second of two opposing messages, is most compelling. There is no conclusive evidence in favor of either primacy or recency. Effects depend on situational factors, such as amount of time that elapses between messages, and audience involvement.

communicators use words and symbols to persuade an audience. Emotional appeals are discussed in the next chapter. The focus is why and when message factors work, and their applications to everyday persuasion.

Message Structure

Just what influences do persuasive messages exert, and how does the structure of the communication influence attitudes? These are time-honored questions, and communication research has offered contemporary insights. There are also practical issues at stake. Communicators want to know how to package their message and the best way to organize arguments. There are two specific issues here.

The first concerns the most persuasive way to conclude the message. The second examines whether communicators should present both sides of the issue or just their own, and some of the implications for contemporary media.

Conclusion Drawing

Should persuaders *explicitly* draw the conclusion? Should they wrap things up for listeners in an unambiguous, forceful fashion, making it 100 percent clear which path they want audience members to pursue? Or should they be more circumspect and indirect, letting audience members put things together for themselves? These questions point to the question of explicit versus implicit *conclusion drawing*. Arguments can be made for both sides. Perhaps, since audience attention wanders, it is best to present a detailed and forceful conclusion. On the other hand, people might prefer that persuaders not tell them explicitly what to do, but instead allow them to arrive at the conclusion on their own.

A meta-analysis of research provides us with an answer to this dilemma. O'Keefe (1997) found that messages clearly or explicitly articulating an overall conclusion are more persuasive than those that omit a conclusion. As McGuire bluntly observed: "In communication, it appears, it is not sufficient to lead the horse to the water; one must also push his head underneath to get him to drink" (1969, p. 209). Making the conclusion explicit minimizes the chances that individuals will be confused about where the communicator stands. It also helps people to comprehend the message, which in turn enhances source evaluations and persuasion (Cruz, 1998). These findings have important implications for health communication. They suggest that doctors should not beat around the bush when explaining complicated medical issues to patients, lest they get lost in the arcane terminology. Instead, they should make certain to draw the conclusions explicitly, clearly, and humanely.

One or Two Sides?

A *one-sided message* presents one perspective on the issue. A *two-sided message* offers arguments on behalf of both the persuader's position and the opposition. Which is more persuasive?

You might argue that it is best to ignore the other side and hammer home your perspective. After all, this lets you spend precious time detailing reasons why your side is correct. On the other hand, if you overlook opposition arguments with which everyone is familiar, you look like you have something to hide. For example, let's say you are one of those individuals who is fed up with people who text and yak on their cell phone when they drive. You have decided, after years of frustration, to take this issue to the city council. Should you present one or both sides of this issue to council members?

A review of *message sidedness* research provides an answer to this question. Two communication scholars conducted *meta-analyses* of research on one- and two-sided messages. A meta-analysis is a study of other studies. A researcher locates all the investigations of a phenomenon and uses statistical procedures to determine the strength of the findings. After exhaustively reviewing the many studies in this area, researchers Mike Allen (1998) and Daniel J. O'Keefe (1999) reached the same conclusion, something that does not always happen in social science research! Researchers O'Keefe and Allen concluded that *two-sided messages influence attitudes more than one-sided messages, provided one very important condition is met: The message refutes opposition arguments.* When the communication mentions, but not does demolish, an opponent's viewpoint, a two-sided message is actually less compelling than a one-sided message.

Refutational two-sided messages, as they are called, gain their persuasive advantage by: (a) enhancing the credibility of the speaker (he or she is perceived as honest enough to discuss both sides of the coin); and (b) providing cogent reasons why opposing arguments are wrong. As O'Keefe (2016) noted, "Persuaders are best advised to meet opposing arguments head-on, by refuting them, rather than ignoring or (worse still) merely mentioning such counterarguments" (O'Keefe, 2016, p. 225).

This has obvious implications for your speech urging a ban on talking on a cell phone while driving. You should present arguments for your side (texting or talking on a handheld cell phone while driving is a deadly distractor) and the other position (there are numerous other distractors, like fiddling with a GPS navigation device or applying makeup, which should also be banned if local government is planning to restrict cell phone use – but we can't ban them all). You should then refute the other side, arguing texting while driving causes more serious accidents than other distractors because it interferes with visual processing skills, and talking on the phone while driving is a prolonged, not temporary, distraction from the road. You could end on a quantitative crescendo by citing data, such as a National Safety Council estimate that some 1.6 million crashes that occur each year – 28 percent of the total – are caused by drivers who are texting or using cell phones, or that drivers are cognitively impaired for as many as 15 seconds after sending a text while driving (e.g., Brody, 2011). Armed with a two-sided argument, you stand a better chance of convincing your city council to adopt a more safety-conscious policy on cell phone use.

Is there ever a time when a persuader should present a one-sided message? Yes – when the message is directed to audiences who strongly agree with the communicator's position. Given what we know about strong attitudes (see Chapter 5), it would be foolhardy to try to present both sides to members of a political group who have passionate feelings about the topic. They would probably contrast the other position, viewing it as more different from their viewpoint than it really is, and would perceive the communicator as biased against their position. For a politician trying to shore up support among allies, delivering a two-sided message that gave the other side credence would be the kiss of political death. However, in most ordinary persuasion situations, where message receivers do not have strong attitudes toward one position, a two-sided message on behalf of Position A that mentions and refutes Position B is likely to be compelling.

On a more philosophical level, the sidedness research leaves us with a reassuring finding about human nature. It tells us that communicators can change attitudes when they are fair, mention both sides, and offer cogent arguments in support of their position. The results celebrate values most of us would affirm: Honesty and intellectual rigor.

Misinformation and Media

There is another aspect to the message sidedness research, one with contemporary implications for mass and social media that raises darker issues for persuasion. The media and Internet are filled with factually inaccurate information on a number of topics, including Iraqi weapons of mass destruction, climate change, and the link between vaccines and autism (see Chapter 5). Sometimes the facts are conveyed truthfully, but turn out to be false later on. Yet individuals tenaciously believe the original facts are true, a case of misinformation. In other instances, the information is false and spread for propagandistic goals in what is known as disinformation (Lewandowsky et al., 2013).

We look to the media to offer an accurate rendition of the facts, but sometimes problems ensue. Journalists feel a professional obligation to present both sides and don't want to be accused of harboring a bias. Thus, when reporters dutifully describe duelling positions in public policy debates, they can treat the position that has no facts in its behalf as equivalent to the viewpoint that is corroborated by scientific evidence. Social media, for its part, can feature posts from both groups, and individuals may assume the facts from both ideas are both true, when one post contains inaccurate information. Here is where the research on two-sided messages takes on intriguing practical importance. A news story that offers balanced claims for and against a proposition can be viewed as presenting a two-sided message. Recall that the research on message sidedness shows that when a communication presents both sides, but fails to refute the opposing side, it has weak effects on attitudes. Thus, when a news story incorrectly presents information that is factually incorrect alongside information that is true, it can cause individuals to treat the information equivalently, thereby misinforming news consumers.

Graham N. Dixon and Christopher E. Clarke (2013) explored this issue, focusing on the controversial claim that vaccines cause autism. Scientific evidence clearly indicates there is no link between vaccines and autism, but some partisan activists and celebrities (see Chapter 10) continue to make this claim, sometimes because of a misunderstanding of scientific research and in other cases because they harbor a cultural suspicion of medical vaccines. In their study, Dixon and Clarke randomly assigned research participants to read one of four articles. A first article correctly observed that an immunization vaccine does *not* cause autism; a second article incorrectly claimed that the vaccine *could* cause autism; the key third article contained information on both sides (pro- and anti-link between the immunization vaccine and autism), and a fourth group, a control, read an article about an unrelated topic.

Intriguingly, individuals who read the article refuting the vaccine–autism link or the unrelated control group message were significantly more certain that the immunization vaccine does not cause autism than participants who read the balanced coverage. They also were less apt than balanced coverage participants to believe that scientific experts are divided on the issue (there is, of course, scientific consensus that vaccines *don't* cause autism). Exposure to factually inaccurate information diluted the effect of the scientific facts. A two-sided message that failed to rebut incorrect information left individuals with the mistaken view that vaccines might cause autism, a belief with problematic consequences for public health. This suggests that news articles can increase misinformation by suggesting that two sides are equivalent when one is factually incorrect. Exposure to social media posts that present false information on a topic, in tandem with posts that offer an accurate rendition of the facts, can unwittingly mislead and misinform. This can have serious consequences if people form false beliefs from non-refutational two-sided messages, concluding that they should not trust vaccines, global warming is not a problem, or (during the time of the Iraq war) that Iraq possessed weapons of mass destruction (WMDs).

Researchers have begun to explore ways to use persuasive communications to prevent increases in misinformation (Dixon et al., 2015; Kortenkamp & Basten, 2015). This is not easy when people have strong attitudes on the subject (Bode & Vraga, 2015; Nyhan & Reifler, 2010). But research offers hope. Empirical work suggests that persuaders hoping to correct mistaken beliefs should refute the other position with compelling evidence and add a couple of persuasive wrinkles. On a controversial issue, where there is misinformation or deliberately disseminated disinformation about the scientific facts, persuaders can point out that the overwhelming number of scientists agree that, for example, vaccines do *not* cause autism, or that global warming *is* an increasing risk to the planet. The source can serve as a decision-making heuristic or catalyze thinking, as noted in Chapter 8. Communicators can highlight source effects by showing reinforcing visual cues, such as the photograph of a group of scientists, who pictorially exemplify scientific consensus on the issue (Dixon et al., 2015). They can also develop persuasive narratives to counteract misinformed beliefs (Sangalang, Ophir, & Cappella, 2019). With misinformation about health and politics proliferating on social media, it behooves us to develop empirically based strategies on how to craft two-sided messages that convincingly convey the facts about contemporary issues.

Message Content

Evidence

- Passive smoking is a major cause of lung cancer. A husband or wife who has never smoked has an approximately 16 percent increased chance of contracting lung cancer if he or she lives with a smoker.
- Median earnings for college graduates are more than $21,000 higher than median salary and wages for high school graduates in a given year and nearly twice as much over the course of a lifetime.
- Over the past few decades, annual average temperature in the United States has increased by 1.2° Fahrenheit and by 1.8°F, compared to the beginning of the last century. Additional rises in annual average temperature of approximately 2.5°F are expected over the next several decades, regardless of future emission levels (USGCRP, 2018).

These diverse arguments have one thing in common: They use evidence to substantiate their claims. Evidence is employed by persuaders working in a variety of settings, including advertising, health, and politics. Evidence, John C. Reinard notes, is a classic "building block of arguments," or "information used as proof" (1991, p. 102). *Evidence* is a broad term, McCroskey (1969) observes. He defined the concept more than 50 years ago and the definition still holds. As McCroskey noted, evidence can be regarded as: "factual statements originating from a source other than the speaker, objects not created by the speaker, and opinions of persons other than the speaker that are offered in support of the speaker's claims" (1969, p. 170).

Evidence consists of factual assertions, quantitative information (like statistics; see Figure 11.1), eyewitness statements, testimonials, or opinions advanced by credible sources. We are all familiar with evidence and have witnessed its use many times. Communication researchers, also intrigued by evidence, have conducted numerous studies over a 50-year period, probing the effects of evidence on attitudes. Does evidence change attitudes?

You bet.

"The use of evidence produces more attitude change than the use of no evidence," Rodney A. Reynolds and J. Lynn Reynolds declare after reviewing the many studies in the area (2002, p. 428). Reinard goes further, observing that "there actually may be more consistency in evidence research than can be found in almost any other area of persuasion. Evidence appears to produce general persuasive effects that appear surprisingly stable" (1988, p. 46).

When Evidence Persuades

Evidence is especially persuasive when attributed to a highly credible source – an outgrowth of principles discussed in previous chapters. Evidence is also more apt to change attitudes, the more plausible and novel it is (Morley & Walker, 1987).

Persuaders must do more than simply mention evidence: Audience members must recognize that evidence has been offered in support of a proposition and perceive the evidence to be legitimate (Parrott et al., 2005; Reynolds & Reynolds, 2002). If individuals are dozing off and don't hear the evidence, or they dispute the legitimacy of the factual assertions, the evidence presented has less impact on attitudes.

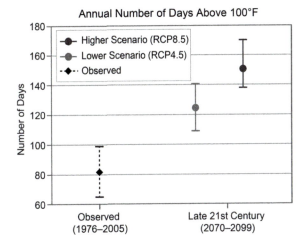

Figure 11.1 This Chart Illustrates How Evidence Can Be Persuasively Harnessed in Persuasion, and on a Topic of Global Importance. The chart depicts the average annual number of days above 100°F in Phoenix, Arizona from 1976–2005 and projections of the average number of days per year that exceed 100°F through the end of this century. The lower scenario is presumably a somewhat more conservative, less serious projection, while the higher scenario projects even more ultra-hot days. Both scenarios, based on expert scientific projections, show the dramatic increase in expected heat waves, raising significant policy issues and showcasing the persuasive power of evidence.

Data from USGCRP (2018, p. 56)

Evidence, in short, must be processed. The ELM reminds us that the ways in which evidence is elaborated determine its effect on persuasion. When people are highly involved in or knowledgeable about the issue, evidence will be processed centrally. Under these circumstances, quality of evidence matters. Cogent evidence can change people's minds. But remember: Even the most compelling evidence is unlikely to change strong attitudes – those that touch on the self-concept or core values.

Evidence can have striking effects under low involvement, but it works through different processes. When people lack motivation or ability to decipher the issue, they rely on peripheral cues. They may go along with arguments that sound impressive because the communicator cites many facts, uses highfalutin statistics, or throws in testimonial statements. The trappings of evidence are more important than the legal or statistical quality of the facts. Evidence operates more as a cue than an argument when people are not motivated or knowledgeable about the issue. In such cases, communicators can use evidence truthfully, or they can lie with statistics (Huff, 1954). This highlights once again the ways persuasion can be used for morally positive, as well as more questionable, purposes.

But let's end this discussion on a hopeful note. Despite its many limits, particularly when people interpret data through the lens of their own biases, evidence can push through the dark scrim of distortion. When communicators are determined to help people appreciate the empirical facts about a topic and individuals are motivated to look at issues, even those where they have strong positions, objectively, evidence can work wonders.

Some years back, James Sutter, a science teacher in a rural Ohio town, drew on the best of his patient pedagogy to reach the many students in his class, who were climate change skeptics. Sutter called on a combination of factual descriptions, humor, and even a field trip to a local stream to show them that recent warming of Earth's climate could be ascribed "to heat-trapping gases released by burning fossil fuels like the coal." Jacynda Patton was one of those skeptics, her doubts instilled by the skepticism of her father, a former coal miner who felt angry at the environmental groups that he believed had cost him his mining job. But one day at the field trip, when Jacynda noticed that water at the local stream had turned neon orange and the pH levels in the water were highly acidic, she took note, began reading, and looking at the evidence in a different light. "O.K., I'm not going to lie. I did a 180," she told her friend, Gwen Beatty, "This is happening, and we have to fix it" (Harmon, 2017, A1, A14).

Sutter, the science teacher, could not work miracles. He could not reach Gwen Beatty, a straight-A student who remained super-skeptical, partly because her mother and uncle doubted climate change. But his painstaking use of evidence changed the beliefs of a number of students, who initially refused to even consider that humans have contributed to global warming.

The same phenomenon has occurred on a broader scale. A majority of Americans say that global warming has exerted some impact on their communities, and relative to a decade ago, they believe that dealing with climate change should be a top government priority (Funk & Kennedy, 2019). How did these attitude changes occur? They occurred partly through messages marshalling evidence. Evidence, as the ELM reminds us, served multiple functions in influencing climate change attitudes: The multitude of facts were centrally processed as arguments; cool, complex graphs worked as peripheral cues; the vast data encouraged people to think over the issues; and the voluminous numbers, buttressed by credible sources, instilled confidence that individuals' global warming concerns were valid. Given the calamitous future that faces us if we don't make pressing changes in our global environment, it is salutary that evidence has had an impact, though its slow, incremental impacts on the public and policymakers continue to worry climate scientists.

Evidence, with its reliable psychological effects, is not the only compelling aspect of the message. The next section continues the discussion of the persuasive message, focusing on an attribute that works through very different psychological processes from evidence.

Narrative

A movie plot spins around in your head for days as you mull over the moral courage the main character displayed in the face of personal danger. A short story presents a compelling portrait of a teenage girl brimming with pride, but also feeling anxious, as she delivers a baby she had once considered aborting. You are moved by a television drama that tells the tale of a young man who joins the Peace Corps and migrates to South Africa to escape his family, only to find himself caught up in the daily suffering experienced by children with HIV. The program offers a nuanced portrait of the kids – their innocence in the face of a global pandemic, but also their streetwise antics as they pick the Peace Corps activist's pockets as he sleeps. The program movingly depicts the stark realities of AIDS in Africa, along with the personal challenges the characters face as they deal with the brutal challenges of everyday life.

The examples – hypothetical, but similar to current media fare – exemplify narrative persuasion (Bilandzic & Busselle, 2013). We are familiar with communications that harness stories in the service of persuasion. They are all around us: On television, in movie theaters, on our Kindles, and sometimes, in glorified form, in video games. As discussed in Chapter 2, these communications fall into the category of borderline persuasion because the communicator typically does not intend to change attitudes so much as to enlighten or agitate. And yet, as Timothy C. Brock and his colleagues note, "Public narratives – the stories we hear every day in the news media and the stories that we consume in books, films, plays, soap operas, and so forth – command a large share of our waking attention" (Brock, Strange, & Green, 2002, p. 1).

What's more, social narratives in books and movies have profoundly affected society. Charles Dickens' descriptions of life in nineteenth-century England awakened people to the plight of children working in dangerous factories. Novels about race (Harriet Beecher Stowe's *Uncle Tom's Cabin*, James Baldwin's *The Fire Next Time*) may have helped raise consciousness about the ills of slavery and racial prejudice, perhaps laying some of the groundwork for political action (see Figure 11.2). The late Toni

Figure 11.2 Narrative Persuasion – the Telling of Stories – Can Powerfully Influence Attitudes. The nineteenth-century novel *Uncle Tom's Cabin* is widely believed to have stirred the conscience of Northerners in the United States, perhaps enhancing empathy for the plight of American Blacks. Narratives depicted in books, movies, songs, and video games can also change beliefs and attitudes. Research is shedding light on the processes and effects of narrative messages

Image courtesy of Getty Images

Morrison's (1987) impassioned *Beloved* moved readers to appreciate the multiple, conflicting ways that slavery depraved humanity and deprived human beings of their dignity.

The list of movies that have influenced beliefs and attitudes is seemingly endless. One thinks of *Schindler's List, American Sniper, Saving Private Ryan, The Help, 12 Years a Slave, Spotlight, The Big Short*, even *Super Size Me*. Television programs like *Breaking Bad* and *Orange is the New Black* also have conveyed compelling visual narratives. Video games increasingly tell heart-rending, evocative stories about a variety of issues. The affecting *Gone Home* employed a first-person shooter perspective to relate the story of two adolescent girls in love (Suellentrop, 2014). Emma Kidwell's games told stories about her personal struggles, from her angst about her biracial identity to watching her grandmother struggle with dementia (Zaveri, 2019).

For years, the academic literature on persuasion neglected the impact of public narratives on attitudes, emphasizing instead the effects of advocacy (e.g., messages deliberately designed to change attitudes). Over the past decade, researchers have discovered narrative and have explored the impact of a multitude of entertainment stories on attitudes and intentions. Researchers have probed effects of narratives on such issues as cancer, unplanned teenage pregnancy, obesity, HIV/AIDS, and the death penalty (e.g., Dunlop, Wakefield, & Kashima, 2010; Moyer-Gusé & Nabi, 2010; Murphy et al., 2011; Niederdeppe et al., 2014; Niederdeppe, Shapiro, & Porticella, 2011; Slater, Rouner, & Long, 2006; Smith, Downs, & Witte, 2007).

What exactly is a narrative? It is a "symbolic representation of events" that employs elements that typically are not used in persuasive messages (Bilandzic & Busselle, 2013). These include characters, plotlines, and dramatic devices that draw more on the features of fiction than on explicit advocacy. Specifically, *narrative* is defined as "any cohesive and coherent story with an identifiable beginning, middle, and end that provides information about scene, characters, and conflict; raises unanswered questions or unresolved conflict; and provides resolution" (Hinyard & Kreuter, 2007, p. 778).

Narrative seems to work through different psychological processes from advocacy messages that employ standard argumentative fare, such as speeches, public service announcements, and blogs. Advocacy communications influence attitudes by evoking central and peripheral processing, calling on social norms, and arousing inconsistencies. Narrative is different.

Transporting Us to Different Places

Transportation, articulated by Melanie C. Green and Timothy C. Brock (Brock et al., 2000, 2002), offers an engaging view of narrative impact. Great novels, artistic works and interactive narratives perused on an iPad (Green & Jenkins, 2014) transport people to different mental arenas – the world of the author's imagination. "The traveler returns to the world of origin, somewhat changed by the journey" (Gerrig, 1993, p. 11). Psychologically transported or immersed in a story, individuals generate mental images of events that, while literally untrue, play out figuratively in their minds, inducing questioning of existing beliefs.

While transfixed by the artist's creation of an imaginary world, individuals may be more open to questioning their ideas than when they are focusing on an ordinary persuasive message. The narrative may inhibit the normal process of counterarguing with a persuasive message, in part because it can be psychologically difficult to offer logical arguments to a panorama of mental images that a story stimulates (Bilandzic & Busselle, 2013; see also Mazzocco & Brock, 2006; Niederdeppe et al., 2012; Skalski et al., 2009).

Alternatively, when narratives transport people, they achieve persuasive effects by working through more emotional processes than those emphasized by the now-familiar Elaboration Likelihood Model – processes that, while not entirely understood, involve shifting a sense of time and location from the everyday world to the transfixing world of the story, with its compelling models of human endeavor (Busselle & Bilandzic, 2008; Quintero Johnson & Sangalang, 2017; see also Shen & Seung, 2018).

Pioneering Study

Transportation captures the experience a lot of us have when we become immersed in a story. In research you have to test your ideas in the real world, and Green and Brock (2000) devised a nifty way to study these issues empirically. They developed a scale to measure the tendency to become transported to the narrative world created by the artist. Their scale includes items like: "I was mentally involved in the narrative while reading it" and "I could picture myself in the scene of the events described in the narrative." Focusing on the reading experience, Green and Brock asked research participants to read an evocative story, "Murder at the Mall," that concerned a college student whose younger sister is brutally murdered by a psychiatric patient at the mall. The researchers then asked participants a series of questions about the story and characters.

Eager to determine the impact of being transported into a narrative world, Green and Brock examined participants' responses to questions, such as those above. Individuals who strongly agreed that transportation scale items described them to a tee were classified as high in transportation. Those who said these statements did not describe their personalities particularly well were classified as low in transportation. Highly transported individuals were more influenced by the story, reporting more beliefs consistent with the narrative. After reading the story, they were more likely than low-transported participants to believe that the world was less just and psychiatric patients' freedoms should be curtailed. They were less inclined to doubt the story, viewing it as more authentic than those low in transportation. Thus, transportation helps us appreciate how stories can transfix and influence. Fiction, which does not literally describe everyday life but offers deeper truths, can persuade and influence attitudes on different topics (Appel & Malečkar, 2012).

Other Research

Emboldened by this perspective and intrigued about its applications to television entertainment, four University of Southern California researchers, located not far from the world's television and movie entertainment capital, explored whether a lymphoma storyline in a Hollywood television drama, *Desperate Housewives*, could transport viewers, helping them to develop more healthy attitudes toward social support for cancer.

Viewers who were psychologically transported by the program were particularly likely to feel positively about the importance of social support during cancer and to talk to family and friends about cancer (Murphy et al., 2011). Similarly, but dramatically, a heart-rending narrative about a patient who lost her battle with melanoma psychologically transported people, increasing intentions to perform a critical skin self-exam (Jensen et al., 2017). Transportation, by lifting people from their ordinary tendency to mentally argue with positions they oppose, can lead to more openness to alternative points of view, perhaps increasing tolerance for different perspectives (Cohen, Tal-Or, & Mazor-Tregerman, 2015).

Over the past two decades, a number of studies have explored transportation, and the findings are clear. Narratives that transport individuals to different psychological places can influence affect, beliefs, and attitudes about a variety of issues (Van Laer et al., 2014). Transportation into conventional genres, like books, as well as into the virtual world of video games, can exert persuasive effects, as documented by an intriguing study that found transportation into a health-focused video game reduced intent to drive after drinking alcoholic drinks (Burrows & Blanton, 2016).

At the same time, narrative being complicated, other processes underlie the effects of compelling stories. Besides transporting people, narratives can change attitudes by encouraging identification with characters, facilitating the perception of similarity between oneself and the protagonist (in this way activating the self more directly), and evoking negative emotions that can motivate attitude change (Banerjee & Greene, 2012; de Graaf et al., 2012; Hoeken, Kolthoff, & Sanders, 2016; Moyer-Gusé, Chung, & Jain, 2011; Moyer-Gusé & Nabi, 2010; Tal-Or & Cohen, 2010; Tal-Or & Tsfati, 2018; Yoo et al., 2014; Zhou & Shapiro, 2017). Taken together, this research has interesting implications for efforts to alleviate social problems.

Teen Pregnancy

With nearly 3 percent of girls between the ages of 15 and 19 giving birth in the United States, a rate that is higher than in any other developed nation, teenage childbearing is clearly a pressing social problem (Kearney & Levine, 2014). As you probably know, MTV, in the past, produced several reality shows that portray the drama, tribulations, and gritty challenges that teenage moms face. First came *16 and Pregnant*; three spinoffs, *Teen Mom*, *Teen Mom 2*, and *Teen Mom 3*, followed. Contrary to expectations, *16 and Pregnant* did not show how cool it could be to be a teen mom. Instead, it described the gritty difficulties adolescents face in caring for and bringing up a child. The program has a moving dramatic narrative, as episodes, produced in reality TV format, follow the emotional roller coaster of six months of pregnancy, childbirth, and parenthood of different teenagers across the country. The conversations are not pretty; they focus on money, religion, gossip, graduating from high school, dreams left behind, care (and love) of a child, and conflicted relationships with the boyfriend-fathers.

Could these narratives exert an impact on beliefs, attitudes, or behavior? Two researchers concluded they could and do.

In an innovative study, Kearney and Levine (2014) found that *16 and Pregnant* was associated with significant spikes in Google searches and tweets about "birth control and abortion." More intriguingly, they discovered that there was a sharper decline in teen childbearing rates in areas with a higher viewership of MTV programs. Kearney and Levine reported a nearly 6 percent drop in teen births in the year-and-a-half after the show was aired. Consistent with scholarship on narrative persuasion, the program's storyline could have induced young women to question the romance they associate with pregnancy, leading to a reduction in teenage birth rates. Of course, we can't be sure the program was the sole cause.

It is possible that other factors could have accounted for the decline in teen birth rates, such as a tendency for adolescents residing in high MTV-viewing areas to be concomitantly exposed to news or other messages about harmful consequences of teen pregnancy. Adolescents' identification with, and perceived similarity to, the teenage moms also influence attitudes toward teen pregnancy (Behm-Morawitz et al., 2019). Clearly, we need more research with different programs and populations. But the findings suggest, with a real-world edge, that narratives can influence deep-seated attitudes and behaviors. Indeed, with a contemporary twist, narratives that allow receivers to customize the story can, under certain conditions, facilitate persuasive effects (Walter, Murphy, & Gillig, 2018).

When Are Narratives Influential?

Narratives are not always effective. They are not a magic bullet. Alas, the impact of particular narrative features depends on the cognitive goal the persuader hopes to accomplish (Zhou & Niederdeppe, 2017). One of the classic issues that bedevil researchers is whether narratives, with their emphasis on personalized, emotionally engaging stories, have a greater impact than another core persuasion variable, evidence, which emphasizes scientifically compelling facts and cold numbers.

Some scholars argue that narratives are more effective than evidence. They observe that persuaders – running the gamut from attorneys to advocacy groups to health practitioners – frequently call on vivid, personalized stories, hoping these will tug at our heartstrings and influence beliefs (see Box 11.1). Never mind that these stories sometimes are based on the experience of just one person, and statistics derive from the experiences of hundreds, maybe thousands. Vivid case histories evoke stronger mental images than abstractly presented information, are easier to access from memory, and are therefore more likely to influence attitudes when the individual is trying to decide whether to accept message recommendations (Rook, 1987). Narratives and graphic images are – let's face it – more interesting than statistical evidence (Green & Brock, 2000). As stories, they engage the imagination and are "intuitively appealing to humans, as we are all essentially storytellers and avid story recipients" (Kopfman et al., 1998, p. 281). The expression "one death is a tragedy, a million deaths is a statistic" captures this viewpoint, highlighting the influence that stories – and vivid images – exert on attitudes. Several years back, a social media image – the heart-rending picture of a dead Syrian child lying face down on a beach – moved many people across the globe, symbolizing the tragedy of the Syrian migrant crisis.

Similarly, in a contemporary update (there is never a let-up in tragic injustice), a 2019 photograph of a father and daughter, both dead, lying side by side, faces down in the muddy river on the Rio Grande banks, stirred emotions worldwide, capturing the hazardous journey migrants experience when they try to travel from Mexico to the United States. It also called attention to governments' failure to figure out ways to save the lives of migrants caught in the crossfire of poverty, gang violence, and political imbroglios, a collective indifference that moved one writer to pin a finger of blame on all of us for looking at the vivid pictures, "secure in our reactions, perennially missing the point," until we put them away and do nothing (Cole, 2019, p. 10).

Vivid messages, themselves mini-narratives, thus galvanize our emotions, influencing us even if they don't always produce behavioral or policy action.

Let's return now to the more prosaic issue of the role of evidence in everyday persuasion situations, and the more narrow scientific comparison of evidence and narrative. Thinking analytically, researchers note that graphic images, such as the single-case exemplars described above, and narratives more generally, are not always effective. Narratives can be so distracting that they interfere with reception of the message. When this occurs, people fail to process message arguments or overlook the merits of the position advocated in the communication (e.g., Frey & Eagly, 1993). According to this view, statistical evidence, dull though it may be, has the upper hand in persuasion. Evidence, as discussed in the previous section and by the ELM, is demonstrably effective, serving multiple functions in the persuasion process.

We need more research to uncover the conditions under which evidence is more effective than narrative, and narrative overpowers evidence. Unquestionably, these factors work through different psychological processes, showcasing the different ways that messages can engage the mind. But the more we appreciate how best to construct a narrative and evidence-based message – for example by focusing more on the present in a more personalized narrative message and more on the future in a more detached, non-narrative message – the more we can change attitudes in helpful ways (Kim & Nan, 2019; see also Ma & Nan, 2018, for a cleverly titled study of the role played by social distance).

BOX 11.1

A Vivid Narrative on Drinking and Driving

Mothers Against Drunk Driving and Students Against Drug Driving frequently rely on vivid anecdotes – commonly a part of narratives – to convey their arguments. They undoubtedly regard these as more persuasive than gray statistics about the number of deaths caused by drunk drivers. Here is one particularly gripping example, supplied by a student. She read it during high school prom week, the narrative poem made an indelible impression, and she kept it over the years. As you read it over, ask yourself if you find this persuasive – and if so, why?

> I went to a party, Mom, I remembered what you said.
> You told me not to drink, Mom, so I drank a coke instead …
> I know I did the right thing, Mom, I know you're always right.
> Now the party is finally ending, Mom, as everyone drives out of sight …
> I started to drive away, Mom, but as I pulled onto the road,
> The other car didn't see me, Mom, it hit me like a load.
> As I lay here on the pavement, Mom, I hear the policeman say
> The other guy is drunk, Mom, and I'm the one who'll pay…
> The guy who hit me, Mom, is walking. I don't think that's fair.
> I'm lying here dying, Mom, while all he can do is stare …
> Someone should have told him, Mom, not to drink and drive.
> If only they would have taken the time, Mom, I would still be alive.

When and Why

With such strong logic on the sides of both narratives and statistical evidence, it should come as no surprise that both have been found to influence attitudes (Allen et al., 2000; Kazoleas, 1993; Major & Coleman, 2012). Evidence seems to carry more weight when persuaders are trying to influence cognitions or when people are sufficiently high in involvement that they are motivated to process more informative, evidence-based messages (Braverman, 2008; Kopfman et al., 1998). Narratives may be more impactful when communicators are trying to shake up people who strongly disagree with the message (Slater & Rouner, 1996). Truth be told, we do not yet know the precise circumstances under which narrative outguns evidence and evidence overpowers stories (Bilandzic & Busselle, 2013). Narrative is a relatively new area of scholarly study, compared with evidence, which has generated considerable research.

In the long run, the differential effectiveness of narrative and evidence is of less consequence than the psychology underlying their effects. Evidence works by stimulating attention and prompting greater cognitive elaboration (McKinley, Limbu, & Jayachandran, 2017). Narrative operates through more affective processes: transportation, identification with characters, and processes ordinarily associated with reading fiction. A narrative – a story with an educational message – can elide the usual resistance people put up in the face of persuasive messages. However, it will influence individuals only if it is believable and immerses individuals in the lives of fictional characters. There is a delicious irony that lies at the heart of narrative persuasion. Sometimes communicators may find that the most effective way to change attitudes about issues steeped in everyday life is to conjure up a universe that exists solely in the spiritual figment known as the human imagination.

There is a caveat to all this. Narratives can exert deleterious, as well as beneficial, effects. Persuasion being what it is, great literary narratives can arouse empathy for the afflicted and enhance appreciation for the downtrodden; vicious, prejudiced narratives can also move bigots to commit crimes of hate. *The Turner Diaries*, a 1978 novel discovered in terrorist Timothy McVeigh's car after the Oklahoma City bombing, relates the story of an underground organization of White Americans who conspire to take their country back from Jews and Blacks, executing Jews and African Americans, ultimately eliminating all non-White races. It is a cautionary tale. We need to remember that narratives can transport individuals to different psychological places; it is up to each of us to make sure that the places where we are transported enshrine goodness and human dignity.

It is also important to remember that, at least in practical situations, we don't have to always choose between evidence and narrative. Returning to the climate, it is instructive to note that the voluminous evidence about climate change – effects on coastlines, glaciers, rising temperatures, droughts, hurricanes, and food shortages – is persuasive, but can be so detailed it can be mind-numbing. Narratives, such as those offered by the international youth activist Greta Thunberg, can be powerful, but vacuous to those who dispute basic premises. If we are to change attitudes and policies on climate change, we need both stories and facts, for, as Jane Goodall (2019, p. 50) reminds us, "the window of time is closing."

Let's now move from these important topics to another core message dimension, one that emphasizes the power of words and the rhetorical frame.

Framing

Several decades ago, just when researchers thought they knew all there was to know about human thought processes, a couple of Israeli psychologists conducted an array of studies that transformed the conventional wisdom. At the time, scholars believed that people were rational information processors who made decisions based exclusively on what would maximize their self-interest. Amos Tversky and Daniel Kahneman turned this assumption on its head, showing that people are susceptible to breath-taking biases in intuition. Even the most intelligent and erudite individuals fell prey to cognitive biases and mental traps, frequently induced by how a message is framed. Consider:

In one study, physicians at the Harvard University Medical School read statistics attesting to the success of two different treatments for lung cancer: Surgery and radiation. They were then asked to indicate whether they preferred surgery or radiation. Although survival rates over five years favored the surgical option, in the short run, surgery has more risks than radiation. Half of the doctors read this statistic about the short-term consequences of surgery:

The one-month survival rate is 90%.

The other half read this statistic about the outcomes of surgery:

There is 10 percent mortality in the first month.

Reread the two outcomes. Which would you choose?

Now note that the outcomes are logically the same. Rational thinkers should make the same decision, regardless of which statement they read. But, defying predictions of rationality, the results showed that 84 percent of the physicians who read the first option chose surgery, compared to just 50 percent in the second group. The way the outcomes were phrased made all the difference. "Ninety percent survival sounds encouraging whereas 10% mortality is frightening," Kahneman (2011, p. 367) notes.

This illustrates the power of a *frame*, or the overarching way an idea is communicated, or phrased. A frame is the slant, focal point, or frame of reference. To frame, communication researcher Robert Entman (1993, p. 52), explained: "is to select some aspects of a perceived reality and make them more salient in a communicating text in such a way as to promote a particular problem definition, causal interpretation, moral evaluation, and/or treatment recommendation." Research has documented that simply varying the way a message is framed can strongly influence attitudes. Different versions contain the same facts, but they communicate the information through different frames of reference.

Kahneman and Tversky's research has been criticized for posing artificial, brain-teasing problems that produce results that would not occur in the real world. It is a reasonable criticism. However, in the main this criticism falls short, because their findings have been obtained consistently and over the course of several decades with different populations and in different experimental tests. Their results have done much to enhance understanding of the automatic, not-so-rational processes that underlie decision-making and attitude change. In 2002, Kahneman and the late Tversky received the Nobel Prize for their work on decision-making.

Message framing effects capitalize on subtle but psychologically important variations in message wording (O'Keefe & Jensen, 2006; Simon & Jerit, 2007; Tewksbury & Scheufele, 2009). Frames work by accessing a particular perspective on an issue. Frames can activate mental frameworks, and when the mental frameworks differ in their implications for decision-making, the results can be dramatic.

Some years back, Europeans learned of a disturbing difference among four countries in the rate of organ donation connected with accidental death. The organ donation rate was almost 100 percent in Austria and 86 percent in Sweden. But in Germany it was 12 percent and in Denmark a mere 4 percent. There is no compelling reason to think that citizens of Austria and Sweden are more inherently compassionate on this issue than their counterparts in Germany and Denmark. So what gives?

Austria and Sweden employ an "opt-out form," in which individuals who prefer not to donate must check a box on a form. Unless they take this step, they are regarded as organ donors. But Germany and Denmark use an "opt-in" form, where individuals have to check a box if they want to donate organs. The first frame makes it difficult for people to say no. They have to expend effort and make a conscious decision to opt out in a context in which peripheral, low-involvement processing may be the norm. The second frame makes it more difficult to opt in. Because many people are ambivalent about organ donation, they may be reluctant to expend the effort necessary to put a checkmark in a box. There may be a variety of other reasons why these countries differ in organ donation rates. However, framing offers a compelling interpretation (Kahneman, 2011; see Figure 11.3).

Framing has other intriguing implications for persuasion. When faced with a persuasive task, most of us access our own values, framing a message by consulting our moral and social compasses (Feinberg & Willer, 2015). After all, we like our cherished beliefs and assume everyone else will too! It turns out this egocentric approach to persuasion is not likely to persuade those with an opposing point of view.

Paying heed to the power of strong attitudes, framing research suggests that persuaders should *not* frame messages on involving topics in terms of their own moral values, but rather should call on

Figure 11.3 How Should a Communicator Frame Requests for Organ Donation? Research in Europe finds that the manner in which organ donation requests are framed, such as the one shown, can strongly influence donation rates

Image courtesy of Getty Images

the frames of the target audience. Drawing on both Haidt's (2013) value theory (see Chapter 4) and cognitive consistency needs (see Chapter 13), persuaders are more likely to change attitudes when they emphasize the ways that the message reaffirms values their receivers hold near and dear.

Suppose you want to convince a conservative to support same-sex marriage and a liberal to endorse military spending, positions which may be inconsistent with their attitudes. Let's say you know that conservatives tend to gravitate to values of group loyalty and patriotism, while liberals favor values like fairness and equality. Research shows that conservatives are more likely to endorse same-sex marriage if same-sex rights are framed in terms of patriotism ("same-sex couples are proud and patriotic Americans" who "contribute to the American economy and society") than if the message emphasizes fairness (Willer & Feinberg, 2015, p. 9). By contrast, liberals are more inclined to support increased military spending if the message highlights fairness – "through the military, the disadvantaged can achieve equal standing and overcome the challenges of poverty and inequality" – than if the message emphasizes patriotism and loyalty (Feinberg & Willer, 2015, p. 1671).

Persuaders can also nudge conservatives toward expressing more concern about climate change by couching the message in terms of their broad values, such as respect for authority, purity of nature, group loyalty, and patriotism. As you can see, the pro-environmental message that Wolsko, Ariceaga, and Seiden (2016) wrote is unabashedly strong in conservative values:

> Show you love your country by joining the fight to protect the purity of America's natural environment. Take pride in the American tradition of performing one's civic duty by taking responsibility for yourself and the land you call home. By taking a tougher stance on protecting the natural environment, you will be honoring all of Creation. Demonstrate your respect by following the examples of your religious and political leaders who defend America's natural environment. SHOW YOUR PATRIOTISM.
>
> (Wolsko et al., p. 10)

As you can see, from purity to patriotism to religion, with overtones of group loyalty and authority, the message screams moral conservatism. And, in line with the framing approach, conservative students who read this message, rather than a passage emphasizing liberal values like caring for the vulnerable environment, adopted more positive environmental attitudes. The authors titled their article optimistically, "Red, white, and blue enough to be green."

So, yes, these finding suggest the wisdom of couching messages in terms of receivers' particular moral values. Although we naturally gravitate to frames we endorse, it is more persuasive to frame arguments with a focus on values the audience affirms, an approach that might actually change important attitudes and increase tolerance of different views.

There is a catch. Conservative participants in the aforementioned study were especially likely to exhibit pro-environmental and climate change attitudes when the message was delivered by an in-group communicator who shared their conservative values. In real-world conditions, many political conservatives oppose climate change initiatives. It would be hard to find an in-group communicator willing to endorse this approach. What's more, conservative receivers, centrally processing this highly involved issue, might not buy the argument that you show your love of country by protecting the environment; they would also question whether taking a tougher stance on the environment really means one is honoring God.

Thus, even frames that are congenial with people's values can face an uphill fight in producing systematically processed, long-term attitude change. And yet, the reality is that frames that come from an opposing position can't even get in the persuasion door. Messages are certainly more likely to change attitudes if they embrace receivers' preferred frames. Communicators also need to know which frames to highlight and the words, pictures, and visual symbols that are most effective in conjuring the values they seek to cultivate.

This brings us back to climate change. Even as the public has become more concerned about climate change, few tangible policy steps have been taken to tackle the problem – "the greatest challenge humanity has collectively faced," as one expert called it (Lanchester, 2019, p. 1). There are many reasons for society's failure to take meaningful steps: Bureaucratic roadblocks, myopic economic self-interest, political opportunism, and intransigence. Complementing these has been society's inability to frame the issue with sufficient urgency, clarity, and linguistic muscle to propel collective action, a shortcoming "that posterity will find it hard to believe, and impossible to forgive" (Lanchester, 2019, p. 20). This speaks to the important role that framing can play in the global challenge to tackle climate change.

Language

An important aspect of framing involves the words persuaders use to frame messages in particular ways. Great persuaders have long known that how you say it can be as important as what you say. Persuasion scholars and speakers alike recognize that the words communicators use can influence attitudes. But just what impact does language have? How can we get beyond the generalities to hone in on the specific features of language that matter most? How can you use language more effectively yourself in your efforts to convince people to go along with what you recommend?

These are social scientific questions – specific inquiries that allow us to explore theories and see how they play out in everyday life. This section examines subtle, fascinating aspects of language, as well as *paralinguistic features*, which convey meaning in ways other than words. This includes speech rate, pitch, volume, and tone of voice (see practical tips in Box 11.2). Guided by the volume of research, the section focuses on speed of speech, powerless vs. powerful speech, with its gender implications, as well as metaphors.

Speed of Speech

Ever since America mythologized the fast-talking salesman, people have assumed that fast speakers are more compelling than slow ones. The character Harold Hill in the American classic *The Music Man* epitomizes our stereotype of the fast-talking peddler of wares. Since then, movies, videos, and songs have rhapsodized about the supposed persuasive effects of fast-talking persuaders.

Leave it to social scientists to study the phenomenon! Does speed of speech enhance persuasion? Early studies suggested it did (Miller et al., 1976; Street & Brady, 1982). However, more recent studies have cast doubt on this glib conclusion. Researchers have discovered that speech rate does not inevitably change attitudes and, under some conditions, may not exert a particularly strong impact on attitudes or beliefs (Buller et al., 1992). Just as you can hypothesize that faster speech should be persuasive because it acts as a credibility cue, you can also reason that it should reduce persuasion if it interferes with message processing or annoys the audience ("Don't y'all know we don't speak as fast as you Yankees down here in ol' Alabama?").

Thus, there are both theoretical and practical reasons to argue that speech rate does not have a uniformly positive or negative effect on persuasion. Instead, the most reasonable conclusion is that effects depend on the context. Several contextual factors are important.

First, speech rate may enhance persuasion when the goal of the persuader is to capture attention. A trendy example is a fast-talking video from the controversial YouTube personality James Charles, where he delivers direct messages to his favorite celebs, asking them to select products for his personal makeup routine, all the while speaking super-fast with few pauses between sentences. His fast speech grabs your attention, taking you away from peripheral thoughts and directing you to his message.

Second, fast speech can be effective when the persuader's goal is to be perceived as competent. Speaking quickly can suggest that the communicator is credible, confident, and possesses expertise (Scherer, London, & Wolf, 1973). Moderately fast and fast speakers are seen as more intelligent, confident, and effective than their slower-speaking counterparts. Speed of speech thus serves as a heuristic or peripheral cue.

Third, speech rate can be effective when audience members are low in involvement (Smith & Shaffer, 1995). Under low involvement, speech rate can serve as a peripheral cue. Invoking the heuristic or cultural stereotype that "fast talkers know their stuff," audience members may go along with fast speakers because they assume they are credible or correct. Fast speech may be a facade, employed to disguise a lack of knowledge, but by the time message recipients discover this, they may have already plunked down their money to purchase the product.

Fourth, speech rate can also enhance persuasion when it is relevant to the message topic. A now-famous advertisement for Federal Express depicted a harried businessman, facing an urgent deadline. The man barked out orders to a subordinate and both spoke quickly.

A more recent ad you may have seen on TV or on YouTube harnessed the FedEx fast-speaking technique. It applied it to a business that, like FedEx, values speed of speech: Jimmy John's Sandwich Shop. The ad goes like this, with each person speaking in a staccato voice at lightning-quick speed:

Employer:	What's on your mind, kid? Make it fast.
Young man:	I'd like to work here at Jimmy John's World's Greatest Gourmet Sandwich Shop, sir.
Employer:	Why do you want to work at Jimmy John's, kid?
Young man:	I'm perfect for Jimmy John's.
Employer:	Doing what?
Young man:	Delivery.
Employer:	Delivery?
Young man:	Delivery.
Employer:	We deliver pretty fast here at Jimmy John's.
Young man:	That's what I heard.
Employer:	What'd you hear?
Young man:	You deliver pretty fast here at Jimmy John's.
Employer:	Then you heard right.
Young man:	I'm a fast study, sir.
Employer:	You know the Jimmy John's slogan?
Young man:	The Jimmy John's slogan?
Employer:	The Jimmy John's slogan is said so fast you'll freak.
Young man:	Said so fast you'll freak is a swell slogan, sir.
Employer:	When people call for a Jimmy John's sandwich, they want it fast.
Young man:	Then I'm your man, sir …
Employer:	Okay, give me some time to think it over.
Young man:	Okay.
Employer:	Okay, I've thought it over. When can you start?
Young man:	Now.
Employer:	Now's good. What's your name, kid?
Young man:	Stephanopolopodopolous.
Employer:	Too long.
Young man:	How about Ed?
Employer:	Ed's fine. Welcome aboard, Ed.

The fast-talker ad may have contributed to the success of the Jimmy John's franchise. The symmetry between the theme of the ad – speed of speech – and a business that hyped fast service may have helped promote the restaurant with consumers.

Under other conditions, fast speech is not so likely to enhance credibility or persuasion. When the audience suspects the speaker is covering something up, fast speech can reinforce this perception, accessing stereotypes of the slick, fast-talking salesman or attorney, attenuating credibility.

In addition, when the message concerns sensitive or intimate issues, a faster speaker may communicate insensitivity or coldness (Giles & Street, 1994; Ray, Ray, & Zahn, 1991). In cases where a message focuses on medical problems, safer sex, or a personal dilemma, slow speech may be preferable. In these situations, slow speech may convey communicator concern, empathy, and goodwill.

This plays out on a national political level as well. When citizens are experiencing a national crisis, they may respond more positively to a slower speaker, whose slower pace conveys calm and reassurance. During the 1930s and 1940s, when Americans faced the Depression and World War II, they found solace in the slow speech – and melodious voice – of President Franklin Delano Roosevelt (Winfield, 1994). Had FDR spoken quickly, he might have made people nervous; his pace might have reminded them of the succession of problems that faced them on a daily basis.

When people are in the throes of sorrow, slower speech can soothe. When former President Obama gave a moving eulogy in June 2015 for the Reverend Clementa Pinckney and other victims of the Charleston, South Carolina murders, he spoke compassionately about the kindness of the reverend and the dignity of the Black church. He also spoke slowly and deliberately, the slowness of his speech a sign of the respect for the occasion and the losses people felt.

Thus, research suggests that faster speech is not inherently or always more effective or appropriate than slower speech. Instead, persuaders must appreciate context, and the audience's motivation and ability to process the message. It would be nice if we could offer a simple prescription, like one your doctor gives the pharmacist. The reality is that speech-rate effects are more complex. For researchers, complexity is not a stopping point, but a sign that more penetrating perspectives are needed to pull together diverse strands in the empirical arena.

Perhaps the most useful framework to help integrate the different issues in speech rate research is an interpersonal communication perspective called *communication accommodation theory* (McGlone & Giles, 2011). The theory is guided by the insight that communicators sometimes adapt their behavior toward others, as when a speaker slows down when talking to an older person. The accommodation perspective looks at when individuals adapt their communication behavior toward others – or accommodate them – and when they diverge from others, or speak in a style that differs from the majority of audience members.

A fast-talking speaker who finds that he is addressing a slower-speaking audience might want to accommodate the audience by slowing his speech rate down. Audience members would appreciate the effort and would also affirm the similarity between the speaker and their own speech style. On the other hand, a speaker could misjudge the situation. For example, she might be talking to an older audience, assume they are slow speakers and reduce her speech rate, only to find the majority are quick-thinking, fast-talking retired neuroscientists, who resent her attempt to pander to them!

From an academic perspective, the communication accommodation framework reminds us that the effects of speech rate on persuasion depend on a host of contextual factors, including: (a) the similarity between the speech rate of the communicator and the audience; (b) the communicator's perceptions of how quickly audience members speak; (c) the audience's perceptions of how quickly the communicator is talking; (d) stereotypes of speech rate that both communicator and audience members bring to bear; and (e) the topic of the message. Complicated stuff, but, as you now appreciate, persuasion is a complicated business.

Powerless Versus Powerful Speech

Has this ever happened to you? You're sitting in class when a student raises his hand and says, "I know this sounds like a stupid question, but ..." and proceeds to ask the professor his question. You cringe as you hear him introduce his query in this manner; you feel embarrassed for your classmate and bothered that someone is about to waste your time with a dumb question. Something interesting has just happened. The student has deliberately undercut his own credibility by suggesting to the class that a query that may be perfectly intelligent is somehow less than adequate. The words preceding the question – not the question itself – have produced these effects, providing another example of the subtle role language plays in communication.

The linguistic form at work here is *powerless speech*. It is a constellation of characteristics that may suggest to a message receiver that the communicator is less than powerful or is not so confident. In contrast, *powerful speech* is marked by the conspicuous absence of these features.

The primary components of powerless speech are:

- *Hesitation forms.* "Uh" and "well, you know" communicate lack of certainty or confidence.
- *Hedges.* "Sort of," "kinda," and "I guess" are phrases that reduce the definitiveness of a persuader's assertion.
- *Tag questions.* The communicator "tags" a declarative statement with a question, as in, "That plan will cost us too much, don't you think?" A tag is "a declarative statement without the assumption that the statement will be believed by the receiver" (Bradley, 1981, p. 77).
- *Disclaimers.* "This may sound a little out of the ordinary, but" or "I'm no expert, of course" are introductory expressions that ask the listener to show understanding or to make allowances.

Researchers have examined the effects of powerless and powerful speech on persuasion. Studies overwhelmingly show that powerless speech is perceived as less persuasive and credible than powerful speech (Burrell & Koper, 1998; Hosman, 2002). Communicators who use powerless speech are perceived to be less competent, dynamic, and attractive than those who speak in a powerful fashion (e.g., Adkins & Brashers, 1995; Erickson et al., 1978; Haleta, 1996; Holtgraves & Lasky, 1999; Hosman, 1989). There are several reasons why powerless communicators are downgraded. Their use of hedges, hesitations, and qualifiers communicates uncertainty or lack of confidence. Powerless speech may also serve as a low-credibility cue, a culturally learned heuristic that suggests the speaker lacks intelligence or knowledge (Sparks & Areni, 2008). In addition, powerless speech distracts audience members, which reduces their ability to attend to message arguments.

This research has abundant practical applications. It suggests that, when giving a talk or preparing a written address, communicators should speak concisely and directly. They should avoid qualifiers, hedges, tag questions, and hesitations. Instead, they should emphasize assertive speech (see Box 11.2).

Other Applications

In politics, decisive speech conveys expertise and political gravitas. Halting, powerless speech can snuff out the oxygen from a potential political moment. Just ask the Congressional Democrats who were hoping that former Special Counsel Robert Mueller (who supervised the investigation into links between Russia's attempt to sabotage the 2016 presidential election and Donald Trump's presidential campaign) would deliver blockbuster, Watergate-style made-for-TV revelations during his testimony before Congressional committees in July 2019.

It didn't work out this way. In his testimony, Mueller's language fell into the hesitant, unassertive speech domain, as he was "shaky," "hesitant about the facts," awkwardly stumbling over a poorly phrased question, "at times struggling to keep up" (Baker, 2019; LaFraniere et al., 2019). He lacked the laser-like precision and combative stance he had as FBI director, causing even supporters to conclude he had failed to deliver the dramatic blast of verbal bombast that Democrats needed to change the public conversation about Trump's missteps. For their part, Republicans were delighted that the tepid Mueller performance had not inflicted any public damage on the president.

Courtroom presentations is another arena with powerful/powerless speech implications. Two experts in the psychology of law argue, based on research evidence, that "the attorney should, whenever possible, come directly to the point and not hedge his points with extensive qualifications" (Linz & Penrod, 1984, pp. 44–45). Witnesses, they add, should be encouraged to answer attorneys' questions as directly and with as few hesitations and qualifiers as possible.

This style was very much in evidence when psychologist Christine Blasey Ford addressed a Senate Judiciary hearing – and a national TV audience – in September 2018, explaining calmly, precisely, with little hesitation or uncertainty, how then-Supreme Court Justice nominee Brett Kavanaugh had sexually assaulted her when they were at a high school party. Speaking resolutely in a high-pitched voice about a traumatic issue, Blasey Ford did not falter, hesitate, or deprecate her memory or credentials. "She was composed, but not practiced," a critic noted (Poniewozik, 2018, p. A16; see Figure 11.4).

Figure 11.4 Dr. Christine Blasey Ford Captivated the Nation in September, 2018 With Her Stunning Testimony Before the Senate Judiciary Committee, Calmly, Assertively, and With Powerful Speech, Describing How Supreme Court Justice Nominee Brett Kavanaugh Had Sexually Assaulted Her When They Were in High School. Kavanaugh offered a more emotional, angry response, categorically denying the incident had happened, displaying an anger that would be stereotypically inappropriate for a woman speaker to convey

Image courtesy of Getty Images

To be sure, there were questions about the truthfulness of Blasey Ford's account. In a rebuttal, Kavanaugh gave an entirely different account, forcefully denying the incident ever happened, his snarling anger an interesting gender-based contrast to Blasey Ford's more measured speaking style. (Note that Blasey Ford gained credibility points because she was perceived as disconfirming knowledge bias-type expectations by displaying a willingness to go public with a deeply embarrassing story, raising the question of why someone would do this, and narrate it credibly, unless the incident had actually happened. However, the fact that she was credible, due to her assertive speech and detailed memory for events, does not, of course, mean that her recollections were factually correct. Supporters *perceived* her to be credible and *presumed* her account was true.)

BOX 11.2

Language Tips

How can you use language to spruce up your persuasive communications? Here are several suggestions, based on research and theory:

1   Avoid "uh," "um," and other non-fluencies.
2   Don't use disclaimers ("I'm no expert, but …"). Just make your point.
3   If you are nervous, think through the reasons you feel that way and try to increase your confidence. You may feel better by sharing your uncertainty with your audience, but the powerlessness you convey will reduce your persuasiveness.
4   Vary your pitch as much as possible. Avoid the boring monotone.
5   Accommodate your speech to listeners' language style. If your audience speaks quickly (and your talk does not concern intimate issues), speak at a faster clip.
6   Accommodate to audience language style, but don't pander. Some years back, an African American student related a story of a White speaker who addressed her high school class. Trying to be hip, he infused his talk with Black lingo (using phrases of the "yo, what's poppin'?" variety). The students laughed, seeing through his insincere attempt to appeal to them.
7   Be careful about using intense or obscene speech. Intense language can work, particularly when the communicator is credible and the topic is of low ego-involvement. Obscenities can be effective, if listeners expect the speaker to use four-letter words and they share his or her political values (see Donald Trump's success with his supporters, but not with his opponents). The international climate change activist Greta Thunberg energized supporters by distributing flyers that read "I am doing this because you adults are shitting on my future" (Kolbert, 2019, p. 19). To be sure, in interpersonal contexts, obscenity can be the norm in certain neighborhoods; if speakers don't swear, they will be disregarded. But in more formal public contexts, obscene speech is risky; it violates audience expectations of what is appropriate and can offend key constituents. What is obscene, of course, changes with the times, so the topic is fraught, fascinating, and volatile.
8   Paralinguistic features can influence persuasion subtly and powerfully. In an intriguing series of studies, titled "How the Voice Persuades," two psychologists examined the impact of vocalic components, such as volume and pitch. Speakers who spoke louder, increasing and varying their volume, were more persuasive. The key reason: They seemed more

confident in themselves, which increased their ability to persuade, another example of the role of confidence in persuasion (Van Zant & Berger, 2020).

9 Be aware of your non-verbal expressions. About 65 percent of the meaning in an interpersonal interaction is communicated non-verbally (Burgoon, 1994). Thus, you may know your stuff, but if you look like you're not happy to be speaking – because you're frowning or clenching your fists – you can erase the positive effects of a well-crafted message. Use facial expressions and a posture that you're comfortable with. Nod your head a little – not in a robotic way – when you are presenting strong arguments; head-nodding can increase your self-confidence (Briñol & Petty, 2003). And unless you're communicating bad news, smile.

Let's return to powerful/powerless speech with one additional caveat. Although powerful speech is usually more persuasive than powerless language, there is at least one context in which powerless speech can be effective. When communicators wish to generate goodwill rather than project expertise or emphasize their sincerity, certain types of unassertive language can work to their advantage (Claeys & Cauberghe, 2014).

Let's say that an authority figure wants to humanize herself and appear more down-to-earth in message recipients' eyes. She may find it useful to end some statements with a question. Physicians and therapists frequently use tags to gain rapport with clients. Tag questions such as "That must have made you feel angry, right?" can show empathy with patients' concerns (Harres, 1998). As researcher Annette Harres observed, after studying physicians' use of language devices, "Affective tag questions were a very effective way of showing that the doctor was genuinely concerned about the patient's physical and psychological well-being … They can indicate to patients that their concerns are taken seriously" (Harres, 1998, pp. 122–123).

Forceful Language

There is another exception to the rule that powerful speech persuades. It is an important one, with practical applications. When powerless language becomes forceful, and is controlling and demeaning, it crosses a line. *Forceful language* thus contains two components: Controlling and demeaning speech (Jenkins & Dragojevic, 2013). Controlling language employs commands, such as advocating that the recommended behavior "must be performed." Demeaning language degrades audience members who take an alternative position, telling them, for example, to "get real and recognize that no other position is defensible." Persuaders – even those who are honestly convinced they are correct and try to guide the audience in their direction – can fail to influence when their powerful messages are filled with forceful speech.

Forceful speech can be problematic for several reasons. First, it arouses an unpleasant emotional state called *reactance*. According to reactance theory, people have a fundamental need for freedom and autonomy. They experience reactance when this need is thwarted (Brehm, 1966; Quick, Shen, & Dillard, 2013). Forceful language, with its controlling, in-your-face directives, can arouse reactance, leading to resistance to persuasion. Second, forceful language is impolite. It threatens aspects of individuals' "face" and self-respect by publicly questioning the person's competence to judge the merits of a persuasive message. Third, forceful speech violates normal expectations of how a persuader should frame an argument in an ordinary situation. Accordingly, research finds that forceful speech, and highly controlling language in particular, can lead people to resist persuasion and negatively evaluate the message (Jenkins & Dragojevic, 2013; Miller et al., 2007, 2013).

Thus, powerful speech is persuasive – provided it does not contain controlling, demeaning, or threatening language. When this occurs, the credibility conferred by powerful speech may be overwhelmed by reactance, and the anger and irritation that forceful speech produces (Richards, Banas, & Magid, 2017). Persuasion is subtle; seemingly small things can make a big difference.

Gender and Public Persuasion

Is there a gender gap in powerless speech?

This is an important question addressed by research. There is some evidence that women use more tentative speech and men gravitate to more powerful speech forms. Yet this does not reflect verbal deficits. Women have a better vocabulary than men (Karpowitz & Mendelberg, 2014). As a result of traditional sex-role socialization, women learn that speech that carries assertive, aggressive overtones is frowned on and not "appropriate" for girls to use. However, there are so many contextual factors at work here – the topic of the conversation, the place where the conversation takes place, the salience of gender, as well as cultural norms – that we need to be wary of concluding that women invariably use more powerless than powerful speech more so than men do.

What is clear is that women tend to be less confident than men about their public persuasive speaking, displaying (at least in U.S. contexts) more anxiety before a public speech, less comfort with asking questions in class, and less interest in pursuing leadership posts, particularly in politics (Karpowitz & Mendelberg, 2014). Given that women, on average, have a better vocabulary than men, these differences would seem to be rooted in what culture teaches women and girls about assertive public speaking.

At the same time, there is suggestive evidence that a double standard may be at work in the powerless/powerful speech domain. In one classic study, Linda L. Carli (1990) found that women were more influential when they used assertive or powerful speech, notably when trying to persuade other women. Women respected a female speaker's use of confident, direct persuasive language. But the tables turned when women spoke with men. When trying to persuade men, women speakers were more persuasive when they spoke tentatively, using tag questions, hedges, and disclaimers. Apparently, men viewed a female speaker's use of dominant, powerful language as inappropriate, even threatening. Thus, women had to play the traditional, coquettish female role, deferring to men in the service of persuasion.

We see this in politics, where Hillary Clinton in 2008 faced criticism for engaging in assertive, political speech. Caustic critics described her with the b-word and derogated her cruelly on television talk shows and websites (Falk, 2010). To be sure, things have changed over the years. Significantly more women have been elected to office, with four well-respected female U.S. senators major contenders for the 2020 Democratic presidential nomination. But gender inequalities persist.

When Brett Kavanaugh responded with anger, pouts, and tears in response to Christine Blasey Ford's quieter, but assertive, accusations of sexual assault, it was considered okay. Had Blasey Ford spoken this way – expressing outrage, emoting with anger, even crying as she recollected the incident – she would have been mocked and viewed as a typically emotional female witness rather than a credible psychologist speaking truth to power (even if there remained unanswerable questions about who was telling the truth).

Given stereotypes that women speakers still face, it is important to develop sensitive strategies to increase gender parity in real-life communication settings. Researchers Christopher F. Karpowitz and Talia Mendelberg proposed a number of suggestions to increase gender role equity, including that organizations:

> make access to the floor easy, require each person to speak some minimum number of times, enforce turn taking, ensure that no one person monopolizes the floor, (and) invite members to indicate explicitly when they agree with a statement immediately after a relatively quiet person talks ... (because) women benefit from hearing others supporting them while they speak.
>
> (2014, pp. 351–352)

Metaphors, Figures of Speech, and Language Intensity

We now move to a different aspect of language, intensity – the feature that most people think of when they free-associate about language effects. *Language intensity* includes a variety of tropes or figures of speech, including metaphors, as well as passionate, strong language, and emotionally charged words. It is the province of political rhetoric, social activism, hate speech, and eloquent public address.

One prominent feature of language intensity is the metaphor. A *metaphor* is "a linguistic phrase of the form 'A is B,' such that a comparison is suggested between the two terms leading to a transfer of attributes associated with B to A" (Sopory & Dillard, 2002, p. 407). For example, former president, Ronald Reagan, liked to describe America as "a torch shedding light to all the hopeless of the world." The metaphor consists of two parts: A (America) and B ("torch shedding light to all the hopeless of the world"). It suggests a comparison between A and B, such that the properties associated with a torch shedding light to the world's hopeless are transferred to America. It was a compelling, affecting metaphor.

In our own age, symbol-laden figures of speech and semantically powerful rhetorical expressions are frequently spread through social media. In the wake of police killings of unarmed Blacks, impassioned activists, savvy with social media and adept at language frames, reached millions of people via semantically rich Twitter posts. Their messages used simple, emotional tweets with hashtags, like "Black Lives Matter" and "I Can't Breathe" (the words Eric Garner spoke as a New York City police officer put him in a chokehold that killed him).

Tweets like "Black Lives Matter" and "I Can't Breathe" are, in one sense, metaphors for racial injustice that condense a great deal of emotion into one phrase. As emotional frames, focusing on anger, they can call information and emotions to mind (Kühne & Schemer, 2015). And when conveyed via Twitter, which reaches millions, these semantically rich hashtags – supplemented by short messages and vivid pictures – can influence attitudes and impel the committed to action (see Figure 11.5). On the other end of the political spectrum, President Trump's iconic "Make America Great Again," encapsulating patriotism and nostalgic hankering for memories of a simpler, controversially idyllic past, packs a great deal of rhetorical punch.

So, do metaphors work? Researchers Pradeep Sopory and James P. Dillard (2002) conducted a meta-analytic review of the empirical research on metaphor and persuasion. They concluded that messages containing metaphors produce somewhat greater attitude change than do communications without metaphors. Metaphors are effective because they evoke strong semantic associations, increasing mental elaboration. Metaphors help people efficiently structure message arguments, in

(a)

(b)

Figure 11.5a–b Symbol-Laden Figures of Speech, Semantically Rich Rhetorical Expressions, and Metaphors, Conveyed through Twitter, Can Arouse Feelings and Sway Attitudes in Ways That Ordinary Language Cannot. The hashtags "Black Lives Matter," which diffused after police killings of unarmed African Americans, and "Love Wins," which spread with lightning speed after the 2015 Supreme Court decision legalizing gay marriage, were harnessed in protests, showcasing the role language plays in political persuasion

Image courtesy of Getty Images

turn strengthening interconnections among the arguments that enhance comprehension and attitude change (Shen & Bigsby, 2013). This offers suggestive evidence that metaphorical or symbol-laden tweets, as well as time-honored political metaphors, can influence attitudes. They may access affect and strengthen bonds among the affective and cognitive elements of attitudes. Research on strong attitudes reminds us that tweets, such as those above, will be singularly ineffective among those who are more sympathetic with the police than with Black Lives Matter activists. At the same time, among many Americans unfamiliar with the issue, the tweets may have increased its salience, encouraging them to frame police violence (a complex, multiple-perspectival problem) in a different way.

Psychologically effective as metaphors are, they are not the only component of intense language (Bowers, 1964; Hamilton & Hunter, 1998; Hosman, 2002). Intense language includes specific, graphic language. It also encompasses emotion-laden words like "freedom" and "beauty," as well as "suffering" and "death." Intense language can also reflect the extremity of the communicator's issue position. A communicator who describes efforts to clone human beings as "disgusting" is using more intense language than one who calls such research "inappropriate." The first speaker's language also points up a more extreme position on the cloning issue.

What impact does such language have on attitudes? Should persuaders deploy vivid, graphic terms? The answer depends on the persuader's goal, his or her credibility, and the audience's involvement in the issue. If the goal is to enhance dynamism, intense language can help speakers achieve this objective. If a communicator is addressing an audience of supporters, intense language can enhance enthusiasm, firing up emotions, leading supporters to feel all the more favorably as they assimilate the message into their latitudes of acceptance. However, intense language can anger opponents and can push neutral observers into the latitude of resistance. More generally, its effects on persuasion depend on a host of factors, including audience members' prior attitudes, ego-involvement, and the speaker's credibility (Hamilton & Hunter, 1998; Hosman, 2002; Blankenship & Craig, 2011; see also Hamilton & Hunter, 1998; Craig & Blankenship, 2011). Intense language inflames, moves, stirs emotions, and arouses antipathy in audiences; it's a worthwhile, if dicey, weapon in the persuasion arsenal.

Applications of Words in Action: The Case of Language and Abortion

Language also plays a potent role in fractious social disputes. Activists are adept at choosing metaphors that can galvanize support for their cause. They recognize that the way they frame the issue – and the linguistic terms they select – can strongly influence attitudes. Case in point: The appeals made by opponents and supporters of abortion (see Figure 11.6).

Abortion foes chose the metaphor "pro-life" to describe their heartfelt opposition to abortion in the United States. Just about everyone loves life. By linking a fetus with life, activists succeeded in making a powerful symbolic statement. It placed those who did not believe that a fetus constituted a full, living human being on the defensive. What's more, pro-life activists deployed vivid visual metaphors to make their case. They developed brochures and movies that depicted powerful images – for example, "a fetus floating in amniotic fluid, tiny fetal feet dangled by a pair of adult hands, [and] a mutilated, bloodied, aborted fetus with a misshapen head and a missing arm" (Lavin, 2001, p. 144). These visual images became the centerpiece of a national anti-abortion campaign that began in the 1960s and 1970s.

Over the ensuing decades, the language became more intense, the rhetoric fiercer. Pro-life activists spent much linguistic energy condemning a specific late-term abortion procedure, called partial-birth abortion. The procedure is unpleasant and controversial, and pro-life supporters have gained rhetorical

(a)

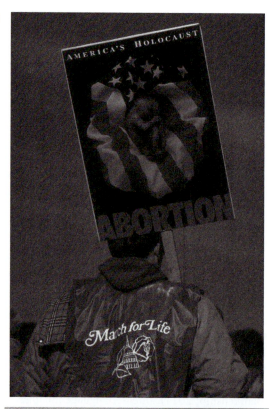

(b)

Figure 11.6a–b Intense Language, Notably Metaphors and Vivid Language, Has Been an Integral Part of Persuasive Battles on the Issue of Abortion. Such language can arouse supporters to action, but it can also polarize people. In some cases it may have helped spark violent confrontations

Image courtesy of Getty Images

punch by promoting the name "partial-birth abortion" rather than employing a formal medical term: Intact dilation and evacuation.

Appreciating the power of language, pro-life advocates have been adept at describing the entity that is removed from the womb as a "baby" rather than a "fetus." The linguistic frame matters. In one study, individuals who read an article on a ban on partial-birth abortion that used the term "baby" registered more opposition to legalizing partial-birth abortion than those who read the same article with the term "fetus" (Simon & Jerit, 2007).

On the other side of the abortion divide, women's groups that favor abortion rights have also exploited the symbolic power of language and pictures. They used a coat hanger dripping blood as a metaphor for "the horrid means and consequences of the illegal abortions that occur when legal abortion is banned" (Condit, 1990, p. 92). They argued that the fetus should be characterized as a lump of tissues rather than a baby. Pro-choice activists went to lengths to frame the issue around favoring choice rather than supporting abortion.

One popular pro-choice pamphlet presented the Statue of Liberty, with the line that "there are no pictures in this pamphlet, because you can't take a picture of liberty." Condit notes that "the statue – as a woman, a symbol of the downtrodden, and a symbol of Freedom, Liberty, and home – embodied the ideal American representation of Choice or Reproductive Freedom" (1990, pp. 93–94).

Although pro-choice appeals to values like freedom helped to shift the focus of the abortion debate, it did not eliminate the rhetorical power of visual images, like mangled fetuses. The coat hanger packs less rhetorical punch than a bloody fetus, and the choice metaphor loses out in the language-intensity war when pitted against graphic images of "aborted babies." As one abortion advocate conceded, "When someone holds up a model of a six-month-old fetus and a pair of surgical scissors, we say 'choice,' and we lose" (Naomi Wolf on abortion, 2013).

The language has become even more intense in recent years. Pro-life activists, outraged about the immorality of abortion, have objected to pro-choice partisans trotting out the phrase "clusters of cells that have not yet developed into a viable human being" to describe a prenatal child. The phrase denies the humanity of the nascent child, hiding "the fact that by the time most surgical abortions take place, a prenatal child has electrical activity in the brain and a beating heart" (Camosy, 2019, A23).

On the other side of the linguistic divide, pro-choice advocates have objected to the graphic nature of the term "heartbeat" legislation used to promote laws that ban abortion as early as the sixth week of pregnancy. Abortion rights supporters argue that the term, which pulls at the emotional heartstrings, is misleading because it conflates an electric pulse in cells "the size of a pencil tip" with a heart that requires a structure and basic neurological system to function (Harmon, 2019, A18). However, pro-choice activists emphasize that the cell lacks this structure and function.

The language wars continue and show no signs of stopping, as both sides remain strongly committed to their position and convinced the other side is cheapening humanity and suffocating life. The language showcases the linguistic creativity of human beings' symbolic powers, while demonstrating the ways rhetoric can become ever-more extreme, reflecting the moral passion of activists, while simplifying the complexity with which many women approach the issues.

Abortion is a heart-rending issue, and intense language can form and shape attitudes, showcasing the ways words – never mere rhetoric – can arouse and activate, as well as pummel and polarize citizens in a democratic society. In a society where violence and prejudice go hand in hand, leaders' use of intense, aggressive rhetoric can leave implicit residues in the minds of hate-filled extremists, perhaps lighting a mental match that propels them to violent action.

Intense language has been a persuasive weapon in a multitude of issues. Proponents and opponents are battling for public opinion. They are trying to change people's attitudes. This is a complex issue. There are many facets, angles, scientific layers, and moral perspectives. As you read about this topic over the coming years, you might take note of the ways in which activists frame the issue. Listen to the words they use. Be cognizant of the words you select to describe the issue to others. Note when the meanings that are evoked demonize and divide rather than heal.

Conclusions

The message is the heart of persuasion – the rhetorical artery of the persuasion process. Scholars from Aristotle to contemporary communication researchers have theorized about the most effective ways to harness messages so as to change attitudes. A hallmark of today's scholarship is the recognition that messages do not have simple influences. Instead, their effects hinge on: (a) the particular facet of the message communicators employ and (b) the ways that receivers think about what they have seen or heard. This chapter has introduced you to different categories of the message: Structure, content, framing, and language.

The concepts discussed in the chapter, intriguing as they are, are less theories than intriguingly rich individual-level concepts. Thus, transportation, evidence, and the linguistic message features all have interesting implications for message effects, but they are not full-blown theoretical frameworks like the Elaboration Likelihood Model. Each of the message factors can be understood as implicating a host of psychological processes, which in turn shed light on communication effects.

Focusing first on message structure, research indicates that: (a) explicit conclusion drawing is usually more effective than implicit drawing of the conclusion and (b) two-sided messages are more persuasive than one-sided messages, provided they refute the opposing side. Two-sided message research takes on particular importance in view of the plethora of factually inaccurate information available on television, the Internet, and social media. When communications present a position that has few facts in its behalf as equivalent to the viewpoint that is backed up by scientific evidence, they can unwittingly convey a two-sided message that misinforms the public on a contemporary policy issue.

Two core message-content factors are evidence and narrative. Evidence is defined as factual statements that originate from a source, other than the communicator, that are offered to verify the communicator's claims. It typically consists of quantitative information, like statistics. Research finds that evidence changes attitudes. Psychologically, evidence works through processes laid out by the ELM. Under conditions of low involvement and ability, evidence serves as a peripheral cue. Under higher involvement and ability, it serves as an argument, catalyst to thought, or factor that bolsters confidence in a receiver's assessment of the message.

Narrative operates very differently. It straddles the line between entertainment and pure persuasion. Narratives are coherent stories that provide information about characters and conflict, raise questions, and offer a resolution to the problem. Unlike advocacy messages, which work primarily through central and peripheral processes or social norms, narratives transport individuals to different psychological realms. In so doing, they immerse audiences in an imaginative domain that may reduce defensive resistance and increase receptivity to new ideas about an issue. Narratives can also deflect the usual resistance that accompanies reception of a persuasive message. Narratives and evidence, when deftly used and working through different psychological processes, can change attitudes, demonstrating their importance in the persuasive communicator's message arsenal.

Framing and language focus on the strong influence that verbal frameworks and words have on attitudes. Attitudes can be steered by subtle changes in emphasis in how problems are defined and phrased. Frames highlight certain concepts, and emphasize particular ways of interpreting ambiguous facts. They are particularly likely to influence attitudes when they jell with the values that guide message receivers' thinking about the issue. While speakers naturally gravitate toward their own frames, research suggests that in this area of persuasion, like many others, they appeal to the frames held by their receivers. Naturally, communicators should not abandon their values, lest they be rightly called opportunistic and violate their own ethical precepts. Instead, they should embrace values like tolerance by trying much as possible to frame messages in terms of ideas their audience will endorse.

Research also indicates that words and sematic features of a message can sway feelings and thoughts. Key language components are speed of speech, powerless/powerful speech, and language intensity. Fast speech can influence attitudes by conveying credibility and distracting audience members from counterarguing with the message. Speech-rate effects on persuasion are complex, with impact depending on the topic and the similarity between the speech rate of the communicator and the audience.

Powerful speech, characterized by the absence of hesitation, hedges, disclaimers, and other unassertive speech forms, can convey credibility and influence attitudes. Audiences may ignore the content of what the speaker is saying and focus instead on how he or she says it, forming an evaluation of the speaker and message based on whether he hedges, hesitates, or qualifies. Thus, a speaker who really knows her stuff may be dismissed if she speaks in a manner that conveys uncertainty. Provided a speaker does not employ controlling and demeaning forceful speech, powerful speech can enhance persuasion. It's a lesson that women communicators, whose vocabulary generally exceeds that of men but who have internalized gender stereotypes, can definitely benefit from.

The rub is that when speakers use forceful – controlling and demeaning – speech, they threaten and irritate the message receiver. Parents, operating from good intentions, can use this speech style in hopes of goading children into taking better care of their health or adopting pro-social behaviors. Research suggests that forceful language can doom their effort from the beginning; they would be better advised, in most instances, to speak assertively, but not in a controlling manner.

Intense language is the feature of language that comes to mind when many of us think about the power of words. We think of charismatic speakers who use language colorfully and metaphorically, or of terse semantically evocative Twitter posts like #LoveWins. Indeed, intense language, notably metaphors, can influence attitudes, increasing motivation and evoking positive mental images. Like all message variables, language intensity works under particular conditions and has been harnessed for good and bad ends. When addressing audiences who share the communicator's attitude, intense language can arouse passions and mobilize individuals to join a partisan cause. But on sensitive issues, intense language can turn people off and cause people to reject a message they might otherwise favor. When delivering two-sided messages to audiences who may disagree with their perspective, persuaders should steer clear of intense verbiage. When appealing to their troops on Twitter, intense, even obscene language (which respects the group's values) is increasingly acceptable in a no-digital-holds barred age. When this language becomes incendiary, egging on true believers with inflammatory rhetoric, it can prime prejudices, translating violent sentiments into action.

The structure, content, and language of a message are weapons in the persuader's arsenal. They are not magical. They work through psychological processes that offer insights into the dynamics of persuasion. Sometimes message effects occur immediately after receipt of the communication. In other cases, effects do not emerge until later, a phenomenon known as *the sleeper effect*, whereby a message initially discounted by message receivers comes to be accepted over time; this in turn has disturbing implications when the message is false, but widely diffused (Gruder et al., 1978; Kumkale & Albarracín, 2004).

All in all, the message continues to be a cornerstone of persuasion, as important today as it was in Aristotle's time, but wielded more fluidly and controversially through the rich panoply of oral, written, televised, and tweeted messages.

It's all the more important, given the critical challenges we face grappling with problems ranging from homelessness to schooling to climate change. While messages directed at individuals can't change public policies, collectively, working on the micro and macro levels, they can make a difference, as discussed on a broader level in Chapter 16. Given the urgent political and existential challenges people of the world face, from immigration to coronavirus to the environment, it is important to be cognizant of the ways that thoughtfully crafted, ethically toned, research-guided messages can change attitudes and behaviors. As Nelson Mandela optimistically noted, "it always seems impossible until it's done" (Machel, 2019, p. 50).

References

Adkins, M., & Brashers, D. E. (1995). The power of language in computer-mediated groups. *Management Communication Quarterly, 8*, 289–322.

Allen, M. (1998). Comparing the persuasive effectiveness of one and two sided messages. In M. Allen & R. W. Preiss (Eds.), *Persuasion: Advances through meta-analysis* (pp. 87–98). Cresskill, NJ: Hampton Press.

Allen, M., Bruflat, R., Fucilla, R., Kramer, M., McKellips, S., Ryan, D. J., & Spiegelhoff, M. (2000). Testing the persuasiveness of evidence: Combining narrative and statistical forms. *Communication Research Reports, 17*, 331–336.

Appel, M., & Malečkar, B. (2012). The influence of paratext on narrative persuasion: Fact, fiction, or fake? *Human Communication Research, 38*, 459–484.

Baker, P. (2019, July 25). Refusal to dramatize findings prevents blockbuster moment. *The New York Times*, A1, A14.

Banerjee, S. C., & Greene, K. (2012). Role of transportation in the persuasion process: Cognitive and affective responses to antidrug narratives. *Journal of Health Communication, 17*, 564–581.

Behm-Morawitz, E., Aubrey, J. S., Pennell, H., & Kim, K. B. (2019). Examining the effects of MTV's 16 and Pregnant on adolescent girls' sexual health: The implications of character affinity, pregnancy risk factors, and health literacy on message effectiveness. *Health Communication, 34*, 180–190.

Bilandzic, H., & Busselle, R. (2013). Narrative persuasion. In J. P. Dillard & L. Shen (Eds.), *The Sage handbook of persuasion: Developments in theory and practice* (2nd ed., pp. 200–219). Thousand Oaks, CA: Sage.

Blankenship, K. L., & Craig, T. Y. (2011). Language use and persuasion: Multiple roles for linguistic styles. *Social and Personality Psychology Compass, 5*, 194–205.

Bode, L., & Vraga, E. K. (2015). In related news, that was wrong: The correction of misinformation through related stories functionality in social media. *Journal of Communication, 65*, 619–638.

Bowers, J. W. (1964). Some correlates of language intensity. *Quarterly Journal of Speech, 50*, 415–420.

Bradley, P. H. (1981). The folk linguistics of women's speech: An empirical examination. *Communication Monographs, 48*, 73–90.

Braverman, J. (2008). Testimonials versus informational persuasive messages: The moderating effect of delivery mode and personal involvement. *Communication Research, 35*, 666–694.

Brehm, J. W. (1966). *A theory of psychological reactance*. New York: Academic Press.

Briñol, P., & Petty, R. E. (2003). Overt head movements and persuasion: A self-validation analysis. *Journal of Personality and Social Psychology, 84*, 1123–1139.

Brock, T. C., Strange, J. J., & Green, M. C. (2002). Power beyond reckoning: An introduction to narrative impact. In M. C. Green, J. J. Strange, & T. C. Brock (Eds.), *Narrative impact: Social and cognitive foundations* (pp. 1–15). Mahwah, NJ: Lawrence Erlbaum Associates.

Brody, J. E. (2011, April 12). Keeping eyes on distracted driving's toll. *The New York Times*, A27.

Buller, D. B., LePoire, B. A., Aune, R. K., & Eloy, S. V. (1992). Social perceptions as mediators of the effect of speech rate similarity on compliance. *Human Communication Research, 19*, 286–311.

Burgoon, J. K. (1994). Nonverbal signals. In M. L. Knapp & G. R. Miller (Eds.), *Handbook of interpersonal communication* (2nd ed., pp. 229–285). Thousand Oaks, CA: Sage.

Burrell, N. A., & Koper, R. J. (1998). The efficacy of powerful/powerless language on attitudes and source credibility. In M. Allen & R. W. Preiss (Eds.), *Persuasion: Advances through meta-analysis* (pp. 203–215). Cresskill, NJ: Hampton Press.

Burrows, C. N., & Blanton, H. (2016). Real-world persuasion from virtual-world campaigns: How transportation into virtual worlds moderates in-game influence. *Communication Research, 43*, 542–570.

Busselle, R., & Bilandzic, H. (2008). Fictionality and perceived realism in experiencing stories: A model of narrative comprehension and engagement. *Communication Theory, 18*, 255–280.

Camosy, C. C. (2019, January 10). The war of words on abortion. *The New York Times*, A23.

Carli, L. L. (1990). Gender, language, and influence. *Journal of Personality and Social Psychology, 59*, 941–951.

Claeys, A.-S., & Cauberghe, V. (2014). Keeping control: The importance of nonverbal expressions of power by organizational spokespersons in times of crisis. *Journal of Communication, 64*, 1160–1180.

Cohen, J., Tal-Or, N., & Mazor-Tregerman, M. (2015). The tempering effect of transportation: Exploring the effects of transportation and identification during exposure to controversial two-sided narratives. *Journal of Communication, 65*, 237–258.

Cole, T. (2019, July 14). Crime scene. *The New York Times Magazine*, 7–10.

Condit, C. M. (1990). *Decoding abortion rhetoric: Communicating social change*. Urbana, IL: University of Illinois Press.

Craig, T. Y., & Blankenship, K. L. (2011). Language and persuasion: Linguistic extremity influences message processing and behavioral intentions. *Journal of Language and Social Psychology, 30*, 290–310.

Cruz, M. G. (1998). Explicit and implicit conclusions in persuasive messages. In M. Allen & R. W. Preiss (Eds.), *Persuasion: Advances through meta-analysis* (pp. 217–230). Cresskill, NJ: Hampton Press.

de Graaf, A., Hoeken, H., Sanders, J., & Beentjes, J. W. J. (2012). Identification as a mechanism of narrative persuasion. *Communication Research, 39*, 802–823.

Dixon, G. N., & Clarke, C. E. (2013). Heightening uncertainty around certain science: Media coverage, false balance, and the autism–vaccine controversy. *Science Communication, 35*, 358–382.

Dixon, G. N., Weberling, M. B., Holton, A. E., Clarke, C., & Eosco, G. (2015). The power of a picture: Overcoming scientific misinformation by communicating weight-of-evidence information with visual exemplars. *Journal of Communication, 65*, 639–659.

Dunlop, S. M., Wakefield, M., & Kashima, Y. (2010). Pathways to persuasion: Cognitive and experiential responses to health-promoting mass media messages. *Communication Research, 37*, 133–164.

Entman, R. M. (1993). Framing: Toward clarification of a fractured paradigm. *Journal of Communication, 43*, 51–58.

Erickson, B., Lind, E. A., Johnson, B. C., & O'Barr, W. M. (1978). Speech style and impression formation in a court setting: The effects of "powerful" and "powerless" speech. *Journal of Experimental Social Psychology, 14*, 266–279.

Falk, E. (2010). *Women for president: Media bias in nine campaigns* (2nd ed.). Urbana, IL: University of Illinois Press.

Feinberg, M., & Willer, R. (2015). From gulf to bridge: When do moral arguments facilitate political influence? *Personality and Social Psychology Bulletin, 41*, 1665–1681.

Frey, K. P., & Eagly, A. H. (1993). Vividness can undermine the persuasiveness of messages. *Journal of Personality and Social Psychology, 65*, 32–44.

Funk, C., & Kennedy, B. (2019, April 19). How Americans see climate change in 5 charts. *Fact Tank: News in the numbers*. Online: www.pewresearch.org/fact-tank/2019/04/19/how-americans-see-climate... (Accessed: July 31, 2019).

Gerrig, R. J. (1993). *Experiencing narrative worlds: On the psychological activities of reading*. New Haven, CT: Yale University Press.

Giles, H., & Street, R. L., Jr. (1994). Communicator characteristics and behavior. In M. L. Knapp & G. R. Miller (Eds.), *Handbook of interpersonal communication* (2nd ed., pp. 103–161). Thousand Oaks, CA: Sage.

Goodall, J. (2019, September 23). The devastation of climate change is real. But there are reasons to be hopeful. *Time*, 50.

Green, M. C., & Brock, T. C. (2000). The role of transportation in the persuasiveness of public narratives. *Journal of Personality and Social Psychology, 79*, 701–721.

Green, M. C., & Jenkins, K. M. (2014). Interactive narratives: Processes and outcomes in user-directed stories. *Journal of Communication, 64*, 479–500.

Gruder, C. L., Cook, T. D., Hennigan, K. M., Flay, B. R., Alessis, C., & Halamaj, J. (1978). Empirical tests of the absolute sleeper effect predicted from the discounting cue hypothesis. *Journal of Personality and Social Psychology, 36*, 1061–1074.

Haidt, J. (2013). *The righteous mind: Why good people are divided by politics and religion*. New York: Vintage Books.

Haleta, L. L. (1996). Student perceptions of teachers' use of language: The effects of powerful and powerless language on impression formation and uncertainty. *Communication Education, 45*, 16–28.

Hamilton, M. A., & Hunter, J. E. (1998). The effect of language intensity on receiver evaluations of message, source, and topic. In M. Allen & R. W. Preiss (Eds.), *Persuasion: Advances through meta-analysis* (pp. 99–138). Cresskill, NJ: Hampton Press.

Harmon, A. (2017, June 5). Obstacle for climate science: Skeptical, stubborn students. *The New York Times*, A1, A14.

Harmon, A. (2019, May 23). Abortion fight is a turf battle in many words. *The New York Times*, A1, A18.

Harres, A. (1998). "But basically you're feeling well, are you?" Tag questions in medical consultations. *Health Communication, 10*, 111–123.

Hinyard, L. J., & Kreuter, M. W. (2007). Using narrative communication as a tool for health behavior change: A conceptual, theoretical, and empirical overview. *Health Education & Behavior, 34*, 777–792.

Hoeken, H., Kolthoff, M., & Sanders, J. (2016). Story perspective and character similarity as drivers of identification and narrative persuasion. *Human Communication Research, 42*, 292–311.

Holtgraves, T., & Lasky, B. (1999). Linguistic power and persuasion. *Journal of Language and Social Psychology*, *18*, 196–205.

Hosman, L. A. (1989). The evaluative consequences of hedges, hesitations, and intensifiers: Powerful and powerless speech styles. *Human Communication Research*, *15*, 383–406.

Hosman, L. A. (2002). Language and persuasion. In J. P. Dillard & M. Pfau (Eds.), *The persuasion handbook: Developments in theory and practice* (pp. 371–390). Thousand Oaks, CA: Sage.

Huff, D. (1954). *How to lie with statistics*. New York: Norton.

Jenkins, M., & Dragojevic, M. (2013). Explaining the process of resistance to persuasion: A politeness theory-based approach. *Communication Research*, *40*, 559–590.

Jensen, J. D., Yale, R. N., Krakow, M., John, K. K., & King, A. J. (2017). Theorizing foreshadowed death narratives: Examining the impact of character death on narrative processing and skin self-exam intentions. *Journal of Health Communication*, *22*, 84–93.

Kahneman, D. (2011). *Thinking, fast and slow*. New York: Farrar, Straus and Giroux.

Karpowitz, C. F., & Mendelberg, T. (2014). *The silent sex: Gender, deliberation, and institutions*. Princeton, NJ: Princeton University Press.

Kazoleas, D. C. (1993). A comparison of the persuasive effectiveness of qualitative versus quantitative evidence: A test of explanatory hypotheses. *Communication Quarterly*, *41*, 40–50.

Kearney, M. S., & Levine, P. B. (2014). Media influences on social outcomes: The impact of MTV's *16 and Pregnant* on teen childbearing. *NBER Working Paper Series*. Cambridge, MA: National Bureau of Economic Research. Online: www.nber.org/papers/w19795 (Accessed: May 22, 2014).

Kim, J., & Nan, X. (2019). Temporal framing effects differ for narrative versus non-narrative messages: The case of promoting HPV vaccination. *Communication Research*, *46*, 401–417.

Kolbert, E. (2019, September 30). A climate change? *The New Yorker*, 19–20.

Kopfman, J. E., Smith, S. W., Ah Yun, J. K., & Hodges, A. (1998). Affective and cognitive reactions to narrative versus statistical evidence organ donation messages. *Journal of Applied Communication Research*, *26*, 279–300.

Kortenkamp, K. V., & Basten, B. (2015). Environmental science in the media: Effects of opposing viewpoints on risk and uncertainty perceptions. *Science Communication*, *37*, 287–313.

Kühne, R., & Schemer, C. (2015). The emotional effects of news frames on information processing and opinion formation. *Communication Research*, *42*, 387–407.

Kumkale, G. T., & Albarracín, D. (2004). The sleeper effect in persuasion: A meta-analytic review. *Psychological Bulletin*, *130*, 143–172.

LaFraniere, S., Schmidt, M. S., Weiland, N., & Goldman, A. (2019, July 25). Mueller defends inquiry and says Russia isn't done: A halting delivery at odds with a laser focus of the past. *The New York Times*, A1, A16.

Lanchester, J. (2019, April 28). World on fire. *The New York Times Book Review*, 1, 20.

Lavin, M. (2001). *Clean new world: Culture, politics, and graphic design*. Cambridge, MA: MIT Press.

Lewandowsky, S., Stritzke, W. G. K., Freund, A. M., Oberauer, K., & Krueger, J. I. (2013). Misinformation, disinformation, and violent conflict: From Iraq and the "War on Terror" to future threats to peace. *American Psychologist*, *68*, 487–501.

Linz, D. G., & Penrod, S. (1984). Increasing attorney persuasiveness in the courtroom. *Law and Psychology Review*, *8*, 1–47.

Ma., Z., & Nan, X. (2018). Friends don't let friends smoke: How storytelling and social distance influence nonsmokers' responses to antismoking messages. *Health Communication*, *33*, 887–895.

Machel, G. (2019, September 23). Africa can be the launchpad for a green-energy revolution. *Time*, 40.

Major, L. H., & Coleman, R. (2012). Source credibility and evidence format: Examining the effectiveness of HIV/AIDS messages for young African Americans. *Journal of Health Communication*, *17*, 515–531.

Mazzocco, P. J., & Brock, T. C. (2006). Understanding the role of mental imagery in persuasion: A cognitive resources model analysis. In L. R. Kahle & C.-H. Kim (Eds.), *Creating images and the psychology of marketing communication* (pp. 65–78). Mahwah, NJ: Erlbaum Associates.

McCroskey, J. C. (1969). A summary of experimental research on the effects of evidence in persuasive communication. *Quarterly Journal of Speech, 55,* 169–176.

McGlone, M. S., & Giles, H. (2011). Language and interpersonal communication. In M. L. Knapp & J. A. Daly (Eds.), *The Sage handbook of interpersonal communication* (4th ed., pp. 201–237). Thousand Oaks, CA: Sage.

McGuire, W. J. (1969). The nature of attitudes and attitude change. In G. Lindzey & E. Aronson (Eds.), *Handbook of social psychology* (Vol. 3, 2nd ed., pp. 136–314). Reading, MA: Addison-Wesley.

McKinley, C. J., Limbu, Y., & Jayachandran, C. N. (2017). The influence of statistical versus exemplar appeals on Indian adults' health intentions: An investigation of direct effects and intervening persuasion processes. *Health Communication, 32,* 427–437.

Miller, C. H., Ivanov, B., Sims, J., Compton, J., Harrison, K. J., Parker, K. A., ... Averbeck, J. M. (2013). Boosting the potency of resistance: Combining the motivational forces of inoculation and psychological reactance. *Human Communication Research, 39,* 127–155.

Miller, C. H., Lane, L. T., Deatrick, L. M., Young, A. M., & Potts, K. A. (2007). Psychological reactance and promotional health messages: The effects of controlling language, lexical concreteness, and the restoration of freedom. *Human Communication Research, 33,* 219–240.

Miller, N., Maruyama, G., Beaber, R. J., & Valone, K. (1976). Speed of speech and persuasion. *Journal of Personality and Social Psychology, 34,* 615–624.

Morley, D. D., & Walker, K. B. (1987). The role of importance, novelty, and plausibility in producing belief change. *Communication Monographs, 54,* 436–442.

Morrison, T. (1987). *Beloved.* New York: Penguin.

Moyer-Gusé, E., Chung, A. H., & Jain, P. (2011). Identification with characters and discussion of taboo topics after exposure to an entertainment narrative about sexual health. *Journal of Communication, 61,* 387–406.

Moyer-Gusé, E., & Nabi, R. L. (2010). Explaining the effects of narrative in an entertainment television program: Overcoming resistance to persuasion. *Human Communication Research, 36,* 26–52.

Murphy, S. T., Frank, L. B., Moran, M. B., & Patnoe-Woodley, P. (2011). Involved, transported, or emotional? Exploring the determinants of change in knowledge, attitudes, and behavior in entertainment-education. *Journal of Communication, 61,* 407–431.

Naomi Wolf on abortion (2013, January 27). *ClinicQuotes.* Online: www.clinicquotes.com/naomi-wolf-on-abortion/ (Accessed: January 12, 2016).

Niederdeppe, J., Kim, H. K., Lundell, H., Fazili, F., & Frazier, B. (2012). Beyond counterarguing: Simple elaboration, complex integration, and counterelaboration in response to variations in narrative focus and sidedness. *Journal of Communication, 62,* 758–777.

Niederdeppe, J., Shapiro, M. A., Kim, H. K., Bartolo, D., & Porticella, N. (2014). Narrative persuasion, causality, complex integration, and support for obesity policy. *Health Communication, 29,* 431–444.

Niederdeppe, J., Shapiro, M. A., & Porticella, N. (2011). Attributions of responsibility for obesity: Narrative communication reduces reactive counterarguing among liberals. *Human Communication Research, 37,* 295–323.

Nyhan, B., & Reifler, J. (2010). When corrections fail: The persistence of political misperceptions. *Political Behavior, 32,* 303–330.

O'Keefe, D. J. (1997). Standpoint explicitness and persuasive effect: A meta-analytic review of the effects of varying conclusion articulation in persuasive messages. *Argumentation and Advocacy*, *34*, 1–12.

O'Keefe, D. J. (1999). How to handle opposing arguments in persuasive messages: A meta-analytic review of the effects of one-sided and two-sided messages. In M. E. Roloff (Ed.), *Communication yearbook 22* (pp. 209–249). New York: Routledge.

O'Keefe, D. J. (2016). *Persuasion: Theory and research* (3rd ed.). Thousand Oaks, CA: Sage.

O'Keefe, D. J., & Jensen, J. D. (2006). The advantages of compliance or the disadvantages of noncompliance?: A meta-analytic review of the relative persuasive effectiveness of gain-framed and loss-framed messages. In C. S. Beck (Ed.), *Communication yearbook 30* (pp. 1–43). Mahwah, NJ: Erlbaum Associates.

Parrott, R., Silk, K., Dorgan, K., Condit, C., & Harris, T. (2005). Risk comprehension and judgments of statistical evidentiary appeals: When a picture is not worth a thousand words. *Human Communication Research*, *31*, 423–452.

Poniewozik, J. (2018, September 29). Two voices with a notable contrast in volume. *The New York Times*, A16.

Quick, B. L., Shen, L., & Dillard, J. P. (2013). Reactance theory and persuasion. In J. P. Dillard & L. Shen (Eds.), *The Sage handbook of persuasion: Developments in theory and practice* (2nd ed., pp. 167–183). Thousand Oaks, CA: Sage.

Quintero Johnson, J. M., & Sangalang, A. (2017). Testing the explanatory power of two measures of narrative involvement: An investigation of the influence of transportation and narrative engagement on the process of narrative persuasion. *Media Psychology*, *20*, 144–173.

Ray, G. B., Ray, E. B., & Zahn, C. J. (1991). Speech behavior and social evaluation: An examination of medical messages. *Communication Quarterly*, *39*, 119–129.

Reinard, J. C. (1988). The empirical study of the persuasive effects of evidence: The status after fifty years of research. *Human Communication Research*, *15*, 3–59.

Reinard, J. C. (1991). *Foundations of argument: Effective communication for critical thinking*. Dubuque, IA: Wm. C. Brown.

Reynolds, R. A., & Reynolds, J. L. (2002). Evidence. In J. E. Dillard & M. Pfau (Eds.), *The persuasion handbook: Developments in theory and practice* (pp. 427–444). Thousand Oaks, CA: Sage.

Richards, A. S., Banas, J. A., & Magid, Y. (2017). More on inoculating against reactance to persuasive health messages: The paradox of threat. *Health Communication*, *32*, 890–902.

Rook, K. S. (1987). Effects of case history versus abstract information on health attitudes and behaviors. *Journal of Applied Social Psychology*, *17*, 533–553.

Sangalang, A., Ophir, Y., & Cappella, J. N. (2019). The potential for narrative correctives to combat misinformation. *Journal of Communication*, *69*, 293–319.

Scherer, K. R., London, H., & Wolf, J. J. (1973). The voice of confidence: Paralinguistic cues and audience evaluation. *Journal of Research in Personality*, *7*, 31–44.

Shen, L., & Bigsby, E. (2013). The effects of message features: Content, structure, and style. In J. P. Dillard & L. Shen (Eds.), *The Sage handbook of persuasion: Developments in theory and practice* (2nd ed., pp. 20–35). Thousand Oaks, CA: Sage.

Shen, L., & Seung, S. Y. (2018). On measures of message elaboration in narrative communication. *Communication Quarterly*, *66*, 79–95.

Simon, A. F., & Jerit, J. (2007). Toward a theory relating political discourse, media, and public opinion. *Journal of Communication*, *57*, 254–271.

Skalski, P., Tamborini, R., Glazer, E., & Smith, S. (2009). Effects of humor on presence and recall of persuasive messages. *Communication Quarterly*, *57*, 136–163.

Slater, M. D., & Rouner, D. (1996). Value-affirmative and value-protective processing of alcohol education messages that include statistical evidence or anecdotes. *Communication Research, 23,* 210–235.

Slater, M. D., Rouner, D., & Long, M. (2006). Television dramas and support for controversial public policies: Effects and mechanisms. *Journal of Communication, 56,* 235–252.

Smith, R. A., Downs, E., & Witte, K. (2007). Drama theory and entertainment education: Exploring the effects of a radio drama on behavioral intentions to limit HIV transmission in Ethiopia. *Communication Monographs, 74,* 133–153.

Smith, S. M., & Shaffer, D. R. (1995). Speed of speech and persuasion: Evidence for multiple effects. *Personality and Social Psychology Bulletin, 21,* 1051–1060.

Sopory, P., & Dillard, J. P. (2002). Figurative language and persuasion. In J. P. Dillard & M. Pfau (Eds.), *The persuasion handbook: Developments in theory and practice* (pp. 407–426). Thousand Oaks, CA: Sage.

Sparks, J. R., & Areni, C. S. (2008). Style versus substance: Multiple roles of language power in persuasion. *Journal of Applied Social Psychology, 38,* 37–60.

Street, R. L., Jr., & Brady, R. M. (1982). Speech rate acceptance ranges as a function of evaluative domain, listener speech rate, and communication context. *Communication Monographs, 49,* 290–308.

Suellentrop, C. (2014, October 26). Can video games survive? *The New York Times* (Sunday Review), 1, 7.

Tal-Or, N., & Cohen, J. (2010). Understanding audience involvement: Conceptualizing and manipulating identification and transportation. *Poetics, 38,* 402–418.

Tal-Or, N., & Tsfati, Y. (2018). Does the co-viewing of sexual material affect rape myth acceptance? The role of the co-viewer's reactions and gender. *Communication Research, 45,* 577–602.

Tewksbury, D., & Scheufele, D. A. (2009). News framing theory and research. In J. Bryant & M. B. Oliver (Eds.), *Media effects: Advances in theory and research* (3rd ed., pp. 17–33). New York: Routledge.

Toulmin, S. (1958). *The uses of argument.* New York: Cambridge University Press.

USGCRP. (2018). *Impacts, risks, and adaptation in the United States: Fourth national climate assessment* (pp. II). Washington, DC: U.S. Global Change Research Program. doi:10.7930/ NCA4.2018. (Accessed: November 13, 2019).

Van Laer, T., Ruyter, K. D., Visconti, L. M., & Wetzels, M. (2014). The extended transportation-imagery model: A meta-analysis of the antecedents and consequences of consumers' narrative transportation. *Journal of Consumer Research, 40,* 797–817.

Van Zant, A. B., & Berger, J. (2020). How the voice persuaders. *Journal of Personality and Social Psychology, 118,* 661–682.

Walter, N., Murphy, S. T., & Gillig, T. K. (2018). To walk a mile in someone else's shoes: How narratives can change causal attribution through story exploration and character customization. *Human Communication Research, 44,* 31–57.

Willer, R., & Feinberg, M. (2015, November 17). The key to political persuasion. *The New York Times* (Sunday Review), 9.

Winfield, B. (1994). *FDR and the news media.* New York: Columbia University Press.

Wolsko, C., Ariceaga, H., & Seiden, J. (2016). Red, white, and blue enough to be green: Effects of moral framing on climate change attitudes and conservation behaviors. *Journal of Experimental Social Psychology, 65,* 7–19.

Yoo, J. H., Kreuter, M. W., Lai, C., & Fu, Q. (2014). Understanding narrative effects: The role of discrete negative emotions on message processing and attitudes among low-income African American Women. *Health Communication, 29,* 494–504.

Zaveri, M. (2019, October 17). Game makers who game changers. *The New York Times,* B6, B7.

Zhou, S., & Niederdeppe, J. (2017). The promises and pitfalls of personalization in narratives to promote social change. *Communication Monographs, 84,* 319–342.

Zhou, S., & Shapiro, M. A. (2017). Reducing resistance to narrative persuasion about binge drinking: The role of self-activation and habitual drinking behavior. *Health Communication, 32,* 1297–1309.

Chapter 12

Emotional Message Appeals

Fear and Guilt

Fear. It's that gyrating feeling you have in the pit of your stomach, the dizziness you feel when the doctor tells you he is not sure why your arm hurts and will need to conduct some tests to evaluate the problem. Fear is the emotion we experience when we learn that our dependence on something or someone could be bad for our health. It's the sinking sensation you have when you suddenly realize that the careening out-of-control car you are driving is going to smash another car and probably injure you and the other driver. Fear. It is part of being human, but it is not pleasant and, except maybe when you are riding a roller coaster you know will return safely to the hub, it is aversive and almost never fun.

Fear is a powerful emotion. For this reason it has been a source of fascination to persuasion researchers, who have sought to understand how it can be harnessed in the service of attitude change. This chapter examines the processes and effects of two emotional persuasive appeals: Fear and guilt. The first section, the thrust of the chapter, explores fear appeals, while the second portion examines guilt. It's a complex chapter because it covers the multitude of studies on fear appeals, with their twists, turns, and contradictions.

Emotions themselves are complex critters. An emotion involves a cognitive assessment of a situation, physiological arousal, a subjective set of feelings, motivation to behave in a certain way, and a motor or facial expression (Nabi, 2009). Given the emotional underpinnings of attitudes, emotions invariably come into play in the conceptualization of communications designed to change attitudes. Unlike positive emotions, like pride or warmth, which are characterized by satisfaction with a mood state, fear motivates people to take action. Unlike anxiety and depression, which can induce indecision or helplessness, fear can be harnessed to change attitudes in a constructive fashion. Let's turn now to the fear factor, the name of an old TV game show and also the concept that has stimulated thousands of persuasion studies across social science disciplines.

Fear Appeals

Some years back, Maureen Coyne, a college senior enrolled in a persuasion class, ruminated about a question her professor asked: Think of a time when you tried to change someone's attitude about an issue. How did you go about accomplishing this task? After thinking for a few moments, Maureen recalled a series of events from her childhood, salient incidents in which she mightily tried to influence loved ones' attitudes. "My entire life," she related, "I have been trying to persuade my lovely parents to quit smoking. It started with the smell of smoke," she said, recollecting:

> I would go to school and kids could smell it on me to the extent that they would ask me if my parents smoked. It was humiliating. Then the lessons began from the teachers. They vehemently expressed how unhealthy this habit was through videos, books, and even puppet shows. In my head, the case against smoking was building. From my perspective, smoking was hurting my parents, my younger brothers, and me. With this in mind, it is understandable that a young, energetic, opinionated child would try and do something to rid her life of this nasty habit. Well, try I did. I educated them constantly about the dangers of first- and second-hand smoke, with help from class assignments. I would tell them about the cancers, carbon monoxide, etc., and remind them every time I saw something on TV or in the paper about smoking statistics. I begged and begged and begged (and then cried a little). I explained how much it hurt my brothers and me. I reminded them that they should practice what they preach (they told us not to smoke).
>
> (Coyne, 2000)

Maureen's valiant attempt called on a variety of emotions and message strategies, not just fear, as frequently happens when fear appeals are employed. She used a subtle threat, as well as direct and indirect interpersonal compliance techniques. Although her plaintive pleas ultimately failed (her parents disregarded her loving advice), she showed a knack for devising a compelling fear appeal to influence attitudes toward smoking. Maureen is hardly alone in trying to scare people into changing a dysfunctional attitude or behavior. Fear appeals are ubiquitous. Consider the following:

- Hoping to deter juvenile criminals from a life of crime, a New Jersey prison adopted a novel approach in the late 1970s. Teenagers who had been arrested for crimes like robbery were carted off to Rahway State Prison to participate in a communication experiment. The teens were seated before a group of lifers, men who had been sentenced to life imprisonment for murder and armed robbery. The men, bruising, brawling criminals, intimidated the youngsters, swearing at them and threatening to hurt them. At the same time, they used obscene and intense language to scare the youngsters into changing their ways. The program, *Scared Straight*, was videotaped and broadcast on national television numerous times over the ensuing decades. Although there is mixed evidence regarding its actual effects in deterring juvenile crime (Finckenauer, 1982), it has become part of popular culture, excerpted on YouTube, parodied in *The Office*, and the focus of a successful A&E reality television show, *Beyond Scared Straight*, that bears little resemblance to the original program.
- Then there all those public service announcements (PSAs), in magazines, on television, and on websites that regularly arouse fear in the hope of convincing young people to stop smoking, quit using dangerous drugs like methamphetamine, quit texting when they drive, and avoid binge-drinking episodes. Some PSAs have become world famous, like the Partnership for a Drug-Free America's "brain on drugs" ad. ("This is your brain. This is drugs. This is your brain on drugs. Any questions?") Many other similar messages appear on YouTube or in texts, using fear to persuade young adults to change risky habits.
- Now consider this all-too-familiar existential threat, global warming. It has been the focus of innumerable fear messengers, pronouncing, as writer David Wallace-Wells duly notes, "the age of climate panic is here" (2019, p. 1). Experts warn that we can expect "heat deaths" through

devastating storms, mass migration, and economic calamities. The time to panic has long past arrived, Wallace-Wells says, adding dramatically that "the longer we wait, the worse it will get," and ending with an aphorism that cuts to the core of this chapter: "What creates more urgency than fear?" (p.7).

Alas, we certainly have seen this urgency with the anxiety and precautions that were taken in the wake of the outbreak of the coronavirus in 2020.

Fear appeals can be international in scope, like these, or narrowly focused on risks taken by particular individuals in contexts from health to technology to consumer product purchases, where the specter of dirty clothes and bad breath are raised. They evoke different reactions – spanning angst, anxiety, and action. When conveyed moralistically, of course, fear messages can remind people of the worst moments of adolescence, when parents warned them that every pleasurable activity would end up haunting them in later life. Some observers, noting that life is full of dangers, approve of and appreciate these communications. Still other observers wonder why we must resort to fear, preferring to just given people the facts, while forgetting that the facts will be constructed differently by those who deny, rather than acknowledge, their fears.

Appealing to people's fears is, to a considerable degree, a negative communication strategy. The communicator must arouse a little pain in the individual, hoping it will produce gain. The persuader may have to go further than the facts of the situation warrant, raising specters and scenarios that may be rather unlikely to occur even if the individual continues to engage in the dysfunctional behavior. In an ideal world, it would not be necessary to arouse fear. Communicators could simply present the facts in a boring, didactic manner, and logic would carry the day. But this is not an ideal world; people are emotional, as well as cognitive, creatures, and they do not always do what is best for them. People are tempted by all sorts of demons – objects, choices, and substances that seem appealing but actually can cause quite a bit of harm. Thus, fear appeals are a necessary persuasive strategy, useful in a variety of arenas of life, and the use of negative emotions can ultimately exert positive effects (see Figure 12.1).

The Psychology of Fear

Before discussing the role that fear plays in persuasion, it is instructive to define our terms. What is fear? What is a fear appeal? Social scientists define the terms in the following ways:

- *Fear*: An internal emotional reaction composed of psychological and physiological dimensions that may be aroused when a serious and personally relevant threat is perceived (Witte, Meyer, & Martell, 2001, p. 20).
- *Fear appeal*: A persuasive communication that tries to scare people into changing their attitudes by conjuring up negative consequences that will occur if they do not comply with the message recommendations.

Over the past half-century, researchers have conducted numerous studies of fear-arousing messages. As a result of this research, we know a great deal about the psychology of fear and the impact of fear appeals on attitudes. The research has also done much to clarify common-sense notions – in some cases misconceptions – of fear message effects.

At first glance, it probably seems like it is very easy to scare people. According to popular belief, all persuaders need do is conjure up really terrible outcomes, get the person feeling jittery and anxious, and wait as fear drives the individual to follow the recommended action. There are two misconceptions

Figure 12.1 People Engage in Lots of Risky Behaviors. Fear appeals are a way to persuade them to change their attitudes toward these problems and adopt a healthier behavioral regimen. However, fear is a dicey weapon in the persuasion arsenal and works only if it is used deftly and sensitively

Image courtesy of Shutterstock

here: First, that fear appeals invariably work, and second, that fear acts as a simple drive. Let's see how these notions oversimplify matters.

Contrary to what you may have heard, it is not easy to scare people successfully. Arousing fear does not always produce attitude change. After reviewing the research in this area, Franklin J. Boster and Paul Mongeau concluded that "manipulating fear does not appear to be an easy task. What appears to be a highly-arousing persuasive message to the experimenter may not induce much fear into the recipient of the persuasive message" (1984, p. 375).

More generally, persuaders frequently assume that a message scares audience members. However, they may be surprised to discover that individuals either are not frightened or did not tune in to the message because they perceived that it was irrelevant to their needs. This has been a recurring problem with automobile safety videos – those designed to persuade people to wear seat belts or not drink when they drive. Message designers undoubtedly have the best of intentions, but their persuasive videos are often seen by audience members as hokey, far-fetched, or just plain silly (Robertson et al., 1974).

Not only can fear appeals fail because they arouse too little fear, but they can also backfire by running up against psychological barriers to change. Fear messages invariably suggest that bad things will happen if individuals continue engaging in dangerous behaviors, like smoking or excessive drinking. None of us likes to admit that these outcomes will happen to us, so we deny or defensively distort the communicator's message. There is considerable evidence that people perceive that bad things are less likely to happen to them than to others (Weinstein, 1980, 1993). In a classic study, Neil D. Weinstein (1980) asked college students to estimate how much their own chances of experiencing negative life events differed from the chances of their peers. Students perceived that they were significantly less likely than others to experience a host of outcomes, including:

- dropping out of college;
- getting divorced a few years after getting married;
- being fired from a job;
- having a drinking problem;
- getting lung cancer;
- contracting venereal disease.

Think of it this way: Remember high school when a friend wanted to be cool and hip, showed up at a party once, drank too much, and embarrassed herself. In her mind, there was zero chance that negative consequences would befall her. Unfortunately, it does not always work that way. Teenagers will boast on Facebook about their social or sexual exploits, only to regret it afterwards or discover that school officials read their messages. Some teens do outlandish pranks, hoping to gain notoriety by videotaping and posting them on YouTube. One New Jersey teen loaded his bathtub with fireworks, layered himself in protective clothing, and turned on a video camera to record the spectacle. The explosion, which the boy said he hoped to place on YouTube, produced a fireball that left the youngster with burns on more than 10 percent of his body (Parker-Pope, 2010).

During the early days of the global coronavirus epidemic, many people understandably minimized the risk, convinced they would not be affected. Some Louisiana women acknowledged they even cracked jokes about it, asking why everyone is "so wigged out" – until a close friend's husband tested positive for the virus. Suddenly, that put "a real face on a real danger," another friend shared (Plott, 2020).

The belief that one is less likely to experience negative life events than others is known as *unrealistic optimism* or the *illusion of invulnerability*. People harbor such illusions for three reasons.

First, they do not want to admit that life's misfortunes can befall them. For instance, many young people routinely accept medications like Ritalin from friends, switch from Paxil to Prozac based on the recommendation of an email acquaintance, or trade Ativan for Ambien (Harmon, 2005). Youthful, assured, and confident of their knowledge, they minimize the risks involved in taking drugs for which they do not have a prescription. Countless young teenage girls, in search of the body-beautifying tan and fantasizing that pale means pretty, spend hours at indoor tanning salons. They plunk down $7 for 20 minutes in a tanning bed at a tanning salon, hoping to beautify their bodies before the prom, attract guys, and increase self-confidence. But indoor tanning carries serious risks, accounting for an estimated 400,000 annual cases of skin cancer. Yet teenage girls don't think it will happen to them, until the price tag comes, as Sarah Hughes, a small-town girl from Alabama sadly discovered, when nine years of tanning left a tumor on her left leg (Tavernise, 2015).

A second reason people harbor an illusion of invulnerability is that they maintain a stereotype of the typical victim of negative events and blithely maintain that they do not fit the mold. For example, in the case of cigarette smoking, they may assume that the typical smoker who gets lung cancer is a thin, nervous, jittery, middle-aged man who smokes like a chimney. Noting that they smoke but do not fit the prototype, individuals conclude they are not at risk. This overlooks the fact that few of those who get cancer from smoking actually match the stereotype.

A third reason is that people, enjoying the pleasures of risky choices, decide to offload the costs of these pleasures to the more mature adults they will become in the future (Holt, 2006). In essence, an individual separates out his present and future selves, then rationalizes pursuit of a risky behavior in the here and now, "making the future self suffer for the pleasure of the moment" (Holt, 2006, pp. 16–17). Exemplifying this view, 22-year-old Elizabeth LaBak, an inveterate indoor tanner, noted that, "If I get skin cancer I'll deal with it then. I can't think about that now" (Tavernise, 2015, p. 16). In adopting this defensive orientation, young adults like Elizabeth choose to minimize the long-term consequences they will endure as adults.

The illusion of invulnerability is a major barrier to fear appeals' success. If I don't believe or don't want to believe that I am susceptible to danger, then I am unlikely to accept the persuader's advice.

A second misconception of fear appeals follows from this tendency. Fear is commonly thought to be a simple drive that propels people to do as the persuader requests.

According to this notion (popularized by early theorists), fear is an unpleasant psychological state, one that people are motivated to reduce. Supposedly, when the message provides recommendations that alleviate fear, people accept the recommendations and change their behavior (Hovland, Janis, & Kelley, 1953). To be sure, fear is an unpleasant emotional state, but, contrary to early theorists, people do not behave in a simple, animal-like manner to rid themselves of painful sensations. Fear is more complicated.

A message can scare someone, but fail to change attitudes because it does not connect with the person's beliefs about the problem, or neglects to provide a solution to the difficulty that ails the individual. The original drive model put a premium on fear, simplifying the processes by which fear induces attitude change (though see Dillard, Li, Meczkowski, Yang, & Shen, 2017 for a useful perspective). We know that persuaders must do more than just arouse fear to change an individual's attitude or behavior. They must convince message recipients that they are susceptible to negative outcomes and that the recommended response will alleviate the threat. Messages must work on a cognitive, as well as affective, level. They must help individuals appreciate the problem and, through the power of words and suggestions, encourage people to come to grips with the danger at hand.

A Theory of Fear Appeals

Devising an effective fear appeal is, to some extent, an art, but it is an art that requires a scientist's appreciation of the intricacies of human behavior. For this reason, theoretical approaches to fear messages are particularly important to develop, and there has been no shortage of these over the years (Dillard, 1994; Rogers, 1975).

Ronald W. Rogers developed an important cognitive-based approach in 1975, called *protection motivation theory*. Departing from the 1950s-style drive model, he argued that a fear appeal must contain information about the amount of threat the problem poses, its probability of occurrence, and the effectiveness of recommended responses. Each of these triggers cognitive mediating responses, which in turn motivate people to protect themselves from danger, ideally leading to attitude change (Rajecki, 1990).

Building on Rogers' work, Kim Witte proposed a more intricate, widely cited framework, the *Extended Parallel Process Model* (EPPM). Her model synthesizes different research strands, with more crystallized predictions. It also emphasizes two parallel processes, or two different mechanisms by which fear appeals can influence attitudes. Like the ELM, the EPPM is a process model, one that calls attention to the ways in which people think and feel about persuasive messages. Reasoning that fear is a complex emotion, Witte (1998) invokes specific terms. She talks about fear, but recognizes that we need to consider other subtle aspects of fear-arousing messages if we are to understand their effects on attitudes.

A fear-arousing message contains two basic elements: *threat* and *efficacy information*, or a problem and solution. A message must first threaten the individual, convincing him or her that dangers lurk in the environment. To do this, a message must contain four key threat-oriented elements.

Harnessing the Four Components of the EPPM

Let's see how plays out if you were devising a message to scare teenagers into quitting that e-cigarette we love to hate, the e-cig puffed on by more than about 3.5 million middle and high school students in the United States over the past year.

Although some research indicates that e-cigarettes like Juul can help people quit the smoking habit, considerable evidence suggests they have addictive properties that can worsen adolescents' health (Hoffman, 2019). In any case, few would argue they exclusively promote health benefits; quite the contrary, critics argue, noting they may have fueled a mini health epidemic among adolescents eager to experiment with new substances, particularly the electronic version of the iPhone, as the thumb-drive resembling Juuls have been called. Juul now accounts for 70 percent of U.S. e-cigarette sales, and it can be hard to kick the vaping habit, with its nicotine-addicting vapers (Hoffman, 2018). So how would you use the EPPM to persuade teens to quit? You would adroitly call on the four core EPPM elements. Let's discuss each in turn.

1 *Severity information: Information about the seriousness or magnitude of the threat.* You could use a combination of evidence and narrative to present severity information persuasively. You could start with evidence, buttressing the effect by noting the information comes from the highly credible former commissioner of the U.S. Food and Drug Administration, Dr. David A. Kessler. Juul has increased the nicotine kick from earlier e-cigarettes by using as much as 5 percent nicotine, adding some flavors to decrease the harshness of the taste. "Each Juul cartridge with 5 percent nicotine delivers 200 puffs, compared to the 10 to 15 puffs of a traditional cigarette," Kessler has said (2019, p. A27). Nicotine dependence can start slowly, is increasingly difficult to stop, and its addictive aspects are more serious for teenagers, whose brains are still developing. You could complement evidence with a story, lending the transportive property of narrative. You might relate the travails of Matt Murphy, a college student from Reading, Massachusetts, who, at 17, loved "the euphoric power-punch of the nicotine … the head rush" it gave him. Before long, he was up

to three or four hits a day, moving to a daily pod, sometimes more, laying out $40 a week (plus his Christmas and birthday money). He couldn't play his sports – hockey and tennis – without getting winded and realized, when he got to college, that he had a problem. He just wanted to be in his room doing Juul, his dependence so bad it came to a head with an emotional argument with his parents, a tearful talk where Matt had to come to terms with a problem he never thought he would have to confront (Hoffman, 2018).

2   *Susceptibility information: Information about the likelihood that the threatening outcomes will occur.* This is among the hardest psychological barriers to penetrate because it taps into people's defensive, distorted beliefs – and need to believe – that they are invulnerable to life's misfortunes. In a small recent study of small-town Ohio high school teens, one of my students discovered that teenagers minimized their susceptibility to Juul's hazards, perceiving other adolescents were more likely than they were to become addicted to Juul, to get in trouble with parents for using Juul, and to experience a stomach ache from puffing the e-cig (Haren, 2019). To combat these perceptions and shatter the all-important illusion of invulnerability, you, as the persuader, could call on tried-and-true communicator principles like similarity. You could patiently explain that more than 20 percent of high school students nationally and more than one in four kids under 18 suffered health consequences, from serious lung illnesses to death (Perloff, 2019; Williams & Del Real, 2019).

   Turning to the high school audience, you could slowly, deliberately, looking directly into the teens' eyes, explain that this fate could befall them too.

After threatening or scaring the person, the message must sensitively, but emphatically, provide a recommended response – a way the individual can avert the threat. It must contain efficacy information or facts about effective ways to cope with the danger at hand. Efficacy consists of two components, which result in two additional elements of a fear appeal:

3   *Response efficacy: Information about the effectiveness of the recommended action.* It is imperative to offer pathways to healing, hope, and solutions to the fear that has been aroused. You, as the persuader, could explain that, with patience, forbearance, and determination, people can gradually reduce their dependence on Juul by gradually replacing Juul with other pleasurable, but less addictive, activities, joining a support group, or working with mental health counselors to help themselves get better. After three weeks, you could relate, Matt found the worst of the pain of nicotine withdrawal had passed.

4   *Self-efficacy information: Arguments that the individual is capable of performing the recommended action.* This final step involves persuading people that they have what it takes, the wherewithal, and gumption to quit and get their bodacious life back. Affirming individuals, helping them get in touch with their best traits, trying to access their inner confidence in themselves, and reminding them of other difficult tasks they have mastered can help build self-efficacy. Matt, now the familiar focus of your story, once addicted, is no longer, you could note. He transferred to another university, majored in business, and moved home for a time to draw on support from his parents. Now *he* is the one trying to help friends quit their dependence on Juul. His friends text him frequently when they're trying to quit, asking if he experienced a particular pain. And Matt emphasizes that "it gets better" (Hoffman, 2018).

   Each of these message components theoretically triggers a cognitive reaction in the person. Severity and susceptibility information should convince the individual that the threat is serious and likely to occur, provided no change is made in the problematic behavior. Response efficacy and self-efficacy information should persuade the individual that these outcomes can be avoided if the recommended actions are internalized and believed.

The operative word is *should*. There is no guarantee a fear appeal will work in exactly this way. Much depends on which of the two parallel processes the message unleashes. The two cognitive processes at the core of the model are danger control and fear control (see Figure 12.2).

Danger control is a cognitive process that occurs when people perceive that they are capable of averting the threat by undertaking the recommended action. When in danger control mode, people turn their attention outward, appraise the external danger, and adopt strategies to cope with the problem.

By contrast, *fear control*, an emotional process, occurs when people face a significant threat, but focus inwardly on the fear, rather than on the problem at hand. They concentrate on ways of containing their fear and keeping it at bay, rather than on developing strategies to ward off the danger. Witte and colleagues invite us to consider how the processes might work:

> Think of a situation in which you were faced with a grave threat. Sometimes, you may have tried to control the danger by thinking about your risk of experiencing the threat and ways to avoid it. If you did this, you engaged in the danger control process. Now, think of times when your fear was so overwhelming that you didn't even think of the threat. Instead, you focused on ways to calm down your racing heart, your sweaty palms, and your nervousness. You may have taken some deep breaths, drunk some water, or smoked a cigarette. These all are fear control strategies. You were controlling your fear, but without any thought of the actual danger facing you.
>
> (2001, pp. 14–15)

Thus, when individuals are in fear control mode, they focus defensively on controlling the fear, reducing anxiety, and calming their nerves – but they don't go outside themselves to try to deal with the danger at hand. Perceiving they are susceptible to the problem, they can be in high-anxiety mode (So,

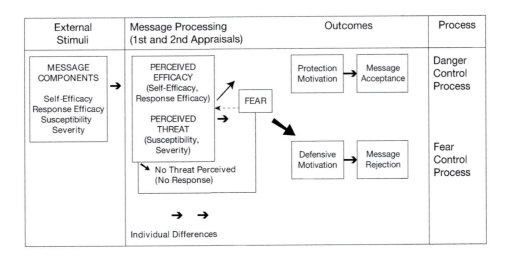

Figure 12.2 Extended Parallel Process Model
From Witte (1998)

Kuang, & Cho, 2016). Feeling helpless to undertake the recommended action, they remain vulnerable to the danger: Getting cancer from smoking, liver disease from drinking, or clogged arteries from too much transfat. When in danger control mode, they find the wherewithal to deal with the external problem and begin taking steps to improve their physical or psychological health. This has important implications for persuasion. It suggests that a fear appeal works if it nudges the individual into danger control and fails if it pushes the person into fear control.

If the message convinces people that they can cope, it can change attitudes. If people are bowled over by their fear and paralyzed by the severity of the threat, the message backfires. Indeed, when people possess unusually high levels of fear, scaring them can be counterproductive. When individuals are terrified about a social problem, scaring them can increase anxiety and render fear appeals ineffective, as in the case of fear appeals about the coronavirus directed at people nervous they had been exposed to someone who tested positive (Muthusamy, Levine, & Weber, 2009; Morris & Swann, 1996). "You can't even cough without people losing their minds," said a student at Yeshiva University in New York in the wake of a report of a student who had positive test results (Gold & Ferré-Sandurní, 2020, p. A16). In these cases fear appeals must be carefully crafted.

Scholars, attempting to advance basic and applied knowledge, emphasize that when threat and efficacy are high, people are motivated to consider changing their attitude (Mongeau, 2013). (To be sure, comparing threat and efficacy, very different constructs, is a tricky empirical proposition.) In general, the theory suggests that when perceived high efficacy equals or exceeds perceived high threat, individuals engage in danger control and adopt recommendations to avert the danger (O'Keefe, 2016; Witte et al., 2001). They feel motivated to protect themselves from danger (protection motivation in the model) and take necessary steps to deal with the problem at hand. However, if perceived threat exceeds perceived efficacy, people shift into fear control mode, obsess about the fear, defensively process the message, and do nothing to alter their behavior. For example, an anti-smoking campaign succeeds if it convinces the smoker that the risk of cancer can be averted if he quits smoking now and begins chewing Nicorette gum instead of smoking Camels. The campaign fails if it gets the individual so worried that he will get cancer that he begins smoking cigarettes just to calm down!

What role does fear play in all this? Fear is probably a necessary condition for messages to succeed. People have to be scared, and messages that arouse high levels of fear can produce significant attitude change (Boster & Mongeau, 1984; Mongeau, 1998). But fear is not enough. In order to change attitudes, a message must harness fear and channel it into a constructive (danger control) direction. This entails "pushing all the right buttons" or, more precisely, convincing people that the threat is severe and real, but that there is something they can do to ward off the danger. Note that messages must contain threats, a different construct than fear. If they trigger the right cognitive and emotional responses, they can change attitudes (see Box 12.1).

Applying Theory to the Real World

Fear appeal theories like Witte's have generated many studies, mostly experiments. Researchers have randomly assigned one group of subjects to watch a video or DVD that contains a very threatening message. They have exposed an equivalent group to a message that raises milder threats. Experimenters have also varied other aspects of the message, such as the effectiveness of the recommended response or self-efficacy. A variety of studies support the EPPM, as well as Rogers' protection motivation model. For example, in one study smokers who were led to believe that there was a high probability that smoking causes cancer indicated an intention to quit only if they believed that the recommended practice (quitting smoking) was highly effective (Rogers & Mewborn, 1976).

BOX 12.1

Understanding Theory: Primer on the Extended Parallel Process Model and Other Fear Appeals Research

1   The model contains specific, testable propositions, emphasizing *processes* that mediate the effects of fear-arousing messages on attitudes.

2   A first set of parallel processes is fear control and danger control. Messages that drive receivers into fear control fail, as individuals focus on the inward fear, not the danger. Messages can succeed when they push individuals into danger control, where they process the danger at hand.

3   A second set of processes is perceived efficacy and perceived threat. When perceived efficacy exceeds perceived threat – when the message convinces individuals that recommendations can avert the danger more than it induces them to worry about the threat – the message can change attitudes toward the problem.

4   Perceived efficacy is important. If the message cannot influence perceived efficacy, and persuade individuals of the effectiveness of the recommendation on a general or personal level, a fear message may not be the most useful way to change attitudes (Maloney, Lapinski, & Witte, 2011).

5   The four broad components of a fear appeal are severity, susceptibility, response efficacy, and self-efficacy.

6   Messages must contain a persuasive *threat* to change attitudes (Dillard & Li, in press). Fear frequently has to be aroused, but it can backfire, leading to defensive rejection of the message. To succeed, messages must contain a credible threat, demonstrate that the threat is severe and can probably occur, and then impress upon people that the message can alleviate the threat.

7   The model does not offer a precise recipe on how to design the optimum fear appeal, or how to accommodate individual differences in emotional responses to the issue.

8   On balance, the EPPM is a helpful model, shedding light on the processes and effects of fear appeals.

Research Support: Gun Control in Michigan

Particularly compelling support for the model was offered in an experiment on gun safety. Firearms are a leading cause of fatal injury in the United States, even surpassing car accidents in several states to become the primary cause of fatal injuries. Concerned about this problem, researcher Anthony J. Roberto and colleagues developed a graphic videotape to influence attitudes toward gun safety (Roberto et al., 2000). Guided by the EPPM, they organized the videotape so that it presented susceptibility, severity, response efficacy, and self-efficacy information.

The video presents heart-rending statements by young men whose physical and emotional lives were shattered by gun accidents. For example, Andy, a 29-year-old Michigan native, relates that one night he was cleaning his gun and accidentally shot himself in the leg. Severely wounded, Andy crawled about 50 feet to his home to get help. Although doctors saved Andy's life, his leg was amputated below the knee.

In the video you are introduced to other young people who were severely injured by gun accidents. They talk openly about what happened and how the accident could have been prevented.

Severity information is persuasively communicated by comments like this one: "If you get shot in the head, there is an 80 percent chance you will die. If you get shot in the body, there is a 90 percent chance you will need surgery."

Susceptibility is displayed through comments like this one, spoken by Andy: "I've been around guns all my life. I knew gun safety. I was always careful. I never thought that I could have an accident with a gun."

Response efficacy is relayed by statements like: "If I just had a trigger lock on the gun, none of this would have happened." Self-efficacy information is relayed by statements like: "A gun safety class takes only a few hours to complete."

In Michigan, 175 individuals enrolled in hunter safety classes participated in the experiment. Participants in the experimental group watched the video and filled out a survey probing perceptions of gun safety. Individuals in the control group answered the gun safety questions first and then watched the video. In dramatic support of the EPPM, experimental group participants (a) perceived that gun injuries resulted in more severe consequences, (b) believed that they were more susceptible to accidental gun injuries, and (c) listed more recommended gun safety practices, such as always using a trigger lock, than individuals in the control group (Roberto et al., 2000). To be sure, we don't know if these beliefs will endure beyond the experimental setting. The Reasoned Action Model suggests that beliefs – and, more precisely, attitudes – influence behavior under a specified set of conditions. Nonetheless, the findings offer support for the EPPM in an important applied setting (see Figure 12.3).

Harnessing the EPPM

The EPPM provides a helpful framework for examining fear appeal effects. Yet, as we have seen with other models, the EPPM, and its research foundation, are imperfect. Researchers, while appreciating the model's organized formulations, have offered a variety of criticisms of the approach.

For one thing, some of the model's conceptual propositions have failed to obtain consistent support from empirical studies (Popova, 2012, though see Shen, 2017). The model also does not provide a precise recipe for how to design the optimum fear appeal. It doesn't specify the impact social context exerts, or how to accommodate a variety of individual differences factors (Nabi, 2002a; Nabi, Roskos-Ewoldsen, & Carpentier, 2008; O'Keefe, 2003; Shen & Dillard, 2014). More generally, the ways in which different mental, emotional, and physiological processes combine and collide when fear is aroused are not entirely understood (e.g., Dillard & Anderson, 2004; Mongeau, 2013; Nabi, 2002a, 2002b; Rimal & Real, 2003; Quick et al., 2018). What's more, fear may not always have a direct, linear effect on persuasion; the effects may be more complex, at times curvilinear, even if linearity is probably the norm (Meczkowski, Dillard, & Shen, 2016; Dillard, Li, & Huang, 2017; Dillard Li, Meczkowski, Yang, & Shen, 2017; Dillard, Li, & Huang, 2017; Dillard & Li, in press).

The emotional effects of fear are probably understated in the model, reflecting persuasion research's tendency to downplay the ways in which affect influences attitudes. So, scholarly work needs to be

Figure 12.3 Gun Accidents Are a Leading Cause of Death in the United States. Even more tragically, accidental gun deaths occur primarily among the young, notably those under nine years old. If we can harness fear to persuade gun owners, particularly those (like the men in Roberto and his colleagues' study) who feel they are invulnerable to gun injury, we can save lives. Gun safety instruction, trigger locks, and smart guns that can only be fired by an authorized user are EPPM recommendations that can alleviate fear and influence gun safety attitudes. While there are political challenges to implementing some of these changes, they represent common sense fear appeals that can reduce tragic firearm injuries and deaths in the United States and across the world

done. But let's not minimize the contributions of the EPPM. Meta-analytic studies offer supportive findings. Scholarship indicates that both the EPPM and its predecessor, the protection motivation approach, preferred by some scholars for its parsimony, have helped elucidate and explain diverse findings on fear appeals (Chen & Yang, 2019; de Hoog, Stroebe, & de Wit, 2007; Lewis, Watson, & White, 2013; Maloney et al., 2011; Peters, Ruiter, & Kok, 2013; Roberto, 2013; Shen, 2019; Shi & Smith, 2016; Witte, 2013; Witte & Allen, 2000; Wong & Cappella, 2009), providing researchers with a framework for appreciating fear appeal processes and effects. The model also offers, albeit general, guidelines for designing health risk communications. Listed below are five practical suggestions that emerge from theory and research.

1 *Communicators must scare the heck out of recipients.* We are frequently tempted to go easy on others, trying not to hurt their feelings. Research suggests that fear enhances persuasion and that high-fear appeals are more effective than low-fear appeals (Boster & Mongeau, 1984). Let's be precise: "Adding additional fear-arousing content to a persuasive message is likely to generate greater levels of persuasion," Paul A. Mongeau concluded after reviewing the research in the area (1998, p. 64). Let's be clear: Fear appeals work. A thorough meta-analysis of fear appeals research found that "fear appeals are effective … (and) were successful at influencing attitudes, intentions, and behaviors across nearly all conditions that were analyzed" (Tannenbaum et al., 2015, p. 1196). As Lijiang Shen (2017) pithily put it, based on a thoroughly crafted experiment, we need to put "the fear back again" in fear appeals.

2 *Persuaders must shatter the illusion of invulnerability.* To persuade people, we must convince them that bad things can happen to them. Individuals can consider the possibility of change only when they acknowledge that their behavior is part of the problem. Communicators can help people appreciate that negative outcomes can befall them by developing appeals that vividly describe consequences of engaging in risky behavior. For example, if you wanted to convince people not to drink when they drive, you might write a message like the one in Box 12.2.

3 *Persuaders must discuss solutions, as well as problems.* Communicators must offer hope, telling individuals that they can avert the dangers graphically laid out earlier in the message, shoring up efficacy and increasing self-confidence (Quick et al., 2018). Communicators must "get 'em well" after they "get 'em sick." They must teach, as well as scare, provide hope, as well as angst, and put people in touch with their concerns about the problem (Nabi & Myrick, 2019; Roskos-Ewoldsen, Yu, & Rhodes, 2004).

4 In short, as Aristotle wrote years ago, people cannot overcome the "anguish of uncertainty" without "some lurking hope of deliverance." After all, "no one deliberates about things that are hopeless" (see Witte & Roberto, 2009, p. 605). A fear appeal must leave the receiver with the prospect of hope and a belief that adversity can be overcome.

5 *Efficacy recommendations should emphasize costs of not taking precautionary actions, as well as benefits of undertaking the activity.* This suggestion draws on framing research. Persuaders frequently must decide whether to frame the message so that it emphasizes benefits of adopting a behavior ("a diet high in fruits and vegetables, but low in fat, can keep you healthy") or costs of not performing the requested action ("a diet low in fruits and vegetables, but high in fat, can lead to cancer") (Salovey & Wegener, 2002). Messages that emphasize benefits of adopting a behavior are *gain-framed*; those that present the costs of not adopting the behavior are *loss-framed* (see Nan, Daily, & Qin, 2018 for a deeply integrative review).

Usually we think of fear messages framed in terms of gain – how you can benefit if you change the problematic behavior. However, they also can be framed on the basis of losses. It may seem strange to emphasize what people lose from not performing a behavior, until you consider that negative information – losses linked with inaction – can be more memorable than benefits associated with action. Beth E. Meyerowitz and Shelly Chaiken (1987) demonstrated this in a now-classic study of persuasive communication and breast self-examination. (At the time the study was conducted, experts believed that the self-exams helped women diagnose breast cancer. Subsequent research has found little evidence that breast self-exams are an effective screening device for early breast cancer detection, although some experts believe that it can help women become familiar with the normal look and feel of their breast so they can be sensitive to possibly problematic changes.)

In their study, Meyerowitz and Chaiken asked one group of undergraduate female subjects to read gain-framed arguments ("by doing breast self-examination now, you can learn what your normal, healthy breasts feel like so that you will be better prepared to notice any small, abnormal changes that might occur as you get older"). Others read loss-oriented arguments ("by not doing breast self-examination now, you will not learn what your normal, healthy breasts feel like, so you will be ill prepared to notice any small, abnormal changes that might occur as you get older"; Meyerowitz & Chaiken, 1987, p. 506). Women who read the loss-framed arguments held more positive attitudes toward breast self-exams and were more likely than gain-oriented subjects to report performing this behavior at a four-month follow-up.

Behavior being complex, there are also cases in which gain-framed arguments are more compelling. Alexander J. Rothman and colleagues (Rothman et al., 1993) compared the effects of gain- and loss-framed pamphlets regarding skin cancer prevention. The gain-framed message emphasized benefits rather than costs, and focused on positive aspects of displaying concern about skin cancer ("regular use of sunscreen products can protect you against the sun's harmful rays"). The loss-framed message stressed risks, rather than benefits ("If you don't use sunscreen products regularly, you won't be protected against the sun's harmful rays"). Of those who read the positive, gain-framed message, 71 percent requested sunscreen with an appropriate sun-protection factor. Only 46 percent of those who read the loss-framed pamphlet asked for sunscreen with an appropriate sun-protection level (see also Reinhart et al., 2007).

Theoretically, gain-framed messages should be more effective in promoting *health-affirming (disease prevention) behaviors*. These are behaviors where gains or benefits are frequently clear, certain, and obvious, as in cases of sunscreen use, physical exercise, or dental hygiene. Emphasizing the positive – what one gains from compliance – is persuasive (Gallagher & Updegraff, 2012). Loss-framed message effects are more complex (O'Keefe & Jensen, 2006; see also, 2009). However, loss-framed messages may be particularly effective when individuals feel vulnerable and outcomes are more uncertain (Harrington & Kerr, 2017; O'Keefe & Jensen, 2007). In these situations, people focus on negative aspects of the issue, leading them to be more susceptible to the negatively oriented, loss-framed communications.

Hyunyi Cho and Franklin J. Boster (2008) obtained evidence consistent with this view. They reported that loss-framed anti-drug ads that emphasized the *disadvantages* of doing drugs exerted a stronger impact on teenagers who reported their friends used drugs than did gain-framed ads that focused on the *benefits* of not doing drugs. If your friends do drugs, you will probably feel anxious or nervous about doing drugs yourself, but worried that your friends may reject you if you don't partake. With negative issues salient in adolescents' minds, loss-framed messages carried greater weight (though see O'Keefe, 2012).

Well, there is little doubt that this is a complex area! If you are faced with a health-persuasion task, the research suggests that you should consider framing the message in terms of benefits when you want to encourage individuals to take positive, proactive steps, like engaging in disease prevention. If there is negativity associated with the situation, risks attached to the recommended action, or the individual habitually focuses more on costs than benefits, a loss-framed message *may* provide a better fit between the message and the person (Cesario, Grant, & Higgins, 2004; Nan, 2007, 2012; Yan, Dillard, & Shen, 2010; see also Shen & Bigsby, 2013). The gain–loss issue is an intriguing one, as it promises to shed light on the best ways to frame health-related fear appeals, as well as intersections with personality factors (e.g., Jensen et al., 2018; Mollen et al., 2017; Shen & Kollar, 2015).

Alas, the effects remain complex – to use that overused, but helpful, term, and it has been hard to pinpoint exactly when gain-framed appeals are more effective than loss-framed appeals. There have been few consistent differences between gain- and loss-framed messages. The best we can say is that persuaders should be flexible, trying out gain appeals when prevention is the goal, showing sensitivity to loss frames when people are negative and uncertain, and modulating both to the message topic, illness, and particular risks in play. Gain or loss may be intriguingly more effective for a certain problem, but it will require adroit sensitivity to the problem to determine which to use. This brings us to the last prescription.

6   Research suggests that *threats and recommendations should be salient – or relevant – to the target audience*. You cannot assume that what scares you also terrifies your target audience. Different fears are salient to different groups (Crano, 2010). If you want to scare middle-class high school girls into practicing safer sex, you should stress that they might get pregnant. These teens don't want to have a baby; pregnancy represents a serious threat. However, if your target audience is poor ethnic women, you should rethink this appeal. To some low-income women, pregnancy is a positive, rather than negative, consequence of sexual intercourse. It produces a human being who depends on them and loves them to bits; it also, at least in the best of worlds, shows that they have a loving, trusting relationship with a man, which provides status and emotional fulfillment (Sobo, 1995; Witte et al., 2001).

BOX 12.2

An Anti-DUI Appeal

Here's what can happen: You attend a small dinner party at your brother's house with your 80-year-old mother, your visiting 74-year-old second cousin from Holland, and assorted other family members. As per family custom, you enjoy hors d'oeuvres and several glasses of wine over a lovely meal full of conversation and laughter.

Around 9 o'clock, after a couple of small cups of coffee, and a little more wine, a thimble's worth of Scotch, you prepare to leave, and do so. Ten minutes later, on a quiet country road near a small town, you notice flashing blue lights behind you; you stop, and you are spoken to by a young officer who asks if you have been drinking.

"Yes," you say, "I had a couple of glasses of wine at a family dinner."

You are asked to step out of the car for some "field sobriety tests" … The officer asks if you are willing to take a Breathalyzer; if you refuse, you will receive an automatic six-month suspended license. You agree, somewhat hopefully: You blow into the tube – very well, and slowly. He repeats the process. There is a pause, and the young man says, rather abruptly: "Put your hands behind your back. You have the right to remain silent …" You feel the cold hardness of your new manacles, and the hardness of the back seat of the police cruiser, which is made of plastic.

You arrive at the police station, where you are processed and re-breathalyzed twice – "point 08," you hear the officer say. In your state it's the lowest measurable illegal amount.

It used to be 0.10. Your license is taken away.

You pay your own bail, $40, and call your brother, who agrees to pick you up. While you wait, you are put in a jail cell, and you lie on a shiny aluminum "bed" under a bright yellow light, feeling dumb and criminal, in the company of a gleaming metal toilet. You use it …

Two weeks later, you are back in court with your brother-in-law lawyer to learn your fate. He negotiates … and the judge reads you your sentence: 45 (more) days' suspended license; one year's probation; 16 weekly alcohol-education classes, including two A.A. meetings and a "victim-impact movie" …

By August, you have completed all 16 classes, and have only seven more monthly checks of $65 to send to your probation officer. In November, a note from your car insurance company informs you that your policy has been cancelled; you call, and they say you can reapply with a subsidiary. Your premium more than doubles.

This is what can happen. And while all this is happening, you find yourself thinking more and more about something else that could have done: you could have crashed and killed someone, including yourself (Updike, 2010, p. 74).

Surprisingly, perhaps, the main drawback of getting pregnant, in the view of inner-city teenage girls, is that you get fat and lose your friends (Witte et al., 2001). Thus, a campaign to promote abstinence or safer sex among inner-city teenagers might emphasize how much weight you gain when you're pregnant. It should also explain that you can lose your friends if you have to spend time taking care of a baby rather than hanging with them (Witte et al., 2001).

Summary

Fear appeals are among the diciest weapons in the persuader's arsenal. This is because they evoke fear, a strong emotion with physiological correlates, touch on ego-involved issues, and attempt to change dysfunctional behaviors that are difficult to extinguish. To succeed, fear-arousing messages must trigger the right emotional reaction, lest they push the message recipient into fear control mode. Kathryn A. Morris and William B. Swann aptly observed that health risk communications must "walk the whisker-thin line between too little and too much – between making targets of persuasive communications care enough to attend to the message but not dismiss the message through denial processes" (1996, p. 70; see also Rhodes, 2017; see also Byrne & Hart, 2009; Taubman Ben-Ari, Florian, & Mikulincer, 1999). The key is balance, maintaining the right measure of fear, danger, threat, and efficacy – scaring individuals enough to get them to think about the dangers that lie ahead, and motivating them to do something to change their behavioral regimen. No one said appealing to fear would be easy. Arousing fear is an art, as well as a science, but models like the EPPM offer useful guidelines for behavioral change.

Guilt Appeals

Guilt is a time-honored appeal. It is a favorite of novelists and Jewish mothers. It is also frequently used by charitable organizations, which employ graphic appeals of deprived children, portraying them as abused, undernourished, and in desperate need of attention (see Figure 12.4). You have seen the pictures – the child's gaunt face, sad eyes, mournful expression. These televised messages are unabashed guilt appeals, attempts to arouse guilt in an effort to induce people to donate money to charitable groups. Do these and related appeals work?

NOTHING
It's what's for dinner.

Figure 12.4 A Graphic Appeal to Help a Hungry Child Tugs at Our Heart Strings, Arousing Guilt. Yet, sadly, appeals like these face many obstacles to success. How do you think we can increase the persuasive power of appeals like these?

Image obtained from Flickr. Taken by Keely Joy Photography, Inc., for the organization Feed My Starving Children

Like fear, guilt is a negative emotional response, one that has affective and cognitive components. Guilt, however, involves "ought" and "should" dimensions. *Guilt* "occurs when an individual notes with remorse that s/he failed to do what s/he 'ought to' or 'should' do – for example, when s/he violates some social custom, ethical or moral principle, or legal regulation," explain Debra Basil and her colleagues (Basil, Ridgway, & Basil, 2008, p. 3).

There is meta-analytic evidence that health-related guilt appeals can change attitudes (Xu & Guo, 2018). The effects are more complicated when one considers guilt messages on a variety of topics, besides health. Although more direct, explicit guilt appeals do evoke more guilt than less explicit messages, the explicit appeals are not more persuasive, perhaps because they unleash negative reactions, like anger, irritation, and resentment (O'Keefe, 2000, 2002). Guilt is a particularly dicey weapon of influence because it can provoke angry responses, as in "Why is she trying to 'guilt' me?" or because it fails to draw the connection between the message and recommendation, as when the individual appreciates there is a problem, but fails to believe he has a responsibility to fix it, as in people's attitudes toward climate change. And yet, as O'Keefe (2002, p. 335) acknowledges, "plainly, aroused guilt can be an important mechanism of influence."

How can you make guilt work? Basil and her colleagues had an idea. Intrigued by the EPPM's approach, they derived a model of guilt that emphasized EPPM processes.

Basil and her colleagues proposed a model of guilt and giving derived from the EPPM. They argue that the two key mechanisms are empathy and efficacy. Just as a fear appeal contains a threat to motivate people to act, a guilt appeal arouses empathy so as to induce individuals to perform a particular helping behavior. Empathizing with the plight of deprived children should remind people of a cultural norm to assist the less fortunate. This in turn should arouse guilt, an unpleasant feeling that people are motivated to reduce – ideally, by donating to charity. Guilt is not a sufficient condition. Basil's model stipulates that people will donate to a charitable organization only if guilt is combined with efficacy, the perception that one can effectively engage in the advocated action. Televised messages frequently contain self-efficacy messages, such as "for less than a $1 a day you can save a child's life."

In experiments to examine guilt appeal effects, Basil and colleagues devised messages to prod individuals to donate to charity. Research participants were randomly assigned to read messages high or low in guilt, empathy, and efficacy. For example, the following message was designed to induce both empathy and guilt:

> *You are Lilia.* You are eight, and curious about books and pens, things that you knew for a few months in your school before it burned. Before your mother became sick, and lost the resources within her care to care adequately for a child. And before you reached the point where you stopped drawing pictures in the dirt with sticks, because you are so tired from doing your mother's job.
>
> As a citizen of the most privileged country in the world, your life couldn't be more different from Lilia's. Not only do you live in America, you also get to go to college. So not having access to elementary education is difficult to imagine. But it's frighteningly common. Please help. Child-reach needs your donation.
>
> (Basil, Ridgway, & Basil, 2006, p. 1052)

There is evidence that guilt appeals like these have positive effects. In line with their model, Basil and colleagues (2008) found that a message promoting empathy with deprived children induced guilt, which in turn led to an increase in intent to donate to a charitable organization. Self-efficacy also spurred donation intentions.

Many of us have viewed heart-rending televised messages such as the one above, yet have not donated a dime. How could this be, if experiments demonstrate that guilt appeals work? There are many reasons. First, the televised appeals may be less impactful than the laboratory messages; the television messages may fail to induce empathy or guilt. Second, research shows only that people intend to donate; many factors determine whether people actually make good on their intentions, such as external constraints and availability of significant others who endorse the norm of giving (Fishbein & Ajzen, 2010). Third, people may distrust charitable organizations, suspecting that they are inefficient or corrupt. Fourth, individuals may not believe it is their responsibility to improve the lives of these needy children.

Like fear appeals, guilt communications are effective only if certain conditions are met. Research suggests that guilt appeals can work if the message: (a) induces empathy, (b) instills a sense of social, normative responsibility to help, (c) convinces individuals that the recommended behavior will reduce guilt, repair the problem or encourage personal responsibility; and (d) transports the individual to a more accepting state (Antonetti, Baines, & Jain, 2018; Basil et al., 2006; Carcioppolo et al., 2017; Graton, Ric, & Gonzalez, 2016; Hibbert et al., 2007). However, if the message goes too far, eliciting reactance and making people angry, it can backfire, making people angry or ashamed (Boudewyns, Turner, & Paquin, 2013; Coulter & Pinto, 1995; O'Keefe, 2002; Turner & Underhill, 2012). And if the individual lacks an ethical compass or can alleviate the guilt in ways other than complying with the persuader's request, guilt can backfire.

Guilt is a complex emotion, and people frequently employ guilt appeals in interpersonal conversations, particularly when relationships are close. But guilt messages do not always persuade message recipients to change their attitude or comply with a request. They can backfire when recipients perceive that the speaker is applying inappropriate interpersonal pressure to induce them to comply. If individuals do not feel guilty about a social wrong – Whites who do not feel governments should make reparations for slavery, a controversial issue – the guilt appeal will fail. If the problem is abstract and seemingly distant – as in a guilt appeal designed to provoke action on global warming – it also can fail to change attitudes. On the other hand, if the message takes into account research prescriptions, guilt can propel attitude change. It can promote helping behavior and, in the long run, perhaps enhance maturity. Appeals to guilt – frequently referred to as the "sinking feeling in the stomach" – can build character (Tierney, 2009, p. D1).

The challenge lies in helping people get beyond initial defensiveness and anger. We need to help individuals appreciate that they need not be diminished by guilt, nor need feel the appeal has struck a dagger at their self-concept. Given interpersonal and social wrongs in need of correction, empathy-based guilt appeals that transport individuals beyond themselves to appreciate the broader societal context can be ethical assets in the persuader's argumentative arsenal. Alas, persuaders must be adroit in using guilt, appreciating its psychological minefields, as well as moral virtues.

Conclusions

This chapter has examined the effects of two message factors designed to arouse emotions. Fear and guilt are important, though tricky, weapons in the persuasive arsenal, harnessed to change attitudes on issues as broad-based as global warming and narrowly, micro-focused as an individual's propensity to take health risks. Research on both fear and guilt has been guided by ideas generated by the Extended Parallel Process Model.

Fear appeals are defined as persuasive communications that try to arouse fear and conjure up negative consequences that will occur if people do not comply with message recommendations. They play on fear, an internal emotion composed of psychological and physiological elements that can be evoked when threats are perceived. Fear is a tricky emotion. It can trigger anxiety, worry, and paralysis. Harnessed effectively, the model suggests ways to persuade teens to take precautions when puffing e-cigarettes or practicing unsafe sex. An influential model, the EPPM, stipulates that fear messages influence attitudes when they convince individuals to rethink the problem and recognize that they are capable of averting the threat by accepting recommendations contained in the message. The EPPM stipulates that a fear message succeeds when it moves people into the zone of danger control. In order for this to happen, the model says, persuaders should devise a message that contains severity, susceptibility, response efficacy, and self-efficacy information. When perceived efficacy exceeds perceived threat, the message can push people into a danger control mode.

Framing research suggests that persuaders should consider whether to frame the message so it emphasizes benefits of adopting a recommended behavior (gain-framing) or focuses on costs of not performing the recommended action (loss-framing). The literature is complicated (no surprise, right!). However, it yields insights, suggesting that gain-framed messages are more influential than loss-framed appeals when you want someone to adopt a health-affirming, illness-prevention behavior. If there is negativity or serious emotional risks associated with the situation, a loss-framed message may be worth contemplating.

The EPPM has generated a number of studies and helps us appreciate diverse findings in this decades-long area of research. And yet, like all approaches, the model is not without problems. For example, it does not offer a precise recipe as to how to design an optimum fear message, offering instead useful, but vague, specifications. What's more, the ways the four components intersect, the role played by fear itself, and moderating influences of social context are not entirely understood. Yet its theoretical postulates – like the emphasis on warding off danger rather than obsessing about fear – can help in the design of health prevention messages, such as in the area of cancer screening (Chae & Lee, 2019). Unquestionably, fear appeal research, guided by the EPPM, has important implications for helping influence individuals to take action to protect both their own health and the broader global environment (Skurka et al., 2018).

Persuasion research also has explored the impact of guilt, also a multifaceted emotion. Unlike fear, guilt contains "should" or "ought" dimensions. Moralistic parents, stern preachers, and attentive mothers are among those who have invoked guilt in the service of persuasion! And, of course, the many PSAs calling attention to the plight of abused or impoverished children abroad and in the United States also call on guilt. Does guilt persuade?

We know much less about guilt appeal than fear appeal influences. There is evidence that guilt appeals can work, but there remain questions about the breadth of the effects. Several investigations, combining EPPM concepts with a focus on empathy, have found that guilt appeals can influence attitudes. Messages designed to arouse guilt, such as PSAs urging viewers to save a poor child from dying of hunger, can backfire by failing to convince individuals that their behavior will make a difference, or even to arouse guilt. This is one reason why all tug-on-the-heartstrings televised appeals don't propel us to donate money. But if a guilt appeal arouses empathy, convinces the recipient that the recommended behavior can repair the problem, perhaps transporting the individual to a more accepting state of mind, and avoids making the person feel angry about being preached to, it can change attitudes.

Guilt is a reliable weapon in a persuader's moral arsenal, but can easily backfire because of its emphasis on the dicey "should" aspects of human behavior. Individuals, being what they are, may not buy into the idea that they have broader responsibilities or may doubt the ability of the message to produce the desired effects. Guilt – good in theory (depending on your perspective) – is truly a fraught persuasive weapon.

Persuasive messages can employ other emotions besides fear and guilt. Messages can evoke positive feelings like pride and warmth, along with negative emotions, such as anger and sadness. Research tells us that when people experience a positive emotion or are in a good mood, they often think in rather simple terms, and avoid heavy details, not wanting anything to put them out of their blissful state (Nabi, 2007). However, invariably, negative emotions motivate more serious attention to a message. When we are scared, worried, or even angry, we can attend more closely to a persuader's arguments, recognizing that a serious problem demands our consideration. The intensity of our emotions, particularly anger, can influence the role arguments play in persuasion (Nathan et al., 2019).

This highlights an important point: Emotions play a useful role in our responses to persuasive communications. We frequently think of persuasion in cognitive terms, emphasizing the most logical, cogent arguments to place in a message. But emotions can be helpful heuristics and can play important roles in health campaigns (Nabi, 2002a; Nan, 2017). When people are worried about a health problem, they are motivated to gather information about the ailment, and this can help them cope with the problem. When individuals are angry about a social injustice, they may formulate strategies to redress the ethical inequity. Emotions are not always barriers – things that obstruct rational message processing. They are part of our personal makeup as human beings and need to be factored in to the persuasion process by receivers, as well as persuaders. As communication researcher Robin L. Nabi (2007) notes, a consideration of both thoughts and feelings is

> essential for progress to be made, and whereas the right combination can motivate effective behavior, the wrong combination will most assuredly backfire. Finding the most effective blending of cognitive and emotional persuasive elements, then, should be both our challenge and our goal.
>
> (p. 394)

References

Antonetti, P., Baines, P., & Jain, S. (2018). The persuasiveness of guilt appeals over time: Pathways to delayed compliance. *Journal of Business Research*, *90*, 14–25.

Basil, D. Z., Ridgway, N. M., & Basil, M. D. (2006). Guilt appeals: The mediating effect of responsibility. *Psychology & Marketing*, *23*, 1035–1054.

Basil, D. Z., Ridgway, N. M., & Basil, M. D. (2008). Guilt and giving: A process model of empathy and efficacy. *Psychology & Marketing*, *25*, 1–23.

Boster, F. J., & Mongeau, P. (1984). Fear-arousing persuasive messages. In R. N. Bostrom (Ed.), *Communication yearbook 8* (pp. 330–375). Beverly Hills, CA: Sage.

Boudewyns, V., Turner, M. M., & Paquin, R. S. (2013). Shame-free guilt appeals: Testing the emotional and cognitive effects of shame and guilt appeals. *Psychology & Marketing*, *30*, 811–825.

Byrne, S., & Hart, P. S. (2009). The boomerang effect: A synthesis of findings and a preliminary theoretical framework. *Communication Yearbook*, *33*, 3–38.

Carcioppolo, N., Li, C., Chudnovskaya, E. V., Kharsa, R., Stephan, T., & Nickel, K. (2017). The comparative efficacy of a hybrid guilt-fear appeal and a traditional fear appeal to influence HPV vaccination intentions. *Communication Research*, *44*, 437–458.

Cesario, J., Grant, H., & Higgins, E. T. (2004). Regulatory fit and persuasion: Transfer from "feeling right". *Journal of Personality and Social Psychology*, *86*, 388–404.

Chae, J., & Lee, C.-J. (2019). The psychological mechanism underlying communication effects on behavioral intention: Focusing on affect and cognition in the cancer context. *Communication Research*, *46*, 597–618.

Chen, L., & Yang, X. (2019). Using EPPM to evaluate the effectiveness of fear appeal messages across different media outlets to increase the intention of breast self-examination among Chinese women. *Health Communication*, *34*, 1369–1376.

Cho, H., & Boster, F. J. (2008). Effects of gain versus loss frame antidrug ads on adolescents. *Journal of Communication*, *58*, 428–446.

Coulter, R. H., & Pinto, M. B. (1995). Guilt appeals in advertising: What are their effects? *Journal of Applied Psychology*, *80*, 697–705.

Coyne, M. (2000). Paper prepared for course on persuasion and attitude change, Cleveland State University, Cleveland, OH.

Crano, W. D. (2010). Experiments as reforms: Persuasion in the nation's service. In J. P. Forgas, J. Cooper, & W. D. Crano (Eds.), *The psychology of attitudes and attitude change* (pp. 231–248). New York: Psychology Press.

de Hoog, N., Stroebe, W., & de Wit, J. B. F. (2007). The impact of vulnerability to and severity of a health risk on processing and acceptance of fear-arousing communications: A meta-analysis. *Review of General Psychology, 11,* 258–285.

Dillard, J. P. (1994). Rethinking the study of fear appeals: An emotional perspective. *Communication Theory, 4,* 295–323.

Dillard, J. P., & Anderson, J. W. (2004). The role of fear in persuasion. *Psychology & Marketing, 21,* 909–926.

Dillard, J. P., Li, R., & Huang, Y. (2017). Threat appeals: The fear-persuasion relationship is linear and curvilinear. *Health Communication, 32,* 1358–1367.

Dillard, J. P., Li, R., Meczkowski, E., Yang, C., & Shen, L. (2017). Fear responses to threat appeals: Functional form, methodological considerations, and correspondence between static and dynamic data. *Communication Research, 44,* 997–1018.

Dillard, J. P., & Li, S. S. (in press). How scary are threat appeals? Evaluating the intensity of fear in experimental research. *Human Communication Research.* doi:10.1093/hcr/hqz008

Finckenauer, J. O. (1982). *Scared straight! and the panacea phenomenon.* Englewood Cliffs, NJ: Prentice Hall.

Fishbein, M., & Ajzen, I. (2010). *Predicting and changing behavior: The reasoned action approach.* New York: Psychology Press.

Gallagher, K. M., & Updegraff, J. A. (2012). Health message framing effects on attitudes, intentions, and behavior: A meta-analytic review. *Annals of Behavioral Medicine, 43,* 101–116.

Gold, M., & Ferré-Sandurní, L. (2020, March 5). State scrambles as nine new cases are connected to Westchester man. *The New York Times,* A16.

Graton, A., Ric, F., & Gonzalez, E. (2016). Reparation or reactance? The influence of guilt on reaction to persuasive communication. *Journal of Experimental Social Psychology, 62,* 40–49.

Haren, P. T. (2019). Adolescents and e-cigarettes: A look into the minds of adolescents and their views of e-cigarettes. *Paper completed for independent study communication class at Cleveland State University (R. Perloff, supervising instructor).*

Harmon, A. (2005, November 16). Young, assured and playing pharmacist to friends. *The New York Times,* A1, A17.

Harrington, N. G., & Kerr, A. M. (2017). Rethinking risk: Prospect theory application in health message framing research. *Health Communication, 32,* 131–141.

Hibbert, S., Smith, A., Davies, A., & Ireland, F. (2007). Guilt appeals: Persuasion knowledge and charitable giving. *Psychology and Marketing, 24,* 723–742.

Hoffman, J. (2018, November 16). The price of cool: A teenager, a Juul and nicotine addiction. *The New York Times.* Online: www.nytimes.com/2018/11/16/health/vaping-juul-teens-addiction-nicotine.html (Accessed: August 9, 2019).

Hoffman, J. (2019, January 31). E-cigarettes offer higher success rate in quitting smoking, study says. *The New York Times,* A16.

Holt, J. (2006, December 3). The new, soft paternalism. *The New York Times Magazine,* 15–17.

Hovland, C. I., Janis, I. L., & Kelley, H. H. (1953). *Communication and persuasion: Psychological studies of opinion change.* New Haven, CT: Yale University Press.

Jensen, J. D., Ratcliff, C. L., Yale, R. N., Krakow, M., Scherr, C. L., & Yeo, S. K. (2018). Persuasive impact of loss and gain frames on intentions to exercise: A test of six moderators. *Communication Monographs, 85,* 245–262.

Kessler, D. A. (2019) The e-cigarettes kids love. *The New York Times*, A27.

Lewis, I., Watson, B., & White, K. M. (2013). Extending the explanatory utility of the EPPM beyond fear-based persuasion. *Health Communication, 28*, 84–98.

Maloney, E. K., Lapinski, M. K., & Witte, K. (2011). Fear appeals and persuasion: A review and update of the Extended Parallel Process Model. *Social and Personality Psychology Compass, 5*, 206–219.

Meczkowski, E. J., Dillard, J. P., & Shen, L. (2016). Threat appeals and persuasion: Seeking and finding the elusive curvilinear effect. *Communication Monographs, 83*, 373–395.

Meyerowitz, B. E., & Chaiken, S. (1987). The effect of message framing on breast self-examination attitudes, intentions, and behavior. *Journal of Personality and Social Psychology, 52*, 500–510.

Mollen, S., Engelen, S., Kessels, L. T. E., & Van Den Putte, B. (2017). Short and sweet: The persuasive effects of message framing and temporal context in antismoking warning labels. *Journal of Health Communication, 22*, 20–28.

Mongeau, P. A. (1998). Another look at fear-arousing persuasive appeals. In M. Allen & R. W. Preiss (Eds.), *Persuasion: Advances through meta-analysis* (pp. 53–68). Cresskill, NJ: Hampton Press.

Mongeau, P. A. (2013). Fear appeals. In J. P. Dillard & L. Shen (Eds.), *The Sage handbook of persuasion: Developments in theory and practice* (2nd ed., pp. 184–199). Thousand Oaks, CA: Sage.

Morris, K. A., & Swann, W. B., Jr. (1996). Denial and the AIDS crisis: On wishing away the threat of AIDS. In S. Oskamp & S. C. Thompson (Eds.), *Understanding and preventing HIV risk behavior: Safer sex and drug use* (pp. 57–79). Thousand Oaks, CA: Sage.

Muthusamy, M., Levine, T. R., & Weber, R. (2009). Scaring the already scared: Some problems with HIV/AIDS fear appeals in Namibia. *Journal of Communication, 59*, 317–344.

Nabi, R. L. (2002a). Discrete emotions and persuasion. In J. P. Dillard & M. Pfau (Eds.), *The persuasion handbook: Developments in theory and practice* (pp. 289–308). Thousand Oaks, CA: Sage.

Nabi, R. L. (2002b). Anger, fear, uncertainty, and attitudes: A test of the cognitive-functional model. *Communication Monographs, 69*, 204–216.

Nabi, R. L. (2007). Emotion and persuasion: A social cognitive perspective. In D. R. Roskos-Ewoldsen & J. L. Monahan (Eds.), *Communication and social cognition: Theories and methods* (pp. 377–398). Mahwah, NJ: Erlbaum Associates.

Nabi, R. L. (2009). Emotion and media effects. In R. L. Nabi & M. B. Oliver (Eds.), *The Sage handbook of media processes and effects* (pp. 205–221). Thousand Oaks, CA: Sage.

Nabi, R. L., & Myrick, J. G. (2019). Uplifting fear appeals: Considering the role of hope in fear-based persuasive messages. *Health Communication, 34*, 463–474.

Nabi, R. L., Roskos-Ewoldsen, D., & Carpentier, F. D. (2008). Subjective knowledge and fear appeal effectiveness: Implications for message design. *Health Communication, 23*, 191–201.

Nan, X. (2007). The relative persuasive effect of gain- versus loss-framed messages: Exploring the moderating role of the desirability of end-states. *Journalism and Mass Communication Quarterly, 84*, 509–524.

Nan, X. (2012). Relative persuasiveness of gain- versus loss-framed human papillomavirus vaccination messages for the present- and future-minded. *Human Communication Research, 38*, 72–94.

Nan, X. (2017). Influence of incidental discrete emotions on health risk perception and persuasion. *Health Communication, 32*, 721–729.

Nan, X., Daily, K., & Qin, Y. (2018). Relative persuasiveness of gain-vs loss-framed messages: A review of theoretical perspectives and developing an integrative framework. *Review of Communication, 18*, 370–390.

Nathan, W., Tukachinsky, R., Pelled, A., & Nabi, R. (2019). Meta-analysis of anger and persuasion: An empirical integration of four models. *Journal of Communication, 69*, 73–93.

O'Keefe, D. J. (2000). Guilt and social influence. In M. Roloff (Ed.), *Communication Yearbook 23* (pp. 67–101). Thousand Oaks, CA: Sage.

O'Keefe, D. J. (2002). Guilt as a mechanism of persuasion. In J. P. Dillard & M. Pfau (Eds.), *The persuasion handbook: Developments in theory and practice* (pp. 329–344). Thousand Oaks, CA: Sage.

O'Keefe, D. J. (2003). Message properties, mediating states, and manipulation checks: Claims, evidence, and data analysis in experimental persuasive message effects research. *Communication Theory, 13,* 251–274.

O'Keefe, D. J. (2012). From psychological theory to message design: Lessons from the story of gain-framed and loss-framed persuasive messages. In H. Cho (Ed.), *Health communication message design: Theory and practice* (pp. 3–20). Thousand Oaks, CA: Sage.

O'Keefe, D. J. (2016). *Persuasion: Theory and research* (3rd ed.). Thousand Oaks, CA: Sage.

O'Keefe, D. J., & Jensen, J. D. (2006). The advantages of compliance or the disadvantages of noncompliance?: A meta-analytic review of the relative persuasive effectiveness of gain-framed and loss-framed messages. In C. S. Beck (Ed.), *Communication yearbook 30* (pp. 1–43). Mahwah, NJ: Erlbaum Associates.

O'Keefe, D. J., & Jensen, J. D. (2007). The relative persuasiveness of gain-framed loss-framed messages for encouraging disease prevention behaviors: A meta-analytic review. *Journal of Health Communication, 12,* 623–644.

O'Keefe, D. J., & Jensen, J. D. (2009). The relative persuasiveness of gain-framed and loss-framed messages for encouraging disease detection behaviors: A meta-analytic review. *Journal of Communication, 59,* 296–316.

Parker-Pope, T. (2010, June 15). Stupid teenage tricks, for a virtual audience. *The New York Times,* D5.

Perloff, R. M. (2019, August 8). We have to do more to curb use of e-cigarettes among youths. *The Sun Press/Sun News,* p. A8.

Peters, G.-J. Y., Ruiter, R. A. C., & Kok, G. (2013). Threatening communication: A critical re-analysis and a revised meta-analytic test of fear appeal theory. *Health Psychology Review, 7*(Supplement 1), S8–S31.

Plott, E. (2020, March 19). Her Facebook friends asked if anyone was actually sick. She had an answer. *The New York Times.* Online: https://www.nytimes.com/2020/03/19/us/politics/coronavirus-heaven-frilot-mark-frilot.html (Accessed: May 26, 2020).

Popova, L. (2012). The extended parallel process model: Illuminating the gaps in research. *Health Education & Behavior, 39,* 455–473.

Quick, B. L., LaVoie, N. R., Reynolds-Tylus, T., Martinez-Gonzalez, A., & Skurka, C. (2018). Examining mechanisms underlying fear-control in the extended parallel process model. *Health Communication, 33,* 379–391.

Rajecki, D. W. (1990). *Attitudes* (2nd ed.). Sunderland, MA: Sinauer Associates.

Reinhart, A. M., Marshall, H. M., Feeley, T. H., & Tutzauer, F. (2007). The persuasive effects of message framing in organ donation: The mediating role of psychological reactance. *Communication Monographs, 74,* 229–255.

Rhodes, N. (2017). Fear-appeal messages: Message processing and affective attitudes. *Communication Research, 44,* 952–975.

Rimal, R. N., & Real, K. (2003). Perceived risk and efficacy beliefs as motivators of change: Use of the Risk Perception Attitude (RPA) framework to understand health behaviors. *Human Communication Research, 29,* 370–399.

Roberto, A. J. (2013). Editor's note for the extended parallel process model: Two decades later. *Health Communication, 28,* 1–2.

Roberto, A. J., Meyer, G., Johnson, A. J., & Atkin, C. K. (2000). Using the Extended Parallel Process Model to prevent firearm injury and death: Field experiment results of a video-based intervention. *Journal of Communication, 50*(4), 157–175.

Robertson, L. S., Kelley, A. B., O'Neill, B., Wixom, C. W., Eiswirth, R. S., & Haddon, W., Jr. (1974). A controlled study of the effect of television messages on safety belt use. *American Journal of Public Health, 64,* 1071–1080.

Rogers, R. W. (1975). A protection motivation theory of fear appeals and attitude change. *Journal of Psychology, 91,* 93–114.

Rogers, R. W., & Mewborn, C. R. (1976). Fear appeals and attitude change: Effects of a threat's noxiousness, probability of occurrence, and the efficacy of coping responses. *Journal of Personality and Social Psychology, 34,* 54–61.

Roskos-Ewoldsen, D. R., Yu, H. J., & Rhodes, N. (2004). Fear appeal messages affect accessibility of attitudes toward the threat and adaptive behaviors. *Communication Monographs, 71,* 49–69.

Rothman, A. J., Salovey, P., Antone, C., Keough, K., & Martin, C. D. (1993). The influence of message framing on intentions to perform health behaviors. *Journal of Experimental Social Psychology, 29,* 408–433.

Salovey, P., & Wegener, D. T. (2002). Communicating about health: Message framing, persuasion, and health behavior. In J. Suls & K. Wallston (Eds.), *Social psychological foundations of health and illness* (pp. 54–81). Oxford: Blackwell.

Shen, L. (2017). Putting the fear back again (and within individuals): Revisiting the role of fear in persuasion. *Health Communication, 32,* 1331–1341.

Shen, L. (2019, August 22). *Personal communication on fear appeals chapter to the author.*

Shen, L., & Bigsby, E. (2013). The effects of message features: Content, structure, and style. In J. P. Dillard & L. Shen (Eds.), *The Sage handbook of persuasion: Developments in theory and practice* (2nd ed., pp. 20–35). Thousand Oaks, CA: Sage.

Shen, L., & Dillard, J. P. (2014). Threat, fear, and persuasion: Review and critique of questions about functional form. *Review of Communication Research, 2,* 94–114. doi:10.12840/issn.2255-4165.2014.02.01.004

Shen, L., & Kollar, L. M. M. (2015). Testing moderators of message framing effect: A motivational approach. *Communication Research, 42,* 626–648.

Shi, J., & Smith, S. W. (2016). The effects of fear appeal message repetition on perceived threat, perceived efficacy, and behavioral intention in the extended parallel process model. *Health Communication, 31,* 275–286.

Skurka, C., Niederdeppe, J., Romero-Canyas, R., & Acup, D. (2018). Pathways of influence in emotional appeals: Benefits and tradeoffs of using fear or humor to promote climate change-related intentions and risk perceptions. *Journal of Communication, 68,* 169–193.

So, J., Kuang, K., & Cho, H. (2016). Reexamining fear appeal models from cognitive appraisal theory and functional emotion theory perspectives. *Communication Monographs, 83,* 120–144.

Sobo, E. J. (1995). *Choosing unsafe sex: AIDS-risk denial among disadvantaged women.* Philadelphia, PA: University of Pennsylvania Press.

Tannenbaum, M. B., Hepler, J., Zimmerman, R. S., Saul, L., Jacobs, S., Wilson, K., & Albarracín, D. (2015). Appealing to fear: A meta-analysis of fear appeal effectiveness and theories. *Psychological Bulletin, 141,* 1178–1204.

Taubman Ben-Ari, O., Florian, V., & Mikulincer, M. (1999). The impact of mortality salience on reckless driving: A test of terror management mechanisms. *Journal of Personality and Social Psychology, 76,* 35–45.

Tavernise, S. (2015, January 11). Warning: That tan could be hazardous. *The New York Times*, 1, 16.

Tierney, J. (2009, August 25). Guilt and atonement on the path to adulthood. *The New York Times*, D1, D3.

Turner, M. M., & Underhill, J. C. (2012). Motivating emergency preparedness behaviors: The differential effects of guilt appeals and actually anticipating guilty feelings. *Communication Quarterly*, 60, 545–559.

Updike, D. (2010, December 5). Lives: Drinking and driving and paying. *The New York Times Magazine*, 74.

Wallace-Wells, D. (2019, February 17). Time to panic. *The New York Times* (Sunday Review), 1, 6–7.

Weinstein, N. D. (1980). Unrealistic optimism about future life events. *Journal of Personality and Social Psychology*, 39, 806–820.

Weinstein, N. D. (1993). Testing four competing theories of health-protective behavior. *Health Psychology*, 12, 324–333.

Williams, T., & Del Real, J. A. (2019, September 18). State actions against e-cigarettes fall short of the biggest concern. *The New York Times*, A15.

Witte, K. (1998). Fear as motivator, fear as inhibitor: Using the Extended Parallel Process Model to explain fear appeal successes and failures. In P. A. Andersen & L. K. Guerrero (Eds.), *Handbook of communication and emotion: Research, theory, applications, and contexts* (pp. 423–450). San Diego, CA: Academic Press.

Witte, K. (2013). Introduction: Pathways. *Health Communication*, 28, 3–4.

Witte, K., & Allen, M. (2000). A meta-analysis of fear appeals: Implications for effective public health campaigns. *Health Education & Behavior*, 27, 591–615.

Witte, K., Meyer, G., & Martell, D. (2001). *Effective health risk messages: A step-by-step guide*. Thousand Oaks, CA: Sage.

Witte, K., & Roberto, A. J. (2009). Fear appeals and public health: Managing fear and creating hope. In L. R. Frey & K. N. Cissna (Eds.), *Routledge handbook of applied communication research* (pp. 584–610). New York: Routledge.

Wong, N. C. H., & Cappella, J. N. (2009). Antismoking threat and efficacy appeals: Effects on smoking cessation intentions for smokers with low and high readiness to quit. *Journal of Applied Communication Research*, 37, 1–20.

Xu, Z., & Guo, H. (2018). A meta-analysis of the effectiveness of guilt on health-related attitudes and intentions. *Health Communication*, 33, 519–525.

Yan, C., Dillard, J. P., & Shen, F. (2010). The effects of mood, message framing, and behavioral advocacy on persuasion. *Journal of Communication*, 60, 344–363.

Chapter 13

Cognitive Dissonance Theory

- When Litesa Wallace packed her bags for college at Western Illinois University some years back, she never harbored any doubt that she would pledge a sorority. The initiation rites for Delta Sigma Theta turned out to be a tad more severe than Litesa expected: doing 3,000 sit-ups, drinking hot sauce and vinegar, and swallowing her own vomit. While some might have quit at this point, Litesa endured the hardship. "She wanted to be in the sorority very badly. It's very prestigious, and she believed that it would be beneficial to her life," her attorney explained. Attorney? That's right: Ms. Wallace sued the sorority for hazing after she was hospitalized for injuries sustained during the initiation period. Yet, even as she awaited the outcome of her suit, Litesa remained a Delta, apparently feeling considerable loyalty to the sorority (Pharnor, 1999).
- Movies strike resonant chords in many people, and the following conversation from the 1982 movie *The Big Chill* sheds light on a phenomenon that many have experienced in everyday life:

   Sam: Why is it what you just said strikes me as a mass of rationalizations?
   Michael: Don't knock rationalizations. Where would we be without it? I don't know anyone who could get through the day without two or three juicy rationalizations. They're more important than sex.
   Sam: Ah, come on. Nothin's more important than sex.
   Michael: Oh yeah? You ever gone a week without a rationalization? (Steele, 1988; see Figure 13.1)

- A week after the 9/11 attacks, a strange development occurred. Five anthrax-laced envelopes were mailed to major media outlets in New York City. Three weeks later, two anthrax-laden envelopes were sent to the offices of two U.S. senators. The anthrax-laden materials ultimately killed five people, caused 17 others to become sick, and led to widespread national panic.

Over a seven-year period, FBI investigators conducted more than 9,000 interviews and close to 100 searches, in the most intricate criminal investigation in FBI history.

Figure 13.1 The 1982 Movie *The Big Chill* Contained a Classic Statement That Called to Mind the Cognitive Dissonance Theory Notion of Rationalization. A character flatly claimed that rationalizations are more important than sex

Image courtesy of Columbia Pictures Corporation

But the emotional costs were high. Federal officials pegged Dr. Kenneth Berry, an emergency room doctor concerned about bioterrorism problems, as a suspect. Although Berry turned out not to be the culprit, the stress took a toll on his career and marriage.

Dr. Steven Hatfill, a physician and former Army researcher, became the focus of the FBI investigation in 2002. FBI agents informed the woman he was living with that he was a murderer, threatening her if she did not talk. Although Hatfill claimed he was innocent, the FBI trailed him for a year and raided his home. Prominent news articles associated him with the case. He sued the U.S. Department of Justice and *The New York Times*. He was subsequently cleared and received $4.6 million from the U.S. government.

Despite all this, authorities steadfastly denied they did anything wrong. Federal officials rejected criticisms from government colleagues, voicing neither regret nor remorse. "I do not apologize for any aspect of the investigation," the FBI director said. It is incorrect to "say there were mistakes" (Broad & Shane, 2008, p. 17; see Figure 13.2).

Figure 13.2 The FBI Pegged Former Army Researcher Steven Hatfill as a Suspect in an Investigation of the Deaths of Five People from Anthrax-Laden Materials in 2001. Hatfill, pictured above, holds a photograph that depicts the inside of his girlfriend's apartment after an FBI search. Although Hatfill was subsequently cleared of wrongdoing, the authorities strongly denied that they had made mistakes; a classic, if dysfunctional, example of dissonance reduction

Image courtesy of Getty Images

What do these richly different examples have in common? They illustrate the powerful role that a phenomenon called cognitive dissonance plays in everyday life. You may have heard the term "cognitive dissonance." No surprise: It has become part of the popular lexicon. Writers, politicians, therapists, and people like you and me use the term to describe conflict or negative feelings about issues. But what exactly does dissonance mean? Why did one psychologist call it the greatest achievement of social psychology (see Aron & Aron, 1989)? How can dissonance principles be harnessed in the service of persuasion? And what insights does cognitive dissonance theory still contribute to everyday life, more than 60 years after it was conceptualized? This chapter, reviewing classic and the latest twenty-first century work on dissonance, examines these issues.

Foundations

Cognitive dissonance is a bona fide theory, one of the oldies but goodies. It contains definitions, hypotheses, explanations, and theoretical statements. It has generated numerous studies; indeed, the concept boasts more than 2,000 citations (Crano, Cooper, & Forgas, 2010). Yet it has provoked profound disagreements among scholars as to just why a particular finding has emerged. It is a psychological theory, one of a wave of 1950s-style approaches that assumed people have an overarching need for cognitive consistency or balance. Leon Festinger developed the theory in 1957, conducted some of the major experiments on dissonance effects, and then departed from the social psychology scene to pursue studies of human perception. That was dissonant – or inconsistent – with what you would expect an established, successful theorist to do. But in a way it was typical of dissonance theory: A counterintuitive "reverse psychology" sort of approach that turned ideas on their head, but in a fashion that stimulated and intrigued scholars across the world.

So what do we mean by cognitive dissonance? Dissonance means discord, incongruity, or strife. Thus, cognitive dissonance means incongruity among thoughts or mental elements. Two cognitions are in a dissonant relationship when the opposite of one cognitive element follows from the other. For example, the idea that "eating junk food is bad for your heart" is ordinarily dissonant with the cognition that "I love junk food." The cognition "I just plunked down $20,000 for a car" is dissonant with the observation that "I just found out you can't accelerate past 60 on the highway in this piece of junk." The cognitions "My boyfriend gets abusive when he's mad" and "I love him and want to stay with him always" are also dissonant. Finally, and most gravely, the cognition "The world is a beautiful and wonderful place" is dissonant with the realization that "evil people can kill thousands of innocent people in a single day."

Dissonance, as these examples suggest, cuts across contexts. It is specifically and formally defined as *"a negative, unpleasant state that occurs whenever a person holds two cognitions that are psychologically inconsistent"* (Aronson, 1968, p. 6). Notice that I say "psychologically inconsistent." Two thoughts can be psychologically – but not logically – inconsistent. The cognition "I love junk food" is not logically inconsistent with the belief that "eating junk food is bad for your heart." Knowing that a junk-food diet increases the risk of heart disease does not make it illogical to eat burgers, fries, and nuggets. However, the two cognitions arouse dissonance because, psychologically, it does not make sense – at least for most people – to engage in a behavior that increases the risk of disease. Dissonance is a complex theory with many hypotheses. It has been refined many times over the years. Its core components remain the following:

1 Dissonance is psychologically uncomfortable, and physiologically, even neurologically, arousing, stimulating the posterior medial frontal cortex, as well as the anterior cingulate cortex, a region of the brain that is activated by conflicts involving behavior and core values (Harmon-Jones &

Harmon-Jones, 2019; Harmon-Jones et al., 2011; Izuma & Murayama, 2019; van Veen et al., 2009). The discomfort arising from dissonance drives individuals to take steps to reduce it.

2   Dissonance occurs when an individual: (a) holds two clearly incongruent thoughts, (b) makes a decision that rules out a desirable alternative, (c) expends effort to participate in what turns out to be a less than ideal activity, or (d) in general is unable to find sufficient psychological justification for an attitude or behavior he or she adopts.

3   Dissonance is set in motion once an individual performs a behavior, propelling the person to rationalize the behavioral choice.

4   The magnitude of dissonance depends on a host of factors, including the number of dissonant elements and the importance of the issue.

5   People are motivated to take steps to reduce dissonance, including changing their attitude in response to a persuasive message.

6   For dissonance arousal to lead to attitude change, the individual must have freely decided to perform the advocated behavior.

7   People may not always succeed in alleviating dissonance, but they are motivated to try.

Dissonance theory is intriguing in an important respect. The theories discussed up to this point have suggested that changes in attitude can produce changes in behavior. Dissonance theory suggests that the opposite can occur – changes in behavior can produce changes in attitude (Cooper & Scher, 1994). For this to happen, a critical requirement of persuasion must be satisfied: People must persuade themselves to adopt a new attitude on the topic. Dissonance theory, as one would expect from a theory of persuasion, assigns central importance to the power of self-persuasion.

Dissonance and Decision-Making

Life is filled with decisions, and decisions (as a general rule) arouse dissonance. For example, suppose you had to decide whether to accept a job in a stunningly beautiful area of the country or to turn down the job so that you could be near friends and family. Either way, you would experience dissonance. If you took the job, you would miss loved ones; if you turned down the job, you would long wistfully for the breathtaking mountains, luscious waterfalls, and lovely evening sunsets. Both alternatives have their good and bad points. The rub is that making a decision cuts off the possibility that you can enjoy the advantages of the unchosen alternative. It also ensures that you must accept the negative elements of the choice you make.

The writer Adam Ross captures the feeling aptly in the ending of a story about Sara, a beleaguered 39-year-old mother of two, whose husband still arouses warmth in her, but not sexual ardor. For this reason, she contemplates flying to L.A. for a rendezvous with Thom, with whom she had a romantic relationship while in college but whom she has not seen until she decides on a lark to meet him again. She meets up with him in Nashville, where they are both doing professional work; they kiss briefly, make plans to meet at 11 that night, but Thom, claiming to be consumed by unexpected professional business, texts her, inviting her to meet him in L.A. tomorrow. Flying from Nashville to L.A., with an intermediary stop in St. Louis, she sits and, as the plane lands in St. Louis, she contemplates whether she should hook up with Thom, knowing whatever she decides will bring about cognitive dissonance:

> Then, with uncanny synchronicity, a call came from Thom. Unknown Number, her screen said, with two choices given below: Answer. Ignore. She pressed the latter and remained seated. Group A was just boarding. She could get off here, in St. Louis, catch a flight to LaGuardia, and be home. She could forgive herself for Thom, for the kiss, for all of it. No harm, no foul. Yet it

was the possible regrets that troubled her most, no matter what choice she made, the ones that would come to her later, in the night, and gnawed at her even now – starting with what you didn't take versus what you did. Not to mention the stories she might tell a future stranger about this moment, and what she'd decided before she was airborne again.

(Ross, 2011, p. 241)

This mirrors choices we all face in real life. In actual situations, people behave like Sara, experiencing conflicts when making a decision and anticipating regrets about whatever choice they make.

It is only after the decision is made that they experience the particular stress known as dissonance (Aronson, 1968). At this point, they truly are faced with two incompatible cognitions: I chose Alternative A, but this means I must forego the benefits of Alternative B. In some cases, simply anticipating making a difficult choice can trigger dissonance (Cooper, Blackman, & Keller, 2016).

We do not experience dissonance after each and every decision. It's the ones that are the most important, personally consequential, and least amenable to change that seem to trigger the greatest amount of cognitive dissonance (Simon, Greenberg, & Brehm, 1995; Wicklund & Brehm, 1976). Thus, choosing between two equally desirable paper towels should ordinarily produce less dissonance than selecting between two attractive and similarly priced apartments. In addition, if you can revise your decision – take it back, so to speak – you should have less dissonance than if you have signed the deal on the dotted line and cannot revisit your choice, except with considerable psychological or financial pain. If you suddenly discover, after you signed your lease, that the apartment you're renting is located in a dwelling built with asbestos, you're apt to experience a good deal of cognitive dissonance.

Just how this would feel would depend on you and how you deal with decisional stress. But there is little doubt that it wouldn't feel good! Scholars have actually studied how dissonance "feels," and they conclude it's a complex amalgamation of physiological arousal, negative affect, and mental anguish (Cooper & Fazio, 1984; Elkin & Leippe, 1986; Elliot & Devine, 1994).

So how do people cope with this discomfort we call dissonance? Theorists argue that they employ a variety of techniques. Consider two examples, the first more consequential, the second rather ordinary, even prosaic. The first illustration involves dissonance about eating meat in view of ethical concerns about killing and morally offensive ways of breeding animals (see Figure 13.3).

To justify eating meat, individuals who have some ethical qualms about meat-eating can eliminate dissonance in a number of ways (Rothgerber, 2014). They can employ language to disassociate the animal from the food they consume, using words like "sirloin" and "bacon" as "substitutes for the animal flesh people consume, allowing omnivores to maintain the illusion that animals are not involved" (Rothgerber, 2014, p. 33). They also can self-protectively call themselves vegetarians, even though they eat chicken and fish. Or they can take a more proactive approach, justifying their meat-eating by exaggerating how much they enjoy it, claiming that God intended for humans to eat meat (even though that is obviously questionable), and convincing themselves that they have no choice – they have to eat meat to survive. By perceiving they have no choice, they do not have to take responsibility for the aversive outcome or for causing harm to animals or the environment, in this way eliminating some of the anguish a more conscious awareness of their choice would bring.

The second example of dissonance reduction in the face of a decision is more familiar. Let's say you invite a close friend to a movie that has garnered favorable reviews. The movie, obligatory popcorn, and soft drinks are expensive, so you hope the film will pan out. It doesn't; the movie turns out to be a real loser, and you find yourself sitting there, hoping it will get better. Hope springs eternal; nevertheless, the movie stinks.

Figure 13.3 People Who have Moral Qualms About Eating Meat Experience Cognitive Dissonance When They Dig into a Steak, Hamburger, or Chicken. Dissonance theory suggests that they must resort to a variety of cognitive strategies, even distortions, to gain peace of mind. In this way, they can justify the dissonance they experience over consuming animal products, perhaps, as in the picture above, exaggerating or overstating the pleasure they take from a summer barbecue

You are in a state of cognitive dissonance. The cognition "I spent a lot of money on this movie" is dissonant with the knowledge that the movie is no good. Or, the thought that "I'm personally responsible for ruining my friend's evening" is dissonant with your positive self-concept or your desire to look good in your friend's eyes. How can you reduce dissonance? Research suggests you will try one or several of these techniques:

1 *Change your attitude.* Convince yourself it's a great flick, on balance – this may be hard if the movie is really bad.
2 *Add consonant cognitions.* Note how cool the cinematography is or decide that one of the actors delivered an especially convincing portrayal.
3 *Derogate the unchosen alternative.* Tell yourself that going to a movie beats sitting at home, endlessly checking Instagram posts.

4 *Spread apart the alternatives.* Convince yourself that the choice you made (sticking with the movie) is much better than shuffling out and doing nothing all night (numerically, on a 1–5 scale, before the decision, both choices were a 3; after the decision, staying at the flick moves up to a 4 and leaving drops down to a 3.2).

5 *Alter the importance of the cognitive elements.* Trivialize the decision by telling yourself that it's only a movie, just two hours of your life.

6 *Suppress thoughts.* Deny the problem and just try to get into the movie as much as you can.

7 *Communicate.* Talk up the movie with your friend, using the conversation to convince yourself it was a good decision.

8 *Alter the behavior.* Leave.

People frequently bolster the chosen option and criticize the rejected choice, spreading apart the alternatives, so there is a greater difference between the choices before than after the decision. Two products that were neck-in-neck, tied for first place, no longer appear this way in people's minds after the decision. The purchased product seems more attractive than the runner-up, a strategy to reduce dissonance. Individuals reduce dissonance in other ways as well, striving for personally adaptive ways to restore psychological consonance. It is amazing how few people seem to avail themselves of the last option: Altering the behavior. Don't we frequently sit through a bad movie, spending our valuable cognitive energy justifying and rationalizing instead of saving ourselves the hardship by walking out? Yet this is consistent with dissonance theory.

Dissonance theorists emphasize that people prefer easier to harder ways of changing cognitive elements (Simon et al., 1995). It is hard to alter behavior. Behavior is well learned and can be costly to modify. Walking out could prove embarrassing. To be sure, sticking through a lemon of a movie is not necessarily rational; it is an example of what psychologists call a sunk cost (Garland, 1990). You are not going to get the money back, no matter how much you convince yourself that it was a great film. However, as dissonance theorists are fond of reminding us, human beings are not *rational* animals, but, rather, rationalizing animals, seeking "to appear rational, both to others and [themselves]" (Aronson, 1968, p. 6). Rather than admit they are wrong, people rationalize. They deny and distort reality, refusing to acknowledge that they made a mistake. As Carol Tavris and Elliot Aronson (2007) note, "most people, when directly confronted by evidence that they are wrong, do not change their point of view or course of action but justify it even more tenaciously" (p. 2).

How apt a description of human decision-making! Immediately after people make up their minds to embark on one course rather than another, they bear an uncanny resemblance to the proverbial ostrich, sticking their heads in the sand to avoid perspectives that might conflict with the option they chose, doing all they can to reaffirm the wisdom of their decision. For example, let's say a friend of yours smokes a pack a day. If you asked her why she smokes, you would hear a long list of rationalizations speaking to the power of dissonance reduction. Her reasons might include: "I know I should quit, but I've got too much stress right now to go through quitting again"; "I guess I'd rather smoke than pig out and end up looking like a blimp"; and "Hey, we're all going to die anyway. I'd rather do what I enjoy." All these reasons make great sense to your friend; they help restore consonance, but they prevent her from taking the steps needed to preserve her health. Such is the power of cognitive dissonance.

Impactful as cognitive dissonance is, it intriguingly intersects with another important social influence: *Culture.* Dissonance should depend on the particular type of cultural inconsistency that is in play. Western cultures emphasize independent thinking, placing a premium on people making rational decisions that reflect their own preferences rather than the dictates of others. In general, Asian cultures stress interdependence among people, with value accorded to decisions that maintain harmony and promote consideration of others' feelings. Thus, individuals from Western societies – the United States and European countries – should have a greater need to reduce dissonance when a decision involves themselves, while those from Asian cultures should experience more need to rationalize dissonance when the decision involves another person, like a close friend. Research supports these propositions (Hoshino-Browne et al., 2005). Yet, even if culture influences the way that people experience dissonance, the need to reduce cognitive dissonance is universal. Individuals from different cultures experience dissonance after making a decision that is personally important, and they feel a need to rationalize or justify the decisions they make.

Dissonance and Expenditure of Effort

Let's explore another facet of cognitive dissonance, one that evokes a series of everyday queries. For example, have you ever wondered why fraternity pledges come to like a fraternity more after they have undergone a severe initiation procedure? Ever been curious why law students who have survived the torturous experience of being asked to cite legal precedent before a class of hundreds come to think positively of their law school professors? Or why medical interns who work 30-hour shifts, with barely any sleep, vigorously defend the system, sometimes viewing it as a grand way to learn the practice of medicine (Kleinfield, 1999)? An explanation of these phenomena can be found in the application of dissonance theory to the expenditure of effort.

The core notion here is quite simple, as Aronson and Mills explained:

> No matter how attractive a group is to a person it is rarely completely positive; i.e., usually there are some aspects of the group that the individual does not like. If he has undergone an unpleasant initiation to gain admission to the group, his cognition that he has gone through an unpleasant experience for the sake of membership is dissonant with the cognition that there are things about the group that he does not like.
>
> (1959, p. 177)

One way to reduce dissonance is to convince oneself that the group has many positive characteristics that justify the expenditure of effort.

Elliot Aronson and Judson Mills tested this hypothesis long ago – in 1959. Yet their findings have been replicated by other experimenters, and continue to shed light on events occurring today. Like many researchers of their era, they preferred to set up a contrived procedure to study dissonance and effort. Believing that they needed to provide a pure test of the hypothesis, they devised an experiment in which female college students were told they would be participating in several group discussions on the psychology of sex. Informed that the group had been meeting for several weeks and they would be replacing a woman who had dropped out due to scheduling conflicts, women in the experimental condition were told they would be screened before gaining formal admission to the group. (The experimenters deliberately chose women, perhaps because they felt that the sexual words they would ask women to read would have a stronger effect on these 1950s co-eds than on male students. Seen through today's ethical lights, the study is sexist and abusive. (Researchers conducting the study in today's more morally sensitive college environment would – and should – employ a different procedure.)

Students assigned to the severe initiation condition read aloud 12 obscene words and two graphic descriptions of sexual activity from contemporary novels. Women in the mild initiation condition read five sex-related words that were not obscene. Subjects in both conditions were then informed they had performed satisfactorily and had been admitted into the group. All the women subsequently listened to a tape-recorded discussion of a group meeting. The discussion was made to seem dull and banal, with group members speaking dryly and contradicting each other.

The discussion was set up this way to arouse dissonance. Female participants in the study had to confront the fact that they had undergone a humiliating experience, reading sexual words in front of some guy they had never met, for the sake of membership in a group that seemed boring and dull.

You might think that women in the severe initiation condition would dislike the group. Indeed, simple learning models would suggest that the unpleasant experience these women underwent would increase antipathy to the group. However, dissonance theory made the opposite prediction. It predicted that women in the severe initiation treatment would evaluate the group most positively. They had the most dissonance, and one way to reduce it would be to rationalize the unpleasant initiation by convincing themselves that the group discussion was not as bad as it seemed and was, in some sense, worth the pain they endured. This is what happened: Women in the severe initiation condition gave the group discussion higher ratings than other subjects did.

Although Aronson and Mills' study was intriguing, it did not convince all researchers. Some suggested that perhaps the severe initiation procedure did not embarrass the women at all, but aroused them sexually! If this were true, women in the severe initiation condition would have liked the group more because they associated the pleasant arousal with the group experience (Chapanis & Chapanis, 1964). To rule out this and other alternative explanations, researchers conducted a different test of the effort justification hypothesis, one that involved not a sexual embarrassment test but, rather, different initiation procedures. Using these operationalizations, experimenters found additional support for the Aronson and Mills findings (Cooper & Axsom, 1982; Gerard & Mathewson, 1966).

Applications

We must be careful not to apply these findings glibly to the real world. People do not always rationalize effort by changing their attitude toward the group; they may reduce dissonance in other ways – for example, by trivializing the initiation rite. In some cases, the effort expended is so enormous and the initiation ceremony so humiliating that people cannot convince themselves that the group is worth it. This helps explain why Litesa Wallace, the young woman mentioned at the beginning of the chapter, sued her sorority (while still remaining a Delta). Nevertheless, effort justification sheds light on real-life situations. And, like all persuasion techniques, it exerts both positive and negative effects.

Jewish children spend much time at synagogue learning Hebrew and reciting the Torah in preparation for their Bar and Bat Mitzvahs. The time spent is dissonant with the knowledge that they could be having more fun doing other things, but in the end the need to reduce dissonance pushes them to evaluate the experience positively. This enables the ritual – and religion – to get passed on to future generations, thus preserving time-honored traditions.

The use of effort justification in other contexts is more controversial. On the one hand, initiation rituals at many college fraternities and sororities, while mildly stressful, are not harmful. Through a process of dissonance reduction, students forge bonds and form a strong commitment to a valued social group. Rites of passage employed by college sports teams and the military can serve similar positive functions. However, when groups initiate new members through physical abuse, verbal harassment, or humiliation, they cross an ethical line, engaging in hazing.

Over the years, young people have been seriously injured and died as a result of hazing rituals at colleges and universities. A Florida A&M band member died in 2011 after participating in a bizarre hazing initiation, called "Crossing Bus C," where band members walk down a parked, dark bus used to transport them to out-of-town football games, as fellow band members pound them with mallets and drumsticks (Alvarez, 2014). In 2013, a 19-year-old freshman at Baruch College in New York, Michael Deng, died during a hazing ritual. Deng, blindfolded and wearing a backpack weighted down by 20 to 30 pounds of sand, walked across a frozen yard while others attempted to tackle him. He was lifted and dropped hard onto the frozen ground, likely causing severe head damage (Rojas & Southall, 2015).

The students complied because they had made a commitment they did not want to break and wanted to justify the effort they expended. Upperclassmen were not cruel by nature, but sought to rationalize the fact that they had complied and undergone the same treatment when they were freshmen or sophomores. They reduced dissonance, enhanced the allure of the ritual, and convinced themselves that hazing built character, regarding it as a valued ritual that needed to be passed on to others (Marklein, 2000; see Figure 13.4).

Figure 13.4 Although Fraternity and Sorority Initiations Rarely Involve Hazing (Illustrated by the Activity Shown Here), Extreme Hazing Does Occur. Cognitive dissonance theory offers a novel explanation for why these practices continue and can, paradoxically, lead initiates to develop a favorable attitude toward the group

Image courtesy of Getty Images

There is an even more tragic twist in the case of the death of Michael Deng. Deng, a young Chinese-American from New York City, sought to be a member of an Asian-American fraternity, whose brothers intended the physical and verbal abuse "to teach him that solidarity with his fellow Asians is his only hope of making it in a white world" (Kang, 2017, p. 33). Their motives were beneficent, but in learning to reduce dissonance by aggrandizing a hazing ritual, they lost sight of their ethical and humane responsibilities to a fellow student, to whom they were even more bonded because of their similar ethnic background.

Induced Compliance

What happens if a person is coaxed to argue publicly for a position he or she does not privately accept? Further, what if the individual is paid a paltry sum to take this position? Suppose you gave a speech that advocated banning cell phone use in cars, although you privately disagreed with this position? Let's say someone paid you a dollar to take this stand. Dissonance theory makes the unusual prediction that, under these circumstances, you would actually come to evaluate the proposal favorably.

This prediction is part of a phenomenon known as *induced compliance*. The name comes from the fact that a person has been induced – gently persuaded – to comply with a persuader's request. The person freely chooses to perform an action that is inconsistent with his or her beliefs or attitude. Such actions are called counterattitudinal.

When individuals perform a counterattitudinal behavior and cannot rationalize the act – as they could if they had received a large reward – they are in a state of dissonance. One way to reduce dissonance is to change one's attitude so that it is consistent with the behavior – that is, convince oneself that one really agrees with the discrepant message.

This hypothesis was elegantly tested and supported by Leon Festinger and J. Merrill Carlsmith in 1959. Students were asked to perform two tasks that were phenomenally boring: (1) placing spools on a tray, emptying the tray, and refilling it with spools; and (2) turning each of 48 pegs on a peg board a quarter turn clockwise, then another quarter turn, and so on for half an hour. In what could have been an episode from the old TV show *Spy TV*, the experimenter then asked students to do him a favor: Tell the next participant in the study that this monotonous experiment had been enjoyable, exciting, and a lot of fun. You see, the experimenter suggested, the person who usually does this couldn't do it today, and we're looking for someone we could hire to do it for us. The whole thing was a ruse: There was no other person who usually performed the task. The intent was to induce students to say that a boring task was enjoyable – a dissonant act. There was also a twist.

Some students were paid $20 for telling the lie that they enjoyed the task. Others were paid $1, and those in a control condition did not tell a lie at all. Participants then rated the enjoyableness of the tasks. As it turned out, those paid $1 said they liked the tasks more and displayed greater willingness to participate in similar experiments in the future than did other students (see Table 13.1).

How can we explain the findings? According to theory, the cognition that "the spool-removing and peg-turning tasks were really boring" was dissonant with the cognition that "I just told someone it was lots of fun." The $20 provided students with external justification for telling the lie. It helped them justify why they said one thing (the tasks were exciting), yet believed another (they were really boring). They received $20; that helped them feel good about the whole thing, and they had no need to change their attitude so as to restore consonance. Like a stiff drink that helps people forget their sorrows, the $20 helped to erase the dissonance, or sufficiently so that students didn't feel any need to change their attitude toward the tasks.

Table 13.1 Results of the Festinger and Carlsmith Study

Question	Experimental Condition		
	$1	$20	Control
How Enjoyable Were Tasks? (Rated from –5 to +5)	1.35	–.05	–.45
Were Tasks Scientifically Important? (Rated from 0 to 10)	6.45	5.18	5.60
Are You Willing to Participate in Similar Experiments? (rated from –5 to +5)	1.20	–.25	–.62

Source: Festinger and Carlsmith (1959)

For students paid $1, it was a different matter. Lacking a sufficient external justification for the inconsistency, they had to turn inward to get one. They needed to bring their private attitude in line with their public behavior. One way to do this was to change their attitude toward the tasks. By convincing themselves that "the thing with the spools wasn't so bad; it gave me a chance to do something, perfect my hand–eye coordination – yeah, that's the ticket," they could comfortably believe that the statement they made to a fellow student ("I had a lot of fun") actually reflected their inner feelings. Dissonance was thus resolved; they had restored cognitive harmony (see Figure 13.5).

Note that these findings are exactly the opposite of what you might expect based on common sense and classic learning theory, notably reinforcement theory (Aronson, 2019). Both would suggest that people paid more money would like something more. Reward leads to liking, right? Not according to dissonance theory. Indeed, the negative relationship between reward and liking, consistent with cognitive dissonance theory, has held up in other studies conceptually replicating the Festinger and Carlsmith experiment (Harmon-Jones, 2002; Preiss & Allen, 1998).

The early research had exciting theoretical implications. As researcher Elliot Aronson eloquently observed, in a triumphal paragraph:

As a community we have yet to recover from the impact of this research – fortunately! ... Because the finding departed from the general orientation accepted either tacitly or explicitly by most social psychologists in the 1950s: [That] high reward – never low reward – is accompanied by greater learning, greater conformity, greater performance, greater satisfaction, greater persuasion ... [But in Festinger and Carlsmith] either reward theory made no prediction at all or the opposite prediction. These results represented a striking and convincing act of liberation from the dominance of a general reward-reinforcement theory.

(Quoted in Aron & Aron, 1989, p. 116)

More generally, the results of this strange – but elegantly conducted – experiment suggested that people could not be counted on to slavishly do as experts predicted. They were not mere automatons whose

Figure 13.5 Classic Dissonance Studies Show That When People Choose to Engage in a Boring Task – Such as Carefully Sharpening a Large Number of Pencils with a Small Pencil Sharpener – and Receive a Meager Reward, They Can Change Their Attitude Toward the Task. To reduce dissonance, they justify their behavior and convince themselves the task was enjoyable

Image courtesy of Shutterstock

thoughts could be controlled by behavioral engineering or psychologists' rewards. Like Dostoyevsky's underground man, who celebrated his emotion and spontaneity, dissonance researchers rejoiced in the study's findings, for they spoke to the subjectivity and inner-directedness of human beings.

Applications

The great contribution of induced compliance research is theoretical, in suggesting new ways to think about human attitudes and persuasion. However, the research does have practical applications. The negative incentive effect – paying people less changes their attitudes more – can be applied to the problem of motivating individuals to engage in positive, healthy acts they would rather not perform. For example, consider the case of a parent who wants to convince a couch-potato child to exercise more. Should the parent pay the kid each time she or he jogs, plays tennis, or swims laps? Dissonance theory says no. It stipulates that children frequently face dissonance after engaging in vigorous physical exercise – for example, "*I just ran a mile, but, geez, did that hurt*"; "*I just ran five laps, but I could have been on Facebook.*" By paying sons or daughters money for exercising, parents undermine children's motivation to change their attitudes. The money provides strong external justification, erasing the dissonance: The child no longer feels a need to change an anti-exercise attitude so that it is compatible with behavior (jogging a mile a day). Instead, the money bridges thought and action and becomes the main thing the child gets out of the event. Thus, the same old negative attitude toward exercise persists.

By contrast, if parents don't pay their children a hefty sum (or give them only a paltry reward), children must reduce the dissonance on their own. To be sure, kids may not restore consonance by developing a positive attitude toward exercise (they could blame their parents for "forcing" them to work up a sweat or just complain about how sore their bodies feel). But it is entirely possible – and I've seen examples of this with parents in my neighborhood, to say nothing of research that backs it up (Deci, 1975) – that children will change their attitude to fit their behavior. They develop a positive attitude toward exercise to justify their behavior. Exercise becomes a positive, not a negative, force in their lives; it becomes associated with pleasant activities; and the attitude motivates, then triggers, behavior. The child begins to exercise spontaneously, on his or her own, without parental prodding (see Figure 13.6).

There is also a more negative sociological implication of the $1 versus $20 study. Employers could capitalize on the finding that people derive more intrinsic satisfaction from getting paid less than more money; why not just pay people less, they might reason? But would employees really be more satisfied if they were paid less than a minimum wage? Of course not. A literal interpretation of Festinger and Carlsmith suggests that workers who perform boring tasks would convince themselves they enjoy their work to rationalize their doing it for paltry wages. However, it defies credulity to think that people would be more satisfied with mundane work performed at a lower, rather than a higher, wage. Dissonance theorists might point out that choice, a requirement for dissonance reduction to kick in, was not involved as employees didn't choose to perform this work. On the other hand, they chose to take the job. So, this does represent a practical issue for dissonance research to wrestle with.

The example raises social justice issues. We wouldn't want to suggest that employers should manipulate workers' tendency to try to rationalize performing boring work at a lower wage. From a theoretical perspective, this application suggests that other factors – like social comparisons with other more highly paid colleagues and the need to make ends meet – intervene, demonstrating that, for all the strengths of the study, it has its limits, or, at least, dissonance reduction needs to be considered in the context of other social and economic forces.

Explanations and Controversies

When a theory is developed, researchers test it to determine if it holds water. If hypotheses generated from the theory are empirically supported, researchers are elated: They have come upon a concept that yields new insights, and they have landed a way to publish studies that enhance their professional reputations. But once all this happens, the question "What have you done for me lately?" comes to mind. The ideas become rather familiar. What's more, scholars begin wondering just why the theory works and come to recognize that it may hold only under particular conditions. These new questions lead to revisions of the theory and advance science. They also help to "keep the theory young" by forcing tests in new eras, with new generations of scholars and different social values.

Figure 13.6 How Can Parents Convince Their Children to Get off the Couch or Put Away Their Electronic Devices and Hit the Jogging Trail? Dissonance theory suggests that they should create a situation of insufficient justification: Encouraging children to agree to get some exercise, while not dispensing any reward. The resultant dissonance may lead children to develop a more positive attitude toward exercising, and they may come to enjoy running with their mom or dad, or by themselves

Image courtesy of Shutterstock

Dissonance theory fits this trajectory. After the studies of the 1950s and 1960s were completed (yes, they were conducted that long ago!), scholars began asking deeper questions about dissonance theory. They began to wonder just why dissonance leads to attitude change and whether there weren't other reasons why individuals seek to restore dissonance than those Festinger posited. Many theorists proposed alternative accounts of dissonance and tested their ideas.

The catalyst for this research was the Festinger and Carlsmith boring-task study previously discussed. Like a Rorschach projection test, it has been interpreted in different ways by different scholars. Their research suggests that when people engage in counterattitudinal behavior, there is more going on than you might think. Four explanations of the study have been advanced. Each offers a different perspective on human nature and persuasion. Yet all four agree on one point: Festinger's thesis – people are driven by an overarching need to reduce inconsistency – is not the only psychological engine that leads to attitude change. Students in the boring-task study may have been bothered by the inconsistency between attitude toward the task and behavior (telling others it was enjoyable). However, there were other reasons why they changed their attitude than the mere discomfort that inconsistency causes. Let's review these four perspectives on cognitive dissonance.

This discussion will help you appreciate that dissonance is complicated and that there are four different, but plausible, ways of looking at the same phenomenon: The Festinger and Carlsmith study. The viewpoints reflect different windows on human nature, and suggest diverse ways of using persuasion to influence people. I begin with the view that the findings in the $1 study stemmed from unpleasant consequences.

1. Unpleasant Consequences + Responsibility = Dissonance

What really bothered students in Festinger and Carlsmith's experiment, researcher Joel Cooper has insightfully suggested, is that they might be personally responsible for having caused unpleasant consequences (Scher & Cooper, 1989). By leading an innocent person to believe that a monotonous study was enjoyable, they had, arguably, caused a fellow student to develop an expectation that would not be met by reality. This realization caused them discomfort. To alleviate the pain, they convinced themselves that the task was really interesting. Thus, it was not inconsistency per se but, rather, "the desire to avoid feeling personally responsible for producing the aversive consequence of having harmed the other participant" that motivated attitude change (Harmon-Jones & Mills, 1999, p. 14) (see also Harmon-Jones & Harmon-Jones, 2019, for an action-based model proposing critical refinements on aversive consequences, with a focus on how making commitments primes individuals to translate intention into action).

2. Dissonance Occurs When You Are Concerned That You Look Bad in Front of Others

This view emphasizes people's need to manage impressions or present themselves positively in front of other people (Tedeschi, Schlenker, & Bonoma, 1971). Theorists argue that students in Festinger and Carlsmith's study did not really change their attitudes, but marked down on the questionnaire that they liked the task only to avoid being viewed negatively by the experimenter. Concerned that the experimenter would look down on them for being willing to breach their ethics for the reward of $1, students in the $1 condition strategically changed their attitude so that it looked as if they really liked the task. Thus, they could not be accused of selling their souls for a trivial sum of money (Cooper & Fazio, 1984).

3. Dissonance Involves a Threat to Self-Esteem

The self-concept is at the center of this interpretation. In Aronson's (1968) view, students in Festinger and Carlsmith's study experienced dissonance between the cognition "I am a good and moral person" and the knowledge that "I just lied to someone, and I won't have a chance to 'set him straight' because I probably won't see him again" (p. 24). Students were not bothered by the mere inconsistency between thoughts but, rather, by the fact that their behavior was inconsistent with – or violated – their positive self-concept. Of course, lying is not dissonant to a pathological liar; yet it was assumed that for most people, telling a fib would be moderately dissonant with their views of themselves as honest individuals. The self-concept is at the center of other contemporary views of dissonance reduction, such as self-affirmation theory (Aronson, Cohen, & Nail, 2019; Steele, 1988), which takes a slightly different approach to the issue (see Box 13.1).

It's Not Dissonance, but Self-Perception

Daryl J. Bem shook things up with a very different account of the classic study. Back in 1970, Bem argued that effects observed in experiments like Festinger and Carlsmith's had nothing to do with cognitive dissonance, but were due to an entirely different psychological process. Unlike the three explanations just discussed, Bem's theory dismisses dissonance entirely. Arguing that people aren't so much neurotic rationalizers as dispassionate, cool observers of their own behavior, Bem suggests that people look to their own behavior when they want to understand their attitudes.

Behavior leads to attitude, Bem (1972) argues, but not because people want to bring attitude in line with behavior so as to gain consistency. Instead, behavior causes attitude because people infer their attitudes from observing their behavior. For example, according to Bem, a young woman forms her attitude toward vegetarian food by observing her behavior: "I'm always eating pasta and vegetables. I never order meat from restaurants anymore. I must really like veggie food." Or a guy decides he likes a girl, not on the basis of his positive thoughts but, rather, because he observes that "I'm always texting her and get excited when she texts back. I must really like her."

Applying this analysis to Festinger and Carlsmith's classic experiment, Bem argued that students paid $20 to say a boring task was interesting quickly looked to the situation, asked themselves why they would do this, and observed that they had just been paid $20 to make the statement. "Oh, I must have done it for the money," they concluded. Having reached this judgment, there was not the slightest reason for them to assume that their behavior reflected an attitude.

Subjects paid $1 looked dispassionately at their behavior to help decide why they told the other student the task was fun. Noting that they had received only a buck to lie, they concluded, "I sure didn't do this for the money." Seeking to further understand why they behaved as they did, the $1 subjects then asked themselves, "Now why would I have told the experimenter the tasks were interesting? I didn't get any big external reward for saying this." Then came the explanation, obvious and plausible: "I must have really liked those tasks. Why else would I have agreed to make the statements?" These inferences – rather than rationalizations – led to the $1 students' forming a favorable attitude toward the tasks.

Resolutions

Who's right? Who's wrong? Which view has the most support or the most adherents? What's the right answer?

These questions probably occur to you as you read the different views of dissonance. However, there is usually not one correct interpretation of a complex phenomenon, but many. Thus, there are various reasons why low reward or counterattitudinal advocacy leads to attitude change. Inconsistency between cognitions, feeling responsible for producing negative consequences, discomfort at looking bad in front of others, perceiving that one has engaged in behavior that is incongruent with one's sense of self, and subsequent self-perceptions all motivate individuals to change attitudes to fit behavior. For a number of years, researchers tried to tease out which explanation explained the $1 vs. $20 findings best. It became so difficult to disentangle the different psychological processes that researchers moved on, concluding that each perspective contributed different insights. Of course, that's a glib conclusion, and leading researchers continue to argue that their particular view of dissonance best accounts for the facts.

More than 60 years after dissonance theory was proposed, there remain persistent – and intriguing – questions about the nature of dissonance. Does dissonance reduction primarily involve coping with aversive arousal from a behavioral choice, as Cooper (2019) argues, or does it represent a subset of the desire to restore self-worth? Dissonance is a bona fide phenomenon, with fascinating implications for persuasion, but its existential nature remains abstruse. Other questions also emerge. Can neuroscience methods help adjudicate this debate by locating different neural responses that co-occur with different psychological mechanisms (Izuma & Murayama, 2019)? What about pesky evidence that attitude change in the service of dissonance reduction doesn't really cause people to feel better (Devine et al., 2019)? And yet, ending on a consensual note, researchers from different camps agree that dissonance, complex as it is, is a fascinating construct, with theoretical, counterintuitive, and practically relevant implications for attitudes and everyday life.

On a real-world note, of the two different approaches advanced above, the two that probably have the most interesting real-world implications are the self-concept and self-perception theories. Self-concept perspectives, such as Steele's (1988) self-affirmation theory, have intriguing implications for persuasion and health (see Box 13.1). Another approach, self-perception theory has helped explain an important interpersonal compliance phenomenon known as foot-in-the-door (see Chapter 14). It has also had broader political implications, suggesting that if government enacts policy changes that force changes in behavior (such as refraining from using plastic bags), more pro-environmental attitudes will follow at the individual level through a process of self-perception.

BOX 13.1

Dissonance and Mental Health

One of the great things about dissonance theory is that over half a century after it was formulated, it continues to contain enlightening ideas about everyday life. Some of these ideas have interesting implications for mental health. Here are five suggestions, culled from theory and research, for how to harness dissonance in the service of a happier, healthier life:

1 *Expect to experience dissonance after a decision.* Don't expect life to be clean and free of stress. If you choose one product or side of the issue instead of another and the selection was difficult, there is bound to be discomfort.

2 *Don't feel you have to eliminate the dissonance immediately.* Some people, uncomfortable with dissonance, mentally decree that no unpleasant thoughts about the decision should enter their mind. But sometimes the more we try to suppress something, the more apt it is to return to consciousness (Wegner et al., 1987). Dissonance can present us with a learning experience; it can help us come to grips with aspects of decisions we didn't like or positions that have more of a gray area than we believed at the outset. The thinking that dissonance

stimulates can help us make better decisions, or deliver more compelling persuasive communication next time around. Of course, it is perfectly natural to want to reduce dissonance that follows a decision or performance of a behavior. However, we should also be open to the possibility that dissonance can be a teaching tool, as well as an annoyance – a phenomenon that can deepen our understanding of human experience.

3   *Don't feel bound to each and every commitment you make.* Dissonance research indicates that once people make a public commitment, they are loath to change their minds, for fear of looking bad or having to confront the fact that they made a mistake, and so on. But there are times – such as undergoing a cruel initiation rite to join a sorority – when backing out of a commitment may be the healthy thing to do. Naturally, we should try to honor our commitments as much as possible, but we also should not feel obligated to do something unhealthy or unethical just because we sunk a lot of time into the project.

4   *Admit your mistakes.* Most of us are loath to admit we made a mistake. Fearing that the mistake would reflect negatively on their self-concept or arouse other dissonant elements, people cling tenaciously to their original decision. But this is not always a mature or helpful response. Understanding why a decision caused dissonance and learning from mistakes can help us grow and avoid similar errors in the future. The Chinese philosopher Lao Tzu said:

> A great nation is like a great man: when he makes a mistake, he realizes it. Having realized it, he admits it. Having admitted it, he corrects it. He considers those who point out his faults as his most benevolent teachers.
>
> (Tavris & Aronson, 2007)

5   *Harness your regret in positive ways.* Regret, which emerges from unresolved dissonance in the wake of a difficult decision, can have salutary aspects. Rather than denying or derogating regret, you can use it as a source of inspiration, as a method to grow and improve. Rather than obsessing about what we have should have done and focusing on the negative parts of regret, it is best to find "a silver lining" in our regret, appreciating that we are human and make mistakes, but can draw lessons from what we've done (Taitz, 2019). By extracting something positive from the experience, we can learn, grow, and approach future situations with more insight and wisdom.

6   *Be creative in your attempts to reduce dissonance.* You may not be able to reduce all the dissonance that results from a decision or performance of behavior. A young woman who smokes, quits for a while, and then starts up again is apt to feel dissonance. A deadbeat dad may finally feel guilt or discomfort after years of leaving and neglecting his kids. According to Claude M. Steele and colleagues, these individuals feel dissonant because they have performed actions that call into question their self-worth or sense of themselves as competent, good people (Aronson, Cohen, & Nail, 1999; Steele, 1988). Given that self-esteem incongruency or related processes are at the root of dissonance, people can alleviate dissonance by doing things that affirm core beliefs or make them look good in their own eyes (e.g., Randles et al., 2015). Thus, although the smoker cannot reduce all the dissonance aroused by her failure to quit smoking, she might restore a sense of self-competence by completing important projects at work or doing other things that show she can follow up on personal promises she makes. Realistically, the deadbeat dad may have alienated his kids so much that he can't do much to regain their trust. However, he might be able to restore a positive sense of self by at least celebrating their major accomplishments, or by opting to spend time with other children in need.

In sum, more than half a century since Festinger invented the concept, cognitive dissonance continues to stimulate scholarly discussion and theorizing about persuasion. There is no question that dissonance produces genuine, abiding changes in attitudes, beliefs, and behavior. However, for dissonance to produce attitude change, the individual must have freely chosen to perform the advocated behavior. Dissonance does not produce attitude change when behavior is coerced; in such situations, the person feels no internal need to rationalize the behavior (for a summary of the theory, see Box 13.2).

This brings us to the final issue in this chapter – an important one for this book: Implications of dissonance theory for attitude change. The next section explores ways in which communication experts can use dissonance theory to influence attitudes in a variety of real-life settings.

Dissonance and Persuasion

Dissonance theorists take a decidedly different approach to persuasion from approaches reviewed in earlier chapters. Rather than trying to accommodate the other person's thinking or speech style,

---

BOX 13.2

Understanding Theory: Primer on Cognitive Dissonance Theory

1. Cognitive dissonance occurs when an individual holds two psychologically inconsistent cognitions.
2. Dissonance is psychologically uncomfortable, physiologically arousing, and drives individuals to take steps to reduce this uncomfortable state.
3. Dissonance occurs under several conditions, such as when an individual: (a) is faced with a psychologically difficult decision; (b) expends effort to participate in what turns out to be a less than ideal task; and (c) in general freely performs a behavior that is inconsistent with an attitude. Individuals are motivated to take steps to reduce dissonance.
4. One method to rid oneself of dissonance is to change the problematic attitude after receiving a persuasive message.
5. The classic $1 vs. $20 induced compliance study found that when individuals freely choose to perform an unpleasant task, they are more likely to feel positively toward the task when they are paid a small amount of money than when they are paid a lot of money.
6. There are a variety of psychological explanations for this finding and for dissonance effects in general. These include an emphasis on aversive consequences, self-presentation, self-esteem, and self-perception. This has created a certain ambiguity, for it is difficult, if not impossible, to determine for sure when one, rather than another, process holds.
7. Cognitive dissonance theory emphasizes the power of self-persuasion. We persuade ourselves that a decision or action is justified.
8. Persuaders can harness dissonance theory to help individuals change attitudes. They can call on the power of commitments, effects of hypocrisy inducement, and self-affirmation.

like the ELM or speech accommodation, dissonance theory has a confrontational streak. It says that persuaders should deliberately arouse cognitive dissonance and then let psychology do its work. Once dissonance is evoked, individuals should be motivated to reduce the discomfort. One way they can do this is to change their attitude in the direction the persuader recommends.

Calling on the major implications of the approaches previously discussed, we can suggest some concrete ways that dissonance theory can be employed in the service of persuasion.

Make a Commitment Public

When we commit ourselves publicly to an action, something interesting happens. We put pressure on ourselves to translate intention into action. If we fail to make good on a promise that others expect us to keep, we face opprobrium from strangers or friends; we also risk a very public blow to our self-esteem. In order to forestall such negative consequences, dissonant as they are, people find it psychologically easier to make good on their commitments. Research indicates that the strategy works. Women who made a long-term *public* commitment to lose weight were especially likely to achieve their goal, losing more weight than women who did not make any commitment (Nyer & Dellande, 2010).

In contemporary life, individuals frequently make commitments by posting details on websites and blogs.

More than 63,000 public commitments have been posted on a website called stickK (Rosenbloom, 2011). The name conjures up the desire to "stick" to your promises, and the capital K is a legal shorthand symbol for the term "contract." Meander through the site and you will see familiar promises to lose weight, exercise, and avoid junk food. But you also will find more idiosyncratic resolutions like practicing perfect pitch daily, quitting reading and writing fiction until medical school applications are complete, only using Facebook once a week for no more than 30 minutes (good luck!), never being mean to a girlfriend, and abstaining from eating meat or fish, except Buffalo chicken wings!

Here is how it works: People publicly resolve to accomplish a goal, make a financial commitment (giving a credit card number, but money is charged only in the case of failure), and indicate where the funds should be allocated if they do not follow through on their commitment. An individual might select a charitable organization she likes, or, to offer additional motivation to succeed, a charity she dislikes. People also choose others to serve as online supporters to cheer them on. Does it work? We can't know for sure. Some people swear by it; others no doubt failed to implement their plans. Public commitment does not guarantee that dissonance will produce attitude change. However, under the right circumstances, commitment can nudge the process along.

There are broader, environmental implications too. In California, which at time of writing is reeling under pressure from a severe drought, the state government mandated a 25 percent cut in urban water consumption. But the state has limited power to enforce the ban, so persuasion is necessary. Naturally, Californians love their verdant lawns, lemon trees, and purple and gold flowering hibiscus plants. Who can blame them? But conservation is key to the state's future, and dissonance-based commitment suggests a promising strategy.

Dissonance theory suggests that the state of California might create a website where homeowners publicly commit to reducing water by 25 percent. Those who make the pledge would receive a lawn sign that points to their less-than-verdant yellow lawn and proclaims, "My lawn is yellow because I took a pledge to help California. Join me at yellowlawns.ca.gov!" (Yoeli et al., 2015, p. 12). By making their commitment public, residents would feel compelled to water their yards less, lest they look bad in the view of their neighbors, passersby, and themselves.

Encourage People to Publicly Advocate a Position with Which They Disagree

Another social problem that afflicts America is prejudice. How can we nudge people into reducing a prejudiced attitude? This, to some extent, draws on time-honored research on advocating a message opposed, or counter, to one's initial attitude (Kim, Allen, Preiss, & Peterson, 2014). A key strategy is to call on the power of public behavior.

If individuals who harbor a prejudiced attitude toward minorities or gays can be coaxed into making a tolerant statement in public, they may feel cognitive dissonance. They privately do not like the particular group, but now, lo and behold, they have delivered a favorable speech in public. This may heighten the dissonance and, in some instances, motivate the individuals to bring attitude in line with public behavior. In a study that tested this hypothesis, Michael R. Leippe and Donna Eisenstadt (1994) gave White students an opportunity to write essays endorsing a scholarship policy that would significantly increase money available to Blacks, presumably at the expense of Whites. White students who believed their essays could be made public became more favorable toward both the policy and African Americans (see also Eisenstadt et al., 2005).

Interestingly, a judge used a variant of this procedure on a bigot who burned a Black doll and a cross in Black residents' yards. In addition to using coercive punishments such as sentencing him to jail, the judge ordered the man to go to the library to research the impact of cross burnings (Martin, 2001). Studying the issue could help the man think through his misguided sentiments. In addition, researching the topic in a public setting might lead the man to come to grips with his racist attitudes, perhaps inducing attitude change.

Confront People with Their Own Hypocrisy

This strategy places dissonance front and center in the individual's mind. A communicator directly confronts the person, letting him know that he has performed a behavior that violates a personal belief. The inconsistency is psychologically disturbing, propelling the individual to alter their attitude.

Stone and his colleagues employed this procedure in an engaging study of safe sex. They recognized that most students believe they should use condoms to prevent the spread of AIDS, but do not always practice what they preach. Stone and colleagues argued that, if they reminded individuals of this fact, "the resulting inconsistency between [students'] public commitment and the increased awareness of their current risky sexual behavior should cause dissonance" (Stone et al., 1994, p. 117). To alleviate dissonance, students might begin to practice safer sex.

Participants in the study were led to believe they were helping to design an AIDS prevention program for use at the high school level. Experimental group subjects wrote a persuasive speech about safer sex and delivered it in front of a video camera. They read about circumstances that made it difficult for people to use condoms and listed the circumstances that surrounded their own previous failures to practice safe sex. This was designed to provoke inconsistency or induce hypocrisy. (Control group subjects did not list these reasons or make the safer-sex speech before a video camera.)

All students were given an opportunity to buy condoms, using the $4 they had earned for participating in the study. As predicted, more students in the hypocrisy condition purchased condoms and bought more condoms than students in the control conditions. Their behavior was apparently motivated by the discomfort and guilt they experienced when they recognized they did not always practice what they preached (O'Keefe, 2000).

As intriguing as Stone and his colleagues' findings are, we need to be cautious about glibly endorsing *hypocrisy induction* as a method for safer-sex induction. First, making people feel hypocritical may make them angry and that may cause the treatment to boomerang. Second, in the case of the study of AIDS and safer sex, it is useful to note that safer-sex requests in real-world situations meet up against a variety of roadblocks, including the pleasures of sex, reluctance to offend a partner by proposing condom use, and even anxiety about being physically assaulted if one suggests using a condom. Hypocrisy induction may change attitudes in an experimental context, but persuasion is apt to be more difficult in actual sexual situations.

At the same time, the strategy has intriguing possibilities. Letting people know that a behavior they perform or position they endorse is incompatible with an important component of their self-concepts can make them feel uncomfortable (Takaku, 2006). Telling someone straight out that she has made a prejudiced remark can reduce the likelihood that this person will behave in a stereotyped way in the future (Czopp, Monteith, & Mark, 2006). Confronting individuals with an instance of their prejudice or self-incongruent behavior can be just the right psychological medicine to goad them into changing their attitudes (see Box 13.3).

Importantly, inducing hypocrisy can produce guilt and reduce prejudice, but probably only among people who are ambivalent about race, harboring egalitarian values, but also implicit, unconscious prejudice toward minority groups (Son Hing, Li, & Zanna, 2002). For Whites who are abjectly racist or proudly prejudiced, telling them that they treated an African American or individual from a minority race negatively would not produce dissonance at all, reminding us once again of the limits of even the most imaginative techniques for attitude change.

Yet hypocrisy induction holds out promise in an array of situations, where extreme attitudes are not involved, but where social change is important, such as safe driving and texting while driving (Fointiat, 2004) and other contexs, where persuading people to take better care of their health is of the essence.

BOX 13.3

90210 Dissonance

This story is about a father and teenage son who lived in the 90210 zip code region of the United States. You may know where that is. It's Beverly Hills, California. All too ordinary in some respects, the story concerns a high school student who was heavily dependent on drugs, and a dad who found out and tried to do something about it. The story, originally broadcast on the National Public Radio program *This American Life* on January 16, 1998, would not be relevant to this chapter except for one small but important fact: The father used dissonance theory to try to convince his son to quit doing drugs. His dad probably had never heard of cognitive dissonance, but his persuasive effort is a moving testament to the ways that dissonance can be used in family crisis situations. Here is what happened:

Joshua, a student at plush Beverly Hills High School, got involved with drugs in a big way.

> I failed English. I failed P.E. even, which is difficult to do, unless, you're, you know, running off getting stoned whenever you're supposed to be running around the track. And I just, you know, I just did whatever I wanted to do whenever I wanted to do it,

he told an interviewer. He stole money from his parents regularly to finance his drug habit.

Joshua had no reason to suspect his parents knew. But strange things began to happen. His dad started to punish him, grounding him on the eve of a weekend he planned to do LSD, offering no reason for the punishment. Claiming there was going to be a drug bust at Beverly Hills High, Josh's dad revealed the names of students who were doing drugs. How could his father know this?, Josh wondered.

About a month later, Josh and a buddy were hanging out in his backyard. The night before, there had been a big wind storm. It ripped off a panel from the side of the house. He and his friend were smoking a joint, like they did every day after school, when his buddy, noticing the downed panel, suddenly said, "Dude, what is this? Come here, dude. Come here, dude. Look at this." Josh saw only a strange piece of machinery inside a wall, when his buddy shocked him. "Dude, your parents are taping your calls."

Suddenly, Josh understood. That explained his dad's punishments and knowledge of the high school drug group. At this point, the radio program switched to Josh's dad, who revealed what had happened. He said he became upset when Josh's grades plunged and his son "started acting like a complete fool." Concerned and noticing that Josh spent a lot of time on the phone, he decided to tape-record Josh's phone calls. The ethical aspects of this appeared not to bother the father.

Aware his dad was taping him, Josh made a decision. He would not quit drugs – that was too great a change – but would tell his friends that he was going straight when they talked on the phone. This worked for a while, until Josh felt guilty about lying to his father. He valued his relationship with his dad and decided to talk to him. He cornered his dad at a party and told him that he knew he had been taping his phone calls.

In a dramatic admission, his father conceded he had been tape-recording Josh's conversations and said he was not going to do it anymore. He then told his son that there was something he didn't know yet, and perhaps would not understand. "Josh," he said,

> you think that because I'm your father and I am in this role of the disciplinarian, that it's between you and me. What you haven't realized yet is that your actions have far more impact on your own life than they will on mine.

He told Josh that he was going to take out the tape recorder the following day. At this point, Josh was waiting for a punishment – a severe punitive action, he assumed, perhaps military school. "I'll take the tape recorder out tomorrow," his dad said, "and there is only one thing I want you to do. I have about 40 tapes. I am going to give them to you, and I want you to listen to them, and that's all I ask."

With this statement, Josh's father hoped to unleash cognitive dissonance in his son. He wanted Josh to hear how he sounded on the tapes – his redundant, frequently incoherent conversations, non sequiturs, his cruel treatment of others. Clearly, his dad wanted to provoke an inconsistency between Josh's self-concept and his behavior on the tapes. And this was exactly what occurred. Josh was embarrassed – appalled – by the conversations that he heard. He listened to a call from his girlfriend, upset that he had ignored her and that he treated her coldly and with indifference. He showed the same indifference with his friends.

"I had no idea what I sounded like and I didn't like what I sounded like at all," Josh said. "I was very self-centered and egotistical and uncaring of other people." After listening to the tapes, over time, Josh changed his attitudes toward drugs, stopped lying, and altered his life's course. His father – who instigated the radical plan – was amazed. "He understood the entire thing that he was doing," he said proudly.

As you undoubtedly noted, technology has come a long way since Josh's father installed a tape recorder to record his son's phone calls. Parents can employ sophisticated apps to secretly monitor their teenagers' texts and posts. Ethical issues clearly arise when parents do this without their children's permission. For our purposes, this reminds us that modern-day parents who choose to track their teenager's activity (ethically, one hopes) can harness dissonance theory to help their child recognize an inconsistency between risky behavior and a more thoughtful self-concept, a step toward meaningful personal change.

Affirm People

People frequently reject messages not just because they are inconsistent with an attitude, but because they threaten a core sense of self. Gun owners dislike gun control because guns are connected in their minds with a valued belief in freedom. Gun opponents reject pro-gun arguments because these undermine an abiding commitment to non-violence. People also resist changing unhealthy habits because addictions to cigarettes, drugs, and gambling have become important parts of their social identities. Self-affirmation, which evolved out of cognitive dissonance theory, suggests an intriguing way to change these attitudes. According to the self-affirmation view, people reject threatening social and health information to preserve a positive sense of self. But if one's self-concept can be elevated in some other fashion, the impulse to react defensively to threatening messages can be diminished (Sherman, Nelson, & Steele, 2000, p. 1048; Steele, 1988; see also Wang & Zhao, 2018).

In a series of studies, researchers induced self-affirmation by asking students to describe experiences in which they implemented values that were personally important. For example, a student who valued a sense of humor discussed an incident where her sense of humor took on importance and led her to feel positively about herself. Control group participants engaged in a neutral activity, listing everything they had eaten or drunk over the past two days. Everyone then read a scientific report that presented arguments critical of their attitude toward capital punishment. Participants who supported the death penalty read an anti-capital punishment scientific report. Those opposed to the death penalty read a pro-capital punishment article. Now here is where self-affirmation kicked in: Students who had earlier affirmed an important value like humor were more open to evidence that opposed their capital punishment position than were those in the control group. Affirmed students actually *changed* their attitudes toward capital punishment – an issue they felt strongly about – more than non-affirmed subjects (Cohen, Aronson, & Steele, 2000).

In a similar fashion, affirmation of an important personal characteristic, when a partisan identity was made salient, led to more openness toward an opposing political position and to compromise on a strongly held position (Cohen et al., 2007). And, in research with health implications, affirming people led to more positive attitudes toward health issues, including stronger intention to reduce unhealthy behaviors, as well as stronger support for water conservation policies (Arpan, Lee, & Wang, 2017; Walter, Demetriades, & Murphy, 2017; Walter, Saucier, & Murphy, 2019; Wang & Zhao, 2018).

"Shoring up global self-worth," Cohen and his colleagues concluded, "takes the sting out of new ideas, making them less painful to accept as true" (Cohen et al., 2000, p. 1161). But if our global self-worth has been validated, we are a tad less defensive and more open to giving the other side another look (see also Sherman & Cohen, 2006).

Thus, if persuaders want to reduce defensiveness to information that threatens a strongly held attitude, they should engage in a little jujitsu. They should affirm people's self-concepts and help them feel good about their values. This will open psychological receptors and give people the strength they need to consider information that questions a habit of mind. But there are limits to how robustly this can work in everyday life. In some situations, it is not clear that just reminding people in the throes of dissonance that they are a good cook or a fast runner will alleviate the stress caused by cognitive discomfort (Cooper, 2019).

Moreover, when people are extraordinarily wedded to an attitude, such as abortion, or are psychologically dependent upon a behavior, like drugs, or distrust the persuader, it will take more than simple praise to change their attitude. Individuals may also not perceive they are hypocritical, resorting to rational or irrational beliefs to defend their attitude against attack. Alas, self-affirmation provides us with clues on how to influence core attitudes, but the trick is how to make it work in dicey everyday situations.

Conclusions

Cognitive dissonance remains an important, intriguing psychological theory with numerous implications for persuasion. Dissonance is an uncomfortable state that arises when individuals hold psychologically inconsistent cognitions. As revised and reconceptualized over the years, dissonance also refers to feeling personally responsible for unpleasant consequences, and experiencing stress over actions that reflect negatively on the self. There are different views of dissonance and diverse explanations as to why it exerts the impact that it does on attitudes.

There is little doubt that dissonance influences attitudes and cognitions. Its effects fan out to influence decision-making, justification of effort, compliance under low reward, and advocating a position with which one disagrees. The theory also helps us understand why people commit themselves to causes – both good and bad ones. It offers suggestions for how to help people remain committed to good causes and how to aid individuals in quitting dysfunctional groups. The theory also has intriguing implications for persuasion. Departing from conventional strategies that emphasize accommodating people or meeting them halfway, dissonance theory recommends that persuaders (either overtly or subtly) provoke inconsistencies in individuals. Dissonance then serves as the engine that motivates attitude change. In this sense, dissonance is a powerful theory of persuasive communication, emphasizing, as it does, the central role that self-persuasion plays in attitude change. It is noteworthy that more than 60 years after the theory was introduced, it continues to intrigue, shedding light on paradoxical aspects of social behavior and offering imaginative perspectives on persuasion. At the same time, its ability to stimulate new studies has peaked, and, if dissonance research is to continue to make contributions, it probably has to focus on three areas: (1) demonstrating the replicability of studies, in view of the replicability issues raised in social psychology (see Chapter 3); (2) pinpointing neural bases of dissonance, teasing out different neural mechanisms for different psychological processes; and (3) looking more broadly at macro issues, such as cultural and class variations, and ways these can be harnessed for social change.

As this chapter has highlighted, dissonance is more complicated and intriguing than it may at first have seemed. It is richly informative, offering insights on contemporary issues, ranging from students' defensive rationalizations for blackout drinking to the persistence of prejudice (Wombacher et al., 2019). Its theoretical postulates continue to excite and engage (Harmon-Jones, 2019), offering up promising, provocative avenues for academic and pragmatically minded students of persuasion.

References

Alvarez, L. (2014, November 1). Florida A&M band member is convicted in hazing death. *The New York Times*, A19.

Aron, A., & Aron, E. N. (1989). *The heart of social psychology: A backstage view of a passionate science* (2nd ed.). Lexington, MA: Lexington Books.

Aronson, E. (1968). Dissonance theory: Progress and problems. In R. P. Abelson, E. Aronson, W. J. McGuire, T. M. Newcomb, M. J. Rosenberg, & P. H. Tannenbaum (Eds.), *Theories of cognitive consistency: A sourcebook* (pp. 5–27). Chicago, IL: Rand McNally.

Aronson, E. (2019). Dissonance, hypocrisy, and the self-concept. In E. Harmon-Jones (Ed.), *Cognitive dissonance: Reexamining a pivotal theory in psychology* (2nd ed., pp. 141–157). Washington, DC: American Psychological Association.

Aronson, E., & Mills, J. (1959). The effect of severity of initiation on liking for a group. *Journal of Abnormal and Social Psychology, 59*, 177–181.

Aronson, J., Cohen, G., & Nail, P. R. (1999). Self-affirmation theory: An update and appraisal. In E. Harmon-Jones & J. Mills (Eds.), *Cognitive dissonance: Progress on a pivotal theory in social psychology* (pp. 127–147). Washington, DC: American Psychological Association.

Aronson, J., Cohen, G., & Nail, P. R. (2019). Self-affirmation theory: An update and appraisal. In E. Harmon-Jones & J. Mills (Eds.), *Cognitive dissonance: Progress on a pivotal theory in social psychology* (2nd ed., pp. 159–174). Washington, DC: American Psychological Association.

Arpan, L. M., Lee, Y. S., & Wang, Z. (2017). Integrating self-affirmation with health risk messages: Effects on message evaluation and response. *Health Communication, 32*, 189–199.

Bem, D. J. (1972). Self-perception theory. In L. Berkowitz (Ed.), *Advances in experimental social psychology* (Vol. 6, pp. 1–62). New York: Academic Press.

Broad, W. J., & Shane, S. (2008, August 10). For suspects, anthrax case had big costs. *The New York Times*, 1, 17.

Chapanis, N. P., & Chapanis, A. C. (1964). Cognitive dissonance: Five years later. *Psychological Bulletin, 61*, 1–22.

Cohen, G. L., Aronson, J., & Steele, C. M. (2000). When beliefs yield to evidence: Reducing biased evaluation by affirming the self. *Personality and Social Psychology Bulletin, 26*, 1151–1164.

Cohen, G. L., Sherman, D. K., Bastardi, A., Hsu, L., McGoey, M., & Ross, L. (2007). Bridging the partisan divide: Self-affirmation reduces ideological closed-mindedness and inflexibility in negotiation. *Journal of Personality and Social Psychology, 93*, 415–430.

Cooper, J. (2019). In search of the motivation for dissonance reduction: The drive to lessen aversive consequences. In E. Harmon-Jones & J. Mills (Eds.), *Cognitive dissonance: Progress on a pivotal theory in social psychology* (2nd ed., pp. 175–193). Washington, DC: American Psychological Association.

Cooper, J., & Axsom, D. (1982). Effort justification in psychotherapy. In G. Weary & H. L. Mirels (Eds.), *Integrations of clinical and social psychology* (pp. 214–230). New York: Oxford Press.

Cooper, J., Blackman, S. F., & Keller, K. T. (2016). *The science of attitudes*. New York: Routledge.

Cooper, J., & Fazio, R. H. (1984). A new look at dissonance theory. In L. Berkowitz (Ed.), *Advances in experimental social psychology* (Vol. 17, pp. 229–266). Orlando, FL: Academic Press.

Cooper, J., & Scher, S. J. (1994). When do our actions affect our attitudes? In S. Shavitt & T. C. Brock (Eds.), *Persuasion: Psychological insights and perspectives* (pp. 95–111). Boston, MA: Allyn and Bacon.

Crano, W. D., Cooper, J., & Forgas, J. P. (2010). Attitudes and attitude change: An introductory review. In J. P. Forgas, J. Cooper, & W. D. Crano (Eds.), *The psychology of attitudes and attitude change* (pp. 3–17). New York: Psychology Press.

Czopp, A. M., Monteith, M. J., & Mark, A. Y. (2006). Standing up for a change: Reducing bias through interpersonal confrontation. *Journal of Personality and Social Psychology, 90,* 784–803.

Deci, E. L. (1975). *Intrinsic motivation.* New York: Plenum Press.

Devine, P. G., Tauer, J. M., Barron, K. E., Elliot, A. J., Vance, K. M., & Harmon-Jones, E. (2019). Moving beyond attitude change in the study of dissonance-related processes. In E. Harmon-Jones & J. Mills (Eds.), *Cognitive dissonance: Progress on a pivotal theory in social psychology* (2nd ed., pp. 247–269). Washington, DC: American Psychological Association.

Eisenstadt, D., Leippe, M. R., Stambush, M. A., Rauch, S. M., & Rivers, J. A. (2005). Dissonance and prejudice: Personal costs, choice, and change in attitudes and racial beliefs following counterattitudinal advocacy that benefits a minority. *Basic and Applied Social Psychology, 27,* 127–141.

Elkin, R. A., & Leippe, M. R. (1986). Physiological arousal, dissonance, and attitude change: Evidence for a dissonance–arousal link and a "don't remind me" effect. *Journal of Personality and Social Psychology, 51,* 55–65.

Elliot, A. J., & Devine, P. G. (1994). On the motivational nature of cognitive dissonance: Dissonance as psychological discomfort. *Journal of Personality and Social Psychology, 67,* 382–394.

Festinger, L., & Carlsmith, J. M. (1959). Cognitive consequences of forced compliance. *Journal of Abnormal and Social Psychology, 58,* 203–210.

Fointiat, V. (2004). "I know what I have to do, but …": When hypocrisy leads to behavioral change. *Social Behavior and Personality: An international journal, 32,* 741–746.

Garland, H. (1990). Throwing good money after bad: The effect of sunk costs on the decision to escalate commitment to an ongoing project. *Journal of Applied Psychology, 75,* 728–731.

Gerard, H. B., & Mathewson, G. C. (1966). The effect of severity of initiation on liking for a group: A replication. *Journal of Experimental Social Psychology, 2,* 278–287.

Harmon-Jones, E. (2002). A cognitive dissonance theory perspective on persuasion. In J. P. Dillard & M. Pfau (Eds.), *The persuasion handbook: Developments in theory and practice* (pp. 99–116). Thousand Oaks, CA: Sage.

Harmon-Jones, E. (Ed.). (2019). *Cognitive dissonance: Reexamining a pivotal theory in psychology* (2nd ed.). Washington, D.C.: American Psychological Association.

Harmon-Jones, E., & Harmon-Jones, C. (2019). Understanding the motivation underlying dissonance effects: The action-based model. In E. Harmon-Jones (Ed.), *Cognitive dissonance: Reexamining a pivotal theory in psychology* (2nd ed., pp. 63–89). Washington, D.C.: American Psychological Association.

Harmon-Jones, E., Harmon-Jones, C., Serra, R., & Gable, P. A. (2011). The effect of commitment on relative left frontal cortical activity: Tests of the action-based model of dissonance. *Personality and Social Psychology Bulletin, 37,* 395–408.

Harmon-Jones, E., & Mills, J. (1999). An introduction to cognitive dissonance theory and an overview of current perspectives on the theory. In E. Harmon-Jones & J. Mills (Eds.), *Cognitive dissonance: Progress on a pivotal theory in social psychology* (pp. 3–21). Washington, DC: American Psychological Association.

Hoshino-Browne, E., Zanna, A. S., Spencer, S. J., Zanna, M. P., Kitayama, S., & Lackenbauer, S. (2005). On the cultural guises of cognitive dissonance: The case of Easterners and Westerners. *Journal of Personality and Social Psychology, 89,* 294–310.

Izuma, K., & Murayama, K. (2019). Neural basis of cognitive dissonance. In E. Harmon-Jones & J. Mills (Eds.), *Cognitive dissonance: Progress on a pivotal theory in social psychology* (2nd ed., pp. 227–245). Washington, DC: American Psychological Association.

Kang, J. C. (2017, August 13). Not without my brothers. *The New York Times Magazine*, 30–35. 45, 49.

Kim, S. Y., Allen, M., Preiss, R. W., & Peterson, B. (2014). Meta-analysis of counterattitudinal advocacy data: Evidence for an additive cues model. *Communication Quarterly*, 62, 607–620.

Kleinfield, N. R. (1999, November 15). For three interns, fatigue and healing at top speed. *The New York Times*, A1, A28.

Leippe, M. R., & Eisenstadt, D. (1994). Generalization of dissonance reduction: Decreasing prejudice through induced compliance. *Journal of Personality and Social Psychology*, 67, 395–413.

Marklein, M. B. (2000, October 11). Ugly truths about hazing. *USA Today*, 6D.

Martin, M. (2001, March 30). Man sentenced to educate himself. *The Plain Dealer*, 1-B, 5-B.

Nyer, P. U., & Dellande, S. (2010). Public commitment as a motivator for weight loss. *Psychology & Marketing*, 27, 1–12.

O'Keefe, D. J. (2000). Guilt and social influence. In M. E. Roloff (Ed.), *Communication yearbook 23* (pp. 67–101). Thousand Oaks, CA: Sage.

Pharnor, A. (1999, May). Breaking the code. *The Source*, 72.

Preiss, R. W., & Allen, M. (1998). Performing counterattitudinal advocacy: The persuasive impact of incentives. In M. Allen & R. W. Preiss (Eds.), *Persuasion: Advances through meta-analysis* (pp. 231–242). Cresskill, NJ: Hampton Press.

Randles, D., Inzlicht, M., Proulx, T., Tullett, A. M., & Heine, S. J. (2015). Is dissonance reduction a special case of fluid compensation? Evidence that dissonant cognitions cause compensatory affirmation and abstraction. *Journal of Personality and Social Psychology*, 108, 697–710.

Rojas, R., & Southall, A. (2015, September 15). 5 from Baruch College face murder charges in 2013 fraternity hazing. *The New York Times*, A19.

Rosenbloom, S. (2011, January 23). I resolve. World, don't fail me now. *The New York Times* (Sunday Styles), 8.

Ross, A. (2011). *Ladies and gentlemen*. New York: Knopf.

Rothgerber, H. (2014). Efforts to overcome vegetarian-induced dissonance among meat eaters. *Appetite*, 79, 32–41.

Scher, S. J., & Cooper, J. (1989). Motivational basis of dissonance: The singular role of behavioral consequences. *Journal of Personality and Social Psychology*, 56, 899–906.

Sherman, D. A. K., Nelson, L. D., & Steele, C. M. (2000). Do messages about health risks threaten the self? Increasing the acceptance of threatening health messages via self-affirmation. *Personality and Social Psychology Bulletin*, 26, 1046–1058.

Sherman, D. K., & Cohen, G. L. (2006). The psychology of self-defense: Self-affirmation theory. In M. P. Zanna (Ed.), *Advances in experimental social psychology* (Vol. 38, pp. 183–242). San Diego, CA: Elsevier.

Simon, L., Greenberg, J., & Brehm, J. (1995). Trivialization: The forgotten mode of dissonance reduction. *Journal of Personality and Social Psychology*, 68, 247–260.

Son Hing, L. S., Li, W., & Zanna, M. P. (2002). Inducing hypocrisy to reduce prejudicial responses among aversive racists. *Journal of Experimental Social Psychology*, 38, 71–78.

Steele, C. M. (1988). The psychology of self-affirmation: Sustaining the integrity of the self. In L. Berkowitz (Ed.), *Advances in experimental social psychology* (Vol. 21, pp. 261–302). San Diego, CA: Academic Press.

Stone, J., Aronson, E., Crain, A. L., Winslow, M. P., & Fried, C. B. (1994). Inducing hypocrisy as a means of encouraging young adults to use condoms. *Personality and Social Psychology Bulletin*, *20*, 116–128.

Taitz, J. (2019, February 11). Regrets can become powerful sources of inspiration. *The New York Times*, B9.

Takaku, S. (2006). Reducing road rage: An application of the dissonance-attribution model of interpersonal forgiveness. *Journal of Applied Social Psychology*, *36*, 2362–2378.

Tavris, C., & Aronson, E. (2007). *Mistakes were made (but not by me): Why we justify foolish beliefs, bad decisions, and hurtful acts*. Orlando, FL: Harcourt.

Tedeschi, J. T., Schlenker, B. R., & Bonoma, T. V. (1971). Cognitive dissonance: Private ratiocination or public spectacle? *American Psychologist*, *26*, 685–695.

van Veen, V., Krug, M. K., Schooler, J. W., & Carter, C. S. (2009). Neural activity predicts attitude change in cognitive dissonance. *Nature Neuroscience*, *12*, 1463–1468.

Walter, N., Demetriades, S. Z., & Murphy, S. T. (2017). Involved, united, and efficacious: Could self-affirmation be the solution to California's drought? *Health Communication*, *32*, 1161–1170.

Walter, N., Saucier, C. J., & Murphy, S. T. (2019). Increasing receptivity to messages about e-cigarette risk using vicarious-affirmation. *Journal of Health Communication*, *24*, 226–235.

Wang, X., & Zhao, X. (2018). The mediating role of temporal considerations on the effects of self-affirmation on responses to organ donation messages. *Health Communication*, *33*, 148–155.

Wegner, D. M., Schneider, D. J., Carter, S. R., III, & White, T. L. (1987). Paradoxical effects of thought suppression. *Journal of Personality and Social Psychology*, *53*, 5–13.

Wicklund, R. A., & Brehm, J. W. (1976). *Perspectives on cognitive dissonance*. Hillsdale, NJ: Lawrence Erlbaum Associates.

Wombacher, K., Matig, J. J., Sheff, S. E., & Scott, A. M. (2019). "It just kind of happens": College students' rationalizations for blackout drinking. *Health Communication*, *34*, 1–10.

Yoeli, E., Bhanot, S., Kraft-Todd, G., & Rand, D. (2015). How to get people to pitch in. *The New York Times* (Sunday Review), 12.

Part Four

Persuasive Communication Contexts

Chapter 14

Interpersonal Persuasion

Their interpersonal persuasion techniques were straight out of the sales playbook: Lure clients to palatial resorts, pay all their expenses, and use emotional selling techniques. Also, make sure you avoid code words that could give clients second thoughts about the pitch.

For years, this was part of the game plan for the billionaire pharmaceutical firm, Purdue Pharma, which manufactured and distributed the addictive drug, OxyContin. Purdue lured some 5,000 doctors, nurses, and pharmacists, through dozens of all-expenses-paid conferences to plush resorts in Florida and Arizona, hoping they would prescribe OxyContin. Sales skyrocketed, as unsuspecting patients died from drug overdoses in the national opioid epidemic. "The doctors started prostituting themselves for a few free trips to Florida," explained a lawyer for the families, whose desperate patients committed crimes to get OxyContin. "The irony of it was, the victims were getting jail time instead of the people who caused it," he added, fingering the pharmaceutical firm that exploited social exchange techniques to increase profits (Macy, 2018, p. 47).

As if that were not enough, Johnson & Johnson, the storied corporation known for its baby shampoo, developed a particular opium poppy that produced a major painkilling component used in OxyContin, as well as one used in its own drug, Tylenol with codeine. Johnson & Johnson, determined to increase its share of the market, coached its sales reps to use "emotional selling" tactics on physician-clients. In their interpersonal conversations with doctors, Johnson & Johnson's sales force claimed that patients were hurt by undertreating their problem. Sales reps used "unbranded promotion," coaxing doctors to keep prescribing opioids. They pushed the idea of "pseudoaddiction," the notion that patients who asked doctors for bigger doses weren't necessarily addicted to the drug, but just required a bigger dosage to reduce their pain (Thomas & Hsu, 2019, p. A14). The company instructed their reps to avoid the "addiction ditch," where the conversation turned to the negative aspects of drug dependence. That was a sure-fire way to lose the sale.

The payoff from persuading physicians to prescribe opioid drugs? Priceless. For their part, Purdue Pharma reps earned as much as $100,000 for a quarter of the year in bonus payments (Macy, 2018). And they weren't the only ones. Sales representatives from a host of big companies could cash in when they persuaded docs to keep prescribing their brands. At Purdue, supervisors were cynically nicknamed "the Wizard of OxyContin" or "the Supreme Sovereign of Pain Management." Reps were known as "royal crusaders and knights" (Macy, 2018, p. 33).

The pharmaceutical companies' sales techniques were part of a piece, some of the tried-and-true interpersonal communication strategies sales agents used on doctors, usually, in fairness, to promote more beneficent products than opioids. But in the case of opioid drugs, their strategies had deadly consequences. Prescription opioids have contributed to an epidemic increase in deaths from drug overdoses, as well as a multitude of other medical and psychological problems (see Figure 14.1). Over the past two decades, some 400,000 Americans have died from opioid overdoses, and the epidemic has run up an annual price tag of more than $78 billion in health care and productivity losses (Make those opioid payments count, 2019). In a ruling with significant legal implications for similar court cases in the United States, an Oklahoma judge ordered Johnson & Johnson to pay more than $500 million for its part in the nation's opioid crisis. Purdue Pharma has said it will settle thousands of similar legal suits.

To be sure, the drug companies were not the only cause of the crisis. Addiction to street drugs like heroin and fentanyl caused overdose deaths. Physicians' initial overreliance on opioids to manage pain, as well as feeble government action, contributed as well. At the same time, the interpersonal

Figure 14.1 Over the Past Decades, Hundreds of Thousands of Americans Have Died From Opioid Overdoses, an Epidemic With a Multitude of Severe Psychological and Economic Effects. Although there are many causes, aggressive, manipulative interpersonal persuasion techniques wielded by pharmaceutical sales agents, to which some doctors succumbed, aggravated the problem

Photo courtesy of Pixabay

sales campaign pushed the process along, by exploiting communication strategies to coax doctors to prescribe opioids, enabling or at least reinforcing a culture of addiction.

There is nothing wrong with using communication techniques to make a sale. And there are many sales reps who harness their expertise to promote safe drugs that help patients. However, the opioid case was a perfect storm, in which sales reps frequently used false and misleading strategies that helped increase America's opioid addiction rate. It is a sad, telling case of persuasion gone awry.

Interpersonal persuasion, a centerpiece in drug companies' opioid marketing campaigns and the subject of this chapter, offers a glimpse into a realm of persuasion that is somewhat different from those discussed so far in the book. Unlike purely psychological approaches, it focuses on the dyad, or two-person unit (persuader and persuadee). In contrast to attitude-based research, it centers on changing behavior – on inducing people to comply with the persuader's requests. Unlike message-oriented persuasion research, which focuses on modifying views about political or social issues, it explores techniques people employ to accomplish interpersonal objectives – for example, how they "sell themselves" to others.

Drawing on the fields of interpersonal communication and social psychology, interpersonal persuasion research examines the strategies people use to gain compliance. It looks at how individuals try to get their way with others (something we all want to do). It examines techniques businesses use to convince customers to sign on the dotted line, strategies charities employ to gain donations, and methods that health practitioners use to convince people to take better care of their health. To gain insight into these practical issues, interpersonal persuasion scholars develop theories and conduct empirical studies – both experiments and surveys. In some ways, this is the most practical, down-to-earth chapter in the book; in other ways, it is the most complicated because it calls on taxonomies and cognitive concepts applied to the dynamic dance of interpersonal communication.

The first portion of the chapter looks at a variety of techniques that have amusing sales pitch names like foot-in-the-door and door-in-the-face. These persuasive tactics are known as *sequential influence techniques*, in which persuasive communications follow one another in a step-by-step fashion. Influence in such cases "often proceeds in stages, each of which establishes the foundation for further changes in beliefs or behavior. Individuals slowly come to embrace new opinions, and actors often induce others to gradually comply with target requests" (Seibold, Cantrill, & Meyers, 1994, p. 560). The second section of the chapter focuses more directly on the communication aspect of interpersonal persuasion. It looks at the strategies that people – you, me, our friends, and parents – use to gain compliance, how researchers study this, and the many factors that influence compliance-gaining.

The Psychology of Communicative Compliance

Foot-in-the-Door

This classic persuasion strategy dates back to the days when salespeople knocked on doors and plied tricks of the trade to maneuver their way into residents' homes. If they could just overcome initial resistance – get a "foot in the door" of the domicile – they felt they could surmount subsequent obstacles and make the sale of an Avon perfume, a vacuum cleaner, or a set of encyclopedias. Going door to door is out of date, but starting small and moving to a larger request is still in vogue. The *foot-in-the-door* (FITD) technique stipulates that an individual is more likely to comply with a second, larger request if he or she has agreed to perform a small initial request.

Many studies have found support for the FITD procedure. Researchers typically ask individuals in an experimental group to perform a small favor, one to which almost everyone agrees. Experimenters next ask these folks to comply with a second, larger request, the one in which the experimenter is actually interested. Participants in the control condition receive only the second request. Experimental group participants are typically more likely than control subjects to comply with the second request. For example:

- In a classic study, Freedman and Fraser (1966) arranged for experimenters working for a local traffic safety committee to ask California residents if they would mind putting a three-inch "Be a safe driver" sign in their cars. Two weeks later, residents were asked if they would place a large, unattractive "Drive Carefully" sign on their front lawns. Homeowners in a control condition were asked only the second request. Seventeen percent of control group residents agreed to put the large sign on their lawns. However, 76 percent of those who agreed to the initial request or had been approached the first time complied with the second request.
- Participants were more willing to volunteer to construct a hiking trail if they had agreed to address envelopes for an environmental group than if they had not acceded to the initial request (Dillard, 1990a).
- Individuals were more likely to volunteer a large amount of time for a children's social skill project if they had initially assisted a child with a small request – helping an eight-year-old get candy from a candy machine (Rittle, 1981).

Emboldened by results like these, researchers have conducted over 100 studies of the FITD strategy. Meta-analytic, statistically based reviews of the research show that the effect is reliable and occurs more frequently than would be expected by chance (e.g., Dillard, Hunter, & Burgoon, 1984). The effect is so robust it even occurs with a robot! An experiment found that when students played a game of trivia with a seemingly autonomous robot, who sported a visually animated face and the synthetic male voice, they were more likely to comply with a larger request (completing 50 pattern recognition tasks) if they first completed 25 tasks (Lee & Liang, 2019). Given its utility, professional persuaders – ranging from telemarketers to university alumni fundraisers – frequently employ FITD.

Why Does It Work?

There are three reasons why the foot-in-the-door technique produces compliance. The first explanation calls on Bem's self-perception theory, described in Chapter 13. According to this view, individuals who perform a small favor for someone look at their behavior and infer that they are helpful, cooperative people. They become, in their own eyes, the kinds of people who do these sorts of things, go along with requests made by strangers, and cooperate with worthwhile causes (Freedman & Fraser, 1966, p. 201). Having formed this self-perception, they naturally accede to the second, larger request.

A second interpretation emphasizes consistency needs. Recalling that they agreed to the first request, individuals find it dissonant to reject the second, target request. Perhaps having formed the perception that they are helpful people, they feel motivated to behave in a way that is consistent with their newly formed view of themselves. In a sense, they may feel more committed to the requester or to the goal of helping others.

A third explanation places emphasis on social norms. When asked to enact a small first request, people become more aware of society's norm of social responsibility – "a norm that prescribes that one should help those who are in need," a scholar notes (DeJong, 1979, p. 2236).

When Does It Work?

The FITD technique does not always produce compliance. It is particularly likely to work when the request concerns a pro-social issue, such as asking for a donation to charity or requesting favors from strangers. Self-perceptions, consistency needs, and social norms are likely to kick in under these circumstances. Foot-in-the-door is also more apt to succeed when the second query is "a continuation," or logical outgrowth, of the initial request, and when people actually perform the requested behavior (Burger, 1999; Dillard et al., 1984).

FITD is not so likely to succeed if the same persuader asks for a second favor immediately after having hit up people for a first request. The bang-bang, request-upon-request approach may create resentment, leading people to say no just to reassert their independence (Chartrand, Pinckert, & Burger, 1999).

Next time you do a favor for someone and are tempted to accede to a second, larger request, check to see if the facilitating factors operating in the situation match those just described. If they do, you may be more apt to go along with the request, and it may be one that you would rather decline.

Door-in-the-Face

This technique undoubtedly gets the award for the most memorable name in the Persuasion Tactics Hall of Fame. It occurs when a persuader makes a large request that is almost certain to be denied. After being turned down, the persuader returns with a smaller request, the target request the communicator had in mind at the beginning. *Door-in-the-face* (DITF) is exactly the opposite of foot-in-the-door. Foot-in-the-door starts with a small request and moves to a larger one. DITF begins with a large request and scales down to an appropriately modest request. Researchers study the technique by asking experimental group participants to comply with a large request, one certain to be denied. When they refuse, participants are asked if they would mind going along with a smaller, second request. Control group subjects receive only the second request.

The DITF technique has been tested in dozens of studies. It emerges reliably and dependably, meta-analytic studies tell us (Feeley, Anker, & Aloe, 2012; O'Keefe & Hale, 1998). Consider the following supportive findings:

- A volunteer, supposedly working for a local blood services organization, asked students if they would donate a unit of blood once every two months for a period of at least three years. Everyone declined this outlandish request. The volunteer then asked experimental group subjects if they would donate just one unit of blood between 8:00 a.m. and 3:30 p.m. the next day. Control group participants were asked the same question. Of those who rejected the first request, 49 percent agreed to donate blood, compared with 32 percent of those in the control group (Cialdini & Ascani, 1976).
- An experimenter working with a boys and girls' club asked students if they would mind spending about 15 hours a week tutoring children. When this request was declined, the experimenter asked if students would be willing to spend an afternoon taking kids to a museum or the movies. Students who turned down the initial request were more likely to agree to spend an afternoon with children than those who only heard the second request (O'Keefe & Figgé, 1999).

Why Does It Work?

Four rather interesting explanations for the DITF strategy have been advanced. One view emphasizes a powerful psychological factor akin to dissonance but more emotion-packed: Guilt. Individuals feel guilty about turning down the first request. To reduce guilt, an unpleasant feeling, they go along with the second request (O'Keefe & Figgé, 1999). There is some evidence that guilt helps explain DITF effects.

A second view emphasizes reciprocal concessions. As a persuader (deliberately) scales down his request, he is seen as having made a concession. This leads the persuadee to invoke the social rule that "you should make concessions to those who make concessions to you" or "you should meet the other fellow halfway." As a result, the persuadee yields and goes along with the second request (Cialdini et al., 1975; Feeley et al., 2017; Rhoads & Cialdini, 2002; Turner et al., 2007). The norm can be particularly effective when people initially turn down a worthwhile cause, inducing a stronger obligation or feeling of social responsibility to comply with the second request (Feeley et al., 2012).

Third, social judgment processes also operate in the DITF situation. The extreme first request functions as an anchor against which the second request is compared. After the outrageous initial request, the second request seems less costly and severe. However, control group participants who are asked to comply only with the smaller request do not have this anchor available to them. Thus, experimental group participants are more apt than control group subjects to go along with the target request.

Fourth, self-presentation concerns may also intervene. People fear that the persuader will evaluate them negatively for turning down the first request. Not realizing that the whole gambit has been staged, they accede to the second request to make themselves look good in the persuader's eyes.

When Does It Work?

Like other persuasion factors discussed, the DITF technique is sensitive to contextual factors (Fern, Monroe, & Avila, 1986; O'Keefe & Hale, 1998). DITF works particularly well when the request concerns pro-social issues. People may feel guilty about turning down a charitable organization's request for a large donation or time expenditure. They can make things right by agreeing to the second request.

DITF effects also emerge when the same individual makes both requests. People may feel an obligation to reciprocate a concession if they note that the person who asked for too much is scaling down her request. If two different people make the requests, the feeling that "you should make concessions to those who make concessions to you" may not kick in.

The DITF strategy is also more apt to work if there is only a short delay between the first and second requests. If too long a time passes between requests, the persuadee's guilt might possibly dissipate. In addition, the more time that passes between requests, the less salient is the contrast between the extreme first request and the seemingly more reasonable second request.

Applications

The FITD and DITF techniques are regularly used by compliance professionals. Noting that you gave $25 to a charity last year, a volunteer asks if you might increase your gift to $50. A representative from the local newspaper calls and asks if you would like to take out a daily subscription. When you tell her you don't have time to read the paper every day, she asks, "How about Sunday?" Or the bank loan officer wonders if you can afford a $100 monthly payment on your student loan. When you decline, he asks if you can pay $50 each month, exactly the amount he had in mind from the beginning.

FITD and DITF, like all persuasion techniques, can be used for unethical, as well as morally acceptable, purposes. Unsavory telemarketers or front organizations posing as charities can manipulate people into donating money through adroit use of these tactics. At the same time, pro-social groups can employ these techniques to achieve worthwhile goals. For example, a volunteer from Mothers Against Drunk Driving might use FITD to induce bar patrons to sign a petition against drunk driving. Sometime later in the evening, the volunteer could ask patrons if they would agree to let a taxi take them home (Taylor & Booth-Butterfield, 1993). In the same fashion, charitable organizations such as the Red Cross or Purple Heart might employ DITF gently to arouse guilt that inevitably follows refusal of the initial request.

The FITD and DITF strategies have generated the most research, and we know the most about when they work and why. A number of other compliance techniques have been described. Reviewing key compliance strategies offers insights into the canny ways that persuaders use communication to achieve their goals (e.g., Pratkanis, 2007).

Pre-Giving

As the name suggests, the persuader who employs this technique gives the target a reward or gift, or does the individual a favor. Subsequently, our persuader asks for help or presents a message that requires the target to return the favor. Like DITF, *pre-giving* assumes that the recipient will feel pressured by the reciprocity norm that emphasizes reciprocal concessions. People feel socially obligated to return a favor that someone has bestowed upon them (Cialdini, 2009). They also do not like to feel indebted to others, as this imposes a psychological burden to reciprocate at a cost that may not be comfortable. However, a gnawing sense of indebtedness is *not* the only reason why pre-giving works. There are also two positive reasons: Gratitude and liking. People feel grateful to someone who does them a favor, and they understandably like the favor-giver. These good feelings lead individuals to want to do something kind to the persuader in return (Goei et al., 2003; Goei et al., 2007; see Figure 14.2).

There is evidence that pre-giving enhances compliance. Bell and his colleagues (1996) solicited money for the Sacramento AIDS Foundation, arranging for their assistants to knock on doors in the state's capital city. For half of the households, the solicitor performed a favor of sorts, explaining the organization's mission and handing the individual a pamphlet describing how HIV spreads, along with places to seek medical information. The other half of the households served as the control and received no pre-giving treatment. Individuals who received the pamphlet were almost twice as likely to give as controls. They gave more money ($1.29 on average, compared with 77 cents).

For pre-giving to succeed, it is necessary that targets accept the favor. If they reject it cold, they feel no obligation to reciprocate (Dillard & Knobloch, 2011). (Unlike DITF, the persuader does not return with a smaller request.) In addition, pre-giving works better when the persuader and target are strangers rather than friends. The norm of reciprocity is less likely to operate between friends, close friends, or family members. When one is close or intimate with another, it is expected that one extends help because one cares for the other, not out of picayune concern that a favor be reciprocated. Interestingly, pre-giving is regularly harnessed by businesses, sometimes in nefarious ways (see Box 14.1).

Figure 14.2 People May Comply with an Interpersonal Request, Such as Signing a Petition for a Pro-Social Cause, If the Persuader Employs Foot-in-the-Door, Door-in-the-Face, Pre-Giving, and Other Interpersonal Persuasion Strategies. The trick is knowing when, for example, a strategy like foot-in-the-door or door-in-the-face is particularly likely to work

Image courtesy of iStock

BOX 14.1

You Scratch My Wallet and I'll Fatten Yours

The docs danced to the resonant thumping of the neon water drums, as fireworks lit up the sky. Luxuriating at an oceanfront pool party, enjoying the breath-taking view of the majestic Ritz-Carlton Hotel in Cancun, they posted videos of beach towels, water bottles, and flip-flops.

The doctors – plastic surgeons and cosmetic dermatologists – were reveling in an expense-paid trip, courtesy of Evolus, the manufacturer of the facial wrinkle-smoothing injectable, Jeuveau. And those poolside videos of beach towels and water bottles showcased the Evolus brand, describing Jeuveau in glowing terms, as "the happy toxin" or "latest and greatest." Dr. Melanie Petro, a plastic surgeon from Alabama, told her 74,000 followers that "everything is coming up BUTTERFLIES," as she posed on a runaway featuring the company's butterfly logo (Thomas, 2019).

The social media posts and doctors' gushing about the poolside party exemplify medical marketing to the tee, a striking, if shameless, example of pre-giving. Evolus hoped that by currying favor with the doctors, it could convince them to recommend their brand, helping it compete against Botox, the leader in the lucrative wrinkle-smoothing injection market. There was also an ethical twist: The dozen or so doctors who bragged about the Cancun event on social media did not bother to tell their followers that Evolus had bankrolled the trip, a violation of medical ethics and possibly Federal Trade Commission policies.

Although the docs pooh-poohed moral issues, insisting that the event would not influence their recommendations, persuasion research views their caveat with a jaundiced eye, noting how interpersonal influence techniques can prey on psychological norms. It works like this:

Person A provides Person B with a tangible, material, or psychological reward. In exchange, when Person A approaches B with a request, B complies (see also Homans, 1961; West & Turner, 2010). The stratagem influences people through the power of obligation, indebtedness, gratitude, and liking.

While the technique can be employed for pro-social purposes, it can also be harnessed for profits-over-people pursuits, as the opioid example at the beginning of the chapter illustrated. Consider these troubling examples in medical marketing:

- Since 2009, a dozen big drug companies have paid doctors and other medical representatives more than $755 million for promotional speaking, consulting, and medical research. Although pharmaceutical firms claim the payments can benefit patients, others worry about a quid pro quo derived from social exchange. As a reporter covering the problem notes, "a growing number of critics say the payments show the extent of the influence drug makers have on doctors. They [critics] are most critical about the speaking payments because the talks, most of which are carefully scripted by drug companies, essentially turn physicians into drug company employees, casting doubt on whether the doctors are placing the interests of the drug companies above patients" (Davis, 2011, p. A8). "You should know that many of these speakers bureaus require the physicians to use slides developed by the company to have just exactly the right sales message," one leading physician said (p. A8). Noted another medical ethics expert, "drug and device companies are very shrewd and very sophisticated. If they did not think this kind of gifting mattered, they wouldn't do it" (see Lyon & Mirivel, 2011).

- "It's not quite brainwashing, but they have a way of influencing your thinking," a doctor said of drug companies' attempts to promote new drugs in another area of medicine (Santora, 2006, p. A13). "You're making [a doctor] money in several ways," explained one former sales manager at Merck. "You're paying him for the talk. You're increasing his referral base so he's getting more patients. And you're helping to develop his name. The hope in all this is that a silent quid quo pro is created. I've done so much for you, the only thing I need from you is that you write more of my products" (Harris & Roberts, 2007, p. A18).

You may ask, "What is wrong with a little quid pro quo, or the old I'll scratch your back if you scratch mine?" However, the unsavory relationship between doctors and drug manufacturers usurps the trust that underlies a relationship between a doctor and patient. Patients trust that doctors will prescribe medications based solely on their medical needs. If physicians, albeit a minority, base pharmaceutical recommendations on their own financial self-interest, they are acting unethically.

In addition to be fair, in the medical realm most doctors are honorable, even beneficent when it comes to their patients. But pre-giving is a popular persuasion tactic among medical marketers. As one addiction specialist noted, doctors "are human just like anybody else and they are affected by marketing," sometimes with ill effects on their patients (Thomas & Hsu, 2019, p. A14).

Low-Balling

This strategy earns its name from the observation that persuaders – most famously, car salespeople – try to secure compliance by "throwing the customer a low ball." In persuasion scholarship, *low-balling* has a precise meaning. It occurs when a persuader induces someone to comply with a request and then "ups the ante" by increasing the cost of compliance. Having made the initial decision to comply, individuals experience dissonance at the thought that they may have to back away from their commitment. Once individuals have committed themselves to a decision, they are loath to change their minds, even when the cost of a decision is raised significantly and unfairly (Cialdini et al., 1978). In addition to commitment, people feel a social obligation to comply with a request politely made by another individual (Dolinksi, 2016). Having complied with an initial request, they don't want to abruptly break off a relationship with another person, even though that person is insidiously trying to change their mind.

Low-balling is similar to FITD in that the persuader begins with a small request and follows it up with a more grandiose alternative. In low-balling, though, the action initially requested is the target behavior; what changes is the cost associated with performing the target action. In the case of FITD, the behavior that the persuader asks the person to initially perform is a setup to induce the individual to comply with the larger, critical request.

Robert B. Cialdini and colleagues have conducted experiments demonstrating that low-balling can increase compliance. Their experimental findings shed light on sales practices in the ever colorful, always controversial, business of selling cars. As the authors explain:

> The critical component of the procedure is for the salesperson to induce the customer to make an *active decision* to buy one of the dealership's cars by offering an extremely good price, perhaps as much as $300 below competitors' prices. Once the customer has made the decision for a specific car (and has even begun completing the appropriate forms), the salesperson removes the price advantage in one of a variety of ways … In each instance, the result is the same: the reason that the customer made a favorable purchase decision is removed, and the performance of the target behavior (i.e., buying that specific automobile) is rendered more costly. The increased cost is such that the final price is equivalent to, or sometimes slightly above, that of the dealer's competitors. Yet, car dealership lore has it that more customers will remain with their decision to purchase the automobile, even at the adjusted figure, than would have bought it had the full price been revealed before a purchase decision had been obtained.
>
> (1978, p. 464; see Figure 14.3)

Over the years, you have undoubtedly heard someone derisively charge that a salesperson "low-balled me." Persuasion research illuminates exactly what this means and why low-balling can be effective.

"That's Not All"

Another tactic that borrows from persuasion practitioners is the "that's-not-all" technique. You have probably heard TV announcers make claims like, "And that's not all – if you call now and place an order for this one-time only collection of '60s oldies, we'll throw in an extra rock and roll CD – so call right away!" Researcher Jerry M. Burger capitalized on such real-life observations. He conceptualized and tested the effectiveness of the *that's-not-all technique*. In theory, Burger explained:

Figure 14.3 Car Salesmen Famously Employ the Low-Balling Persuasion Tactic to Make a Sale
Photograph by William C. Rieter

The salesperson presents a product and a price but does not allow the buyer to respond immediately. Instead, after a few seconds of mulling over the price, the buyer is told "that's not all"; that is, there is an additional small product that goes along with the larger item, or that "just for you" or perhaps "today only" the price is lower than that originally cited. The seller, of course, had planned to sell the items together or at the lower price all along but allows the buyer to think about the possibility of buying the single item or the higher priced item first. Supposedly, this approach is more effective than presenting the eventual deal to the customer in the beginning.

(1986, p. 277)

Burger demonstrated that the "that's-not-all" tactic can influence compliance. In one experiment, two researchers sat at tables that had a sign promoting the university psychology club's bake sale. Cupcakes were featured at the table. Individuals who wandered by sometimes expressed interest in the cupcakes, curious how much they cost. Those assigned to the experimental group were told that cupcakes cost 75 cents each. After listening to a seemingly impromptu conversation between the two experimenters, these individuals were told that the price included two medium-sized cookies. By contrast, subjects in the control group were shown the cookies when they inquired about the cost of the cupcakes. They were told that the package cost 75 cents. Even though people got the same products for the identical cost in both conditions, more experimental group subjects purchased sweets (73 percent) than did control group subjects (40 percent).

That's-not-all relies on a semantic ploy, the suggestion that the buyer is getting something for nothing. In addition, like DITF, the technique plays on the reciprocity norm. Thus, participants in Burger's experimental group naively assumed the persuader had done them a favor by throwing in two cookies. Not knowing that this was part of the gambit, they acquiesced.

Fear-Then-Relief

This is somewhat different from the other techniques in that the persuader deliberately places the recipient in a state of fear. Suddenly and abruptly, the persuader eliminates the threat, replaces fear with kind words, and asks the recipient to comply with a request. The ensuing relief pushes the persuadee to acquiesce.

Dolinski and Nawrat (1998) demonstrated *fear-then-relief* in several clever experiments. In one study, the researchers placed a piece of paper that resembled a parking ticket behind a car's windshield wiper. When drivers arrived at their cars, they experienced that telltale feeling of fear on noticing what looked to be a parking ticket. In fact, the paper was a leaflet that contained an appeal for blood donations. As drivers' anxiety was replaced with reassurance, an experimenter asked them if they would mind taking 15 minutes to complete a questionnaire. Sixty-eight percent of experimental group subjects complied with the request, compared with 36 percent of control group participants.

Fear-then-relief works for two reasons. First, the relief experienced when the threat is removed is reinforcing. It becomes associated with the second request, leading to more compliance. Second, the ensuing relief places people in a state of "temporary mindlessness." Preoccupied with the danger that could have snared them, and their own supposed carelessness, individuals are distracted. They are less attentive, and more susceptible to the persuader's request.

The technique has interesting implications for a powerful domain of persuasion, yet one infrequently discussed – interrogation of prisoners. We often think that compliance with captors results from the induction of terror and fear. Fear-then-relief suggests that a more subtle, self-persuasion dynamic is in operation. Captors initially scream at a prisoner, threaten him or her with torture, and begin to hurt the prisoner physically. Suddenly, the abuse ends and is replaced by a softer tone and a nice voice. In some cases, "the sudden withdrawal of the source of anxiety intensifies compliance" (Dolinski & Nawrat, 1998, p. 27; Schein, 1961).

Fear-then-relief is used in peacetime situations too – by parents, teachers, and other authority figures who replace the stick quickly with a carrot. Like other tactics (e.g., Aune & Basil, 1994), it capitalizes on the element of surprise, which succeeds in disrupting people's normal defenses.

Advertisers also use surprise in ads capitalizing on fear-then-relief. An advertisement for Rogaine raises the specter of thinning hair or loss of hair and then promotes the hair growth product. A commercial for a law firm scares viewers by reminding them of an automobile accident that left them injured and promises relief by contacting the law firm to sue the other driver. Success of these ads is not guaranteed, but hinges on presenting just the right dose of relief and fear.

Pique and Disrupt-then-Reframe

Surprise is the key in a couple of other techniques that psychologists have studied, ones no doubt used by compliance professionals. The first is known as the *pique technique*. It involves "making the request in an unusual and atypical manner so that the target's interest is piqued, the refusal script is disrupted, and the target is induced to think positively about compliance" (Santos, Leve, & Pratkanis, 1994, p. 756; Guéguen & Lamy, 2016). In an experimental demonstration of the technique, Santos and colleagues reported that students posing as panhandlers received more money from passersby when they asked, "Can you spare 17 cents (or 37 cents)?" than when they asked if the people could spare a quarter or any change. When was the last time that a panhandler asked you for 37 cents? Never happened, right? Therein lies the ingenuity – and potential lure – of the pique technique.

The pique procedure works because it disrupts our normal routine. It engages and consumes the conscious mind, thereby diverting it from the resistance that typically follows a persuader's request. Piquing people with an unusual request focuses attention on the distinctive appeal, particularly when they stop to inquire about the request rather than falling back on a standard refusal script (Burger et al., 2007).

Disruption of conscious modes of thought plays a critical role in acquiescence to persuasion, in the view of Eric S. Knowles and his colleagues (2001). Knowles emphasizes that persuaders succeed when they devise clever ways to break down our resistance (see Box 14.2). Intriguingly, he and his colleagues have shown that persuaders can disrupt resistance by subtly changing the wording of requests. Employing what they call the *disrupt-then-reframe* technique, Knowles and his colleagues have shown that they can dramatically increase compliance by first mildly disrupting "the ongoing script of a persuasive request" and then reframing the request or encouraging the listener to "understand the issue in a new way" (Knowles et al., 2001, p. 50).

BOX 14.2

Resistance and Compliance

The orchids caught her attention. She was reeling in pain after a man had crashed into her bike while she was cycling, brutally beat her, pulled her into his car and later tried to suffocate her. Nathalie Birli, terrified but keeping what few wits she had left about her, noticed the orchids. On a lark she dropped that into the conversation, telling him "his orchids were so beautiful" (Eddy, 2019, p. A10). Suddenly, her kidnapper turned into a different person, talking about how he cared for the orchids with water from his aquarium.

He told her about his cats, which he also took care of, but were taken from him, about his grandparents, the girlfriends who had double-crossed him, and his mother, who drank too much. She then shared that she had a little baby, a "little guy" who needed his mother to take care of him, asking how her aggressor would have felt if he had grown up without his mom. The conversation turned again. He asked if she could help him.

With this persuasive jujitsu, a combination of pique, empathy, similarity, and reassurance, the man let down his guard and released her. Nathalie persuaded her kidnapper, not by changing his attitude, but by breaking down his resistance. While this example is sadly not the norm in cases of kidnapping, it intriguingly highlights a neglected area of persuasive communication effects, one that focuses not on convincing others to comply with requests, but on overcoming their resistance to persuasive requests, a notion developed by Eric S. Knowles and Jay A. Linn (2004).

Knowles and Linn note that most interpersonal persuasion research has focused on devising ways to make a message more appealing rather than on the obverse: Figuring out how best to overcome people's resistance to persuasive messages. By understanding why individuals resist messages, researchers can do a better job of formulating strategies to increase compliance.

There are many aspects to resistance. One issue is how people resist messages: Do they systematically think through all the weak points of the message, or does resistance operate more peripherally, as when someone simply refuses to listen to a speaker because of religious or ethnic differences? Are some people more resistant to persuasion than others – i.e., more inclined to reject a position, regardless of the merits of the arguments? (Briñol et al., 2004)? What are the most effective ways to overcome resistance?

Scholarly research suggests that persuaders can neutralize resistance in several ways, including: (a) framing the message to minimize resistance, (b) acknowledging and confronting resistance head-on, (c) reframing the message, and (d) disrupting resistance to the message (Knowles & Linn, 2004).

In the bold tradition of interpersonal persuasion research, the researchers went door to door selling Christmas cards. They explained that money from the sales would go – as indeed it did – to a non-profit center that helps developmentally disabled children and adults. The experimenters told some residents that the price of a Christmas card package was $3. They informed others that the price was $3 and then added, "It's a bargain." In the key disrupt-then-reframe condition, the experimenter stated, "This package of cards sells for 300 pennies" (thereby shaking up the normal script for a door-to-door request). She then added, after pausing, "That's $3. It's a bargain" (reframe). Of respondents who purchased cards, 65 percent were in the disrupt-then-reframe treatment, compared with 35 percent in the other groups. Other experiments obtained similar findings, demonstrating that a small, but subtle, variation in a persuasive request can produce dramatic differences in compliance (Davis & Knowles, 1999).

Application

Con artists have long known how to disrupt and reframe, harnessing the technique to disarm and then exploit vulnerable targets. Twelve-year-old Glenn Sparks fell prey to a thief's cunning persuasion as a youngster working in his dad's doughnut shop. Sparks, now a successful professor of communication at Purdue University, relates the incident, based loosely on disrupt-then-reframe, in an enjoyable book aptly called *Rolling in Dough*:

One man bought two coffee rolls and paid the 70 cent sale with a $20 bill. I gave him some coins and 19 single bills and prepared to move on to another customer. But, before I could do so, the man asked me if he could have two $10 bills for the $20 in singles that he was now briskly counting out on the counter between us. He asked me to count it to make sure there was $20. He had pulled a $1 bill from his pocket and added it to the $19 in bills that I had just given him. I am not sure what in the world I was thinking (that was part of the flimflam art), but instead of taking the $20 to the register, depositing it, and getting the two tens, I went to the register first and retrieved the two tens and came back to the counter.

The man was quick. He added the two $10 bills I had given him to the small pile of $20 that was sitting between us. He quickly picked it up and counted it out. Forty dollars. Then, he asked me to count it out to see if there was $40 in the pile. There was. Somehow, the fact that I was able to agree with him about this helped me ignore my feeling that something wasn't going right about this transaction. He asked me if he could have eight $5 bills for the pile of $40. Again, I went to the register to retrieve the money, leaving the pile on the counter. And once again, the man took the bills that I gave him with one hand and scooped up the pile of cash sitting between us with the other, counting furiously. He asked me for another transaction and we repeated the ritual. One more transaction later, and on my way down the counter to the second register to get more cash (because there were no bills left in the first register), I realized that something was very wrong ... When I turned around to challenge the man, he was gone ... I had been flimflammed.

(Sparks, 2010, pp. 29–30)

The con artist first disrupted, distracting Sparks by counting bills and then asking him to count them too. He then implicitly reframed his request, asking for eight $5 bills. Only later did Sparks appreciate the con that had been perpetrated!

A meta-analysis of empirical studies of disrupt-then-reframe documents the success of the technique (Carpenter & Boster, 2009), although the authors caution that only a relatively small number of experiments have examined this technique. Interestingly, their review indicates that disrupt-then-reframe is especially effective when the request concerned a non-profit organization, perhaps because the reframing then seems more sincere. More broadly, these studies attest to the power of framing in persuasion. Disrupt-then-reframe, after all, works in part because of the subtle influence exerted by an alteration in the persuader's framework.

Other Subtle Verbal Sleights of Hand

All the techniques discussed in this section play on what Freedman and Fraser (1966) called "compliance without pressure." They are soft-sell, not hard-ball, tactics that worm their way through consumers' defenses, capitalizing on social norms, emotions, and sly disruption of ordinary routines. Used adroitly by canny professionals, they can be remarkably effective. They also work because people respond automatically to many such requests, employing heuristics that persuaders exploit for their own advantage.

Underlying a number of the persuasion strategies discussed above are subtle, sometimes sneaky, uses of language. In a review of research on wording the social influence request, Dolinksi (2016) extended knowledge by highlighting several additional compliance strategies, along with the psychological processes that underlie their effects.

1   Research shows that asking someone *"how you are feeling?"* can increase persuasion (Howard, 1990), partly because when the recipient responds by explaining how he or she is feeling, this helps forge a cordial relationship between persuader and persuadee. The dialogue between the two parties lays a social trap for the persuadee, invoking a norm that we should help others with whom we have a connection, even if this connection was actually manufactured by the persuader.

2   Persuaders can lay another social trap by adroit use of words and cultural meanings. "By implying that a minute favor is acceptable but not necessarily desirable, a requester could make it difficult for a target to refuse to provide some measure of help," Cialdini and Schroeder (1976, p. 600) argued. When persuaders have added the phrase, "Even a penny will help," they have obtained high rates of compliance in charity drives. That's it! Just saying that even a small amount of money can have beneficial results legitimizes the request. Thus, the technique is called the *legitimization of paltry contributions*. It's subtle, but reliable, as meta-analytic studies have documented its impact (Andrews et al., 2008; Bolkan & Rains, 2017). Interestingly, a key reason why this works is impression management concerns. Failing to fork over even a penny can make it hard for a person to avoid leaving the impression that he or she is selfish and uncaring (e.g., Bolkan & Rains, 2017). In order to make sure one does not leave that negative impression, people donate.

3   Another clever technique exploits the value that people place on freedom and the reactance they feel when their freedom is thwarted. By just adding a phrase to a persuasive request – "*But you are free to accept or to refuse*" – persuaders play on this freedom, reminding individuals that they can refuse a request. In some cases, this can increase compliance (Guéguen & Pascual, 2005). It's amazing! Just reminding people that they are free to reject the request can secure agreement, perhaps because it (cleverly) affirms the receiver's dignity. Meta-analytic evidence confirms this: The "But you are free" technique is an effective way to enhance compliance, its effect size consistent with those of other techniques in compliance research (Carpenter, 2013).

Alas, words are tricky and the meanings conveyed differ, depending on the situation. A polite request that includes the word "please" can nudge people into agreeing with the request. However, the word "please" does not always have this impact, Dolinksi reminds us. Let's say it is used in a request to help the needy, as in "Will you purchase a cookie to help those suffering from hunger, please?" The "please" deflects attention away from the needy and onto the persuader himself, contaminating the purity of the request. The recipient no longer forms a perception of herself as an altruistic, good person who is willing to help the less fortunate, but, instead, as someone who is being pushed into "please" helping a local persuader she barely knows.

This research is quite interesting and suggestive of how subtle changes in wording can influence compliance (Dudczak, 2016). A caveat needs to be added, however. Although these psychological studies are well executed and have advanced knowledge, they are primarily experimental in nature. For the most part, we do not know how these social influence phenomena operate in actual situations, and the ways real-life parameters intervene. The research tells us that gambits like foot-in-the-door, low-balling, and other verbal sleights of hand can work, if conditions are ripe, everything being equal. But everything is never equal. Context and the relationship between the communicator and message recipient unquestionably moderate the effectiveness of sequential influence techniques. The next section takes up such real-world concerns in more detail, with a focus on compliance in everyday, interpersonal settings between friends, acquaintances, and strangers.

Compliance-Gaining

You want to dine out with someone, but you disagree about which restaurant it is going to be; someone in the department must do an unpleasant job, but you want to make sure that in any case it will not be you; you want to make new work arrangements, but you are afraid your boss will not agree; you want to get your partner to come with you to that tedious family party, but you suspect that he or she does not want to come along.

(van Knippenberg et al., 1999, p. 806)

Add to these more serious requests for compliance: An effort to convince a close friend to return to school after having dropped out for a couple of years, a doctor's attempt to persuade a seriously overweight patient to pursue an exercise program, a husband's effort to persuade his wife to quit hitting the bottle. Such requests are pervasive in everyday life. They speak to the strong interest human beings have in getting their way – that is, in persuading others to comply with their requests and pleas. This section of the chapter moves from an exploration of how professional persuaders achieve their goals to an examination of us – how we try to gain compliance in everyday life. The area of research is appropriately called compliance-gaining.

Compliance-gaining is defined as "any interaction in which a message source attempts to induce a target individual to perform some desired behavior that the target otherwise might not perform" (Wilson, 2002, p. 4). Notice that the focus of compliance-gaining is on communication. It examines not only the psychology of the individual's request for compliance, but also the broader interaction, the dyadic (one-on-one) conversation between people, or among individuals. This is important because it calls attention to the dynamic interpersonal dance that characterizes so much of everyday persuasion. Interpersonal communication scholars, who have pioneered research in this area, have sought to understand how individuals try to get others to go along with their requests in social situations. They have probed the strategies people use, the impact of context on compliance-gaining strategies, and the goals individuals pursue to gain compliance from others.

How We Study Compliance-Gaining

One of the daunting issues researchers face is how to empirically study a broad area, like compliance-gaining. They could devise experiments of the sort conducted by psychologists researching FITD and DITF. Although these would allow researchers to test hypotheses, they would not tell them how compliance-gaining works in the real world that lies outside the experimenter's laboratory. Scholars could observe people trying to gain compliance – on the job, at school, or in social settings like bars (that might be fun!). However, this would provide an endless amount of data, too much to code meaningfully. Dissatisfied with these methodologies, scholars hit on the idea of conducting surveys that ask people how they would gain compliance, either in situations suggested by the researcher or in an open-ended manner, in the individuals' own words.

The first survey method is *closed-ended* in that it provides individuals with hypothetical situations and asks them to choose among various strategies for compliance. For example, researchers have asked participants to imagine that they have been carrying on a close relationship with a person of the opposite sex for two years. Unexpectedly, an old acquaintance happens to be in town one evening. Desirous of getting together with their old friend, but mindful that their current boyfriend or girlfriend is counting on getting together that night, respondents are asked to indicate how they would try to convince their current steady to let them visit their former acquaintance (Miller et al., 1977).

Respondents have also been asked to imagine that their neighbors, whom they do not know very well, own a dog that barks almost all night. This in turn incites the other local canines to do the same. Students are asked how they would attempt to convince the neighbors to curb their dog's night-time antics (Cody, McLaughlin, & Jordan, 1980). Individuals are provided with a list of strategies, such as friendly appeals, moral arguments, manipulative tactics, and threats. They are asked to indicate on a Likert scale how likely they would be to use these techniques. (See Box 14.3 for a practical example of a closed-ended compliance-gaining measurement technique.)

A second way to tap compliance-gaining is to use *open-ended* survey techniques. If a researcher wanted to employ an open-ended strategy, he or she might hand each respondent a sheet of paper. On the top of the page would appear the words:

On this page, write a paragraph about "How I Get My Way." Please be frank and honest.

(Falbo, 1977)

Some years back, one of my students, Karen Karp, visited a local health club and talked to salespeople in search of an answer to this question. Karp pretended she was interested in joining and listened as the salesperson made his spiel. She then categorized his responses using a classic scheme devised by Marwell and Schmitt (1967). Based on what the salesman had said and her extrapolations from the interview, she and I developed an exemplar of each of the 16 Marwell and Schmitt tactics. Key examples are:

1   Promise (If you comply, I will reward you):
    "If you begin your membership today, you'll receive a bonus of three free months."
2   Liking (Actor is friendly and helpful to get target in "good frame of mind" so that he will comply with request):
    "I think it's great that you've decided to begin an exercise program. The staff is here to help you reach your fitness goals."
3   Moral appeal (You are immoral if you do not comply):
    "Fitness is so important. I think it's almost immoral not to take good care of your health."
4   Self-feeling, Positive (You will feel better about yourself if you comply):
    "Why don't you sign up right now? You'll feel so good about yourself once you begin a workout program."
5   Altercasting, Negative (Only a person with "bad" qualities would not comply): "It's only laziness that keeps people from joining, but that's not you, is it?"
6   Esteem, Negative (People you value will think worse of you if you do not comply): "Do not disappoint your family. Didn't you promise them that you would start taking better care of yourself?"

What would you say? How *do* you get your way? Are you rational, arguing incessantly like one of the nerds on the television program *The Big Bang Theory?* Are you a charmer, acting "sweety-sweet" until you get what you want? What *do* you do to get what you want? Researchers would classify the open-ended responses, placing them into a smaller number of categories that cut across different respondents' answers.

Closed- and open-ended techniques each have advantages and drawbacks. The closed-ended selection technique provides an efficient way to gather information. It also provides insights on how people try to gain compliance in representative life situations. Its drawback is that people frequently give socially desirable responses to closed-ended surveys. They are reluctant to admit that they sometimes use brutish, socially inappropriate tactics to get their way (Burleson et al., 1988).

The strength of the open-ended method is that it allows people to indicate, in their own words, how they get compliance. There is no speculation about hypothetical behavior in artificial situations. A drawback is that researchers must make sense of – and categorize – subjects' responses. This can be difficult and time-consuming. Scholars may not fully capture or appreciate an individual's thought processes.

What We Know About Compliance-Gaining

Despite their limitations, when taken together, open- and closed-ended questionnaires have provided useful insights about compliance-gaining. Researchers, using both types of procedures, have devised a variety of typologies to map out the techniques people use to gain compliance. These typologies have yielded insights about the major strategies individuals (at least on American college campuses) use to influence others. Strategies can be classified according to whether they are:

1 *Direct versus indirect.* Direct techniques include assertion (voicing one's wishes loudly) and persistence (reiterating one's point). Indirect tactics include "emotion-target" (putting the other person in a good mood) and thought manipulation (trying to get your way by making the other person feel it is his idea) (Falbo, 1977; see also Dillard, Kinney, & Cruz, 1996).

2 *Rational versus non-rational.* Rational techniques include reason (arguing logically) and doing favors. Non-rational tactics include deceit (fast talking and lying) and threat (telling her I will never speak to her again if she doesn't do what I want) (Falbo, 1977).

3 *Hard-sell versus soft-sell.* Hard-sell tactics include yelling, demanding, and verbal aggression. Soft-sell techniques include kindness, flattery, and flirting (Kipnis & Schmidt, 1996).

4 *Dominance-based versus non-dominance-based.* Dominance-oriented strategies emphasize the power the communicator has over the target, while the latter employ a more egalitarian, conciliatory approach (Dillard, Wilson, Tusing, & Kinney, 1997).

5 *External versus internal.* Tactics can be externally focused, such as rewards or punishments. To motivate a child to study, a parent could use a carrot, like promise ("I'll raise your allowance if you study more"), or a stick, like aversive stimulation ("You're banned from driving until you hit the books"). Techniques can also be internally focused – that is, self-persuasion-type appeals designed to engage the recipient. These include positive self-feeling ("You'll feel good about yourself if you study a lot") and negative self-feeling ("You'll be disappointed with yourself in the long run if you don't study more"; see Marwell & Schmitt, 1967; Miller & Parks, 1982).

Notice that the same techniques can be categorized in several ways. Threat could be direct, non-rational, hard-ball, and external. Positive self-feeling could be indirect, rational, and soft-sell, as well as internal. This cross-categorization occurs because there is not one but a variety of compliance-gaining taxonomies, constructed by different scholars, for different purposes. Nonetheless, these five sets of labels provide a useful way of categorizing compliance-gaining behavior.

Contextual Influences

People are complex creatures. They use different techniques to gain compliance, depending on the situation. In one situation, a person may use reason; in another she may scream and yell, employing verbal aggression. We are all chameleons, to a degree. Which situations are the most critical determinants of compliance-gaining? Scholars have studied this issue, delineating a host of important contextual influences on strategy selection. The following factors are especially important.

Intimacy

Contexts differ in the degree to which they involve intimate associations between persuader and persuadee. As you move along the continuum from stranger to acquaintance to friend to lover or family member, you find that the same individual can behave very differently, depending on which of these "others" the person is trying to influence. In an old but still engaging study, Fitzpatrick and Winke (1979) reported that level of intimacy predicted use of conflict-reducing strategies. Focusing on people casually involved in romantic relationships, those in serious relationships, and married partners, the investigators found that married persons were especially likely to employ emotional appeals or personal rejections ("withholding affection and acting cold until he or she gives in") to resolve differences. "You always hurt the one you love," Fitzpatrick and Winke observed. They explained:

Individuals in a more committed relationship generally have less concern about the strengths of the relational bonds. Consequently, they employ more spontaneous and emotionally toned strategies in their relational conflicts … In the less committed relationships, the cohesiveness of the partners is still being negotiated … Undoubtedly, it would be too risky for them to employ the more open conflict strategies of the firmly committed.

(1979, p. 10)

This is not to say that everyone uses more emotional or highly manipulative tactics in intimate settings than in everyday interpersonal encounters. These findings emerged from one study, conducted at one point in time. However, research indicates that intimacy can exert an important impact on compliance-gaining behavior (Cody & McLaughlin, 1980).

Here is an intriguing social media wrinkle on these findings: People sometimes use very emotional, personal, even mean-spirited compliance-gaining strategies when they are trying to influence strangers (non-intimates) on social networking sites or the Internet. Some blogs have a great deal of incivility, insults, and vulgarities, what Seely (2015) called "virtual vitriol," directed at people users do not know. Freed of ordinary inhibitions that operate in interpersonal situations, some verbally aggressive individuals may use insulting language in an effort to influence or persuade. This suggests an exception to the interpersonal rule that individuals shy away from emotionally toned compliance-gaining messages when they are dealing with strangers. Reconciling these ideas, it seems as if individuals ordinarily may be reluctant to use harsh, emotional messages on individuals they have met, but do not know well. When separated by electronic barriers, a different dynamic occurs.

Dependency

We use different strategies to gain compliance, depending on whether we are dependent on the person we are trying to influence. People are more reluctant to use hard-ball tactics when the other has control over important outcomes in their lives (van Knippenberg et al., 1999). Graduate teaching assistants who say they "dominate arguments" and "argue insistently" with disgruntled undergraduate students acknowledge that they prefer to use non-confrontational techniques, even sidestepping disagreements, when discussing job-related conflicts with the professor (Putnam & Wilson, 1982). It is only natural to be more careful when trying to gain compliance from those who have control over important outcomes in your life. Thus, when people lack power, they are more likely to employ rational and indirect tactics "because no other power base is available to them" (Cody & McLaughlin, 1985).

Rights

People employ different tactics to get their way, depending on whether they believe they have the right to pursue a particular option. If they do not feel they have the moral right to make a request, they may use softer tactics. However, if they believe they have the right to make a request, or if they feel they have been treated unfairly, they are more apt to employ hard rather than soft techniques (van Knippenberg et al., 1999).

Consider the marked change in tactics employed by people trying to convince smokers to quit smoking in public places. Decades ago, individuals who objected to smokers polluting public space said little, afraid they would offend smokers. Nowadays, non-smokers, redefining the meaning of public space and feeling they have the right to insist that smokers not puff in public, frequently use uncompromising, even non-rational, tactics to induce smokers to put out a cigarette. This change in compliance-gaining strategies resulted from years of social protest against smoking. Protests against problematic social norms, and subsequent changes in the law, can empower ordinary people, encouraging them to use feistier techniques to get their way.

Cultural and Individual Differences

Individuals differ dramatically in how they go about trying to get their way. Some people are direct; others are shy. Some individuals worry a great deal about hurting others' feelings; other individuals care not a whit. Some people respect social conventions; other people disregard them.

If individuals differ in their compliance-gaining strategies, can research elucidate or specify the differences? You bet! Scholars have focused on two factors that influence compliance-gaining choices: The macro factor, culture; and a micro variable: The personality factor, self-monitoring (see Chapter 6).

One important aspect of culture is the degree to which the society emphasizes individualism or collectivism. Individualism stresses independence, self-determination, and pursuit of one's self-interest. Collectivism emphasizes concern with group harmony, maintaining positive interpersonal relationships, and a "we" rather than "I" identification. On a cultural level, Western nations like the United States are individualistic, while Asian societies, such as South Korea and Japan, tend to be more collectivist.

In intriguing studies, Min-Sun Kim and colleagues have found that culture influences choice of compliance-gaining strategies. When asked to identify the most important determinants of whether a request is effective, South Korean students emphasized the degree to which the request is sensitive to the other individual's feelings and does not create disapproval. By contrast, U.S. students maintained that a request is more effective when it is made as clearly and directly as possible. South Korean students regard an indirect strategy like hinting as relatively effective for gaining compliance, while American students put a higher premium on direct statements (Kim & Bresnahan, 1994; Kim & Wilson, 1994). Naturally, there are additional differences within Western and Asian cultures that complicate matters. Regardless of country of origin, students whose self-concepts revolve around independence place more emphasis on being clear and direct. Students whose self-concepts center on interpersonal harmony put a higher premium on not hurting the other individual's feelings (Kim & Sharkey, 1995). Under certain conditions (perhaps more than frequently acknowledged), these individual factors overwhelm broad cultural differences.

A second factor that influences compliance-gaining is the personality factor, self-monitoring. High self-monitors, attuned as they are to the requirements of the situation, tend to adapt their strategy to fit the person they are trying to influence (Caldwell & Burger, 1997). Low self-monitors are more apt to use the same technique with different people. High self-monitors are more likely to develop elaborate strategic plans prior to the actual influence attempt (Jordan & Roloff, 1997). In keeping with their concern with image management, high self-monitors are more apt than low self-monitors to include in their plans a consideration of how they could manipulate their personal impression so as to achieve their goals. However, they were not more likely than low self-monitors to build rapport, a pro-social strategy to influence others. High self-monitors may be more elaborate strategists, but low self-monitors can also can bring distinctive approaches to the interpersonal persuasion encounter.

What about you? Do you use the same techniques with different people and across different situations? If so, you may be a low self-monitor. Do you vary your strategies to fit the constraints of the situation? In this case, you could be a high self-monitor. Research provides facts about compliance-gaining in everyday life and can also offer insights into our own behavior.

Application

Compliance-gaining richly explains people's choice of behavioral persuasion techniques in a variety of situations, ranging from the amusing – how individuals try to convince people not to give them traffic tickets (see Box 14.4) – to the serious: Communication that occurs in medical settings. Compliance-gaining research has particularly enriching implications for health. It offers guidelines to doctors on how they can improve their style of communicating medical information, provides clues on how young adults can convince their partners to practice safe sex, and suggests ways that pre-teens can, say, turn down shady requests to experiment with drugs (Burgoon et al., 1989; Perloff, 2001). Although context is important, a general guideline is tailoring the message to the needs of the recipient, showing goodwill, and maintaining a committed, resolute attitude toward the advocated position.

BOX 14.4

Compliance and the Cops

You're driving home one evening, speeding a little because you've got to get ready for a party later that night. The radio's blaring and you're feeling good as you tap your fingers and sing the words of a song you've heard many times before. Out of the corner of your eye you see a couple of lights, but ignore them until you see them again – the telltale flashing light of a police car. Your heart skips a beat as you realize the police car is following you. The siren is sounding now and you get that terrible sinking feeling and agonizing fear that something bad is going to happen.

At this point, many of us faced with the impending possibility of a speeding ticket search our minds ferociously for an excuse, an extenuating reason, a white or black lie, a rhetorical rabbit we can pull out of the hat to convince the officer not to give us a ticket (see Figure 14.5). Of course, in an ideal world, if one ran afoul of the law, he or she would admit it and graciously take responsibility for the mistake. But this is not an ideal world, and many individuals are probably more willing to shade the truth a little than to come clean and suffer the indemnity of a fine and points on their record. Thus, many people try to persuade the police officer not to ticket them, relying on a variety of compliance-gaining techniques.

How do people try to secure compliance from a police officer when they are stopped for traffic violations? Jennifer Preisler and Todd Pinetti, students in a communication class some years back, explored this issue by talking with many young people who had found themselves in this predicament.

Their research, along with my own explorations, uncovered some interesting findings, including the following responses from young people regarding how they have tried to persuade a police officer not to ticket them:

- "I will be extra nice and respectful to the officer. I will apologize for my negligence and error. I tell them about the police officers I know."
- "I flirt my way out of it, smile a lot. [Or I say] 'My speedometer is broken. Honestly, it hasn't worked since August.'"
- "When I am stopped for speeding, I usually do not try to persuade the officer to not give me a ticket. He has the proof that I was speeding, so I don't try to insult his intelligence by making up some stupid excuse. I do try to look very pathetic and innocent, hoping maybe he will feel bad for me and not give me a ticket."

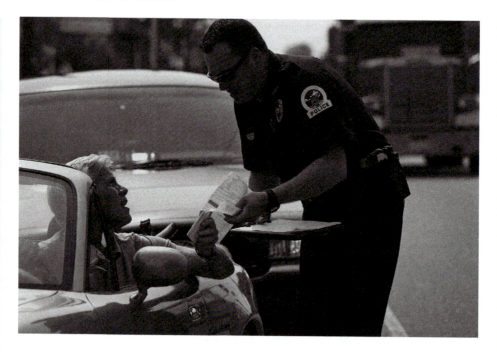

Figure 14.5 When a Police Officer Turns on the Flashing Light and Signals for a Driver to Pull Over, People Frequently Dream Up Lots of Reasons – Some Based in Fact, Others Much Less So – to Persuade the Officer Not to Give Them a Ticket. Individuals differ in the compliance-gaining techniques they employ (and their success in avoiding the ticket). Understandable as it is to try to persuade your way out of a ticket, the more prudent and safety-conscious approach is to acknowledge the error and try to be a better driver
Image courtesy of Getty Images

- "I turn on the dome light and turn off the ignition, roll down the window no matter how cold it is outside. I put my keys, driver's license, and proof of insurance on the dashboard, and put my hands at 10 and 2 on the wheel. I do all this before the officer gets to the window. I am honest and hope for the best. I have tried three times and all three were successful."
- "The officer said, 'I've been waiting for an idiot like you [who he could pull over for speeding] all night.' I told him, 'Yeah, I got here as fast as I could.' He laughed for about two minutes straight and let us go."
- "I gain compliance by smiling [big] and saying, 'Officer, what seems to be the problem?'"
- "I'm on my way to church."
- "The line that I have used to get out of a ticket is 'My wife's in labor.'"

- "My technique is when I am getting pulled over, I reach into my glove compartment and spray a dab of hair spray onto my finger. Then I put it in my eyes and I start to cry. I have gotten pulled over about 15 to 20 times and I have only gotten one ticket."

Many people suspect that gender intervenes – that is, male police officers are more forgiving of females than of males who violate a traffic law. Research bears this out. Male police officers issued a greater percentage of citations to male drivers than did female police officers. In a similar fashion, female police officers issued a greater percentage of their traffic citations to female drivers than did male officers (Koehler & Willis, 1994). Police officers may be more lenient with opposite-sex than same-sex offenders; they may find the arguments provided by opposite-sex individuals to be more persuasive because they are attracted sexually to the drivers. Or they may be less apt to believe excuses offered by members of their own gender.

Unfortunately, there is a more negative side to compliance and police, one that extends beyond pleasant persuasion to the more serious issue of racial attitudes. Police officers are more likely to demand compliance from African American than White drivers, frequently pulling Black drivers over for traffic violations far more than would be expected based on their share of the population in a city. In four states, African American drivers were more likely to be searched for contraband than Whites, even though the police found guns, drugs, and illegal materials more frequently when the driver was White (LaFraniere & Lehren, 2015). Try as they might, Black drivers could not persuade officers of their innocence, reminding us of the ways that coercion overlaps with persuasion and the role that prejudice plays even in contexts that seem far removed from the stain of racial discrimination.

To gain additional insight into the ways compliance-gaining research can shed light on social problems, I invite you to consider another issue that has become so commonplace we have become desensitized to its serious effects. The problem is child abuse. Child abuse and neglect are important problems both in the United States and abroad. Parents can abuse their children through physical, sexual, and verbal aggression, as well as through outright neglect. Abusive parents employ a battery of cruel and aggressive strategies to induce their children to comply with their requests. Lynn Oldershaw and her colleagues (1986) conducted an observational study to examine whether abusive mothers differed from non-abusive moms in their compliance-gaining strategies.

The researchers focused on ten physically abusive mothers and ten non-abusive moms, videotaping them as they interacted for about 40 minutes with one of their children: A two- to four-year-old. They videotaped the interactions and carefully classified the mothers' ways of seeking compliance from their toddlers, categorizing them into power-assertive techniques, such as threat, humiliation, and negative physical touch, and positive pro-social strategies like modeling, reasoning, and bargaining. There were stark and disturbing differences between abusive and comparison moms.

For abusive mothers, the interaction was all about their power over the child. They employed power-assertive strategies, like those used above, or were more likely than comparison mothers to command their children to engage in a particular behavior. They tended to issue their commands without offering any positive rationale and without conveying a favorable vocal tone. Not only were the abusive mothers' techniques cruel, they were ineffective. Abused children were less likely to obey their mothers' requests for compliance than non-abused children. Even when their kids did comply, abusive mothers were as likely to respond with criticisms, as with compliments. Comparison mothers typically complimented their kids when they complied (see Wilson, 2010).

The study leaves a powerful imprint. One feels terrible for the kids, just two- to four-year-olds. But the implications are as important as the findings are heart-rending. If mothers could be taught to seek compliance in more humane ways, perhaps future abuse could be halted. We need to persuade mothers, and fathers as well, to seek compliance in different ways. This is not an easy task. But, thanks to Oldershaw and her associates' study, we have some clues as to where to begin (see Figure 14.6).

Beyond Compliance-Gaining

Compliance-gaining research has richly informed our knowledge of interpersonal persuasion. Unfortunately, the area reached an impasse because of a series of procedural problems. For all the advantages that compliance-gaining typologies offer practitioners, they are filled with methodological problems. Strategies are frequently defined ambiguously, inconsistently, or so specifically that it is difficult to know what the strategies mean (Kellermann & Cole, 1994; see also Wilson, 2002). Critics have also noted that much of the research involves responses to hypothetical situations, rather than actual compliance-gaining behavior.

Figure 14.6 Compliance-Gaining Research Offers Clues About How Parents Can Gain Compliance From Their Children Without Resorting to Power-Assertive Techniques Like Threat or Physical Aggression

Image courtesy of Shutterstock

The good news is that the intuitive strength of the area – a down-to-earth explanation of how people go about gaining compliance – has generated exciting research. An important framework focuses on the persuasion objectives individuals seek to attain in interpersonal situations.

Interpersonal Persuasion Goals

The research begins with the insight that people do not approach compliance-gaining with a blank slate. Instead, they define a situation in a particular way, pursuing goals and enacting plans. People have primary and secondary goals (Dillard, Segrin, & Harden, 1989; Wilson, 2010). A primary goal structures the interaction, propelling individuals to seek a particular behavior from the target. Primary or key influence goals include:

- Asking a favor ("Can you drive me to the airport?");
- Giving advice ("I think you should quit drinking");
- Obtaining permission ("Professor, can I get an extension on my paper?");
- Sharing activity ("Let's see a movie");
- Enforcing obligations ("You promised to clean the kitchen. Come on, it's not fair if you don't do your part.")

(Dillard & Knobloch, 2011)

These are everyday, down-to-earth influence objectives. So too are secondary goals. Secondary goals determine how people approach their primary goal. Focusing on the interpersonal dynamics of the situation, secondary goals influence individuals as they pursue their primary objectives. Secondary goals include:

- Maintaining a positive public impression, or face;
- Avoiding behaviors that would tarnish another person's image or face;
- Maintaining interpersonal relationships;
- Avoiding resource risks, such as wasting time or money.

It is a complex dance. People have multiple, sometimes conflicting, goals they want to accomplish in a particular situation (Dillard, 1990b). What's more, people are always balancing intrapersonal and interpersonal needs. They want to maintain their autonomy, yet need approval from others (Brown & Levinson, 1987). They want to get their way, but recognize that this can threaten another's image, autonomy, or "face" (Wilson, Aleman, & Leatham, 1998). They don't want to hurt the other's feelings, but recognize that if they are too nice they may kill the clarity of their request with politeness and ambiguity.

People frequently must balance their desire to achieve a *primary goal* – influencing the target's behavior – with an attempt to meet a *secondary goal* also, such as maintaining a good public impression, not damaging a friendship, or doing the morally right thing (Dillard et al., 1989; Meyer, 2007; Wilson, 2002). There is a yin and yang between primary goals, which push the persuader toward action, and secondary goals, which pull or constrain the individual from going too far. We all have been in situations where we want to get our way, but realize that if we are too argumentative or dismissive of the other person's feelings, we will destroy a valued relationship.

Scholars have studied how people process these matters and go about balancing conflicting needs. Their models emphasize that people have elaborate cognitive structures regarding compliance-gaining and ways to achieve their goals (Wilson, 1999). This is fascinating because we all go about the business of trying to get our way, but rarely give any thought to how we think about trying to gain compliance or how we process, in our own minds, "all that stuff going on in the situation." Interpersonal communication models and research shed light on such issues.

Theoretical frameworks have focused on communicators' face or interpersonal presentation needs. People want to gain important others' approval of their interpersonal behavior (positive face), while not wanting to lose their autonomy or have their actions restricted without reason (negative face; see Brown & Levinson, 1987).

A core model that offers an integrative perspective to goals and interpersonal interaction is James P. Dillard's (1990b) goal-driven approach. According to a goals approach, when persuaders are more concerned with achieving primary than secondary goals, they will interpersonally engage the target, generating and editing plans to help implement the goal. When the primary and secondary goals are equally important, persuaders will choose an influence strategy that takes into account their concern about not thwarting secondary goals. In these cases, the dynamics of influence are more complex. Seeking a strategy that will not interfere with secondary goals, they may mentally consider or reformulate their plans before confronting the other person.

Application

To appreciate how all this works in real life, consider the following example:

> Professors sometimes require group projects, in which students work together on a task and complete a group paper. While opinions are divided on group projects – some students find them unfair, others like group interaction – they have been a consistent part of university classes for a long time. The primary goal is successful completion of the project. A secondary goal arises when one student in the group fails to pull his weight and other students must decide how to communicate their dissatisfaction to the slacker in a way that preserves their reputation, does not unduly threaten the slacker's face, and does not destroy the relationship. If the primary goal is paramount, other students may tell the slacker off, demanding he put in his fair share of the work, with little concern about offending him. If primary and secondary goals are weighed equally – perhaps because the slacker is a friend – then the other students will tread more carefully, mentally mulling over strategies before they act, balancing bluntness with politeness, and perhaps avoiding a strategy that would totally embarrass their friend.

It is a dicey situation. Researchers find that when people possess incompatible goals such as trying to convince a target to do something she most definitely does not want to do, while at the same time not hurting her feelings in the slightest – they pause more and don't communicate as effectively (Greene et al., 1993). The incongruity of goals puts stress on the mental system. Thus, the best advice in this situation may be not to beat around the bush. Persuaders may be most effective when they honestly and unambiguously share their objection to the slacker, in a way that respects their friend's autonomy, but also communicates the importance of the primary goal.

Of course, as any of us who have valiantly embarked on this strategy only to be ignored or criticized by our slacker friend will attest, this technique is not guaranteed to work. Much depends on the content of the request, the manner in which it is implemented, and the personality of the persuader and target. The nature of the relationship also matters. Strategies will vary, depending on so-called intimacy (how well you know the slacker and nature of the interpersonal relationship), dominance (whether one of you has power over the other), and the benefits that the paper and the relationship offer both parties.

If this strikes you as interesting but vague, you are right! The strength of interpersonal persuasion research has been in articulating the cognitive and situational dynamics of interpersonal influence contexts. Its shortcoming has been in laying out predictions or hypotheses about optimum strategies to achieve persuasion goals. Nevertheless, the interpersonal goals approach helpfully advances knowledge by shedding light on the cognitive and interpersonal dynamics of everyday compliance-gaining situations. It underscores the emotional messiness of everyday persuasion. By articulating goals and the mental activities in which persuaders engage, it helps to clarify the nature of interpersonal persuasion.

Ethical Issues

"Communication is founded on a presumption of truth," two scholars aptly note (Buller & Burgoon, 1996, p. 203). Yet persuasion commonly involves some shading of truth, a tinting that is rationalized by persuaders and lamented by message receivers. Interpersonal persuasion – from the sequential influence techniques discussed earlier in the chapter to the endless variety of compliance-gaining tactics just described – sometimes seems to put a premium on distorting communication in the service of social influence. Distorting communication in the service of social influence? A blunter, more accurate way to describe this is "lying."

Lying is remarkably common in everyday life. In two diary studies, college students reported that they told two lies a day. They admitted they lied in one of every three of their social interactions (DePaulo et al., 1996). To be sure, some of these lies were told to protect other people from embarrassment, loss of face, or having their feelings hurt. However, other lies were told to enhance the psychological state of the liars – for example, to make the liars appear better than they were, to protect them from looking bad, or to protect their privacy. Many of these were white lies that we have told ourselves; others were darker distortions, outright falsehoods (DePaulo et al., 1996). On the other hand, another survey obtained more optimistic results, finding that most people subjectively report relatively little lying, and that only a small minority of individuals, with psychopathic predispositions, lie frequently (Halevy, Shalvi, & Verschuere, 2014).

Lying is a complex, many-layered entity, with its definition and evaluation depending on intentions and consequences. Still, there is little doubt that interpersonal compliance-gaining (as opposed to everyday communication) is fraught with lies, or at least greasing the truth. Even flattery involves a certain amount of shading of truth, a convention that many people admittedly enjoy and cherish (Stengel, 2000). All this has stimulated considerable debate among philosophers over the years. As discussed in Chapter 2, utilitarians argue that a lie must be evaluated in terms of its consequences. Deontological thinkers tend to disapprove of lies in principle because they distort truth. Related approaches emphasize that what matters is the motivation of the liar – a lie told for a good, virtuous end may be permissible under some circumstances (Gass & Seiter, 2014).

We cannot resolve this debate. In my view, social discourse – and the warp and woof of social influence – contain much truth, shading of truth, and lies. They also contain certain corrective mechanisms. Those who lie habitually run the risk of earning others' disapproval, or finding that even their truthful statements are disbelieved. Social norms operate to discourage chronic lying. So too do psychodynamic mechanisms that have evolved over human history. Guilt and internalized ethical rules help regulate people's desire to regularly stretch the truth.

However, a certain amount of lying is inevitable, indeed permissible, in everyday interpersonal communication. Social influence – and persuasive communication – are human endeavors, part of the drama of everyday life, in which people are free to pursue their own ends, restrained by internalized moral values and social conventions (Scheibe, 2000). Democratic, civilized society enshrines people's freedom to pursue their own interests and celebrates those who can exert influence over others. The downside of this is that some people will abuse their freedom and seek to manipulate others, distorting truth and using deceitful tactics. Human evolution has not yet evolved to the point that ethics totally trumps (or at least restrains) self-interest, and perhaps it never will. The best hope is education: Increased self-understanding, development of humane values, and (trite as it may sound) application of the time-honored, but always relevant, Golden Rule that emphasizes the intrinsic value of telling the truth and respecting our fellow human beings.

Conclusions

This chapter has examined interpersonal persuasion – the many techniques individuals use to influence one another in dyadic or one-on-one interactions. Social psychological research has documented that gambits like foot-in-the-door and door-in-the-face can be especially effective in securing compliance. Make no mistake: These tactics do not always work, and many consumers have learned to resist them. However, they are used regularly in sales and pro-social charity work; under certain conditions, for various psychological reasons, they can work handily. Other tactics employed by professional persuaders – pre-giving exchange, low-balling, "that's-not-all," fear-then-relief, pique, and disrupt-then-reframe – can also influence compliance. So too do strategies that play in different ways on words and psychological needs, including those where the persuader asks "How are you feeling?," adds "Even a penny will help," or suggests that "You are free to accept or to refuse." Compliance strategies work through different psychological processes, such as self-perception, reciprocal concessions, impression management, and arousal of reactance. The more that communicators appreciate these processes – the "whys" of persuasion – the more successful they will be in gaining compliance. For example, if a persuader appreciates that foot-in-the-door works partly because the persuader has caused message receivers to view themselves as the kind of people who cooperate with others, he or she should make certain to call on this self-perception when making the second request. If communicators recognize that door-in-the-face works by activating a pro-social responsibility norm of reciprocating concessions, they can highlight this when appealing to message receivers the second time around. If the verbally clever "even a penny will help" activates a desire not to look like an insensitive cheapskate, the persuader can use impression management appeals to nudge the individual toward compliance. As with all persuasion, compliance techniques can be used for deceptive, manipulative ends, as well as for pro-social causes. Such is the rub of interpersonal persuasion.

In everyday life, we employ a variety of tactics to get our way. Interpersonal communication scholars have developed typologies to categorize these techniques. Strategies vary in their directness, rationality, and emphasis on self-persuasion. Different strategies are used in different situations, and the same person may use a direct approach in one setting and a cautious, indirect technique in another. Culture and personality factors like self-monitoring also place limits on compliance-gaining choices. Compliance-gaining research has illuminated knowledge of interpersonal persuasion. Its strength is its rich exploration of dyadic interactions. Its shortcomings include absence of theory and lack of precision in strategy measurement.

Other approaches have extended interpersonal persuasion research, notably, those that explore the nature of primary and secondary goals. A primary goal structures an interaction between people, while a secondary objective focuses on the interpersonal dynamics of the situation. In some instances, what began as a secondary goal – maintaining a positive public face or not hurting someone's feelings – can become the preeminent goal in the situation.

Everyday interpersonal persuasion is complex and dynamic. Persuaders are constantly editing and reformulating plans so that they can balance primary and secondary goals. Compliance choices vary as a function of whether a primary or secondary goal is paramount, the nature of the situation, and the feelings that the compliance-gaining elicits. Research, focusing on ever-more cognitive aspects of individuals' strategic choices, is shedding light on the dynamics of everyday interpersonal persuasion.

It is important to remember that culture plays a key role in compliance-gaining choices (Fitch, 1994). Research, with its focus on American college students, tends to underestimate the degree to which culture influences the ways we think about persuasion and try to persuade others. Effective persuasion in an interconnected world requires an appreciation for cultural morays – the ways that persuasion differs across cultures, as well as the verities that make for constancy, even in very different cultural settings.

In sum, given the central role that interpersonal persuasion plays in everyday life and in business transactions, it behooves us to understand and master it. A practical strategy that experts suggest is to look to the behavior of highly effective persuaders. Successful persuaders recognize that persuasion requires give and take, flexibility, and ability to see things from the other party's point of view (Cody & Seiter, 2001; Delia, Kline, & Burleson, 1979; Waldron & Applegate, 1998). "Effective persuaders have a strong and accurate sense of their audience's emotional state, and they adjust the tone of their arguments accordingly," observes Jay A. Conger (1998, p. 93). He notes that they plan arguments and self-presentational strategies in advance and "enter the persuasion process prepared to adjust their viewpoints and incorporate others' ideas. That approach to persuasion is, interestingly, highly persuasive in itself" (p. 87).

References

Andrews, K. R., Carpenter, C. J., Shaw, A. S., & Boster, F. J. (2008). The legitimization of paltry favors effect: A review and meta-analysis. *Communication Reports, 21*, 59–69.

Aune, R. K., & Basil, M. D. (1994). A relational obligations approach to the foot-in-the-mouth effect. *Journal of Applied Social Psychology, 24*, 546–556.

Bell, R. A., Cholerton, M., Davison, W., Fraczek, K. E., & Lauter, H. (1996). Making health communication self-funding: Effectiveness of pregiving in an AIDS fundraising/education campaign. *Health Communication, 8*, 331–352.

Bolkan, S., & Rains, S. A. (2017). The legitimization of paltry contributions as a compliance-gaining technique: A meta-analysis testing three explanations. *Communication Research, 44*, 976–996.

Briñol, P., Rucker, D. D., Tormala, Z. L., & Petty, R. E. (2004). Individual differences in resistance to persuasion: The role of beliefs and meta-beliefs. In E. S. Knowles & J. A. Linn (Eds.), *Resistance and persuasion* (pp. 83–104). Mahwah, NJ: Lawrence Erlbaum Associates.

Brown, P., & Levinson, S. C. (1987). *Politeness: Some universals in language usage*. Cambridge, UK: Cambridge University Press.

Buller, D. B., & Burgoon, J. K. (1996). Interpersonal deception theory. *Communication Theory, 6*, 203–242.

Burger, J. M. (1986). Increasing compliance by improving the deal: The that's not all technique. *Journal of Personality and Social Psychology, 51,* 277–283.

Burger, J. M. (1999). The foot-in-the-door compliance procedure: A multiple process analysis and review. *Personality and Social Psychology Review, 3,* 303–325.

Burger, J. M., Hornisher, J., Martin, V. E., Newman, G., & Pringle, S. (2007). The pique technique: Overcoming mindlessness or shifting heuristics? *Journal of Applied Social Psychology, 37,* 2086–2096.

Burgoon, M., Parrott, R., Burgoon, J., Birk, T., Pfau, M., & Coker, R. (1989). Primary care physicians' selection of verbal compliance-gaining strategies. *Health Communication, 2,* 13–27.

Burleson, B. R., Wilson, S. R., Waltman, M. S., Goering, E. M., Ely, T. K., & Whaley, B. B. (1988). Item desirability effects in compliance-gaining research: Seven studies documenting artifacts in the strategy selection procedure. *Human Communication Research, 14,* 429–486.

Caldwell, D. F., & Burger, J. M. (1997). Personality and social influence strategies in the workplace. *Personality and Social Psychology Bulletin, 23,* 1003–1012.

Carpenter, C. J. (2013). A meta-analysis of the effectiveness of the "But You Are Free" compliance-gaining technique. *Communication Studies, 64,* 6–17.

Carpenter, C. J., & Boster, F. J. (2009). A meta-analysis of the effectiveness of the disrupt-then-reframe compliance gaining technique. *Communication Reports, 22,* 55–62.

Chartrand, T., Pinckert, S., & Burger, J. M. (1999). When manipulation backfires: The effects of time delay and requester on the foot-in-the-door technique. *Journal of Applied Social Psychology, 29,* 211–221.

Cialdini, R. B. (2009). *Influence: Science and practice* (5th ed.). Boston, MA: Pearson Education.

Cialdini, R. B., & Ascani, K. (1976). Test of a concession procedure for inducing verbal, behavioral, and further compliance with a request to give blood. *Journal of Applied Psychology, 61,* 295–300.

Cialdini, R. B., Cacioppo, J. T., Bassett, R., & Miller, J. A. (1978). Low-ball procedure for producing compliance: Commitment then cost. *Journal of Personality and Social Psychology, 36,* 463–476.

Cialdini, R. B., & Schroeder, D. A. (1976). Increasing compliance by legitimizing paltry contributions: When even a penny helps. *Journal of Personality and Social Psychology, 34,* 599–604.

Cialdini, R. B., Vincent, J. E., Lewis, S. K., Catalan, J., Wheeler, D., & Darby, B. L. (1975). Reciprocal concessions procedure for inducing compliance: The door-in-the-face technique. *Journal of Personality and Social Psychology, 31,* 206–215.

Cody, M. J., & McLaughlin, M. L. (1980). Perceptions of compliance-gaining situations: A dimensional analysis. *Communication Monographs, 47,* 132–148.

Cody, M. J., & McLaughlin, M. L. (1985). The situation as a construct in interpersonal communication research. In M. L. Knapp & G. R. Miller (Eds.), *Handbook of interpersonal communication* (pp. 263–312). Beverly Hills, CA: Sage.

Cody, M. J., McLaughlin, M. L., & Jordan, W. J. (1980). A multidimensional scaling of three sets of compliance-gaining strategies. *Communication Quarterly, 28,* 34–46.

Cody, M. J., & Seiter, J. S. (2001). Compliance principles in retail sales in the United States. In W. Wosinska, R. B. Cialdini, D. W. Barrett, & J. Reykowski (Eds.), *The practice of social influence in multiple cultures* (pp. 325–341). Mahwah, NJ: Lawrence Erlbaum Associates.

Conger, J. A. (1998, May–June). The necessary art of persuasion. *Harvard Business Review, 76,* 84–95.

Davis, B. P., & Knowles, E. S. (1999). A disrupt-then-reframe technique of social influence. *Journal of Personality and Social Psychology, 76,* 192–199.

Davis, D. (2011, September 8). NE Ohio doctors got $5.8M from drug makers for talks. *The Plain Dealer,* A1, A8.

DeJong, W. (1979). An examination of self-perception mediation of the foot-in-the-door effect. *Journal of Personality and Social Psychology, 37,* 2221–2239.

Delia, J. G., Kline, S. L., & Burleson, B. R. (1979). The development of persuasive communication strategies in kindergartners through twelfth graders. *Communication Mono graphs*, *46*, 241–256.

DePaulo, B. M., Kashy, D. A., Kirkendol, S. E., Wyer, M. M., & Epstein, J. A. (1996). Lying in everyday life. *Journal of Personality and Social Psychology*, *70*, 979–995.

Dillard, J. P. (1990a). Self-inference and the foot-in-the-door technique: Quantity of behavior and attitudinal mediation. *Human Communication Research*, *16*, 422–447.

Dillard, J. P. (1990b). A goal-driven model of interpersonal influence. In J. P. Dillard (Ed.), *Seeking compliance: The production of interpersonal influence messages* (pp. 41–56). Scottsdale, AZ: Gorsuch-Scarisbrick.

Dillard, J. P., Hunter, J. E., & Burgoon, M. (1984). Sequential request persuasive strategies: Meta-analysis of foot-in-the-door and door-in-the-face. *Human Communication Research*, *10*, 461–488.

Dillard, J. P., Kinney, T. A., & Cruz, M. G. (1996). Influence, appraisals, and emotions in close relationships. *Communication Monographs*, *63*, 105–130.

Dillard, J. P., & Knobloch, L. K. (2011). Interpersonal influence. In M. L. Knapp & J. A. Daly (Eds.), *The Sage handbook of interpersonal communication* (4th ed., pp. 389–422). Thousand Oaks, CA: Sage.

Dillard, J. P., Segrin, C., & Harden, J. M. (1989). Primary and secondary goals in the production of interpersonal influence messages. *Communication Monographs*, *56*, 19–38.

Dillard, J. P., Wilson, S. R., Tusing, K. J., & Kinney, T. A. (1997). Politeness judgments in personal relationships. *Journal of Language and Psychology*, *16*, 297–325.

Dolinksi, D. (2016). *Techniques of social influence: The psychology of gaining compliance*. New York: Routledge.

Dolinski, D., & Nawrat, R. (1998). "Fear-then-relief" procedure for producing compliance: Beware when the danger is over. *Journal of Experimental Social Psychology*, *34*, 27–50.

Dudczak, C. A. (2016). Dariusz Dolinski, *Techniques of social influence: The psychology of gaining compliance*. (Book review). *Southern Communication Journal*, DOI: 10.1080/1041794X.2015.1124915.

Eddy, M. (2019, July 31). Austrian woman softens her kidnapper with kindness. *The New York Times*, A10.

Falbo, T. (1977). Multidimensional scaling of power strategies. *Journal of Personality and Social Psychology*, *35*, 537–547.

Feeley, T. H., Anker, A. E., & Aloe, A. M. (2012). The door-in-the-face persuasive message strategy: A meta-analysis of the first 35 years. *Communication Monographs*, *79*, 316–343.

Feeley, T., Fico, A. E., Shaw, A. Z., Lee, S., & Griffin, D. J. (2017). Is the door-in-the-face a concession? *Communication Quarterly*, *65*, 97–123.

Fern, E. F., Monroe, K. B., & Avila, R. A. (1986). Effectiveness of multiple request strategies: A synthesis of research results. *Journal of Marketing Research*, *23*, 144–152.

Fitch, K. L. (1994). A cross-cultural study of directive sequences and some implications for compliance-gaining research. *Communication Monographs*, *61*, 185–209.

Fitzpatrick, M. A., & Winke, J. (1979). You always hurt the one you love: Strategies and tactics in interpersonal conflict. *Communication Quarterly*, *27*, 1–11.

Freedman, J. L., & Fraser, S. C. (1966). Compliance without pressure: The foot-in-the-door technique. *Journal of Personality and Social Psychology*, *4*, 195–202.

Gass, R. H., & Seiter, J. S. (2014). *Persuasion: Social influence and compliance gaining* (5th ed.). Boston, MA: Pearson.

Goei, R., Lindsey, L. L. M., Boster, F. J., Skalski, P. D., & Bowman, J. M. (2003). The mediating roles of liking and obligation on the relationship between favors and compliance. *Communication Research*, *30*, 178–197.

Goei, R., Roberto, A., Meyer, G., & Carlyle, K. (2007). The effects of favor and apology on compliance. *Communication Research*, 34, 575–595.

Greene, J. O., McDaniel, T. L., Buksa, K., & Ravizza, S. M. (1993). Cognitive processes in the production of multiple-goal messages: Evidence from the temporal characteristics of speech. *Western Journal of Communication*, 57, 65–86.

Guéguen, N., & Pascual, A. (2005). Improving the response rate to a street survey: An evaluation of the "But you are free to accept or to refuse" technique. *Psychological Record*, 55, 297–303.

Guéguen, N., & Lamy, L. (2016). The pique technique: A goal-oriented effect?

Halevy, R., Shalvi, S., & Verschuere, B. (2014). Being honest about dishonesty: Correlating self-reports and actual lying. *Human Communication Research*, 40, 54–72.

Harris, G. R., & Roberts, J. (2007, March 21). A state's files put doctors' ties to drug makers on close view. *The New York Times*, A1, A18.

Homans, G. C. (1961). *Social behavior: Its elementary forms*. New York: Harcourt: Brace.

Howard, D. J. (1990). The influence of verbal responses to common greetings on compliance behavior: The foot-in-the-mouth effect. *Journal of Applied Social Psychology*, 20, 1185–1196.

Jordan, J. M., & Roloff, M. E. (1997). Planning skills and negotiator goal accomplishment: The relationship between self-monitoring and plan generation, plan enactment, and plan consequences. *Communication Research*, 24, 31–63.

Kellermann, K., & Cole, T. (1994). Classifying compliance-gaining messages: Taxonomic disorder and strategic confusion. *Communication Theory*, 4, 3–60.

Kim, M. S., & Bresnahan, M. (1994). A process model of request tactic evaluation. *Discourse Processes*, 18, 317–344.

Kim, M. S., & Sharkey, W. F. (1995). Independent and interdependent construals of self: Explaining cultural patterns of interpersonal communication in multicultural organizational settings. *Communication Quarterly*, 43, 20–38.

Kim, M. S., & Wilson, S. R. (1994). A cross-cultural comparison of implicit theories of requesting. *Communication Monographs*, 61, 210–235.

Kipnis, D., & Schmidt, S. (1996). The language of persuasion. In E. J. Coats & R. S. Feldman (Eds.), *Classic and contemporary readings in social psychology* (pp. 184–188). Upper Saddle River, NJ: Prentice Hall.

Knowles, E. S., & Linn, J. A. (2004). Approach-avoidance model of persuasion: Alpha and omega strategies for change. In E. S. Knowles & J. A. Linn (Eds.), *Resistance and persuasion* (pp. 117–148). Mahwah, NJ: Lawrence Erlbaum Associates.

Knowles, E. S., Butler, S., & Linn, J. A. (2001). Increasing compliance by reducing resistance. In J. P. Forgas & K. D. Williams (Eds.), *Social influence: Direct and indirect processes* (pp. 41–60). Philadelphia, PA: Taylor & Francis.

Koehler, S. P., & Willis, F. N. (1994). Traffic citations in relation to gender. *Journal of Applied Social Psychology*, 24, 1919–1926.

LaFraniere, S., & Lehren, A. W. (2015, October 28). The disproportionate risk of driving while Black. *The New York Times*, 1(18), 19.

Lee, S. A., & Liang, Y. (2019). Robotic foot-in-the-door: Using sequential-request persuasive strategies in human-robot interaction. *Computers in Human Behavior*, 90, 351–356.

Lyon, A., & Mirivel, J. C. (2011). Reconstructing Merck's practical theory of communication: The ethics of pharmaceutical sales representative–physician encounters. *Communication Monographs*, 78, 53–72.

Macy, B. (2018). *Dopesick: Dealers, doctors, and the drug company that addicted America*. New York: Little, Brown and Company.

Make those opioid payments count. (2019, August 29). (Editorial.) *The New York Times*, A26.

Marwell, G., & Schmitt, D. R. (1967). Dimensions of compliance-gaining behavior: An empirical analysis. *Sociometry*, 30, 350–364.

Meyer, J. R. (2007). Compliance gaining. In D. R. Roskos-Ewoldsen & J. L. Monahan (Eds.), *Communication and social cognition: Theories and methods* (pp. 399–416). Mahwah, NJ: Erlbaum Associates.

Miller, G. R., Boster, F., Roloff, M., & Seibold, D. (1977). Compliance-gaining message strategies: A typology and some findings concerning effects of situational differences. *Communication Monographs*, 44, 37–51.

Miller, G. R., & Parks, M. R. (1982). Communication in dissolving relationships. In S. Duck (Ed.), *Personal relationships 4: Dissolving relationships* (pp. 127–154). Orlando, FL: Academic Press.

O'Keefe, D. J., & Figgé, M. (1999). Guilt and expected guilt in the door-in-the-face technique. *Communication Monographs*, 66, 312–324.

O'Keefe, D. J., & Hale, S. L. (1998). The door-in-the-face influence strategy: A random-effects meta-analytic review. In M. E. Roloff (Ed.), *Communication yearbook 21* (pp. 1–33). Thousand Oaks, CA: Sage.

Oldershaw, L., Walters, G. C., & Hall, D. K. (1986). Control strategies and noncompliance in abusive mother–child dyads: An observational study. *Child Development*, 57, 722–732.

Perloff, R. M. (2001). *Persuading people to have safer sex: Applications of social science to the AIDS crisis*. Mahwah, NJ: Lawrence Erlbaum Associates.

Pratkanis, A. R. (2007). Social influence analysis: An index of tactics. In A. R. Pratkanis (Ed.), *The science of social influence: Advances and future progress* (pp. 17–82). New York: Psychology Press.

Putnam, L. L., & Wilson, C. E. (1982). Communicative strategies in organizational conflicts: Reliability and validity of a measurement scale. In M. Burgoon (Ed.), *Communication yearbook 6* (pp. 629–652). Beverly Hills, CA: Sage.

Rhoads, K. V. L., & Cialdini, R. B. (2002). The business of influence: Principles that lead to success in commercial settings. In J. P. Dillard & M. Pfau (Eds.), *The persuasion handbook: Developments in theory and practice* (pp. 513–542). Thousand Oaks, CA: Sage.

Rittle, R. H. (1981). Changes in helping behavior: Self versus situational perceptions as mediators of the foot-in-the-door effect. *Personality and Social Psychology Bulletin*, 7, 431–437.

Santora, M. (2006, November 25). In diabetes fight, raising cash and keeping trust. *The New York Times*, A1, A13.

Santos, M. D., Leve, C., & Pratkanis, A. R. (1994). Hey buddy, can you spare seventeen cents? Mindful persuasion and the pique technique. *Journal of Applied Social Psychology*, 24, 755–764.

Scheibe, K. E. (2000). *The drama of everyday life*. Cambridge, MA: Harvard University Press.

Schein, E. H. (1961). *Coercive persuasion: A socio-psychological analysis of the "brainwashing" of the American civilian prisoners by the Chinese communists*. New York: W. W. Norton.

Seely, N. K. (2015). Virtual vitriol: A comparative analysis of incivility in discussion forums of online mainstream news outlets and political blogs. In *Paper presented to the annual conference of the Midwestern Association for Public Opinion Research*, Chicago.

Seibold, D. R., Cantrill, J. G., & Meyers, R. A. (1994). Communication and interpersonal influence. In M. L. Knapp & G. R. Miller (Eds.), *Handbook of interpersonal communication* (2nd ed., pp. 542–588). Thousand Oaks, CA: Sage.

Sparks, G. G. (2010). *Rolling in dough: Lessons I learned in a doughnut shop*. Amherst, MA: White River Press.

Stengel, R. (2000). *You're too kind: A brief history of flattery*. New York: Simon & Schuster.

Taylor, T., & Booth-Butterfield, S. (1993). Getting a foot in the door with drinking and driving: A field study of healthy influence. *Communication Research Reports*, 10, 95–101.

Thomas, K. (2019, May 15). A rival to Botox invites doctors to party in Cancun, with fireworks, confetti and social media posts. *The New York Times*. Online: www.nytimes.com/2019/05/15/health/evolus-wrinkles-toxin-jeaveau.html (Accessed: August 24, 2019)

Thomas, K., & Hsu, T. (2019, August 28). Opioid penalty is latest blow for old brand. *The New York Times*, A1, A14.

Turner, M. M., Tamborini, R., Limon, M. S., & Zuckerman-Hyman, C. (2007). The moderators and mediators of door-in-the-face requests: Is it a negotiation or a helping experience? *Communication Monographs*, 74, 333–356.

van Knippenberg, B., van Knippenberg, D., Blaauw, E., & Vermunt, R. (1999). Relational considerations in the use of influence tactics. *Journal of Applied Social Psychology*, 29, 806–819.

Waldron, V. R., & Applegate, J. L. (1998). Person-centered tactics during verbal disagreements: Effects on student perceptions of persuasiveness and social attraction. *Communication Education*, 47, 53–66.

West, R., & Turner, L. H. (2010). *Introducing communication theory: Analysis and application* (4th ed.). Boston, MA: McGraw-Hill Higher Education.

Wilson, S. R. (1999). Developing theories of persuasive message production: The next generation. In J. O. Greene (Ed.), *Message production* (pp. 15–44). Mahwah, NJ: Lawrence Erlbaum Associates.

Wilson, S. R. (2002). *Seeking and resisting compliance: Why people say what they do when trying to influence others*. Thousand Oaks, CA: Sage.

Wilson, S. R. (2010). Seeking and resisting compliance. In C. R. Berger, M. E. Roloff, & D. R. Roskos-Ewoldsen (Eds.), *The handbook of communication science* (2nd ed., pp. 219–235). Thousand Oaks, CA: Sage.

Wilson, S. R., Aleman, C. G., & Leatham, G. B. (1998). Identity implications of influence goals: A revised analysis of face-threatening acts and application to seeking compliance with same-sex friends. *Human Communication Research*, 25, 64–96.

Chapter 15

Advertising, Marketing, and Persuasion

You have seen it in hundreds of commercials and on all types of clothing – shirts, jackets, and hats. It is an oversized check mark, a smoker's pipe that juts outward, a "curvy, speedy-looking blur" (Hartley, 2000). Take a look below. It's the Nike "swoosh" – the symbol of Nike products, promoted by celebrity athletes; an emblem of Nike's television advertising campaigns; and, to many, the embodiment of speed, grace, mobility, and cool. The swoosh is a major reason why Nike is the major player in the sneaker market, and a testament to the success of commercial advertising (Goldman & Papson, 1996).

Advertising. That's a topic we know something about, though if you asked, we would probably politely suggest that it's everyone else who's influenced. Yet if each of us is immune to advertising's impact, how come so many people instantly connect slogans like "Just do it" and "It's finger lickin' good" to Nike and KFC respectively.

Advertising – the genre we love to hate, the quintessential symbol of American society from the eyes of Doctor T. J. Eckleburg in *The Great Gatsby* to TV's *Mad Men* – is showcased every day on television and each time you glance at Instagram or your Facebook News Feed. It's on buses and billboards, elementary school classrooms, YouTube, and cell phones. It is on subway turnstiles, which bear messages for Geico car insurance; in bus shelters, where "Got milk?" billboards emit the smell of chocolate chip cookies; and even in major league baseball stadiums, where, in a deal concocted by the New York Life Insurance Company, a player who is called safe at home plate triggers the appearance of the company's logo on the TV screen and the announcer must state, "Safe at home. Safe and secure. New York Life" (Sandel, 2012; Story, 2007). As if this were not enough, marketers are pervasively present on social media, with promoted brand tweets on Twitter, and personalized location-sensitive alerts on smartphones that let consumers know when they are approaching a store carrying branded merchandise (Wingfield, 2014).

Image courtesy of Nike

Advertising: It is the most real of communications, for it promotes tangible objects – things, stuff, and goods. It's also the most surrealistic, most unreal of mass communications. It shows us "a world where normal social and physical arrangements simply do not hold," critic Sut Jhally (1998) observes. "A simple shampoo brings intense sexual pleasure, nerdy young men on the beach, through the wonders of video rewind, can constantly call up beautiful women walking by, old women become magically young, offering both sex and beer to young men," he notes.

Advertising has been universally praised and condemned. It has been cheered by those who view it as emblematic of the American Dream – the notion that anyone with money and moxie can promote a product to masses of consumers, along with the promise, cherished by immigrants, that an escape from brutal poverty can be found through purchase of products and services not available in more oppressive economies. Advertising has been roundly condemned by those who despise its attack on our senses, its appropriation of language for use in a misty world located somewhere between truth and falsehood, and its relentless, shameless exploitation of cultural icons to sell goods and services (Cross, 1996, p. 2; Schudson, 1986; see Figure 15.1). The "all-seeing eye" of tailored advertising is a target of criticism in George Saunders' novel, *In Persuasion Nation*, depicted as devices embedded in the sidewalk that extract digital information from strips in two characters' shoes, the images beseeching them to visit a Burger King restaurant nearby (Saunders, 2006; Marantz, 2019, p. 107).

Figure 15.1 Advertising, Which Has Been Widely Praised for Its Ingenuity and Condemned for Its Attack on Our Sensibilities, Works by Exploiting a Sophisticated Understanding of the Social Psychology of the Mind
Image courtesy of Shutterstock

Advertising, a focus of this chapter, is a complex, colorful arena. It is paid materialist speech – messages for which companies pay in order to shape, reinforce, and change attitudes. (And they pay handsomely for these messages, to the tune of more than $5 million per 30-second ad during the Super Bowl.) Advertising operates on a micro level, subtly influencing consumer behavior. It also works on the macro level, serving as the vehicle by which capitalist society promotes goods to masses of consumers.

In recent years, advertising, notably on TV, has struggled, with national sales of television ads peaking in 2016, and companies redirecting their advertising dollars to Google, Facebook, and YouTube (Maheshwari & Koblin, 2018). Kylie Cosmetics, the beauty and skin care brand launched by Kylie Jenner, generates enormous social media engagement on Instagram, but reportedly spends little or nothing on paid advertisements (Williams, 2019). Increasingly advertising has given way to *marketing*, the broader term that refers to the activities and processes by which a society communicates products and services of value to masses of consumers.

Marketing is pervasive on social media. We see it pervasively with influencer marketing that capitalizes on young savvy, entertaining YouTube personalities, subtly or transparently promoting products, along with peer influencers, kid influencers, mom influencers, super-influencers, and even virtual influencers, the latter raising ethical concerns. Digital marketing is now the norm, a pastiche of strategies to recruit attention, shape attitudes, and build loyalty to that quintessential marketing concept: The brand. A *brand* is the core of a product, service, or organization that communicates meaning to consumers. *Branding* is the process of defining a commercial entity so that it is perceived as unique and different, and can be quickly called to mind (Newman & Newman, 2018). You know brands. Apple, Amazon, Google, Disney, Netflix, Starbucks, Budweiser, and Hershey's are among many popular brands that have molded consumer attitudes. Persuasion is at the heart of this, offering theories and research that underpin the ways advertising, marketing, and branding influence attitudes and behavior.

This chapter covers a lot of territory. I begin by discussing the complexities of subliminal advertising, debunking a common myth, move on to discuss two psychological theories of advertising effects, and ethical quandaries. The next portions of the chapter focus on marketing, particularly the psychology of influencer marketing, practical implications, and the ethical conundrums of privacy-encroaching online marketing.

The Subliminal Myth

It began, appropriately enough, in the 1950s, a decade in which post-World War II Americans were bewildered by all manner of things, ranging from reports of flying saucers to the successful Soviet launching of a space satellite. In 1957, the same year the Soviets sent up Sputnik, an enterprising marketer named James Vicary reported an equally jarring set of facts. He arranged for a drive-in movie theater in Fort Lee, New Jersey, a suburb of New York City, to beam the words "Drink Coca-Cola" and "Eat popcorn" for less than a millisecond during the romantic movie *Picnic*. Vicary immediately proclaimed success. He claimed an 18 percent rise in Coke sales and a 58 percent increase in popcorn purchases, compared with an earlier period.

The nation's media were shocked, *shocked*. Minds have been "broken and entered," *The New Yorker* (somewhat facetiously) declared on September 21, 1957. The National Association of Broadcasters forbade its members from using subliminal ads. One writer, convinced that subliminal messages had dangerous effects, wrote several best-selling books on the subject. Wilson Bryan Key claimed that subliminal stimuli were everywhere! "You cannot pick up a newspaper, magazine, or pamphlet, hear radio, or view television anywhere in North America without being assaulted subliminally," Key announced (1974, p. 5). He claimed that advertisements for cigarettes, liquor, and perfume contained embedded erotic pictures that caused people to march off and buy these products, like brainwashed automatons from the old film *Coma* (see Figure 15.2).

You yourself may have heard the term *subliminal* or *subliminal advertising*. It's easy to locate the words on the Web. There are dozens of websites with names like "Subliminal Advertising and Modern Day Brainwashing" and "7 Sneaky Subliminal Messages Hidden in Ads." Reflecting this belief in the power of subliminal ads, over 70 percent of respondents in scientific surveys maintain that subliminal advertisements are widely used and are successful in promoting products (Rogers & Smith, 1993; Zanot, Pincus, & Lamp, 1983). In a similar fashion, many people believe that subliminal messages in rock songs manipulate listeners. Some years back, parents of two men who committed suicide charged that the rock group Judas Priest had induced their sons to kill themselves. The parents claimed that Judas Priest had subliminally inserted the words "Do it, do it" underneath the lyrics in a morbid song called "Beyond the Realms of Death." (The parents lost the case.)

Beliefs are powerful entities. In the case of subliminal advertising, they can drive fears and influence emotions. Researchers, curious about subliminal message effects, have long studied the impact of

Figure 15.2 Advertising Images That Play Up Sexuality are Commonly Assumed to Contain Embedded Subliminal Messages. They almost never do. In fact, advertised sexual appeals influence consumers not through "subliminal seduction," but because they psychologically connect with individuals in subtle, yet powerful, ways
Image courtesy of Shutterstock

subliminally embedded words and pictures. Their conclusion: *There is little evidence to support the claim that subliminal ads influence attitudes or behavior.* To appreciate how scholars arrived at this judgment and what it tells us about the psychology of advertising, we need to examine the research on this issue.

Definition

In the popular view, subliminal advertising means powerful advertising that appeals to emotional, even unconscious, needs. Given this broad definition, it is not surprising that many people believe advertising is subliminal. Scholars define "subliminal" differently – and far more precisely. *Subliminal perception* occurs when stimuli are "discriminated by the senses," but are transmitted in such a way that they fail "to reach conscious awareness and cannot be reported verbally" (Dijksterhuis, Aarts, & Smith, 2005, p. 80).

More simply, subliminal perception is perception without awareness of the object being perceived. It is "sublimen," or below the "limen" or threshold of conscious awareness. Making matters more complicated, the limen is a hypothetical construct, not one that is always easy to pinpoint.

Applying this perceptual concept to advertising is not a simple matter and is far more complicated than glib commentators like Key assume. But if one struggles to apply it to advertising, in order to put popular ideas to the test, we could say that a *subliminal advertisement* is one that includes a brief, specific message (picture, words, or sounds) that cannot be perceived at a normal level of conscious awareness. This definition excludes many appeals commonly associated with subliminal ads. Commercials that contain sexy models, erotic images, vibrant colors, haunting images, or throbbing music are not, in themselves, subliminal. Why? Because the erotic or colorful image appeal is right there – you see it or hear it and, if someone asks, you could tell her what you saw or heard. Product images that have been strategically placed in movies are not necessarily or inherently subliminal (see Box 15.1). A subliminal ad – or, more precisely, one that contains a message that eludes conscious awareness – is a very different animal.

BOX 15.1

Product Placements

Placement of products into movies, television shows, and video games has become so commonplace it is difficult to imagine an era in which anyone raised eyebrows about the practice. Products are placed increasingly into video games, like the automobile racing game *Gran Turismo*, and have been enhanced by online streaming (Shoenberger & Kim, 2019). Annual spending on product placement stretches into the billions.

What is a *product placement*? It is defined as a paid communication about a product that is designed to influence audience attitudes about the brand through the deliberate and subtle insertion of a product into media entertainment programming. Product placements are similar to advertisements in that they are paid attempts to influence consumers. However, unlike advertising, which identifies the sponsor explicitly, product placements do not indicate that a sponsor has paid for the placement of a product into the media program. Because product placements disguise the attempt of a persuader to influence attitudes, they are regarded by some scholars as less ethical than advertising (Nebenzahl & Jaffe, 1998), and advertising is a medium that has not exactly been free of ethical condemnation.

The issue of disguised attempts to influence raises the question of whether product placements are subliminal messages. One could argue that product placements are so incidental to the plot that they are processed on a subliminal level. But recall that subliminal perception occurs when stimuli are detected by the senses but fail to reach conscious awareness, even when attention is directed at them. Product placements are usually transmitted above the threshold of conscious awareness, and people are ordinarily aware they saw a branded candy bar or automobile that was inserted into a movie.

Theories offer insights as to why placements can be effective (Cowley, 2012). Mere exposure and association (discussed later in this chapter) have interesting implications. Repeated exposure to the product over the course of a movie, TV show, or video game can promote positive attitudes. Conditioning and association processes operate, producing a favorable linkage between an attractive character and the brand. ELM processes also can operate. For low-involvement products, the placement serves as a peripheral cue. When consumers already harbor an attitude toward the product or can elaborate on the brand, the placement might stimulate thinking about the product.

Narrative perspectives suggest that consumers may elaborate more on placements when they are integrated into the plot or dramatic theme of the entertainment program (see McCarty, 2004). In a study of placements of beverage and candy products in several movies (e.g., *The Client* and *Legally Blonde*), Yang and Roskos-Ewoldsen (2007) found that viewers recognized the brand more when it was central to the story or was used by the main character than when it was shown in the background. Greater involvement with characters or enjoyment of the program in which the brand is embedded can enhance positive attitudes toward the product, as well as influence children's snack consumption (Nelson & Waiguny, 2012; Matthes & Naderer, 2015; for other research, see Trifts & Aghakhani, 2019; Guo et al., 2019).

There are, of course, limits to product placement effects. Just because viewers recognize or recall a product does not mean they will choose the brand. What's more, it is possible that psychologically memorable product placements can have a boomerang effect. Vividly recalling the placement, viewers may recognize that an advertiser is trying to influence them, resent this influence, and feel reactive toward the product (Nabi & Moyer-Gusé, 2013). And yet marketers' ability to devise ever-more-clever product placements should not be underestimated. As advertisers increasingly promote products in native advertising, influencer marketing, and social media apps, promotional content merges seamlessly with other content on the site, as when influencers, with the skill of a magician, mention a branded product as they talk about the emotional ups and downs of their day. These can make promotions more difficult to recognize for what they are – product promos, hawked by persuaders wielding old wine in new digital bottles.

Subliminally embedded messages exist, though. The key question is: How common are they? A study of advertising executives found that few, if any, advertising agencies strive to develop subliminal ads (Rogers & Seiler, 1994). In view of the powerful impact that ordinary ads exert, it doesn't make much sense for advertisers to rack their brains to embed subliminal messages in commercials. Besides, if the news media ever found out that an agency had slipped a subliminal spot into an ad, the bad press the advertiser would receive would overwhelm any potential benefits of the subliminal message.

Does this mean there are no subliminals anywhere in the media? Not quite. In a country as big as the United States or as cosmopolitan as nations in Europe, with so many creative, ambitious (and slippery) characters, it seems likely that a handful of advertising practitioners subliminally embed sexy messages in ads. (They could do this by airbrushing or using high-powered video editing techniques to insert subliminals in ads, including those that pop up on the Internet.) The major question is: What impact do subliminal messages have on consumers' attitudes or behavior?

Effects

It is important to distinguish between subliminal perception in theory and subliminal perception in the reality of advertising. People can perceive information on a subliminal level and, under certain circumstances, stimuli processed subliminally can affect judgments (Bargh & Pietromonaco, 1982; Bornstein, 1992). But just because something can happen in a rarefied laboratory setting does not mean it does or is likely to happen in the noisy, cluttered world of advertising. Let's review the research.

The first evidence of subliminal advertising effects came in Vicary's report on the effects of "Drink Coca-Cola" and "Eat popcorn" messages. At the time, his study seemed to suggest that subliminals could potently shape human behavior. But when scholars peered beneath the surface, they discovered that his research had serious flaws. In the first place, there was no control group, an essential requirement of a scientific experiment. Thus, there is no way of knowing whether moviegoers bought more popcorn and Cokes because they happened to be hungry and thirsty that particular day. It is even possible that the movie itself stimulated sales; it was named "Picnic" and showed scenes of people enjoying food and drinks!

More seriously, Vicary never released his data or published his study. Publication and open inspection of data are basic principles in scientific research, and Vicary's reluctance to do so casts doubt on the validity of his results. Shortly after Vicary's findings were revealed, a respected psychological firm tried to replicate his study under controlled conditions. Using more rigorous procedures, the psychologists reported no increase in purchases of either Coke or popcorn. In 1958, a Canadian broadcast network subliminally transmitted the message "Phone now" 352 times during a Sunday night TV show. Telephone calls did not rise during this period, and no one called the station (Pratkanis, 1998).

These results cast doubt on the subliminal thesis, but do not disprove it. A more rigorous test involves evaluating results from dozens of carefully conducted experiments. Researchers have designed and conducted such studies, embedding messages in ads at levels that elude conscious awareness, making sure subjects could not consciously recognize the subliminal primes to which they had been exposed. Researchers also have compared the responses of experimental group participants who received the subliminal stimuli with control group subjects who viewed a similar message without subliminals. The findings have stimulated lively debate among scholars. Although a handful of researchers make the case for subliminal advertising effects, they frequently confuse subliminal perception or processing with subliminal advertising effects. They also ignore the preponderance of data that show subliminal messages have few negligible influences on consumer attitudes or behavior (Theus, 1994; Trappey, 1996).

But – some curious readers may object – isn't it possible that the instantaneity and interactivity of social media might make it easier for subliminal messages to penetrate the mind? Indeed, there is experimental evidence that subliminals embedded in new technological formats can exert an impact, particularly when they match individuals' levels of motivation (Bermeitinger et al., 2009; see also Karremans, Stroebe, & Claus, 2006; Fennis & Stroebe, 2010). For example, Bermeitinger and her colleagues found that exposure to a subliminally presented brand logo for a dextrose, sugar-type pill increased pill consumption, but only when participants were tired.

This is interesting research and we need to keep an open mind. People can perceive or process stimuli at subliminal levels and theoretically can be affected by what they see, though apparently only in the short run and when particular conditions are met (Strahan, Spencer, & Zanna, 2002). However, it is one thing to say that subliminal perception occurs and quite another to jump – no, leap – to the conclusion that subliminally embedded stimuli in ads affect purchase intentions or, as is commonly believed, that advertising mainly works through subliminal, unconscious, even Freudian, processes. The handful of studies demonstrating subliminal effects were well-crafted laboratory experiments, but these create surroundings that are very different from the multifaceted, multitasking-focused real world of media in which consumers live. The effects occurred in the short term only and did not mirror the contexts in which people must decide which products to purchase.

Do online ads encourage subliminal effects? Despite understandable speculation that online plat-forms might exert subliminal effects, there are shortcomings in the thesis. It is not clear that individuals should be more susceptible to subliminal advertising messages relayed online rather than on television or film, with their immersive qualities. Given the sheer volume of other activities people do while online, the chances that a subliminal message seeps into the mind are relatively low. There is also pre-ciously little evidence to substantiate this claim. This may seem surprising, in view of what you may have read on this topic. However, it makes good psychological sense. More generally, there are five reasons why one should not expect subliminally transmitted messages to influence consumer attitudes or behavior:

- *There is little documented evidence that subliminal messages are embedded in advertisements.* Claims that ads are subliminal frequently confuse subliminal and supraliminal messages. Yes, ads have plenty of sex – but it is right out there on the surface, arousing, appealing, and associated with the product. Sexual appeals are not inherently subliminal. YouTube videos that purport to show subliminal effects can be cleverly photoshopped. Why would advertisers include a sexual message in an advertisement, knowing their actions could be unmasked, publicized, and ridiculed on Twitter?
- *People have different thresholds for conscious awareness of stimuli.* To influence a mass audience, a subliminal message would have to be so discreetly beamed that it reached those with normal thresholds of awareness without catching the "attention" of those who are exquisitely sensitive to such stimuli. This would be difficult, perhaps impossible, to achieve using contemporary media. Screen sizes and clarity levels vary greatly. A message that is perceived at subliminal levels on tele-vision might never be noticed on small smartphone screens.
- *There is no guarantee that consumers "see" or interpret the message in the manner that advertisers intend.* (For example, "Drink Coca-Cola" and "Eat popcorn" moved so quickly across the screen that some moviegoers may have seen "Stink Coke" or "Beat popcorn." This could have had the opposite impact on some viewers.)
- *For a subliminal message to influence attitudes, it must, at the very least, command the viewer's absolute attention.* This can happen in the experimenter's laboratory (Cooper & Cooper, 2002), but is not so likely to occur in the real world. People are frequently distracted or doing other things when they watch TV, or are second screening on their mobile devices, switching from one platform to another.
- Let me be clear: It *is* possible that a subliminal message could be perceived on a subconscious level. A sexy picture might "enter" a subterranean portion of the mind. Big deal. *For soon after the picture is*

processed, it is apt to be overwhelmed by the more powerful images or sounds depicted in the advertisement – the luscious features of the model that can be processed instantly on a conscious level, the obvious beauty of a mountain scene, or jingle-jangle of the advertiser's song. These attention-grabbing pictures and sounds will swamp the subliminal embed. Just because a message is "in" an ad does not mean it gets "inside" consumers for very long – or at all. It would be hard for a subliminal embed that matches individuals' motivation – a subliminally embedded soft drink ad presented when consumers are thirsty – to exert the same impact it might have in the laboratory because the image could be easily swamped either by competing messages or by potent superliminal ads for the thirst-quenching drink. After all, if subliminal persuasion were this easy, subliminals would be in every ad in every technological medium, and all the creative directors at advertising agencies would be very rich.

Placebo Effects and Beyond

There is continued debate about the impact of subliminal advertising, and this is as it should be. Recent studies make it clear that such effects are theoretically possible, making this a matter of continued psychological interest. But the absence of real-world evidence, coupled with the daunting impediments to meaningful subliminal effects, casts doubt on the thesis that subliminally presented advertisements are a major influence on brand attitudes or behavior. The more interesting question is whether the *belief* that subliminals are powerful might itself influence attitudes toward a product. Anthony G. Greenwald and colleagues suspected that it could. As true-blue social scientists, they decided to test their intuition. They examined attention on a different kind of persuasive communication: Therapeutic self-help audio tapes (they would be health care apps now). The researchers focused on the tapes' claim that subliminally embedded messages could help listeners solve personal problems.

Greenwald and his associates observed that some self-help tapes promise to enhance self-esteem by subliminally beaming messages like "I have high self-worth and high self-esteem" (Greenwald et al., 1991). Others attempt to improve memory skill by claiming to subliminally transmit messages like "My ability to remember and recall is increasing daily." These words might be embedded underneath sounds, like waves lapping against a shore. Knowing the research as they did, Greenwald and colleagues doubted that such subliminals would have any impact. However, they suspected that consumers' expectations that the subliminals were effective might strongly influence beliefs.

In an elaborate study using careful scientific procedures, Greenwald and his associates (1991) obtained strong support for their hypothesis. Individuals who heard an audiotape that contained the subliminal message "I have high self-worth" did not exhibit any increase in self-esteem. In addition, those who listened to the tape that contained the "My ability to remember is increasing" message did not display improvements in memory. But the belief in subliminals' impact exerted a significant effect. Subjects who thought they had been listening to a tape designed to improve self-esteem (regardless of whether they actually had) believed their self-esteem had improved. Individuals who thought they had been listening to a memory audiotape (regardless of whether they had) were convinced their memory had gotten better!

The researchers argued that what they had discovered was "an illusory placebo effect – placebo, because it was based on expectations; illusory, because it wasn't real" (Pratkanis, 1998, p. 248). Indeed, the findings exemplify a classic *placebo effect*, where a placebo, an artificial or inauthentic treatment, influences behavior because individuals, assuming it is real, attribute power to the treatment. A placebo effect occurs when individuals' expectations about a treatment cause them to alter their cognitions or behavior in a way that leads to an actual impact on behavior or thoughts.

Notice that a placebo effect operates on the conscious level, not the secretive, subconscious level at which subliminal ads are supposed to work. And, ironically, it is the conscious level at which subliminal ads may have their greatest impact. Actually, it is not the ads that exert the impact, but rather the *perceptions* of their effects that are influential. Thus, perceiving that memory and self-esteem tapes would improve their memory and self-esteem (because of the assumed, magical power of subliminals), participants in Greenwald's study figured their memory and self-esteem had gotten better. Conscious expectations, not subconscious perceptions, carried the day.

In view of the exaggerated notions of subliminal message effects, the interesting question is not the objective impact of subliminal stimuli, but the subjective issue. Why do so many people continue to be convinced that these teeny-tiny, sometimes-weird, messages have so strong an impact on attitudes and behaviors? Laura A. Brannon and Timothy C. Brock put forth several explanations for the persistence in belief in subliminal communications, including the assumption that "if something exists it must be having an effect" (1994, p. 289). People also yearn for simple explanations of complex phenomena like advertising, and the subliminal thesis gives them a foolproof, conspiracy-type theory that seems to explain all of advertising's powerful influences on consumers.

With this in mind, perhaps next time you read that liquor ads contain subliminally embedded faces or bikini-clad women, you might step back a moment and ask yourself a few questions. First, what evidence is there that these faces or scantily dressed women are actually in the ads, rather than a figment of the writer's sexually active imagination? Second, even if they are "there," what evidence exists that they influence perceptions? Third, assuming that the stimuli influence perceptions (a large "if"), how realistic is it to assume that they influence consumers' attitudes or behavior? By approaching advertising this way, you will quickly recognize that the mad search for subliminals takes you down the wrong trail in the quest to understand advertising effects. By the same token, it is important not to dogmatically take a diametrically opposite approach, in which we assume that consumers are consciously aware of every feature of an advertisement.

Gray Areas

Even though subliminal advertising messages do not influence viewers in real-world contexts, other subtle commercial appeals *can* affect individuals' feelings and thoughts, without awareness. Sometimes product placements and clever ads that tell heartrending stories can tug on the heartstrings. These are not necessarily subliminal appeals, because viewers can tell you the gist of what they consciously saw. But viewers may not realize how Super Bowl ads that seamlessly associated a man's love of a Clydesdale horse with Budweiser, linked the goodness of a farmer with a Dodge Ram truck, or blended patriotic images of soldiers with a Chrysler Jeep instantly aroused their emotions. People can be conscious of the literal message they saw, but not be entirely aware of how immersed they were in the deeper emotional subtext of the advertisement, or of the meaning they attach to the ad, let alone the reason they were affected by the commercial.

As L. J. Shrum and his colleagues (2013) point out, when consumers saunter through a store, they may be consciously aware that music is being piped into the background. But they may not appreciate that the musical tempo can influence the speed at which they shop for goods. A department store may play slower music to induce consumers to shop for a longer amount of time and shell out more money, while a fast-food restaurant may play fast-paced rock and roll to induce people to leave and increase the turnover of customers (see also Nurit, 2019).

In these instances, the stories employ priming appeals (see Chapter 5). They use music to prime feelings they hope will be connected with the retail establishment. Note that these aren't direct appeals, with overt messages on behalf of the store or brand, and they don't contain embedded subliminal messages, as would be suggested by the popular, simplistic subliminal thesis. We need to differentiate between *subliminal content* embedded in a message, which these stimuli do not contain, and *subliminal or less-than-conscious processing* of marketing messages, which can happen and sometimes influences consumer behavior. The latter concept – subliminal processing – is much different than the popular idea that messages with subliminally hidden content seduce, even brainwash consumers.

In sum, there are a variety of ways that marketing and advertising appeals can influence consumers' thoughts and feelings. Some of these work on a conscious level, others on a less conscious level. Sorting out what is very conscious from what is less conscious is a complicated business. From a persuasion perspective, the important point is that advertising appeals can influence the mind in many different ways, cleverly tapping into a variety of mental and emotional processes. In the next sections, I examine theories that help pinpoint these processes, helping us appreciate the many, seemingly magical but actually psychological, ways that advertising influences consumers (see Table 15.1).

Mere Exposure

More than 40 years ago, a news story appeared that has nothing – yet everything – to do with advertising:

> A mysterious student has been attending a class at Oregon State University for the past two months enveloped in a big black bag. Only his bare feet show. Each Monday, Wednesday, and Friday at 11:00 A.M. the Black Bag sits on a small table near the back of the classroom. The class is Speech 113 – basic persuasion ... Charles Goetzinger, professor of the class, knows the identity of the person inside. None of the 20 students in the class do. Goetzinger said *the students' attitude changed from hostility toward the Black Bag to curiosity and finally to friendship.*
>
> (Zajonc, 1968, p. 1)

Table 15.1 Concepts Explaining Advertising and Marketing Effects

ADVERTISING

- Mere Exposure
- Association Principles
  - Classical Conditioning
  - Semiotics
  - Accessibility

MARKETING (INFLUENCER MARKETING)

- Similarity
- Likability
- ELM: Cognitive Elaboration and Heuristics

This story illustrates a fundamental postulate of Robert B. Zajonc's *mere exposure* theory: Through repeated exposure to a neutral stimulus, an individual comes to evaluate the stimulus more favorably. According to the theory, all that is necessary is repetition. The more frequently an individual is exposed to a novel object, the more favorably he or she evaluates it.

Mere exposure has emerged as a robust theory of advertising effects. According to the theory, simple exposure to communications can influence attitudes. Merely seeing a message repeated over and over again leads to liking (Zajonc, 1968). This is a familiar experience. The longer you gaze at a painting in a museum, the more times you hear a hip-hop song on your Apple iPhone, and the more frequently you see an advertisement on TV, the more you come to like these stimuli.

Notice that mere exposure makes a prediction opposite to common sense. You have probably heard that "familiarity breeds contempt" or that "absence makes the heart grow fonder." Mere exposure theory suggests that those are nice ideas, but they do not accurately describe how advertising shapes attitudes.

The first studies of mere exposure examined responses to nonsense words, Chinese characters, and photographs – all of which were totally unfamiliar to student participants. Zajonc (pronounced zyance) deliberately chose to manipulate exposure to unfamiliar stimuli in order to provide as pure a test as possible of mere exposure theory. In this way he could be sure that whatever treatment differences were obtained were entirely due to the manipulation of mere exposure.

In a classic study (Zajonc, 1968), subjects were asked to pronounce a variety of nonsense words (e.g., afworbu, civrada, jandara, nansoma, iktitaf). Frequency of exposure was varied and order was counterbalanced so that each word was pronounced 0, 1, 2, 5, 10, or 20 times. The results supported mere exposure: The more frequently a word was pronounced, the more positively it was evaluated. Incredibly, although these words were absolutely incomprehensible to the subjects, with each repetition the words (like the student encased in the black bag) came to elicit a more positive reaction (see Figure 15.3).

Other studies obtained similar findings. With repeated exposure, Chinese characters, men's graduation pictures, and even Pakistani music (a genre unfamiliar to most students outside Kabul) gained in positive affect (Rajecki, 1982). Research over the past decades has provided continued support for the theory, with evidence suggesting that repeated exposure to advertising also enhances favorable attitudes (Grush, McKeough, & Ahlering, 1978).

Why Mere Exposure Works

Mere exposure places more importance on form than content. It is the format – repeated exposure to a neutral stimulus – that matters, not the content of the ad. All that is needed is *mere* exposure.

There are a variety of explanations of the mere exposure effect (see Fang, Singh, & Ahluwalia, 2007). One possibility is cognitive – that messages are easier to process and encode when they have been seen or heard before (Bornstein, 1992). Other researchers argue that people attribute higher credibility to messages they repeatedly receive, believing these message recommendations are more likely to be correct (Koch & Zerback, 2013; Montoya et al., 2017). This may be because they rely on a heuristic that "what has been repeated at different times is true," or because they assume that if the communicator has the resources to repeatedly advertise, he or she has developed a credible product.

A related explanation is more complex: Consumers infer that advertisements that come more quickly to mind as a result of mere exposure are ones they like a lot. Another view is simpler, emphasizing accessibility (Courbet et al., 2014). With greater exposure to an ad, a positive attitude may simply be more accessible.

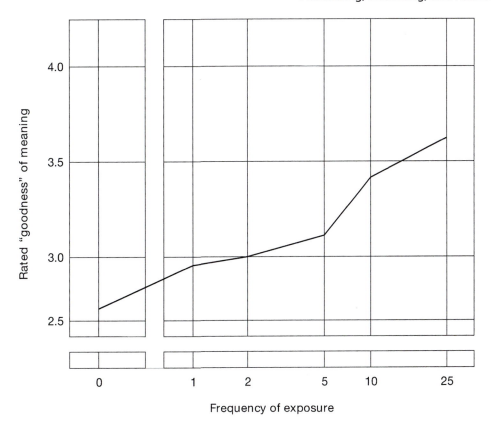

Figure 15.3 Mere Exposure to Nonsense Words
Image from Zajonc (1968).

A final explanation is more affective, emphasizing the pleasures that come from increased familiarity with an advertisement. According to this view, the first exposure brings an uncomfortable sense of unfamiliarity as different cognitive responses compete for attention. Over time, one settles in on a particular reaction and the ensuing calm is pleasant. The first time television viewers saw the old Taco Bell ad in which the little Chihuahua utters, "Yo quiero Taco Bell" ("I want Taco Bell"), they probably were a little confused by the phrase and put off by the presence of a smirking, talking dog in an ad for a fast-food franchise. But with repetition, they got used to the ad, adjusted to the smug little dog, and developed a sense of what would occur as the quirky ad unfolded. The more they saw the ad, the more comfortable they felt and the more they liked it.

A similar process could have occurred for the "Can you hear me now?" ads for Verizon cell phones; MasterCard's cute, but incessant, repetition of "For everything else, there's MasterCard"; and McDonald's "I'm lovin' it." In all these cases, the more people saw the ads, the more comfortable they felt, the more they resonated to the ensuing feeling of predictability and calming sensations. People made fun of the old Charmin toilet paper ads ("Please don't squeeze the Charmin"). However, the ads apparently worked, as Charmin, never known to consumers before, captured a significant share of the market after its non-stop advertising campaigns. People ridiculed Charmin, but the company's executives had the last repeated laugh, en route to the bank!

When Mere Exposure Is Effective

Is repetition a panacea, a factor that always works? No way! Mere exposure is most effective under certain conditions. First, it works best for neutral products and issues, those to which we have not yet developed a strong attitude. It explains how advertising forms attitudes toward products, not how it *changes* them.

Second, once people have developed an especially negative attitude toward a product, company, or politician, repetition cannot change the attitude. In fact, it may have the opposite effect, producing more negative affect toward the issue as people ruminate about how much they hate the fast-food product, big corporation, or obnoxious politician (Tesser, 1978).

Third, mere exposure works only up to a certain point. After a certain number of exposures, repetition leads to boredom, tedium, and irritation. A phenomenon known as *wear-out* occurs (Bornstein, 1989; Solomon, 1999). Early in the mere exposure curve, repetition is a positive experience, reducing uncertainty, inducing calm, and bringing on a certain amount of pleasure. After a certain point, repetition has the opposite effect, and people become annoyed with the ad or come to resent its attempt to persuade them (Koch & Zerback, 2013). Repetition ceases to induce positive affect; it may produce reactance, negative feelings toward the ad or product, and a curvilinear relationship between exposure and liking (Monotya et al., 2017; see Figure 15.4). This is one reason why companies like McDonald's

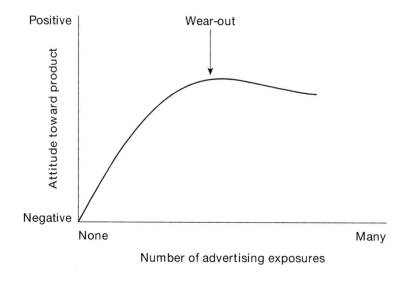

Figure 15.4 Repetition, Advertising, and Wear-Out. After a certain number of repetitions, advertising can lead to wear-out

and Coke frequently switch slogans and change advertising agencies. They want to prevent wear-out and preserve the effect of a novel campaign slogan.

It is not just television or traditional media that capitalize on mere exposure principles. Sports marketing specialists cash in all the time. Brands like Toyota exploit the concept when they pay $80,000 to have their logos shown on video scoreboards during a college football game. Coca-Cola does the same when it pays at least $100,000 to own the branding in the tunnels and corner boards at a University of Alabama football game (Drape, 2015).

Social media also can be a tributary for the flow of repetition effects. Many companies now have geofilters on Snapchat, images or branded tags that appear when users snap a picture of themselves at a restaurant, store, theme park, or commercial location. Overlaid on photos or videos individuals post on Snapchat, the digital stickers are linked with particular locations, so that individuals can decorate a post of themselves or friends at McDonald's with an illustration of the Golden Arches, a visit to Disney World with a picture of Mickey Mouse, or a date at the ballpark with a photo of the verdant baseball field. The location-specific digital emblems show up when individuals or others check their Snapchat app, offering a bonanza of repeated exposures to the brand. Of course, the brands are already well known to users – they're not neutral stimuli. But theory suggests that, until wear-out occurs, these branded snaps can add luster and positive affect to attitudes toward McDonald's, Disney World, and a host of companies that capitalize on these digital imprints.

The Magic of Association

There is a marvelous McDonald's ad that was popular some years back. When students watch it, they invariably smile warmly. The ad begins with a football coach lecturing a team of eight-year-old boys. He intones, "A great man once said, 'Winning, gentlemen, isn't everything, it's the only thing.'" Suddenly we hear one of the boys, obviously oblivious to the coach's serious tone, shout, "Look, a grasshopper." All the youngsters jump up to take a look. The coach throws down his hat in mock despair. Another coach, kneeling down, says seriously to one of the boys: "I-formation, 34 sweep, on 2. Got it?" When the boy, doing his best to understand but obviously bewildered, shakes his head, the coach says, "Just give the ball to Matt. Tell him to run for his daddy, okay?" The boy nods happily.

As the camera pans the oh-so-cute boys in their blue uniforms, shows us the misty, but picture-perfect, football day, and lets us watch the players do push-ups while fathers feverishly peer through video cameras to record their sons' every movement, we hear the narrator say, "It starts every September with teams like the Turkey Creek Hawks and the Bronx Eagles." Alas, these September days are about more than just winning football games, the narrator goes on to suggest; they're about dads and sons, good times, and – now the pitch – where you go after the game. Soft, sentimental music builds as the scene slowly shifts to what must be a later point in time – the boys smiling and enjoying themselves at McDonald's, no doubt chomping down burgers and fries. And so, the narrator intones, the scene moving back to football, McDonald's would like to salute the players, coaches, and team spirit that are part of these fall September rituals. The visual then profiles a boy, looking up at the "winning isn't everything" coach. "Can we go to McDonald's now, Coach?" he asks. Patiently, kindly, but firmly, the coach notes, "Sit down, Lenny. It's only halftime." The music, playing softly in the background, trails off and fades, as the ad gently comes to a close.

The advertisement illustrates the principle of association. It associates the good feelings produced by football, boys playing pigskin on weekend afternoons, and autumn with the fast-food franchise, McDonald's. McDonald's has not told us the reasons why its hamburgers are tasty (that might be a hard sell, given what we know about fast-food diets!). It has not provided cogent arguments that dining at McDonald's is a healthy, useful activity for budding athletes. In fact, the ad has provided neither argument nor logic. Instead, it has employed the rich language of emotion, telling us a story, associating McDonald's with positive, pleasant images that are peripheral to the purchase decision. If you tried the same technique in a job that required you to provide arguments why clients should purchase your product, trying to associate your product with good times while humming a sentimental tune, you might be fired! Yet McDonald's succeeds because the world of advertising is not purely or primarily rational. It invariably prefers emotion to syllogistic logic. It frequently favors Aristotle's pathos to his deductive logos.

Association and Branding in Action

There are a multitude of examples of the use of association in advertising, illustrating the harnessing and exploitation of psychological concepts (see Figure 15.5).

(a)

(b)

(c)

Figure 15.5a–c Association Is Used All the Time in Advertising. By associating products with pleasant, exciting, and beautiful images, advertisers hope the products will take on these desirable attributes. As these examples illustrate, advertising can promote associations for healthy and unhealthy products by calling up an associative memory network of images, fantasies, and feelings

Advertisements fundamentally try to build in positive associations between the product and positive images. Super Bowl ads for Jeep, Ram Trucks, and Coca-Cola are classics, blending emotional images with their products. Fast-food chains like McDonald's, Burger King, and Kentucky Fried Chicken harness association all the time, linking the company brand with kids, birthday parties, and health (yes, you read that right, they try to persuade consumers that their products are healthy). In this way they try to build what psychologists call an associative memory network, so that consumers will call up these positive images when thinking about a fast-food restaurant (Kimmel, 2013).

Without question the most noteworthy and graphic example of advertised associations is sex. Displays of nudity, sexual allusions, sexual behavior, and physical attractiveness are … everywhere, it seems – in ads on television, in magazines, and on the Internet, the latter employing virtual models that are drop-dead gorgeous and spectacularly thin (Lambiase, 2003; Reichert, 2003).

Advertisers dream up product names by appeals to association, implicitly calling on linguistic aspects of brand names, psycholinguistic theories of word meaning, and the ways phonemes in a name can communicate meaning, an idea that dates back to Plato (Johnson, 2011, p. 71; Surowiecki, 2016). As one writer observed, calling on the original meanings of the words, "Corvette is a light, speedy attack ship; Tesla was an inventor of genius … Lexus evokes luxurious; Viagra conjures virility and vitality" (Surowiecki, 2016, p. 35). These are only the tip of the iceberg (also a semantically rich phrase). There's also Juul, a semantic creation based on two homophones: The splendiferous "jewel" and scientific "joule" (a unit of energy; Jackler et al., 2019). One study even found that consumers who ate ice cream called "Frosh," with its creamy-sounding vowel, liked it better than people who consumed the same ice cream, called "Frish," with its frigid connotations (Surowiecki, 2016).

There are also the more familiar examples: *Ivory* soap, *Cheer* detergent, *Splash* iced tea, and in the technology area, the internationally famous *Apple*, *BlackBerry*, and *Twitter*. Explaining how product names call on the associational power of metaphor, linguist Christopher Johnson, who helped coin names like these, notes that:

> the names Apple and BlackBerry metaphorically use the look and feel of fruits to add vividness to technological products. The name Twitter uses the cheerful sound of birds as an instantly recognizable aural image for a new multivocal form of communication.
>
> (Johnson, 2011, p. 71)

Association techniques constantly evolve, adapted to the tastes of a current generation. Young adults like brands to express values, displaying a conscience on issues spanning climate change, environmental protection, and social justice. While conscience is not exactly the kind of attribute one thinks of when conjuring corporations, the yearning for a brand with values pushes companies to advertise their association with environmentally friendly choices, like wildlife, as the dishwashing liquid, Dawn, has done with "Tough on grease, yet gentle on feathers" or Nike did, embracing controversy by selecting Colin Kaepernick, the former San Francisco 49ers quarterback, famous for kneeling during the national anthem to protest Black oppression, as the face of the 30th anniversary of its "Just Do It" campaign (see Figure 15.6). Of course, associating a brand with au courant social values (frequently, it seems, more of the left-wing variety) dates back decades, and it remains in play today.

Associating a brand with one side of a controversial issue is not without risks. It may work for international companies like Nike, which have long been linked with hot-button issues, or niche firms that make their business from products, like feminine hygiene and reproductive health. Failing to take a stand with customers who buy these politically laced products may be perceived as pusillanimous,

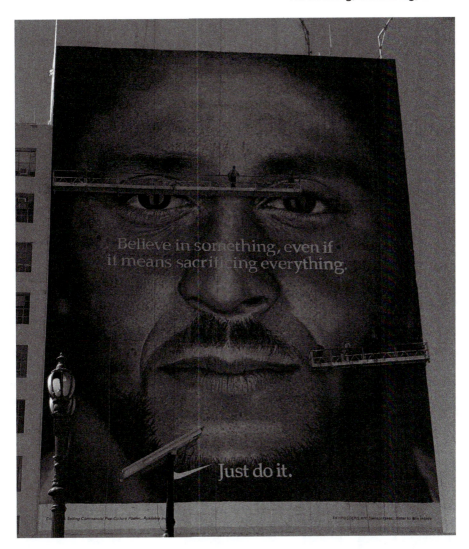

Figure 15.6 Brands Sometimes Invite Controversy, Believing That It Showcases Social Conscience, Melding With the Values or Edginess of the Company. Nike did this by selecting Calvin Kaepernick, the former San Francisco 49ers quarterback, famous for kneeling during the national anthem to protest racism against Blacks, as the face of the 30th anniversary of its "Just Do It" campaign. The compelling tagline, "Believe in something, even if it means sacrificing everything," fits Nike's marketing-sculpted image and trumpeted a stirring commitment to social justice

Photo courtesy of Getty Images

the death knell of authenticity that conveys a jaw-dropping insensitivity. But a symbolic relationship with an unpopular figure can also polarize consumers. Indeed, there is evidence that a third of the people who disagree with a company's political stance would boycott the company, and over half would make fewer purchases, illustrating the power that associations (of a less positive kind) exert on brand behavior (Perloff, 2019).

Branding Unhealthy Products

There is also a dark side. As a weapon of persuasion, association has been exploited in morally offensive ways, as in the classic twentieth century ads that paired deadly cigarettes with relaxing images, and more recently, e-cigarette promos that linked the ever-popular Juul with a variety of pleasant, life-is-great images. Juul created sleek, association-based ads and trendy posts, with messages that promoted e-cigs to young people on Twitter, Facebook, and Instagram. Juul's posts, colorful and catchy with its name in bold trademark capital letters, featured cool-looking young people posing flirtatiously with their Juuls, attractive young women with taglines like "Vaporized," and a couple rapturously kissing, Juul in hand (Richtel & Kaplan, 2018; Jackler et al., 2019; see also Jo et al., 2019; Paek et al., 2014).

Its campaigns, capitalizing on suggestive sexual images, social media influencers, highly publicized launch parties, and youth-oriented appeals that evolved to meet the changing market, are classic association appeals. Eerily calling on the same strategies as ads for tobacco-stained cigarettes which preceded them, appeals for e-cigarettes on YouTube and other domains link the product with sexuality freedom, and independence (e.g., Willis, Haught, & Morris, 2017; see Figure 15.7). The reality is much bleaker, of course. E-cigarette use can provoke vomiting, damage lungs, and cause addictions, even death – and they have, in increasing numbers (Kaplan & Richtel, 2019). No matter. The campaigns helped launch the product, established the brand, and recruited an immense young audience, some of whom used

(a)

(b)

(c)

Figure 15.7a–c These Juul Ads, Calling on Some of the Same Association Strategies Tobacco Commercials Used to Hook Smokers, Linked Juul With Youth, Sexuality, Freedom, and Good Times With Friends, Using Trendy Images and Slogans. The ads, distributed on YouTube or other media outlets, helped promote Juul as the desirable anti-cigarette for millions of young adults – until reality set in, and harmful, even deadly, consequences ensued

Juul to dump cigarettes, others who minimized its risks, and still others who suffered serious physical ailments (Kim et al., 2019). Indeed, even though Juul halted print, broadcast and digital advertising in the wake of bad publicity the e-cigarette received, it had already cultivated a positive association with youth and fun, quite the opposite of some of the e-cigarette's lingering effects. Such is the nefarious power of association.

Thus, association is perhaps the most important reason why advertising succeeds. It explains why things – including those with no inherent value – acquire powerful meanings in consumers' eyes. Scholars have advanced several theories to explain how association works. They include *classical conditioning*, *semiotics*, and *accessibility*.

Classical Conditioning

The granddaddy of association concepts, conditioning, dates back to Pavlov. "Does the name Pavlov ring a bell?" Cialdini (2009) asks humorously, reminding us of the Russian psychologist's century-old study that paired an unconditioned stimulus (food) with a conditioned stimulus (bell) to produce a conditioned response (salivation to the bell). Psychologists have long applied classical conditioning to social learning, particularly attitude acquisition (Staats & Staats, 1958).

In a similar fashion, consumer psychologists have shown that attitudes toward products can be classically conditioned through association with pleasant images. Stuart, Shimp, and Engle (1987) paired a neutral stimulus ("Brand L toothpaste") with higher-order stimuli (nature scenes such as a mountain waterfall or a sunset over an island). For experimental group participants, the toothpaste and beautiful nature scenes were linked over the course of a number of conditioning trials. For control subjects, the toothpaste and nature scenes were presented in random order with respect to each other. The researchers found that experimental group subjects who were exposed to the pairing of toothpaste and beautiful natural scenes displayed significantly more positive attitudes toward Brand L toothpaste than did control group subjects (see also Till, Stanley, & Priluck, 2008).

Classical conditioning processes, complex as they are, help us understand how people develop favorable attitudes toward products (Bouton, 2016). However, they have drawbacks. Conditioning employs a rather clunky, mechanistic terminology that does not capture the ways that contemporary advertising operates. Focused as it is on unconditioned stimuli and conditioned responses, it does not appreciate the powerful role that symbols play in advertising or the mental processes by which people come to link images with brands. Advertising does not stamp in associations in the way that Pavlovian learning conditions behavioral responses, even if contemporary conditioning research acknowledges the role cognition plays. Ads form associations in a much more fluid and complicated process that involves a dynamic, complex cognitive network of associated images, constructions of meaning, and affect. Classical conditioning is a real and important phenomenon. However, it has limited utility in explaining contemporary advertising, let alone the interactive world of online marketing. Thus, to appreciate the way association works in advertising, we need to consider other perspectives.

Semiotics

Semiotics is the study of signs and symbols. It helps us understand how signs – visual objects or geometric shapes with no inherent meaning – take on a rich tapestry of social and cultural meaning. A symbol is a sign with substance – a sign that bursts with value and emotional signification. The Cross and Star of David are shapes, but as symbols they are much more. The Cross symbolizes Jesus's crucifixion and redemption – an emblem of Christian love. The Star of David, a six-pointed star formed by superimposing two equilateral triangles, is a symbol of Judaism and Jewish culture.

Advertising thrives on signs. It transforms signs into symbols that give a product its meaning or "zip" (Goldman & Papson, 1996). Take a look at the signs in Figure 15.8. Glance first at Coca-Cola, closing your eyes to gain a clearer fix on the image. Do the same for McDonald's, the Nike swoosh, and the iPhone. What comes to mind? Images, feelings, pictures, people? I'd be willing to bet they did, even if you don't like the products or purchase them. Such is the power of advertising. It attempts to fill commodity signs with meaning, to give value to brands, and to stamp imagery onto products that sometimes differ only trivially from their competitors. Consider that classic entry in the sneaker wars, the Nike swoosh, which was discussed earlier in the chapter.

Figure 15.8a–d Well-Known Signs and Symbols in American Advertising (see also Goldman & Papson, 1996)

Robert Goldman and Stephen Papson offer a historical perspective:

> Once upon a time, the Nike swoosh symbol possessed no intrinsic value as a sign, but value was added to the sign by drawing on the name and image value of celebrity superstars like Michael Jordan. Michael Jordan possesses value in his own right – the better his performances, the higher his value. The sign of Nike acquired additional value when it joined itself to the image of Jordan.
>
> (1996, p. 10)

This was the Nike "advertising sign machine" of the late 1980s and 1990s, featuring associations between the swoosh and Jordan; Bo Jackson, the professional athlete; and movie director Spike Lee. Since then, Nike has embarked on numerous ad campaigns, including ones that feature commercials resembling MTV videos – brilliant, but blatant, attempts to associate the swoosh with images resonant with a younger market. Nike, innovatively blurring fashion and athletic wear, has increasingly positioned itself as a fashion brand, with ad campaigns showing super-models like Karlie Kloss working out in Nike sportswear (Friedman, 2016). Nike, like other advertisers, strives constantly to redefine its image in the eyes of new market segments through ever-inventive ways of combining signs with in-vogue celebrities, trends, and images, exemplified by its release of an inspirational ad shortly after the U.S. women's soccer team won the World Cup in 2019 that depicted the victorious players not just as athletes, but as advocates of equal rights.

From a more theoretical perspective, semiotics, the underpinning of ads like these, does not explain how advertising creeps into the minds of consumers. It is a theory of message content, not message effects. To understand associative advertising impact, we must turn to cognitive psychological concepts. Consider that advertising shapes attitudes toward products by helping to forge an association between the product and a pleasant, memorable image. Once the attitude is formed, it must be retrieved or accessed, particularly at the moment when consumers are making a product decision.

Accessibility

If you want to see accessibility in action, consider an old-fashioned appeal that appears on a here-and-now social media network, Twitter. The ad begins with a series of images of children frightened and looking to their mothers for support: An African American girl terrified by a tornado, as sirens sound, consoled by her mother; a White girl riding in a car as it swerves, unnerved and afraid, told by her mother "you're okay, you're okay"; an Asian boy and his mother shaken by an electric malfunction in an elevator, the boy gaining solace from his mother's support. After each childhood image, the scene switches to the child, now an Olympic athlete, anxious at the start of a gymnastics, volleyball, or diving event, visualizing these moments, gaining confidence from the comfort their mothers long ago offered, performing with excellence to the roars and adulation of the crowd, as the child's eyes meet the mom's at the moment of victory, as piano chords softly tingle in the background. The tagline, simple, saccharine, but remarkably effective, is: "It takes someone strong to make someone strong. Thank you, Mom." The montage of images, the commonality of mother–child love all the more poignant because of the racial diversity emblematic in the ad, elicits goose bumps and near-tears of joy, as the ad ends, somewhat awkwardly but gracefully, with a display of different products – Tide, Bounty, Pampers, all made by Proctor and Gamble. The announcer intones "P&G, Proud Sponsor of Moms."

The ad is all about accessibility – the notion, at least in its elemental form, that when people access product attitudes from memory, the affect and attitudes stick with them and can push them to buy the product. Research discussed in Chapter 5 more pragmatically suggests that the more exposure consumers have to advertisements that plant the association between a product and image, the more they can quickly get in touch with their attitude when they are trying to decide which soft drink, fast food, or sneakers to purchase. Advertisers recognize this and design messages to encourage consumers to call up attitudes from memory (see Shrum et al., 2013).

Thus, McDonald's ads try to induce consumers who are in the mood for fast food to call up the feelings they had when they watched an ad like the one described earlier in the chapter. Coke tries to access years of internalized associations between its product and positive images. These include mid-twentieth-century linkages between Coca-Cola and patriotic appeals that call to mind artist Norman Rockwell; the classic 1971 song that associated Coke with global, ethnic diversity ("I'd like to buy the world a Coke and keep it company. It's the real thing"); and current multicultural campaigns that span Egypt, Saudi Arabia, and South Africa.

Other advertisements employ similar strategies. The American commercial icon Campbell's Soup spent much of the twentieth century building powerful linkages between its product and down-home days with Mom and Dad (albeit of the White variety). Campbell's ads seemingly left an imprint, as one consumer acknowledged:

> Campbell's tomato soup is the only one that will do. It's like a cozy, comforting thing. It tastes good mainly because you associate it with what it did for you when you were a kid. Maybe it doesn't even taste that good, but somehow it works on a level beyond just your taste buds.
>
> (Langer, 1997, p. 61)

Association appeals can even succeed in convincing consumers to buy products that have no distinctive qualities. Case in point: Bottled water. Blind taste tests reveal that most people cannot tell the difference between bottled and tap water. One researcher arrayed ten bottles of water on a table, including one filled with water from the tap. He asked participants in his informal study to rate samples from each bottle for flavor, aftertaste, feel, and appearance. The majority could not discriminate among the group; indeed, they could not correctly identify the bottle that contained tap water (Standage, 2005). If taste is not the reason why millions buy Aquafina, Evian, Fiji, and other brands, why has bottled water become so popular? A major reason is that bottled water has become fashionable, linked with purity, cleanliness, and good health. "Advertisers used words (*pure, natural*) and imagery (waterfalls, mountains) to imply that bottled water tasted better and was healthier than tap," a writer notes (Royte, 2008, p. 34).

The images that advertising calls up are represented as webs of associations, or associative memory networks, in our minds. Figure 15.9 shows an associative memory network for several fast-food chains, suggesting the advertising and marketing images these restaurants try to access to induce consumers to purchase food at these restaurants.

Summary

In these diverse ways, marketing builds associations into signs, products, and brands. It transforms things into symbols of hope, desire, and status (Langrehr & Caywood, 1995; McCracken, 1986). Nike shoes are not sneakers but, rather, emblems of excellence, pronouncements of athletic ability, exemplifying "the idea of transcendence through sports" (Hess, 2018). Objects gain this majesty through associational appeals in advertising and the projections of consumers.

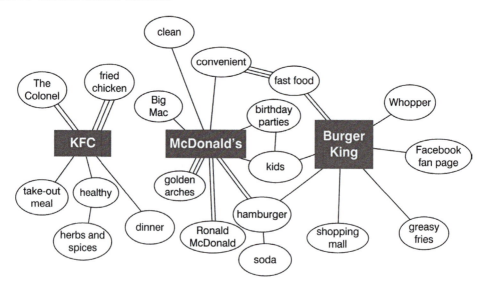

Figure 15.9 Associative Memory Network Depicting Images Called Up by Three Fast-Food Restaurant Chains

From Kimmel (2013, p. 107)

Although ads do not always exert this impact – the floors of advertising agencies are littered with footage from unsuccessful media campaigns – ads can potently influence affect toward products via the power of association. In light of advertising's widely recognized ability to shape product attitudes – through association and mere exposure – it is little wonder that people unschooled in advertising effects leapt onto the subliminal seduction bandwagon. They presumed the effects had to be subliminal, with all its sexual connotations, neglecting the role that more psychologically substantial factors exert on brand attitudes. Ads aren't always effective, as noted above – and their effects are the subject of complex studies in the psychology of advertising. But when they influence consumers, they have exquisitely activated principles of association, as well as accessing, priming, and the duller, but influential, mere exposure. But there is also another concept that also comes to the fore in contemporary marketing, one that calls on all these theoretical ideas in different ways.

Celebrities as Persuasive Cues

When consumers are in a low-involvement mode – as most are when they encounter ads for soft drink, lip balm, paper towel, and toothpaste – celebrities can serve as compelling peripheral cues. Celebrities or other endorsers are particularly apt to enhance consumer attitudes when their characteristics "match up with" or are relevant to the product being promoted (Chew, Mehta, & Oldfather, 1994; Lynch & Schuler, 1994). This is known as *the advertising match-up hypothesis*. It has received considerable research attention and has empirical support (Wright, 2016). The match between celebrity and product can involve athletic success (tennis star Venus Williams endorsing Reebok sneakers), looks (Kylie Jenner's full lips as a cue for her lipstick), and qualities created strictly through fictional entertainment (Jim Parsons, the geeky nerd of *Big Bang Theory* fame, promoting Intel).

Celebrities exert complex match-up effects. They can work via peripheral cues or through the central route by offering a strong argument for an endorsed product when the celebrity's expertise matches up with, or is relevant to, the product (Lee & Koo, 2016). At the same time, there are times when a moderate mismatch between a celebrity and product (Brad Pitt promoting a candy bar) can generate interest, sometimes enhancing the associative transfer from the celebrity to the brand (Lee & Thorson, 2008). The success of a match or moderate mismatch between a celebrity and product depends both on the advertised association and the ways consumers relate to the celebrity, pointing up the role that receivers' construction of meaning plays in advertising effects.

Match-ups can be very effective, if crafted creatively. Nike famously and imaginatively has harnessed match-ups. Its brand conveys athleticism and grace, and the company has selected a legion of sports stars to serve as product representatives. Endorsers, who often simply wear a hat with a salient swoosh, include American basketball stars LeBron James, as well as international tennis greats like Serena Williams, and U.S. soccer star Megan Rapinoe (see Figure 15.10).

Celebrity characteristics can net advertisers millions, but they also can be persuasive liabilities. After Olympic swimmer Ryan Lochte fabricated a story of being robbed at gunpoint in Rio de Janeiro in 2016, Speedo USA and the luxury clothing company Ralph Lauren ended their endorsement deals with Lochte.

In a similar fashion, ex-New England quarterback Tom Brady – who endorsed Ugg, the fancy sheepskin footwear, and Under Armour, a sports clothing company – experienced a drop in his trust ratings in the wake of news reports that he probably participated in the tampering with footballs

(a)

(b)

(c)

Figure 15.10a–c Celebrities Can Pack a Powerful Persuasive Punch in Advertising. Celebrity, superstar athletes like LeBron James, Serena Williams, and Megan Rapinoe influence consumer attitudes by tapping into positive associations, accessing preeminent symbolic connections (like the globally iconic Nike swoosh) and serving as peripheral cues. Celebrities, being celebrities, can also lose their luster, which can tarnish the allure of the brand, though not among uber-loyal followers

Images courtesy of Getty Images

during an American Football League Conference Championship game in 2015. With news reporting over a period of months that Brady was probably aware that the Patriots deliberately under-inflated footballs, which can make the ball easier to hurl and catch, his image plummeted.

On the other hand, considering the ways morally blemished celebrities of yore, like Winona Ryder (arrested for shoplifting) and Kate Moss (allegations of cocaine use), reinvented themselves, it is possible that Brady's brush with Deflategate, as the football scandal is known, may have elevated his brand, lending a certain risqué edge to his image (Friedman, 2015).

At the same time, when celebrities utter bigoted remarks – as when YouTube megastar PewDiePie made virulent anti-Semitic remarks – corporate brands like Disney and Google cut their ties (Friedman, 2017). However, loyal followers, who help sustain YouTube influencers' reputations on social media, can maintain faith in their favorite celebrity, derogating corporations for their decisions to cut off YouTube celebs like PewDiePie, holding fast to their beliefs in ways that are psychologically predictable, but morally offensive.

Ethical Issues

Research has established that advertising and marketing shape attitudes toward products. But, as philosophers remind us, "is" does not constitute "ought": Just because media exert effects does not mean these impacts are ethically or normatively good. Let's explore the ethical conundrums and normative issues surrounding advertising, with a focus on social media issues examined later in the chapter.

It is helpful to begin with philosophy. A utilitarian perspective emphasizes the balance between pleasure and pain, the positive and negative consequences of modern marketing. It highlights how advertising creates memorable images that convince consumers to purchase high-tech products they love, but also the litany of cigarette (and later e-cigarette) advertisements that sowed the psychological seeds of addiction; mediated messages extolling an ultra-thin physique that have pushed young teenage girls to become dissatisfied with their body images; and ubiquitous fantasy sports ads of DraftKings and FanDuel that can propel risk-taking young men to become addicted to online gambling.

Complementing these utilitarian criticisms, a deontological approach emphasizes that the test of ethical communication is whether it treats individuals as an ends, not a means, and operates from honorable motives. Viewed in this way, advertising can fall drastically short of an ethical ideal. Advertisers develop ads that make promises they know products can't deliver. Cigarettes don't offer hedonistic pleasure; cars don't make you rich or famous; and making pancakes for your kids on Saturday won't assuage your guilt about neglecting them all week, despite the plaintive plea of a Bisquik pancake commercial. And while many people experience lots of pleasure from their smartphones – even to the point of falling in love with an intelligent operating system in the movie, *Her* – advertising for personalized gadgets may promise human rewards, but can't deliver on the emotions that make us happy.

Advertisers want consumers to project fantasies onto products in order to hook individuals on the image of the brand. Viewed from a Kantian perspective, advertising is not ethical because advertisers are not truthful. If the decency of the communicators' motives is the criterion for ethical communication, advertising fails. Advertisers deliberately construct fantasies to serve their clients' needs, not to aid the customer in living a healthier, happier life.

In response to these criticisms, defenders of advertising emphasize that consumers recognize that advertising creates untruths. They do not expect ads to tell them "the way things really are in society," Messaris (1997) notes. "Almost by definition," he says, "the portrayals of the good life presented in ads carry with them the implicit understanding that they are idealizations, not documentary reports"

(p. 268). In effect, advertising defenders say, "Don't worry; be happy." Advertising is capitalism's playful communication, an attempt to give people an outlet for universal human fantasies.

In the view of defenders, advertising and marketing offer a wealth of positive utilitarian outcomes. They convey information about how to possess nifty things that people desire. Marketers argue that advertising does not create a need for products, but responds to consumers' craving for the latest gadget or thing. Relax, chill out, marketers say; ads aren't forcing people to buy things they don't like. Advertising does not coerce consumers, defenders remind us; instead, ads and online promotions merely give people what they want. On a macro level, advertising keeps the engines of the free market economy rolling. It increases demand and allows companies to sell products, prosper, and employ managers and workers. Yes, critics say; we don't object to advertising as a macro institution, and we know people bear responsibility for their decisions. But what if company executives who know tobacco or fantasy sports have addictive effects continue to aggressively market their products, placing the profit margin ahead of the health of vulnerable consumers? When does business bear responsibility for ads that exert harmful effects? Where do you draw the line between individual choice and corporate responsibility?

The Psychology of Social Media Persuasion

With international e-commerce sales surpassing more than $1 trillion annually, you have to believe that persuasion is involved, and in some practically important ways (DeAndrea et al., 2018). Social media companies like Facebook sell data – yours, mine, our friends' – to marketers, who develop specific microtargeted messages based on this information, harnessing facts about consumers to develop persuasive appeals (Kosinski, 2018). As a Facebook engineer noted, "We know who you are as a person …We know what pages you've 'Liked.' We know what ads you have hidden in the past or said that you didn't want to see more of. We can combine all that to ensure that the ads you do see are relevant" (Metz, 2015). These raise ethical questions, as will be discussed later in the chapter.

From a persuasion perspective, it's basic: Marketers tailor promotional messages to the psychological profile of an individual consumer, using digital technology to make the connection between message and mind more psychologically salient, as well as exploiting the geometric fact that there is less room for ads on mobile phone screens than laptops, affording ads a more pronounced position on ubiquitous smartphones (Metz, 2017). Instead of gearing a message to a super-broad demographic, online promoters engage in *microtargeting*, in which they tailor a message so it is in sync with particular consumers' interests or, ideally, a particular consumer's specific buying, social, and political preferences.

Microtargeting isn't a theory, and its effectiveness undoubtedly varies. The underlying psychological postulate is this: The more your message matches the psychology of the target, the more likely he or she will perceive personal connections with the product, elaborating more centrally and feeling more affect toward the ad or product itself. Although microtargeting gets lots of buzz and is assumed to work, of course it doesn't always or perhaps even most of the time. Nonetheless, the concept is consistent with classic persuasion principles and is continuing to evolve in more sophisticated ways.

Influencer Marketing

This is the face and voice of contemporary marketing. Ceili Lynch, an enterprising teenage girl from Mount Vernon, New York, sits at her computer in her bedroom, tweeting about a big bombshell film release, hoping to promote the flick with her online peers across the world. As Ceili explains, "basically, it's just, like, one person finds out, it goes to … two more people, and then it just kind of, like, multiplies" (Generation Like-Transcript, 2014).

Except there is more to the marketing campaign than this. Ceili is not liking and sharing posts so avidly simply because she really loves the movie. Ceili is both consumer and marketer, a promoter who hopes to gain get online rewards for her tweets, presumably from the movie studio that has put her to work, in what it hopes will be a two-way conversation that will generate buzz online. What seems oh-so-spontaneous tweeting has been manipulated from afar. In marketing parlance, it is all about influence, part of what is called influencer marketing. Yes, the techniques are different than in the past, with new technological overlays and a strategic attempt to make a highly managed, manipulated campaign seem like a spontaneous online brushfire. However, the concepts that underline contemporary social media campaigns call on classic persuasion theories that span source attributes and the ELM.

In the era of digital marketing, companies rely much less on traditional advertising to promote their products, exquisitely aware that television ratings have declined and the bulk of their young adult audience is online, comfortable with new forms of commercial outreach. Into this breach has stepped *influencer marketing*, a promotional strategy that calls on communicators who have clout and resonance with their audience, signified by a substantial social media following. Influence marketers include celebrities (like Bella Hadid, with 25.8 million Instagram followers), "super-influencers" (like beauty sage Negin Mirsalehi, 5.5 million Instagram fans), and the ever-disclosing, infectiously likable Emma Chamberlain (8 million YouTube followers; see Figure 15.11).

Influencers also include ordinary, marketing-savvy young people who connect the brand and consumer through sponsored blog posts, as well as young adults with as few as 1,000 followers, who are willing to post on behalf of brands on Instagram or serve as on-campus brand ambassadors in exchange for a modest commission or free samples. There are loads of influencers who promote prosaic products like lawnmowers, as well as YouTube fitness influencers (like Jeff Nippard) who peddle fitness programs and nutritional plans to body building aficionados.

Psychological Processes

Influencer marketing is a fancy term with digital bells and whistles that emphasizes a time-honored strategy: Use credible, socially attractive communicators who activate positive thoughts, as well as feelings about the brand.

Similarity is seen as a persuasion plus. Just as a movie franchise hoped that Ceili Lynch's earnest posts would appeal to fellow teens, Johnson & Johnson called on adolescent Instagram users with about 500 followers to endorse its Clean & Clear product line, presuming that teenager influencers who struggle with acne themselves would be perceived as more believable than clearer-skinned celebrities who peddle different products (Marikar, 2019; see also Maheshwari, 2018a).

Similarity is big on the college marketing circuit, as literally thousands of college students across the U.S. harness their Instagram accounts to promote corporate brands online. Companies have long turned to college students to serve as ambassadors for their clients, but now the focus is online promotion, giving marketers a double whammy: Similarity of promoter to college student consumer, coupled with a complementary visual message (product promotion that adjoins the student promoter's photos of friends and family). It's an effort to cash in on students' perceptions that if a similar other endorses a product, it would be a good bet they will like it too.

Isabel Senior, a Duke University student, posted one Instagram photo, an Instagram story, and a message on another social media platform about LaCroix for six weeks. The company hoped that students who incessantly checked their Instagram, Snapchat, and Facebook accounts would notice the down-to-earth persuasive appeals, enhanced by their narrative effects, and feel more positively toward the brands. (Intriguingly, Isabel was paid for her work, but if she didn't complete an assignment, she was docked some pay; see Ballentine, 2018).

Research shows that online messages sent by personal communicators – those who are part of individuals' personal networks, like friends, family members, and classmates, who were on one of their social media accounts – significantly influence willingness to participate in online social activism-related activities (Nekmat et al., 2019). Interestingly, *cognitive elaboration* mediated these effects, indicating, in accord with the *ELM*, that personal communicators induce greater online thinking about the message, which in turn bolstered behavioral intentions.

The most subtle – and insidious – influencer marketing ploy that derives from theory is the familiar harnessing of "likes" and favorable online responses. Recognizing that people rely on a *heuristic* that "what is popular is good," marketers have sought to aggressively manipulate the number of "likes" a product obtains, using online reps like Ceili Lynch to recommend a product. It's all based on

(a)

Figure 15.11a–c Influencers and super-influencers like Emma Chamberlain, Bella Hadid, and Negin Mirsalehi, with very different persuasion styles, are the new cutting edge of online marketing, until the next trend comes along.

(b)  (c)

Figure 15.11a–c *(continued)*

the ELM insight that people rely on peripheral processes to make judgments when they lack the ability or, more likely, motivation to make a decision (Chang, Yu, & Lu, 2015). It may seem silly or foolish to rely on "likes" when making your decision, but, as the ElM reminds us, we can be peripheral processors, susceptible to others' ministrations.

Corporate brands harness these heuristics, hoping that consumers scanning Instagram will think to themselves, "If 10,000 people online are following them" (the youthful influence marketers), "maybe I should start paying attention to them, too" (Maheshwari, 2017). It is complex, as you may recall from Chapter 8. The number of online followers can theoretically fulfill different functions, serving as an argument, catalyst for thinking, or a factor enhancing confidence in consumers' cognitive assessments of the message. In any case, strictly from a logical reasoning perspective, the fact that 10,000 or 100,000 people follow a product is not a particularly worthwhile or diagnostic reason to purchase the brand.

Number of followers has drawbacks as a persuasion technique. An influencer with thousands or millions of followers may reduce perceptions that the brand is unique and right for "me." If so many people follow the brand influencer, consumers may reason, maybe it's just a clichéd popular brand – one that does not fit *my* unique needs (De Veirman, Cauberghe, & Hudders, 2017).

Other conditional effects have also emerged. Intriguingly, research indicates that online customer reviews may have a greater impact on less well-known and less-established brands in a product category than on their better known and more regarded counterparts (Ho-Dac, Carson, & Moore, 2013).

Stronger, more valued brands tend to be systematically processed, with consumers holding stronger attitudes that are insulated from online comments. Weaker, less well-known brands may benefit from online tweets, which can serve as peripheral cues and helpful heuristics in decision-making.

In any case, the sheer number of tweets or followers is not the only process by which influencers shape attitudes. Message and source content matters, including the visual appeal of posts, influencers' expertise, physical attractiveness, and ability to relate with fans (Ki & Kim, 2019). Influencer can attract followers, in turn shaping brand attitudes through their online spontaneity and likability, which encourages adolescent followers to engage in the ultimate form of flattery toward these product endorsers: purchasing the product online (Ki & Kim, 2019).

It's psychologically intricate. Consider how Kim Kardashian famously marketed her SugarBearHair gummy vitamins, designed to improve the gloss and glisten of women's hair (see Figure 15.12). Kardashian, with an eye-popping 149 million Instagram followers, a celebrity influencer par excellence,

Figure 15.12 Celebrity Influencer Kim Kardashian Has Marketed SugarBearHair Gummy Vitamins, With Her Famous Hair Serving Multiple Branding Functions, As Suggested by the ELM. This illustrates the ways celebrities call on their credibility to influence millions of followers (with varying degrees of success, of course), as well as the way that a venerable psychological theory sheds light on the magic of marketing

serves as a peripheral cue for those low in involvement in taking care of their hair, an argument (Kim's own gorgeous hairstyle and texture) for those highly involved in grooming their hair, a catalyst for processing among those in moderate elaboration likelihood, and an endorser whose recommendations bolster followers' confidence that purchasing gummy vitamins is the right decision for them. The psychology is complicated, but the apparent success of the vitamins due to Kim Kardashian's ELM-based endorsements is priceless, even as questions remain about the vitamins' bona fide effects on the sheen of women's hair.

Practical Implications

It's not just Kim.

Influencer marketers are on the front lines of countless campaigns dreamed up by advertising agencies in cities across the nation. Some years back, the innovative Cleveland-based advertising and marketing agency, Marcus Thomas, developed a social media campaign to persuade 18–34 year-old women to remove their makeup before going to sleep. Their marketing research showed that only about half of young adult women take off their makeup before they fall asleep, which can clog pores, aggravate acne, and irritate the skin. And voila, this became the foundation – no pun intended – of a campaign for Swisspers makeup removal wipes. (It isn't clear, by the way, that sleeping with makeup presents any dangers, from a dermatology perspective, though it may contribute to some irritation or block pores. The marketers clearly wanted to make this case to promote the product.)

And so, calling on a little verbal jujitsu, the marketing gurus dubbed the campaign "Sleep Naked," using "naked" as a double entendre to call attention to the perceived importance of sleeping with no makeup covering the face. They recruited five well-known, attractive female influencers with a sizable following to promote the campaign, placed their makeup-free photographs on social media, eliciting lots of fan tweets, and followed this up with a National Sleep Naked Night event on Twitter, with six beauty bloggers and the five influencers adding their endorsements. Fans voted for the makeup blogger they liked best and shared content online. A follow-up campaign featured two competing teams in a Sleep Naked Face-Off – the familiar, but ever-popular, blondes versus brunettes competition.

And guess what? The hashtag #SleepNaked began trending, captured attention from you-know-who (the Kardsashian sisters), and garnered more than 70 million social media impressions, all on behalf of a relatively unknown brand. A subsequent study found that about 25 percent of young adult women said they remembered the campaign, and 8 percent recalled specific posts (Ewing, Engler, & Modarelli-Frank, 2015). The campaign – coordinated by agency specialists, including Jim Sollisch, Heidi Modarelli-Frank, and Scott Chapin, and a host of others – won a national award for the best social media advertising, and enhanced Swisspers' reputation (Orsini, 2019). You can see why; that "Sleep Naked" motif is catchy.

Psychologically, the campaign called on mere exposure (message repetition for a novel product), similarity, physical attractiveness, and evidence that online campaigns can work more effectively on unfamiliar brands (Ho-Dac et al., 2013). Its long-term effects are more difficult to assess, as it is methodologically challenging to demonstrate that media campaigns influence consumers' brand attitudes. Indeed, there is voluminous research on how to empirically assess marketing campaigns, with measures running the gamut from trending on social media metrics to semantic differential-measured brand attitudes. The Sleep Naked campaign may have enhanced short-term brand awareness, but that's only the first step in building a successful brand. Whatever the ambiguities of measurement, there is little question that the influencers created some Swisspers buzz, highlighting the importance of circumventing traditional advertising via influencers and reliance on mobile phones to reach young consumers.

And yet, like all marketing strategies, influencer marketing is no panacea; it does not always work. Influencer endorsements interact with dozens of factors, including consumers' preexisting product attitudes, receivers' ability or motivation to process the message, functions the product serves, and the particular heuristics employed. But it capitalizes on persuasion and is a big business, creating wealthy influencer YouTube celebrities.

(It turns out that – channel eye roll – that becoming a YouTube celebrity may require hard work, e.g., Bromwich, 2019. See also the wickedly funny YouTube satires of comedian Colleen Ballinger – YouTube nom de plume Miranda Sings – that make fun of narcissistic, verbally inept YouTube personalities.)

As natural or self-taught persuaders, influencers hone their theatrical skills, tailoring their message to a target audience, exemplifying the endless, creative ways people devise to promote themselves, playfully and artfully. The down and difficult side is ethics, the ways influencers wittingly or unwittingly can manipulate consumers. Federal Trade Commission guidelines state that if there is a tangible connection between an endorser – or influencer – and the brand that could influence how consumers evaluate the endorsement, the influencer should disclose this openly (The FTC's Endorsement Guides, 2017). Of course, influencers may not always do this explicitly, or do so in a blurred-line, deceptive way that exploits followers' trust.

Ethical Quandaries

The diffusion of digital technologies has led to increasing penetration of consumers' personal space. Digital advertisers use start-ups to track consumers online, employing sophisticated devices that allow them to track consumers' locations as frequently as 5,000 times over a two-week period (Zuboff, 2019). A student shopping for a durable backpack can now thumb through backpack websites and before she knows it, an advertisement for an "awesome" backpack brand will follow her everywhere online, loading in her Facebook feed, showing up on Instagram on her phone, and even popping up on news sites in her web browser that have no connection with backpacks (Chen, 2018).

Ever-more savvy tech companies, like the ubiquitous Facebook, harness an array of data-mining software, enhanced by artificial intelligence, that collect biometric facial information. This allows advertisers to monitor users' online activities, encompassing their purchasing preferences, political interests, and their geographical location, tracked by their app, at a given time in the day (like the time they attended a yoga session), all the more useful for the yoga mat company to hit them up later with an online ad (Singer, 2018a; Valentino-DeVries et al., 2018).

Marketers maintain that these techniques, felicitously called "personalized retargeting," are morally acceptable, noting that they have been used for years in one form or another and are not especially intrusive. Some consumers confess that they are delighted when they learn of a new gadget, wardrobe, or hot product through an adroitly targeted online ad. It saves them time and money they would otherwise have spent shopping online or at the mall.

Others beg to differ, raising philosophical objections.

Retargeting or personalization "illustrates that there is a commercial surveillance system in place online that is sweeping in scope and raises privacy and civil liberties issues," said one privacy advocate (Helft & Vega, 2010, p. B2). One mother and father who recently purchased a software program to keep track of their children's activities online were appalled when they learned the company was selling information about their kids to third-party marketing companies.

It is a classic case of weighing the utilitarian benefit to companies (and consumers) against the psychological costs experienced by individuals when they realize their privacy has been hijacked. It involves considering whether the many opportunities consumers receive from an Internet that minimizes privacy exceed the social drawbacks. Ultimately, one must balance a desire not to intrude on the free market with an appreciation that privacy violations raise deontological issues, telegraphing disrespect for an individual's right to withhold information about the self from strangers with unknown motives. Although Google and Facebook argue that we need to adapt to the inevitability of an all-is-public online world, others worry that the rich and powerful businesses "know a lot more about us than we know about each other – and sometimes, more than we know about ourselves" (Pariser, 2011, p. 147). What concerns critics is the lack of symmetry between what the powerful know about the powerless and the powerless know about the powerful.

In recent years, the imbalance has slid much more palpably toward the powerful, in the wake of revelations about tech companies' ability to extract personal information from consumers, running the gamut from their relationship status to their biometric facial data, invariably without their formal consent. As Peter Eckersley, the chief computer scientist at a digital rights firm noted:

> Facebook can learn almost anything about you by using artificial intelligence to analyze your behavior. That knowledge turns out to be perfect both for advertising and propaganda. Will Facebook ever prevent itself from learning people's political views, or other sensitive facts about them?
>
> (Singer, 2018a)

It is a fair question, and so far the answer for Facebook and other technology, is No, or at least not voluntarily.

Facebook has shared user information with Microsoft and Amazon without gaining explicit permission. It has given third-party apps access to personal data, even though the social networking company said the apps could only get information they needed to run their programs. Google lets businesses share data from users' Gmail accounts, using consumers' smartphones to scrutinize their behavior. Target permits companies to gather information from people who visit their websites or mobile apps (Turow, 2018). AT&T can discover which customers have indigestion, or purchased over-the-counter medications to help treat it, presumably so they can tailor persuasive messages to these consumers (see Maheshwari, 2018b; Singer, 2018b, 2018c). For this we can thank the digital marketing business, which "transforms latent attention into real money that pays for many truly useful inventions," but also "collects and constantly profiles data about our behavior, creates incentives to monetize our most private desires and frequently unleashes loopholes that the shadiest of people are only too happy to exploit" (Manjoo, 2018).

Ethical persuasion requires that consumers willingly agree to provide personal information that may later be used to try to influence them. However, many Americans do not realize that even if a website has a privacy policy, it will share user information without their permission. Most Americans do not know that brands can legally collect personal information on 13-year-olds, treating them like adults, because the relevant legal statute applies only to children who are 12 years and under (Maheshwari, 2018b). Indeed, about three-fourths of Facebook's users are not aware that the tech company makes available information about personal interests they have shared on Facebook to advertisers (Maheshwari, 2019). In our surveillance society, big companies have access to information most people would rather keep private because people don't read the fine print on privacy policies, make benign assumptions about how companies collect information, or process all this information peripherally and superficially. You could say: Let the buyer beware, it is people's responsibility to protect their privacy. But this dismisses how difficult it is for people to appreciate these complex fine points, and the capacity of technological companies to legally – not necessarily ethically – exploit their vulnerabilities.

Case in point: Some years back, a Missouri man suffering from a spreading cancer sued Facebook, charging that the company had infringed on his privacy by collecting information about his medical options – presumably providing the data to marketing firms – without his permission. Facebook countered that monitoring users for advertising purposes was a standard business procedure, one users had consented to when enrolling in its service (Singer, 2018a). But this seems a highly questionable argument that flies in the face of most users' experiences, eliding the ways tech companies can devise consent procedures that are difficult to decipher and easy to exploit.

The ethical implications are both deontological, treading on moral duties to respect the dignity of each individual, and consequence-based, as utilitarian theory emphasizes. Harms are tangible, invading a person's privacy by giving information he or she might not want others to know about (like attending an AA meeting or seeing a psychiatrist). They are also symbolic:

> (the) societal impact of having people targeted with divisive and exploitative ads … the collective impact of consumers' being stripped of control over information they own and having intimate details of their life, like relationship status and political views, shared with countless entities.
>
> (Guliani, 2019, p. A23)

Advertisers and consumers obviously derive benefits from social media, both in terms of profit and social pleasure, but the ethical questions speak to the disturbing moral areas of what Zuboff (2019) calls "the age of surveillance capitalism." While defenders of the new marketing defend the rights of companies to pursue their own economic interests, extolling surveillance-based marketing's benefits to consumers, others are more wary, suggesting the broader dangers implicit in the invasive aspects we quietly come to accept, pushing for remedies spanning breaking up tech companies, tighter regulation, and taking Facebook to court (Guliani, 2019), all ambitious, but politically fraught ideas.

Finally, the time-honored ethical issues in subtle, secretive manipulation come to the fore in different ways in social media-based advertising, as marketers push the limits of consumer heuristics, heisting users' profile pictures to artificially inflate the popularity of products, devising automated accounts with millions of faux Twitter followers, even creating computer-generated super-models, virtual influencers like Lil Miquela, with more than 1.5 million Instagram followers (Hsu, 2019).

Solutions are always daunting when one balances the virtues of a free enterprise economy with the inevitable ethical harm that comes from unfettered capitalism. We as a society are always trying to thread the needle, but we can do better. Promising ideas are afoot, such as a state or federal privacy law that let people "access, correct, delete and download their data," protecting privacy, yet allowing "companies to develop products people love" (Beckerman, 2018, p. A26). Inevitably, there will be free speech questions when the people who want to restrict the data are companies and the data bear on the public interest. But these issues can be worked out, for a more ethical persuasive framework is sorely needed in an age of influencers and a surveillance economy.

Conclusions

We all assume we're not affected in the slightest by advertising or marketing messages. We can see through those ploys, we tell ourselves; it's everyone else – the audience, the unwashed masses, who are vulnerable. But this is a fallacy, an illusion (Sagarin et al., 2002). If you are right that other people are influenced by advertisements, then it certainly stands to reason that you, too, should be swayed. On the other hand, if you are correct that you are not influenced and everyone else presumably claims the same lack of influence, then you exaggerate the effects of advertising on others (Perloff, 2009). "In either case," Tiedge and colleagues note, "most people appear to be willing to subscribe to the logical inconsistency inherent in maintaining that the mass media influence others considerably more than themselves" (Tiedge et al., 1991, p. 152). (Communication researchers call this the *third-person effect*: The notion that persuasive media do not affect "you" or "me" – but, rather, "them" – the third persons; see also Andsager & White, 2007.)

The reality is that, of course, we are influenced by advertising – sometimes subtly, other times quite directly. Indeed, advertising is such a pervasive part of American culture that it is difficult to conjure up mental images of products that have not been formed through advertising. If you were asked to free-associate about Coca-Cola, Budweiser, Nike, classy perfumes, or cars running the gamut from Mustangs to minivans, your mental images would undoubtedly contain ideas and pictures gleaned from commercials. It is physically difficult, if not impossible, to call to mind an advertising-free image of products. In fact, advertising effects are so deep-seated that exposure to a celebrity who commonly appears in ads and comes across as an expert elicits specific brain activity (Klucharev, Smidts, & Fernandez, 2008).

Little wonder that critics have charged that advertising's power comes from subliminally embedded messages that elude conscious awareness. Although there is some evidence that subliminally presented images can influence short-term behavior, these effects emerged in laboratory studies that differ vastly from the actual situations in which consumers view product advertisements. There is virtually no evidence that subliminally presented images can influence brand attitudes in actual situations, and there are strong psychological impediments to obtaining real-world subliminal effects. Still, the debate about subliminal influences is sufficiently titillating that it continues more than a half-century after the issue first surfaced at an obscure drive-in theater in New Jersey. This is as it should be, of course.

At present, the accumulated evidence and reasoning strongly indicate that subliminal-presented stimuli in ads (few and far between as they are) exert little or no impact on real-world consumer preferences. However, the conscious belief that a message contains a subliminal message can influence attitudes. On the other end of the spectrum, marketers can employ, sometimes successfully, promotional techniques that elude conscious awareness, priming attitudes. They're just not sneakily embedding a specific subliminal message in an ad, although the lines between conscious and unconscious are complex and not always easy to delineate.

As suggested by the ELM, advertising works through different pathways under low and high involvement. When viewing ads for low-involvement products, consumers process information peripherally. Mere or repeated exposure is particularly impactful, exerting stronger effects under particular conditions and working through an intriguing variety of processes. Association, which encompasses classical conditioning, semiotics, and accessibility, is a potent weapon in advertising campaigns.

When considering more personally consequential purchases, consumers process ads centrally, taking into account the benefits that products offer and the psychological functions that products serve. When directing ads at highly involved consumers, advertisers use factual messages and symbolic appeals targeted to particular attitude functions. Of course, central and peripheral processes messily interact, given that a seemingly peripheral cue, like number of tweets, can be processed centrally. As you know, the same branded factor can serve in different capacities – as an argument, catalyst for thought, or cognitive confidence builder – depending on individual and social conditions.

Influencer marketing, a recent craze, calls on communicators with clout with their target audience (from mega-models to everyday college students). Influencers (the name begging the question of whether they actually influence) cash in on time-honored communicator techniques, such as likability and similarity. Influencer marketing works not simply through time-worn appeals, like number of tweets, but through the visual content of posts and their ability to inspire young followers to identify with influencers' distinctive online shtick.

As au courant as these techniques are, these is no guarantee they will succeed just because they are relayed digitally with social networking glitz. Marketing effectiveness depends on just the right dose of psychology, creative marketing, and aesthetic appeal. We still do not understand exactly what makes for a successful marketing campaign, for it involves a number of elusive psychological and communication strategies, working in just the right manner, until it becomes passé. And, truth be told, it can be fiendishly difficult to determine the precise impact a television, YouTube, or social media marketing campaign has on consumer attitudes or behaviors. Researchers have to isolate the effects of a particular marketing appeal from all the other factors that influence brand choices. But theory and research suggest that artfully designed, scientifically tested ads and marketing messages can shape product attitudes and behaviors.

Needless to say, as an instrument of contemporary capitalism, with its economic strengths and social inequities, advertising has generated considerable criticism. Long controversial, advertising has been condemned on deontological grounds by those who point to the obvious falsehoods that ads contain. Other critics lament that advertising inculcates a strange philosophy of life that places great faith in the ability of products to satisfy universal human desires.

Advertising's defenders are nonplussed. Chill out, they say. People don't believe all of what advertising says and they enjoy watching the clever "magic tricks" ads employ, for example on Super Bowl Sunday. Besides, defenders note, humans' desire to acquire cool gadgets drives advertising. If people did not love things and the status products convey, advertising could not prosper.

Some years back, people around the world were shocked by revelations of government surveillance of citizens' phone calls, yet seem to be more forgiving of corporations, which probably know more about their personal preferences than does the government. This has created a privacy conundrum, where tech companies provide an online cornucopia of commercial extravaganzas – cool ads, sponsored posts, ability to purchase products with the press of a finger on a mobile device – in exchange for relinquishing, frequently without their informed consent, privacy to advertisers. The inequity of the exchange has bothered critics, who have proposed a variety of remedies, including breaking up tech companies, enacting federal privacy legislation, or requiring advertisers to reveal the precise information they use about a consumer to devise a particular ad (Turow, 2011).

In the final analysis, advertising and commercial marketing remain ethically problematic, but necessary, parts of capitalist society. Needed to differentiate and promote products, advertising increases demand, helping businesses to sell products, and employ workers. But questions about falsehood and manipulation persist. Advertising remains, in Schudson's (1986) memorable phrase, an "uneasy persuasion." As we balance the pleasant moments of perusing product posts against the increasingly subtle manipulations and invidious intrusions on privacy, the use of the "adjective" uneasy feels like an increasingly quaint understatement.

References

Andsager, J. L., & White, H. A. (2007). *Self versus others: Media, messages, and the third-person effect*. Mahwah, NJ: Lawrence Erlbaum Associates.

Ballentine, C. (2018, September 1). Their homework: Pushing brands online. *The New York Times*, B1, B2.

Bargh, J. A., & Pietromonaco, P. (1982). Automatic information processing and social perception: The influence of trait information presented outside of conscious awareness on impression formation. *Journal of Personality and Social Psychology, 43*, 437–449.

Beckerman, M. (2018, December 15). To protect online privacy. *The New York Times* (Letter to the Editor), A26.

Bermeitinger, C., Goelz, R., Johr, N., Neumann, M., Ecker, U. K. H., & Doerr, R. (2009). The hidden persuaders break into the tired brain. *Journal of Experimental Social Psychology, 45*, 320–326.

Bornstein, R. F. (1989). Exposure and affect: Overview and meta-analysis of research, 1968–1987. *Psychological Bulletin, 106*, 265–289.

Bornstein, R. F. (1992). Subliminal mere exposure effects. In R. F. Bornstein & T. S. Pittman (Eds.), *Perception without awareness: Cognitive, clinical, and social perspectives* (pp. 191–210). New York: Guilford.

Bouton, M. E. (2016). *Learning and behavior: A contemporary synthesis* (2nd ed.). Sunderland, MA: Sinauer.

Brannon, L. A., & Brock, T. C. (1994). The subliminal persuasion controversy: Reality, enduring fable, and Polonius's weasel. In S. Shavitt & T. C. Brock (Eds.), *Persuasion: Psychological insights and perspectives* (pp. 279–293). Needham Heights, MA: Allyn & Bacon.

Bromwich, J. E. (2019, July 11). What if being a YouTube celebrity is actually backbreaking work? *The New York Times*, D1, D4.

Chang, Y. T., Yu, H., & Lu, H. P. (2015). Persuasive messages, popularity cohesion, and message diffusion in social media marketing. *Journal of Business Research, 68*, 777–782.

Chen, B. X. (2018, August 16). Targeted ads stalking you? You can make them go away. *The New York Times*, B5.

Chew, F., Mehta, A., & Oldfather, A. (1994). Applying concept mapping to assess the influence of celebrity message dynamics on communication effectiveness. In K. W. King (Ed.), *Proceedings of the 1994 Conference of the American Academy of Advertising* (pp. 26–39). New York: American Academy of Advertising.

Cialdini, R. B. (2009). *Influence: Science and practice* (5th ed.). Boston, MA: Pearson Education.

Cooper, J., & Cooper, G. (2002). Subliminal motivation: A story revisited. *Journal of Applied Social Psychology, 32*, 2213–2227.

Courbet, D., Fourquet-Courbet, M.-P., Kazan, R., & Intartaglia, J. (2014). The long-term effects of e-advertising: The influence of Internet pop-ups viewed at a low level of attention in implicit memory. *Journal of Computer-Mediated Communication, 19*, 274–293.

Cowley, E. (2012). As a backdrop, part of the plot, or a goal in a game: The ubiquitous product placement. In L. J. Shrum (Ed.), *The psychology of entertainment media: Blurring the lines between entertainment and persuasion* (2nd ed., pp. 37–63). New York: Routledge.

Cross, M. (1996). Reading television texts: The postmodern language of advertising. In M. Cross (Ed.), *Advertising and culture: Theoretical perspectives* (pp. 1–10). Westport, CT: Praeger.

De Veirman, M., Cauberghe, V., & Hudders, L. (2017). Marketing through Instagram influencers: The impact of number of followers and product divergence on brand attitude. *International Journal of Advertising, 36*, 798–828.

DeAndrea, D. C., Van Der Heide, B., Vendemia, M. A., & Vang, M. H. (2018). How people evaluate online reviews. *Communication Research*, 45, 719–736.

Dijksterhuis, A., Aarts, H., & Smith, P. K. (2005). The power of the subliminal: On subliminal persuasion and other potential applications. In R. R. Hassin, J. S. Uleman, & J. A. Bargh (Eds.), *The new unconscious* (pp. 77–106). New York: Oxford University Press.

Drape, J. (2015, November 6). Rolling in cash, Crimson Tide lifts all boats. *The New York Times*, A1, B12–13.

Ewing, M. E., Engler, S., & Modarelli-Frank, H. (2015, October). Swisspers® Sleep Naked social media campaign: A case study exploring the role of online influencers. *Research Journal of the Institute for Public Relations*, 2, 2. Online: https://prjournal.instituteforpr.org/wp-content/uploads/SwisspersSSSMCaseStudyCompetition-FIXED11132015-1.pdf (Accessed: November 21, 2019).

Fang, X., Singh, S., & Ahluwalia, R. (2007). An examination of different explanations for the mere exposure effect. *Journal of Consumer Research*, 34, 97–103.

Fennis, B. M., & Stroebe, W. (2010). *The psychology of advertising*. New York: Psychology Press.

Friedman, V. (2015, January 22). After a tragedy, the memorabilia. *The New York Times*, E5.

Friedman, V. (2016, March 17). Game on. *The New York Times*, D1, D2.

Friedman, V. (2017, May 10). The rise and (maybe) fall of influencers. *The New York Times*. Online: nytimes.com/2017/05/10/fashion/kendall-jenner-fyre-festival-pepsi-bella-hadid-influencers.html (Accessed: September 14, 2019).

The FTC's endorsement guides: What people are asking. (2017, September). Online: ftc.gov/tips-advice/business-center/guidance/ftcs-endorsement-guides-what-people-are-asking (Accessed: September 16, 2019).

Generation Like-Transcript. (2014, February 18). *Frontline*. Online: www.pbs.org/wgbh/frontline/film/generation-like/transcript/ (Accessed: September 5, 2019).

Goldman, R., & Papson, S. (1996). *Sign wars: The cluttered landscape of advertising*. New York: Guilford Press.

Greenwald, A. G., Spangenberg, E. R., Pratkanis, A. R., & Eskenazi, J. (1991). Double-blind tests of subliminal self-help audiotapes. *Psychological Science*, 2, 119–122.

Grush, J. E., McKeough, K. L., & Ahlering, R. F. (1978). Extrapolating laboratory exposure research to actual political elections. *Journal of Personality and Social Psychology*, 36, 257–270.

Guliani, N. S. (2019, January 7). See you in court, Facebook. *The New York Times*, A23.

Guo, F., Ye, G., Hudders, L., Lv, W., Li, M., & Duffy, V. G. (2019). Product placement in mass media: A review and bibliometric analysis. *Journal of Advertising*, 48, 215–231.

Hartley, R. E. (2000). *Marketing mistakes* (8th ed.). Wiley: New York.

Helft, M., & Vega, T. (2010, August 30). Seeing that ad on every site? You're right. It's tracking you. *The New York Times*, A1, B2.

Hess, A. (2018, May 1). What happens when people and companies are both just "brands"? *The New York Times Magazine*. Online: nytimes.com/2018/05/01/magazine/what-happens-when-people-and-companies-are-both-just-brands.html (Accessed: September 14, 2019).

Ho-Dac, N. N., Carson, S. J., & Moore, W. L. (2013). The effects of positive and negative online customer reviews: Do brand strength and category maturity matter? *Journal of Marketing*, 77, 37–53.

Hsu, T. (2019, June 18). 1.6 million follow her online. She doesn't exist. *The New York Times*, A1, A16.

Jackler, R. K., Chau, C., Getachew, B. D., Whitcomb, M. M., Lee-Heidenreich, J., Bhatt, A. M., … Ramamurthi, D. (2019, January 31). JUUL advertising over its first three years on the market. *Stanford University School of Medicine*. Online: tobacco.stanford.edu/tobacco_main/publications/JUUL_Marketing_Stanford.pdf (Accessed: September 1, 2019).

Jhally, S. (1998). *Advertising and the end of the world* (video). Northampton, MA: Media Education Foundation.

Jo, C. L., Noar, S. M., Southwell, B. G., & Ribisl, K. M. (2019). Efforts of e-cigarette advertising message form and cues on cessation intention: An exploratory study. *Journal of Health Communication*, 24, 570–580.

Johnson, C. (2011). *Microstyle: The art of writing little*. New York: W. W. Norton.

Kaplan, S., & Richtel, M. (2019, September 1). Vaping one day, then on a ventilator the next. *The New York Times*, 1, 16.

Karremans, J. C., Stroebe, W., & Claus, J. (2006). Beyond Vicary's fantasies: The impact of subliminal priming and brand choice. *Journal of Experimental Social Psychology*, 42, 792–798.

Key, W. B. (1974). *Subliminal seduction*. New York: Signet Books.

Ki, C.-W. C., & Kim, Y.-K. (2019). The mechanism by which social media influencers persuade consumers: The role of consumers' desire to mimic. *Psychology & Marketing*, 36, 905–922.

Kim, M., Popova, L., Halpern-Felsher, B., & Ling, P. M. (2019). Effects of e-cigarette advertisements on adolescents' perceptions of cigarettes. *Health Communication*, 34, 290–297.

Kimmel, A. J. (2013). *Psychological foundations of marketing*. New York: Routledge.

Klucharev, V., Smidts, A., & Fernandez, G. (2008). Brain mechanisms of persuasion: How "expert power" modulates memory and attitudes. *Social Cognitive and Affective Neuroscience*, 3, 353–366.

Koch, T., & Zerback, T. (2013). Helpful or harmful? How frequent repetition affects perceived statement credibility. *Journal of Communication*, 63, 993–1010.

Kosinski, M. (2018, December 13). Facebook's data sleight of hand. *The New York Times*, A27.

Lambiase, J. J. (2003). Sex—Online and in Internet advertising. In T. Reichert & J. Lambiase (Eds.), *Sex in advertising: Perspectives on the erotic appeal* (pp. 247–269). Mahwah, NJ: Lawrence Erlbaum Associates.

Langer, J. (1997). What consumers wish brand managers knew. *Journal of Advertising Research*, 37(6), 60–65.

Langrehr, F. W., & Caywood, C. L. (1995). A semiotic approach to determining the sins and virtues portrayed in advertising. *Journal of Current Issues and Research in Advertising*, 17, 33–47.

Lee, J.-G., & Thorson, E. (2008). The impact of celebrity–product incongruence on the effectiveness of product endorsement. *Journal of Advertising Research*, 48, 433–449.

Lee, Y., & Koo, J. (2016). Can a celebrity serve as an issue-relevant argument in the elaboration likelihood model? *Psychology & Marketing*, 33, 195–208.

Lynch, J., & Schuler, D. (1994). The matchup effect of spokesperson and product congruency: A schema theory interpretation. *Psychology & Marketing*, 11, 417–445.

Maheshwari, S. (2017, June 6). How bots are inflating Instagram egos. *The New York Times*. Online: nytimes.com/2017/06/06/business/media/instragram-bots.html (Accessed: September 7, 2019).

Maheshwari, S. (2018a, November 11). Are you ready for the nanoinfluencers? *The New York Times*. Online: nytimes.com/2018/11/11/business/media/nanoinfluencers-instragram-influencers.html (Accessed: September 10, 2019).

Maheshwari, S. (2018b, December 25). Giving up data privacy with a sigh. *The New York Times*, B1, B4.

Maheshwari, S. (2019, January 17). Facebook's ad profiles remain mystery to many, survey reveals. *The New York Times*, B3.

Maheshwari, S., & Koblin, J. (2018, May 14). No choice for marketers but to rethink TV ads. *The New York Times*, B1, B4.

Manjoo, F. (2018, January 31). Tackling the Internet's central villain: The advertising business. *The New York Times*. Online: www.nytimes.com/2018/01/31/technology/internet-advertising-business.html (Accessed: September 10, 2019).

Marantz, A. (2019). *Antisocial: Online extremists, techno-utopians, and the hijacking of the American conversation*. New York: Viking.

Marikar, S. (2019, February 3). The sneaky side of Instagram. *The New York Times* (Sunday Review), 2.

Matthes, J., & Naderer, B. (2015). Children's consumption behavior in response to food product placements in movies. *Journal of Consumer Behaviour, 14*, 127–136.

McCarty, J. A. (2004). Product placement: The nature of the practice and potential avenues of inquiry. In L. J. Shrum (Ed.), *The psychology of entertainment media: Blurring the lines between entertainment and persuasion* (pp. 45–61). Mahwah, NJ: Lawrence Erlbaum Associates.

McCracken, G. (1986). Culture and consumption: A theoretical account of the structure and movement of the cultural meaning of consumer goods. *Journal of Consumer Research, 13*, 71–84.

Messaris, P. (1997). *Visual persuasion: The role of images in advertising*. Thousand Oaks, CA: Sage.

Metz, C. (2015, September 21). How Zuck's old TA helped Facebook master mobile ads. *Wired*. Online: www.wired.com/2015/09/zucks-old-ta-helped-facebook-master-mobile-ads/ (Accessed: September 14, 2019).

Metz, C. (2017, October 16). Blurring lines: How the ad system on your Facebook news feed works. *The New York Times*, B3.

Montoya, R. M., Horton, R. S., Vevea, J. L., Citkowicz, M., & Lauber, E. A. (2017). A re-examination of the mere exposure effect: The influence of repeated exposure on recognition, familiarity, and liking. *Psychological Bulletin, 143*, 459–498.

Nabi, R. L., & Moyer-Gusé, E. (2013). The psychology underlying media-based persuasion. In K. Dill (Ed.), *Oxford handbook of media psychology* (pp. 285–301). New York: Oxford University Press.

Nebenzahl, I. D., & Jaffe, E. D. (1998). Ethical dimensions of advertising executions. *Journal of Business Ethics, 17*, 805–815.

Nekmat, E., Gower, K. K., Zhou, S., & Metzger, M. (2019). Connective-collective action on social media: Moderated mediation of cognitive elaboration and perceived source credibility on personalness of source. *Communication Research, 4*, 62–87.

Nelson, M. R., & Waiguny, M. K. J. (2012). Psychological processing of in-game advertising and advergaming: Branded entertainment or entertaining persuasion? In L. J. Shrum, *The psychology of entertainment media: Blurring the lines between entertainment and persuasion* (2nd ed., pp. 93–144). New York: Routledge.

Newman, B., & Newman, T. (2018). *Brand*. Dubuque, IA: Kendall Hunt.

Nurit, T.-O. (2019). The relationship between viewing environment, narrative environment, and involvement with narratives: The case of temperature. *Human Communication Research, 45*, 395–426.

Orsini, E. (2019, November 20). Invited talk to class in Psychological Processing of Media, Cleveland State University.

Paek, H.-J., Kim, S., Hove, T., & Huh, J. Y. (2014). Reduced harm or another gateway to smoking? Source, message, and information characteristics of e-cigarette videos on YouTube. *Journal of Health Communication, 19*, 545–560.

Pariser, E. (2011). *The filter bubble: What the Internet is hiding from you*. New York: Penguin Press.

Perloff, C. (2019, April). Nike scored big with Colin Kaepernick. Should your company talk politics? *Inc.* Online: inc.com/magazine/201904/catherine-perloff/should-company-take-political-stand-values-controversy-authentic.html (Accessed: September 16, 2019).

Perloff, R. M. (2009). Mass media, social perception, and the third-person effect. In J. Bryant & M. B. Oliver (Eds.), *Media effects: Advances in theory and research* (3rd ed., pp. 252–268). New York: Taylor & Francis.

Pratkanis, A. R. (1998). Myths of subliminal persuasion: The cargo-cult science of subliminal persuasion. In K. Frazier (Ed.), *Encounters with the paranormal: Science, knowledge, and belief* (pp. 240–252). Amherst, NY: Prometheus Books.

Rajecki, D. W. (1982). *Attitudes: Themes and advances.* Sunderland, MA: Sinauer Associates.

Reichert, T. (2003). What is sex in advertising? Perspectives from consumer behavior and social science research. In T. Reichert & J. Lambiase (Eds.), *Sex in advertising: Perspectives on the erotic appeal* (pp. 11–38). Mahwah, NJ: Lawrence Erlbaum Associates.

Richtel, M., & Kaplan, S. (2018, August 27). A goal to hook youths for life? F.D.A. investigates vaping ads. *The New York Times*, A1, A13.

Rogers, M., & Seiler, C. A. (1994). The answer is no: A national survey of advertising industry practitioners and their clients about whether they use subliminal advertising. *Journal of Advertising Research*, 34(2), 36–45.

Rogers, M., & Smith, K. H. (1993, March–April). Public perceptions of subliminal advertising: Why practitioners shouldn't ignore this issue. *Journal of Advertising Research*, 33, 10–18.

Royte, E. (2008). *Bottlemania: How water went on sale and why we bought it.* New York: Bloomsbury.

Sagarin, B. J., Cialdini, R. B., Rice, W. E., & Serna, S. B. (2002). Dispelling the illusion of invulnerability: The motivations and mechanisms of resistance to persuasion. *Journal of Personality and Social Psychology*, 83, 526–541.

Sandel, M. J. (2012). *What money can't buy: The moral limits of markets.* New York: Farrar, Straus and Giroux.

Saunders, G. (2006). *In persuasion nation: Stories.* New York: Riverhead Books.

Schudson, M. (1986). *Advertising, the uneasy persuasion.* New York: Basic Books.

Shoenberger, H., & Kim, E. (2019). Product placement as leveraged marketing communications: The role of wishful identification, brand trust, and brand buying behaviours. *International Journal of Advertising*, 38, 50–66.

Shrum, L. J., Liu, M., Nespoli, M., & Lowrey, T. M. (2013). Persuasion in the marketplace: How theories of persuasion apply to marketing and advertising. In J. P. Dillard & L. Shen (Eds.), *The Sage handbook of persuasion: Developments in theory and practice* (2nd ed., pp. 314–330). Thousand Oaks, CA: Sage.

Singer, N. (2018a, April 11). What you don't know about how Facebook uses your data. *The New York Times.* Online: www.nytimes.com/2018/04/11/technology/facebook-privacy-hearings.html (Accessed: September 12, 2019).

Singer, N. (2018b, September 23). Just don't call it privacy. *The New York Times* (Sunday Review), 4–5.

Singer, N. (2018c, December 24). Why privacy at Facebook is eyed anew by the F.T.C. *The New York Times*, B1, B3.

Solomon, M. R. (1999). *Consumer behavior: Buying, having, and being* (4th ed.). Boston, MA: Allyn & Bacon.

Staats, A. W., & Staats, C. K. (1958). Attitudes established by classical conditioning. *Journal of Abnormal and Social Psychology*, 57, 37–40.

Standage, T. (2005, August 1). Bad to the last drop. *The New York Times*, A17.

Story, L. (2007, January 15). Anywhere the eye can see, it's now likely to see an ad. *The New York Times*, A1, A14.

Strahan, E. J., Spencer, S. J., & Zanna, M. P. (2002). Subliminal priming and persuasion: Striking while the iron is hot. *Journal of Experimental Social Psychology*, 38, 556–568.

Stuart, E. W., Shimp, T. A., & Engle, R. W. (1987). Classical conditioning of consumer attitudes: Four experiments in an advertising context. *Journal of Consumer Research*, 14, 334–349.

Surowiecki, J. (2016, November 14). What's in a name? *The New Yorker*, 35.

Tesser, A. (1978). Self-generated attitude change. In L. Berkowitz (Ed.), *Advances in experimental social psychology* (Vol. 11, pp. 181–227). New York: Academic Press.

Theus, K. T. (1994). Subliminal advertising and the psychology of processing unconscious stimuli: A review of research. *Psychology & Marketing*, *11*, 271–290.

Tiedge, J. T., Silverblatt, A., Havice, M. J., & Rosenfeld, R. (1991). Discrepancy between perceived first-person and perceived third-person mass media effects. *Journalism Quarterly*, *68*, 141–154.

Till, B. D., Stanley, S. M., & Priluck, R. (2008). Classical conditioning and celebrity endorsers: An examination of belongingness and resistance to extinction. *Psychology & Marketing*, *25*, 179–196.

Trappey, C. (1996). A meta-analysis of consumer choice and subliminal advertising. *Psychology & Marketing*, *13*, 517–530.

Trifts, V., & Aghakhani, H. (2019). Enhancing digital entertainment through personalization: The evolving role of product placements. *Journal of Marketing Communications*, *25*, 607–625.

Turow, J. (2011). *The daily you: How the new advertising industry is defining your identity and your worth*. New Haven, CT: Yale University Press.

Turow, J. (2018, August 21). Privacy policies don't work. *The New York Times*, A21.

Valentino-DeVries, J., Singer, N., Keller, M. H., & Krolik, A. (2018, December 10). Your apps know where you've been, and can't keep a secret. *The New York Times*, A1, A20–21.

Williams, R. (2019, September 12). Kylie Cosmetics show highest social media engagement and no ad spending, study says. *Mobile Marketer*. Online: www.mobilemarketer.com/news/kylie-cosmetics-shows-highest-social-media-engagement-and-no-ad-spending-s/562751/ (Accessed: November 21, 2019).

Willis, E., Haught, M. J., & Morris, D. L., II (2017). Up in vapor: Exploring the health messages of e-cigarette advertisements. *Health Communication*, *32*, 372–380.

Wingfield, N. (2014, January 31). Another Super Bowl ad fest, this time on the cellphone. *The New York Times*, A1, A19.

Wright, S. A. (2016). Reinvestigating the endorser by product matchup hypothesis in advertising. *Journal of Advertising*, *45*, 26–32.

Yang, M., & Roskos-Ewoldsen, D. R. (2007). The effectiveness of brand placements in the movies: Levels of placements, explicit and implicit memory, and brand-choice behavior. *Journal of Communication*, *57*, 469–489.

Zajonc, R. B. (1968). Attitudinal effects of mere exposure. *Journal of Personality and Social Psychology Monographs Supplement*, *9*(2, Pt. 2), 1–27.

Zanot, E. J., Pincus, J. D., & Lamp, E. J. (1983). Public perceptions of subliminal advertising. *Journal of Advertising*, *12*, 39–45.

Zuboff, S. (2019). *The age of surveillance capitalism: The fight for a human future at the new frontier of power*. New York: PublicAffairs.

Chapter 16

Health Communication Campaigns

Bill Alcott and Sy Graham were horrified. They were aghast at what people did to their bodies, day after day shoveling unhealthy, even dangerous, food into their mouths. Didn't people know the damage that meat, fried foods, and butter did to the stomach and heart? Convinced that Americans needed to change their diets, Alcott and Graham organized a health food store that supplied fresh fruits and vegetables. A proper diet, in their view, consisted of wheat bread, grains, vegetables, fruits, and nuts. By eating healthy food and avoiding anything that harmed the body, Graham and Alcott emphasized, people could live longer, healthier lives.

Sound familiar? Another example of contemporary activists trying to convince consumers to give up junk food? Well – not exactly. Alcott and Graham were committed health reformers, but they communicated their message some time ago. More than 150 years ago, to be precise! William Alcott and Sylvester Graham, born in the late 1700s, promoted their nutrition reform campaign in the 1830s. They were early advocates of health education, pioneers in a clean-living movement that began in the United States in the 1800s and continues to this day. Alcott's writings can be found in scattered libraries across the country. Graham – or at least his name – is known worldwide through his Graham cracker (Engs, 2000).

Long before it became fashionable to tout one's opposition to smoking or drugs, activists were pounding the pavement, preaching and proselytizing. Campaigns to improve the public health date back to the early 1800s, with Alcott and Graham's vegetarianism, health reformers' condemnation of the "evil, deadly" tobacco, and the Temperance Movement's efforts to promote abstinence from alcohol. Clean-living movements, as Ruth Clifford Engs (2000) calls them, took on special urgency during the 1830s and 1840s, with the outbreak of cholera, an infectious disease that spread through filthy water, a common problem during a time when drainage systems were poor or non-existent and pigs roamed the streets feeding on uncollected garbage. Although the causes of cholera could be traced to the social environment, cholera (like AIDS a century and a half later) was viewed as "God's punishment for vice, sin, and moral flaws" (Rushing, 1995, p. 168).

Health campaigns flourished in the twentieth century, with the proliferation of television and realization that activists could change institutions through a combination of persuasion and protest. In the public health arena, campaigns continue apace, with interventions designed to convince people to adopt healthy eating habits, take steps to avert breast cancer, quit bullying (see Figure 16.1), and

(a)

(b)

(c)

IT'S SO NOT COOL!

Figure 16.1a–c Contemporary Campaigns Employ a Host of Persuasion Strategies to Change Health-Related Attitudes and Behavior. As shown here, a healthy eating campaign employs a slogan and a famous credible source, Michelle Obama. A breast cancer awareness rally promotes the iconic, and sometimes-controversial, pink ribbon, while an anti-bullying intervention employs a contemporary appeal

Images courtesy of Getty Images

prevent suicide (Pirkis et al., 2019). Nowadays, campaigns frequently target a specialized audience of young people, relying on websites, social media, and text messages. Yet although campaigns adopt a more niche, targeted approach today, they remain socially important and illuminated by persuasion perspectives. Just think for a moment about the urgent need that faced nations during the outbreak of the coronavirus, when government leaders harnessed media and psychological resources to change the health habits of their citizens.

Campaigns – colorful, vibrant, and controversial – are the focus of this final chapter. The chapter is organized into several sections. The first describes the nature of campaigns. The second portion reviews major theories of campaign effects, with emphasis on applications to online and texting interventions. The third section focuses on campaign effects and a contemporary approach to health campaigns, one particularly relevant to university settings. The final segment describes ethical issues surrounding campaigns.

As you read the chapter, keep in mind that blockbuster media, state, and national health campaigns – and research evaluations – are far less common today than in decades past. This is the result of the decline of federal government funding for campaign development and evaluation. Other factors that have led to a decrease in nationally based campaigns include increased awareness of health risks, compared to the knowledge-darker decades of the mid- to late twentieth century, the decline of mass media, and, of course, proliferation of online social media channels directed at specific audiences. However, social marketing, online, and text campaigns (as well as one-time interventions) are proliferating in the United States and across the world, calling on a variety of strategies to improve the public health. The chapter presents different frameworks to help you appreciate and critically review the application of persuasion principles to these broader public interventions.

Thinking about Campaigns

This is your brain on drugs ... Parents: The antidrug ... Welcome to Loserville. Population: You ... Friends don't let friends drive drunk.

These are some of the most famous emblems of public information campaigns in the United States (see Figure 16.2). However, campaigns involve more than clever slogans. They are systematic,

Figure 16.2 This Classic, Decades-Old Antidrug Campaign Advertisement Is Still Well Known Today. Although its effectiveness in reducing drug use has not been conclusively documented, the ad attracted attention, due to its memorable visuals and clever use of parallel phrases. In fact, the ad's "Any questions" motif inspired a new PSA that invites kids to ask adults a variety of questions about drugs. Sadly, drug abuse continues to be a problem, and campaigns are needed to reduce their impact

Image obtained from Partnership for a Drug-Free America

organized efforts to mold health or social attitudes through the use of communication. More formally, *communication campaigns* can be defined broadly as:

> (1) purposive attempts, (2) to inform, persuade, or motivate behavior changes, (3) in a relatively well-defined and large audience, (4) generally for noncommercial benefits to the individuals and/or society at large, (5) typically within a given time period, (6) by means of organized communication activities involving mass media and Internet, and (7) often complemented by interpersonal support.
>
> (Adapted from Rice & Atkin, 2009, p. 436)

People do not devise campaigns with the flick of a wrist. Campaigns require time and effort. Typically, activists or professional organizations hatch a campaign concept. They sculpt the idea, working with marketing and communication specialists; pretest messages; and take their communications to the real world in the hope they will influence behavior.

Like advertising and marketing, health information campaigns apply theories to practical concerns. However, classic advertising campaigns differ from their public information counterparts in a variety of ways:

- Commercial advertising is designed to make a profit for companies. Information campaigns are not purely capitalistic undertakings. They are designed to promote social ideas or improve public health. Typically, pro-social projects have smaller budgets than advertising campaigns. This can limit their effectiveness. What's more, advertising can work at cross-purposes with health campaigns. Campaigns designed to promote healthy eating are thwarted by glitzy advertisements that hype junk food.
- Interpersonal and organizational communication play a more important role in health campaigns than in commercial advertising. The McGruff "Take a bite out of crime" campaign supplemented media messages with supportive communication from community groups, businesses, and local police forces (O'Keefe et al., 1996; see Figure 16.3). The Stanford cardiovascular risk reduction project involved multiple communication efforts, including hundreds of educational sessions and distribution of thousands of nutrition tip sheets to grocery stores. The D.A.R.E. (Drug Abuse Resistance Education) campaign developed an elaborate school curriculum, with police officers teaching children ways to say no to drugs.
- Advertising campaigns try to induce people to do something, like buying a six-pack of beer or soft drinks. Information campaigns often try to convince consumers *not* to perform a particular activity (*not* to smoke, litter, or drive after imbibing).
- Information campaigns invariably face more daunting obstacles than does commercial marketing. It is usually easier to convince someone to buy a commercial product than to "buy into" the idea that she should quit smoking or change her diet.
- Campaigns frequently target their messages at the 15 percent of the population that is least likely to change its behavior (Harris & Sanborn, 2014). These may be the poorest, least educated members of society, or the most down-and-out intravenous drug users who continue to share HIV-infected needles. By contrast, commercial campaigns focus on the mainstream – on those who are shopping for a product or a dream.
- Information campaigns involve more highly charged political issues than do commercial efforts. Campaigns frequently encounter strong opposition from powerful industries, such as tobacco companies, beer distributors, oil companies, or gun manufacturers. Anti-tobacco campaigns, for example, have become embroiled in the politics and economics of tobacco production.

Figure 16.3 An Advertisement from a Classic Communication Campaign, the McGruff "Take a bite out of crime" Campaign. The campaign featured an animated trench-coated dog, called McGruff, who urged viewers to take steps to reduce crime. Through media and community activities, the campaign led to increases in crime prevention behaviors

Reprinted with permission of the National Crime Prevention Council

Locating Effects

What impact do campaigns and media have on public health? That's a big question; thus, you need big ideas to help you grapple with it. Communication scholars Kim Walsh-Childers and Jane D. Brown (2009) developed a framework to help explain media influences on personal and public health. They proposed that mass media effects fall into three categories: (a) intention of the message communicator (intended/unintended), (b) level of influence (personal/public), and (c) outcome (positive/negative).

An effect can be intended, as when MTV's reality series *16 and Pregnant* was associated with a sharp decrease in teenager childbearing (Kearney & Levine, 2014), and unintended, when a high school girl rethinks her desire to get pregnant after coming across a sobering exchange between a pregnant teen and her mom on YouTube. The bulk of effects discussed in this chapter are intended, since they emanate from campaigns designed to influence attitudes.

A campaign effect can occur at the personal level (a public service ad convinces parents to buy a new child safety seat to protect their infant), or at the public level (a legislator decides, after watching campaign ads, to introduce a bill requiring that all new cars have a special anchoring device to keep the safety seat in place). Finally, effects can be positive, for example, producing primarily healthy outcomes, or negative, leading to mainly unhealthy consequences.

Viewed in this way, campaigns are multifaceted phenomena. They are complex events that can be examined from different points of view. A good way to begin this examination is to look at theories articulated to explain campaign effects.

Theoretical Perspectives

Three major models of campaigns have been developed. The first is a psychological, individual-level perspective. The other two approaches focus on the bigger picture, viewing campaigns from a macro, community-level orientation.

Psychological Approach

The psychological perspective emphasizes that you can't expect a campaign to change behavior instantly, lickety-split. Instead, change occurs gradually, in stages, in line with the ancient Chinese proverb that "a journey of a thousand miles begins with a single step." For example, J. O. Prochaska and colleagues note that people progress through different stages of change, including pre-contemplation, during which they are not aware that they have a psychological problem, contemplation, in which they begin considering how to make a change in behavior, and action, in which they actually modify risky behaviors (Prochaska, DiClemente, & Norcross, 1992; see also Hampton et al., 2009).

The preeminent psychological approach to campaigns combines stages of change with persuasive communication theory. According to McGuire (1989), persuasion can be viewed as a series of input and output steps. In Figure 16.4, the input column labels refer to standard persuasion variables out of which messages can be constructed. The output row headings correspond to the steps that individuals must be persuaded to take if the message is to have its intended impact.

As the figure shows, a message must clear many hurdles if it is to successfully influence attitudes and behavior. An antidrug campaign may not clear the first hurdle – exposure – because it never reaches the target audience, or alternatively because receivers, finding the message threatening, tune it

INPUT: Independent (Communication) Variables / OUTPUT: Dependent Variables (Response Steps Mediating Persuasion)	SOURCE				MESSAGE					CHANNEL			RECEIVER				DESTIN-ATION		
	number	unanimity	demographics	attractiveness	credibility	type of appeal	type of information	inclusion/omission	organization	repetitiveness	modality	directness	context	demographics	ability	personality	lifestyle	immediacy/delay	prevention/cessation	direct/immunization
1. Exposure to the communication																				
2. Attending to it																				
3. Liking, becoming interested in it																				
4. Comprehending it (learning what)																				
5. Skill acquisition (learning how)																				
6. Yielding to it (attitude change)																				
7. Memory storage of content and/or agreement																				
8. Information search and retrieval																				
9. Deciding on basis of retrieval																				
10. Behaving in accord with decision																				
11. Reinforcement of desired acts																				
12. Post-behavioral consolidating																				

Figure 16.4 Persuasion and Campaign Stages
From McGuire (1989)

out as soon as they view it. Or the message may pass the first few steps, but get knocked out of the box when it threatens deeper values or psychological needs.

The input–output matrix has an optimistic side. It says that campaigns can succeed even if they do not lead to major changes in behavior. Indeed, such changes are not always reasonable to expect, based only on short-term exposure to communications. Campaigns can be regarded as successful if they get people to remember an antidrug ad (Step 4) or if they teach them how to say no to attractive drug-using peers (Step 5). Over time, through subsequent interventions, people can be persuaded to make long-term behavioral changes (Steps 10–12).

Stage-based psychological models are useful. Indeed, when people are in a stage where they are actively trying to change their behavior, as when smokers have a strong desire to quit, they can be particularly influenced by tobacco education campaigns (Davis et al., 2017). As helpful as the insights stage campaigns offer on the individual level, their individual-level focus has its limits. It ignores the larger context – the community and society in which campaigns take place. The next two theories address these domains.

Diffusion Theory

Developed by Everett M. Rogers (1995), *diffusion theory* examines the processes by which innovations diffuse, or spread through, society. Campaigns are viewed as large-scale attempts to communicate innovative ideas and practices through mass media and interpersonal communication. The following can be regarded as innovations:

- seat belts;
- child safety seats;
- designated drivers;
- low-cholesterol diets;
- sunscreen lotion;
- pooper scoopers;
- Fitbits.

Think for a moment of all the important knowledge about health you take for granted: If you drink too much at a party, you recognize you should give the keys to someone else; you know all too well that you should not text when you drive; and you're well aware that a healthy diet is low in saturated fat and transfat. This information didn't come out of thin air. It was widely disseminated through the media; it was, at least partly, via media that individuals came to acquire beliefs or attitudes that helped them take steps to protect their health and well-being.

While media-relayed interventions do not always influence behavior or behavioral intentions (Kruvand & Bryant, 2015), in view of the challenges of translating attitudes into behavior, their impact on awareness is important. Awareness is a first step to influencing attitudes and behavior. Diffusion theory emphasizes that concerted interpersonal communication, in conjunction with media, can lead to changes in health behavior, mediated by the host of persuasion factors – credibility, identification, central processing, and fear – discussed in this text.

On a broad scale, diffusion theory calls attention to the ways that bold ideas from innovative change agents can lead to societal changes in health and social behavior. On a more specific level, it stipulates the conditions that make health innovation more likely to occur. One key factor is *compatibility of the health innovation with prevailing values*. The less compatible that an innovation is with prevailing values and societal norms, the less rapidly it is accepted. For example, dropping litter in trash cans, environmental recycling, and energy efficiency did not take hold back in the 1960s and '70s because they diverged from the dominant ideologies: "Bigger is better" and "Commercial growth supersedes environmental change." It took several decades for the ideas, promoted through communication, persuasive arguments, and institutional changes, to take hold. In a similar fashion, policy reforms and changes in public attitudes toward e-cigarettes occurred much more quickly than they did in the case of cigarette smoking in the 1950s and '60s, as the public opinion climate was much more favorable toward smoking restrictions by the time e-cigarettes became popular.

Another attribute of an innovation is the degree to which it promises *a clear, salient reward to the individual*. A barrier to condom use is that condoms do not offer an immediate reward. The advantage condoms offer – preventing pregnancy or HIV infection – is not visible immediately after the consummation of sex. As Rogers notes, "The unwanted event that is avoided … is difficult to perceive because it is a non-event, the absence of something that otherwise might have happened" (1995, p. 217). Partly because the benefits of condom use are not readily apparent, safer-sex practices have not always been a quick, easy sell.

Diffusion theory originally stipulated that mass media are most influential in enhancing knowledge of the innovation, while interpersonal communication is more effective in changing attitudes toward the innovation. Newer approaches suggest that campaigns affect interpersonal communication, which in turn can influence campaign outcomes, depending on the nature of the health topic, and the people with whom receivers converse (Jeong & Bae, 2018; see Hwang, 2012). Communication processes blur all the more today when interpersonal communication occurs so frequently on social media, requiring revision of the old-fashioned media versus interpersonal dichotomy.

A Downside of Diffusion

Now the bad news: It is not all blue skies and rosy fields when it comes to media and campaigns. Consider that poor people or those with little education frequently know less about health issues than people who are wealthier or have more education under their belts (Freimuth, 1990). One objective of campaigns is to narrow the gap between the advantaged and disadvantaged members of society. Unfortunately, just the opposite can occur. Campaigns can widen the disparity so that, by the end of the campaign, the rich and better-educated people are even more knowledgeable of the problem than their poorer, less educated counterparts (Gaziano, 1983; Viswanath & Finnegan, 1996). This is known as the *knowledge gap*, the tendency for campaigns to increase cognitive differences between haves and have-nots in society (see Figure 16.5).

For example, despite the wide diffusion of information on the Affordable Health Care Act (in the news and YouTube videos), a law that greatly expands health care for the poor, many poor, uninsured Americans have not heard of the law (MacGillis, 2015; see also Kelley, Su, & Britigan, 2016). As a result of the gap in, or lack of, knowledge, these poor Americans are unlikely to take the steps necessary to gain health insurance.

In another arena of health, smoking cessation, knowledge gaps can also occur among lower socio-economic status (SES) individuals. As Jeff Niederdeppe and his colleagues (2008a) noted, in a thorough analysis of smoking cessation media campaigns, smokers lower in SES may be less likely than their higher SES counterparts to gain meaningful exposure to anti-smoking messages, less motivated to attend to messages, and have fewer opportunities, due to everyday stressors, to implement their intentions to quit smoking.

There are a number of reasons why knowledge gaps persist, even in the face of the abundance of health-related digital information. One key reason is that the health information is less likely to reach, or be cognitively accepted by, disadvantaged individuals. Those who have been disadvantaged by society may be so preoccupied with tangible survival needs that they neglect to focus on health issues that are of long-term personal importance. Low SES individuals may also lack the time or motivation to translate beliefs into action, given societal-level constraints, as the theory of planned behavior

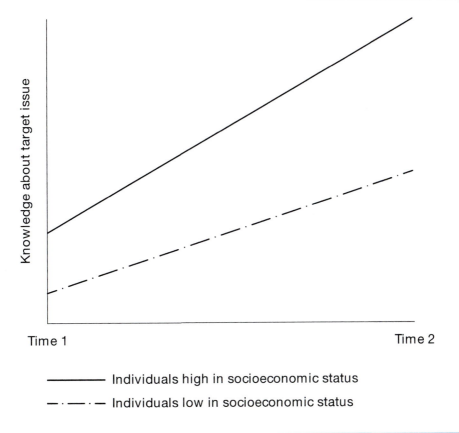

Figure 16.5 Schematic Diagram of the Knowledge Gap. Communication occurs between Time 1 and Time 2, in some cases increasing informational disparities between socioeconomic groups

notes. Researchers have identified ways to reduce knowledge gaps – for example, by targeting low-income individuals through tailored messages, employing channels that are most germane to low-income respondents. Nonetheless, the knowledge gap is a downside – or inevitable negative consequence – of communication campaigns.

Social Marketing

Pink

If you want to understand social marketing, think *pink*. The classic social marketing campaign is breast cancer awareness, originally symbolized by a pink ribbon and now by pink earrings, pink umbrellas, pink tote bags, and even pink clothing donned by performers during a Dallas Cowboys halftime show.

Pink was originally chosen to represent breast cancer because the color symbolizes femininity. But during October, marketed as National Breast Cancer Awareness Month, "'pink' becomes more than a color." It becomes a ubiquitous brand designed to call up concerns about breast cancer, convince women to get mammograms, and raise money for research (Singer, 2011, p. 1). Over the past decades, organizations like the Susan G. Komen for the Cure have successfully harnessed techniques pioneered by commercial marketers, ranging from handing out free products to sponsoring races, all designed to raise consciousness about breast cancer. By employing pink marketing, Komen "has rebranded an entire disease by putting an upbeat spin on fighting it" (Singer, 2011, p. 6).

It is vintage social marketing, though its ubiquity in October – police officers employing pink handcuffs, Ford selling "pink warrior" car decals – that has emboldened marketers, while causing some women to view it as just a cheap "feel-good catchall" (Kolata, 2015, p. A16). Over the past decade, the "pink" mantra has become the victim of its own success and overreach. Critics have argued that the pink ribbon trivializes the fight against breast cancer, masking the pain breast cancer victims experience and the ways corporations profit from branding themselves with pink breast cancer awareness campaigns (Jaggar, 2014; Weller, 2013). In an era of widespread distrust of established institutions and pervasive social media, social marketing of health can itself become a focus of controversy.

Social marketing, a core concept in the study of communication campaigns, has a specific definition in the academic literature. The concept's architect, Philip Kotler, defines it as "a process that uses marketing principles and techniques to change priority audience behaviors that will benefit society as well as the individual" (Lee & Kotler, 2020, p. 25). As James Dearing elaborates, it is also "a process of designing, implementing, and controlling programs to increase the acceptability of a pro-social idea among population segments of consumers" (Dearing et al., 1996, p. 345). Social marketing is an intriguing concept. It says, in effect: "You know all those great ideas developed to sell products? You can use them to sell people on taking better care of their health. But to do that, you must understand marketing principles."

Social marketing is not a theory in the analytical sense emphasized by theoretical perspectives discussed in this book – theories that make specific testable predictions (Truong, 2014). It is more of a systematic framework that draws on constructs from different disciplines and, at its best, helps guide campaign development. Its lack of a theoretical focus is a shortcoming. However, its broad sweep allows it to incorporate a variety of conceptual processes, albeit inexactly. And yet social marketing, broadly guided by commercial marketing principles, has stimulated a multitude of campaigns and campaign ideas, spanning HIV/AIDS testing, environmental protection, teen pregnancy, obesity, organ donation, and breast cancer screening, some more successful than others.

Let's examine social marketing in depth. There are five strategic steps in a social marketing campaign: (a) planning, (b) theory, (c) communication analysis, (d) implementation, and (e) evaluation and reorientation (Maibach, Kreps, & Bonaguro, 1993; see Figure 16.6).

Planning

During this first phase, campaigners make the tough choices. They select campaign goals. They decide whether to focus on creating cognitions or changing existing ones. They deliberate about which beliefs to target and whether to focus on attitudes or behaviors.

Theory

Models, concepts, and theories are the backbone of campaigns (Slater, 2006). You cannot wage a campaign without some idea of what you want to achieve and how best to attain your objectives. The central issue is whether your idea is sound, based on concepts, and of sufficient breadth so as to suggest

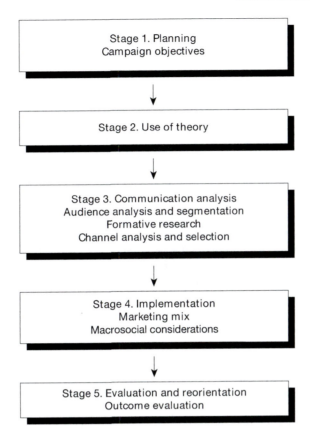

Figure 16.6 A Strategic Health Communication Campaign Model
Adapted from Maibach, Kreps, and Bonaguro (1993)

specific hypotheses. Ideas may be cheap, but good ideas are invaluable. One thing that frequently differentiates unsuccessful from successful campaigns is that ineffective interventions are based only on "seat of the pants" intuitions, while effective campaigns draw carefully on theoretical principles.

Communication Analysis

After suitable theory and concepts are selected, they must be aptly applied to the context. This occurs during the down-to-earth communication analysis phase of the campaign. Early on, campaign specialists conduct formative research to explore audience perceptions (Atkin & Freimuth, 2001). They probe targeted audience members' beliefs prior to conducting the campaign, so that they can make sure message arguments will be in sync with audience concerns. In social judgment theory terms, they want to make sure their messages fall within the latitude of acceptance and nudge people toward rethinking risky behaviors.

Implementation

During this phase, the campaign is designed, finalized, and launched. Marketing principles play a critical role here. Of particular importance are the four Ps of marketing: *product*, *price*, *placement*, and *promotion*.

Product? Most of us do not associate products with health campaigns. Yet *products* can be prosocial, as well as commercial. Products are the constellation of benefits that a campaign-suggested behavior offers target audience members, from tangible physical objects, such as Neighborhood Crime Watch posters, child safety seats, gun trigger locks, and pink ribbon wristbands, to services pro-abstinence agencies provide to ideas, like safer sex or suggestions on how to exercise more regularly. Products are fraught with meaning, and meanings can change.

Decades ago, the pink ribbon had a simple, feel-good meaning; nowadays, as you know, it calls up images of corporatization, where corporations make money from sponsoring breast cancer causes, making more in profits than is given back to charity or cancer research (Frieswick, 2009; Lieber, 2014). The iconography is complex. The symbol of pink as breast cancer awareness remains, raising questions as to how marketers can promote a product that is part commodification (and even a form of War-holesque pop art) yet at the same time an indelible emblem of caring – a product that, when translated to the very real health arena, has many beneficent, but also negative, connotations.

Thus, products come with a *price*. The price can be cultural and symbolic, or social psychological. In the AIDS context, planners debate whether to charge a price for condoms (dispensing them free of charge saves people money, but it also can make the product seem "cheap" or "unworthy"). Psychologically, the price of using condoms may be less pleasurable sex or fear of offending a partner. Campaigns strive to devise messages to convince people that these costs are more than offset by the benefits that safe sex provides over the long haul. Taking into account the monetary or psychological prices points up the need to consider the multiple meanings consumers attach to products, and the importance of devising messages that counteract perceived price with arguments about benefits, material or symbolic.

Place involves the channel in which the message is diffused. This is critically important, as correct placement can ensure reaching the target audience; incorrect placement can mean that a good message misses its target. The favorite weapon in communication campaigns is the public service advertisement (PSA), a promotional message placed in news, entertainment, or interactive media. Once novel, PSAs are now part of the media landscape – informational sound bites that savvy young people have come to enjoy or ignore. Clever, informative PSAs get noticed and can shatter illusions of invulnerability; dull – or obnoxious – ones are mentally discarded. Cheesy, preachy PSAs can elicit negative reactions, like reactance (Andsager, Austin, & Pinkleton, 2001).

The channel – for example, television, Internet, or social media – is a key factor in placement decisions. Television allows campaigners to reach lots of people and to arouse emotions through evocative messages. However, it is very expensive. Interactive media offer several advantages. They are usually cheaper than other media, permit upgrading of messages, and allow campaigns to tailor messages to audience subgroups (Kreuter et al., 2000; Lieberman, 2001).

Other health interventions capitalize on text messages (e.g., York & Loeb, 2014). Given the sheer number of texts that teens send, texting is a natural distribution channel to reach adolescents (Gregory, 2015). Thus, Sex-Ed Loop, a Chicago program, provides weekly texts on disease prevention and contraception. ICYC (In Case You're Curious), a text-chat service coordinated by Planned Parenthood of the Rocky Mountains, can text teens back with answers to their questions on sexually transmitted diseases (Hoffman, 2011).

Curious about the effects of texted health messages, a group of California researchers examined perceptions of text messages sent by a health service called the Hookup. The messages were explicit, and terse:

> Condom broke? Emergency contraception can prevent pregnancy if taken w/in 5 days – ASAP is best.
> Think ur clear if u don't have symptoms? Most STDs don't show. Get tested. Text clinic + ur zipcode to 61827.
> Scared to talk to ur parents about sex. It might not be so bad. Some ideas on how to start @ www.teensource.org.
> Don't assume a sexy pic u send will remain private. Think twice before u hit send.
> (Perry et al., 2012, p. 221)

The researchers reported that a small sample of 26 young people, ages 15–20 years old from the Los Angeles area, reacted favorably to the messages, saying they were informative, relevant, and easily shared with friends (Perry et al., 2012). In a similar vein, other research, such as on text message effects on reports of unprotected sex while on meth, found texts exerted positive influences on HIV risk behaviors (Reback et al., 2012). However, there remain important methodological questions about the generalizability of studies such as these, with small samples, and on whether those most influenced by texts were already predisposed to reduce risky sexual behaviors.

Pros and Cons of Texts. From a social marketing perspective, texts as a distribution channel offer several key benefits. They are: (1) simple; (2) convenient; (3) easy to share; (4) don't cost much; and (5) can reach people at any time, particularly when they are tempted to indulge in a risky behavior (Reback et al., 2012). On the other hand, clutter and competing posts can prevent campaign texts from capturing receivers' attention (Metzger, 2009). Texts can also be impersonal and cold, as well as lacking the kinds of arguments and emotional resonance required to help people come to terms with unhealthy behaviors. They also have a self-selection bias: People must choose to receive the texts. Those who choose to receive them may already agree with the message texts convey. Thus, texts may not reach those individuals in most need of the information, perpetuating knowledge gaps. Viewed from McGuire's and other stage approaches, text messages are a first step in the arduous process of behavior change, helping individuals realize they have a problem or offering a recommendation. But they need to be supplemented by more extensive interpersonal or mediated communications to change behavior in the long run. Still, it is important to remember that digital channels offer communication benefits that were unavailable or unimaginable in the twentieth century. In the wake of the outbreak of the coronavirus, nations created websites and used mobile apps that gave specific information, such as locations where people could be tested, as well as information about patients who had been infected and locales they visited before they tested positive (Cave, 2020). Yet the knowledge gap reminds us there could be key socioeconomic and educational differences in who accessed these sites, with the poor comparatively less informed, despite their high risk of contracting the virus.

Promotion is the final marketing P, and it is a key part of the planning process. Promotion involves persuasion – application of theories discussed in this book and implemented in a macro campaign setting (e.g., Garnett et al., 2014). As noted above, there is no substitute for theory in devising effective campaigns. Theory offers specific predictions, helps researchers explain complex phenomena, articulates underlying micro and macro processes, pinpoints messages practitioners should develop, identifies particular subgroups messages should target, and offers suggestions on how to revise campaigns when they do not meet initial objectives.

The reasoned action model, along with planned behavior processes, suggest ways to appreciate salient beliefs and norms of targeted audience members. The EPPM offers helpful strategies to guide a variety of fear-based campaigns, such as those against texting-while-driving, a focus of EPPM research (Cismaru, 2014; see Figure 16.7). Narratives and transportation, with a focus on harnessing stories, are a natural approach for health campaigns (for an interesting study, see Niederdeppe and colleagues, 2019). The venerable ELM also suggests strategies to facilitate cognitive elaboration under high involvement (Oh & Sundar, 2015), along with more contemporary approaches that try to involve target audience members in the active co-creation of campaign messages. Indeed, van den Heerik and colleagues (2017) did just this, asking individuals to complete the slogan "smoking is sooo ..." on social networking sites with an outdated phrase that conveyed its irrelevance to young people today.

A more up-to-date example involves the coronavirus outbreak, where persuasion offered important suggestions on how best to help mitigate the problem. Evidence about the number of people exposed to the virus, as well as moving narratives about individuals who gave of themselves to help others, undoubtedly helped influence attitudes.

Clearly, the Extended Parallel Process model has important implications, such as that persuaders should convince people the problem was severe (not a problem once news spread), and that they were susceptible to the virus, particularly if they were very old, or could spread the virus to others, even if their younger age shielded them from harmful personal consequences. As we know, it is always difficult to shatter the illusion of invulnerability, but explaining how individuals similar to the target audience had contracted the virus or calling on celebrities, like Tom Hanks and his wife, who announced that they had been diagnosed with the virus, probably helped convince people to take necessary preventive steps.

The EPPM also highlights the importance of clearly explaining ways people could protect themselves and family members – by frequent hand washing and using certain hand sanitizers – and emphasizing that people were capable of changing their habits, as it might be a matter of life and death. The handwashing message diffused widely. However, not all these messages reached or impacted individuals at risk, as indicated by young people still congregating in New York City bars in March, 2020 before the mayor shut down thousands of bars in the city. There is also much we don't know about the ways fear was harnessed helpfully or poorly in the coronavirus case. Yet calling on promotion, and the other Ps, can help campaigns about deeply problematic health issues achieve some of their objectives.

Revisiting the 4Ps. The 4Ps, however, are not without problems. Over the years, social marketing scholars have discussed the strengths and shortcomings of these classic, but dated, 4Ps (Edgar, Huhman, & Miller, 2017). While appreciating their parsimony, scholars have highlighted their limits in contemporary social marketing contexts. The term "product," for example, doesn't describe the host of less tangible recommendations social marketers offer, some not focused on a physical product at all. Social marketing campaigns frequently emphasize services or activities, like increased exercise, rather than products per se (Eagle et al., 2013).

Researchers have observed that it can be difficult to locate a clear-cut product when marketers want individuals to *refrain* from performing a problematic behavior. For these reasons, scholars have suggested the term product be replaced with another "P": Proposition, a general, but perhaps more useful, term (Peattie & Peattie, 2003). Others have suggested two other potent Ps be promulgated: Political power and public opinion influence. From an alphabetical perspective, marketing scholars have even suggested that the 4Ps be replaced entirely – by 4Cs, like concept mix, cost mix, channels mix, and communication mix – or by 4Rs, relevance, response, relationships, and results (Eagle et al., p. 32).

(a)

(b)

Figure 16.7a–b Harnessing Theory in Distracted Driving Campaigns. Texting while driving is a major cause of distracted driving, longer reaction times, and accidents. Thousands of people have been killed and hundreds of thousands have been injured in car crashes caused by mentally impaired driving. Fear appeals, guided by the EPPM have been a major focus of campaigns to curb texting-while-driving. While it is a challenge to devise effective EPPM-based interventions to risk groups in the real world, the theory's postulates offer helpful suggestions for message planners

Images courtesy of Getty Images.

The 4Cs emphasis on channels and communication has merit, given the awkward application of the original term, "place," with its emphasis on physical locations, to the current multimedia online environment. On the other hand the 4Rs that have been proposed seem a little unwieldy.

In sum, the 4Ps have an alliterative simplicity, but understate the unique properties of health marketing contexts. Clearly, some adaptation of these older terms to the current era are welcome.

Evaluation and Reorientation

Contemporary campaign communications sites trumpet the success of campaigns, boasting that they have had whopping, incredible success. They reduce smoking! They curb drug abuse! Before the campaign, things were terrible, and now lives have improved!

It is important to remember that campaigns frequently have a vested interest in heralding success. If the campaign shows improvement, the organizations that spearheaded it can make a forceful case that they should get more money to wage another campaign. This is why it is important to evaluate campaigns as objectively as possible, hopefully using outside agencies that are not connected to the intervention. Campaigns are evaluated through careful empirical studies that use *comparisons* as the basis for judging success.

Evaluators frequently compare those who had exposure to the campaign with a control group of others who did not have exposure. They also make over-time comparisons, looking to see if the problem has declined since the advent of the campaign. Researchers evaluate campaigns on three specific levels: *individual*, *community*, and *state*.

At the individual level, evaluators compare people who viewed or heard many campaign messages with those who were exposed to few, if any. If the intervention worked, individuals with exposure to many campaign communications should change their attitude more in the intended direction than those who were exposed to a handful or none at all.

Researchers also evaluate campaigns at the community level. One town is randomly assigned to be the treatment group. Its citizens receive promotional materials – let's say to persuade people to buckle up when they drive. An equivalent community serves as the control; its residents are not exposed to campaign messages. Researchers then compare the communities, for example, by enlisting police officers to stand on street corners counting the number of drivers wearing safety belts. If a higher proportion of drivers in the treatment community wear safety belts than in the control town, the campaign is declared a success (Roberts & Geller, 1994).

Campaigns can also be assessed at the state level. Let's assume that the number of casualties drops in Indiana shortly after the conclusion of a media campaign promoting seat belt use in the Hoosier state. Let's also assume that casualties in Iowa, a state that shares some demographic features with Indiana, do not decline over a similar time period. These data give us confidence that the Indiana campaign exerted a causal impact on seat belt behavior.

Evaluation is critical because it shows whether campaign objectives have been met. It can provide campaign specialists with feedback that can be used to reorient or adjust the campaign midstream if messages are not exerting their desired impact. But evaluation is not a perfect science. In individual-level surveys, one never knows for sure whether those who saw campaign messages were the same in all other ways as those who did not happen to view the campaign. In community evaluations, researchers can never be 100 percent certain that the treatment and control towns are exactly alike. If the treatment community in the safety belt study had more drivers who were older (and therefore more safety conscious) than the control community, the older age of drivers, rather than the campaign, could have produced the observed effects. In a similar fashion, if the Indiana news media extensively covered an automobile accident that involved the governor's wife, the news coverage – not the campaign – could have caused the concomitant decline in traffic casualties. Researchers take precautions to factor in these extraneous variables, quantifying their contributions in statistical tests.

Online media campaigns pose a different set of procedural problems. It can be difficult to convince individuals, who are randomly assigned to a particular intervention, to attend to an Internet-based campaign. Sites that house campaigns can disappear or change without warning, and different subgroups in a particular sample may answer different portions of the questionnaire (Rice & Atkin, 2009). On a positive note, new evaluation strategies, geared to social media, are opening up new avenues to assess campaigns. Researchers can gain access to Twitter data, allowing them to assess the content of tweets on a health topic. Emery and her colleagues (2014) did exactly this, carefully analyzing some 193,000 tweets in response to an anti-smoking campaign and discovering more than 85 percent showed acceptance of the campaign message. Methodologically imaginative as such a post-campaign analysis of tweets is, it is limited, alas, to individuals who choose to tweet. It does not tell us the impact of the campaign on the entire, or targeted members of the, campaign audience.

More broadly, the study underscores the important role evaluation research plays in campaigns. Evaluation documents campaign effects. It pinpoints campaign failures. It offers specialists useful feedback for future campaigns. Evaluation also serves an important political function. Private and public groups spend hundreds of thousands of dollars on campaigns. They are entitled to know if they have gotten their money's worth. When government spends taxpayer money on anti-smoking or antidrug campaigns, the public has a right to know if socially valuable goals – reducing smoking or drug use – have actually been achieved. A final example, involving a campaign to persuade young people not to try a deadly drug, illustrates the strengths and complexities of campaign assessment.

Evaluation in Action: Montana Meth Project

Methamphetamine is an addictive synthetic drug that can wreak devastating effects. In Montana the state government has spent close to $50 million each year, trying to deal with costs of meth abuse. In an effort to remedy the problem, a non-profit organization launched an anti-meth campaign some years back, blitzing the airwaves and plastering billboards with hard-hitting, graphic ads. The ads are compelling, capitalizing on fear and vividness appeals (to view them, see www.montanameth.org/ads). The Montana Meth Project says the campaign has significantly reduced meth use and meth-related crimes.

But has it? A systematic evaluation, published in a scientific journal, offers a more skeptical conclusion (Erceg-Hurn, 2008). The study concludes that there is no evidence that the campaign reduced use of methamphetamine. Showcasing the important role comparisons play in research, the researcher noted that any reductions in meth usage in Montana could have occurred *not* because of the advertisements, but for another reason. Stricter laws were adopted in 2005, around the time the campaign began. These laws reduced the availability of meth in Montana communities and may have been responsible for some of the positive effects that proponents attributed to the campaign. This is not to say the campaign had no effects. It may have raised awareness about the problem and changed some people's attitudes, perhaps via increasing conversations about meth (Richards, 2014; Southwell & Yzer, 2009). However, it does not appear to have exerted the striking effects that its planners claimed. This highlights the importance of conducting hard-nosed empirical evaluations of campaigns (see Figure 16.8).

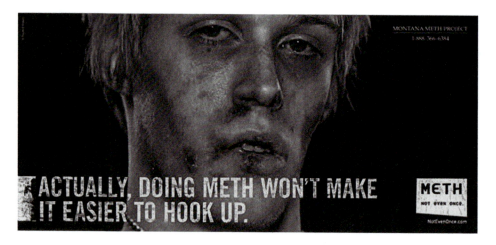

Figure 16.8 There Are Many Campaign Message Appeals Out There That Are Designed To Convince Young People Not to Use Methamphetamine. Some campaigns may be effective, others less so. As evaluation research makes clear, we cannot assume campaigns work unless there is evidence documenting their effects

Image obtained from Montana Meth Project

Real-World Constraints and Societal Forces

Campaigns may be based on theory, planned according to marketing principles, and evaluated through high-powered statistics. However, they take place in the real world, with its rough edges, cultural norms, and political constraints. Societal norms and macrosocial factors influence campaigns in a variety of ways. Anti-smoking campaigns had little chance of changing attitudes so long as most Americans trusted the tobacco companies or doubted that smoking caused cancer. As evidence mounted that smoking causes cancer and Americans learned that tobacco companies withheld knowledge that smoking was addictive, anti-smoking campaigns faced a more receptive audience to their messages. Even so (and not surprisingly), anti-smoking campaigns attempting to increase public support for regulation of the tobacco industry have faced daunting opposition from the tobacco industry, as the gripping, factually based movie *The Insider* documented.

In a similar vein, the alcohol industry – for example beer manufacturers – fought efforts, spearheaded by grassroots groups like Mothers Against Drunk Driving (MADD), to reduce drunk driving. In the 1980s, the industry opposed an innocuous bill that aimed to force states to approve laws that banned the sale of alcohol to individuals under the age of 21 (Lerner, 2011). President Ronald Reagan signed the bill into law, but only after extensive lobbying from MADD.

For much of the twentieth-century American culture promoted or tolerated drunk driving with a wink and a nod. Anti-drunk driving campaigns, such as those eventually developed by MADD, initially had a hard cultural road to hoe. Little by little, MADD made inroads on cultural beliefs about drinking and driving, harnessing the impassioned, personal appeals of its founder, Candy Lightner, whose daughter was tragically killed by a drunk driver, through: Community events; a national media campaign, with the brainchild slogan "Friends don't let friends drive drunk"; and messages conveyed in entertainment news that brandished a new alliterative phrase, "designated driver." The message, reframing drunk driving from an acceptable problem to shameful moral behavior, diffused widely through American culture in the 1980s, leading to legal changes and punishments for driving while drunk.

MADD's campaigns have been stunningly effective over the course of the past decades, but they had to overcome initial cultural and political resistance.

Thus, there are many social and cultural factors that determine campaign success. You cannot understand communication campaigns without appreciating the larger milieu in which they take place. Big corporations that produce and distribute unhealthy products like tobacco, sugary soft drinks, and fast food have many more economic and political resources at their disposal than do social marketing groups. Ads for soft drinks and unhealthy food appear during prime time on television, while messages discussing the health risks of obesity appear on less credible channels that do not reach as many people.

For example, Coca-Cola gave $3 million to the city of Chicago to promote the deceptive message that Coke products "can be part of an active, healthy lifestyle that includes a sensible, balanced diet and regular physical activity" (Schatzker, 2015, p. 15). The message suggests that as long as you eat healthy food and exercise, it is healthy to drink Coke. But it takes lots of exercise to rid oneself of the calories contained in the number of Cokes many Americans drink each day, and the sugar content in soft drinks contributes to the death of more than 180,000 people each year (Schatzker, 2015). What's more, the people most likely to consume sugar-sweetened soft drinks are frequently young, poorly educated, and already overweight. It is frequently more difficult to reach and influence poorer and less educated individuals, because they do not have the time, inclination, or ability to contemplate and act on health recommendations (though see Jacobs, 2018).

Taking note of the many macro barriers to campaign success, Niederdeppe and his colleagues (2008b) pulled these issues together, identifying key challenges that face health communication campaigns. One challenge is economic self-interest: It is hard to mobilize policymakers with a stake in the status quo to make changes if they stand to lose financial benefits. Second, campaigns emphasize making individual changes, which are important, but minimize the significance of economic, structural, and cultural factors, which, as we saw with soft drink companies, can potently determine individual behavior. Yet campaigns are inevitably waged and distributed in a capitalist society, with inequities as well as benefits, and they are, for better or worse, usually targeted at individuals and groups.

Campaign Effects

Do campaigns work? Do they influence targeted attitudes and behaviors? After reading this and thinking about the issues, what do you think? What is your best guess?

There is little question that campaigns face an uphill battle, even on the individual, psychological, level of analysis. As McGuire's matrix stipulates, interventions must first attract the target audience and capture its attention. This can be difficult. For a variety of psychological reasons, Caroline Schooler and colleagues note, "Those whom a campaign most seeks to reach with health information are the least motivated to pay attention to it" (1998, p. 414). The last thing addicted smokers, drug users, or gamblers want to do is pay attention to moralistic messages that tell them to stop doing what makes them happy.

Today's teenagers have grown up with health campaigns and have been lectured and hectored by well-meaning, but sometimes overbearing, adults. When a media campaign tells them that they are engaging in unhealthy behavior, they can become resistant and reactive. The message may evoke a threat to their freedom, leading them to embrace the unhealthy behavior that the communicator condemns (see Burgoon et al., 2002; Dillard & Shen, 2005; Rains, 2013; Shen, 2010).

Psychological reactance theory suggests that an overly moralistic health message can threaten an individual's freedom and self-determination, arousing *reactance*. Reactance is the emotional state experienced when one's valued freedom is threatened. When a campaign arouses reactance, people sometimes do precisely the opposite of what the communicator recommends (Brehm, 1966). This may be especially likely when the threatened freedom is important (Quick, Shen, & Dillard, 2013). (As parents sang in a song from the musical, *The Fantasticks*: "Why did the kids put beans in their ears? No one can hear with beans in their ears. After a while the reason appears. They did it "cause we said no!" Or, as a character in the movie *Hudson Hawk* said, "I hated cigarettes until I saw my first No Smoking sign!")

There is no guarantee a campaign will work. It may fail, and plenty do. There are five major barriers to the success of a health information campaign:

1 Campaigns do not reach or influence those most affected by the problem, whose social media feeds can favor the allure of unhealthy products.
2 Campaign messages may be lost in the clutter of social media.
3 Although aims are well-intentioned, messages may not be in sync with how the target audience thinks or feels about the problem.
4 Campaigns may arouse reactance, turning target audience members off with preachy messages that may smack of middle-aged adult values, or threatening freedom through overly graphic imagery on cigarette or e-cigarette packages (LaVoie et al., 2017).
5 Campaign messages are swamped by the prevailing values of mass culture, as when an anti-obesity campaign cannot compete with marketing for fast food and high-calorie junk food.

Okay – but I wouldn't be devoting an entire chapter to this topic if campaigns failed consistently and repeatedly! In fact, more than a half-century of research indicates that if practitioners know their stuff, apply theory deftly, and utilize principles of social marketing, they can wage effective campaigns (Noar, 2006).

Campaigns have changed health-related attitudes. The most noteworthy example is cigarette smoking, which has declined dramatically over the years. It has dropped by about two-thirds over the past half-century (see Cigarette smoking among U.S. adults hits all-time low, 2019). One cause of this decline is the multitude of campaigns that have influenced beliefs (Peracchio & Luna, 1998; Pfau & Van Bockern, 1994), employed emotional appeals, such as fear and disgust (Clayton et al, 2017; Leshner, Bolls, & Thomas, 2009), and drawn on social learning theory in behavioral interventions (Maccoby & Farquhar, 1975; Hornik, 2002; see Figure 16.9).

To be sure, it is hard to quantify the precise impact anti-smoking campaigns have exerted on smoking decrements because one has to link particular campaigns with an overall drop in smoking. Certainly there are other causes, such as changing interpersonal norms toward cigarette smoking. At the same time, methodologically savvy evaluations have offered strong evidence connecting declines in cigarette consumption with communication campaigns (Burgoon, Hendriks, & Alvaro, 2001; Emery et al., 2012; Farrelly et al., 2009; Pierce, Emery, & Gilpin, 2002; Siegel & Biener, 2002; Worden & Flynn, 2002; see Figure 16.9).

(a)

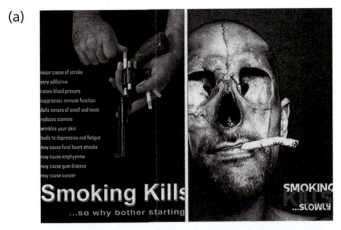

(b)

(c)

Figure 16.9a–c Anti-smoking Campaigns Have Employed an Endless Variety of Appeals to Change Attitudes Toward Smoking. Over the long haul, the campaigns have helped to reduce smoking levels in the United States

Images obtained from Tobacco News

Emboldened by studies like these, researchers have identified a number of concrete steps that campaign planners should take to maximize the likelihood of success in health campaigns. These studies help us appreciate the types of effects campaigns can exert. Health interventions are particularly likely to succeed when practitioners:

1 Begin with a theory to generate hypotheses about target audience message processing and messages that should have optimal impact.
2 Understand the audience and tailor messages so they connect with audience members' needs, pre-existing attitudes, and the functions those attitudes serve (Cesario, Grant, & Higgins, 2004; Wan, 2008). (One way to do this is to choose communicators who have credibility with the target audience, as seen in the U.S. Surgeon General's recognition that influencers like Kylie Jenner would be more effective in persuading young people to take preventive steps on the coronavirus than a stodgy government doc. Jenner's post, communicated in social media influencer argot – "Hey guys. Happy self-quarantine" – was totally in sync with the pandemic moment.)
3 Target messages so they are grounded in the cultural characteristics of a particular subgroup, connect with community channels, are developed by community members, and are tailored as much as possible to the unique traits of the target audience (Kreuter et al., 2000; Jensen et al., 2012; Noar, Benac, & Harris, 2007; Dutta et al., 2019; Hecht & Lee, 2008; Hecht & Miller-Day, 2009; Pope, Pelletier, & Guertin, 2018).
4 Refine messages so that they are relevant, cogent, and of high production value; this is particularly important when targeting young people, who have grown up with savvy, interactive media.
5 Coordinate efforts across media, and repeat messages over time and in different media and interpersonal channels.
6 Supplement media materials as much as possible with community contacts and participation (McAlister & Fernandez, 2002; Rice & Atkin, 2002).
7 Appreciate that it is frequently easier to promote a new behavior than to convince people to stop a dysfunctional behavior (Snyder, 2001).
8 Design messages so that they cultivate social norms regarding appropriate behavior. (For example, anti-smoking campaigns capitalized on social norms that it is neither healthy nor cool to smoke. During the coronavirus outbreak, celebrities like Justin Bieber appealed to a widely-diffused social norm to stay at home and keep away from others, calling on both moral and conformity pressures.)
9 Concentrate on building awareness. Theory and research suggest that the most consistent effect campaigns exert is on beliefs – creating awareness and knowledge of risks of cigarette smoking, drug use, drunk driving, texting while driving, failure to wear seat belts, unhealthy high-fat diets, and HIV/AIDS. Televised and social media campaigns can diffuse information about health risks to large numbers of people. While campaigns ordinarily cannot produce long-term behavioral change in and of themselves, they can start the ball rolling, building a branded health image associated with positive affect, and helping people to think about changing the risky behavior (Prochaska et al., 1992).
10 Maintain flexibility. Campaigns sometimes have to recalibrate if they do not reach the target audience, the message is not memorable, or the message offends individuals. In addition, once campaigns have proceeded over a number of years, they need to reassess their approach. (For example, breast cancer campaigns seem to have succeeded in creating awareness of the risks of breast cancer. Thus, they need to get beyond pink ribbons and "pinkification" to the more challenging tasks of propelling individuals to take steps to change their diets, get tested, and consider how best to be treated; see Kolata, 2015.)

These prescriptions and conclusions about campaigns are based primarily on cognitive and affective, individual-level perspectives. Another theoretical approach to campaigns focuses on interpersonal, social norms appeals. It is interesting, relevant to university settings, and not without problems. The next section examines this contemporary perspective.

Social Norm Campaign Approach

We all care about the environment and public health, right? We all want to live in a cleaner, less polluted environment. Well, perhaps not everybody, but it is a norm – a widely held prescriptive belief, or socially accepted behavior in society – that people should do their part to keep the social surroundings free of litter and should also maintain their personal hygiene. The presence of strong social norms has implications for persuasion. It suggests that persuasive campaign specialists could harness these normative beliefs and unleash their psychological power in the service of attitude change. And that is exactly what communication campaign practitioners have done.

The psychological principle underlying the social norm perspective is that people like to be in sync with what others do; they feel more comfortable when they go along with their peers, their social compatriots. As discussed in Chapter 6, one of the functions that attitudes serve is social adjustive: They help us adjust to reference groups, or the views of significant others. By communicating the social norms on an issue, communicators can subtly encourage individuals to change their attitudes so they are more in keeping with the sentiments of the larger group. There is a conformity – or, less pejoratively, "desire to fit in" – basis to these ideas. Although they are loath to admit it, people (some more than others) frequently feel comfortable taking positions that bind them to the larger group. We humans are social animals.

The social norms approach is decidedly indirect, unlike the direct fear appeals and hard-hitting messages used in anti-smoking campaigns. It does not say: "You should do this or you will suffer unpleasant outcomes down the line," or "Here are three reasons why you should *not* perform this behavior." Instead, it softly holds out the behavior of others and suggests, "Consider doing this, in light of your social obligations." The idea is that once people learn about a salient social norm, social pressures or personal obligations will kick in, and they will persuade themselves to carry out the action.

You can find echoes of a social norms perspective in Fishbein and Ajzen's Reasoned Action Model (see Chapter 6). Remember that the model emphasizes the influences of injunctive normative beliefs, beliefs that significant others endorse a targeted behavior, and descriptive normative beliefs, beliefs that important others actually perform the behavior. Kallgren and his colleagues have shown that communicators can call on norms to encourage people not to litter in public places. Norms are particularly impactful when individuals are induced to focus attention on the social obligation to not litter (Kallgren, Reno, & Cialdini, 2000).

Another normative behavior that a social norms approach can influence is one you may not have thought about: Hand-washing. Perhaps it seems prudish and cleanliness-obsessive to encourage people to wash their hands! But public health experts emphasize that regular washing of hands can prevent the spread of infectious diseases and viruses, particularly the infamous coronavirus. Although 91 percent of Americans say they wash their hands after using a public restroom, just 82 percent of individuals whose behaviors were publicly observed actually did so (Bakalar, 2005). Men are less likely to wash their hands than women. So, now we have a problem in persuasion, one that campaigns can help combat. How do you convince people to wash their hands without arousing reactance or sounding prudish, like everybody's meddling mother?

Maria Knight Lapinski and her colleagues (2013) theorized that a social norms approach could be helpful, and they dreamed up an imaginative study to demonstrate normative impact. Given that men are less likely to wash their hands in public restrooms than women, they directed their messages at men. They developed color posters that displayed the backs of five guys, who looked like college students, in a restroom facing urinals. To increase realism, the posters showed the men wearing backward baseball caps with university insignia. One experimental group of participants viewed a message that said, "Four out of five college students wash their hands EVERY time they use the bathroom"; a second group saw the message, "One out of five college students wash their hands EVERY time they use the bathroom"; and a third group served as a no-message control.

How do you think the researchers assessed message effects on hand-washing? Very directly! Once a man entered the washroom, an experimental confederate would follow him in, stand near the sinks, and pretend to clean a stain on his shirt. The observer surreptitiously recorded whether men washed their hands after they were done with their business and, if so, how long their hands were under water (the amount of time the water ran).

The results indicated that men who viewed the messages emphasizing that four of five *and* one of five college students wash their hands every time they use the bathroom were more likely than no-message controls to wash their hands and to wash them for a longer time. Interestingly, guys in the one-of-five-college-students-wash-their-hands group were more likely than those in the four-of-five group to wash their hands, either because they didn't believe that four of five men actually wash their hands or, perhaps feeling shamed that only 20 percent of fellow men washed their hands, decided to right the wrong by engaging in a hand-wash themselves. However, participants in the four-of-five condition did display more favorable attitudes toward hand-washing than other men. To be sure, we do not know whether the message-induced change in hand-washing would hold over time. Undoubtedly, to produce longer-term changes, the posters would have to be supplemented by regular, supportive messages by peers interpersonally or via social media. But they suggest that a theory-based appeal to social norms is an effective prod to influence actions that have important implications for public health.

Social norms marketing can influence behaviors in addition to those that bear on littering and personal hygiene. Campaign practitioners have devised social norm appeals in hopes of influencing a troubling campus activity: Alcohol abuse.

Social Norms and Binge Drinking

It isn't clear whether Leslie Baltz, who was in her fourth year [at the University of Virginia], wanted to drink that much. The 21-year-old honor student, who had a double major in art history and studio art, liked to paint and sketch. Once, at the age of 11, she wrote 31 poems for her mother, one for each day of the month, about love, dreams, and impermanence.

At a party that Saturday, Ms. Baltz drank enough booze-spiked punch that she decided to lie down at a friend's house while her buddies went out. When they returned that night after U. Va.'s 34–20 upset of Virginia Tech, they found her unconscious at the foot of a stairway. Ms. Baltz's blood alcohol level was 0.27%, more than triple the state's legal limit for drivers, but probably survivable if not for her fall … She was declared dead of head injuries. Thus, Ms. Baltz became the fifth Virginia college student to die of alcohol-related causes that autumn, and the 18th at U. Va. since 1990.

(Murray & Gruley, 2000, p. A10)

Unfortunately, Leslie is not the only student to die as a result of alcohol abuse. Accidents due to drinking claim too many students' lives each year. Drinking, of course, is common on campus. Some students can be viewed as "binge drinkers" – men who consume at least five, and women who drink four or more, drinks in one sitting (see Figure 16.10). As many as 40 percent of college students, the number depending on the campus, have engaged in binge drinking (Galbicsek, 2019).

For years, universities used a pastiche of anti-drinking appeals, ranging from scare tactics to pictures of cars destroyed by drunk drivers. Convinced that these did not work and searching for something new, they opted to employ a technique based on communication research and social marketing.

Figure 16.10 Binge Drinking Has Been a Major Problem on Some College Campuses. One strategy to alleviate the problem is social norms marketing, as shown in this example. The strategy has met with mixed success

Image obtained from the Penn State University Collegian

Called social norms marketing, the strategy draws on the psychology of norms – what we think important others are doing or what we think important others believe we *should* do (Fishbein & Ajzen, 2010; Goldstein & Cialdini, 2007; Park et al., 2009). In the case of drinking, it targets students' perceptions that others drink a lot. The idea is that students overestimate how much alcohol their peers consume. Believing that everyone else drinks a lot and wanting to fit into the dominant college culture, they drink more than they would like. The solution follows logically: "If students' drinking practices are fostered, or at least maintained, by the erroneous perception that other students feel more positively toward these practices than they do," two scholars noted, "then correcting this misperception should lower their alcohol consumption" (Schroeder & Prentice, 1998, p. 2153).

Social norms marketing, appealing to a desire to fit in with the peer culture, devises campaign messages suggesting that students hold incorrect social norms about drinking, believing drinking is more common than it actually is.

A number of universities have adopted this approach in an effort to curb alcohol abuse. The University of Virginia placed posters in the blue and orange school colors in freshman dorms. "Most U. Va. 1st years have 0 to 4 drinks per week," posters declared. A Rutgers University "RU SURE?" campaign devised messages listing the top ten misperceptions on campus, ranging from the humorous ("It's easy to find a parking place on campus") to the critical ("Everyone who parties gets wasted"). The latter was followed with the answer that two-thirds of Rutgers students stop at three or fewer drinks (Lederman et al., 2001).

What's the verdict? Do social norm campaigns work? The evidence is mixed. Northern Illinois University implemented a social norms campaign in an attempt to reduce the number of students who thought binge drinking was the campus norm. Prior to the campaign, 70 percent of the students believed binge drinking was common practice. By the campaign's conclusion, the percentage had dropped to 51 percent. Self-reported binge drinking decreased by nearly 9 percent during this period (Haines & Spear, 1996). Other studies, using more finely tuned scientific methods, have reported similar findings (Godbold & Pfau, 2000; Jang, 2012; Perkins & Craig, 2003; Schroeder & Prentice, 1998).

These results have intrigued scholars, but raised questions. Some wonder whether students genuinely changed their views or were just saying they had, in order to comply with the norm of pleasing the faculty investigator. Other scholars doubt that simply providing correct information is sufficient to overcome the more emotional reasons why people choose to drink (Austin & Chen, 1999). Polonec and colleagues (2006) raised more serious questions. In a study of Penn State undergraduates' perceptions of social norms, they discovered that over 70 percent of respondents did not believe that most students drank "0 to 4" drinks when they partied. If the social norm is not credible with students, the message will not persuade them. The researchers also found that social norms messages are singularly ineffective in reaching an important target of the campaign: Hard-core drinkers. Other carefully conducted studies have also cast doubt on the effectiveness of various university-based social norms campaigns (Cameron & Campo, 2006; Campo & Cameron, 2006; Russell, Clapp, & DeJong, 2005; Yanovitzky, Stewart, & Lederman, 2006).

Thus, we glimpse the complex issues surrounding social norms campaign persuasion. A social norm approach can be a remarkably effective tool in the campaign message arsenal. It has a solid track record in influencing public health-oriented behaviors, such as littering and hand-washing. Indirect appeals can elide defensive mechanisms and appeal to a desire to conform to prosocial societal norms. On the other hand, social norms appeals are not always effective in curbing binge drinking. Drinking is a more emotion-packed behavior than littering or hand-washing, freighted with psychological needs and addictive elements. In addition, students may doubt the validity of social norm estimates, either because their peer group drinks more or they need to believe that binge drinking is the cool thing to do. Thus, social norm-based appeals to curb drinking require an exquisite appreciation of the target audience and precise tailoring of message to receivers, the success of which depends on an apt integration of theory, message pretesting, and ongoing evaluation research.

Social Media Implications

Social norms can intersect with social media-based health campaigns in interesting ways (Rimal & Lapinski, 2015). A social media site can promote health behavior by publicizing descriptive norms. For example, research indicates that the amount of physical exercise reported on an individual's social networking site and the size of the person's social network can increase individuals' physical exercise over time (Carpenter & Amaravadi, 2019). If people think others are engaging in healthful behavior – and their friends are the ones reporting the healthy activities – they may feel a social pressure, triggered by social norms and dissonance reduction, to perform these actions.

You could argue that a campaign that appeals to subtle social pressures – "I'll join the health club because all my friends are" – is relying on conformity appeals, employing a questionable means for a positive end. Perhaps in the long run, it's morally problematic to reinforce social conformity to get people to take better care of their health. Or perhaps this is a good way to get a foot in the door, a realistic way to induce people to reduce problematic behaviors, triggering central processing that instigates deeper long-term changes.

Values and Ethics

You may know the game "Where's Waldo?" Perhaps you played it as a child. You would try to spot the cagey character, Waldo, who was hiding somewhere in the picture of a house or outdoors scene. He was always there; you just had to locate his whereabouts. So it is with values and ethical aspects of campaigns, an issue touched on but not directly broached in this chapter. Noted one ethicist, "They are always there, the value judgments: the choices in policy decisions. There are always choices made" (Guttman, 2000, p. 70).

It is nice to think of campaigns as these objective entities, planned by scientifically minded behavioral engineers, implemented by marketing specialists, and evaluated by statisticians. To be sure, campaigns are devised by social science and communication professionals who call on the science and art of persuasive communication in the development of health messages. Yet inevitably, choices must be made. Values and ethics are an inescapable part of persuasion, all the more so in the case of health campaigns which involve larger social and cultural issues. These are six key, value-based issues that face health campaign practitioners:

● *What is the locus of the dilemma?* Planners of a childhood obesity campaign may perceive that the source of the problem is children and their parents. In this case, they would direct messages at kids, moms, and dads, employing media channels they use at home, individually or as a family. Campaign organizers may contend instead that the problem lies with schools that serve lunches kids love – cheeseburgers and fries – but which are filled with transfats. If they locate the dilemma at this level, they would direct messages to school boards and school administrators, as well as to children in the school setting. Alternatively, planners may believe the problem is more social-structural, rooted in American culture's infatuation with fast food and the money restaurants make from serving fatty meals. If so, they might decide to focus their energies on convincing the city board of health to ban the use of transfats in restaurant cooking.

Similarly, in the climate change arena, the locus of the dilemma can be on the individual, with campaigns trying to persuade people not to buy paper straws, drive gas-guzzling cars less, buy more electric cars, use less hot water, and recycle more. Alternatively, one could argue the onus should be on the macro level. According to this view, climate change campaigns should work to persuade auto companies to make more electric cars and restaurants to use more climate-friendly meat. On a political level, they should work with policy-makers to persuade governments to insist on stricter emission and fuel economy standards for cars, as well as signing international global warming agreements that commit countries to strict environmental policies on greenhouse gas emissions. Alas, this is a highly political issue, in which partisan attitudes and politicians' emphasis on their own electoral fortunes can overwhelm the efforts of persuasion campaigns. Nonetheless, hope springs eternal, and deciding on the optimal locus of the problem can help determine the most effective social marketing strategies on climate change and related issues (Dutta, 2006; Dutta-Bergman, 2005).

- *If the goal is to benefit the public good, is the campaign designed to do more good for certain members of the public than for others?* There is no absolute definition of "public good." Instead, the definition inevitably reflects value judgments. Should good be defined in utilitarian terms – a cardiovascular risk reduction campaign designed to reach the greatest number of people? Or should it be viewed in a more deontological fashion, emphasizing values like justice – as when planners of a blood pressure screening campaign, acknowledging that poverty induces stress that can elevate blood pressure, choose to focus primarily on poor people?

  Should campaign specialists direct the campaign at a large, heterogeneous population, knowing full well the intervention may increase knowledge gaps? Or should the campaign focus critical attention at low socioeconomic individuals to reduce the likelihood of enhanced gaps in knowledge? As Nurit Guttman asks, "Should campaign resources be devoted to target populations believed to be particularly needy or those who are more likely to adopt its recommendations?" (1997, p. 181). Given scarce resources, which strategy makes more sense?

- *Are the costs of focusing on a particular audience segment worth the benefits?* Segmenting campaign audiences into different demographic groups is usually a worthwhile strategy. Segmentation can make it more likely that the campaign will reach the target audience. However, it can also lead to stigmatization, as when a well-publicized HIV/AIDS campaign focuses particular efforts at gay men in a particular city, or an anti-teen pregnancy campaign directs considerable attention on low-income minorities in particular neighborhoods. Campaign planners might reason that the campaign should focus efforts on particular groups from a public health perspective. But if the intervention produces more stigmatization than health gains, were the benefits worth the cost? (See Hornik & Ramirez, 2006 for engaging discussion of these and related issues.)

- *How are values implicated in the solutions campaigners recommend?* The recommended solution inevitably reflects a particular set of values. A teen pregnancy prevention campaign that urges people to practice safer sex has opted not to communicate the values of abstinence, or waiting to have sex until you are married. Social norm-based anti-drinking campaigns advocate moderate drinking, an option that some parents oppose. Are these the best options?

- *How do values influence criteria used to proclaim success?* Evaluators must devise benchmarks that can be used to determine if a campaign has succeeded. Values come into play here. For example, an intervention to promote breast cancer screening could be deemed successful if it increased the number of women who had mammograms yearly. However, given that those most likely to get mammograms are women with insurance that covers the procedure, the criterion for success may exclude poor women (Guttman, 2000). Once again, the evaluator may reason that a campaign cannot do everything and note that increases in mammography, even among those with insurance policies, is an achievement. That may be a reasonable call, but it reflects a certain set of value judgments.

- Although different values shape campaigns, all campaigns are based on a core assumption: *The world will be a better place if social interventions try to change individual behavior.* Campaigns assume that social marketing interventions to change behavior and improve the public health are worthwhile ventures. However, in some cases campaigns launched with good intentions may have unintended or dysfunctional effects. Consider the case of campaigns to increase awareness of prostate cancer. These campaigns have caused false alarms, leading people to overestimate their chances of dying from cancer, in turn creating unnecessary anxiety (Singer, 2009).

Consider also the controversy that has surrounded breast cancer campaigns. The ubiquitous use of "pink," originally a creative marketing device, may have exerted some negative influences, leading the public to assume that awareness is the main objective, while neglecting a focus on more substantive actions needed to prevent the spread of breast cancer (Jaggar, 2014). The color "pink" may also access gender stereotypes, perhaps implicitly suggesting to some women that satisfactory recovery from breast cancer requires breast construction or "perfect" breasts (Lerner, 2010).

The admirably optimistic fitness focus, colorfully communicated by a pastiche of pink as runners partake in the Susan G. Komen Race for the Cure, may delegitimize other perspectives, such as more realistic feelings of anger, chaos, and pain that breast cancer victims experience when undergoing treatments, as well as diverting attention from structural problems, like lack of access to health care (Gatison, 2015; Lerner, 2001; Sulik, 2011). Finally, critics argue that a relatively small amount of the profits made from sales of breast cancer awareness products, like pink caps, marketed by organizations like the National Football League, goes toward actual research on cancer (Weller, 2013). "Breast cancer," Sulik (2011) tellingly observes, "is an illness that now functions as a concept brand" (p. 22).

On the other hand, campaigns do need corporate sponsors to raise funds for health programs, and the "pink" label has done wonders, transforming breast cancer from a relatively little-known disease into a socially significant problem affecting hundreds of thousands of women, and raising a great deal of money for the cause. How can breast cancer campaigns balance these conflicting objectives, offering optimism but not false hopes, promoting a positive, branded message while maintaining truth in advertising? How can social marketing promote healthy behavior without co-opting the social cause? These are important questions that today's marketing-focused health campaigns must address.

A final thematic issue emerges in the study of health campaigns, one with core philosophical implications. Campaigns are heavy on social responsibility, placing them at odds with a classic libertarian perspective that regards individual liberty as an unshakeable first principle. Libertarians would question why we need campaigns, since people know that smoking causes cancer but choose to smoke, or know all about the risks of HIV but prefer to practice unsafe sex because it's fun. Don't people have a right to make their own choices and live life according to their own rules, even those that strike others as self-destructive? It is a good question, one that philosophers have been asking in one fashion or another for centuries. Campaigns must necessarily balance individual liberties and the public good. Both are important values.

Clearly, when your liberty (to smoke) threatens my good health by exposing me to second-hand smoke, it's a no-brainer for many people. But how far should you go in infringing on smokers for the sake of the larger whole? Is it right to finance public health projects by increasing the tax on cigarettes rather than on other products like candy, salt, or butter, which also cause adverse health outcomes? Should schools become the food police, banning even the most innocuous fatty food from children's diets? From a libertarian perspective, should the government ban e-cigarettes when this infringes on people's freedom, may produce reactance, and might cause users to turn to deadlier conventional cigarettes? Should they ban advertising for e-cigarettes, or restrict advertising, and how should this be implemented? Or should we oppose any limits on e-cigarettes, prizing freedom to indulge in personally gratifying activities?

Although one can appreciate this libertarian perspective, increasingly, when one considers the many preventable risks people take and the many deaths that could be prevented by successful health campaigns (Sanger-Katz, 2016), the public benefits campaigns achieve may, from a utilitarian view, considerably outweigh these hoary philosophical concerns. Indeed, the bigger value-based conundrum is that campaigns usually focus on persuading individuals to change unhealthy habits, when more enduring change occurs on the macro level, when government enacts health policy reform. Even as public health interventions persuade young people about the dangers of vaping, there lurks behind these efforts a long-dormant federal government apparatus (the Food and Drug Administration that bowed to political pressures), enabling the growth of an unregulated e-cigarette industry that helped addict a generation of young people to nicotine-laden liquids (Thomas & Kaplan, 2019).

In a similar fashion, climate change initiatives can influence individuals' environmental actions, an accomplishment to be sure, but these attainments pale if governments refrain from taking concerted actions to address global warming. The ideal, alas, is to work on both the micro and macro efforts simultaneously, designing campaigns that can influence individual behaviors, while complementing these efforts with broader policies designed to protect the public health. It's a difficult task, but that's what ideals are for.

Conclusions

Communication campaigns are vital interventions that call on mass media and interpersonal communication to make improvements in public health. They have a long, proud history in this country and abroad. Campaigns are broader in scope than most persuasion discussed in this book. They are designed to influence the health and social attitudes of a large audience within a specified amount of time, by means of mediated and interpersonal messages. Unlike commercial campaigns, health campaigns are not designed to make a profit for the sponsoring organizations. They face more daunting obstacles than commercial campaigns, frequently targeting the 15 percent of the population that is least likely to change.

Three theoretical approaches guide campaigns: A step-by-step psychological approach and two macro perspectives: Diffusion, and social marketing. Diffusion calls on theoretical ideas regarding the spread of new ideas throughout society. Social marketing applies the venerable 4Ps of commercial marketing – product, price, place, and promotion – to prosocial interventions, with increased recognition that the Ps need refinement to adapt more effectively to contemporary health contexts.

Persuasion theories can usefully complement these perspectives, as diffusion and social marketing do not always suggest specific implications for message design.

One cannot assume that campaigns succeed without conducting empirical evaluations. Campaigns are assessed at the individual, community, and state levels. Individuals or groups exposed to the intervention are compared with an equivalent group with little or no exposure to campaign messages. Real-world political factors can influence campaigns, as entrenched, powerful groups can reframe issues, offering competing messages.

Campaigns can face long odds, typified by the difficulty in reaching target audience members who would rather persist in, rather than change, a harmful health habit. Nonetheless, they can succeed when based on theory, and practitioners develop messages congruent with audience needs, employ media messages with high production value, and supplement media materials with community contacts. Campaigns are particularly adept at forming beliefs about a problem, creating awareness, linking affect with health problems, and building branded images.

It is tempting to view campaigns as all-powerful weapons in the health communication arsenal. They are not. They can fail if messages are executed poorly. They can fail if individuals fail to internalize the campaign message, and succumb to temptation at a later point in time.

Social and cultural norms play a role in campaign effectiveness. What works in one culture will not succeed in another. Campaign organizers can have brilliant ideas, but if they don't gel with cultural norms or lack the support of prominent opinion leaders, they are unlikely to succeed. And yet research has made it abundantly clear that well-conceptualized, well-executed campaigns can convince people to rethink their resistance to innovation and adopt healthier lifestyles. A generation of anti-smoking interventions offers strong empirical evidence that communication interventions can alter behavior.

Campaigns are ever-changing. The mass media-based anti-smoking campaigns of the 1980s have given way to new interventions, focused on social problems like obesity and bullying. Television PSA-dominated campaigns still exist, but are increasingly supplemented or even replaced by Web, social media, and text-based campaigns, calling on time-honored concepts, but requiring novel methodological applications and involving new challenges.

Some wonder if campaigns will continue in a niche, social media era, where it is difficult to attract a mass audience. The likelihood is that, given the importance of reaching vulnerable individuals with the technology du jour, campaigns will evolve, tailored to more specialized markets using more focused media. The days of campaigns transmitted solely through evening and late-night TV PSAs are over. Hello YouTube, social media, and text messages containing the argot of the young. Welcome also to campaigns supplementing memorable videos with favorable comments from opinion leaders and friends, relayed via social media texts.

These campaigns will require an adaptation of theory to contemporary technologies, with their short messages, catchy graphics, and interactive features. We may see more specialized campaigns, transmitted on particular social media platforms, that may be stunningly successful or run the risk of failing to connect with hard-to-reach target audiences due to the abundance of social networking sites. Still, given the multitude of health problems facing society, potential of communication to change behavior, and dedication of passionate change agents, we can expect health campaigns to continue, perhaps even thrive in new formats. The question, as always, is whether creative efforts in message design bear fruit, achieving their intended objectives.

This brings us to values and ethics, the spiritual foundation of persuasion research. Values are a core component of health campaigns. A host of ethical issues present themselves, such as determining the locus of the dilemma, deciding if the campaign should be designed to appeal to certain sectors of the public rather than the public-as-a-whole, and favoring one set of morally tinged recommendations rather than another. Values inevitably and appropriately intersect with campaigns. We want campaigns to be guided by enlightened moral principles. Researchers should try to appreciate how their value judgments, as well as those of community organizers and corporate sponsors, influence the choice of strategies. It is best to think through these issues, carefully and with as many different perspectives brought to the table as possible, at the outset rather than after the campaign has been launched.

Remember also that even as campaigns are relayed via social media and text, ethical issues remain. Technology does not wipe out moral dilemmas. It merely alters the platforms on which ethical lapses occur.

Postscript

We now have reached the end. This chapter and the book as a whole have argued that if we understand how people think and feel about communication, we have a pretty good chance of changing their views in socially constructive ways. Stated somewhat differently, the more communicators understand the dynamics of the mind, the better their chances of constructing attitude-altering messages. This is a centerpiece of contemporary persuasion scholarship and seems to have a great deal of empirical support. Yet it is always worth playing devil's advocate with oneself and noting that there are individuals whose attitudes are not amenable to change. There are people who will smoke, no matter how many times they are exposed to an anti-smoking message, and others who will abuse drugs even after you tell them they can get busted, precisely because they enjoy the thrill of testing the law. Still others will drink and drive, even when they have been arrested time and again.

Persuasive communication, like all forces in life, has limits, a point emphasized at various times in this text. Yet the fact that communication has limits does not mean it is powerless or ineffectual or necessarily plays into the hands of the vile or corrupt. Persuasion can have these effects, of course, but it can also be an instrument of self-insight, healing, and social change.

In the final analysis, it is up to us to harness persuasion for prosocial, humane purposes. We – you, me, the readers of this book – know the theories and the strategies. We also know what constitutes the morally appropriate action. We intuitively know how we want to be treated and how to treat others. As persuaders, it is up to us to communicate in ways that help people make wise choices, avoid perilous undertakings, and do all they can to live enriching, uplifting lives.

References

Andsager, J. L., Austin, E. W., & Pinkleton, B. E. (2001). Questioning the value of realism: Young adults' processing of messages in alcohol-related public service announcements and advertising. *Journal of Communication, 51*(1), 121–142.

Atkin, C. K., & Freimuth, V. S. (2001). Formative evaluation research in campaign design. In R. E. Rice & C. K. Atkin (Eds.), *Public communication campaigns* (3rd ed., pp. 125–145). Thousand Oaks, CA: Sage.

Austin, E. W., & Chen, Y. J. (1999, August). The relationship of parental reinforcement of media messages to college students' alcohol-related behaviors. Paper presented to the annual convention of the Association for Education in Journalism and Mass Communication, New Orleans.

Bakalar, N. (2005, September 27). Many don't wash hands after using the bathroom. *The New York Times.* Online: www.nytimes.com/2005/09/27/health/27wash.html?_r=0 (Accessed: February 7, 2016).

Brehm, J. W. (1966). *A theory of psychological reactance.* New York: Academic Press.

Burgoon, M., Alvaro, E., Grandpre, J., & Voulodakis, M. (2002). Revisiting the theory of psychological reactance: Communicating threats to attitudinal freedom. In J. P. Dillard & M. Pfau (Eds.), *The persuasion handbook: Developments in theory and practice* (pp. 213–232). Thousand Oaks, CA: Sage.

Burgoon, M., Hendriks, A., & Alvaro, E. (2001, May). *Tobacco prevention and cessation: Effectiveness of the Arizona tobacco education and prevention media campaign.* Paper presented to the annual convention of the International Communication Association, Washington, DC.

Cameron, K. A., & Campo, S. (2006). Stepping back from social norms campaigns: Comparing normative influences to other predictors of health behaviors. *Health Communication, 20,* 277–288.

Campo, S., & Cameron, K. A. (2006). Differential effects of exposure to social norms campaigns: A cause for concern. *Health Communication, 19,* 209–219.

Carpenter, C. J., & Amaravadi, C. S. (2019). A big data approach to assessing the impact of social norms: Reporting one's exercise to a social media audience. *Communication Research, 46,* 236–249.

Cave, D. (2020, March 13). In Australia, where getting a virus test isn't a problem. *The New York Times,* A4.

Cesario, J., Grant, H., & Higgins, E. T. (2004). Regulatory fit and persuasion: Transfer from "feeling right". *Journal of Personality and Social Psychology, 86,* 388–404.

Cigarette smoking among U.S. adults hits all-time low. (2019, November 14). CDC Newsroom. Online: www.cdc.gov/media/releases/2019/p1114-smoking-low.html. (Accessed: November 27, 2019).

Cismaru, M. (2014). Using the extended parallel process model to understand texting while driving and guide communication campaigns against it. *Health Communication, 20,* 66–82.

Clayton, R. B., Leshner, G., Bolls, P. D., & Thorson, E. (2017). Discard the smoking cues – keep the disgust: An investigation of tobacco smokers' motivated processing of anti-tobacco commercials. *Health Communication, 32,* 1319–1330.

Davis, K. C., Duke, J., Shafer, P., Patel, D., Rodes, R., & Beistle, D. (2017). Perceived effectiveness of antismoking ads and association with quit attempts among smokers: Evidence from the Tips from Former Smokers Campaign. *Health Communication, 32,* 931–938.

Dearing, J. W., Rogers, E. M., Meyer, G., Casey, M. K., Rao, N., Campo, S., & Henderson, G. M. (1996). Social marketing and diffusion-based strategies for communicating with unique populations: HIV prevention in San Francisco. *Journal of Health Communication, 1,* 343–363.

Dillard, J. P., & Shen, L. (2005). On the nature of reactance and its role in persuasive health communication. *Communication Monographs, 72,* 144–168.

Dutta, M. J. (2006). Theoretical approaches to entertainment education campaigns: A subaltern critique. *Health Communication, 20,* 221–231.

Dutta, M. J., Collins, W., Sastry, S., Dillard, S., Anaele, A., Kumar, R., … Bonu, T. (2019). A culture-centered community-grounded approach to disseminating health information among African Americans. *Health Communication, 34,* 1075–1084.

Dutta-Bergman, M. J. (2005). Theory and practice in health communication campaigns: A critical interrogation. *Health Communication, 18,* 103–122.

Eagle, L., Dahl, S., Hill, S., Bird, S., Spotswood, F., & Tapp, A. (2013). *Social marketing.* Harlow, UK: Pearson.

Edgar, T., Huhman, M., & Miller, G. A. (2017). Where is the toothpaste? A systematic review of the use of the product strategy in social marketing. *Social Marketing Quarterly, 23,* 80–98.

Emery, S., Kim, Y., Choi, Y. K., Szczypka, G., Wakefield, M., & Chaloupka, F. J. (2012). The effects of smoking-related television advertising on smoking and intentions to quit among adults in the United States: 1999–2007. *American Journal of Public Health, 102,* 751–757.

Emery, S. L., Szczypka, G., Abril, E. P., Kim, Y., & Vera, L. (2014). Are you scared yet? Evaluating fear appeal messages in tweets about the Tips campaign. *Journal of Communication, 64,* 278–295.

Engs, R. C. (2000). *Clean living movements: American cycles of health reform*. Westport, CT: Praeger.

Erceg-Hurn, D. M. (2008). Drugs, money, and graphic ads: A critical review of the Montana Meth Project. *Prevention Science, 9*, 256–263.

Farrelly, M. C., Nonnemaker, J., Davis, K. C., & Hussin, A. (2009). The influence of the national truth campaign on smoking initiation. *American Journal of Preventive Medicine, 36*, 379–384.

Fishbein, M., & Ajzen, I. (2010). *Predicting and changing behavior: The reasoned action approach*. New York: Psychology Press.

Freimuth, V. (1990). The chronically uninformed: Closing the knowledge gap in health. In E. B. Ray & L. Donohew (Eds.), *Communication and health: Systems and applications* (pp. 171–186). Hillsdale, NJ: Lawrence Erlbaum Associates.

Frieswick, K. (2009, October 4). Sick of pink. *Boston Globe Sunday Magazine*. Online: http://archive. boston.com/bostonglobe/magazine/articles/2009/10/04/s (Accessed: April 14, 2016).

Galbicsek, C. (2019, July 24). College alcoholism. *Alcohol Rehab Guide*. Online: www. alcoholrehabguide.org/resources/college-alcohol-abuse/ (Accessed: November 27, 2019).

Garnett, B. R., Buelow, R., Franko, D. L., Becker, C., Rodgers, R. F., & Austin, S. B. (2014). The importance of campaign saliency as a predictor of attitude and behavior change: A pilot evaluation of social marketing campaign Fat Talk Free Week. *Health Communication, 29*, 984–995.

Gatison, A. M. (2015). The pink and black experience: Lies that make us suffer in silence and cost us our lives. *Women's Studies in Communication, 38*, 135–140.

Gaziano, C. (1983). The knowledge gap: An analytical review of media effects. *Communication Research, 10*, 447–486.

Godbold, L. C., & Pfau, M. (2000). Conferring resistance to peer pressure among adolescents: Using inoculation theory to discourage alcohol use. *Communication Research, 27*, 411–437.

Goldstein, N. J., & Cialdini, R. B. (2007). Using social norms as a lever of social influence. In A. R. Pratkanis (Ed.), *The science of social influence: Advances and future progress* (pp. 167–191). New York: Psychology Press.

Gregory, A. (2015, February 9). R U there? *The New Yorker*, 30–35.

Guttman, N. (1997). Ethical dilemmas in health campaigns. *Health Communication, 9*, 155–190.

Guttman, N. (2000). *Public health communication interventions: Values and ethical dilemmas*. Thousand Oaks, CA: Sage.

Haines, M., & Spear, S. F. (1996). Changing the perception of the norm: A strategy to decrease binge drinking among college students. *Journal of American College Health, 45*, 134–140.

Hampton, B., Brinberg, D., Peter, P., & Corus, C. (2009). Integrating the unified theory and stages of change to create targeted health messages. *Journal of Applied Social Psychology, 39*, 449–471.

Harris, R. J., & Sanborn, F. W. (2014). *A cognitive psychology of mass communication* (6th ed.). New York: Routledge.

Hecht, M. L., & Lee, J. K. (2008). Branding through cultural grounding: The *keepin' it REAL* curriculum. In W. D. Evans & G. Hastings (Eds.), *Public health branding: Applying marketing for social change* (pp. 161–179). Oxford, UK: Oxford University Press.

Hecht, M. L., & Miller-Day, M. (2009). Drug resistance strategies project: Using narrative theory to enhance adolescents' communication competence. In L. R. Frey & K. N. Cissna (Eds.), *Routledge handbook of applied communication research* (pp. 535–557). New York: Routledge.

Hoffman, J. (2011, December 31). New medium for sex education is text message. *The New York Times*, A1, A3.

Hornik, R. (2002). Public health communication: Making sense of contradictory evidence. In R. Hornik (Ed.), *Public health communication: Evidence for behavior change* (pp. 1–19). Mahwah, NJ: Lawrence Erlbaum Associates.

Hornik, R. C., & Ramirez, A. S. (2006). Race/ethnic disparities and segmentation in communication campaigns. *American Behavioral Scientist*, 49, 868–894.

Hwang, Y. (2012). Social diffusion of campaign effects: Campaign-generated interpersonal communication as a mediator of antitobacco campaign effects. *Communication Research*, 39, 120–141.

Jacobs, A. (2018, February 8). Waging a sweeping war on obesity, Chile slays Tony the Tiger, *The New York Times*. A1, A10.

Jaggar, K. (2014, October 1). Think before you pink: Stop the distraction. HuffPost Impact. Online: www.huffingtonpost.com/karuna-jaggar/think-before-you-pink- (Accessed: April 10, 2016).

Jang, S. A. (2012). Self-monitoring as a moderator between descriptive norms and drinking: Findings among Korean and American university students. *Health Communication*, 27, 546–558.

Jensen, J. D., King, A. J., Carcioppolo, N., & Davis, L. (2012). Why are tailored messages more effective? A multiple mediation analysis of a breast cancer screening intervention. *Journal of Communication*, 62, 851–868.

Jeong, M., & Bae, R. E. (2018). The effect of campaign-generated interpersonal communication on campaign-targeted health outcomes: A meta-analysis. *Health Communication*, 33, 988–1003.

Kallgren, C. A., Reno, R. R., & Cialdini, R. B. (2000). A focus theory of normative conduct: When norms do and do not affect behavior. *Personality and Social Psychology Bulletin*, 26, 1002–1012.

Kearney, M. S., & Levine, P. B. (2014). Media influences on social outcomes: The impact of MTV's *16 and Pregnant* on teen childbearing. *NBER Working Paper Series*. Cambridge, MA: National Bureau of Economic Research. Online: www.nber.org/papers/w19795 (Accessed: May 22, 2014).

Kelley, M. S., Su, D., & Britigan, D. H. (2016). Disparities in health information access: Results of a county-wide survey and implications for Health Communication. *Health Communication*, 31, 575–582.

Kolata, G. (2015, October 31). Some breast cancer activists assail rampant "Pinkification" of October. *The New York Times*, A16.

Kreuter, M., Farrell, D., Olevitch, L., & Brennan, L. (2000). *Tailoring health messages: Customizing communication with computer technology*. Mahwah, NJ: Lawrence Erlbaum Associates.

Kruvand, M., & Bryant, F. B. (2015). Zombie apocalypse: Can the undead teach the living how to survive an emergency? *Public Health Reports*, 130, 655–663.

Lapinski, M. K., Maloney, E. K., Braz, M., & Shulman, H. C. (2013). Testing the effects of social norms and behavioral privacy on hand washing: A field experiment. *Human Communication Research*, 39, 21–46.

LaVoie, N. R., Quick, B. L., Riles, J. M., & Lambert, N. J. (2017). Are graphic cigarette warning labels an effective message strategy? A test of psychological reactance theory and source appraisal. *Communication Research*, 44, 416–436.

Lederman, L. C., Stewart, L. P., Barr, S. L., Powell, R. L., Laitman, L., & Goodhart, F. W. (2001). RU SURE? Using communication theory to reduce dangerous drinking on a college campus. In R. E. Rice & C. K. Atkin (Eds.), *Public communication campaigns* (3rd ed., pp. 295–299). Thousand Oaks, CA: Sage.

Lee, N. R., & Kotler, P. (2020). *Social marketing: Behavior change for social good* (6th ed.). Los Angeles, CA: Sage.

Lerner, B. H. (2001). *The breast cancer wars: Hope, fear, and the pursuit of a cure in twentieth-century America*. New York: Oxford University Press.

Lerner, B. H. (2010, October 11). Pink ribbon fatigue. *International New York Times*. Online: http://well.blogs.nytimes.com/2010/10/11/pink-ribbon-fatigue/?modu (Accessed: April 12, 2016).

Lerner, B. H. (2011). *One for the road: Drunk driving since 1900*. Baltimore, MD: Johns Hopkins Press.

Leshner, G., Bolls, P., & Thomas, E. (2009). Scare 'em or disgust 'em: The effects of graphic health promotion messages. *Health Communication, 24*, 447–458.

Lieber, C. (2014, October 22). The very pink, very controversial business of breast cancer awareness. *Racked*. Online: www.racked.com/2014/10/22/7572161/breast-cancer-awareness (Accessed: April 14, 2016).

Lieberman, D. A. (2001). Using interactive media in communication campaigns for children and adolescents. In R. E. Rice & C. K. Atkin (Eds.), *Public communication campaigns* (3rd ed., pp. 373–388). Thousand Oaks, CA: Sage.

Maccoby, N., & Farquhar, J. W. (1975). Communication for health: Unselling heart disease. *Journal of Communication, 25*, 114–126.

MacGillis, A. (2015). Who turned my blue state red? *The New York Times* (Sunday Review), 1, 4.

Maibach, E. W., Kreps, G. L., & Bonaguro, E. W. (1993). Developing strategic communication campaigns for HIV/AIDS prevention. In S. Ratzan (Ed.), *AIDS: Effective health communication for the 90s* (pp. 15–35). Washington, DC: Taylor & Francis.

McAlister, A. L., & Fernandez, M. (2002). "Behavioral journalism" accelerates diffusion of healthy innovations. In R. Hornik (Ed.), *Public health communication: Evidence for behavior change* (pp. 315–326). Mahwah, NJ: Lawrence Erlbaum Associates.

McGuire, W. J. (1989). Theoretical foundations of campaigns. In R. E. Rice & C. K. Atkin (Eds.), *Public communication campaigns* (2nd ed., pp. 43–65). Thousand Oaks, CA: Sage.

Metzger, M. J. (2009). The study of media effects in the era of Internet communication. In R. L. Nabi & M. B. Oliver (Eds.), *The Sage handbook of media processes and effects* (pp. 561–576). Thousand Oaks, CA: Sage.

Murray, S., & Gruley, B. (2000, November 2). On many campuses, big brewers a play a role in new alcohol policies. *The Wall Street Journal*, A1, A10.

Niederdeppe, J., Bu, Q. L., Borah, P., Kindig, D. A., & Robert, S. A. (2008b). Message design strategies to raise public awareness of social determinants of health and population health disparities. *The Milbank Quarterly, 86*, 481–513.

Niederdeppe, J., Connelly, N. A., Lauber, T. B., & Knuth, B. A. (2019). Effects of a personal narrative in messages designed to promote health fish consumption among women of childbearing age. *Health Communication, 34*, 825–837.

Niederdeppe, J., Kuang, X., Crock, B., & Skelton, A. (2008a). Media campaigns to promote smoking cessation among socioeconomically disadvantaged populations: What do we know, what do we need to learn, and what should we do now? *Social Science & Medicine, 67*(9), 1343–1355.

Noar, S. M. (2006). A 10-year retrospective of research in health mass media campaigns: Where do we go from here? *Journal of Health Communication, 11*, 21–42.

Noar, S. M., Benac, C. N., & Harris, M. S. (2007). Does tailoring matter? Meta-analytic review of tailored print health behavior change interventions. *Psychological Bulletin, 133*, 677–693.

O'Keefe, G. J., Rosenbaum, D. P., Lavrakas, P. J., Reid, K., & Botta, R. A. (1996). *Taking a bite out of crime: The impact of the National Citizens' Crime Prevention Media Campaign*. Thousand Oaks, CA: Sage.

Oh, J., & Sundar, S. S. (2015). How does interactivity persuade? An experimental test of interactivity on cognitive absorption, elaboration, and attitudes. *Journal of Communication, 65*, 213–236.

Park, H. S., Klein, K. A., Smith, S., & Martell, D. (2009). Separating subjective norms, university descriptive and injunctive norms, and U. S. descriptive and injunctive norms for drinking behavior intentions. *Health Communication, 24*, 746–751.

Peattie, S., & Peattie, K.J. (2003). Ready to fly solo? Reducing social marketing's dependence on commercial marketing theory. *Marketing Theory*, 3, 365–385.

Peracchio, L. A., & Luna, D. (1998). The development of an advertising campaign to discourage smoking initiation among children and youth. *Journal of Advertising*, 27, 49–56.

Perkins, H. W., & Craig, D. W. (2003). The Hobart and William Smith Colleges experiment: A synergistic social norms approach using print, electronic media, and curriculum infusion to reduce collegiate problem drinking. In H. W. Perkins (Ed.), *The social norms approach to preventing school and college age substance abuse: A handbook for educators, counselors, and clinicians* (pp. 35–64). San Francisco, CA: Jossey-Bass.

Perry, R. C. W., Kayekjian, K. C., Braun, R. A., Cantu, M., Sheoran, B., & Chung, P. J. (2012). Adolescents' perspectives on the use of a text messaging service for preventive sexual health promotion. *Journal of Adolescent Health*, 51, 220–225.

Pfau, M., & Van Bockern, S. (1994). The persistence of inoculation in conferring resistance to smoking initiation among adolescents: The second year. *Human Communication Research*, 20, 413–430.

Pierce, J. P., Emery, S., & Gilpin, E. (2002). The California tobacco control program: A longterm health communication project. In R. Hornik (Ed.), *Public health communication: Evidence for behavior change* (pp. 97–114). Mahwah, NJ: Lawrence Erlbaum Associates.

Pirkis, J., Rossetto, A., Nicholas, A., Ftanou, M., Robinson, J., & Reavley, N. (2019). Suicide prevention media campaigns: A systematic literature review. *Health Communication*, 34, 402–414.

Polonec, L. D., Major, A. M., & Atwood, L. E. (2006). Evaluating the believability and effectiveness of the social norms message "Most students drink 0 to 4 drinks when they party". *Health Communication*, 20, 23–34.

Pope, J. P., Pelletier, L., & Guertin, C. (2018). Starting off on the best foot: A review of message framing and message tailoring, and recommendations for the comprehensive messaging strategy for sustaining behavior change. *Health Communication*, 33, 1068–1077.

Prochaska, J. O., DiClemente, C. C., & Norcross, J. C. (1992). In search of how people change: Applications to addictive behaviors. *American Psychologist*, 47, 1102–1114.

Quick, B. L., Shen, L., & Dillard, J. P. (2013). Reactance theory and persuasion. In J. P. Dillard & L. Shen (Eds.), *The Sage handbook of persuasion: Developments in theory and practice* (2nd ed., pp. 167–183). Thousand Oaks, CA: Sage.

Rains, S. A. (2013). The nature of psychological reactance revisited: A meta-analytic review. *Human Communication Research*, 39, 47–73.

Reback, C. J., Ling., G. D., Fletcher, J. B., Branson, C. M., Shoptaw, S., Bowers, J. R., ... Mansergh, G. (2012). Text messaging reduces HIV risk behaviors among methamphetamine-using men who have sex with men. *AIDS Behavior*, 16, 1993–2002.

Rice, R. E., & Atkin, C. K. (2002). Communication campaigns: Theory, design, implementation, and evaluation. In J. Bryant & D. Zillmann (Eds.), *Media effects: Advances in theory and research* (2nd ed., pp. 427–451). Mahwah, NJ: Lawrence Erlbaum Associates.

Rice, R. E., & Atkin, C. K. (2009). Public communication campaigns: Theoretical principles and practical applications. In J. Bryant & M. B. Oliver (Eds.), *Media effects: Advances in theory and research* (3rd ed., pp. 436–468). New York: Routledge.

Richards, A. S. (2014). Predicting attitude toward methamphetamine use: The role of antidrug campaign exposure and conversations about meth in Montana. *Health Communication*, 29, 124–136.

Rimal, R. N., & Lapinski, M. K. (2015). A re-explication of social norms, ten years later. *Communication Theory*, 25, 393–409.

Roberts, D. S., & Geller, E. S. (1994). A statewide intervention to increase safety belt use: Adding to the impact of a belt use law. *American Journal of Health Promotion*, 8, 172–174.

Rogers, E. M. (1995). *Diffusion of innovations* (4th ed.). New York: Free Press.

Rushing, W. A. (1995). *The AIDS epidemic: Social dimensions of an infectious disease*. Boulder, CO: Westview.

Russell, C. A., Clapp, J. D., & DeJong, W. (2005). Done 4: Analysis of a failed social norms marketing campaign. *Health Communication, 17*, 57–65.

Sanger-Katz, M. (2016, April 11). Despite large income disparity, New York's poor are living longer. *The New York Times*, A11.

Schatzker, M. (2015, November 22). Things go worse. *The New York Times* (Book Review), 15.

Schooler, C., Chaffee, S. H., Flora, J. A., & Roser, C. (1998). Health campaign channels: Tradeoffs among reach, specificity, and impact. *Human Communication Research, 24*, 410–432.

Schroeder, C. M., & Prentice, D. A. (1998). Exposing pluralistic ignorance to reduce alcohol use among college students. *Journal of Applied Social Psychology, 28*, 2150–2180.

Shen, L. (2010). Mitigating psychological reactance: The role of message-induced empathy in persuasion. *Human Communication Research, 36*, 397–422.

Siegel, M., & Biener, L. (2002). The impact of antismoking media campaigns on progression to established smoking: Results of a longitudinal youth study in Massachusetts. In R. Hornik (Ed.), *Public health communication: Evidence for behavior change* (pp. 115–130). Mahwah, NJ: Lawrence Erlbaum Associates.

Singer, N. (2009, July 17). In push for cancer screening, limited benefits. *The New York Times*, A1, A15.

Singer, N. (2011, October 16). Welcome, fans, to the pinking of America. *The New York Times* (Sunday Business), 1, 6.

Slater, M. D. (2006). Specification and misspecification of theoretical foundations and logic models for health communication campaigns. *Health Communication, 20*, 149–157.

Snyder, L. B. (2001). How effective are mediated health campaigns? In R. E. Rice & C. K. Atkin (Eds.), *Public communication campaigns* (3rd ed., pp. 181–190). Thousand Oaks, CA: Sage.

Southwell, B. G., & Yzer, M. C. (2009). When (and why) interpersonal talk matters for campaigns. *Communication Theory, 19*, 1–8.

Sulik, G. A. (2011). *Pink ribbon blues: How breast cancer culture undermines women's health*. New York: Oxford University Press.

Thomas, K., & Kaplan, S. (2019, October 14). The F.D.A. had a decade to rein in the vaping industry. It failed. *The New York Times*, A1, A16.

Truong, V. D. (2014). Social marketing: A systematic review of research 1998-2012. *Social Marketing Quarterly, 20*, 15–34.

van den Heerik, R. A. M., van Hooijdonk, C. M. J., Burgers, C., & Steen, G. J. (2017). "Smoking is sóóó … sandals and white socks": Co-creation of a Dutch anti-smoking campaign to change social norms. *Health Communication, 32*, 621–628.

Viswanath, K., & Finnegan, J. R., Jr. (1996). The knowledge gap hypothesis: Twenty-five years later. In B. R. Burleson (Ed.), *Communication yearbook 19* (pp. 187–227). Thousand Oaks, CA: Sage.

Walsh-Childers, K., & Brown, J. D. (2009). Effects of media on personal and public health. In J. Bryant & M. B. Oliver (Eds.), *Media effects: Advances in theory and research* (3rd ed., pp. 469–489). New York: Routledge.

Wan, -H.-H. (2008). Resonance as a mediating factor accounting for the message effect in tailored communication—Examining crisis communication in a tourism context. *Journal of Communication, 58*, 472–489.

Weller, C. (2013, October 16). Pinkwashing: Only 8% of NFL pink breast cancer awareness merchandise sales goes toward actual cancer research. *Medical Daily*. Online: www.medicaldaily.com/pinkwashing-only-8-nfl-pink-breast-can (Accessed: April 10, 2016).

Worden, J. K., & Flynn, B. S. (2002). Using mass media to prevent cigarette smoking. In R. Hornik (Ed.), *Public health communication: Evidence for behavior change* (pp. 23–33). Mahwah, NJ: Lawrence Erlbaum Associates.

Yanovitzky, I., Stewart, L. P., & Lederman, L. C. (2006). Social distance, perceived drinking by peers, and alcohol use by college students. *Health Communication*, 19, 1–10.

York, B.N., & Loeb, S. (2014). One step at a time: The effects of an early literacy text messaging program for parents of preschoolers. Cambridge, MA: National Bureau of Economics. Online: https://www.nber.org/papers/w20659 (Accessed: March 27, 2020).

Glossary

Accessibility   the degree to which an attitude can be automatically activated from memory.

Acquiescence   a pitfall in attitude measurement that occurs when respondents agree with items, regardless of their content.

Advertising deception   a representation that contains a message likely to mislead consumers behaving reasonably under the circumstances and likely to influence consumer decision making about a product or service.

Assimilation   perceptual distortion that occurs when an individual assumes that a message is more similar to one's attitude than it actually is.

Attitude   learned global evaluation of an object (person, place, or issue) that influences thought and action.

Authority   power that derives from the communicator's role in a social structure and his or her ability to dispense rewards or punishments.

Balance theory   three-component model of attitude structure that stipulates that people prefer balance or harmony among the components of their attitudes.

Belief   cognition about the world; subjective probability that an object has a particular quality or that an action will lead to a particular outcome.

Branded message   a strategic communication designed to evoke tangible or symbolic benefits that are linked with the identity of a commercially marketed or socially marketed brand.

Branding   the process of defining a commercial entity so that it is perceived as unique and different, and can be quickly called to mind.

Central route   processing path characterized by substantial thinking, or consideration of how a message relates to the receiver's values.

Charisma   a certain quality of a communicator that sets him or her apart from ordinary individuals and, in the perceiver's mind, endows him or her with supernatural, exceptional qualities.

Classical conditioning   Pavlov's theory of association that holds that pairing a conditioned stimulus with an unconditioned stimulus produces a conditioned response.

Coercion   an influence process that occurs when the influence agent delivers a credible threat, raising the prospect of negative physical or emotional consequences; attempts to induce the individual to act contrary to her preferences, and deprives the individual of some measure of freedom or autonomy.

Cognitive dissonance negative, unpleasant state that occurs whenever an individual holds two thoughts that are psychologically incompatible. Cognitive dissonance theory has intriguing implications for persuasion.

Cognitive response approach to persuasion emphasizes the role of thoughts, such as counterarguments and proarguments, in the persuasion process.

Communication accommodation theory an interpersonal communication perspective that examines processes by which individuals adapt their communication behavior toward others—or accommodate them—and the consequences of accommodation on subsequent communication.

Communication campaign large-scale communicative intervention characterized by purposive attempts to persuade a well-defined audience for non-commercial benefits, typically within a given time period by means of organized communication involving mass media and Internet, and often complemented by interpersonal support.

Compatibility principle attitude–behavior perspective that says general attitudes predict behaviors across situations, and specific attitudes forecast a specific behavior at a particular time and place.

Compliance-gaining any communicative interaction in which a communicator tries to convince a message recipient to perform a behavior that he or she would not otherwise perform.

Conclusion drawing message factor that compares effects of a message that draws a conclusion either explicitly or implicitly.

Contrast perceptual distortion that occurs when an individual assumes that a message is more different from one's attitude than it actually is.

Credibility the message receiver's attitude toward the source of a communication; his or her perception of the communicator's qualities.

Cult a group of individuals who are excessively devoted to a charismatic leader (who is himself or herself an object of worship), effectively isolated from the rest of society, denied access to alternative points of view, and subjected to exploitative social influence techniques.

Danger control psychological process whereby a fear appeal leads people to focus on the underlying threat and to therefore consider adopting strategies to ward off the danger.

Deontological thought normative ethical theory that emphasizes universal moral imperatives, such as duty and obligation. Morality is judged in terms of moral obligations, not the consequences of actions.

Diffusion theory communication theory that describes and explains the process by which innovations spread through society.

Disrupt-then-reframe a persuader disrupts the message recipient's cognitive view of a persuasion encounter with an entertaining gambit and then reframes the request.

Distraction process by which environmental distractions can block receivers' cognitive responses to a message, under certain circumstances producing more persuasion.

Door-in-the-face technique a persuader can gain compliance to a second, smaller request by inducing individuals to turn down an outrageously large initial request.

Elaboration Likelihood Model a dual-processing model that highlights the processes by which persuasion occurs. It stipulates that there are two distinct ways people process communications: The central and peripheral routes, with the routes differing in the likelihood that people will elaborate on the message.

Evidence message factor that consists of factual assertions, quantitative information, eyewitness statements, and testimonials advanced by credible sources.

Expectancy–value approach   model of attitude structure that says attitudes are composed of two components (a cognition about the object, an expectation), and an evaluation of this attribute (value).

Extended Parallel Process Model   four-step process model that emphasizes severity, susceptibility, response efficacy, and self-efficacy of a fear-arousing message. The model articulates the processes that a fear appeal must evoke in order to persuade.

Fear appeal   persuasive communication that tries to scare people into changing their attitudes by conjuring up negative consequences that will occur if they do not comply with message recommendations.

Fear control   psychological process whereby a fear appeal leads people to focus on containing their fear rather than developing strategies to ward off danger.

Fear-then-relief   a persuader deliberately places the message recipient in a state of fear, quickly eliminates it, and makes a pitch for the targeted request.

Focus group   a qualitative research strategy that probes the rich meaning people attach to social issues.

Foot-in-the-door technique   a persuader can secure compliance to a second large request by inducing an individual to first go along with a small initial request.

Forewarning   process that occurs when a persuader warns people they will soon be exposed to a persuasive communication. Forewarning can stiffen resistance to persuasion, although the effects can be complex.

Frame   message characteristic that induces persuasion through subtle changes in wording or perspective. To frame is to emphasize a particular definition of the problem or treatment recommendation.

Functional magnetic resonance imaging   neuroscience-based methodology that illuminates brain activity, offering a snapshot of the brain's functioning and structure.

Functional theory   theory of attitudes that argues that people adopt attitudes because they fulfill particular psychological functions.

Gain-framed argument   message that emphasizes benefits of adopting a behavior.

Guttman scale   questionnaire measurement of attitude that progresses from easy-to-accept to difficult-to-accept items.

Heuristic   a simple decision-making strategy.

Heuristic-Systematic Model   a dual-process model of persuasion stipulating that individuals process persuasion through two mechanisms: The systematic and heuristic routes. These dual processes have implications for cognitive processing and persuasion.

Hypocrisy induction   a procedure by which individuals are confronted with examples of their own inconsistency in an effort to harness dissonance to produce attitude change.

Ideological approach to attitudes   model of attitude structure that says attitudes are guided by broad ideological principles.

Illusion of invulnerability   perception that others are more likely to experience negative life outcomes than we are ourselves.

Implicit Association Test   instrument to assess implicit attitude through response time techniques, with the attitude object linked to good and bad labels. The IAT has emerged as a robust measure of prejudice, but has also stimulated considerable controversy.

Implicit attitude   an evaluation that has an unknown origin, is activated automatically, and can influence implicit, uncontrollable responses.

Induced compliance phenomenon that occurs when an individual freely decides to comply with a dissonance-producing request, sometimes agreeing to perform a counter-attitudinal behavior for a small reward.

Influencer marketing a promotional strategy widely used on social media that calls on communicators who have clout and resonance with their audience. It is both a contemporary strategy and classic technique rooted in communicator credibility and social attractiveness principles.

Inoculation persuasion strategy that induces resistance to persuasion by exposing individuals to a small dose of arguments against an idea, followed by criticism of those arguments.

Intense language evocative speech that includes metaphors, vivid language, emotionally charged words, and obscenities.

Knowledge bias audience member's perception that a communicator has a biased view of an issue.

Latitudes the perceived range of psychological acceptability of message positions, derived from social judgment theory, encompassing latitudes of acceptance, rejection, and non-commitment.

Likert scale questionnaire measurement of attitude that asks respondents to indicate agreement or disagreement with a statement along an equal-interval numerical scale.

Loss-framed argument message that emphasizes costs of not performing the requested action.

Low-balling a persuader gains compliance by inducing an individual to comply with an initial request and then "ups the ante" by increasing the costs of compliance.

Manipulation a persuasion technique that occurs when a communicator disguises his or her true persuasive goals, hoping to mislead the recipient by delivering an overt message that belies its true intent.

Marketing activities and processes by which a society communicates products and services of value to masses of consumers.

Mere exposure repeated exposure to a novel, neutral message produces a positive attitude.

Message sidedness message factor that compares effects of a one-sided message that presents one perspective on the issue with a two-sided message that presents arguments on behalf of both the persuader's position and the opposing side.

Narrative a coherent story with a clear beginning, middle, and end that offers plot and characters and provides a resolution.

Need for cognition personality factor that taps individual differences in the tendency to enjoy thinking and to engage in abstract deliberation.

Neuroscience perspective on persuasion an approach that examines the biological and brain-based underpinnings of attitudes. It can help shed light on neurological processes underlying persuasion and ways in which body and mind exert complementary influences on attitude change.

Norm an accepted, recommended social behavior in a society. A perceived norm is perceived social pressure to perform a particular action.

Perceived behavioral control perception of controllability of an action, or the degree to which individuals believe they are capable of performing a particular behavior.

Peripheral route processing path characterized by superficial thinking and consideration of factors irrelevant or peripheral to the message.

Persuasion a symbolic process in which communicators try to convince other people to change their attitudes or behaviors regarding an issue through the transmission of a message in an atmosphere of free choice.

Physiological measurements inference of an attitude from physiological responses such as galvanic skin response, pupil dilation, and facial electromyographic techniques.

Pique technique a persuader makes the request in an unusual fashion, piquing the target's curiosity.

Placebo effect a phenomenon that occurs when a fake, inauthentic treatment, has a positive effect on an individual's thoughts or behavior simply because the individual expects that the treatment will exert positive influences.

Powerless/powerful speech speech that varies in the degree to which it expresses such factors as hesitation, hedges, tag questions, and disclaimers.

Pre-giving persuader provides the receiver with a reward and then follows this up with the targeted persuasive request.

Priming automatized social influence process, whereby exposure to an initially, frequently socially charged, message accesses or primes thoughts psychologically associated with the message.

Product placement paid communication about a product that is designed to influence audience attitudes about the brand through deliberate and subtle insertion of a product into media entertainment programming.

Propaganda a system of communicating information, in which the communicator has near or total control over the transmission of information, and relies on media to reach masses of individuals with false, deceptive, frequently covert messages; the term evokes negative connotations in others.

Reactance motivational state that occurs when an individual's freedom is eliminated or even threatened with elimination. When a perceived freedom is taken away or threatened with elimination, people are motivated to restore the valued freedom.

Reasoned Action Approach a comprehensive theory of attitude and behavior stipulating that behavior can be predicted by inclusion of attitude, norms (descriptive and injunctive), perceived behavioral control, and behavioral intention.

Replication the ability to obtain the same findings when a study is conducted under identical or extremely similar circumstances, using the same procedures, materials, and measuring instruments. Research that has failed to replicate a variety of findings that bear on persuasion has questioned the validity of the original research. Critics have questioned the breadth of these conclusions, while acknowledging the importance of replication in science.

Reporting bias audience member's perception that the communicator has opted not to report or disclose certain points of view.

Response time measurements measurement of attitude by assessing latency or length of time that it takes people to indicate agreement with a statement.

Rhetoric classic concept dating back to ancient Greece that examines the content of argumentation and language in persuasion.

Self-affirmation theory a psychological perspective that argues individuals are motivated to take a variety of steps to affirm the self.

Self-monitoring personality trait with persuasion implications that views individuals as varying in the extent to which they are concerned with displaying appropriate behavior in social situations.

Self-perception theory a psychological theory stipulating that an individual acts as a dispassionate observer of the self, inferring attitudes from behavior.

Semantic differential questionnaire measurement of attitude that taps meaning assigned to an object using bipolar adjectives.

Semiotics   the study of signs and symbols.

Sequential influence techniques   influence techniques that proceed in stages, in which a prior request creates the communicative foundation for requests that follow.

Sleeper effect   a persuasive message impact increases with the passage of time. A message initially discounted by message receivers, due to its attribution to a low-credibility source, comes to be accepted over the longer haul.

Social bot   an automated software that is capable of automatically generating messages and advocating positions by appearing to be a follower or fake account that may solicit followers.

Social judgment theory   attitude theory that emphasizes people's subjective judgments about social issues. People do not evaluate a message purely on its merits, but instead compare the advocated position with their own attitude and determine, on this basis, whether they should accept or reject the message.

Social marketing   a process of creating and implementing programs to enhance the acceptability of a prosocial idea by applying marketing principles to health promotion.

Social norms persuasion   an appeal to descriptive or injunctive social norms that is designed to influence perceptions of socially appropriate behavior in hopes of motivating behavioral change.

Strong attitude   an attitude of personal importance characterized by such aspects as ego-involvement, extremity, certainty, accessibility, knowledge, and hierarchical organization.

Subliminal perception   perception without awareness of the object being perceived.

Subliminal advertisement   an advertisement that includes a brief, specific message that cannot be perceived at a normal level of conscious awareness.

Symbol   a form of language in which one entity represents a concept or idea, communicating rich psychological and cultural meaning.

Symbolic attitude approach   model of attitude structure that stipulates that large emotional evaluations, prejudices, and symbolic attachments are the core of an attitude.

"That's-not-all" technique   a persuader stipulates that purchase of a product or acceptance of an offer will be accompanied by receipt of an additional product that is also part of the deal.

Theory of planned behavior   Theoretical perspective on attitude-behavior consistency that added the construct, perceived behavioral control, to the reasoned action approach, calling attention to the impact of personal and environmental control on behavioral intentions.

Third-person effect   distorted perception that persuasive media do not affect "me" or "you", but "them" – everyone else, the third persons.

Transportation   the process whereby fiction imaginatively takes people to different psychological places, sometimes producing a change in attitude or perspective.

Unobtrusive measure   indirect attitude assessment technique in which a researcher observes individuals' behavior without their knowledge.

Utilitarianism   normative ethical theory that judges actions based on whether they produce more positive than negative outcomes, or consequences.

Value   a guiding principle; the idealized conception of desirable outcomes.

Yale Attitude Change Approach   early influential model of persuasion that focused on sources, messages, channels, and receivers of messages and emphasized role of learning in persuasion.

Subject Index

Please note references to figures are in *italic*; references to tables are in **bold**.

Author Index

Please note references to figures are in *italic*; references to tables are in **bold**.

9780367185794